Encyclopedia of the United Nations

Second Edition

ENCYCLOPEDIA OF THE UNITED NATIONS

SECOND EDITION

Volume I

JOHN ALLPHIN MOORE, JR.
California State Polytechnic University

JERRY PUBANTZ
University of North Carolina at Greensboro

Facts On File
An imprint of Infobase Publishing

Encyclopedia of the United Nations, Second Edition

Copyright © 2008, 2002 by John Allphin Moore, Jr., and Jerry Pubantz

Facts On File, Inc.
An imprint of Infobase Publishing
132 West 31st Street
New York NY 10001

Library of Congress Cataloging-in-Publication Data

Moore, John Allphin, 1940–
Encyclopedia of the United Nations / John Allphin Moore, Jr., Jerry Pubantz—2nd ed.
v. cm.
Includes bibliographical references and index.
ISBN-13: 978-0-8160-6913-2 (hc: alk. paper)
1. United Nations—Encyclopedias. 2. International relations—Encyclopedias. I. Pubantz, Jerry,
1947–II. Title.
KZ4968.M66 2008
341.2303—dc22   2007029559

Facts On File books are available at special discounts when purchased in bulk quantities for businesses, associations, institutions, or sales promotions. Please call our Special Sales Department in New York at (212) 967-8800 or (800) 322-8755.

You can find Facts On File on the World Wide Web at http://www.factsonfile.com

Text design by Cathy Rincon
Cover design by Salvatore Luongo
Illustrations by Patricia Meschino
Compoosition by Hermitage Publishing Services
Cover printed by Yurchak Printing, Landisville, Pa.
Book printed and bound by Yurchak Printing, Landisville, Pa.
Printed in the United States of America

This book is printed on acid-free paper and contains 30 percent postconsumer recycled content.

Dedicated
To Mailinda Moore, Timothy Peterson, and Nora Britt,
and to the hope that their generation
may make a better world

Contents

Appendices:

PREFACE TO
THE SECOND EDITION

The preface to the original edition of this encyclopedia follows immediately, and because it is a reliable statement of the editors' persisting sentiment about their work and also remains accurate as a comprehensive guide about how to use this encyclopedia, we commend a reading of it.

The new and expanded rendition found in the following pages is approximately 50 percent larger than the 2002 edition. We have added many new entries, edited every one of the existing ones to bring them up to date and refine them, inserted late citations, and expanded considerably the appendices and bibliography. In the process we have added several new Web sites and checked every original Web site to ensure that it was current or required updating. Rather than indicate the date of access for each Web site, we inform the reader here that all Web sites cited were accessed during the period of August 2006 through June 2007, the time during which we were composing the renovated text.

As would be expected, given world developments that have occurred since the publication of the first edition, users should be alerted to some variations and added emphases in the present edition. Some new entries, for example, will highlight the steady drift of the UN toward being a part of—even central to—an apparently emerging global governance system. Entries such as "globalization," "democratization," "international civil society," and "SARS" will underscore the theme, and they may be considered in tandem with updated entries such as those for "international criminal court," "international law," and "subsidiarity." Additionally, there are a number of new biographical entries that we trust will bring a deeper human dimension to an organization that is often described in technical and dry language. There are as well new entries that point to the relationship of the UN with freshly emerging international challenges, such as additions and expanded entries on terrorism and related topics. The new edition takes cognizance of the issue of UN reform, which gained added urgency following the U.S. invasion of Iraq in 2003, and the concurrent concern with providing peacekeeping and even peacebuilding mechanisms for newly dysfunctional areas of the world. Additionally, we

need to alert the reader to some alternate spellings sprinkled throughout the text that foreign usage or changes over time necessitate. For example, the current spelling Tehran—the capital of Iran—will not obtain in the very few instances when we reference the historic Teheran Conference of 1943. Finally, we have added to the acronym list appearing early in the manuscript. We would caution that this listing—which appears daunting at first glance—is designed not for pleasurable reading but simply as a reference tool to collate the numerous UN acronyms and place them next to full titles.

Despite these augmentations, the essential organization of the encyclopedia is the same as for the first edition. Moreover, all acknowledgments forwarded in the original preface continue to be relevant for this edition. Contributing essayists are listed under the "contributors" section of the text, and, although we have been energetic in editing all entries for this new volume in order to maintain stylistic consistency and to provide the latest data, we stand in their bountiful debt. Appreciations for colleagues at California State Polytechnic University contained in the original preface deserve reemphasis here, with a couple of added notables—Georgia Mickey and Daniel Lewis, each of the History Department, have been helpful and encouraging. One of us has moved to another academic institution since publication of the encyclopedia's first edition and, in addition to enduring gratitude from a memorable tenure at Salem College, Professor Pubantz would add his appreciation for the encouragement of his colleagues in the Department of Political Science at the University of North Carolina at Greensboro. Special recognition is due Matthew Jeffreys, who, in his capacity as the graduate research assistant on this project, tracked down all of the changes in UN agencies during the past five years, made invaluable suggestions on editorial changes to the text, and wrote two extraordinary entries for the second edition. Readers of the last edition will note that UNCG has also offered up its best expert on African politics, Robert J. Griffiths, as a new contributor to the volume. Finally, thanks must go to the department chair, Ruth DeHoog, who masterfully reworked the teaching schedule to allow Professor

Pubantz the necessary blocks of time to complete this project. More than indirect sustenance has come from Michael Eaton, executive director of the National Collegiate Conference Association, and Taina Järvinen, who has served as a field officer with UN monitoring teams in the most exotic of places as well as participated with us on scholarly endeavors.

Although he is mentioned in our earlier preface, we wish to underscore yet again our appreciation of editor Owen Lancer, who has, for the third time, guided us to publication. And, of equal merit, and thus deserving of another tender of approbation, are our wives—Linda and Gloria—who, gratefully, still show genial and supportive forbearance for our scholarly passion.

We are pleased to accept the support, advice, and encouragement that have come our way, however we concede that errors that may appear in the following pages are the responsibility alone of the editors.

—John Allphin Moore, Jr.
Pomona, CA
—Jerry Pubantz
Greensboro, NC
November 2007

Preface to
the First Edition

On September 11, 2001, the United Nations was due to convene the 56th session of the General Assembly in New York City. That meeting would have opened, as it had every September since 1981, with a moment of silence in recognition of the Assembly's self-proclaimed International Day of Peace. That act of reverence for 20 years had commemorated "the ideals of peace both within and among all nations and peoples." At the appointed moment of 3 P.M., however, the Assembly Hall stood silent and empty, its expected occupants tragically focused on the gruesome events unfolding just 50 blocks south, where the smoking rubble of the World Trade Center towers lay as reminder that peace was hardly secure at the beginning of the new millennium.

The terrorism from the air that wreaked that terrible calamity was a very different insult to the world's peace than the ashes of war out of which the United Nations had been born. Yet, in those harrowing hours, if anyone thought to ask whether the 56-year-old institution would likely address this new global challenge as it had so many other threats to international peace and security since 1945, that person would have predicted "of course." It is an extraordinary thing that, while other international organizations, alliances, and even states of the cold war era have vanished or have had to remake themselves wholly, the United Nations shows the durability that makes it as potentially relevant today as when Franklin Roosevelt, Joseph Stalin, and Winston Churchill first agreed to replace the far more mortal League of Nations. With all of its warts and weaknesses, the United Nations simply is part of our expected reality and an expression of our hoped-for future. It is, as well, a universal focus of what is called "globalization." So, if terrorism has been globalized, then whatever global antidotes are available must of necessity absorb the attention of the wider world. In fact, at the millennium, this suggestion obtains for any number of issues, including rescuing disintegrating states, addressing economic dislocations, extending human rights, avoiding environmental degradation, containing arms races, resolving border disputes, calming ethnic and religious hatreds, and

more. These are not issues isolated in parochial locales. They belong to the entire globe.

Thus, in a new era of international politics, the United Nations has taken on new visibility. Its expansion of peace-keeping operations, the reinvigoration of great power cooperation in the Security Council, and the organization's central role in contemporary international diplomacy have revived interest in UN affairs unparalleled since its founding in 1945. The transformation in world politics brought on by the breakup of the Soviet Union raised the promise and expectations of the United Nations that now require a careful understanding by policy makers and the general public of the world body. The United Nations, unlike any comparable multistate organization in history, has remained with us for an unprecedented half century, expanding its membership to virtual universality. For many it has sustained the hope of a future democratic and peaceful world; for others it has served as the arena or agent for the pursuit of national interests. It is in the firm belief that the United Nations has been, and will continue to be, central to world politics that we have crafted this encyclopedia in order to provide an authoritative source on the UN's structure, functions, and history.

An encyclopedia differs from a dictionary in that the latter is primarily devoted to words; an encyclopedia is, of course, dependent on words, but it is necessarily committed to the use of words for the transmission of comprehensive information. This encyclopedia, in the tradition of those of the past, aspires to a particular kind of breadth, that is, to the compilation of extensive and useful knowledge about the United Nations. We hasten to add that while encyclopedias must be complete, they must also be selective. Everything cannot be described, because then nothing can be highlighted. This reference volume provides a comprehensive guide to the UN's institutions, procedures, policies, specialized agencies, historic personalities, initiatives, and involvement in world affairs. We intend that it set into context the past six decades of major world happenings and the role the United Nations has played in them. We also intend to demonstrate to the careful reader that there is a "new" United Nations. Secretary-

General Kofi Annan best captured its transformation when he talked about it as part of an emerging international civil society. In this volume we present the new UN through thematic essays on topics that would not have been part of an encyclopedia on the institution during its first few decades. Women, environment, human rights, globalization, sustainable development, indigenous peoples, and terrorism, among other topics, have joined traditional UN concerns such as disarmament and the development of international law.

Laid out in alphabetical order for easy access, entries include brief references, longer explanatory essays, and detailed data on the United Nations. For many of the entries we have provided references to some of the most current scholarship and also seminal works on the topic. This is enhanced by a lengthy bibliography divided by subject fields. And in this Internet age, many entries provide Web sites to which students of the institution may turn for even more current information.

The truly lasting encyclopedic works since the time of the Enlightenment have been collections of scholarship by a community of scholars. We have attempted to follow in that tradition. The strength of this work arises from the genius and expertise of its 25 contributors. Their thoughtful essays on critical topics, agencies, people, and themes are each noted by their names at the end of the entry. Their affiliations can be found in the list of Contributors. Three shared qualities bind our contributors: their scholarship, their willingness to let us liberally edit their work to give the volume a consistent style and tone, and their empathy for the institution. This last attribute has been shown in many ways, not the least of which is that several of the contributors are Model United Nations advisers. They have worked together as colleagues, most particularly in the setting of the National Model United Nations in New York, the oldest simulation of its kind in the world. More important, they have taught generations of students the merits, demerits, and broad possibilities for the United Nations in a diverse but globalized world. Those who have not served as Model UN advisers have written extensively in their fields, have been advocates for international cooperation, or have tended to the vineyards of international life in UN agencies, related bodies, or non-governmental organizations. We are deeply in their debt for their contribution to this project. Entries not attributed to a specific author were written by the editors.

As in any effort to put together a meaningful encyclopedia, we found one of our most daunting tasks to be deciding what to put in and what to leave aside. We trust that we have compensated for missed opportunities by providing a useful set of appendices, including important UN documents such as the Charter of the United Nations, the Universal Declaration of Human Rights, and the Statute of the International Court of Justice. Also in the appendices readers will find (1) a list of the member states and their years of accession, (2) a list of the UN's Secretaries-General, their terms, and

their biographical dates, and (3) an index of resolutions that either changed the ways in which the United Nations works (e.g., Uniting for Peace Resolution) or were overwhelmingly critical to world affairs (e.g., Security Council Resolutions 242 and 678). A chronology of important UN dates and the events associated with them is also provided, with capitalization of items that have their own entries in the volume. This should assist the student who wishes to construct a history on a specific UN topic.

Of all the Web sites available on the "net," none is more comprehensive than that offered by the United Nations. "www.un.org" opens an unending cornucopia of information, topics, and links to all the nooks and crannies of the world. But like most things on the Internet, "more" is often confusing and beguilingly misdirecting. To help guide the interested student, we have provided an extensive table of the most useful Web sites. Of course, we know that some will disappear, and some will change their URLs, but at least the serious searcher now can know where to start.

Because the entries are organized alphabetically, a user of the encyclopedia should have little trouble making contact with a specific topic. For further guidance, we have included within entries a wealth of cross-references indicated by capitalization, and at the conclusion of most entries a specific bibliography and directions for the reader to "see also" related entries. In most cases the cross-reference directs the student to a full entry, in others to yet more entries that further describe the topic. The cross-referenced entry will appear in exactly the same form in the alphabetical listing, with only two exceptions to this rule. When the cross-referenced item appears in an entry in the plural form, we have placed that item in small capitals (e.g., treaties), however, the reader should turn to the entry in its singular form (e.g., Treaty). Second, sometimes a cross-referenced entry will be preceded by "UN" (e.g., UN Environment Programme) for the purposes of making the entry more readable. Unless the cross-reference is to a resolution (e.g., UN Security Council Resolution 242) readers should assume that "UN" abbreviates "United Nations" and should turn to the entry with that in mind (e.g., United Nations Environment Programme).

As the previous sentence demonstrates, from time to time the reader will discover a word spelled differently from that normally found in American English. This occurs because the United Nations by tradition and formal agreement employs certain words such as "programme" and "labour" in all of its English-language texts. While the encyclopedia generally employs American usage and spelling, we have conformed to the UN practice of British or French spelling when referring to official UN bodies with these words in their names or when quoting from UN documents. This may appear strange to the American reader, or even inconsistent, since two different forms of the same word (*program* or *programme,* for instance) will be used at different points in this volume. Nonetheless, it is important to record accurately UN practice in this regard.

This large project owes much to many. Along with our contributors we owe primary thanks to the efforts of the editorial staff at Facts On File, most particularly to our gifted editor Owen Lancer. We have worked with Owen on other projects in the past and, frankly, we have been spoiled by the alertness, direction, and subtle if humane pressure only the best of editors can bring to bear on their authors. We have savored our meetings in New York with Owen. And we owe a debt of gratitude to the copy editor, marketing people, and diligent staff at Facts On File. Colleagues at California State Polytechnic University who offered dependable insight, help, and encouragement include Mahmood Ibrahim, Steve Englehart, Griet Vankeerberghen, Zuoyue Wang, John Lloyd, Amanda Podany, and Gayle Savarese. The dean's office at the College of Letters, Arts, and Social Sciences graciously provided partial release time in the fall term of 2000 to allow concentrated work on the project, and the library staff at the university, as always, provided steady support to the enterprise. Wide-ranging, accessible research material was at our fingertips because of librarian Kate Seifert's unfailing and good-natured tutoring on uses of the library's unsurpassed Web site. Once again, John Stephen Moore proved indispensable as an expert computer escort. The researcher at Salem College is always assured success if he or she has the talented assistance of Susan Taylor, Salem's reference librarian. Her devoted help on this project has given it a richness and an accuracy that every author and editor hopes for. Also at Salem the Faculty Affairs Committee generously provided research funds that made possible many happy and useful hours of study at UN headquarters. While he is duly listed among the expert contributors for his superb historical entries in the encyclopedia, Errol Clauss, professor of history at Salem, pro-

vided invaluable counsel throughout the project. And finally, the unerring hand of Fran Swajkoski, Salem faculty secretary, assured that all drafts and final documents arrived where they needed to be, and when they needed to be there.

The manuscript simply could not have appeared in its final form without the substantial contribution of the Dag Hammarskjöld Library at the UN Headquarters in New York. We spent several hours on separate occasions in the alluring setting of the library, making full use of the photographic library with its unprecedented collection of pictures. Several reproductions from this historic collection grace the pages of this encyclopedia. We extend our appreciation to Mr. Pernacca Sudhakaran, head of the Photography Unit. A very special "thank you" must go to Ms. Anne Cunningham in the UN Department of Public Information. Her graciousness, her intercessions on our behalf, her advice, and her support all made working with the UN Secretariat a professional and delightful experience.

Finally, in a shared spirit that we think will not fade from the present moment, we acknowledge the city of New York. As faculty advisers to the National Model UN conference, we first met in New York some quarter of a century ago. We have visited regularly since then, attending to the UN Headquarters at least once a year for that quarter of a century. We do research and turn in manuscripts in New York. We met most of our contributors there. There we have celebrated successes and commemorated tragedy. In New York the United Nations endures and from New York this encyclopedia issues forth. If it carries omissions, oversights, or errors, those belong alone to the editors.

—John Allphin Moore, Jr.
Pomona, CA
—Jerry Pubantz
Winston-Salem, NC

INTRODUCTION

The United Nations and World History

Perhaps the most famous encyclopedia, the French rendition of the late 18th century, edited by Denis Diderot, surfaced during a period later generations called "enlightened." If the Enlightenment brought modern rationality to learning, it also imposed upon international affairs fresh notions that eventually would sway world leaders and lead to the United Nations. Eighteenth-century developments in politics, economics, international law, science, and conceptions of individual rights led to what some have called modern liberal democratic nationalism.[1] In turn, influenced by liberals in the American and French revolutionary traditions, and by German philosopher Immanuel Kant, thinkers envisioned a peaceful world that would be characterized by democracy, economic interdependence, and international law and institutions.[2] Such notions may strike the 21st century reader as commonplace examples of what the current age calls "globalization." But it would take some two centuries, sanguinary conflict, and agonizing efforts to effect a world organization that conformed to the prescriptions of enlightened notions of diplomacy. And still the world would not be perfect.

However, with the subtle deception nonaligned history can on occasion tease, world affairs by the early 1990s conspired to suggest the triumph of Kant's vision. The year 1989 brought the end of the Berlin Wall, the Warsaw Pact, and the cold war. A united Security Council authorized military action against Iraq, pushing the aggressor out of tiny Kuwait. U.S. president George H. W. Bush proclaimed a "New World Order," by which he and his listeners meant a world more nearly conforming to the political and economic norms we associate with enlightened Western society: the rule of law, democratic elections, market economics, rising standards of living, and the advancement of human rights, all within the context of a world of interdependent, cooperating sovereign

nations. Accordingly, in the early 1990s the United Nations was seen as the energizing institution of that new world, just as its founders had intended, and just as it had only recently, against the aggressor Saddam Hussein, proved it could be. By 2007 the United Nations could count 192 member states and numerous international organizations and non-governmental organizations that considered themselves part of the UN family. Composed of and dependent on individual nation-states, it nonetheless seemed poised to transcend distinct state desires for more wide-ranging global purposes.

Crisis at the Millennium

Yet, as the first decade of the new millennium drew to a close the heady assessment of the decade ending the last millennium seemed unhappily premature. Early unpleasantness in Somalia, Bosnia, Chechnya, and Cambodia was followed by the specter of other states around the globe disintegrating—in Indonesia, the former Yugoslavia, and elsewhere in Africa. The Arab-Israeli dispute, calmed by the Oslo Agreement of 1993 and mutual Palestinian-Israeli recognition and the onset of negotiations, degenerated by the early 21st century into a mutual bloodbath. World economic and financial crises emerged in Asia and Latin America, AIDS became an epidemic in much of sub-Saharan Africa, and angry protesters showed up in larger and larger numbers at meetings of international financial and economic organizations to voice strong opposition to globalization. On September 11, 2001, the unimaginable happened as terrorists commandeered four American airplanes on the east coast and slammed two of them into New York's World Trade Center and one into the Pentagon in Washington, D.C., causing unspeakable death and destruction. By the end of the year an internationally endorsed force led by the United States had invaded Taliban-ruled Afghanistan and defeated that government and scattered its allied al-Qaeda operatives, who had announced their complicity in the September 11 attack. But international collaboration forged in the face of novel terrorist threats faded when the government of U.S. president George W. Bush determined to invade

---

[1] Jack C. Plano and Robert E. Riggs, *Forging World Order* (New York: Macmillan, 1967), 7.

[2] Bruce Russett and John R. Oneal, *Triangulating Peace; Democracy, Interdependence, and International Organizations* (New York: Norton, 2001), 10, 29, 35.

Iraq in the spring of 2003, against the will of the Security Council. Secretary-General Kofi Annan, who viewed the invasion as a violation of international law, lamented the crisis confronting the United Nations as its most powerful member (and key founder) appeared to reject the UN Charter's principle of collective security, initiated a blunt foreign policy of unilateralism, and, for the moment at least, inveighed against an ineffectual United Nations.

Although the United Nations remained for many in the world as an institution accepting of appeal to still the noise and to medicate the victims, the euphoric moment of the early 1990s seemed long ago, and much more pessimistic appraisals of international possibility entered the public discourse. Some, such as former U.S. secretary of state Henry Kissinger, simply dismissed the United Nations as an insignificant factor for addressing the world's pains.[3] Professor Samuel P. Huntington provided an even darker assessment, beginning with his stunning essay "The Clash of Civilizations?" Huntington challenged the notion of a universal liberalism ever organizing the world. Instead he offered a more disquieting suggestion, namely, that the future world would be plagued by serious clashes between and among deeply different "civilizations" and cultures. Western civilization was but one of some seven or eight distinct civilizations, each with its own unique cluster of political and social ideas, standards of behavior, and, above all, religion. He predicted the certain and perilous collision of incompatible and suspicious civilizations and urged an end to soft optimism, including any expectation that a flawed United Nations could somehow gloss over such differences.[4] Huntington experienced something of a revival after 2001, as tension between Islamic and Western nations materialized following the terrorist actions in the United States and the U.S. military response, the Arab-Israeli situation deteriorated, religious and ethnic violence erupted in Southeast Asia and across the larger Middle East, and the Balkans split along religious lines.

Other critics were equally depressing. Princeton professor Paul Kennedy, in his widely read book *Preparing for the Twenty-first Century,*[5] offered up a dreary recital of unmanageable worldwide demographic explosion, rampant environmental despoliation, risky biotechnological advances, malnutrition, uncured diseases, ethnic strife, and more. Journalist Robert Kaplan's *The Ends of the Earth* added more misery to the picture. Traveling in remote areas in Africa, the Middle East, and South and Southeast Asia, Kaplan found a nether world in perilous disintegration, plagued by overpopulation,

lack of education, disease, environmental disasters, rampant crime and corruption, anarchy, and civic collapse. "The idea," he insisted, "that a global elite like the UN can engineer reality from above is . . . absurd."[6] In the midst of the tension between the United Nations and Washington over the Iraq imbroglio, some U.S. writers—less concerned with scholarly detachment than the authors mentioned just above—wrote critical screeds against the world organization that appealed to an apparently growing minority of detractors.[7]

Toward Internationalism

Undoubtedly, as we proceed to face the new century more crises will occur and more voices will be raised to find wanting any claim that human society collectively and through international organizations can reasonably address world problems and make life for the world's inhabitants a bit better. We must concede that conflict in the formal relations between and among nations, empires, and peoples has characterized human activity since the millennia before the common era.[8] The diffusion and ultimate availability of texts and treaties dealing with such relations suggests a pattern in world history, however, of cross-cultural intercourse among political elites the world over that led in time to what might be called international relations. Basic principles and precedents emerged as different communities sought to impose order on their mutual relations and to resolve disagreements without the resort to force, unless those principles or their interests might allow or require it.

Empire

Still, for most of history public order was maintained by hierarchical imperial administrations whose dominance was punctuated by sporadic uprisings and dissolution, too often resulting in violence.[9] As a rule the great periods of Chinese history are considered to be those times when powerful consolidating empires brought pervasive peace, some prosperity, Confucianist (or later, Maoist) standards of conduct, artistic grandeur, and systematic rule to a society that nonetheless

---

[3] Henry Kissinger, *Diplomacy* (New York: Simon and Schuster, 1994), 249–50.

[4] Samuel P. Huntington, *The Clash of Civilizations and the Remaking of World Order* (New York: Simon and Schuster, 1996).

[5] Paul Kennedy, *Preparing for the Twenty-first Century* (New York: Random House, 1993). Kennedy's later book, *The Parliament of Man: The Past, Present, and Future of the UN* (New York: Random House, 2006) offers, however, a positive assessment of the UN.

[6] Robert Kaplan, *The Ends of the Earth* (New York: Random House, 1996), 436.

[7] See, for example, Eric Shawn, *The UN Exposed: How the United Nations Sabotages American Security and Fails the World* (New York: Sentinel, 2007).

[8] See Raymond Cohen and Raymond Westbrook, eds., *Amarna Diplomacy: The Beginnings of International Relations* (Baltimore: Johns Hopkins 2000); and James B. Pritchard, ed., *Ancient Near Eastern Texts Relating to the Old Testament* (Princeton, N.J.: Princeton University Press, 1969), 199–206, 529–41.

[9] Here and elsewhere in this Introduction liberal use has been made of chapter 1 of John Allphin Moore, Jr., and Jerry Pubantz, *To Create a New World? American Presidents and the United Nations* (New York: Peter Lang Publishers, 1999).

intermittently plunged into chaotic and disruptive civil strife. The Roman Empire is the prototypical administrative unit of the Western legacy. Rome brought stability, peace (the Pax Romana), law, infrastructure, a common language, and eventually Christianity to the known Western world. Byzantium was the imperial reflection of Rome in much of Eastern Europe, and it lasted longer and left an impressive legacy of Slavic orthodox culture neither nationalist nor liberal in configuration. The Ottoman Empire imposed a flexible bureaucracy on a wide swath of land with an extremely diverse population. And great Russian empires, whether Romanov or Bolshevik, brought to heel the squabbling medley of ethnic groups covering its large landmass. As a rule, when the imperial power was challenged the consequence was unwelcome disruption (the 19th-century Taiping rebellion in China provides an example). Empire, whether imposed willingly and brutally or reluctantly and benignly, seemed the common solution to international disorder. In fact, as late as the turn of the last century, international diplomacy was something characteristically conducted among empires (Romanovs in Eurasia, Manchus in China, Ottomans in the Middle East, Hapsburgs in south-central Europe, Hohenzollerns in Germany and east-central Europe, and the British and French worldwide).

Nation-States

What might be termed the "post-empire" era of political organization is more familiar to the modern world. The idea of "national sovereignty" provided nation-states the ultimate authority over populations within discernible boundaries. The nation-state, considered to have originated in Europe in the 15th and 16th centuries, heralded what some scholars have called "international anarchy." Since no commanding sovereign authority rested above the nations, international order depended on the good faith of its individual sovereign members. In the West this phenomenon led to the development of modern international relations and international law. Scholars and practitioners such as Hugo Grotius (1583–1645) and Emmerich de Vattel (1714–67) sought to codify rules of international behavior, on the understanding that each sovereign state would determine whether to abide by them. This "state of nature" in international matters posited an underlying possibility of conflict. An initial response to this problem was the theory of "balance of power." This meant that if any one nation were to gain overwhelming power so as to represent a danger to others, they would join together to restrain—that is balance—the powerful entity. In addition to balance of power, early European theorists proffered notions of what we might call international human rights law. The earliest approaches to this issue came from alarm about the treatment of civilians during the brutal religious wars, particularly the Thirty Years' War (1618–48). Grotius and Vattel, and their readers in Europe and America, sought to codify into an embryonic international law

accepted practices against what we have come to call "war crimes." Moreover, by way of the Peace of Westphalia that ended the Thirty Years' War, sovereignty became the criterion for authority in any political entity. Thus, sovereign rulers were authorized to determine the religion of any state, in order to avoid internal wars between competing religions, which too often had drawn in outside forces. As a consequence, by the "Westphalian" settlement, Europe came to be characterized by sovereign nation-states theoretically abiding by an international law regarding the rules of war.

Following World War I, new nation-states surfaced in central Europe. In 1947 India and Pakistan became independent of Great Britain, while various states emerged out of the former Ottoman Empire and the mandates administered there by Britain and France. By the 1960s many new states in the "developing world" gained independence. The nation-state had become the accepted mode of political organization.

The Concert of Europe

The American and French Revolutions brought to world politics the idea of universal principles applicable at all times and to all peoples. The idea that all human beings were, by nature, equal inspired but also disturbed existing politics. The French Revolution culminated in a long world war and the age of Napoleon. The victorious allies who finally defeated the French general met at Vienna during 1814–15 and restructured Europe and its diplomatic practices in an attempt to bring order to the continent and avoid another descent into violence. The Congress of Vienna crafted a complex plan to build a peaceful Europe. Diplomats agreed on a new and transformed balance of power, complemented by territorial compromise among all the former belligerents, monarchical legitimacy and restoration, and an agreement to meet in the future to consult on actions to take to meet disruptive crises (signaling the so-called congress system of European affairs).[10] Often considered a conservative settlement, the Vienna program was followed by a reasonably tranquil 19th century, which experienced a creative expansion of international organizations. Early river commissions, such as the Central Rhine Commission (1815) and the European Danube Commission (1856), were examples. The International Red Cross was in place by the middle of the century, and the International Telegraphic Union (1865) and the Universal Postal Union (1874) paved the way for numerous future international agencies in fields as diverse as narcotic drugs, agriculture, health, weights and measures, railroads, time zones, and tariffs. The 1883 Paris Convention for the Protection of Industrial Property and the Berne Convention for the Protection of Literary and Artistic Works (1886) brought issues of protecting patents and copyrights into the larger

---

[10] Paul W. Schroeder, *The Transformation of European Politics, 1763–1848* (Oxford: Clarendon, 1994).

realm of international law. In 1899 and 1907, the Hague conferences marked a culminating phase in the arbitration movement, establishing the Permanent Court of Arbitration and expanding rules governing arbitral procedures.

Twentieth-Century Crisis

But crises challenged the arrangements of the Concert of Europe and the progress in international cooperation right up to the plunge into the Great War of 1914–18. When that disastrous war ended, a new participant encroached into the club of the more traditional great powers to attempt a solution to the disorder that had caused the war. American president Woodrow Wilson joined others at the Paris Peace Conference in 1918–19. He brought with him positions he had earlier articulated in his Fourteen Points, including an outline for a new worldwide organization—a League of Nations—committed to collective security and to the elimination of war. When the peacemakers arrived in the Paris suburb of Versailles to sign the completed agreement, there were several compromises that troubled Wilson's most resolute supporters. Wilson, who had been welcomed to Europe as a savior, became by the end of the negotiations the target of nationalist frustrations abroad and partisan bickering at home. Almost no one was happy with the final national boundaries, and opponents in the United States complained that the president had made too many compromises in Paris and feared that he had overcommitted the country to international collective security. In September 1919, campaigning for Senate approval of the League, the president collapsed following a stroke in Colorado. His resulting illness and the growing opposition to his plans resulted in the Senate's refusal to ratify the peace agreement and thus deny U.S. entrance into the new League of Nations. Still, without doubt the Wilsonian principles of "self-determination" and "internationalism," though from a certain perspective ominously antipodal, had been clearly presented to the world's peoples.

The Versailles settlement may have been doomed to failure irrespective of the American snub. Statesmen at Paris had before them a dangerously disintegrating world. Most of the major organizing empires of the previous century were gone. The Manchu dynasty in China had collapsed in 1911, replaced by a weak republican government, and a disruptive civil war followed. In Russia, a Bolshevik revolution ended the rule of the Romanovs but found itself in control of a truncated state, the former empire having lost considerable territory to the Germans months before the war ended. By war's end, the Hohenzollerns in Germany and the Hapsburg rulers of the Austro-Hungarian Empire were likewise gone, as was the Ottoman Empire, now completely dissolved. Within the resulting vacuums in the center of Europe, in the Middle East, and elsewhere left by these disappearances were a variety of religions and a myriad of ethnic entities that now demanded sovereign national independence along religious and ethnic lines. From a certain perspective, world leaders

have since 1918 been trying to restore order out of the chaos left by World War I.

Despite the American rebuff, the League, guided by its Covenant (its founding document), came into being and functioned until the world descended into the next round of world discord in the late 1930s. Three permanent organs marked the originality of the new experiment—an Assembly with equal representation from all member states, a Council of four permanent members (Britain, France, Italy, and Japan) comprising at first four and then six nonpermanent seats, and a Secretariat. Each of these signified advances in the development of international institutions. Although earlier international conferences had made some use of secretariats, the League Secretariat, providing centralized administration, expert advice, and day-to-day coordination, embodied a novel concept of a permanent international civil service. Outside the Covenant framework, but related to the League, were a Permanent Court of International Justice (the so-called World Court) and the International Labour Organization. Despite its ultimate failure, the League's organizational structure and its various activities provided a basis for its UN progeny.

By the end of the 1930s the League became effectively inoperative and World War II erupted. Seeds for a new organization were planted in the Atlantic Charter of August 14, 1941, issued by U.S. president Franklin Roosevelt and British prime minister Winston Churchill. The document obliquely referred to the future "establishment of a wider and permanent system of general security." On January 1, 1942, with the United States now in the war, 26 nations joined in signing a Declaration by United Nations (a term coined by Roosevelt), reaffirming the principles of the Atlantic Charter and committing themselves to defeat of the Axis powers. At a meeting in Moscow in October 1943, the foreign ministers of the United States, the Soviet Union, Great Britain, and China signed the Moscow Declaration on General Security, explicitly recognizing "the necessity of establishing at the earliest practicable date a general international organization." Planning for the new body had been centered in the U.S. State Department, where Secretary of State Cordell Hull organized a special committee of advisers to draft a proposal as the new organization's governing document. The committee's draft charter became the outline that subsequently was crafted into the final UN Charter. Talks in August and September 1944, at Dumbarton Oaks, an estate in Washington, D.C., furthered planning. At the crucial Yalta Conference, held in the Russian Crimea in February 1945, Roosevelt, Churchill, and Stalin hammered out the final compromises that became the basis for the San Francisco Conference on International Organization, which, in June 1945, witnessed the signing of the completed charter. With sufficient ratifications, the United Nations came into being at 4:50 P.M. on October 24, 1945.

The challenges confronting the UN's founders were not the same as those facing the world community in the early 21st century, but they were no less momentous: Western leaders needed to assuage Russian suspicions of any Western-bred organization to which Moscow would be asked to commit; the United States was obliged to convince its own people and the rest of the world that it would not again retreat from leadership in this postwar period; Britain required encouragement to complete the Wilsonian dream of the dismantling of worldwide empires, the largest of which was administered from London; the defeated nations needed to be reconstructed and fused into the new global framework; urgent rebuilding and rehabilitation of a war-devastated world required action; displaced persons and roaming refugees had want of immediate attention; the world's economy demanded restitution and rational orderliness; and the globe awaited a general, broad, and forceful commitment to those fundamental human rights so long promised by enlightened liberals and so clearly desecrated in recent times. Whatever criticisms can be mounted against the early United Nations, we must remark that it—and its associated organs—met and resolved every one of those challenges within a few short years following the most destructive war in history.

To the Millennium

Although the League of Nations was a model for the United Nations, in important respects the new organization was different from its predecessor. The League had been ensconced in the full Treaty of Versailles; thus to reject the League a nation had to reject the entire peace agreement, as was the case in 1919 with the United States. The United Nations, conversely, was purposely separated from the peace treaties that ended World War II; President Roosevelt, informed by Wilson's lack of success, determined on a separate process of ratification to assure U.S. participation in the new world organization. The League Covenant had been a traditional agreement among governments, called in the Covenant "The High Contracting Parties." The Preamble of the later Charter begins, "We the *peoples* of the United Nations."[11] The League required unanimous votes in both the Assembly and the Council, but decision making in the United Nations is more flexible.[12] Parties to a dispute before the League were prohibited from voting because of the obvious conflict of interest. In the United Nations, in a concession to the realities of power politics, member states had no such limitations. When coupled with the veto, this meant that a permanent member of the Security Council could block UN action.

The organization of the United Nations, which was initially something of a mystery to Soviet leader Stalin, rings familiar to citizens of the Western world or those conversant with presidential or Westminster-style parliamentary systems of government. For example there are legislative (the General Assembly), executive (the Secretariat combined with the Security Council), and judicial (the International Court of Justice) branches, and the Charter emphasizes equal trade and the "territorial and administrative integrity" of sovereign states (Article 2) and, supplemented by the Universal Declaration of Human Rights, individual freedoms.

All this notwithstanding, the United Nations too often is marginalized in discussions of world affairs. Part of this disregard undoubtedly is due to certain misconceptions about the organization. It is useful to remember that the United Nations is a "confederation," not a unitary or federally organized government. That is, it is made up of sovereign members; it has no overarching authority apart from those states, and it is then only what its members make of it. Thus it acts effectively only by way of consensus, not majoritarianism. Moreover, it cannot fulfill "utopian notions" of world peace and order because, as former Israeli representative Abba Eban reminded, it is an "international organization . . . a *mechanism,* not a policy or principle."[13] Or, as Secretary-General Dag Hammarskjöld once explained: "The United Nations is not . . . a superstate, able to act outside the framework of decisions by its member governments. It is an instrument for negotiation . . . [it] can serve, but not substitute itself for the efforts of its member governments."[14]

Also, it may be instructive to note that in the aftermath of the cold war, the United Nations is not alone at a pinnacle above all other institutions that connect the world; rather, it serves as a consolidating axis for all those organizations. The intricate international order purposely crafted following World War II has proved durable and mature. By 2008, the General Agreement on Tariffs and Trade (GATT) had become the World Trade Organization (WTO); the World Bank and the International Monetary Fund (IMF) had extended their activities; at Vienna in 1993 human rights were proclaimed and accepted by most nations as "universal"; the North Atlantic Treaty Organization (NATO) was expanding its membership far to the east; other regional groupings from the North American Free Trade Association (NAFTA) to the Association of Southeast Asian Nations (ASEAN) to the Asian Pacific Economic Cooperation Organization (APEC) to the European Union (EU) linked sovereign states into ever-widening and more closely knit international units. And the United Nations, unlike any comparable multistate organization in history, remained operative for an unprecedented six decades, expanding its membership to virtual universality. As this expansion continued well into the new millennium, the organization found itself at the forefront in some of the most significant international developments. Apart from the oft-remarked activities of UN agencies in bringing about social and health reforms, consider, just for example, the

---

[11] See the entries for "Charter" and "Covenant."

[12] See the entry for "Voting."

[13] "The U.N. Idea Revisited," *Foreign Affairs* (September–October 1995), 40.

[14] *New York Times Magazine* (September 15, 1957), 21. Quoted in Plano, *Forging World Order,* 8.

following: (1) Israel came into being by the Jewish Agency's unilateral implementation of a UN resolution, initiating the modern Middle East quandary; the UN has been the central institution in defining, in international legal terms, the nature of the Middle East problem. From the establishment of Israel to the crisis of 1956, UN Resolutions 242 and 338, the Camp David Accords, the handshake at the White House in 1993, the impasse of 2001, and the formation of the "Quartet" of Russia, the United States, the EU, and the UN, the internationally recognized legal basis of any possible resolution of this seemingly intractable dilemma rests in a long-term connection with the United Nations. (2) The remarkable developments in South Africa and Namibia over the last decade of the 20th century, resulting in the purging of apartheid and the introduction of democratic government in South Africa and full independence of Namibia, were conditional upon UN resolutions. (3) The 1993 elections in troubled Cambodia took place under the legal rubric of UN resolutions and with UN administration, and again in 1998 international monitors returned to watch over another election and the United Nations remained involved as part of the international effort to establish a war crimes tribunal to address the forced deaths of some 1.5 million Cambodians during the 1970s. (4) The ongoing negotiations to settle the Cyprus problem are based in UN resolutions. (5) By the mid 1990s the United Nations, by passing resolutions and establishing observer groups to provide supervision, guided the end of civil wars and the ultimate general elections in three beleaguered Central American countries: Nicaragua, El Salvador, and Guatemala. (6) The Gulf War in 1991, which removed Iraqi forces from Kuwait, was based on UN Security Council resolutions (particularly 678); thus, the war was a genuine "collective security" operation designed to uphold the sovereignty of a UN member. (7) The Dayton Accords of 1995 were U.S.-led impositions to implement the UN's insistence on ending the brutal fighting in the former Yugoslavia; as of the turn of the century, the UN Mission in Bosnia and Herzegovina was still in place, coordinating a wide range of responsibilities, including provision of humanitarian and relief supplies, human rights enforcement, removal of land mines, monitoring of elections, and rebuilding infrastructure. (8) In Kosovo, the UN Kosovo Force (KFOR), starting in spring 1999, supervised the final peace settlement following the NATO war against Serbian domination of the province, and the UN Interim Administration for Kosovo, which monitored the relatively peaceful municipal elections in the province in October 2000, was considered an example of successful nation-building by the United Nations. (9) In 1999 the United Nations took over administration in the embattled territory of East Timor, setting up a transitional authority in the area as it proceeded to separate from Indonesia; in late August, 2001, UN monitors administered a trouble-free election for East Timor, providing self-rule—and independence in May 2002—for its

inhabitants for the first time since the Portuguese arrived 400 years earlier. (10) UN war crimes tribunals were, as of 2007, active in The Hague, in Phnom Penh, Cambodia, in Freetown, Sierra Leone, and in Arusha, Tanzania, prosecuting and trying alleged war criminals from the Balkan, Cambodian, Sierra Leonean, and Rwandan civil wars. In each case, the United Nations legitimized a new era in international politics that defended victims against their own governments despite traditional claims of state sovereignty. (11) In 2000 the United Nations, with broad worldwide consensus, embarked on its most ambitious, if problematic, collective effort—the Millennium Development Goals to combat poverty and child mortality, to achieve gender equality and basic education for the world's youth, and to bring sustainable and environmentally sound development to the poorest regions of the globe.[15]

It is almost trite to say that something called "globalization," which began long ago, has accelerated in our own time, conforming to a conscious policy initiated in the bleak year of 1945 to attract the world into a cooperative international diplomacy. Today the world and individual nations are characterized by both integrating and fragmenting pressures, occasionally at the same time. Along with alarming evidence of ethnic tension, national rivalries, religious fanaticism, ancient prejudices, and powerful grievances, we also have centripetal forces such as the World Wide Web, extensive travel, CNN International and Al-Jazeera television networks, unprecedented mixing of peoples and cultures, and a substantive, developing, credible set of international norms, agreed to at least rhetorically by most nations. The United Nations finds itself at the pivot of this maelstrom.

Of course the human experiment is problematic. Whether we are on the verge of unmitigated disaster or not remains questionable. Whether we are capable of grasping with sharp discernment the challenges to our existence, and dealing with them sensibly, while providing a life just a little bit better for just a few more of our fellow human beings, remains open to debate. Cassandras always have the advantage, since misery and disappointment are constants. Idealists, or even realists who seek orderliness and progress in human affairs, can never be satisfied. And, of course, in the end, as J. M. Keynes so famously reminded us, we are all dead.

But we must insist on applauding united efforts to relieve the downtrodden, expand opportunity to ever more of our earth's citizens, promote self-government, assure human rights everywhere, and provide peace, so that all of us, individually if we wish, and collectively if we will, can savor our moment on Earth. The dense web of international connection represented by the United Nations and its affiliated institutions is, in our time, perhaps the principal mechanism for performing these commendable labors.

---

[15] See "Millennium Development Goal" entry.

CONTRIBUTORS

Douglas J. Becker
University of Southern California

Marjorie W. Bray
California State University, Los Angeles

Marie I. Chevrier
University of Texas, Dallas

Errol MacGregor Clauss
Salem College

Cynthia C. Combs
University of North Carolina, Charlotte

Patrick M. Grady
Global Economics Ltd.

Kenneth J. Grieb
University of Wisconsin, Oshkosh

Robert J. Griffiths
University of North Carolina at Greensboro

Annette Skovsted Hansen
Columbia University

Matthew A. Jeffreys
University of North Carolina at Greensboro

Irina Kebreau
Pace University

Daniel K. Lewis
California State Polytechnic University, Pomona

Michael S. Lindberg
Elmhurst College

Andrei I. Maximenko
Benedict College

Sean F. McMahon
University of Alberta

Robert E. McNamara
Sonoma State University

Amy S. Patterson
Calvin College

Megan E. Reif
University of Michigan

Sandra C. Rein
University of Alberta

Donna M. Schlagheck
Wright State University

G. Sidney Silliman
California State Polytechnic University, Pomona

Malinda S. Smith
Athabasca University

Karen J. Vogel
Hamline University

Thomas J. Weiler
University of Bonn

Shelton L. Williams
Austin College

ACRONYMS

A21	Agenda 21	CAB	Conventional Arms Branch, DDA
ACABQ	Advisory Committee on Administrative and Budgetary Questions	CABEI	Central American Bank for Economic Integration
ACC	Administrative Committee on Coordination	CAT	Committee on Torture
ADF	African Development Fund	CBD	Convention on Biological Diversity
AfDB	African Development Bank	CCAQ	Consultative Committee on Administrative Questions, ACC
AFRC	Armed Forces Revolutionary Council, Sierra Leone	CCD	Conference of the Committee on Disarmament
AFTRCW	African Training and Research Centre for Women	CCD	Convention to Combat Desertification
ALD	Assignment of Limited Duration (short-term UN contract)	CCPCJ	Commission on Crime Prevention and Criminal Justice
AMIS	African Union Mission in Sudan	CCPOQ	Consultative Committee on Programme and Operational Questions, ACC
AOSIS	Alliance of Small Island States	CCSA	Inter-Agency Committee for the Coordination of Statistical Activities, CEB
APEC	Asia-Pacific Economic Cooperation		
AsDB	Asian Development Bank	CCW	Convention on Certain Conventional Weapons
ASEAN	Association of Southeast Asian Nations		
ASP	Assembly of State Parties, International Criminal Court	CD	Conference on Disarmament
		CDB	Caribbean Development Bank
ASPAC	Asian and Pacific Council	CDF	Comprehensive Development Framework, World Bank
ATA	Afghan Transitional Authority		
BC	Basel Convention on the Control of Transboundary Movements of Hazardous Wastes and Their Disposal	CDP	Committee for Development Policy, ECOSOC
		CEB	United Nations System Chief Executives Board for Coordination
BDPA	Beijing Declaration and Platform for Action		
BINUB	United Nations Integrated Office in Burundi	CEDAW	Committee on the Elimination of Discrimination Against Women, also Convention on the Elimination of All Forms of Discrimination Against Women
BIRPI	United International Bureaux for the Protection of Intellectual Property		
BOAD	West African Development Bank		
BONUCA	United Nations Office in the Central African Republic	CEMAC	Central African Economic and Monetary Community
BPOA	Barbados Programme of Action	CERD	Committee on the Elimination of All Forms of Racial Discrimination
BWC	Convention on the Prohibition of the Development, Production and Stockpiling of Bacteriological (Biological) and Toxin Weapons and on their Destruction	CERF	Central Emergency Response Fund, OCHA
		CESCR	Committee on Economic, Social and Cultural Rights
BWIs	Bretton Woods Institutions		
C24	Committee of Twenty-Four	CFA	Committee on Freedom of Association, ILO

CHR	Commission on Human Rights
CIA	United States Central Intelligence Agency
CICP	Centre for International Crime Prevention
CIDIE	Committee of International Development Institutions on the Environment
CITES	Convention on International Trade in Endangered Species of Wild Fauna and Flora
CLCS	Commission on the Limits of the Continental Shelf
CMS	Convention on the Conservation of Migratory Species of Wild Animals
CMW	Committee on the Protection of the Rights of All Migrant Workers and Members of Their Families
CND	Commission on Narcotic Drugs
CO	Country Office
COMESA	Common Market for Eastern and Southern Africa
CONGO	Conference on Non-governmental Organizations
COP	Conference of the Parties to a UN convention
COPUOS	Committee on the Peaceful Uses of Outer Space
CPA	Comprehensive Peace Agreement
CPC	Committee for Programme and Co-ordination
CPF	Collaborative Partnership on Forests
CPR	Committee of Permanent Representatives, UNEP
CPU	Civilian Police Unit
CRC	Convention on the Rights of the Child
CROC	Committee on the Rights of the Child
CSD	Commission on Sustainable Development
CSocD	Commission for Social Development
CSTD	Commission on Science and Technology for Development
CSW	Commission on the Status of Women
CTBT	Comprehensive Test Ban Treaty
CTBTO	Comprehensive Test Ban Treaty Organization
CTC	Counter-Terrorism Committee of the Security Council
CTED	Counter-Terrorism Executive Directorate, CTC
CTITF	Counter-Terrorism Implementation Task Force
CWC	Convention on the Prohibition of the Development, Production, Stockpiling and Use of Chemical Weapons
DAC	Development Assistance Committee
DAM	Department of Administration and Management

DAW	Division for the Advancement of Women, DESA
DDA	Department for Disarmament Affairs
DDRR	Disarmament, Demobilization, Rehabilitation, and Reintegration Programme in Liberia
DDSMS	Department for Development Support and Management Services
DESA	Department of Economic and Social Affairs
DESD	Department of Economic and Social Development
DFID	Department of International Development, Great Britain
DGAACS	Department of General Assembly Affairs and Conference Services
DHA	Department of Humanitarian Affairs
DOALOS	Division for Ocean Affairs and the Law of the Sea
DOMREP	Mission of the Special Representative of the Secretary-General in the Dominican Republic
DPA	Department of Political Affairs, or Darfur Peace Agreement
DPAD	Development Policy and Analysis Division, Department of Economic and Social Affairs
DPCSD	Department for Policy Coordination and Sustainable Development
DPI	Department of Public Information
DPKO	Department of Peacekeeping Operations
DSB	Dispute Settlement Board/WTO
DSG	Deputy Secretary-General
DSU	Understanding on Rules and Procedures Governing the Settlement of Disputes, Marrakesh Protocol
EADB	East African Development Bank
EBRD	European Bank for Reconstruction and Development
ECA	Economic Commission for Africa
ECCC	Extraordinary Chambers in the Courts of Cambodia
ECE	Economic Commission for Europe
EC-ESA	Executive Committee on Economic and Social Affairs
ECLAC	Economic Commission for Latin America and the Caribbean
ECOFIN	Second Committee: Economic and Financial
ECOMOG	Economic Community of West African States Monitoring Group
ECOSOC	Economic and Social Council
ECOWAS	Economic Community of West African States
ECWA	Economic Commission for Western Asia
EIB	European Investment Bank

EIT	Economy in Transition
ENDC	Eighteen Nation Disarmament Committee
ENRIN	Environment and Natural Resources Information Networking, UNEP
EPTA	Expanded Program of Technical Assistance
ESAF	Enhanced Structural Adjustment Facility, IMF
ESCAP	Economic Commission for Asia and the Pacific
ESCWA	Economic and Social Commission for Western Asia
ESP	Committee on Employment and Social Policy, ILO
EU	European Union
EVI	Economic Vulnerability Index
FAO	Food and Agriculture Organization
FCTC	Framework Convention on Tobacco Control
FMCT	Fissile Material Cutoff Treaty
FYROM	Former Yugoslav Republic of Macedonia
G8	Group of Eight
G-21	Group of Twenty-One in the Conference on Disarmament
G-77	Group of developing states in the United Nations Conference on Trade and Development
GA	General Assembly
GAINS	Gender Awareness Information and Networking System, INSTRAW
GATT	General Agreement on Tariffs and Trade
GCD	General and Complete Disarmament
GDP	Gross Domestic Product
GEF	Global Environment Facility
GEMS	Global Environment Monitoring System, UNEP
GICHD	Geneva International Centre for Humanitarian Demining
GLEWS	Global Warning and Response System for SARS
GNP	Gross National Product
GPA	Global Programme on AIDS
GONGO	Government-sponsored Non-governmental Organization
GRIPP	*Global Review and Inventory of Population Policies*, DESA
GRULAC	Regional Group for Latin America and Caribbean
GSDF	Global Sustainable Development Facility
HABITAT	United Nations Centre for Human Settlements
HAI	Human Assets Index
HIPC	Heavily Indebted Poor Country
HLCM	High Level Committee on Management, ACC

HLCOMO	High Level Committee of Ministers and Officials, UNEP
HLCP	High Level Committee on Programmes, ACC
HLP	High Level Panel on Threats, Challenges and Change
HONLEA	Subcommission on Illicit Drug Traffic Enforcement Agencies
IACSD	Inter-Agency Committee on Sustainable Development
IACWGE	Inter-Agency Committee on Women and Gender Equality
IANDRDCCP	Inter-Agency Network for Demand Reduction, Drug Control and Crime Prevention, CEB
IANWGE	Inter-Agency Network on Women and Gender Equality, CEB
IADB	Inter-American Development Bank
IAEA	International Atomic Energy Agency
IATF	Inter-Agency Task Force
IBE	International Bureau of Education
IBRD	International Bank of Reconstruction and Development (World Bank)
IACSD	Inter-Agency Committee on Sustainable Development
IASC	Inter-Agency Standing Committee
ICANN	Internet Corporation for Assigned Names and Numbers
ICAO	International Civil Aviation Organization
ICBL	International Campaign to Ban Landmines
ICC	International Computing Centre
ICC	International Criminal Court
ICCPR	International Covenant on Civil and Political Rights
ICD	Islamic Corporation for the Development of the Private Sector, Islamic Development Bank
ICESCR	International Covenant on Economic, Social, and Cultural Rights
ICGFI	International Consultative Group on Food Irrigation
ICIEC	Islamic Corporation for the Insurance of Investment and Export Credit, Islamic Development Bank
ICJ	International Court of Justice
ICPD	International Conference on Population and Development
ICRC	International Committee of the Red Cross
ICS	International Centre for Science and High Technology
ICSC	International Civil Service Commission
ICSID	International Centre for Settlement of Investment Disputes
ICTR	International Criminal Tribunal for Rwanda

ICTs	Information and Communications Technologies
ICTY	International Criminal Tribunal for the Former Yugoslavia
ICU	Islamic Courts Union in Somalia
IDA	International Development Association
IDB	Inter-American Development Bank, or Islamic Development Bank
IDNDR	International Decade for Natural Disaster Reduction
IDP	Internally Displaced Person
IEFR	International Emergency Food Reserve
IFAD	International Fund for Agricultural Development
IFC	International Finance Corporation
IFOR	Implementation Force: Yugoslavia
IGAD	Inter-governmental Authority on Development
IGF	Internet Governance Forum
IGO	Inter-Governmental Organization
IHR	International Health Regulations of WHO
ILC	International Law Commission
ILO	International Labour Organization
ILOAT	International Labour Organization Administrative Tribunal
IMCO	Inter-Governmental Maritime Consultative Organization
IMF	International Monetary Fund
IMG	International Management Group
IMIS	Integrated Management Information System
IMO	International Maritime Organization
INC	Intergovernmental Negotiating Committee for the UNFCCC
INCB	International Narcotics Control Board
INCD	Intergovernmental Negotiating Committee on Desertification
ICNRD	International Conferences of New and Restored Democracies
INSTRAW	International Research and Training Institute for the Advancement of Women
INTERFET	International Force in East Timor
IOC	Intergovernmental Oceanographic Commission, UNESCO
IPCC	Intergovernmental Panel on Climate Change
IPF	Intergovernmental Panel on Forests
IPTF	United Nations International Police Task Force, UNMIBH
IRPTC	International Register for Potentially Toxic Chemicals
IRTI	Islamic Research and Training Institute, Islamic Development Bank
ISBA	International Seabed Authority
ISCC	Information Systems Coordination Committee, ACC
ITC	International Trade Centre UNCTAD/WTO
ITFC	International Islamic Trade Finance Corporation, Islamic Development Bank
ITLOS	International Tribunal for the Law of the Sea
ITTA	International Tropical Timber Agreement
ITTO	International Tropical Timber Organization
ITU	International Telecommunications Union
IWY	International Women's Year
JAG	Joint Advisory Group, International Trade Centre UNCTAD/WTO
JEM	Justice and Equality Movement
JIAS	Joint Interim Administrative Structure, UNMIK
JIU	Joint Inspections Unit
JSAP	Judicial System Assessment Program, UNMIBH
JUNIC	Joint United Nations Information Committee, ACC
JUSSCANNZ	Non-EU industrialized states
KFOR	Kosovo Force
KPCS	Kimberley Process Certification Scheme
LDC	Less Developed Country, and Least Developed Country
LDCR	Least Developed Country Report
LILS	Committee on Legal Issues and International Labour Standards, ILO
LLDC	Land-locked Least Developed Country
MCC	Management Coordination Committee
MDG	Millennium Development Goal
MDI	Monitoring, Database and Information Branch, DDA
MDRI	Multilateral Debt Relief Initiative
MERCOSUR	Mercado Común del Sur (Southern Common Market)
MICAH	United Nations Civilian Support Mission in Haiti
MICIVIH	International Civilian Mission to Haiti
MIF	Multinational Interim Force (Haiti)
MIGA	Multilateral Investment Guarantee Agency
MINUCI	United Nations Mission in Côte d'Ivoire
MINUGUA	United Nations Verification Mission in Guatemala
MINURCA	United Nations Mission in the Central African Republic
MINURSO	United Nations Mission for the Referendum in Western Sahara
MINUSAL	United Nations Mission in El Salvador
MINUSTAH	United Nations Stabilization Mission in Haiti
MIPONUH	United Nations Civilian Police Mission in Haiti
MONUA	United Nations Observer Mission in Angola
MONUC	United Nations Organization Mission in the Democratic Republic of the Congo
MOP	Meeting of the Parties to a UN convention
MOU	Memorandum of Understanding

NAM	Non-Aligned Movement
NATO	North Atlantic Treaty Organization
NBC	Nuclear, Biological, and Chemical (Weapons)
NDF	Nordic Development Fund
NEEP	National Emergency Employment Programme (Afghanistan)
NEPAD	New Partnership for Africa's Development
NGLS	United Nations Non-Governmental Liaison Service
NGO	Non-governmental Organization
NIB	Nordic Investment Bank
NIDS	New International Development Strategy
NIEO	New International Economic Order
NIIO	New International Information Order
NIICO	New International Information and Communication Order
NNWS	Non-Nuclear Weapons State
NPT	Non-Proliferation of Nuclear Weapons Treaty
NTBs	Non-Tariff Barriers
NWS	Nuclear Weapons State
OAS	Organization of American States
OAU	Organization of African Unity
OC	Organizational Committee, ACC
OCHA	Office for the Coordination of Humanitarian Affairs
ODA	Official Development Assistance
ODCCP	Office for Drug Control and Crime Prevention
OECD	Organization for Economic Cooperation and Development
OECS	Organization of Eastern Caribbean States
OEOA	Office of Emergency Operations in Africa
OFFP	Oil-for-Food Programme
OHCHR	Office of the United Nations High Commissioner for Human Rights
OHR	Office of the High Representative for Bosnia and Herzegovina
OHRLLS	Office of the High Representative for the Least Developed Countries, Landlocked Developing Countries, and Small Island Developing States
OIC	Organization of the Islamic Conference
OIE	Organization for Animal Health
OIOS	Office of Internal Oversight Services
OIP	Office of Iraq Program
OLA	Office of Legal Affairs
ONUB	United Nations Operation in Burundi
ONUC	United Nations Operation in the Congo
ONUCA	United Nations Observer Group in Central America
ONUMOZ	United Nations Operation in Mozambique
ONUSAL	United Nations Observer Mission in El Salvador
ONUVEH	United Nations Observer Mission to Verify the Electoral Process in Haiti
ONUVEN	United Nations Observer Mission to Verify the Electoral Process in Nicaragua
OOSA	Office for Outer Space Affairs
OPANAL	Organization for the Prohibition of Nuclear Weapons in Latin America and the Caribbean
OPCW	Organization for the Prohibition of Chemical Weapons
OPE	Office for Projects Execution, UNDP
OSAA	Office of the Special Adviser on Africa
OSAGI	Office of the Special Adviser on Gender Issues and Advancement of Women
OSCAL	Office of the Special Coordinator for Africa and the Least Developed Countries, DESA
OSCE	Organization for Security and Cooperation in Europe
OSGAP	Office of the Secretary-General in Afghanistan and Pakistan
OSRSGCAAC	Office of the Special Representative of the Secretary-General on Children and Armed Conflict
P-5	Permanent Five Members of the Security Council
PACD	Plan of Action to Combat Desertification
PAERD	Programme of Action for African Economic Recovery and Development
PAHO	Pan-American Health Organization
PAROS	Preventing an Arms Race in Outer Space
PAS	Performance Appraisal System
PCA	Permanent Court of International Arbitration
PCB	Programme Coordinating Board, UNAIDS
PDMs	Practical Disarmament Measures
PFA	Programme, Financial and Administrative Committee, ILO
PKO	Peacekeeping Operation
POPIN	*Population Information Network*, DESA
PrepCom	Preparatory Committee
PRGF	Poverty Reduction and Growth Facility, IMF
PUNE	Peaceful Uses of Nuclear Energy
R2P	Responsibility to Protect
RAMSAR	Convention on Wetlands
RCD	Congolese Rally for Democracy
RDB	Regional Disarmament Branch, DDA
RDMHQ	Rapid Deployable Mission Headquarters
ROEs	Rules of Engagement
SAARC	South Asian Association for Regional Cooperation
SADC	Southern African Development Community
SAF	Structural Adjustment Facility, IMF
SALW	Small Arms and Light Weapons
SARS	Severe Acute Respiratory Syndrome
SC	Security Council

SCITECH	Commission on Science and Technology
SCN	Standing Committee on Nutrition, CEB
SCSL	Special Court for Sierra Leone
SDR	Special Drawing Right
SEATO	Southeast Asia Treaty Organization
SFOR	Stabilization Force: Yugoslavia
SG	Secretary-General
SHIRBRIG	Multinational Standby Forces High Readiness Brigade
SIA	Special Initiative in Africa
SIDS	Small Island Developing States
SLM	Sudanese Liberation Movement
SMG	Senior Management Group, SG
SNPA	Substantial New Programme of Action
SOCHUM	General Assembly Third Committee: Social, Cultural, and Humanitarian
SPECPOL	Fourth Committee: Special Political
SPLOS	States Parties to the Law of the Sea Convention
SRII	Swedish Research Institute in Istanbul
SRPGMA	Office of the Special Representative for the Prevention of Genocide and Mass Atrocities
SRSG	Special Representative of the Secretary-General
SSOD	Special Session on Disarmament
SUNFED	Special United Nations Fund for Economic Development
SU/TCDC	Special Unit/Technical Cooperation Among Developing Countries
SWAPO	South West Africa People's Organization
TC	Trusteeship Council
TFAP	Tropical Forestry Action Plan
TICAD	Tokyo International Conference on African Development
TNC	Trans-national Corporation
TPB	Terrorism Prevention Branch, UNODC
TSZ	Temporary Security Zone
UDHR	Universal Declaration of Human Rights
UN/NGLS	United Nations Non-Governmental Liaison Service
UNA	United Nations Association
UNAIDS	Joint United Nations Programme on HIV/AIDS
UNAKRT	United Nations Assistance to the Khmer Rouge Trials
UNAMA	United Nations Assistance Mission in Afghanistan
UNAMET	United Nations Mission in East Timor
UNAMI	United Nations Assistance Mission for Iraq
UNAMIC	United Nations Advance Mission in Cambodia
UNAMID	United Nations/African Union Hybrid Operation in Darfur
UNAMIR	United Nations Assistance Mission for Rwanda
UNAMIS	United Nations Advance Mission in the Sudan
UNAMSIL	United Nations Mission in Sierra Leone
UNASOG	United Nations Aouzou Strip Observer Group
UNAT	United Nations Administrative Tribunal
UNAVEM	United Nations Angola Verification Mission
UNCAST	United Nations Conference on Applications of Science and Technology for the Benefit of Less Developed Areas
UNCC	United Nations Compensation Commission
UNCCD	United Nations Convention to Combat Desertification
UNCDF	United Nations Capital Development Fund
UNCED	United Nations Conference on Environment and Development (Earth Summit)
UNCF	United Nations Command in Korea
UNCG	United Nations Convention on the Prevention and Punishment of the Crime of Genocide; or United Nations Communications Group, CEB
UNCHS	United Nations Centre for Human Settlements
UNCI	United Nations Commission for Indonesia
UNCIO	United Nations Conference on International Organization (San Francisco Conference)
UNCIP	United Nations Commission for India and Pakistan
UNCITRAL	United Nations Commission on International Trade Law
UNCJS	United Nations Criminal Justice Standards for Peacekeeping Police
UNCLOS	United Nations Convention on the Law of the Sea
UNCOD	United Nations Committee on Desertification
UNCRO	United Nations Confidence Restoration Operation
UNCTAD	United Nations Conference on Trade and Development
UNDAC	United Nations Disaster Assessment and Coordination System
UNDAFs	United Nations Development Assistance Frameworks
UNDC	United Nations Disarmament Commission
UNDCP	United Nations International Drug Control Programme
UNDG	United Nations Development Group
UNDOF	United Nations Disengagement Observer Force
UNDP	United Nations Development Program
UNDRO	United Nations Disaster Relief Coordinator
UNEF	United Nations Emergency Force
UNEP	United Nations Environment Programme
UNEPRO	United Nations Relief Operation in East Pakistan

UNESCO	United Nations Educational, Scientific and Cultural Organization
UNFCCC	United Nations Framework Convention on Climate Change
UNFF	United Nations Forum on Forests
UNFICYP	United Nations Force in Cyprus
UNFIP	United Nations Fund for International Partnerships
UNFPA	United Nations Population Fund
UNFSDT	United Nations Fund for Science and Technology for Development
UNGIWG	United Nations Geographical Information Working Group, CEB
UNGOMAP	United Nations Good Offices Mission in Afghanistan and Pakistan
UNHCHR	United Nations High Commissioner for Human Rights
UNHCR	United Nations High Commissioner for Refugees
UNICEF	United Nations Children's Fund
UNICPO	United Nations Open-ended, Informal, Consultative Process on Ocean Affairs
UNICRI	United Nations Interregional Crime and Justice Research Institute
UNIDIR	United Nations Institute for Disarmament Research
UNIDO	United Nations Industrial Development Board
UNIFEM	United Nations Development Fund for Women
UNIFIL	United Nations Interim Force in Lebanon
UNIIMOG	United Nations Iran-Iraq Military Observer Group
UNIKOM	United Nations Iraq-Kuwait Observation Mission
UNIOSIL	United Nations Integrated Office in Sierra Leone
UNIPOM	United Nations India-Pakistan Observation Mission
UNISPACE	United Nations Conferences on the Exploration and the Peaceful Uses of Outer Space
UNISPAL	United Nations Information System on the Question of Palestine
UNITAF	Unified Task Force
UNITAR	United Nations Institute for Training and Research
UNITeS	United Nations Information Technology Service
UNKRA	United Nations Korean Reconstruction Agency
UNLDC	United Nations Conference on Least Developed Countries
UNMA	United Mission in Angola
UNMAS	United Nations Mine Action Service
UNMEE	United Nations Mission in Ethiopia and Eritrea
UNMIBH	United Nations Mission in Bosnia and Herzegovina
UNMIH	United Nations Mission in Haiti
UNMIK	United Nations Interim Administration Mission to Kosovo
UNMIL	United Nations Mission in Liberia
UNMIN	United Nations Mission in Nepal
UNMIS	United Nations Mission in the Sudan
UNMISET	United Nations Mission of Support in East Timor
UNMIT	United Nations Integrated Mission in Timor-Leste
UNMOGAP	United Nations Good Offices Mission in Afghanistan and Pakistan
UNMOGIP	United Nations Military Observer Group in India and Pakistan
UNMOP	United Nations Mission of Observers in Prevlaka
UNMOT	United Nations Mission of Observers in Tajikistan
UNMOVIC	United Nations Monitoring, Verification and Inspection Commission
UN-NADAF	United Nations New Agenda for the Development of Africa in the 1990s
UNOA	United Nations Office in Angola
UNOB	United Nations Office in Burundi
UNOCHA	United Nations Office for the Coordination of Humanitarian Assistance to Afghanistan
UNOCI	United Nations Operation in Côte d'Ivoire
UNODC	United Nations Office on Drugs and Crime
UNOG	United Nations Office at Geneva
UNOGBIS	United Nations Peace-building Support Office in Guinea-Bissau
UNOGIL	United Nations Observer Group in Lebanon
UNOIP	United Nations Office of the Iraq Programme
UNOL	United Nations Peace-building Support Office in Liberia
UNOMB	United Nations Observer Mission in Bougainville
UNOMIG	United Nations Observer Mission in Georgia
UNOMIL	United Nations Observer Mission in Liberia
UNOMSIL	United Nations Observer Mission in Sierra Leone
UNOMUR	United Nations Observer Mission for Uganda-Rwanda
UNON	United Nations Office at Nairobi
UNOOSA	United Nations Office for Outer Space Affairs
UNOPS	United Nations Office for Project Services
UNOSOM	United Nations Operations in Somalia
UNOTIL	United Nations Office in Timor-Leste
UNOV	United Nations at Vienna
UNOWA	UN Office of the Special Representative of the Secretary-General for West Africa

UNPAN	United Nations Public Administration Network
UNPFII	United Nations Permanent Forum on Indigenous Issues
UNPKO	United Nations Peacekeeping Operations
UNPOB	United Nations Political Office in Bougainville
UNPOS	United Nations Political Office for Somalia
UNPREDEP	United Nations Preventive Deployment Force in the former Yugoslav Republic of Macedonia
UNPROFOR	United Nations Protection Force
UNPSG	United Nations Civilian Police Support Group
UNPSOG-B	United Nations Peacebuilding Support Office in Guinea-Bissau
UNRFNRE	United Nations Revolving Fund for Natural Resources
UNRISD	United Nations Research Institute for Social Development
UNROD	United Nations Relief Operation in Dacca
UNRRA	United Nations Relief and Rehabilitation Administration
UNRWA	United Nations Relief and Works Agency
UNSAS	United Nations Standby Arrangements System
UNSCEAR	United Nations Scientific Committee on the Effects of Atomic Radiation
UNSCO	Office of the United Nations Special Coordinator for the Middle East
UNSCOB	United Nations Special Committee on the Balkans
UNSCOM	United Nations Special Commission on Iraq
UNSCOP	United Nations Special Commission on Palestine
UNSD	United Nations Statistical Division, DESA
UNSDRI	United Nations Social Defence Research Institute
UNSECOORD	Office of the United Nations Security Coordinator
UNSF	United Nations Security Force
UNSIMIC	United Nations Settlement Implementation Mission in Cyprus
UNSMA	United Nations Special Mission to Afghanistan
UNSMIH	United Nations Support Mission in Haiti
UNSO	United Nations Office to Combat Desertification/United Nations Sudano-Sahalian Office
UNTAC	United Nations Transition Authority in Cambodia
UNTAES	United Nations Transitional Authority in Eastern Slavonia, Baranja and Western Sirmium
UNTAET	United Nations Transition Administration in East Timor
UNTAG	United Nations Transition Assistance Group
UNTCOK	United Nations Temporary Commission on Korea
UNTEA	United Nations Temporary Executive Authority
UNTMIH	United Nations Transition Mission in Haiti
UNTOP	United Nations Tajikistan Office of Peacebuilding
UNTSO	United Nations Truce Supervision Organization
UNU	United Nations University
UNV	United Nations Volunteers
UNWCHR	United Nations World Conference on Human Rights
UNWTO/OMT	World Tourism Organization
UNYOM	United Nations Yemen Observation Mission
UPOV	International Union for the Protection of New Varieties of Plants
UPU	Universal Postal Union
USG	Under Secretary-General
V4D	Volunteerism for Development
VERs	Voluntary Export Restrictions
WAEC	West African Economic Community
WB	World Bank
WCED	World Commission on Environment and Development
WEOG	Western European and Other States Group
WFC	United Nations World Food Council
WFP	World Food Programme
WFUNA	World Federation of United Nations Associations
WGIG	Working Group on Internet Governance
WHO	World Health Organization
WIPO	World Intellectual Property Organization
WMD	Weapons of Mass Destruction
WMO	World Meteorological Organization
WP/SDG	Working Party on the Social Dimension of Globalization, ILO
WSC	World Summit for Children
WSIS	World Summit on the Information Society
WSSD	World Summit for Social Development
WTO	World Trade Organization
WWF	World WAQF Foundation, Islamic Development Bank
WWW	World Weather Watch
ZC	Zangger Committee

abstention from voting   *See* VOTING.

accession

The term *accession,* in international parlance, refers to adherence to or formal acceptance of a TREATY, CONVENTION, international organization, or other form of international agreement. Thus new members may "accede" to an intergovernmental organization—such as the United Nations—or to an international statute. For example, the six original members of the European Economic Community signed a Treaty of Accession to the European Communities in 1972, and in September 2000 the UN MILLENNIUM SUMMIT in New York witnessed several accessions by member states to major international treaties.

See also CONVENTION ON THE PROHIBITION OF THE USE, STOCKPILING, PRODUCTION AND TRANSFER OF ANTI-PERSONNEL MINES AND THEIR DESTRUCTION.

Acheson, Dean (1893–1971)

An imposing figure in mid-20th century American diplomacy, Dean Acheson was the quintessential American realist. The most important of President Harry S. Truman's "Wise Men" who shaped postwar U.S. foreign policy, he served as assistant secretary of state during World War II, undersecretary of state under James Byrnes and George Marshall from 1945 to 1947 and as secretary of state from 1949 to 1953. Acheson was (as he said in his autobiography) indeed "present at the creation" of the post–World War II Pax Americana.

An unlikely intimate of President Truman, the aristocratic Acheson was instrumental in creating the postwar international financial institutions at BRETTON WOODS, in organizing the Marshall Plan to restore the economic viability of Western Europe, and in drafting the Truman Doctrine to contain any Soviet advance into the Middle East and Mediterranean. He provided the administration's geopolitical rationale for the North Atlantic Treaty Organization (NATO) as well as Truman's decision to confront North Korean AGGRESSION in 1950.

Although perceived as a rigid cold warrior by many, Acheson also endured the wrath of the McCarthyites for his initial pragmatic attitudes toward Moscow, Beijing, and the need to avoid a nuclear arms race. Secretary of State Byrnes put Acheson in charge of a committee to draft a proposal for the international control of atomic energy, to be submitted to the United Nations Atomic Energy Commission (UNAEC). The undersecretary convened a working group of experts and politically savvy individuals who drafted what became known as the ACHESON-LILIENTHAL REPORT. The plan envisaged an Atomic Development Authority (ADA), which would own and control all uranium mines, fissionable materials, and processing facilities around the world. Acheson proposed phasing the plan in. The United States would not turn over its weapons until all states had submitted their facilities and resources to the authority. The proposal became the basis for the BARUCH PLAN, which was submitted to the UN and summarily rejected by the Soviet Union.

Acheson eventually adopted a rhetoric of anticommunism designed to make his proposals "clearer than truth" to a reluctant Congress. As a realist, he frowned on a "crusade against any ideology." He declined to attend the San Francisco Conference where the CHARTER OF THE UNITED NATIONS was crafted in the spring of 1945. Despite his skepticism about the UN's ability to resolve great international conflicts, and his stern opposition to a cabinet seat for the UN ambassador, Acheson dutifully lobbied for congressional approval of the Charter. He regarded the creation of the United Nations as the most recent example of "the nineteenth-century faith in the perfectibility of man and the advent of universal peace and law." Acheson blamed Woodrow Wilson for the "grand fallacy" that democratic procedures and institutions could be applied effectively to international relations. For Dean Acheson, the United Nations was at best "an aid to diplomacy."

Acheson continued to be influential in Democratic circles after he left the State Department. He consulted with the JOHN F. KENNEDY administration (1961–63) on foreign policy issues and his numerous publications included autobiographical works highlighting international affairs.

Further Reading: Acheson, Dean. *Present at the Creation: My Years in the State Department.* New York: W.W. Norton, 1969. Beisner, Robert. *Dean Acheson: A Life in the Cold War.* New York: Oxford University Press, 2006. Chace, James. *Acheson: The Secretary of State Who Created the American World.* New York: Simon and Schuster, 1998. McGlothlen, Ronald. *Controlling the Waves: Dean Acheson and U.S. Foreign Policy in Asia.* New York: W.W. Norton, 1993.

— *E. M. Clauss*

Acheson-Lilienthal Report

Submitted by the UNITED STATES to the inaugural meeting of the United Nations Atomic Energy Commission (UNAEC) in June 1946, the report served as the basis for early UN deliberations on the control of nuclear weapons. Written by a committee headed by U.S. undersecretary of state DEAN ACHESON and David Lilienthal, the former head of the Tennessee Valley Authority, the American proposal called for the creation of a new UN body, the Atomic Development Authority (ADA). The authority would own and control all uranium mines, processing facilities, and fissionable materials worldwide. The ADA would then distribute "denatured" nuclear materials to national governments for peaceful uses. Acheson and Lilienthal envisioned the transfer of American, Soviet, and all other national nuclear assets to the United Nations in a phased process.

The U.S. representative to the UNAEC, Bernard Baruch, incorporated the elements of the Acheson-Lilienthal Report

into his own BARUCH PLAN, calling for penalties against states that violated ADA authority. The Soviet Union rejected the American initiative as an effort to maintain the U.S. monopoly on nuclear capability. While the UNAEC approved the U.S. plan by a vote of 10 to 0 in December 1946, the Soviet Union abstained, making any further progress impossible.

In December 1953 President Eisenhower revised the American position, calling on nuclear powers to transfer a small percentage of their nuclear materials to a new INTERNATIONAL ATOMIC ENERGY AGENCY (IAEA) under the ultimate authority of the United Nations but largely independent of its control. He suggested that as trust among the nuclear powers and in the agency increased more and more plutonium could be transferred to the United Nations, ultimately meeting the goals of the Acheson-Lilienthal Report. He offered to transfer U.S. stockpiles at a rate of 5 to 1 of that turned over by the USSR. Although the Soviet Union rejected the proposal, Eisenhower's initiative led to the establishment of an IAEA Preparatory Committee and the creation of the UN agency in 1957.

See also DISARMAMENT.

Further Reading: Acheson, Dean. *Present at the Creation: My Years at the State Department.* New York: W.W. Norton, 1969. Clarfield, Gerard H., and William M. Wiecek. *Nuclear America.* New York: Harper and Row, 1984.

Administrative Committee on Coordination (ACC)   *See* CHIEF EXECUTIVE BOARD FOR COORDINATION.

administrative tribunals

Employees who work for the United Nations and its associated bodies are international civil servants. As such, they are not regulated or protected by the labor laws of their own countries. In order to protect their rights and to impose common personnel policy, the UNITED NATIONS SYSTEM has several administrative tribunals to which employees, who believe the terms of their contract or appointment have been violated, may appeal.

There are three significant administrative tribunals in the United Nations System. The UN Administrative Tribunal (UNAT), created by the GENERAL ASSEMBLY in 1949, has seven members appointed for three-year terms by the Assembly on the recommendation of the FIFTH COMMITTEE. The tribunal of the INTERNATIONAL LABOUR ORGANIZATION (ILOAT) is the oldest of the three, founded by the ILO in 1946 as the successor to the High Administrative Tribunal of the LEAGUE OF NATIONS. ILOAT hears appeals from personnel at more than 45 international organizations. The WORLD BANK and INTERNATIONAL MONETARY FUND maintain an administrative tribunal that hears appeals not only from their employees but also appointees at the INTER-NATIONAL FINANCE CORPORATION and the INTERNATIONAL DEVELOPMENT ASSOCIATION. UNAT and ILOAT serve both the employees within their organizations and the workforce of several other SPECIALIZED AGENCIES. UNAT is available to the employees of the INTERNATIONAL CIVIL AVIATION ORGANIZATION and the INTERNATIONAL MARITIME ORGA-NIZATION in addition to UN SECRETARIAT staff. The ILO has similar agreements with the following agencies: FOOD AND AGRICULTURE ORGANIZATION, UNITED NATIONS EDUCA-TIONAL, SCIENTIFIC, AND CULTURAL ORGANIZATION, WORLD HEALTH ORGANIZATION, INTERNATIONAL TELECOMMUNICA-TIONS UNION, WORLD METEOROLOGICAL ORGANIZATION, WORLD INTELLECTUAL PROPERTY ORGANIZATION, INTERNA-TIONAL ATOMIC ENERGY AGENCY, and UNIVERSAL POSTAL UNION. These tribunals, although established by major bod-ies of the UN system, are not considered "subsidiary" bodies, but rather "judicial" organs. They are, therefore, independent of their parent organizations, and their decisions may not be reversed by those organizations. The INTERNATIONAL COURT OF JUSTICE (ICJ) decided this question in 1954, when it issued an advisory opinion in the case of 11 employees who had been awarded $180,000 in compensation by UNAT for illegal dismissal. The Court held that the General Assembly could not reverse the tribunal's award and had to autho-rize payment. On the other hand, employees have an appeal process from the tribunal that allows their cases to be taken to the ICJ. In 2003 the General Assembly reinforced the Administrative Tribunal's independence by directing the Sec-retary-General to separate the tribunal's secretariat from the UN OFFICE OF LEGAL AFFAIRS.

In the 1954 ICJ case UNAT found itself caught up in the politics of McCarthyism in the UNITED STATES. SECRETARY-GENERAL TRYGVE LIE had fired 18 American nationals in 1952 for exercising their Fifth Amendment right against self-incrimination by refusing to testify before the U.S. Senate's Internal Security Subcommittee. They had been accused of being members of the American Communist Party. Lie argued that their behavior violated the requirement that they act in a manner "befitting their status as international civil servants." On appeal to UNAT the fired employees were exonerated and compensated. The United States led the fight in the General Assembly to bar the compensation, but the Court eventually upheld the UNAT decision. That judgment gave the administrative tribunals an independence not enjoyed by other UN-created bodies.

Further Reading: Simma, Bruno, ed. *The Charter of the United Nations. A Commentary.* 2nd ed. New York: Oxford University Press, 2002. Stoessinger, John G. *The United Nations and the Superpowers: China, Russia, and America.* 4th ed. New York: Random House, 1977. United Nations Depart-ment of Public Information. *United Nations Juridical Year-book.* New York: The United Nations, 1962– .

admission of members

In addition to the founding members of the United Nations, as defined in Article 3 of the CHARTER, the UN, in keep-ing with the idea of universality, is open to new members, provided the applicant is a peace-loving state, accepts the obligations of the Charter, is able to carry out these obliga-tions, and is willing to do so. In an opinion on May 28, 1948, the INTERNATIONAL COURT OF JUSTICE (ICJ) ruled that "All these conditions [of Art. 4 para 1] are subject to the judg-ment of the Organization, i.e., of the SECURITY COUNCIL (SC) and of the GENERAL ASSEMBLY (GA) and, in the last resort, of the members of the organization." In this context, the ICJ declared that an application request cannot be denied for any reason other than those stated in Article 4. The ICJ further held in an advisory opinion on March 3, 1950, that the GA could not admit a member without a recommenda-tion given by the Security Council. As of 2008 the number of member states was 192.

Applicants for MEMBERSHIP are evaluated by the Commit-tee on Admission of New Members, a standing committee of the Security Council. Based on its findings, new members may be recommended by the Security Council to the General Assembly, which then votes on their admission. A two-thirds majority in the GA is required to admit new members.

Especially during the first decade of the UN, permanent members' VETOs blocked admission of new members in the Security Council. Given the parliamentary nature of GA procedures, it was important for both the UNITED STATES and the Soviet Union to secure working majorities in the body. For this reason the USSR sought an expansion of UN membership to overcome the initial advantage the United States had among the founding members. The PERMANENT FIVE were also under pressure from the UN's first SECRE-TARY-GENERAL TRYGVE LIE and his successor DAG HAMMAR-SKJÖLD to make the world body truly universal by adding new members. Finally, the newly liberated states themselves conducted public diplomacy toward that end.

In December 1955 the logjam was broken by both sides agreeing to admit 16 nations, 4 from the Soviet bloc and the rest from the ranks of Africa, Asia, and the Arab world. For the first time since INDONESIA's admission in 1950, the Gen-eral Assembly had enlarged its membership. The first wave of new members was quickly followed by other success-ful applicants, such that African and Asian nations achieved a majority of seats in the General Assembly in 1963. The enlargement meant new voices, points of view, and policy emphases would now be advanced in the United Nations. The problems of the LESS DEVELOPED COUNTRIES—poverty, political instability, NORTH-SOUTH trade, and multilateral aid—all moved to the forefront.

A particularly heated controversy was the admission of the People's Republic of CHINA. It was critical to the Soviet Union to seat the representatives of the People's Republic in place of the delegation from the Republic of China (Taiwan).

The USSR had boycotted the Security Council for a good part of 1950 over this issue, with the consequence of letting the United States achieve Council support for intervention in Korea. The admission of "Red China" was an emotional issue in American politics. Mao's introduction of troops in the KOREAN WAR, coupled with the anticommunist mood of the country, produced overwhelming opposition to the seating of a Beijing delegation in New York. If the Mainland Chinese took China's seat in the Security Council it would also mean another certain veto of Western proposals in that body. The American administration sought to maintain a GA majority in opposition to seating the Beijing government. When that no longer seemed achievable, Washington was willing to use all parliamentary procedures available toward this end. This American tactic continued until the presidency of Richard Nixon. Faced with an overwhelming majority in favor of China's admission, and seeking accommodation with the Chinese government itself, the United States sought to accede to the admission of the PRC while maintaining membership of the Republic of China in the General Assembly. In October 1971 the GA majority rejected that approach and gave Taiwan's seat in the UN, and particularly on the Security Council, to the government in Beijing.

Rights and privileges of membership may be suspended and a state can be excluded from the United Nations if the member state either is subject to ENFORCEMENT MEASURES imposed by the Security Council or has "persistently" violated the principles of the Charter (Articles 5 and 6). In the case of EXCLUSION, readmission is possible under the provisions of Article 4. A suspension of UN rights and privileges was imposed on Yugoslavia during the 1990s for the violation of UN RESOLUTIONS pertaining to the Balkans. The Socialist Federal Republic of Yugoslavia was an original member of the United Nations until its dissolution during the crisis in that region. Following the overthrow of President SLOBODAN MILOŠEVIĆ, the Republic of Yugoslavia in the form of a union of Serbia and Montenegro, was readmitted on November 1, 2000. In 2006, Montenegro voted in a plebiscite to secede from the union, leaving Serbia alone, and marking the final dissolution of one of the UN's original members. On June 21, the Security Council voted to recommend Montenegro's admission to the United Nations as its 192nd member.

See also COLD WAR.

Further Reading: Simma, Bruno, ed. *The Charter of the United Nations: A Commentary.* 2nd ed. New York: Oxford University Press, 2002.

— *T. J. Weiler*

Advisory Committee on Administrative and Budgetary Questions (ACABQ)

At its first session in 1946 the UN GENERAL ASSEMBLY created two standing committees to assist with its work during and between regular Assembly meetings. They were the Advisory Committee on Administrative and Budgetary Questions and the COMMITTEE ON CONTRIBUTIONS. The first of these advises the Assembly, by way of its FIFTH COMMITTEE, on financial and budgetary matters related to the administration of the United Nations and its programs. ACABQ has 16 members, who are nominated by their governments but serve as private individuals. They are elected by the Assembly to three-year renewable terms based on their expertise, with due regard for geographical representation. Their terms expire on a rotating basis in order to assure continuity. In 2006, ACABQ's chairman was Rajat Saha of INDIA. He was joined on the Committee by members from Poland, Barbados, the UNITED STATES, the Ivory Coast (Côte d'Ivoire), CHINA, JAPAN, Botswana, Nepal, Honduras, the Netherlands, Canada, Argentina, the RUSSIAN FEDERATION, Cameroon, and FRANCE. The committee is administered by a SECRETARIAT of 11 appointees. Executive Secretary Jules A. Corwin headed the secretariat in 2006. The committee meets several times a year and in different places around the world. In June 2000 alone, it met in Geneva, Switzerland; Turin, Rome, and Brindisi, Italy; Pristina, Yugoslavia; and Vienna, Austria.

Given its expertise and longevity, the committee has achieved increased authority and prestige within the UN STRUCTURE. It can call upon the Secretary-General's office and the heads of UN PROGRAMMES AND FUNDS to meet with it and provide needed information. With regard to those programmes financed with voluntary funds, ACABQ reports to their governing bodies on the programmes' administrative budgets, personnel, and procedures. Its functions also include the examination of the regular UN BUDGET, and of extra-budgetary expenditures. It evaluates and reports on the financing of PEACEKEEPING operations and international tribunals and carries out any other assignments given to it by the SECRETARY-GENERAL. It has the decision-making authority to authorize start-up expenditures by the Secretary-General on peacekeeping operations that need rapid implementation even though related budgetary matters have not yet been resolved. As an example, in July 2000, the SECURITY COUNCIL established the UNITED NATIONS MISSION IN ETHIOPIA AND ERITREA (UNMEE), calling for the deployment of 4,200 troops. While it would have taken some months for the General Assembly process to approve the estimated $199 million budget through June 2001, ACABQ released an immediate $50 million for the dispatch of reconnaissance and liaison teams to the region, and for the creation of an initial UN presence. It also made recommendations to the Fifth Committee on permanent personnel and spending allocations for the mission.

The Advisory Committee played a key role in the implementation of Secretary-General KOFI ANNAN's REFORM program. It promoted "results-based budgeting" throughout the UNITED NATIONS SYSTEM. Particularly in the SPECIALIZED AGENCIES ACABQ urged new cost-accounting procedures, the use of cost-saving technologies, and the sharing of administrative experiences to enhance efficiency. It recommended that the various UN bodies develop common terminology for practices and phenomena so that communication and documentation could be standardized. It also became a major advocate of enhanced support services within the United Nations, including improvement in physical facilities. It argued that continued reductions in spending on UN buildings, including HEADQUARTERS in New York, were shortsighted savings that would reduce UN effectiveness in the long term. Following the terrorist attack on New York City on September 11, 2001, the committee supported Secretary-General Annan's requests for additional funding for security measures throughout the UN System. The reputation of the committee for professional expertise generally produces endorsement of its recommendations by the Fifth Committee, the Assembly as a whole, the Secretary-General, and the rest of the UN system.

Further Reading: See the reports of ACABQ and the remarks of its members to the GA Fifth Committee at the Fifth Committee Web site: <www.un.org/ga/56/fifth/>. For preceding and succeeding years, substitute the GA session number in the Web site URL.

advisory opinion *See* INTERNATIONAL COURT OF JUSTICE.

Afghanistan

Afghanistan became a member of the United Nations on November 19, 1946. Active UN involvement in Afghanistan began on January 5, 1980, when the SECURITY COUNCIL met to consider the Soviet Union's December 27, 1979, invasion of the country. Claiming that the Afghan government requested Soviet assistance under terms of their 1978 friendship TREATY, the USSR vetoed a RESOLUTION condemning the intervention. Invoking the General Assembly's 1950 UNITING FOR PEACE RESOLUTION, the Council moved the question to the GENERAL ASSEMBLY, which voted on January 14, 1980, for withdrawal of foreign troops and soon thereafter authorized the SECRETARY-GENERAL to seek a solution to the conflict.

In February 1981, Secretary-General KURT WALDHEIM named a personal representative on Afghanistan, JAVIER PÉREZ DE CUÉLLAR, who—after becoming Secretary-General himself in 1982—appointed Diego Cordovez to succeed him as personal representative. In April 1988, after 12 rounds of negotiations, the governments of Pakistan and Afghanistan signed the Geneva Accords, with the UNITED STATES and USSR as guarantors. The accords provided for Soviet troop withdrawal, noninterference in Afghanistan's internal affairs, and the voluntary return of refugees. On February

15, 1989, the UN Good Offices Mission in Afghanistan and Pakistan (UNGOMAP) verified the Soviet withdrawal, but civil conflict continued with Soviet assistance to the communist regime and U.S. aid to resistance groups.

In November 1989, the General Assembly encouraged the Secretary-General to facilitate internal settlement, resulting in the 1991 appointment of Benon Sevan, head of the Office of the Secretary-General in Afghanistan and Pakistan (OSGAP), as personal representative. The superpowers agreed in 1991 to end aid to all parties by January 1, 1992, and supported a transition plan in accordance with the Secretary-General's May 1991 statement calling for an "intra-Afghan dialogue" ultimately leading to "free and fair elections." For the first time, some Afghan resistance groups were involved in and supported the UN negotiations, but the Soviet Union collapsed and resistance forces captured Kabul in April 1992 before the communist regime's planned abdication to a transitional council. Soviet-sponsored president Najibullah obtained sanctuary at the UN's Kabul office and, on May 6, 1992, resistance groups established the Afghan Interim Government, headed for two months by Sebghatullah Mujadeddi before he transferred power to Burhanuddin Rabbani, whose government continued to hold Afghanistan's UN seat through the 1990s with annual approval by the CREDENTIALS COMMITTEE.

Factional fighting intensified and UN efforts lapsed until December 1993, when a General Assembly resolution established the UNITED NATIONS SPECIAL MISSION TO AFGHANISTAN (UNSMA). UNSMA was headed by Mahmoud Mestiri (February 1994–May 1996) and later by Norbert Holl (May 1996–October 1997). Secretary-General KOFI ANNAN elevated UN involvement with the appointment of a special envoy, a position held first by Lakhdar Brahimi (July 1997–October 1999), and assumed in February 2000 by Francesc Vendrell. In 1997, with Brahimi's support, Annan convened the "Six-Plus-Two" group, comprised of Afghanistan's six neighbors—CHINA, IRAN, Pakistan, Tajikistan, Turkmenistan, and Uzbekistan, as well as Russia and the United States. From 1984, the UN COMMISSION ON HUMAN RIGHTS regularly renewed the mandate of the SPECIAL RAPPORTEUR for Afghanistan and became increasingly involved in direct investigation of specific rights violations. Yet these UN efforts brought limited achievements and a civil war continued through the 1990s. The Taliban Islamic movement originated in 1994 and gained military ascendance over competing Afghan parties in 1996.

Sometimes lauded as a UN success, the Geneva Accords, accompanied by the Secretary-General's GOOD OFFICES, have been credited with maintaining a critical CONFLICT RESOLUTION mechanism during a period when a PERMANENT MEMBER's VETO (the Soviet Union's) paralyzed the Security Council. However, the troop withdrawal was the only fully implemented element of the accords and, some argue, an inevitable result of a changed international system—that is, a thaw in the COLD WAR—and internal Soviet politics. The accords' exclusion of Afghan resistance parties—either as direct participants or as signatories—the absence of MECHANISMS for enforcement and intra-Afghan settlement, and the guarantors' immediate violation of the agreement through continued aid to their clients contributed to the failure of the UN missions that followed.

The UN missions—some more than others—also were criticized for misapprehending Afghanistan's complexities, for reluctance to address misbehavior of UN member states, and for inconsistent coordination with the UN's humanitarian operations. The UNITED NATIONS HIGH COMMISSIONER FOR REFUGEES, which began assisting refugees in 1978, appeared to reinforce U.S.-supported elements of the Afghan resistance to Soviet occupation and may have undermined the neutrality of UN MEDIATION. During the 1990s, a group of UN committees adopted Afghanistan as a test case for strengthened coordination of UN crisis operations, including the application of a unitary funding mechanism and "principled common programming" on gender, minorities, and other issues. Yet the effort to unify UN humanitarian and political efforts met with limited success.

Afghanistan presented obstacles to UN humanitarian operations, including limited UN access to WOMEN imposed by the Taliban's gender restrictions, looting of UN offices, and violent reaction for the August 1998 U.S. missile attacks on the suspected residence of Osama bin Laden. The attacks were carried out in retaliation for bin Laden's alleged complicity in the terrorist bombing of two U.S. embassies in Africa. In 1999 the Security Council placed SANCTIONS on Afghanistan. Meantime, frequent evacuations and suspensions of operations, although usually justified, compromised the UN's image when agencies such as the International Red Cross remained in Kabul. Nevertheless, UNOCHA, the United Nations Office for the Coordination of Humanitarian Assistance to Afghanistan, as the longest standing UN special body charged with promoting and coordinating assistance in a complex emergency, came to serve as a model for other global humanitarian efforts.

Successive UN missions argued with increasing vigor that their ultimate ineffectiveness was a result of the absence of international political and financial support and a lack of interest in ending the fighting on the part of some Afghans and influential regional powers. In November 1997, Kofi Annan said "it could be argued that . . . the role of the United Nations in Afghanistan is little more than that of an alibi to provide cover for the inaction—or worse—of the international community at large." He later questioned the usefulness of the Six-Plus-Two process when a major Taliban offensive followed the July 1999 Tashkent Declaration on Fundamental Principles for a Peaceful Settlement of the Conflict in Afghanistan, in which Afghanistan's neighbors for the first time pledged publicly to cease military interference in Afghanistan.

With the post–cold war convergence of member interests in the region, the Security Council, in an unprecedented direct action, passed a resolution on October 15, 1999, banning nonhumanitarian flights and freezing Taliban assets to persuade the regime to extradite U.S.-indicted terrorist Osama bin Laden. As it gained increasing control of much of Afghanistan's territory by September 2000, the Taliban renewed efforts to obtain Afghanistan's UN seat and proposed alternatives to the extradition of bin Laden, while the Security Council contemplated further sanctions.

On September 11, 2001, hijackers, reputedly part of bin Laden's AL-QAEDA terrorist network, seized control of four U.S. civilian airliners. They crashed two of them into the World Trade Center towers in New York City, bringing both towers to the ground and killing approximately 3,000 people. The third plane crashed into the U.S. Pentagon in Arlington, Virginia, after circling major government sites in Washington, D.C. The fourth airliner crashed in western Pennsylvania with the loss of all on board. President GEORGE W. BUSH declared the events "acts of war" and made harsh demands on the Taliban government in Afghanistan, believing that the regime was harboring bin Laden.

The United States sought UN support for any actions it might take in reprisal. On September 12 the Security Council unanimously adopted Resolution 1368, condemning the assault and finding it a threat to international peace and security. Council members invoked CHAPTER VII, making the resolution's provisions mandatory on all member states. The General Assembly, once it convened on September 13, followed with a condemnation of the attack. The Council also passed Resolution 1373 on September 28, calling on all states to "prevent and suppress the financing of terrorist acts."

The United States issued an ultimatum to the Taliban demanding the extradition of bin Laden and his senior associates, the closing of his training bases in Afghanistan, and the stationing of U.S. personnel on Afghan territory to investigate and destroy terrorist camps. The regime in Kabul rejected these demands, closed all international aid programs in the country, requested proof of bin Laden's complicity, and seized UN facilities. The Bush administration organized a large coalition in support of its demands, including Afghanistan's neighboring states of Pakistan and Uzbekistan. The North Atlantic Treaty Organization declared the attack on the United States an act requiring COLLECTIVE SELF-DEFENSE. On October 7, 2001, the United States and Great Britain launched intensive air attacks on major cities, military targets, and training areas inside Afghanistan.

Under pressure from the attacks, the Taliban leaders called on all Muslim nations to defend Afghanistan from American "AGGRESSION." At the same time they offered to negotiate turning over Osama bin Laden to a third country in return for a cessation of the bombing. The offer was rejected by Washington. Faced with a growing refugee and humanitarian crisis, and with calls from UN officials among others to assist innocent Afghan victims of the attack, the U.S. administration made airdrops of food rations and offered to assist with humanitarian relief. Also recognizing the need to assure stability in Afghanistan if the Taliban was driven from power, President Bush lent support to future UN efforts at NATION-BUILDING in Afghanistan, reversing the position of the administration on this aspect of contemporary UN PEACEKEEPING activities.

Washington received extensive support—in the United Nations, from NATO, and elsewhere—to remove the Taliban from power in Afghanistan, curtail al-Qaeda activities there, and seek the reconstruction of the country. The Taliban, after all, had been the sponsoring government of al-Qaeda, the alleged force behind the 9/11 attacks. The United Nations, indeed most of the world, supported intervention. By early 2002, Afghanistan was liberated from Taliban rule through a cooperative effort, yet it faced deep problems of political instability and economic despair. Regional warlords remained and the drug trade persisted. In outlying areas the Taliban rematerialized as a threat to the government in Kabul. Still, by early 2004, with international encouragement the Afghans had convened a traditional *loya jirga* and had agreed to a constitution and democratic elections. In late 2004, the country elected Hamid Karzai president, and, in September 2005, it held parliamentary elections. Abiding by a post-Taliban blueprint negotiated at an international conference in Bonn in 2001, warlords began to turn in heavy WEAPONS to the central government. There was a visible UN presence in the country. The organization monitored the historic elections of 2004 and 2005. UN SPECIAL REPRESENTATIVE Lakhdar Brahimi, along with the UN High Commissioner for Refugees and a variety of staff personnel plied their trade with uncommon dedication. Hampered by a lack of money, the slow inflow of promised funds, and the diversion of attention to IRAQ, the UN contingency worked to distribute an international aid disbursement, to increase security, to develop infrastructure, and to strengthen the government. In August 2003 NATO took command of the International Security Assistance Force, which consisted of some 10,000 forces from 37 countries (the first time NATO had acted outside of Europe), and in June 2006, NATO's defense ministers reaffirmed their commitment to deploy about 7,000 troops in southern Afghanistan. By mid 2006 American deaths in Afghanistan were one-10th of those in U.S.-occupied Iraq, even though the international presence in Afghanistan had begun over a year earlier. Furthermore, despite UN and allied efforts, both bin Laden and Mullah Omar, leader of the previous Taliban government, remained in hiding, and resurgent Taliban forces posed an ongoing threat to international political and economic reconstruction in Afghanistan.

Further Reading: Khan, Riaz M. *Untying the Afghan Knot: Negotiating Soviet Withdrawal.* Durham, N.C.: Duke University Press, 1991. Maley, William. "The UN and Afghanistan: 'Doing Its Best' or Failure of a Mission?" In *Fundamentalism Reborn: Afghanistan and the Taliban,* 182–98. Edited by William Maley. New York: New York University Press, 1998. Rashid, Ahmed. *Jihad: The Rise of Militant Islam in Central Asia.* New Haven, Conn.: Yale University Press, 2002. Rubin, Barnett R. *The Search for Peace in Afghanistan: From Buffer State to Failed State.* New Haven, Conn.: Yale University Press, 1995.

— M. E. Reif

Africa   See AFRICAN UNION, ANGOLA, APARTHEID, CONFLICT DIAMONDS, CONGO, DEPARTMENT OF PEACEKEEPING OPERATIONS, DESERTIFICATION, ECONOMIC COMMISSION FOR AFRICA, ECONOMIC COMMUNITY OF WEST AFRICAN STATES, DARFUR, GROUP OF 77, HIV/AIDS, LEAST DEVELOPED COUNTRIES, MILLENNIUM DEVELOPMENT GOALS, NAMIBIA, NATIONAL LIBERATION, NEW PARTNERSHIP FOR AFRICA'S DEVELOPMENT, PEACEKEEPING, RWANDA CRISIS, SIERRA LEONE, SOMALIA.

Africa Industrialization Day

Celebrated annually on November 20, the day is meant to generate support in the international community for the industrialization of Africa.

African Development Bank (ADB)   See REGIONAL DEVELOPMENT BANKS.

African Union (AU)

In 2002 the ORGANIZATION OF AFRICAN UNITY (OAU) became the African Union (AU). The transformation began with the OAU's Sirte Declaration in 1999, which called for the establishment of a more comprehensive body. The 2000 Lomé Summit approved the Constitutive Act, and the 2001 Lusaka Summit mapped out the implementation procedures for the establishment of the new REGIONAL ORGANIZATION. The 2002 Durban Summit marked the formal inauguration of the African Union with the convocation of the first AU Assembly meeting. Among the stated objectives of the organization were greater African unity and solidarity; defense of the SOVEREIGNTY; territorial integrity; and independence of member states; acceleration of the political and socioeconomic integration of the continent; the promotion of peace, security, stability, democratic principles and institutions; and the protection of HUMAN RIGHTS.

Modeled on the European Union, the AU had a MEMBERSHIP of 53 nations by fall 2006. Its structure consisted of the Assembly, the Executive Council, the Permanent Representatives Committee, and the Commission. Composed of heads of state who meet once a year, the AU Assembly is the AU's main decision-making body and is headed by a chairman who is elected annually for a 12-month term. The Executive Council is made up of the foreign ministers of the member states; it meets twice a year and is responsible to the Assembly. The Permanent Representatives Committee is made up of permanent representatives to the AU HEADQUARTERS in Addis Ababa and meets every month. The AU Commission consists of a chairman, elected for a four-year term, a deputy chairman, and eight commissioners who hold portfolios in the functional areas of peace and security, political affairs, infrastructure and energy, social affairs, human resources, science and technology, trade and industry, rural economy and agriculture, and economic affairs. The commission implements AU policies and acts as the SECRETARIAT, coordinating the AU's activities and meetings. In 2004, the AU inaugurated the Pan-African Parliament that initially had only consultative and advisory powers but was intended to evolve into a continental legislature. An African Court of Justice was also due to be established.

One of the critical tasks of the AU is to deal more effectively with the problem of conflict on the continent. To that end, the PROTOCOL establishing the Peace and Security Council entered into force on December 26, 2003, and replaced the OAU MECHANISM for Conflict Prevention, Management and Resolution. The council is composed of 15 members and meets twice a month at the permanent representative level and annually at the minister or head of government level. Leaders expressed their intention to create an early warning system and a stand-by force in order to respond to conflict situations more promptly and to overcome the OAU's reticence to intervene in member states. At the 2004 Second Extraordinary Assembly meeting, AU heads of state took another step toward unity and adopted a DECLARATION on a common defense and security policy.

The AU's first military intervention came when it assumed temporary responsibility for a PEACEKEEPING mission in Burundi in April 2003. A UN force replaced the African Union in June 2004. The mission had a total strength of 3,335 troops drawn from South Africa, Ethiopia, and Mozambique as well as observers from Burkina Faso, Gabon, Mali, Togo, and Tunisia.

The AU also provided a peacekeeping force for the DARFUR region of Sudan. In April 2004, a cease-fire between the government and the rebels resulted in agreement to allow African Union observers to be deployed. An initial force of 3,200 troops was committed with the number rising eventually to 7,000. The mandate allowed the troops to monitor the cease-fire but did not extend to the protection of civilians except in cases of imminent danger. Inadequate funding and logistical problems compromised the effectiveness of the African Union Mission in Darfur (AMIS). Moreover, the 7,000 AU troops were simply inadequate to patrol such a large area. In an effort to bring an end to the conflict the AU brokered the Darfur Peace Agreement (DPA) in May

2006. The peace agreement failed to gain the support of all rebel factions and the conflict continued. The UN SECURITY COUNCIL authorized a peacekeeping mission in August 2006 but the government of Sudan rejected the deployment. With the AU mandate scheduled to expire at the end of September 2006, there was grave concern that the withdrawal of the force would leave the civilian POPULATION even more vulnerable. In mid-2007 Sudan accepted deployment of a "hybrid" UN-AU peacekeeping operation. By early 2008 Darfur waited to see if the new force would materialize and bring relief.

To address its goals of promoting socioeconomic integration and democratic principles, the AU adopted the NEW PARTNERSHIP FOR AFRICAN DEVELOPMENT (NEPAD). NEPAD sought to eradicate poverty in Africa and support efforts to achieve sustainable growth and DEVELOPMENT, and to promote greater African involvement in the global economy. Through its peer review mechanism, NEPAD also encouraged governments to adopt democratic principles and operate in a transparent fashion. The NEPAD Implementation Committee reports to the AU summit on an annual basis.

See also APPENDIX G, BRAHIMI REPORT, ECONOMIC COMMISSION FOR AFRICA, TREATY OF PELINDABA.

Further Reading: African Union Web site: <www.africa-union.org>.

— *R. J. Griffiths*

Agenda for Development

The Agenda for Development, adopted by a special meeting of the GENERAL ASSEMBLY on June 20, 1997, was the result of more than four years of extensive deliberations by member states and the SECRETARIATs of the UNITED NATIONS SYSTEM. The final document represented the product of a special working group of the General Assembly established in December 1994 to provide a forum among UN members for the exchange of views on DEVELOPMENT.

The idea for an agenda for development emerged in 1992, in the wake of SECRETARY-GENERAL BOUTROS BOUTROS-GHALI's elaboration of *AN AGENDA FOR PEACE*. At that time, there had been a strong feeling by many in the global south that development was being marginalized in favor of peace and security. These DEVELOPING NATIONS felt that there was a continued need to assert the United Nation's primacy in the area of development. The South had demanded an agenda for development and Boutros-Ghali made an attempt to produce one. The Secretary-General's own vision of development was set out in May 1994 in a report to the General Assembly entitled *An Agenda for Development*. The report addressed peace, the economy, the ENVIRONMENT, society, and democracy as the five foundations of development. The Secretary-General also examined the multiplicity of actors engaged in development work and outlined his vision of the role of the United Nations in development in an increasingly complex world. His report declared that universal respect for and protection of HUMAN RIGHTS was an integral part of development, and that particular human rights, including group rights such as those of INDIGENOUS PEOPLES, WOMEN, children, and the disabled, should be emphasized. In November 1994, in response to the request of the General Assembly, the Secretary-General issued his recommendations for the implementation of *An Agenda for Development*. However, some nations considered the recommendations incomplete. As a result, member states chose to negotiate key parameters of the agenda. To facilitate this effort, a working group on an agenda for development was established on December 19, 1994, by UN resolution GA 49/126.

Given the background of concern about the development partnership between the North and South, reaching agreement on broad desirable outcomes was a significant achievement. The working group saw its main task as forging a framework for a partnership that would hold together, rather than trying to articulate plans with great detail. The working group hoped that under such a partnership specifics could be sorted out as it developed agreed-upon goals. One of the key stumbling blocks was the fear among Southern states that the emphasis on protecting the environment might stifle their economic growth. As a result of compromise, the document attempted to balance the need for SUSTAINABLE DEVELOPMENT with the need for sustained economic growth.

In UN Secretary-General KOFI ANNAN's words, the Agenda for Development, adopted after intense and extended consultations, "represent[ed] one of the most far-reaching agreements on the central issue of development ever attained by the international community." He reiterated many of the agenda's themes in his report to the MILLENNIUM SUMMIT in 2000, and affirmed the essential connection between human rights and developments in *IN LARGER FREEDOM*, his 2005 UN REFORM proposals. Developing countries, fearing that the United Nations had become marginalized by the BRETTON WOODS institutions, saw the core thrust of the agenda as reaffirming the importance of development for the United Nations, and they sought to resituate the organization's central role toward the encouragement of development. The agenda not only addressed the familiar components of development, such as economic growth, trade, finance, science and technology, poverty eradication, employment and human resources development, but also placed new emphasis on the role of democracy, human rights, popular participation, good governance, and the empowerment of women. As such, it provided, according to Annan, "an all-encompassing framework for international cooperation on development—a central and evolving concern of the United Nations since its inception." Many of the agenda's general recommendations were incorporated in the specific MILLENNIUM DEVELOPMENT GOALS approved by the world community in September 2000.

See also SUSTAINABLE HUMAN DEVELOPMENT.

Further Reading: Agenda for Development Web site: <www.un.org/Docs/SG/ag_index.htm>. Bergesen, Helge Ole, Goerg Parmann, and Oystein B. Thommessen. *Yearbook of International Cooperation on Environment and Development, 1999/2000*. London: Earthscan Publications, 1999. Weiss, Thomas G., David P. Forsythe, and Roger A. Coate. *The United Nations and Changing World Politics*. Boulder, Colo.: Westview Press, 2000.

— *A. I. Maximenko*

Agenda for Peace

In January 1992 a unanimous SECURITY COUNCIL requested that the SECRETARY-GENERAL prepare a report that included "analysis and recommendations on ways of strengthening and making more efficient within the framework and provisions of the CHARTER the capacity of the United Nations for preventive diplomacy, for peacemaking and for PEACEKEEPING." The result of the request was *An Agenda for Peace*. Secretary-General BOUTROS BOUTROS-GHALI authored and released the report in June 1992.

An Agenda for Peace detailed a REFORM agenda. It sought to reinvigorate the United Nations in the post–COLD WAR era. Boutros-Ghali recommended that the United Nations identify "at-risk" states and act early to avoid the collapse of state SOVEREIGNTY and internal order. He proposed that military forces be placed at the disposal of the United Nations for rapid action in times of crisis. The report outlined problems in the LESS DEVELOPED COUNTRIES and the need for a humanitarian, political, economic, and military response by the United Nations. As a result of the report, new terms such as "preventive diplomacy," "state-building," and "peace making" entered the lexicon of potential UN activities.

The report highlighted four concepts: preventive diplomacy, peace making, peacekeeping, and post-conflict peace-building. Preventive diplomacy attempted to resolve intra- and interstate conflicts before violence erupted, or to limit the spread of violence; it was intended to be proactive peacekeeping. Peace making sought to bring hostile parties to agreement through negotiation and MEDIATION. Peacekeeping was defined as UN deployment into potential or actual zones of conflict. Post-conflict peace-building was popularized by this report. Peace-building aimed to construct an environment that sustained durable peace. Peace-building missions addressed the economic, social, cultural, and humanitarian problems that underpinned violent conflict. Preventive diplomacy tried to avoid crisis; peace-building strove to prevent a recurrence.

A supplement to *An Agenda for Peace* was presented in 1995. It reviewed UN experience with peace operations over a two-and-one-half-year period following the original report. Among these missions were peacekeeping operations in SOMALIA (1992–94) and RWANDA (1994), both perceived as failures. Critics accused Boutros-Ghali of overextending UN responsibilities, and argued that the financial and political requirements necessitated by the *Agenda* were beyond the organization's capabilities.

See also AGENDA FOR DEVELOPMENT, CONFLICT RESOLUTION, NATION-BUILDING, PEACEBUILDING COMMISSION.

Further Reading: Boutros-Ghali, Boutros. *An Agenda for Peace.* 2d ed. New York: United Nations Department of Public Information, 1995. Kars, D. "The [UN] Agenda for Peace: A 1995 Evaluation." *European Security* 5, no. 1 (Spring 1996): 98–112. Weiss, Thomas. "New Challenges for UN Military Operations: Implementing an Agenda for Peace." *Washington Quarterly* 16, no. 1 (Winter 1993): 51–66.

— *S. F. McMahon*

Agenda 21

Agenda 21 was the Plan of Action approved by the 1992 UNITED NATIONS CONFERENCE ON ENVIRONMENT AND DEVELOPMENT (UNCED) that provided a set of objectives and strategies for attaining SUSTAINABLE DEVELOPMENT in the 21st century. Filling more than 800 pages, Agenda 21 was the most comprehensive statement of international consensus as of 1992 on the intersections between environmental protection and DEVELOPMENT in the LESS DEVELOPED COUNTRIES (LDCs) of the world. It struck a pragmatic balance between the needs of states in early stages of development and the developed states of the North that sought to avoid environmental damage from unwise development practices.

Agenda 21 was divided into four substantive sections comprising 40 chapters on environmental and development topics. Each chapter outlined the environmental/developmental challenge, set international and national objectives, and provided programmatic activities meant to achieve the objectives. Section I (Chapters 1–8: preamble; international cooperation to accelerate sustainable development; combating poverty; changing consumption patterns; demographic dynamics and sustainability; promoting and protecting human health; promoting sustainable human settlement; integrating ENVIRONMENT and development in decision making) presented the "Social and Economic Dimensions of Sustainable Development." Section II on "Conservation and Management of Resources for Development" included Chapters 9–22 (protection of the atmosphere; planning and management of land resources; combating deforestation; combating DESERTIFICATION and drought; sustainable mountain development; promoting sustainable agriculture and rural development; conservation of biological diversity; environmentally sound management of biotechnology; protection of the oceans and the protection and rational development of their living resources; protection of freshwater resources; environmentally sound management of toxic chemicals; environmentally sound management of hazardous wastes; environmentally sound management of solid wastes;

sound management of radioactive wastes). Section III (Chapters 23–32) on "Strengthening the Role of Major Groups" included among those groups WOMEN (24), children and youth (25), INDIGENOUS PEOPLES (26), NON-GOVERNMENTAL ORGANIZATIONS (27), local authorities (28), workers and trade unions (29), business and industry (30), the scientific and technological community (31), and farmers (32). Section IV (Chapters 33–40) identified the means of implementation for the whole agenda. Most important, chapter 33 established the financial mechanisms to be encouraged and chapter 38 called for the creation of the COMMISSION ON SUSTAINABLE DEVELOPMENT (CSD). Other chapters encouraged education (36), the transfer of environmentally friendly technology (34), and the creation of science for sustainable development. They also promoted national capacity building (37) and the development of international environmental law (39).

In Agenda 21, Earth Summit participants committed UN bodies to incorporating sustainable development into their areas of responsibility. In particular, Agenda 21 assigned strategic planning, the development of international environmental law, and the provision of scientific/technical/legal advisory services to the UNITED NATIONS ENVIRONMENT PROGRAMME (UNEP). The UNITED NATIONS DEVELOPMENT PROGRAMME (UNDP) was given the lead role in obtaining donor assistance, accumulating expertise in sustainable development, working on desertification and drought, and developing new capacities in poor countries for sustainable development. Agenda 21 called for a network of cooperation among UNEP, UNDP, the WORLD BANK, the UNITED NATIONS CONFERENCE ON TRADE AND DEVELOPMENT (UNCTAD), the GLOBAL ENVIRONMENT FACILITY (GEF), the INTERNATIONAL DEVELOPMENT ASSOCIATION (IDA), and REGIONAL DEVELOPMENT BANKS in the effort to carry out more than 1,000 specific recommendations. Most importantly, UNCED's Plan of Action urged the GENERAL ASSEMBLY to create a new functional Commission on Sustainable Development (CSD) under the auspices of the ECONOMIC AND SOCIAL COUNCIL (ECOSOC) that would give continuing international attention to the problems associated with the environment and development. The Assembly fulfilled its charge in this regard the following year.

The negotiations on Agenda 21 were long and difficult. Three sets of issues limited a stronger and more specific list of recommendations. First, the growing conflict between developed states with an interest in global environmental protection and less developed states that did not want any environmental limitations on their development programs meant that consensus on recommendations was only possible if they were vague, or if contradictory recommendations were included in the document. Second, the effort to protect the global environment naturally impinged on the sovereign rights of states to pursue their own internal policies. Agenda 21 generally protected the latter at the expense of the former.

Third, the estimated costs of the recommendations to make sustainable development a reality went far beyond the will of the donor states to give. LDCs had hoped for the creation of a "Green Fund" at UNCED with the major industrialized powers making substantial contributions. The conference SECRETARIAT estimated the cost of Agenda 21's proposals at $600 billion annually, well beyond the then current combination of domestic spending and assistance to the developing world. While Europe and JAPAN announced at the conference that they would increase funding by $5 billion per year, there was no major contribution from the UNITED STATES. Of the total amount estimated by the secretariat, $125 billion was foreign assistance 10 times the 1992 levels of global concessional aid. That figure, however, was close to the official UN target for Official Development Assistance (ODA) of 0.7 percent of rich countries' GNP. This being so, chapter 33 called on states to achieve the 0.7 percent figure "as soon as possible," and made the GEF the interim mechanism for Agenda 21 funding.

The General Assembly's 1997 SPECIAL SESSION (Earth Summit +5) and the WORLD SUMMIT ON SUSTAINABLE DEVELOPMENT (WSSD), held in Johannesburg, South Africa, in late summer 2002 reaffirmed the participants' commitment to the principles of Agenda 21. The WSSD declared 2005 through 2015 the United Nations Decade of Education for Sustainable Development, and named the UNITED NATIONS EDUCATIONAL, SCIENTIFIC AND CULTURAL ORGANIZATION (UNESCO) as the lead agency to organize educational activities around the world.

See also RIO DECLARATION.

Further Reading: Brenton, Tony. *The Greening of Machiavelli: The Evolution of International Environmental Politics.* London: Earthscan Publications, 1994. Campiglio, Luigi, Laura Pineschi, Domenico Siniscalco, and Tullio Treves. *The Environment after Rio.* London: Graham and Trotman, 1994. Grubb, Michael, Matthias Koch, Koy Thomson, Abby Manson, and Francis Sullivan. *The 'Earth Summit' Agreements: A Guide and Assessment.* London: Earthscan Publications, 1993.

aggression

Since one of the principal purposes of the United Nations is to maintain international peace and security, identifying nations that commit aggression constitutes a basis for SECURITY COUNCIL action. CHAPTER VII, Article 39, of the CHARTER states that "The Security Council shall determine the existence of any threat to the peace, breach of the peace, or act of aggression, and shall make recommendations or decide what measures shall be taken." Unfortunately, the Charter contains no definition of aggression, and reaching agreement on a meaningful definition has proven difficult. Various actions can be construed as aggression. While all agree that the unjustified or improper use of force against another nation constitutes aggression, there is always room for debate about whether the use of force was provoked by actions of the other party. While there is widespread agreement that aggression is wrong, nations engaged in armed conflict consistently contend that they act in self-defense. Even Adolf Hitler claimed that Poland attacked GERMANY at the start of World War II in 1939. Only twice has the Security Council, under the provisions of Article 39, identified an aggressor and then used force to halt the aggression. The first was North Korea in 1950. The second was IRAQ in 1990, when it invaded Kuwait.

Since Security Council decisions often entail determining which of the parties to a conflict is the aggressor, it is scarcely surprising that the GENERAL ASSEMBLY established a commission to write a definition shortly after it began functioning. Reaching agreement among all member states on exactly what constituted aggression proved so difficult that the commission negotiated for almost 30 years before arriving at a consensus in 1974. It required almost 500 words to define aggression, and achieving accord required language of such ambiguity and extensiveness that the commission produced an umbrella definition subsuming almost all possible acts as well as exceptions, providing the Security Council with little guidance. The definition stated that "the use of force against the SOVEREIGNTY, territorial integrity or political independence of another state, or in any other manner inconsistent with the Charter of the United Nations" constituted aggression. The definition applied particularly to the state first resorting to force. However, it also described several uses of force that did not constitute aggression, such as "acts by and in support of peoples struggling to achieve self-determination, freedom, and independence" from "colonial and racist regimes or other forms of alien domination."

The broad 1974 definition left each member state to reach its own conclusions about what constituted aggression and effectively left the Security Council to reach a determination on a case-by-case basis. It proved impossible to define the term more effectively, and no new commissions have attempted to grapple with the issue since. The United Nations, and for that matter the world, has no working definition of aggression that is binding under INTERNATIONAL LAW, or is accepted by more than a few nations.

See also APPEALS TO THE SECURITY COUNCIL; BUSH, GEORGE W.; COLLECTIVE SECURITY; COLLECTIVE SELF-DEFENSE; FOURTEEN POINTS; GULF WAR; IRAN-IRAQ WAR; *JUS COGENS;* KOREAN WAR; SOUTHEAST ASIA TREATY ORGANIZATION; TEHERAN CONFERENCE; UNITING FOR PEACE RESOLUTION.

Further Reading: Nyiri, Nicolas. *The United Nations' Search for a Definition of Aggression.* New York: Peter Lang, 1989. Simma, Bruno, ed. *The Charter of the United Nations: A Commentary.* 2nd ed. New York: Oxford University Press, 2002.

— *K. J. Grieb*

AIDS *See* HIV/AIDS, JOINT UNITED NATIONS PROGRAMME ON HIV/AIDS.

al-Qaeda *See* QAEDA, AL-.

Amendments to the Charter of the United Nations *See* CHARTER OF THE UNITED NATIONS.

An Agenda for Development *See* AGENDA FOR DEVELOPMENT.

Angola

Located on the southwest coast of Africa, Angola was colonized by the Portuguese in 1583. Portugal began settling the colony in earnest in the early 20th century and relied heavily on the wealth, particularly oil and diamonds, found within the colony. Beginning in the 1960s, insurgent groups demanded Angola's independence. After 15 years of guerrilla warfare, Portugal left Angola in January 1975. However, a brutal civil war, complicated by differences among several ethnic groups (Ovimbundi, at about 35 percent, represented the largest single group), ensued between the guerrilla groups, further fueled by support from external sources, namely, the UNITED STATES, the Soviet Union, South Africa, and CUBA. The Movimento Popular de Libertação de Angola (MPLA), a Marxist-oriented party, successfully achieved power over the Frente Nacional de Libertação de Angola (FNLA) and the União Nacional para a Independência Total de Angola (UNITA) in November 1975 and established the first independent government in Angola.

The MPLA's dominance, however, did not end the civil war within Angola's borders, nor did it successfully terminate the external COLD WAR interests that continued to support insurgency movements within Angola. UNITA, under the leadership of Jonas Savimbi, an Ovimbundi, and supported by South Africa and the United States, became the foremost threat to the MPLA's hold on power (the MPLA enjoyed the support of Cuba and the Soviet Union). As the United States and the Soviet Union played out their rivalry by proxy, Angola became one of the most heavily landmined regions in the world. By the close of the 1980s, cold war tensions had diminished significantly and the United Nations was invited to verify the withdrawal of Cuban troops in 1988.

Although the Cuban withdrawal signaled an important opportunity to realize peace in Angola, progress was slow. In 1991, the MPLA and UNITA negotiated a set of peace accords, which were intended to lead to national reconciliation and democratic elections. Elections were subsequently held in 1992, under UN observation; however, Savimbi

alleged widespread electoral fraud and refused to accept the results—which clearly favored the MPLA over UNITA. In an attempt to salvage the peace process, a series of negotiations were held between UNITA and the government of Angola (under the leadership of President Jose Eduardo dos Santos) that resulted in the Lusaka PROTOCOL (May 1994, effective November 1994).

Between 1988 and 1999, the United Nations initiated three verification missions to the country (UNAVEM I, II, III) and one observer mission, UN OBSERVER MISSION IN ANGOLA (MONUA). At best, these operations provided short buffer periods between intensified conflict. One of these respites came to an end with particularly tragic consequences for the United Nations. During the last week of 1998 rebel forces shot down two UN cargo airplanes, killing more than 20 passengers and crew. In 1999, the government of Angola indicated that it no longer believed such UN missions were productive. On February 26, the SECURITY COUNCIL ended MONUA's presence in Angola, after a total expenditure of $1.5 billion and the loss of 60 staff members trying to bring peace to the country.

Under pressure from the NON-GOVERNMENTAL ORGANIZATION Human Rights Watch, the Council agreed to open a small UN Office in Angola (UNOA) in October 1999. UNOA's purpose was to liaise with military, police, political, and civilian authorities. UNITA, however, continued to control significant territory and showed no real commitment to peace. General elections were scheduled for 2002, but without a significant improvement in domestic security, the possibility for free and fair elections was severely compromised.

If there was some small cause for hope, it arose from the Security Council's commitment to enforcing SANCTIONS against UNITA and from the growing international condemnation of the purchasing of diamonds from groups such as UNITA. Sponsored by the Canadian representative on the Security Council, the Council unanimously approved in April 2000 a CHAPTER VII monitoring MECHANISM to investigate violations of the diamond ban and to penalize countries that circumvented the sanctions. Constraining UNITA's ability to profit from illegal diamond and resource exchange held the potential of eventually forcing Savimbi to surrender. Also, by the turn of the century the Angolan government indicated that it was willing to consider amnesty for former UNITA activists—a move that could help the cause of national reconciliation. In February 2002, Savimbi was killed in a fire fight with government troops, raising hopes of an end to the fighting, ending Africa's longest running civil war. Combatants signed a cease-fire in April of that year. Dos Santos promised to hold national elections by 2009, with the caveat that inaccessible roads and railways will need to be repaired and some built before a vote can take place.

See also CONGO; NAMIBIA; PÉREZ DE CUÉLLAR, JAVIER; UNITED NATIONS ANGOLA VERIFICATION MISSION.

Further Reading: Ciment, James. *Angola and Mozambique: Postcolonial Wars in Southern Africa.* New York: Facts On File, 1997. Hodges, Tony. *African Issues: Angola from Afro-Stalinism to Petro-Diamond Capitalism.* Bloomington: Indiana University Press, 2001.

— *S. C. Rein*

Annan, Kofi Atta (1938–)

The seventh SECRETARY-GENERAL, Annan was the first person to be elected to the office from the ranks of the United Nations staff, the first black, and the first from sub-Saharan Africa. *Time* magazine called Annan "a miracle of our internationalized world." Born in Ghana, educated in the UNITED STATES and Europe, Annan became a career diplomat with the United Nations, spent much of his career in Europe, Africa, and New York, and ascended to the position of Secretary-General in 1997. This well-traveled international civil servant was born in 1938 in Kumasi, Ghana—at the time a British colony called the Gold Coast. His father, Henry Reginald Annan—whose first and second names were a legacy of British colonialism—was a highly respected noble of the Fante tribe. The son studied at the University of Science and Technology at Kumasi and then, in 1961, completed a bachelor's degree in economics at Macalester College in St. Paul, Minnesota. He pursued graduate studies at the Institut Universitaire des Hautes Ètudes Internationales in Geneva, and in 1971–72 was a Sloan Fellow at the Massachusetts Institute of Technology where he earned a Master of Science degree in management. Fluent in English, French, and several African languages, Annan in 1984 married his second wife, the Swedish artist and lawyer, Nane Lagergren, whose uncle, Swedish diplomat Raoul Wallenberg, helped thousands of Hungarian Jews escape from the Nazis during World War II.

Annan began his career with the United Nations in 1962 as an administrative and budget officer with the GENERAL AGREEMENT ON TARIFFS AND TRADE (GATT)—now the WORLD TRADE ORGANIZATION (WTO)—in Geneva. He went on to serve in a number of posts around the world. For a brief time in the mid-1970s he directed the Ghana Tourist Development Company, but then returned to UN service, rising to assistant secretary-general for human resources management and security coordinator for the UNITED NATIONS SYSTEM from 1987 to 1990 and assistant secretary-general for programme planning, BUDGET and finance, and controller from 1990 to 1992. Secretary-General BOUTROS BOUTROS-GHALI appointed him to a special assignment to negotiate safe passage for some half-million stranded Asian workers and release of hostages during the GULF WAR of 1990–91. In 1993 he became assistant secretary-general for peacekeeping operations and then, in early 1994, UNDER SECRETARY-GENERAL. As under secretary he witnessed the considerable growth in size and scope of UN PEACEKEEPING operations and oversaw 17 military operations and a $3.5 billion budget,

Secretary-General Kofi Annan during the 60th anniversary of the United Nations ceremony at UN Headquarters. (UN PHOTO 99602/ESKINDER DEBEBE)

15 times larger than the budget of 1988. He also supervised the removal of UN forces from SOMALIA in 1995 and served as Boutros-Ghali's SPECIAL REPRESENTATIVE to the FORMER YUGOSLAVIA, in which capacity he worked to organize peacekeeping efforts with the UN ambassadors from the United States, Britain, FRANCE, and Russia and, thus, he oversaw the transition in BOSNIA and Herzegovina from the United Nations Protection Force (UNPROFOR) to the multinational Implementation Force (IFOR), led by NATO (North Atlantic Treaty Organization).

By late 1996 it was clear that the United States, alone among the PERMANENT MEMBERS of the SECURITY COUNCIL, unalterably opposed reappointment of Boutros-Ghali, forcing the Council to consider other candidates. There was high interest in considering sub-Saharan African diplomats, since no Secretary-General had ever come from the region. Annan's reputation, his long residence in New York, and perhaps as important, his acceptability to conservative forces in the United States (led by North Carolina senator Jesse Helms, chair of the Senate Foreign Relations Committee) gained him the firm support of the Clinton administration and made him the consensus favorite, although the French would have preferred a leader from a francophone country. By late December, France withdrew its reticence when all three African nations on the Security Council indicated their support of Annan, who was chosen by the Council on December 17, 1996. After election by the GENERAL ASSEMBLY, Annan assumed the post on January 1, 1997.

The Secretary-General's first major initiative was his REFORM plan, *RENEWING THE UNITED NATIONS*. Unveiled in July 1997, the plan called for restructuring and pruning the UN's bureaucracy. He recommended consolidating and reorganizing 24 agencies into five divisions, to report to the Secretary-General but also to a new position called DEPUTY SECRETARY-GENERAL. (In January 1998, LOUISE FRÉCHETTE, Canada's deputy minister of national defense, became the first deputy secretary-general.) In November 1997 the General Assembly approved the first package of reforms, designed to save the United Nations some $123 million. Although there continued to be critics in American political circles, the U.S. Congress, in response, passed budget legislation in November 1999 appropriating $819 million for partial repayment of the $1 billion back dues owed by Washington.

By early 1998 the issue of WEAPONS inspections in IRAQ brought the threat of confrontation between Baghdad and the United States. SADDAM HUSSEIN insisted that he would deny access to weapons inspectors unless the UN-imposed economic SANCTIONS on his country were lifted. The United States threatened air strikes on Iraq unless the country cooperated with the inspectors. Annan, in an attempt to resolve the standoff diplomatically, met with Hussein. Although criticized in the West, Annan was able to gain from the Iraqi leader the so-called Memo of Understanding of February 22, 1998, whereby Iraq accepted all previous Security Council RESOLUTIONS pertaining to the issue and agreed to "unconditional and unrestricted" inspections. As a consequence the Security Council lifted the annual limit on Iraqi oil sales, on condition that the extra income be used to buy food and medicine and pay for repairs to the country's infrastructure. But in August 1998, Hussein again halted inspections and the unresolved standoff persisted.

The new Secretary-General tirelessly set out to address other stubborn problems facing the United Nations. In March 1998 he visited the Middle East. Speaking to the Palestinian Legislative Council in Gaza City, he urged nonviolence and patience regarding peace talks with Israel; then he spoke to the Israeli Foreign Relations Council in Jerusalem, where he apologized for past unfair UN actions toward Israel but criticized settlements in Palestinian areas and undue hardships imposed on Palestinians. In April of the same year he presented a detailed report to the Security Council entitled "The Causes of Conflict and the Promo-

tion of Durable Peace and SUSTAINABLE DEVELOPMENT in AFRICA." When the peace process collapsed in the Middle East in October 2000, Annan led a feverish diplomatic shuttle among the parties and brokered an emergency summit at Sharm El-Sheik, Egypt, where he brought together Israeli prime minister Ehud Barak, Palestinian Authority chairman YASSER ARAFAT, U.S. president BILL CLINTON, and Egyptian president Hosni Mubarak.

In April 1998 the Secretary-General traveled to his native Africa, visiting eight countries. In Rwanda, before that country's parliament, he sought to repair an abiding ill-will by acknowledging the delinquency of the United Nations in responding to the horrific massacre of Tutsis during disturbances in 1994, a time when he was Under Secretary-General. And, in September 1998, at the opening of the General Assembly, he recommended intervention in the escalating conflict between Serbs and Albanians in KOSOVO. By June 1999 the Security Council approved the NATO-led peacekeeping force in Kosovo, and the UN INTERIM ADMINISTRATION MISSION TO KOSOVO (UNMIK) acquired the difficult responsibility of forming a multinational police force, setting up a justice system, and restoring order in that unhappy province. The Secretary-General also welcomed the establishment of the INTERNATIONAL CRIMINAL COURT (ICC), seated in the Hague in 2002, to bring justice to those committing "crimes against humanity." When, in the fall of 1999, EAST TIMOR voted to secede from INDONESIA, violence erupted as pro-Jakarta militias fought against independence, and a fearful chaos descended over multiethnic and religiously diverse Indonesia. Annan negotiated with the government of President Habibie, who had recently replaced long-ruling General Suharto, to allow UN forces to enter the province. Eventually a UN-sanctioned force, led by Australians, did begin to restore order. But as late as 2006 the United Nations found itself once again in the difficult position of trying to sustain civil order in a dangerous place. The island of Timor remained devastated, and an ominous, seemingly uncontrolled gangs continued to threaten Timorese.

These and other problems related to the challenge of disintegrating states led the Secretary-General to support and build upon certain ideas regarding peacekeeping that were associated with his predecessor, Boutros Boutros-Ghali. In the fall of 2000 the United Nations issued a report, drawn from an international panel of experts, headed by Lakhdar Brahimi, that had been appointed by the Secretary-General, reflecting Annan's vision for peacekeeping. The BRAHIMI REPORT recommended formalizing the UN's peacekeeping activities and ending ad hoc deployments. One of the central recommendations was to create a new information-gathering and analysis office within the United Nations to assemble databases and act as a professional policy planning staff. The panel further recommended the establishment of an integrated task force for each mission, combining analysis, military operations, civilian police, aid programs, finance, electoral assistance, and more. The panel also urged that definitions of self-defense be stretched to allow UN peacekeeping missions to take a more offensive posture in dangerous situations. The expert group that drew up these proposals was made up of members from 10 nations, including the United States and Russia, and its recommendations were praised by, among others, Richard C. Holbrooke, U.S. ambassador to the United Nations.

The forward recommendations for improved UN peacekeeping were ready for timely presentation at the moment of the historic meeting of the MILLENNIUM SUMMIT. This largest gathering of world leaders in history was the brainchild of Secretary-General Annan. Meeting at the UN's New York HEADQUARTERS in September 2000, the meeting entertained some 200 speeches from about 150 prime ministers, presidents, and potentates from most of the world's countries, plus other diplomats. Delegates, in both formal sessions and informal meetings, discussed, and occasionally attempted to resolve, many of the greatest challenges to the world, including reforming peacekeeping, eliminating poverty, reversing the spread of AIDS, promoting DISARMAMENT, advancing the Middle East peace process, making certain that economic globalization left no one behind, and more. When the summit ended on September 8, delegates from countries of often divergent views adopted a wide-ranging DECLARATION containing six "fundamental values" deemed essential to international relations: freedom, equality, solidarity, tolerance, respect for nature, and a sense of shared responsibility. Although some critics scoffed at the apparent ambiguity of the document, the very fact that the United Nations had been able to command the attendance of such a large number of world leaders and keep the summit on the front pages of most major newspapers and on the screens of television and Internet news outlets must have pleased the conference's initiator, Kofi Annan.

And his pleasure must have been enhanced many fold on the following June 27, six months before his first term was to conclude, when the Security Council unanimously renominated Annan and forwarded his name to the General Assembly, where, on June 29, 2001, he was reelected to his post by enthusiastic acclamation. Annan's reelection broke UN tradition. The vote for a Secretary-General normally occurs at the very end of the year, and according to an implicit rotation schedule, Asia could have expected a nominee from its region that December. But Bangladeshi ambassador Anwarul Chowdhury, SECURITY COUNCIL PRESIDENT for June, with the full concurrence of his colleagues, proposed moving the nomination process forward one-half year. This move signaled the growing regard that had been reaped by the Secretary-General and also, of symbolic significance, allowed a developing country to preside over the selection. He had succeeded in meeting the expectations of member states, rich and poor, North and South. Richard Holbrooke captured the attitude of many people around the world, when he referred to Annan as "the international rock star of diplomacy." That stardom received further credence when the Secretary-General and the United Nations garnered the Nobel Peace Prize in 2001, the 100th anniversary of the award. The prize committee praised Annan for "bringing new life to the organization."

During his second term, Annan faced the difficult crises brought on by the terrorist attacks in the United States on September 11, 2001. By the end of 2001 a Security Council sanctioned coalition had invaded AFGHANISTAN seeking to root out AL-QAEDA terrorists and help establish order in the country. In 2002–03, however, the coalition collapsed when the United States decided to go to war with Iraq and topple the regime of Saddam Hussein. The United States did so on the basis of a new foreign policy doctrine—preemption—that challenged the underlying UN principle of COLLECTIVE SECURITY. Secretary Annan feared that the effectiveness of the United Nations was in jeopardy. At the opening session of the General Assembly in September 2003, Annan expressed his fear to the gathered national representatives that the United Nations had reached "a fork in the road." The Secretary-General was also worried about the recent divisions in the Security Council over the war in Iraq. To address the possible need for deep structural reform in the world body, Secretary Annan appointed the HIGH-LEVEL PANEL ON THREATS, CHALLENGES AND CHANGE, chaired by Anand Panyarachun, former prime minister of Thailand, to make recommendations on ways to strengthen the United Nations in the new era.

More difficulties would arise for the Secretary-General as scandals associated with the "OIL-FOR-FOOD" program in Iraq tarnished his reputation. Independent investigations revealed that his son Kojo had benefited financially from the program and that persons close to him may have been involved in criminal conduct. Annan was accused of lax leadership, which led to calls by critics of the United Nations for his resignation. Nonetheless he persisted in serving out his term. In 2005 he put forward a sweeping list of reform proposals in a report entitled *IN LARGER FREEDOM,* urging an expansion of the Security Council to 24 members, the abolition of the TRUSTEESHIP COUNCIL, the replacement of the COMMISSION ON HUMAN RIGHTS with a smaller HUMAN RIGHTS COUNCIL directly elected by the General Assembly, the creation of a PEACEBUILDING COMMISSION, and other reforms. He urged the UN MEMBERSHIP to enact the reforms at the WORLD SUMMIT scheduled for September. The summit, however, refused to act on Security Council reform, and only gave endorsement to the idea of a peacebuilding commission and the replacement of the Commission on Human Rights with a smaller Council. It would be several months before those entities were fully negotiated. Secretary-General Annan's second term drew to a close with far less enthusiasm from the UN member states than his first term had concluded.

See also ADVISORY COMMITTEE ON ADMINISTRATIVE AND BUDGETARY QUESTIONS, GLOBAL COMPACT, SENIOR MANAGEMENT GROUP, SOVEREIGNTY, SUBSIDIARITY.

Further Reading: Annan, Kofi. *Renewing the United Nations: A Programme for Reform.* UN Document A/51/950, July 16, 1997. ————. *We the Peoples: The Role of the United Nations in the 21st Century.* New York: United Nations Department of Public Information, 2000. ————. *In Larger Freedom: Towards Development, Security and Human Rights for All.* UN Document A/59/2005. New York: United Nations, 2005. Farley, Maggie. "Annan Nominated for 2nd Term as Secretary-General," *Los Angeles Times.* June 28, 1901. Miller, Judith. "Annan Says His Son's Payments Created a 'Perception Problem.'" *New York Times,* November 30, 2004. Moore, John Allphin, Jr., and Jerry Pubantz. *To Create a New World?: American Presidents and the United Nations.* New York: Peter Lang Publishers, 1999. *New York Times Magazine.* March 29, 1998. "Secretary General Kofi Annan's Reform Agenda 1997 to Present," <www.globalpolicy.org/reform/initiatives/1997.htm> *Time.* September 4, 2000. Traub, James. *The Best of Intentions: Kofi Annan and the UN in the Era of American World Power.* New York: Farrar, Straus and Giroux, 2006.

Antarctic Treaty

The Antarctic Treaty was signed in Washington, D.C., on December 1, 1959. Its 14 articles came into force on June 23, 1961, upon ratification by all signatory states—Argentina, Australia, Belgium, Chile, FRANCE, JAPAN, New Zealand, Norway, South Africa, the USSR, the United Kingdom, and the UNITED STATES. Under this legal framework, Antarctica, which was defined in the TREATY as the area "south of 60 degrees South Latitude" (Article 6), could only be used for peaceful purposes (Article 1). WEAPONS testing was forbidden, and military personnel and equipment could be used only for scientific research or other peaceful purposes. Article 5 prohibited nuclear tests and explosions and the disposal of nuclear waste, making Antarctica the first NUCLEAR-WEAPONS-FREE ZONE Articles 2 and 3 guaranteed scientific freedom and encouraged scientific cooperation and exchange. Under Article 7, treaty-state observers were given free access to all stations and installations and could conduct inspections of any facility. Contracting parties agreed to undertake efforts consistent with the UN CHARTER to ensure that no one engaged in activities contrary to the principles or purposes of the treaty (Article 10). Should a dispute arise it was to be settled peacefully by the parties concerned. If necessary, it could be submitted to the INTERNATIONAL COURT OF JUSTICE (ICJ).

As of June 2006, there were 45 treaty members: 27 consultative and 18 acceding. The consultative (that is, VOTING) members included those seven nations (Argentina, Australia, Chile, France, New Zealand, Norway, and GREAT BRITAIN) that claimed portions of Antarctica as their national territory and 20 nonclaimant nations (Belgium, Brazil, Bulgaria, People's Republic of CHINA, Ecuador, Finland, GERMANY, India, Italy, Japan, South Korea, the Netherlands, Peru, Poland, Russia, South Africa, Spain, Sweden, Uruguay, and the United States). Parties to the treaty have held regular consultative meetings at which new PROTOCOLs have been considered, with more than 200 adopted.

Among the additions to the treaty, the parties approved the following accords: Agreed Measures for the Conservation of the Antarctic Flora and Fauna (1964), the CONVENTION for the Conservation of Antarctic Seals (1972), the Convention on the Conservation of Antarctic Marine and Living Resources (1980), and a Protocol on Environmental Protection (1991). This last agreement was also known as the Madrid Protocol, entering into force on January 14, 1998. Its aim is to preserve the status of Antarctica as a "natural reserve devoted to peace and science." The protocol prohibited all activities relating to mineral resources unless they were of a scientific research nature. The Antarctic ENVIRONMENT was to be protected further through specific annexes on marine pollution, fauna, flora, waste management, protected areas, and environmental impact assessments. These measures were taken in part because of scientific warnings that tourism—despite heavy penalties assessed for damaging the ecosystem—increasingly threatened the continent.

See also DISARMAMENT, TREATY OF TLATLELOCO.

Further Reading: Joyner, Christopher C. "Recommended Measures under the Antarctic Treaty: Hardening Compliance with Soft International Law." *Michigan Journal of International Law* 19 (Winter 1998): 401–28. Simma, Bruno. "The Antarctic Treaty as a Treaty Creating an 'Objective Regime." *Cornell International Law Journal* 19, no. 2 (1986): 189–209. Stokke, Olav Schram, and Davor Vidas, eds. *Governing the Antarctic: The Effectiveness and Legitimacy of the Antarctic Treaty System.* New York: Cambridge University Press, 1996.

apartheid

From 1946 to 1994, the United Nations addressed the issue of apartheid in more than 220 GENERAL ASSEMBLY resolutions and with a mandatory arms embargo. During this period, UN bodies such as the ECONOMIC AND SOCIAL COUNCIL and the ECONOMIC COMMISSION ON AFRICA, and SPECIALIZED AGENCIES like the WORLD HEALTH ORGANIZATION, the INTERNATIONAL LABOUR ORGANIZATION, and the INTERNATIONAL ATOMIC ENERGY AGENCY voted to restrict South Africa's MEMBERSHIP. The General Assembly also recognized diplomats from the African National Congress and Pan African Congress liberation movements, granting them legitimacy and providing them with needed financial assistance. Over time, South Africa became increasingly ostracized in the United Nations.

South Africa's racial policies were first debated in the United Nations in 1946, when INDIA raised the issue of the treatment of Indian nationals in the Union of South Africa. In response, South Africa invoked the UN CHARTER's principle of noninterference in matters of "domestic JURISDICTION" (Article 2, paragraph 7), and was supported by the UNITED STATES, several European countries, and six Latin American countries. Even though South Africa requested that the INTERNATIONAL COURT OF JUSTICE issue an advisory opinion on the UN's competency, the Indian-sponsored resolution passed the General Assembly. In 1952, India introduced another RESOLUTION specifically concerning the practice of apartheid. By 1960, after the Sharpeville massacre, in which 69 people were killed, the General Assembly passed Resolution 1598, almost unanimously, which rejected apartheid as "reprehensible and repugnant to human dignity." Because of increasing global acceptance of racial equality, and the growing number of African states in the UN, support for South Africa's call for noninterference in the face of UN action declined. In 1962, the General Assembly set up the Special

Segregated sports arena in South Africa, 1969 (UN PHOTO 177913/ H. VASSAL)

Committee on the Policies of Apartheid of the Government of South Africa, which played a crucial role in keeping the apartheid issue before both the General Assembly and the SECURITY COUNCIL. In Resolution 1761 (1962), the General Assembly placed voluntary SANCTIONS on South Africa, including breaking diplomatic relations, boycotting South African goods, and refusing landing rights to South African aircraft. General Assembly Resolution 2398 (1968) discouraged immigration into South Africa and advocated the end of economic linkages with the country. Though voluntary, these sanctions served to heighten South Africa's ostracism by the global community. By 1983, the General Assembly stridently condemned the "illegitimate racist minority regime" of South Africa and termed apartheid a "crime against humanity."

The Security Council also addressed the issue of apartheid. In 1961, the Council considered a resolution to expel South Africa from the United Nations, but it was defeated by several PERMANENT MEMBERS. In 1963, with abstentions by FRANCE and the United Kingdom, the Council called on South Africa to abandon apartheid, claimed these policies seriously disturbed international peace and security, and set a voluntary arms embargo on the country (Res. 181). With no abstentions, the Council passed Resolution 418 in 1977 to make the arms embargo mandatory. Though the Council condemned apartheid and domestic violence in the wake of the 1976 Soweto riots (Res. 417), the permanent members justified the arms embargo by citing South Africa's confrontational foreign policy toward its neighbors. Yet, the Security Council continued to reject mandatory economic sanctions, even when the 1985 South African state of emergency received international condemnation. Several Security Council draft resolutions on sanctions reached the VOTING stage, but they were always rejected by the United States, United Kingdom, and France. In addition to their concerns about COLD WAR confrontations in southern Africa if South Africa was economically weakened, these permanent members expressed a belief that economic sanctions violated the norm of non-interference and would be ineffective.

In February 1990, the new prime minister of South Africa, Frederik W. de Klerk, ordered the release of the black nationalist leader Nelson Mandela, who had been incarcerated for almost three decades. A year later, de Klerk, in compliance with UN resolutions, announced the end of all apartheid laws. Mandela went on to be elected the first black president of South Africa on May 10, 1994. On May 24, the Security Council terminated the arms embargo against South Africa. In June 1994, the General Assembly approved the credentials of the South African delegation, terminated the mandate of the Special Committee Against Apartheid, and removed from its agenda the item on the "elimination of apartheid and the establishment of a united, democratic and non-racial South Africa." Within days, the Security Council removed the item on "the question of South Africa" from its agenda.

Despite the unwillingness of the Security Council to act more forcefully against the South African apartheid regime, the UN did much to shape international opinion about South Africa and the larger norms of racial equality. Between 1946 and 1990, no issue was more enduring, more debated, or more time consuming within the UN than apartheid.

See also NAMIBIA.

Further Reading: Bissell, Richard. *Apartheid and International Organizations.* Boulder, Colo.: Westview Press, 1977. Boutros-Ghali, Boutros, and Nelson Mandela. *The United Nations and Apartheid.* New York: United Nations Department of Public Information, 1996. Stultz, Newell. "Evolution of the United Nations Anti-Apartheid Regime." *Human Rights Quarterly,* no. 13 (1991): 1–23.

— A. S. Patterson

Appeal to the Security Council

Article 35 of the UN CHARTER allows any member state of the United Nations to bring "any dispute or any situation" that is likely to endanger the maintenance of international peace and security to the attention of the SECURITY COUNCIL. Non–member states may also bring disputes as long as they accept in advance the obligations of pacific settlement laid out in CHAPTER VI. While the Council is not obligated to discuss or act on every complaint brought to it, the use of Article 35 has been one of the usual means by which international conflicts have been placed on its agenda.

IRAN's complaint in 1946 that, in the aftermath of World War II, Soviet troops still occupied its northernmost province, was the first appeal to the Council under Article 35. In Africa, states often appealed to the Council to end colonialism or to resolve conflicts between neighboring states. Great powers have also used the procedure to obtain UN endorsement for collective or unilateral action against another state. Conversely, small states have appealed to the Security Council to condemn the actions of major powers. GUATEMALA in 1954 and CUBA in 1960 used this procedure against the UNITED STATES, alleging AGGRESSION in each case.

The question of whether to include an item on the Council's agenda is a procedural matter. It may not be vetoed by one of the PERMANENT MEMBERS. While most appeals are accepted for Council discussion, some have not been. Often prolonged debate occurs over the wisdom of Council action or its JURISDICTION under the Charter. If the Council accepts the appeal, it may invite non-Council members to participate in the debate. It must allow parties to the dispute to address the Council. Once the item is on the Council agenda, the GENERAL ASSEMBLY may make no recommendations concerning it (Article XII), unless the UNITING FOR PEACE RESOLUTION is successfully invoked. In several cases the dispute has remained on the Council's agenda for more than five years.

The Security Council may suggest a traditional means of settling the dispute, including negotiation, INQUIRY, MEDIATION, CONCILIATION, or ARBITRATION. It may also refer the parties to the other bodies of the United Nations, including sending legal disputes to the INTERNATIONAL COURT OF JUSTICE, or to REGIONAL ORGANIZATIONS. In the most serious cases, when it appears that pacific methods are insufficient, it may invoke CHAPTER VII ENFORCEMENT MEASURES and use force to settle the dispute. One strategy, not mentioned in the Charter, but used regularly by the Council when the parties are already locked in battle, has been to call upon the combatants to honor a cease-fire. In a number of Middle East crises this was the approach adopted by the Council, halting the fighting in order to allow for behind-the-scenes diplomacy to find at least a temporary resolution of the conflict.

See also KOREAN WAR.

Further Reading: Bennett, A. LeRoy. *International Organizations: Principles and Issues.* 4th ed. Englewood Cliffs, N.J.: Prentice Hall, 1988. Riggs, Robert E., and Jack C. Plano. *The United Nations: International Organization and World Politics.* Pacific Grove, Calif.: Brooks/Cole Publishing Co., 1988. Simma, Bruno, ed. *The Charter of the United Nations: A Commentary.* 2nd ed. New York: Oxford University Press, 2002.

Arab-Israeli dispute

The struggle between the state of Israel and the Palestinian community, the latter supported by surrounding Arab states in the Middle East, has been the longest running conflict facing the United Nations. The British government first handed the problems of the area over to the fledgling UN when it announced in 1947 its intention to withdraw from its LEAGUE OF NATIONS mandate in Palestine. The central problem then, and over the following 60 years, was the conflict between two peoples who claimed one land—the struggle between the indigenous Palestinian Arabs and the Zionist Jews who had been settling in the region since the late 19th century. Between 1948 and 2007 the United Nations found itself embroiled in six international wars, several local uprisings and civil conflicts, terrorist acts, refugee flows, and superpower politics because of the dispute.

Waves of Jewish immigrants poured into Palestine in the first decades of the 20th century and were further encouraged by a British policy statement in 1917 (the Balfour DECLARATION) committing the United Kingdom to the eventual creation of a Zionist state in the mandate. Faced with British departure the following year, the United Nations established the Special Commission on Palestine (UNSCOP) in 1947 to find a solution to the growing conflict between the two peoples. The commission recommended the partition of Palestine into Jewish and Arab states with Jerusalem under international administration. The GENERAL ASSEMBLY approved Resolution 181 on November 29, 1947, endorsing UNSCOP's proposals. In order to give each side approximately the same amount of land while not requiring the massive movement of local populations, the proposed states were carved out of the territory with irregular borders and separated regions. Zionist leaders of the Jewish Agency quickly accepted the plan, but Palestinians and regional Arab leaders rejected it as the "theft" of Palestinian land. Despite the strategic difficulties of the borders proposed by the partition plan, and the lack of Arab support, both the UNITED STATES and the Soviet Union voted for the RESOLUTION.

Violence escalated dramatically in Palestine following passage of Resolution 181. As tensions led to open warfare in the spring of 1948, both sides frantically prepared for the imminent end of British control. On May 14, Zionist leaders declared the independence of the new Israeli state within its assigned borders of the UN partition plan. The United States and the USSR granted diplomatic recognition within hours.

Arab states responded with military intervention. Armies from Egypt, Transjordan, IRAQ, and Syria joined Palestinian fighters in an effort to reclaim the land for the Arab community. Despite their overwhelming advantage in numbers, the Arab militaries proved no match for the determined Israelis. During the summer the United Nations attempted to establish a cease-fire through the diplomacy of its mediator, Swedish count Folke Bernadotte. His efforts met with only temporary success. In June the SECURITY COUNCIL created the UNITED NATIONS TRUCE SUPERVISION ORGANIZATION (UNTSO), the UN's first observer mission. UNTSO was directed to assist the UN mediator in his efforts to strengthen the cease-fire. Tragically, Bernadotte was assassinated in Jerusalem on September 17 by Israeli ultranationalists. His successor, RALPH BUNCHE, finally achieved an armistice in spring 1949. By the time the fighting ended, Israel's forces were in control of nearly all of Palestine, with the exceptions of East Jerusalem, the West Bank of the Jordan River, parts of the Golan Heights, and the Gaza Strip.

Equally as important, huge flows of Palestinian refugees, numbering nearly 700,000 individuals, were created by the war, leading to the establishment of refugee camps in surrounding Arab states. On November 19, 1948, the General Assembly created UN Relief for Palestine Refugees (UNRPR), sought $25 million in voluntary contributions for it, and gave the effort nine months to assist the refugees. When it became obvious that refugee assistance would have to extend well into the future, UNRPR was replaced by the UNITED NATIONS RELIEF AND WORKS AGENCY FOR PALESTINE REFUGEES IN THE NEAR EAST (UNRWA). It began operation on May 1, 1950, and its mandate, which included the provision of education and work projects in addition to humanitarian assistance, was regularly renewed through 2002.

The uneasy peace following the 1948 war lasted until 1956. Anti-Israeli policies became a staple of Arab foreign policy. The regional opposition to Israel was spearheaded by Egypt and its nationalist leader, GAMAL ABDEL NASSER. He had come to power in 1952 with a group of army officers who had staged a coup in the name of national independence and Egyptian modernization. Much of Nasser's domestic support came from his antagonistic stand against the powers that had controlled Egypt for more than 100 years. The most egregious symbol of European imperialism in Egypt was the Suez Canal, built by Napoleon III and controlled later by the British. Unable to obtain American assistance for significant development projects, Nasser first threatened, then nationalized the Suez Canal (July 26, 1956) in order to secure the income from operating the waterway. Both GREAT BRITAIN and FRANCE saw the seizure of the canal as a mortal threat to their presence not only in the Middle East but also in Asia. Egyptian control of the canal was also perceived as constituting a death grip on the Israeli economy, given the amount of shipping that passed through it on its way to the port of Eilat on the Gulf of Aqaba.

Collusion among Britain, France, and Israel produced a secret arrangement that called for an invasion of Egypt by the latter and a reaction from the European powers that would involve the stationing of an Anglo-French contingent of troops in the canal zone. Israel invaded Egypt on October 29, 1956, and the European forces landed at Port Said and Port Faud on November 5 and 6. Egypt made an APPEAL TO THE SECURITY COUNCIL that led to a resolution vetoed by Britain and France. In response, the Soviet Union invoked the UNITING FOR PEACE RESOLUTION, calling for an emergency session of the General Assembly.

The EMERGENCY SPECIAL SESSION urged a cease-fire, the withdrawal of invading forces, and the reopening of the canal. Canada proposed to the Assembly that it replace foreign forces along the canal with a UN force. On November 4, the Assembly approved Resolution 998 (ES-1) directing SECRETARY-GENERAL DAG HAMMARSKJÖLD to submit within 48 hours a plan "for the setting up, with the consent of the nations concerned, of an emergency international United Nations force (later known as UNEF) to secure and supervise the cessation of hostilities." The intent of the operation was to place a neutral force between the combatants and to monitor the cease-fire. Thus was born on November 5, 1956, the United Nations's first PEACEKEEPING operation. The UN effort, combined with pressure from the United States, led to a British and French announcement on December 3 that they would withdraw, and a similar Israeli announcement on March 1, 1957.

UNEF's presence on Egyptian soil (Israel would not allow the peacekeeping force on its territory) ended direct conflict between Israel and its most important Arab neighbor. The next decade witnessed an evolution in the violence to terrorist attacks, bombings, and brief border skirmishes. The Arab states sponsored new Palestinian organizations. Nasser, in particular, made the Palestinian cause a central tenet of his efforts to mobilize a pan-Arab movement in the Middle East. He took the lead in the creation of the Palestine Liberation

Organization (PLO) in 1964. With Arab support, Palestinian groups such as al-Fatah launched increasingly severe attacks on Israeli domestic sites.

Hostilities reached a critical point between Israel and two of its foes, Egypt and Syria, in the spring of 1967. There were armed Israeli-Syrian clashes in April. On May 16 Nasser asked UN Secretary-General U THANT to remove from the Sinai the peacekeepers who had been there since the armistice of 1956. Thant acceded, much to the consternation of many world leaders. On May 22 Egypt closed the Strait of Tiran and the Gulf of Aqaba, putting a death grip on Israel's economy. Although U Thant had been warning for several months about the rising threat of violence in the Middle East, the PERMANENT MEMBERS OF THE SECURITY COUNCIL did little prior to the outbreak of war in June.

The MIDDLE EAST WAR OF 1967 began June 5 and ended June 10. It was initiated by Israel's preemptive attack on Egypt, Iraq, Jordan, and Syria in which Israeli forces seized the Sinai Peninsula, Syrian territory in the Golan Heights, and the land designated by the 1947 UN partition plan as the territory for the Arab state in Palestine. Israel's air force simultaneously attacked 17 major Egyptian air bases, destroying the bulk of Egypt's airpower within hours of the initiation of hostilities. Similar success against its other Arab enemies led to Israeli occupation of East Jerusalem and the West Bank, producing new waves of Palestinian refugee emigration and adding the issues of Jerusalem's future and that of the occupied territories to the general dispute between Israel and the Arabs.

Israel accepted a UN cease-fire on June 10. It was not until November that the Security Council was able to arrive at a resolution acceptable to all of the parties. RESOLUTION 242, adopted unanimously on November 22, called for a withdrawal of Israel's forces from occupied territories to safe and secure borders, a termination of the state of belligerency and mutual recognition, freedom of navigation, and a settlement of the refugee problem. The recalcitrance of both the Israelis and the Arabs required strong pressure from both the United States and the Soviet Union on their respective allies to get this agreement. Later, there would be acrimony among the parties over the meaning of Resolution 242, specifically concerning whether it required the Israelis to withdraw from ALL occupied territories or only from those that would not jeopardize Israel's security. The resolution was premised on the idea of "land for peace," which became one of the cornerstones for all subsequent regional peace negotiations.

The 1967 war marked the emergence of the Arab-Israeli dispute as a central issue in COLD WAR politics between the two superpowers. LYNDON JOHNSON would be the last U.S. president of the 20th century to believe that this region, as it had been in 1948, was essentially a responsibility of the world's representatives in New York. The "War of Attrition," as it was called, which followed the 1967 conflict, witnessed the division of the region into ideological camps with the Arabs largely dependent on the USSR. In the Soviet-American confrontation each side attempted to manipulate the dispute to its own advantage.

In 1970 Egyptian president Nasser died and was succeeded by Anwar Sadat. In the wake of a confrontation with Egypt's patron, the Soviet Union, Sadat decided that the return of the Sinai depended on a successful demonstration of his country's military strength against Israel and a shift in diplomatic alliances, which would lead to a new and positive relationship with the United States. In Washington the new Nixon administration was pleased that Sadat had removed more than 10,000 Soviet advisers, and it hoped to supplant both Soviet and UN influence over the Arab-Israeli dispute.

At the United Nations, support for Israel, which was increasingly seen as the aggressor and illegal occupier of Arab lands by the growing Third World majority in UN MEMBERSHIP, declined precipitously after 1967. The world body steadily shifted toward support for the Palestinian cause, culminating in the recognition of the Palestine Liberation Organization as the "legitimate representative of the Palestinian people" in 1974, and its achievement of "OBSERVER STATUS" at the UN. Anti-Israeli sentiment peaked with the passage of the ZIONISM IS RACISM RESOLUTION in November 1975. The General Assembly resolution passed by a large majority and equated Israel with the racist regimes then in power in Zimbabwe and South Africa.

The hesitant peace after the 1967 war lasted only until October 6, 1973. On Yom Kippur, the Day of Atonement in the Jewish calendar, Syria and Egypt opened two fronts against Israel seeking to liberate lands captured in the previous conflict. Egypt established a line across the Suez Canal, allowing President Sadat to claim a rare Arab victory against Israeli forces. Within 10 days, however, the balance of forces had shifted and both Syria and Egypt were in retreat. In a daring move Israeli forces crossed the canal, surrounded Suez City, and threatened to march north toward Cairo. The change in military fortune gave incentive to both sides to seek a cease-fire. At the United Nations the USSR offered a draft Security Council resolution calling for (1) a cease-fire in place, (2) withdrawal of Israeli forces to borders implied in Resolution 242, and (3) the commencement of consultations on a peace agreement. After lengthy negotiations between the Soviets and the Nixon administration the Security Council passed Resolution 340, calling for a "return" to the original cease-fire lines as provided in Resolution 338. Following a meeting in the Sinai between Israeli and Egyptian negotiators under UN auspices, a cease-fire was restored.

President Nixon and Secretary of State Kissinger wanted the United States to play the dominant role in bringing a settlement to the troubled area. Despite American sponsorship of Resolution 338, and the Sinai talks under UN auspices, the administration largely ignored the UN machinery in succeeding years as Kissinger launched "Shuttle Diplomacy," hurrying among Middle East capitals, offering American

GOOD OFFICES, and brokering several interim peace arrangements. By the time Kissinger left office in 1977, he had engineered a military disengagement between the Egyptians and the Israelis on the Sinai Peninsula (January 1974) and a similar agreement between the Israelis and the Syrians on the Golan Heights (May 1974). In the Golan Heights the United Nations Disengagement Observer Force (UNDOF) monitored the agreement. On September 4, 1975, Kissinger successfully cobbled together an acceptable buffer zone in the Sinai, originally to be maintained by U.S. civilian technicians stationed between the antagonists. U.S. domination of international efforts to resolve the Arab-Israeli dispute continued into the presidency of JIMMY CARTER. While a strong advocate of the United Nations, Carter played the central role in the negotiation of the Camp David accords, which included a "Framework for Peace" between Israelis and Palestinians and a draft peace TREATY between Israel and Egypt.

Anwar Sadat surprised the world in November 1977 when he became the first Arab leader to make a visit to Israel. In an effort to advance the American-shepherded peace process, in which he had invested much political capital, Sadat addressed the Israeli Knesset and declared his desire for peace. Determined not to let the momentum provided by Sadat's visit slip, Carter invited Sadat and Israeli prime minister Menachem Begin to convene at Camp David, the presidential retreat in rural Maryland. Meetings commenced on September 5, 1978, and lasted 13 days. In the end, the two antagonists agreed to two documents: first, a historic peace agreement between Israel and Egypt, by which the two nations would exchange ambassadors and the Israelis would return occupied portions of the Sinai Peninsula to Egypt; and second, a "Framework for Peace," based on UN Resolutions 242 and 338, detailing procedures to complete a comprehensive peace for the region. The framework called for negotiations involving the United States, Egypt, Israel, and Jordan for the purposes of granting a "homeland" to the Palestinians and securing the border of Israel. In the framework agreement the parties recognized the right of Palestinian representatives to participate in negotiations aimed at establishing an "elected self-governing authority in the West Bank and Gaza." The framework called on the UN Security Council to ensure that its provisions were carried out. The framework laid the basis for a political settlement of the land dispute between Israelis and Palestinians, but it left the question of Jerusalem to future negotiations.

Final approved treaties were scheduled to be completed within three months. But they were not. In the ensuing months, the parties quibbled, and Begin backpedaled on crucial details of the accords. His government also pursued a controversial policy of creating Jewish settlements on the West Bank, drastically changing the demographic and political character of the territory. Rejectionists among Palestinians and the Arab states condemned the framework. Matters were not made easier in March 1978 when Begin ordered an invasion of LEBANON in retaliation for attacks on Israel from guerrilla bases in the southern regions of that tormented country. In the attack, Israel had used American-supplied cluster bombs. Carter was irate, and the United States took the lead in proposing Security Council Resolution 425, which condemned the invasion.

In March 1979, Carter traveled to Cairo and Jerusalem. Once again he used considerable personal pressure to force the parties to an agreement. On March 26, 1979, at the White House, with Carter between them, Sadat and Begin signed the two documents, the first such PACT between an Arab country and Israel since the latter's founding more than 30 years earlier.

In an effort to disrupt the Camp David Accords, the PLO stepped up guerrilla attacks on Israel from southern Lebanon and Syrian territory. In response the Israeli government annexed the Golan Heights in December 1981. Then, on June 6, 1982, it launched a full-scale invasion of Lebanon and headed to Beirut to rout the Palestinians. That same day, the UN Security Council passed Resolution 509, demanding that "Israel withdraw all its military forces forthwith and unconditionally to the internationally recognized boundaries of Lebanon." Ignoring the UN action, Israeli forces within a few days had advanced to the outskirts of Beirut and occupied most of the southern half of the country.

The United States, which had brokered the peace process since the 1973 war, found itself pressured by moderate Arab states to save the Palestine Liberation Organization from complete defeat. The new U.S. secretary of state, George Shultz, and his special envoy in Lebanon, Philip Habib, worked out a plan for the PLO to evacuate the capital city under the protection of a multinational force made up of French, Italian, and American marines. On September 1, President RONALD REAGAN articulated a new American Middle East policy. He proposed a formula of "peace in exchange for territory," with Israel giving up the West Bank, which would become a Palestinian "homeland" to be confederated with Jordan. The Arab states endorsed the Reagan autonomy plan as a good first step. The Israeli government, however, rejected it outright. With no agreement on the Palestinian issue, Israel was bogged down in Lebanon with no obvious way to declare victory and leave.

The frustrations of continued iron-fisted Israeli occupation on the West Bank and Gaza, coupled with new Jewish settlements in the territories and no signs of progress in the peace process, produced the 1987 intifada, a persistent, spontaneous, and widely supported uprising by Palestinians under occupation. Fearing the loss of allegiance from Palestinians in the territories, the PLO indicated its readiness to accept the legitimacy of, and negotiate directly with, Israel. At the end of July 1988, King Hussein announced that Jordan would cut all legal and administrative ties to the West Bank. There was, then, by late summer, considerable activity around the Israeli-Palestinian issue, much of which seemed to suggest the possibility of positive movement. Added to this was the new friendliness between the Soviet Union and the United States, which made senseless any continuing interpretation of the Middle East problem as part of the cold war.

In the fall of 1988, the PLO representative at the United Nations, Zehdi Terzi, informed the Security Council that he would request a visa for YASSER ARAFAT to come to the regular session of the General Assembly. By treaty with the United Nations, the United States had agreed not to block such visas unless a security risk was involved. At the same time, U.S. law forbade representatives of the PLO from visiting unless the secretary of state recommended an exception. This Shultz was unwilling to do, unless the PLO renounced TERRORISM and accepted the provisions of Resolution 242. While Arafat did not attend the General Assembly meeting, in December he met American conditions that Shultz indicated could result in negotiations with the United States. The new administration of GEORGE H. W. BUSH, thus, opened direct talks with the PLO the following year.

The American-orchestrated peace process was put on hold by SADDAM HUSSEIN's invasion of Kuwait in August 1990. The allied victory in the ensuing GULF WAR, however, gave the United States new persuasive power in both Israel and the Arab states, as well as with the PLO. Secretary of State James Baker shuttled between capitals in hope of a breakthrough, an effort culminating in the Madrid Conference in 1991. PLO representatives from the occupied territories joined Israeli government officials and representatives of the Arab states at the negotiating table with President Bush and Soviet president MIKHAIL GORBACHEV. Bush also urged the full participation of the United Nations in the conference, a position adamantly opposed by the Israeli government. In the end the UN was granted a meager "observer" status. The conference operated on two tracks: direct negotiations between Israel and its individual Arab adversaries, and multilateral talks on broader regional issues. Importantly, the Madrid Conference provided the umbrella structure for secret talks between the PLO and the Israeli government, largely conducted away from the Madrid venue. These talks culminated in the Oslo Accords of 1993, which formally accepted the long-endorsed UN principle of partition in Palestine.

As part of the accords, formally signed in Washington on September 13, the PLO conceded Israel's right to exist, and Israel recognized the Palestine Liberation Organization as the representative of the Palestinian people. The Declaration of Principles established a Palestinian Authority in the Gaza Strip and in the West Bank city of Jericho, where Arafat then established his new government. The accords contemplated the eventual transfer of most of the occupied territories to Palestinian control, the negotiation of a final status agreement on Jerusalem, and the refugees' right of return. The momentum of the agreement led to a peace

treaty between Israel and Jordan in 1994. A second Oslo Agreement, encouraged by the United States, was negotiated in September 1995.

The peace process suffered a severe blow when Yigal Amir shot Israeli prime minister Yitzhak Rabin to death on November 4, 1995. A fanatical religious nationalist, Amir admitted at his trial that he assassinated the prime minister in an effort to halt the movement toward peace. He reflected the deep animosity in segments of both the Israeli and the Palestinian communities against the terms established in the Oslo Accords. Most of the opposition in Palestinian society came from Hamas and other Islamic fundamentalist groups. While the interim government of Shimon Peres attempted to move ahead on the peace process, Israeli elections brought to power Benjamin Netanyahu, who opposed any additional concessions to the Palestinian Authority. The new Likud government emphasized security and settlements in the territories. In the spring of 1997 the United States found it necessary to VETO a Security Council resolution condemning the construction of an Israeli settlement at Har Homa. President BILL CLINTON, however, went to great lengths to explain this veto, arguing that the insertion of the United Nations into the issue could jeopardize the ongoing peace negotiations between the Israelis and the Palestinians.

Clinton convened a second Camp David Summit in the summer of 2000, bringing together Arafat and Ehud Barak, Netanyahu's successor. All three leaders had conveyed optimism that a final agreement resolving all of the remaining issues of the Arab-Israeli dispute could be reached. Unfortunately, the meeting ended in failure. While Barak made major concessions on land and Palestinian control over the Holy Sites, Arafat refused to accept an agreement that did not recognize the refugees' right of return and did not grant full SOVEREIGNTY in Jerusalem. The collapse of the summit contributed to the disenchantment in the territories, which in turn produced a second intifada in the fall. Sparked by Israeli politician Ariel Sharon's untimely appearance in September atop the holiest (and most contentious) site in Jerusalem—the Temple Mount, or Haram al-Sharif—Palestinians took to the streets and attacked Israeli security forces and settlers. Israel responded with heavy military force.

As hostilities grew in the streets of the West Bank, U.S. secretary of state Madeleine Albright hurried to Paris and tried to convince assembled Middle East leaders to do something to salvage the faltering peace process. She had no success. On another front, for the first time since 1973 an American administration sought the active leadership of the UN Secretary-General. KOFI ANNAN, who had been shuttling between Jerusalem, Tel Aviv, and Gaza City, and traveling elsewhere in the Middle East, in a quest to ease tensions, stepped into the US/Israeli/Palestinian standoff. With a calm persistence that had become his trademark, Annan persuaded Barak, Arafat, and Egyptian president Hosni Mubarak to convene a summit at Sharm al-Sheik on October 14, 2000. The Israeli government and the Palestinian Authority had come to trust Annan. According to Israel's ambassador to the United Nations, Yehuda Lanery, Annan had "opened the door to Israel. He [was] perceived by Israel as a man of reason, displaying the greatest moral authority possible." The Israeli confidence in Annan was based in part on his expression of regret for the tone of past UN resolutions toward Israel, which he had made during a visit to Jerusalem early in his term. Annan particularly had expressed pleasure at the repeal of the 1975 "Zionism is Racism" resolution in 1991.

At Sharm al-Sheik the United States and the United Nations worked in tandem. President Clinton served as chairman of the summit and Secretary-General Annan provided the quiet diplomacy that led to a tenuous agreement. Arafat and Barak agreed, orally—not in signed form—to call for a halt to the violence; Barak agreed to withdraw Israeli military forces to positions held before the beginning of the unrest, to lift the closure of the West Bank and Gaza, and to reopen the Gaza airport. Security forces from both sides agreed to resume a dialogue that had been interrupted by the crisis. Clinton also announced the creation of a U.S.–controlled fact-finding committee to investigate the causes of the crisis. Clinton appointed the members of the commission after consulting with the parties and Annan. The president designated George Mitchell, former U.S. senator and negotiator of the "Good Friday" agreement in Northern Ireland, as the chairman of the commission. The text of the commission's report, then, was to be shown to Annan and UN officials before being published, and the final decision on the wording of the report was to be made by the United States. A new triangulation had emerged among the White House, UN headquarters, and Middle East leaders.

Unfortunately, the Sharm al-Sheik accord only produced a brief pause in the violence, which soon took the form of Palestinian attacks on settlers and retaliatory Israeli security measures. Faced with opposition from within Palestinian ranks, and with no evidence his commitments at Sharm al-Sheik on their own could halt protests in the streets, Arafat proposed a UN PEACEKEEPING presence in the territories. He sought 2,000 UN peacekeepers to separate the parties on the West Bank and particularly in Gaza, and to limit police actions by the Israeli occupation forces. Tel Aviv immediately rejected the idea. Arafat, however, found support for the proposal not only in Arab capitals but also in Paris, London, and Moscow. Only the threat of a U.S. veto in the Security Council held Britain, France, and Russia to a mere abstention on the final resolution. The resolution failed by only one vote on December 18.

The Israeli electorate chose Ariel Sharon as its new prime minister in the spring of 2001, largely on his promise to end the intifada. Sharon refused to negotiate further with Arafat until the Palestinian Authority controlled the violence. Arafat was hesitant to do so until there was an Israeli promise to withdraw its security forces as agreed at the summit. When the Mitchell Commission issued its report, it called for an end to the violence and a halt to the Israeli construction of settlements in the territories. Both UN and U.S. officials endorsed the commission's recommendations. The new administration of GEORGE W. BUSH sent Secretary of State Colin Powell to the region. On June 28, he announced a change in American policy, endorsing the placement of an observer mission to monitor a cooling-off period until peace negotiations could resume. The creation of such a monitoring force would likely mean a new level of UN involvement in the Middle East crisis. Powell's announcement seemed to foretell a new model of cooperation between New York and Washington in trying to end the Arab-Israeli dispute, which the United Nations first addressed more than 50 years earlier.

Powell's statement came amidst a summer of rising violence in the region. American efforts coupled with significant UN diplomatic involvement proved incapable of moving the peace process forward as Palestinian suicide bombings inside Israel and Israeli reprisal military assassinations of Palestinian leaders became the norm. Particularly in the wake of the September 11, 2001, terrorist attacks on Washington, D.C., and New York City, negotiations between the two sides collapsed. The government of Ariel Sharon depicted Israel's unwillingness to negotiate with Araft and its use of military force to eliminate the suicide attacks as part of the general war on TERRORISM declared by U.S. president Bush. Sharon's position gained credence in January 2002 when his government intercepted a large arms shipment destined for the Palestinian Authority. Israel retaliated by moving forces into the occupied territories, among other intrusions surrounding and bombing Arafat's headquarters in the West Bank. The Palestinian president was unable to leave the compound, which no longer had water or electricity.

In other parts of the territories Israeli military forces carved out "buffer zones" between Palestinian communities and Jewish settlements. In some cases, such as the city of Jenin, this strategy led to heavy bombardment of civilian communities. Part of the separation policy was the announced Israeli intention to construct a 625-mile wall in the West Bank that would provide security from suicide bombers attempting to get into Israel and would impose a unilateral final division of the territories between Israelis and Palestinians. Arab nations introduced a Security Council resolution condemning Israel's actions, and a court case was begun in the INTERNATIONAL COURT OF JUSTICE (ICJ) to block the wall's construction. The Council rejected the Arab initiative but passed Resolution 1397 calling for the restoration of order and the establishment of two states living side-by-side. In an advisory opinion on July 9, 2004, the ICJ ruled the barrier illegal under INTERNATIONAL LAW. The Tel Aviv government rejected the ruling and continued with its construction.

Palestinian claims of GENOCIDE in Jenin put pressure on Secretary-General Annan to intervene in the growing confrontation. He proposed a fact-finding commission, but with no support from the United States, the primary outside power involved in the region, he could not proceed. Instead, Washington sent Ambassador Anthony Zinni to restart the peace process, but he was directed not to include Yasser Arafat in the negotiations. The United States called on the Palestinian Authority to appoint a new prime minister to whom Arafat could transfer many of his presidential powers including control over the security services, and with whom the United States and Israel could negotiate. The United States also blocked a resolution sponsored by Egypt and Tunisia that would have condemned the excessive use of force by Israel and would have established a UN "monitoring MECHANISM" in accordance with the Mitchell Commission's recommendations.

The American decision to go to war in Iraq in March 2003 brought strong Arab and Islamic objection. To blunt criticism the U.S. administration launched a diplomatic offensive to solve the Arab-Israeli dispute. In June President Bush expressed an interest in developing a "Road Map for Peace" that would lay out a timetable for the restoration of security and the emergence of two states. Working with the UN leadership, the United States, Russia, and the European Union formed the "QUARTET," and on September 18 produced "a performance-based roadmap to a permanent two state solution." The plan called for a number of simultaneous steps by both sides including Israeli withdrawal from the territories and the end of its settlements policy. Palestinians were charged with ending all terrorist activity against Israel. But the Road Map proved to be stillborn as the Israeli government decided on a unilateral resolution of the confrontation. Ariel Sharon announced his decision to withdraw Jewish settlements from the Gaza Strip and to impose a final demarcation line in the West Bank.

Isolated and no longer able to control events, President Arafat died in November, 2004. He was succeeded by Mahmoud Abbas, also known as Abu Mazen. Abbas quickly acquired the confidence of President Bush and Ariel Sharon as a serious negotiating partner. In February 2005, Abbas met with President Hosni Mubarak of Egypt, King Abdullah II of Jordan, and Sharon at Sharm el-Sheik. In October, he was rewarded with a visit to the White House. President Bush praised Abbas as a man devoted to peace, and he expressed confidence that the Quartet's Road Map could be fulfilled.

However, President Abbas faced a serious challenge in Palestine from Hamas, the reputed Islamic terrorist organization. For several years it had been gaining political support among the Palestinian people. By January 2006, Hamas had gained a parliamentary majority in the Palestinian government. Thus, Abbas found himself sharing power with a Hamas prime minister. Hamas officially declared that it did not recognize the state of Israel and that it had no intention of negotiating with Israeli leaders.

The United States moved in UN bodies and through diplomatic channels to isolate the Hamas government, calling for economic SANCTIONS and a cutoff of aid to the Palestinian Authority until Hamas recognized Israel's right to exist and dismantled its armed insurgency against the Israelis. Hamas seemed undeterred by the American efforts but did agree to a cease-fire with Israel. Tensions rose during the spring of 2006 as Palestinian bombers resumed efforts to attack civilians in Israel and the Tel Aviv government retaliated with airstrikes against Palestinian targets. When Palestinian radicals abducted an Israeli soldier in June, the Israelis moved troops into northern parts of the Gaza Strip and also arrested several members of the Hamas government. Hezbollah militants from Lebanon then seized two Israeli soldiers in cross-border raids. Israel responded with air and land attacks on southern Lebanon. The United Nations, European Union, France, and GERMANY all expressed deep concern about the escalation in fighting. Kofi Annan called for the release of the soldiers and condemned Israel's retaliatory strikes.

Following the war, the Israeli government of prime minister Ehud Ohlmert sought to reopen negotiations with Palestinian president Abbas. However, Abbas was weakened by a growing rift between his Fatah Movement and Hamas. Arab intermediaries, particular Saudi Arabia, tried to work out a unity Palestinian government, but the situation descended into civil war by late spring 2007. In June, Hamas seized control of the Gaza Strip. The United States moved to cut off all aid to the Palestinians in Gaza, and to end past economic SANCTIONS on the Palestinian Authority under Abbas. Trying to isolate further Hamas and strengthen Abbas's political position, the Bush administration proposed a regional conference to convene in late fall. Other than the Palestinian leader and the Israeli government, there seemed little enthusiasm in Middle East capitals for the summit. After 60 years of continuing conflict a peaceful resolution of the crisis based on the original UN scheme of partition seemed at once the only viable solution and yet elusively out of reach.

See also MIDDLE EAST WAR OF 1973, SUEZ CRISIS.

Further Reading: Bailey, Sydney D. *Four Arab-Israeli Wars and the Peace Process.* London: Macmillan, 1990. Bickerton, Ian, and Carla Klausner. *A Concise History of the Arab-Israeli Conflict.* 2d ed. Englewood Cliffs, N.J.: Prentice Hall, 1995. Laqueur, Walter, and Barry Rubin. *The Israel-Arab Reader: A Documentary History of the Middle East Conflict.* New York: Penguin Books, 2000. Moore, John Allphin, Jr., and Jerry Pubantz. *The New United Nations: International Organization in the Twenty-first Century.* Upper Saddle River, N.J.: Prentice Hall, 2006. Moore, John Allphin, Jr., and Jerry Pubantz. *To Create a New World?: American Presidents and the United Nations.* New York: Peter Lang Publishers, 1999. Ross, Dennis. *The Missing Peace: The Inside Story of the Fight for Middle East Peace.* New York: Farrar, Straus and Giroux, 2005. Rubin, Barry M., and Judith Colp Rubin. *Yasir Arafat: A*

Political Biography. New York: Oxford University Press, 2003. Shlaim, Avi. *The Iron Wall. Israel and the Arab World.* New York: W.W. Norton, 2001.

Arafat, Yasser (1929–2004)

In 1957, Yasser Arafat initiated the Fatah (in Arabic, "opening" or "conquest") guerrilla movement in Palestine to resist the recently created state of Israel. During a long and active life, Arafat became a visible fixture in the world's media, perhaps the single most conspicuous advocate for the rights of the Palestinian people, by definition, those Arabs who lived in the small, geographically triangular area called Palestine, bordered by LEBANON and Syria on the north, Jordan on the east, Egypt on the south, and the Mediterranean Sea on the west. The area had been a British Mandate until 1947, when the United Nations made arrangements to divide it into Arab and Jewish states. The Arab POPULATION resisted, and, following a war won by Israelis, the new nation of Israel assumed control of most of the area. Arafat's Fatah movement eventually metamorphosed into the dominant political party within the Palestine Liberation Organization (PLO, founded in 1964 by the Arab League to remove Israel from the Middle East). Arafat served as Chairman of the PLO from 1969 until his death, and also as president of the Palestinian National Authority (PNA) from 1993 until 2004, and was corecipient (with Israeli Prime Minister Yitzhak Rabin and Foreign Minister Shimon Peres) of the Nobel Peace Prize for negotiating the 1993 Oslo Accords, calling for a two-state solution to the ongoing ARAB-ISRAELI DISPUTE in Palestine. While in 1990 he would marry Suha Tawil, an Orthodox Christian, his personal life would always be secondary to his work on behalf of the Palestinian people. Arafat's life-long cause would be among the most important ongoing matters facing the United Nations.

Born August 24, 1929 (probably in Cairo, although he always insisted that his birth city was Jerusalem), as Mohammed Abdel-Raouf Arafat al-Qudwa (he would also acquire the Arabic honorific name Abu Ammar, used by intimate associates), Arafat was part of a large family of a textile merchant father and a mother from a distinguished Palestinian family. His mother died when he was five, and he spent early years in both Jerusalem and Cairo. He attended Cairo University and, by the end of World War II, seeing the incursion of Jewish refugees into his native land with an intention of establishing a Jewish state, became an opposing Arab guerrilla warrior. For a brief time he was a member of the Muslim Brotherhood and a leader of militant Arab students. He received his college degree in 1956 in civil engineering, joined the Egyptian army, and fought in the 1956 Suez War. He then moved to Kuwait to take a job as a civil engineer, but his heart remained in the Palestinian movement. By the late 1950s he became convinced that Palestinians would have to mount an aggressive resistance on their own and not depend on Arab states to reclaim the lost land. This led him to join with a few colleagues to found Fatah. Fatah initially sought an independent Palestinian state, eventually endorsed the concept of a single, secular state for all of Palestine, and then, by 1993, conceded a two-state solution that would accept both a Palestinian and Israeli state on the land of the former mandate.

In the 1960s, the Middle East was a volatile region, and Fatah's bloody struggle against Israel, usually initiated from Jordanian bases, attracted a growing number of young men to the ranks and elevated Arafat to hero status. In 1969, Arafat became leader of the PLO. The next year, King Hussein's Jordanian government determined to disarm the PLO militias in its midst. A war erupted between Palestinians and the Jordanian army; by late September (called "Black September" by Palestinians), Jordan had suppressed the militias and Arafat was to be exiled to Lebanon. From Beirut Arafat responded to the 1972 assassination of Israeli athletes at the Munich Olympics by disavowing the act and attempting to restrict guerrilla violence to Palestine itself. He officially disbanded the "Black September" militia that had been responsible for the Munich TERRORISM. However, the PLO's reputation had been severely tarnished, and much of the world held Arafat responsible. Yet, within two years, and to the chagrin of many Western nations, the UN GENERAL ASSEMBLY invited Arafat to address its 1974 fall session, where he garnered a GA RESOLUTION declaring the PLO as "the sole legitimate representative of the Palestinian people." In 1976, the PLO obtained full MEMBERSHIP in the Arab League. These triumphs had to be measured against some serious setbacks. The PLO had become enmeshed in the complex Lebanese civil war, and, in 1982, in the aftermath of the Israeli invasion of Lebanon, Arafat found himself once again on the move, being exiled to Tunisia.

In 1988, under considerable diplomatic pressure from the UNITED STATES, he recognized the legitimacy of SECURITY COUNCIL RESOLUTION 242, which envisaged a two-state solution for Palestine. Following the GULF WAR, Arafat's Palestine Authority was invited by U.S. President GEORGE H. W. BUSH to participate in the Madrid talks, which brought together all of the parties to the Arab-Israeli dispute. In parallel secret discussions with Israel Arafat negotiated a dramatic settlement of several outstanding issues. In 1993, he appeared on the White House lawn with President BILL CLINTON and Israeli Prime Minister Yitzhak Rabin to sign the historic Oslo Accords. In compliance with the Accords, which called for the establishment of a "Palestinian Authority" (PA) to carry forth the diplomatic provisions agreed to in 1993, Arafat was elected president of the new PA in January 1996 by 88 percent of those participating in what international observers saw as a free and fair vote (the radical Islamic group Hamas boycotted the election). In following years, however, an aging Arafat came under increasing criticism for practicing cronyism in his appointments and looking aside when obvious corruption began to characterize the PLO. In 2000, Arafat, Clinton, and Israeli Prime Minister Ehud Barak met first at Camp David, and later, in January 2001, at the Taba summit, in a final effort to hammer out a comprehensive settlement to all outstanding issues between the two sides. Although they came tantalizingly close, the negotiations ultimately failed, and some in the West held Arafat responsible for refusing at the last minute to accept unconditionally a workable solution. New U.S. President GEORGE W. BUSH early in his term distanced himself from the Palestinian-Israeli issue, called Arafat "an obstacle to the peace," and attempted to marginalize the PLO leader. Under increasing pressure from the Israeli military, and lacking support from the United States, Arafat became a virtual prisoner in his compound headquarters in Ramallah on the West Bank, where he suffered a serious decline in health, finally dying on November 11, 2004. For the time, his last wish—to be buried in East Jerusalem—was denied, as his remains were interred in Ramallah.

See also MIDDLE EAST WAR OF 1967, MIDDLE EAST WAR OF 1973, MILLENNIUM SUMMIT, NATIONAL LIBERATION, ROAD MAP FOR PEACE.

Further Reading: Gowers, Andrew, and Tony Walker. *Arafat: The Biography.* London: Virgin, 1994. Pubantz, Jerry, and John Allphin Moore, Jr. "Best of Times, Worst of Times: The Fortunes of the United Nations in the Middle East." In *War in the Gardens of Babylon,* edited by Bülent Aras. New York: Tasam Publications, 2004, pp. 89–106. Ross, Dennis. *The Missing Peace: The Inside Story of the Fight for Middle East Peace.* New York: Farrar, Straus and Giroux, 2005. Rubin, Barry M., and Judith Colp Rubin. *Yasir Arafat: A Political Biography.* New York: Oxford University Press, 2003.

arbitration

Arbitration is the process of settling a dispute by using an impartial party or tribunal chosen by the opposing sides that decides the differences between them and adjudicates a solution. Adversaries usually agree in advance to accept the arbitrator's judgment (so-called compulsory arbitration). In international disagreements, arbitrators may be selected from the PERMANENT COURT OF INTERNATIONAL ARBITRATION (PCA), created by the Hague Peace Conferences of 1899 and 1907, or may be selected ad hoc by the disputants. Arbitration is typically conducted on the basis of the rules, practices, and precedents of INTERNATIONAL LAW.

Arbitration is an antique arrangement, used most notably from the late 18th century into the interwar period of the 20th century. The Jay TREATY of 1794, negotiated by GREAT BRITAIN and the UNITED STATES, introduced the modern practice of arbitration as a means of peaceful dispute resolution between two states, and the procedure was used on a few occasions, most notably in the settlement of an American claim from the Civil War period, resulting in the so-called Alabama Arbitration of 1872. Between 1900 and 1932, 20 international disputes utilized the PCA procedures. Since then, only three cases have been resolved in this manner. The proliferation of established arrangements for international judicial settlement, such as the INTERNATIONAL COURT OF JUSTICE, a range of international tribunals, the European Court of Justice, the INTERNATIONAL CRIMINAL COURT, and various MEDIATION procedures in regional and trade organizations, rendered arbitration less practical by the late 20th century.

In 1958 the United Nations GENERAL ASSEMBLY adopted the Model Rules on Arbitral Procedure, formulated by the INTERNATIONAL LAW COMMISSION. The most serious use of arbitration in the contemporary period was the establishment of the Iran–United States Claims Tribunal in 1981 to adjudicate property claims by nationals in each country against the other government. The tribunal was a component in the resolution of the IRAN HOSTAGE CRISIS.

See also AFRICAN UNION CHAPTER VI, CONCILIATION, CONFLICT RESOLUTION, GOOD OFFICES, INDONESIA, UNITED NATIONS CONFERENCE ON THE LAW OF THE SEA.

arms control   *See* DISARMAMENT.

arms race   *See* DISARMAMENT.

Asian Development Bank (ADB)   *See* REGIONAL DEVELOPMENT BANKS.

assessments   *See* SCALE OF ASSESSMENTS.

Atlantic Charter

The Atlantic Charter was the joint DECLARATION of purpose issued by FRANKLIN DELANO ROOSEVELT and WINSTON CHURCHILL at the Atlantic Conference held at Placentia Bay, Newfoundland, on August 9–12, 1941. FDR desired a public statement of fundamental American political convictions regarding a just and peaceful international order that would rally public support for an increasingly dangerous foreign policy in both the Atlantic and the Pacific regions. He also sought a joint statement with GREAT BRITAIN (unlike Woodrow Wilson's unilateral FOURTEEN POINTS) that could serve as a rallying point for an anti-Axis coalition.

The UNITED STATES and Britain pledged territorial nonaggrandizement, self-determination, freedom of trade, freedom of the seas, the abandonment of the use of force, DISARMAMENT, and ultimately, in some form, a world security organization. The joint declaration was not a state paper in the

Winston Churchill and Franklin Roosevelt at Atlantic Conference
(UN/DPI PHOTO)

usual sense of the term. Technically, it was nothing more than a press release, of which there was no official copy.

Nevertheless, the Charter was cabled to JOSEPH STALIN for his endorsement and on January 1, 1942, at U.S. secretary of state CORDELL HULL's suggestion, 26 nations pledged their support for the principles of the Charter in the "DECLARATION BY UNITED NATIONS." This document not only avoided the troubling domestic issue of a formal alliance with Great Britain but also it served as the foundation stone for the later United Nations Organization. The first four signatures on the DECLARATION were those of the representatives of the UNITED STATES, the United Kingdom, the Soviet Union, and CHINA, privately referred to by FDR as the "FOUR POLICEMEN."

Further Reading: Dallek, Robert. *Franklin D. Roosevelt and American Foreign Policy 1932–1945.* New York: Oxford University Press, 1979. Hoopes, Townsend, and Douglas Brinkley. *FDR and the Creation of the U.N.* New Haven, Conn.: Yale University Press, 1997. Kimball, Warren. *The Juggler.* Princeton, N.J.: Princeton University Press, 1991. Langer, William, and S. Everett Gleason. *The Undeclared War. 1940–1941.* New York: Harper and Brothers, 1953.

— E. M. Clauss

Atomic Energy Commission (United Nations Atomic Energy Commission) *See* DISARMAMENT.

Atoms for Peace proposal

U.S. president DWIGHT D. EISENHOWER addressed the UN GENERAL ASSEMBLY on December 8, 1953, and proposed that the nuclear powers gradually transfer a percentage of their fissionable materials to a new INTERNATIONAL ATOMIC ENERGY AGENCY (IAEA), which would be under the ultimate authority of the United Nations. The proposed agency, according to Eisenhower, would safeguard the plutonium deposits and look for ways to use them for the "peaceful pursuits of mankind," such as the generation of electricity "in the power-starved areas of the world." He envisioned scientists and experts mobilized to transform the materials of nuclear destruction into the assets of peaceful world construction. He offered to put U.S. stockpiles under IAEA control at a ratio of 5 to 1 of that turned over by the Soviet Union. Eisenhower's speech provided impetus to UN DISARMAMENT negotiations that led to the 1957 creation of the IAEA and its "safeguards" system for monitoring nuclear material used for peaceful purposes.

During the previous April, the president had directed his advisers to draft a major speech for him on the destructive potential of atomic and hydrogen bombs. In an address that same month to the American Society of Newspaper Editors, he argued that there was a "chance for peace" in the COLD WAR if the USSR was willing to follow a policy of "goodwill." In that case, the two sides could pursue nuclear disarmament, and the savings from that cooperative course of action could be used by the United Nations for a "total war . . . on the brute forces of poverty and need." He laid out the prospect that the end of the arms race could produce the resources for "roads and schools, hospitals and homes, food and health" and could "make the United Nations an institution that can effectively guard the peace and security of all peoples."

It was this formula of responsible Soviet behavior, superpower disarmament, and UN use of armaments savings for humanitarian and development assistance in the Third World that underlay Eisenhower's proposal to the General Assembly in December of his first year in office. Moscow's immediate reaction to the "Atoms for Peace" proposal was negative, as it had been to the Truman administration's BARUCH PLAN. That proposal had also contemplated the transfer of national nuclear assets to UN supervision. Any reduction, however, in nuclear stockpiles by the two sides, even if it drew more heavily from the American arsenal, would still have left the UNITED STATES with an advantage, and consequently the Soviet government was opposed to it. Nonetheless, the United Nations established an IAEA Preparatory Commission in 1954, and the Soviet Union agreed to serve on it, along with the United States, Czechoslovakia, the Vatican, India, and Australia. Eisenhower's speech also created sufficient momentum for the convocation of the first UN Conference on the "Peaceful Uses of Nuclear Energy" (PUNE) in the summer of 1955. After lengthy negotiations the Statute of the IAEA was approved on October 23, 1956, and the agency began operations in 1957. It had no authority to take possession of fissionable materials, but it was authorized to develop nuclear safety standards, and, based on those standards, to assist its member states in the use of nuclear science and technology for peaceful purposes. The agency, which was an outgrowth of Eisenhower's proposal, encompassed 140 member states as of June 2006.

See also ACHESON-LILIENTHAL REPORT.

Further Reading: Ambrose, Stephen E. *Eisenhower. The President*. Vol. 2. New York: Simon and Schuster, 1984. Pruden, Caroline. *Conditional Partners: Eisenhower, the United Nations, and the Search for a Permanent Peace*. Baton Rouge: Louisiana State University Press, 1998. Atoms for Peace Speech Web site: <www.iaea.org/worldatom/About/atoms.html>.

B

bacteriological weapons   *See* DISARMAMENT, WEAPONS OF MASS DESTRUCTION.

Ban Ki-moon (1944–   )

Ban Ki-moon, formerly South Korea's foreign minister, assumed the position of SECRETARY-GENERAL in January 2007 upon the completion of KOFI ANNAN's term. Ban's path to the UN position was surprisingly smooth and his rapid surfacing as the UN's choice was not only swift, but occurred with virtually no interfering diplomatic rancor or debate. Six of the seven candidates placed before the SECURITY COUNCIL were Asians, and Ban, who had declared his candidacy in February 2006, was the clear front runner. He became the second Secretary-General from Asia (U THANT of Burma served from 1961 to 1971). By early October 2006, in an informal straw poll, he had received positive votes from all of the five PERMANENT MEMBERS OF THE SECURITY COUNCIL. On October 9 the Council voted formally and then sent his name to the GENERAL ASSEMBLY, where his appointment was approved.

Ban Ki-moon was born in Chungju, Korea, on June 13, 1944, during the last days of World War II, when Korea was occupied by JAPAN. When he was one year old, the war's victors split the country in two at the 38th parallel, creating an ideologically divided peninsula that, in 2007, was the last of such divided nations so crafted after the war. In the spring of 1950, as Ban turned six, North Korea invaded the South, ini-tiating the KOREAN WAR, in which UN military forces, made up chiefly of U.S. soldiers, fought a sustained battle against the North and its allies—including the People's Republic of CHINA—that ultimately left the country divided exactly as before the war. North Korea remained a one-party communist state well into the 21st century, while the South evolved into an economically successful, democratic, Western-oriented nation. Nonetheless, serious strains remained between North and South, particularly as Kim Jong-Il, son of long-serving dictator KIM IL-SUNG, continued to rule the North with an iron fist. The strain intensified when North Korea announced its intention to build nuclear WEAPONS and Kim, in 2006, declared that his country was prepared to conduct nuclear weapons tests. Secretary Ban was unusually situated to try to cope with this particular predicament. In 1992, following the adoption of the Joint DECLARATION on the Denuclearization of the Korean Peninsula, he served as vice chairman of the South-North Nuclear Control Commission. In addition to serving as South Korea's foreign minister from January 2004 until his selection as Secretary-General, Ban was his country's chief negotiator in the six-nation (South Korea, North Korea, the UNITED STATES, China, Japan, and the RUSSIAN FEDERATION) nuclear talks regarding the crisis.

Ban, who is married and has three children, pursued an educational and diplomatic vocation that recommended him for his UN post. In 1970 he received a bachelor's degree in international relations from Seoul National University and in 1985 he earned a Master of Public Administration from the John F. Kennedy School of Government at Harvard. His diplomatic career spanned three decades. He was posted to INDIA, Washington, D.C., and Austria. He is familiar with the United Nations, where, from 1974 to 1978 he was first secretary for the Mission of the Republic of Korea. In 2001 he was chief assistant (*Chef de Cabinet*) to the president of the General Assembly, Han Seung-soo, and also served as director of the UN Division for the South Korean Foreign Ministry. In 1996, he became National Security Advisor to the President of the Republic of Korea, and three years later, while serving as ambassador to Austria, he was elected as chairman of the Preparatory Commission for the COMPREHENSIVE NUCLEAR TEST BAN TREATY ORGANIZATION (CTBTO). Ban became vice minister for foreign affairs in 2000, ascending to the foreign minister position in January 2004.

See also OFFICE FOR THE COORDINATION OF HUMANITARIAN AFFAIRS, SECRETARIAT, SENIOR MANAGEMENT GROUP, SMART SANCTIONS.

Further Reading: Biography of the Minister, Ministry of Foreign Affairs and Trade, Republic of Korea Web site: <http://www.mofat.go.kr/me/me_a001/me_b002/me_c007/me01_02_sub01.jsp>.

Baruch Plan

This proposal, presented to the United Nations ATOMIC ENERGY COMMISSION (UNAEC) on June 14, 1946, by American industrialist Bernard Baruch, the U.S. representative to the commission, was the first plan ever proposed for the control of nuclear weapons. The commission itself had been created by the UN's first RESOLUTION as an effort to rid "national armaments of atomic WEAPONS and all major weapons adaptable to mass destruction."

The Baruch proposal derived from a committee appointed by President Harry S. Truman, and headed by DEAN ACHESON and David Lilienthal (the administrator of the Tennessee Valley Authority). The ACHESON-LILIENTHAL REPORT provided for an international body to control the raw materials and the production facilities used for atomic energy. Truman then appointed Baruch to present the plan to the UN Atomic Energy Commission. The industrialist altered the original proposal by inserting a VOTING procedure that in effect would have given the UNITED STATES considerable influence over every step in the plan—including the peaceful use of atomic energy in countries like the Soviet Union. On December 30, 1946, the commission approved the Baruch Plan, thereby rejecting an alternative proposal, the so-called Gromyko Plan (named for Soviet ambassador to Washington Andrei Gromyko) that the USSR had offered. The two sides' objections to the other's plan hardened into a pattern that permeated arms control and DISARMAMENT negotiations between the two superpowers throughout almost the entirety of the COLD WAR.

Specifically, the Baruch Plan called for the creation of an International Atomic Development Authority (IADA) that would own and manage all aspects of atomic energy "potentially dangerous to world security." According to the plan no nation would be allowed nuclear weapons and the SECURITY COUNCIL VETO would not extend to the IADA's decisions. The IADA would verify compliance of the peaceful uses of nuclear materials by on-site inspection and any state refusing inspections would suffer economic SANCTIONS. Once the IADA was operating and the inspections regime was in place, the United States would destroy its own atomic stockpile. The Soviets resisted allowing the United States even momentary exclusive control over atomic weaponry and found distasteful the inspections regime. The Gromyko Plan, conversely, called for a speedy abolition of the U.S. nuclear arsenal, rejected the inspection provisions, and demanded the extension of the veto power to the new authority. The United Nations Atomic Energy Commission suspended its meetings on July 29, 1947, due to the deadlock between the United States and the Soviet Union, and the Baruch Plan was never implemented.

Further Reading: Baruch, Bernard M. *Baruch.* Vol. 2. *The Public Years.* New York: Holt, Rinehart and Winston, 1960. Bechhoefer, Bernard. *Postwar Negotiations for Arms Control.* Washington, D.C.: Brookings Institution, 1961. Herken, Gregg. *The Winning Weapon: The Atomic Bomb in the Cold War, 1945–1950.* New York: Vintage Books, 1980. Holloway, David. *The Soviet Union and the Arms Race.* New Haven, Conn.: Yale University Press, 1984.

— *S. L. Williams*

Basel Convention on the Control of Transboundary Movements of Hazardous Wastes and Their Disposal (BC)

Public disclosure in the 1980s that Western industrialists had been dumping toxic wastes in the developing world, mostly in African countries, led to an international effort to ban or regulate the practice. Sponsored by the UNITED NATIONS ENVIRONMENT PROGRAMME (UNEP), the 1987 Cairo Guidelines on Waste Management were drafted to assist states in their own development of waste policies. Two years later a UNEP conference in Basel, Switzerland, adopted the Basel Convention, which did not ban transboundary movement of hazardous waste, but did place stiff regulations on the practice and created a SECRETARIAT to implement its provisions. UNEP provided financing and staffing for the CONVENTION, with the Secretariat's HEADQUARTERS in Geneva. On January 28, 2001, Dr. Sachiko Kuwabara-Yamamoto of JAPAN became the new BC executive secretary. In the summer of 2006, Dr. Kuwabara-Yamamoto presided over a secretariat of some 25 public servants.

The objectives of the convention were to reduce the production, transboundary movement, and distant disposal of hazardous waste, including materials containing arsenic, lead, mercury, asbestos, and other dangerous chemicals. BC also prohibited shipment of this type of waste to countries without the legal, administrative, and technical capability to handle it safely. In addition, the secretariat assisted states with the development of environmentally sound management practices.

As of May 2006, 168 nations had joined the convention. Signatories were obligated to put in place national enforcement measures to fulfill the aims of the PACT. Each transboundary shipment of hazardous waste had to be accompanied by a movement document from the exporting state to the national authorities of the importing nation. Moreover, states were required to identify appropriate disposal and storage sites with sufficient environmental safeguards and to provide enforcement personnel trained in the identification of hazardous waste, with a knowledge of normal companies' operations and a familiarity with international documentation requirements. The Basel Convention established regional centers in Argentina, CHINA, Egypt, EL SALVADOR, INDIA, INDONESIA, Nigeria, Senegal, Slovak Republic, South Africa, RUSSIAN FEDERATION, Trinidad and Tobago, and Uruguay in order to assist governments in these tasks.

The convention created a Conference of the Parties (COP) to meet biennially as the governing body. COP-7 met in GENEVA in October 2004. In previous sessions the COP had added new PROTOCOLS to the convention, strengthening its regulatory functions. The most important of these was the 1995 Ban Amendment, which prohibited export of hazardous waste for any purpose from EU and OECD countries and from Liechtenstein to any other signatory states. In order to enter into force, the ban required ratification from 62 of the parties present at the time of adoption (that is, three quarters of the 82 states). Although exactly 62 states had ratified by May 2006, the amendment had not been effected. The U.S. government had announced in August 2001 that it would not seek Senate ratification for the 1995 amendment. (As of early 2007, the U.S. Senate had not yet ratified the 1989 convention, although Washington had been a signatory since 1990). Without American support the prospects for the ban were seriously diminished.

See also AGENDA 21, COMMISSION ON SUSTAINABLE DEVELOPMENT, ENVIRONMENT.

Further Reading: Eco'Diagnostic, Geneva. *International Geneva Yearbook, 2000–2001.* Geneva: United Nations, 2000. BC Web site: <www.basel.int>.

Beijing Conference   *See* WORLD CONFERENCES ON WOMEN.

Beijing Declaration   *See* WORLD CONFERENCES ON WOMEN.

Beijing +5

In June of 2000, a SPECIAL SESSION of the UN GENERAL ASSEMBLY convened in New York to appraise and assess the progress achieved in the implementation of the Nairobi Forward-looking Strategies for the Advancement of WOMEN and the Beijing Declaration and Platform for Action. The Special Session became known as "Beijing +5" since it was intended to consider what had been accomplished and what was still needed following the Beijing Global Conference on Women, which had been held in 1995. Participants in the Special Session included UN member states, associate members of REGIONAL ECONOMIC COMMISSIONS, UN SPECIALIZED AGENCIES, and NON-GOVERNMENTAL ORGANIZATIONS (NGOs) intergovernmental organizations (IGOs), in CONSULTATIVE STATUS with the ECONOMIC AND SOCIAL COUNCIL (ECOSOC), including NGOs that were accredited to the FOURTH WORLD CONFERENCE ON WOMEN in Beijing, and new NGOs that had achieved accreditation since 1995.

Delegates to Beijing +5 considered 12 areas of concern cited in the Beijing Platform for Action. The topics were poverty, education and training, health, violence, armed conflict, economy, decision making, institutional mechanisms, HUMAN RIGHTS, media, ENVIRONMENT, and the plight of the girl-child. The Platform for Action had spelled out strategic objectives and actions to be taken by governments, non-governmental organizations, the private sector, and the international community. Beijing +5 provided the opportunity to reflect, compare experiences, review commitments, and examine problems and obstacles faced as well as useful practices achieved in putting the Platform of Action into effect. The report of the Special Session recognized the accelerated progress made in some areas of the platform and the problems of discrimination and human rights yet to be addressed.

See also BEIJING +10; WORLD CONFERENCES ON WOMEN.

Further Reading: Beijing +5 Web site: <http://www.un.org/womenwatch/daw/followup/bfbeyond.htm>.

— *K. J. Vogel*

Beijing +10

The UN COMMISSION ON THE STATUS OF WOMEN (CSW) held a 10-year review of the Beijing Platform for Action during the period of February 28–March 11, 2005. The purpose of the review was to note successes, disappointment, and challenges in implementing the Beijing Platform for Action and the BEIJING +5 DECLARATION. Conducted as an expanded meeting of the regular 49th session of the CSW, the gathering featured panels and roundtable discussions, exchanges of ideas, and news regarding the status of the Platform for Action. Government representatives (Ambassador Ellen Sauerbrey represented the UNITED STATES) and several international WOMEN's groups participated. Beijing +10 reaffirmed the Platform for Action and forwarded 10 new RESOLUTIONs covering topics such as gender mainstreaming, HIV/AIDS, and women in AFGHANISTAN. The commission also suggested the usefulness of having a SPECIAL RAPPORTEUR for women's legal rights be appointed in 2006. Several NGOs in attendance expressed concern at losing traction in efforts to implement all the goals of the earlier meetings and even questioned the value of regular WORLD CONFERENCES to deal with such issues. Some participants suggested that subregional meetings might prove more effective in the future.

Bellamy, Carol (1942–)

From 1995 to 2005 Carol Bellamy was the fourth executive director of UNICEF (UNITED NATIONS CHILDREN'S FUND), appointed initially by SECRETARY-GENERAL BOUTROS BOUTROS-GHALI and reappointed by KOFI ANNAN in 2000.

Bellamy was born on January 14, 1942, in New York. She graduated from Gettysburg College in 1963, earned a law degree from New York University in 1968, and was awarded an honorary doctorate of humane letters from Bates College in 2003. Prior to assuming her 10-year position with UNICEF, Ms. Bellamy was engaged in an energetic public life. She was a Peace Corps volunteer in GUATEMALA from 1963 to 1965, New York State senator from 1973 to 1977, and president of the New York City Council from 1978 to 1985. In addition to her public service, she realized a notable private sector career, working as an associate in the law firm of Cravath, Swaine and Moore in the late 1960s and early 1970s, serving as a principal at Morgan Stanley and Company from 1986 to 1990, and as a managing director of Bear Stearns and Company in the early 1990s. U.S. President BILL CLINTON appointed her director of the Peace Corps in 1993, a position she left to become executive secretary of UNICEF.

At UNICEF Bellamy gave primary concentration to suppressing the spread of HIV/AIDS, particularly among young people, protecting children from abuse and violence, striving to immunize every child, working to ensure that all girls and boys received adequate basic education, encouraging early childhood programs in every country, and urging global investment in children. While she was executive director, UNICEF's funding more than doubled, from about $800 million to over $1.8 billion, and considerable progress for children occurred. For example, the child mortality rate worldwide was cut 16 percent (the exception to this positive news being in Africa). Other significant reductions included: polio (down 99 percent from 1988), measles (40 percent from 1999), and diarrhea deaths (50 percent from 1990). In May 2002, in response to Ms. Bellamy's urgings,

the UN SPECIAL SESSION on Children invited hundreds of children to attend, meet with delegates, and influence the goals adopted at the session. In 2005, Ms. Bellamy's term as executive director ended and she was replaced by Ann M. Veneman, formerly U.S. secretary of agriculture. In 2005 Bellamy was appointed to the New York State Board of Regents. As of late 2006, Ms. Bellamy was also serving as president and CEO of World Learning and president of its School for International Training.

Further Reading: UNICEF Web site: <http://www.unicef.org>. UNICEF biography Web site: <http://unicef.org/about/who/index_bio_bellamy.html>. UN Special Session on Children (2002) Web site: <http://www.unicef.org/specialsession/>.

Bernadotte, Folke   *See* ARAB-ISRAELI DISPUTE.

Bertini, Catherine Ann (1950–)

In November 2002 SECRETARY-GENERAL KOFI ANNAN appointed Catherine Bertini as UNDER SECRETARY-GENERAL for Management. In January 2003 she succeeded Joseph Connor in the post and she served until 2005. Prior to this appointment, Ms. Bertini had been for a decade executive director of the Rome-based UN WORLD FOOD PROGRAMME (WFP), the largest international humanitarian agency in the world.

Ms. Bertini was born on March 30, 1950, in Syracuse, New York. She graduated from the State University of New York, Albany, in 1971 with a degree in political science. Long active in Republican Party politics in the UNITED STATES, Bertini ran unsuccessfully for a U.S. congressional seat from Illinois in 1982, worked as campaign manager for other Republican candidates, and sat on the Republican National Committee. For a decade she was a public affairs officer for Container Corporation of America in Chicago, and was a member of the Illinois HUMAN RIGHTS Commission in the late 1980s. Before her appointment to the WFP in 1992, Ms. Bertini was assistant secretary of agriculture for food and consumer services in the U.S. Department of Agriculture and acting assistant secretary of the Family Support Administration in the U.S. Department of Health and Human Services. On the recommendation of U.S. president GEORGE H. W. BUSH, Secretary-General BOUTROS BOUTROS-GHALI appointed her executive director of the World Food Programme and, endorsed by U.S. president Bill CLINTON and the GROUP OF 77, she was reappointed by Secretary Annan in 1997, completing five years later the two five-year terms to which the director is limited. Her terms were challenged by devastating wars and natural disasters. By the end of her service WFP was providing food aid to some 77 million people in 82 countries around the globe. She received plaudits for her efforts to contain famine in North Korea, to provide food during the crises in BOSNIA and KOSOVO, to ward off starvation in the civil conflict–plagued Horn of Africa in 2000 and 2001 (when she served additionally as the Secretary-General's special envoy for Drought in the Horn of Africa), and for delivering needed food aid to AFGHANISTAN in 2001. The WFP Executive Board also lauded her efforts at internal REFORM, including the remarkably low level of administrative overhead costs she was able to achieve. By the end of her service, WFP, dependent on voluntary funding, had attained its highest level of support ever—$1.9 billion. In mid 2002 Ms. Bertini commenced a two-year term as chair of the UN System Standing Committee on Nutrition and also represented the Secretary-General as his Personal Humanitarian Envoy to Israel and the Palestinian territories. In 2003 she was accorded the World Food Prize. During her two-year appointment as Under-Secretary for Management, she was responsible for overseeing the UN's human, physical, and financial resources and for achieving reform of worldwide staff security. These years were marked by rising costs for the United Nations and growing arrearages by member states in their required dues payments. She was forced into cross-borrowing from the PEACEKEEPING account in order to meet regular UN financial obligations. In 2004 Bertini estimated the UN shortfall at nearly $100 million. In the event, she was able to increase UN pension fund investments by 50 percent. She was also deeply involved in seeking additional financing for security at UN venues, and the refurbishment of UN HEADQUARTERS as well as the construction of new facilities. In 2005 Catherine Bertini assumed a professorship of public administration at the Maxwell School, Syracuse University. In September 2006 she was the invited Distinguished Lecturer at the International Union of Food Science and Technology's 13th World Congress held in Nantes, FRANCE.

See also DEVELOPMENT, FOOD AND AGRICULTURE ORGANIZATION.

Further Reading: Bertini CV Web site: <http://classes.maxwell.syr.edu/ppa730/about%20the%20professor/CV/Bio/resumeCATHERINE%20ANN%20BERTINI.pdf#search='Bertini%2C%20Catherine%20CV'>. UN biography website: <http://www.un.org/News/ossg/sg/stories/catherine_bio.asp>.

biological weapons (BW)

Biological WEAPONS are living organisms, most commonly bacteria and viruses, deliberately disseminated to cause death or disease in humans, animals, or plants. Biological weapons are considered WEAPONS OF MASS DESTRUCTION because they have the potential to destroy life equaled only by nuclear weapons. They could also be used for much smaller scale effect and in clandestine operations. An important distinction between biological weapons and nuclear weapons is that the former do not have the ability to destroy a country's infrastructure or industrial capacity. Despite the concern

about BW TERRORISM in recent years, the power of governments to build, maintain, and hide offensive BW programs still constitutes the most serious biological weapons' threat to international peace and security. Advances in the biological sciences in the last quarter century have added to the risk that such expertise could be misused.

The 1925 Geneva PROTOCOL prohibited the use of biological weapons in warfare. The 1972 CONVENTION ON THE PROHIBITION OF THE DEVELOPMENT, PRODUCTION, AND STOCKPILING OF BACTERIOLOGICAL (BIOLOGICAL) AND TOXIN WEAPONS AND ON THEIR DESTRUCTION (BWC) went further by prohibiting their development and possession. The United Nations provides conference services for the BWC and has strongly encouraged its members to strengthen the TREATY's effectiveness through a legally binding protocol. The UN SECRETARY-GENERAL has the authority to investigate the alleged use of biological weapons, ascertain facts regarding such alleged use, and report his findings to the member states.

Prior to the 20th century and the widespread understanding of the role of germs in causing disease, the use of biological weapons was extremely rare. In certain instances, however, their use was well documented, most notably in the deliberate spread of disease among the INDIGENOUS PEOPLE in North America. The 20th century was characterized by state efforts to develop, produce, and, to a lesser extent, use biological weapons. GERMANY used veterinary biological weapons for sabotage purposes in World War I. JAPAN had a sophisticated BW program directed against humans with large-scale experimentation and use in CHINA in the 1940s. The UNITED STATES, United Kingdom, Canada, and FRANCE all had BW research, development, and production programs in the years preceding and/or during World War II, but none of these countries used the weapons they developed.

A number of countries violated their obligations under the BWC by initiating or continuing to develop and produce biological weapons following the treaty's entry into force. The Soviet Union maintained a massive secret BW program, South Africa produced biological weapons in the 1980s and 1990s, and IRAQ, while a signatory of the BWC, developed an offensive biological program in the 1980s. In 1991 the UN SECURITY COUNCIL required Iraq to accept the unconditional destruction of its biological weapons and all components of its BW program. For many years Iraq's BW program could be neither confirmed nor denied, despite international inspection and the accumulation of evidence and documentation. After the overthrow of SADDAM HUSSEIN's government in 2003, inspectors were unable to find any evidence of residual BWs in the country. Following complaints from CUBA to the Secretary-General that the United States had used these types of weapons against it, a formal consultative meeting took place in 1997. The meeting was officially inconclusive; however, substantial credible evidence contradicted Cuba's claim.

See also DISARMAMENT.

Further Reading: "Biological Weapons: From the BWC to Biotech." *Disarmament Forum* no. 4 (2000): 7–50. Geissler, Erhard, and John Ellis van Courtland Moon, eds. *Biological and Toxin Weapons: Research, Development and Use from the Middle Ages to 194,* Stockholm Peace Research Institute (SIPRI) Chemical & Biological Warfare Studies, no. 18. Oxford, U.K.: Oxford University Press, 1999. Lederberg, Joshua, ed. *Biological Weapons: Limiting the Threat.* Cambridge, Mass.: MIT Press, 1999. Zilinskas, Raymond A., ed. *Biological Warfare: Modern Offense and Defense.* Boulder, Colo.: Lynne Rienner, 2000.

— *M. I. Chevrier*

Biological Weapons Ban   *See* BIOLOGICAL WEAPONS (BW), DISARMAMENT.

Blix, Hans (1928–)

Dr. Hans Blix served as DIRECTOR-GENERAL of the INTERNATIONAL ATOMIC ENERGY AGENCY (IAEA) from 1981 to 1997 and as executive chairman of the UNITED NATIONS MONITORING, VERIFICATION AND INSPECTION COMMISSION (UNMOVIC) from March 2000 to June 2003. In the latter position he became one of the most visible UN officials in the world's media as the U.S. war with IRAQ approached in the spring of 2003.

Dr. Blix was born in the university town of Uppsala, Sweden, in 1928. He attended the University of Uppsala, did graduate studies at Columbia University in New York City, and earned a Ph.D. at Cambridge University. In 1960 he began teaching INTERNATIONAL LAW at Stockholm University. He has written several books in the general fields of international law and international relations. From 1963 to 1976 Dr. Blix was legal adviser on international law in the Swedish Foreign Ministry, becoming under secretary of state in 1976 and minister of foreign affairs for the years 1978–79. He was a member of the Swedish delegation to the UN GENERAL ASSEMBLY for two decades beginning in 1961, and between 1962 and 1976 was also a member of his country's delegation to the CONFERENCE ON DISARMAMENT in Geneva. As director-general of the IAEA for almost two decades, he was a focal international official during the years that covered the ending of the COLD WAR and the post–cold war arrangements by the Soviet Union and the UNITED STATES to accelerate nuclear DISARMAMENT. As director general, he made frequent visits to Iraq to inspect the country's nuclear reactor at Osiraq prior to attempted destruction by IRAN in 1980 (during the long IRAN-IRAQ WAR) and its ultimate demolition when the Israeli air force bombed it in 1981. Following the first GULF WAR (1991) the extent of Iraq's nuclear programs, based on highly enriched uranium rather than on plutonium, became known, and, following the military success of the coalition forces in the 1991 war, the UN SECURITY COUNCIL passed RESOLUTIONS (687 in April, 1991, 707 in August, 1991, 715 in October, 1991, and several during the 1990s) that imposed upon Iraq severe limitations on its WEAPONS programs and insisted on international inspections. In early 2000 SECRETARY-GENERAL KOFI ANNAN called Blix back from retirement and appointed him to head the UN MONITORING, VERIFICATION AND INSPECTION COMMISSION (UNMOVIC; he was succeeded by Demetrius Perricos in 2003). In 2002, the Security Council passed RESOLUTION 1441, directing the commission to begin searching Iraq for WEAPONS OF MASS DESTRUCTION, a process that continued through the early spring of 2003. Although grumbling about Iraqi cooperation, Blix and the monitoring commission found no such weapons. Nonetheless, the United States initiated war against Baghdad in March 2003 on the unyielding assumption that such weapons in fact existed. Following the American defeat of SADDAM HUSSEIN and the occupation of Iraq, further inspections confirmed Blix's earlier findings that no WMDs existed in the country. In a BBC interview in February 2004, Blix, who—because his investigations in Iraq had led to questions about claims of the GEORGE W. BUSH administration in 2003—had been widely criticized by supporters of Washington's war policy, remarked that the United States and the United Kingdom had overstated the threat of WMDs in Iraq in order to buttress the case for war. After retiring from UN service, Blix was appointed chair of the Weapons of Mass Destruction Commission, an independent organization based in Stockholm and sponsored by the Swedish government. Blix presented Secretary-General Annan with the commission's recommendations on June 1, 2006. Among other proposals the group suggested the convocation of a world summit on disarmament and a revision of VOTING rules in the CONFERENCE ON DISARMAMENT to allow something less than unanimity to move international disarmament efforts forward.

See also NUCLEAR NON-PROLIFERATION TREATY; SANCTIONS; UNITED NATIONS SPECIAL COMMISSION ON IRAQ (UNSCOM).

Further Reading: Blix, Hans. *Disarming Iraq.* New York: Pantheon, 2004. ———. *Sovereignty, Aggression and Neutrality.* Stockholm: Dag Hammarskjöld Foundation and Almqvist and Wiksell, 1970. UN biography Web site: <http://www.un.org/Depts/unmovic/ExecChair/ExeChBi.htm>.

Blue Helmets

Military personnel serving as UN peacekeepers wear a familiar blue helmet to distinguish themselves from all other military or PEACEKEEPING operations. Increasingly joined by civilian colleagues, the mandates of these so-called Blue Helmets became more challenging as the world moved into the 21st century. Blue-helmeted UN peacekeeping forces administered cease-fires, managed the separation of hostile forces, aided in encouraging national and ethnic reconciliation, promoted HUMAN RIGHTS, monitored elections, and became involved in "NATION-BUILDING," as in AFGHANISTAN, TIMOR-LESTE, the FORMER YUGOSLAVIA, the Middle East, and many other locales. Blue Helmets have been active since 1948, when they were dispatched to Palestine. In 1988, the UN's Blue Helmets—that is its peacekeeping forces—won the Nobel Peace Prize.

See also CHAPTER VI ½ PROVISIONS, SUEZ CRISIS, UNITED NATIONS EMERGENCY FORCE.

Further Reading: *The Blue Helmets.* 3d ed. New York: United Nations Department of Public Information, 1996. Hillen, John. *Blue Helmets: The Strategy of UN Military Operations.* 2d ed. Washington, D.C.: Brassey's, 2000.

Board of Chief Executives of the United Nations System   *See* CHIEF EXECUTIVES BOARD FOR COORDINATION.

Bolton, John R. (1948–   )

U.S. president GEORGE W. BUSH appointed Bolton the U.S. ambassador to the United Nations on August 1, 2005. The appointment came in the aftermath of a period of strained relations between Washington and the United Nations; the UNITED STATES had not had an official representative at the organization since January 2005. (John Danforth resigned in December 2004 after serving five months.) An outspoken critic of the United Nations, Bolton became a controversial diplomat at the New York HEADQUARTERS.

John R. Bolton was born in Baltimore, Maryland, on November 20, 1948. He earned a B.A. summa cum laude and an ensuing law degree (JD), both from Yale University. Early in his professional career he practiced law in Washington, D.C., and he returned to law practice during the 1990s. Prior to assuming the position of ambassador to the United Nations he accumulated an extensive public employment record, serving during the presidency of RONALD REAGAN as, first, general counsel and then assistant administrator for program and policy coordination for the U.S. Agency for International Development, followed by an assignment as assistant U.S. attorney general. While practicing law during the administration of Democratic president BILL CLINTON, Bolton also assumed the post of senior vice president of the American Enterprise Institute (AEI), a conservative think tank in Washington, D.C. President George W. Bush chose him to be under secretary of state for arms control and international security, a position he held from May 2001 to May 2005.

When Secretary of State Condoleezza Rice announced Bolton's nomination to the United Nations she called him a "tough-minded diplomat" with a "proven track record of multilateralism." However, critics, including a consequen-

tial minority of Republicans in the U.S. Senate, saw Secretary Bolton as abrasive and anti-multilateral. Once his nomination was made, previous remarks he had made were publicized to his disadvantage in the Senate confirmation process. Among those was a statement he uttered in a 1994 speech asserting that "there is no such thing as the United Nations. . . . [moreover] If the UN SECRETARIAT building in New York lost ten stories, it wouldn't make a bit of difference." Bolton was a visible and expressive opponent of two multilateral agreements signed by President Clinton but never ratified: the COMPREHENSIVE TEST BAN TREATY (CTBT) and the Rome Statute creating the INTERNATIONAL CRIMINAL COURT (ICC). Because of his brazen demeanor and hawkish reputation, he was unable to garner sufficient votes for confirmation in the U.S. Senate, even though it contained a majority of Republicans. Thus President Bush had to make a "recess" appointment (that is, made while the Senate was in recess and unavailable for VOTING; the consequence was that Bolton was allowed to serve no longer than the end of the next congressional session, by which time the Senate would have to confirm him as U.S. permanent representative or he would have to leave his post).

Upon assuming his position, Bolton immediately made an impact by issuing a series of demands regarding the pre-summit negotiations for the 2005 WORLD SUMMIT, a follow-up to the MILLENNIUM SUMMIT of 2000. Among his stipulations was that the summit drop the words "MILLENNIUM DEVELOPMENT GOALS (MDG)." As it happens, President Bush, in a speech before the summit, announced his *acceptance* of the MDGs, for the moment easing the melancholy caused by his new appointee. Although Bolton continued to be a lightening rod and sparred pugnaciously with members of the Secretariat, he settled into a vigorous regime at the United Nations. He worked with Secretary Rice as well as with his colleagues on the SECURITY COUNCIL trying to craft mutually acceptable RESOLUTIONs to address the challenge of nuclear program development in IRAN and North Korea.

Working in the environment of UN diplomacy, Ambassador Bolton, while often expressing biting rhetorical commentary on the organization's capabilities, adjusted to the nuances of multilateral decision-making. In mid July, 2006, Bolton, who had worked diligently to achieve consensus among the PERMANENT MEMBERS OF THE SECURITY COUNCIL (P5) on collective action to halt North Korea's nuclear program, voted for the unanimously approved SC Resolution 1695, which condemned the country's recent missile launchings, demanded a suspension of all ballistic missile programs, required all countries to prevent North Korea from receiving or transferring missile-related items, and insisted that the country return to the six-nation talks (North and South Korea, RUSSIAN FEDERATION, JAPAN, CHINA, and the United States) designed to end her NUCLEAR WEAPONS program. Bolton called the Council's action "unequivocal, unambiguous and unanimous" and referred to the Council session as "historic." He then voted with a unanimous Security Council in mid October 2006 on follow-up Resolution 1718 which called for SANCTIONS on North Korea.

Ambassador Bolton also appeared to make progress on obtaining a Council consensus on Iran. The United States had taken a strong position in opposition to Iran's nuclear enrichment program. Initially, the Russian Federation and China had opposed any significant sanctions against Iran, and Western European states had promoted negotiations rather than confrontation with Tehran. Bolton worked to bridge the differences among the major powers so as to achieve a Security Council resolution that would not only demand a halt to the Iranian program (Resolution 1696, passed 14-1 in late July, did just that) but would in addition provide for hard-nosed sanctions. Security Council Resolution 1737, passed unanimously by the Council in late December 2006, did impose sanctions on Iran to pressure that country into halting its nuclear enrichment program. However, by the time this delicately negotiated resolution had passed Bolton was no longer at the United Nations. The congressional elections of November 2006 brought a majority of Democrats into both houses of the Congress, ending Bolton's chances of receiving formal Senate confirmation, and he resigned.

Further Reading: Bolton, John R. *Surrender is not an Option: Defending America at the United Nations and Abroad.* New York: Threshold Editions, 2007. Bumiller, Elisabeth, and Sheryl Gay Stolberg. "President Sends Bolton to U.N.; Bypasses Senate." *New York Times,* August 2, 2005, A1. U.S. Department of State Biography Web site: <http:www.state.gov/r/pa/ci/biog/53920.htm>.

Bonn Convention   *See* CONVENTION ON THE CONSERVATION OF MIGRATORY SPECIES OF WILD ANIMALS (CMS).

Bosnia

Bosnia is one of the former Yugoslav republics born out of the Yugoslav civil war of the 1990s. It declared its secession following a plebiscite in February 1992. On May 22, 1992, Bosnia and Herzegovina was officially recognized as a member state of the United Nations. But its three largest communities—Muslims (44 percent of the POPULATION), Croats (17 percent), and Serbs (31 percent)—disagreed about the future of an independent Bosnia, resulting in a bloody civil war.

In the early days of Yugoslavia's breakup, the Yugoslav National Army (JNA), comprised mostly of Serbs, sought to maintain the territorial integrity of the nation. But with the successes of Slovenia and Croatia in establishing their independence, the JNA shifted its emphasis to aiding Serb irredentist sentiment (that is, the JNA insisted that all Serbs should be united under the same government—the postwar "rump" Yugoslavia). When Bosnia attempted to estab-

lish an independent government headed by President Alija Izetbegović, the Serbs within Bosnia revolted and sought to establish their own state or to join their territories with the rest of Yugoslavia. The difficulty of this task, and the ensuing ethnic violence, arose from the interconnectedness of the two communities within Bosnia. In an effort to assure Serb majorities in the parts of Bosnia they controlled, Serbs engaged in ethnic cleansing. They imprisoned many Bosnian Muslims, killed others, and terrorized the rest, forcing them to leave their homes for predominately Muslim areas.

In response to the violence and to Serb policies, the United Nations deployed the UN Protection Force (UNPROFOR) and sought to create "safe havens" in which Muslims would be protected from Serb assaults. The United Nations was unsuccessful at protecting the enclaves. Perhaps the greatest atrocity of the war occurred at the "safe haven" of Srebrenica. During July 1995, Serb forces entered the town, took UN peacekeepers hostage, and systematically murdered hundreds of Muslim men and boys. Out of concern for the remaining foreign peacekeepers' safety, neither European governments nor UN officials would accept American proposals for military retaliation.

In the midst of the fighting, the United Nations and the European Union (EU) collaborated on a peace proposal, authorizing former U.S. secretary of state Cyrus Vance to negotiate for the United Nations, and former British foreign minister Lord David Owen to negotiate for the EU. The Vance-Owen peace plan, however, proved ineffective, due in part to its territorial complexity as well as to the Serb determination to continue fighting the war. In August 1995 Bosnian Serb forces carried out a particularly heinous attack on Sarajevo, shelling the marketplace and killing 35 people. To protect Bosnian Muslims, the North Atlantic Treaty Organization (NATO) began bombing Serb positions within Bosnia. In the wake of the NATO bombing the Croats attacked the Serbs in Croatia along the Krajina strip and retook much of the land the Serbs had won in battle in 1992. The West did little to oppose this Croatian attack, revealing how isolated the Serbs were. Additionally, Bosnian Muslims and Croats agreed to a federated Bosnia, meaning each ethnic group would have autonomous powers within its region should they agree to the territorial integrity of Bosnia. Under intense international pressure, including economic SANCTIONS that created record inflation in Yugoslavia, the Serbian leader, SLOBODAN MILOŠEVIĆ, agreed to accept an American invitation to meet in Dayton, Ohio, with Izetbegović and Croatian president Franjo Tudjman. In November 1995 the DAYTON PEACE ACCORDS ended the civil war in Bosnia.

The Dayton Accords had a number of important provisions: (1) that all nationals be repatriated to their original homes, so that ethnic cleansing would not be rewarded, (2) that the Serbs recognize the SOVEREIGNTY of the Muslim-led government of President Izetbegović, (3) that the United Nations send a PEACEKEEPING force (first called IFOR, for Implementation Force, later SFOR, for Stabilization Force) to monitor the peace, (4) that all war criminals indicted by the INTERNATIONAL CRIMINAL TRIBUNAL FOR THE FORMER YUGOSLAVIA be extradited to The Hague for trial and (5) that the Office of the High Representative (OHR, appointed by the UN SECURITY COUNCIL) oversee the civilian provisions of the accords. NATO troops totaling 60,000 were to supervise the implementation of the agreement. The long process of building the Bosnian nation had begun.

That same year, the SECURITY COUNCIL established the UN International Police Task Force as part of a larger UNITED NATIONS MISSION IN BOSNIA AND HERZEGOVINA (UNMIBH), which supervised the demilitarization of the region and organized elections. In October 1996 Bosnia and Yugoslavia established diplomatic relations. Serious problems, however, continued to confront Bosnia and Herzegovina at the turn of the century, including resettling refugees, rebuilding the economy, establishing a working government, locating indicted war criminals who were still at large, and dealing with the fact of a rump Serbian entity within the country (the Srpska Republic). In a positive move, however, in October 2001 the parliament of the Bosnian Serb enclave approved the arrest of individuals under indictment by the international tribunal in The Hague. And there continued to be a steady return of refugees to their homes. In October 2002 complex elections were held for a three-man presidency, for a parliament, and for the parliaments of the two separate member republics. Nonetheless, Bosnia continued to be administered via the OHR. In December 2004 European Union peacekeeping troops replaced NATO forces in the country. In support of the High Representative, the Security Council created the UN MISSION IN BOSNIA AND HERZEGOVINA (UNMIBH), which was charged with reforming the police system and helping with the development of a professional judiciary. The European Union then took over UNMIBH's functions. On July 11, 2003, the Council passed Resolution 1491 indicating that it "remained seized with the matter" of Bosnia and Herzegovina, but acknowledging and lauding the role of other entities in the administration of the country. By 2006, direct UN involvement was largely conducted through its related agencies—the UN DEVELOPMENT PROGRAMME, the WORLD BANK, and the INTERNATIONAL MONETARY FUND—that served on the OHR's primary advisory panel, the Board of Principals.

See also FORMER YUGOSLAVIA, LAND MINES, RUSSIAN FEDERATION, WAR CRIMES TRIBUNALS.

Further Reading: Daalder, Ivo H. *Getting to Dayton: The Making of America's Bosnia Policy.* Washington: Brookings Institution, 1999. Holbrooke, Richard. *To End a War.* New York: Random House, 1999. Rieff, David. *Slaughterhouse: Bosnia and the Failure of the West.* New York: Simon and Schuster, 1996. Rohde, David. *Endgame: The Betrayal and Fall of Srebenica, Europe's Worst Massacre since World War II.* Boulder, Colo.: Westview Press, 2000. Woodward, Susan L. *Balkan Tragedy: Chaos and Dissolution After the Cold War.* Washington, D.C.: Brookings Institution, 1993. Dayton Peace Accords Web sites: www1.umn.edu/humanrts/icty/ Dayton/daytoncompl.html and www.state.gov/www/regions/ eur/Bosnia/bosagree.html. UNMIBH Web site:www.un.org/ Depts/dpko/Missions/unmibh/.

— D. J. Becker

Boutros-Ghali, Boutros (1922–)

The sixth SECRETARY-GENERAL, Boutros Boutros-Ghali was the first Arab and first African to hold the post. He was born in Cairo, Egypt, in 1922 into a distinguished Coptic Christian family. His grandfather had been prime minister of Egypt and his father finance minister. Boutros-Ghali studied political science, economics, and law at Cairo University, where he received a Bachelor of Law degree in 1946. In 1949 he earned a Ph.D. in INTERNATIONAL LAW from the University of Paris (Sorbonne). He then held professorships at Cairo University and lectured on international law and international affairs at several universities in Europe, the UNITED STATES, INDIA, the Middle East, and Africa. He also authored numerous scholarly books and articles on international affairs—most written in French—was a Fulbright scholar at Columbia University in New York for the 1954–55 academic year, and was a director of the HAGUE ACADEMY OF INTERNATIONAL LAW in the Netherlands, 1963–64.

Boutros-Ghali, appointed as minister of state for foreign affairs in 1977, accompanied Egyptian president Anwar Sadat that year on the historic trip to Jerusalem, and he is considered one of the main architects of the Camp David Accords of 1978, which led to the Egyptian-Israeli peace TREATY of the following year. By 1991, he had been elevated to deputy prime minister of Egypt.

When JAVIER PÉREZ DE CUÉLLAR's retirement neared in late 1991, Boutros-Ghali emerged as one of several possible successors. The ORGANIZATION OF AFRICAN UNITY (OAU) pressed for appointment of an African to the position of Secretary-General. Breaking with tradition, Boutros-Ghali openly campaigned for nomination. Although he was an Arab, he was acceptable to Israel (and the United States) because of his work on the Egyptian-Israeli peace negotiations and because he had married into a prominent Egyptian-Jewish family. The OAU, preferring a sub-Saharan choice, nonetheless accepted Boutros-Ghali as an adequate alternative. Egyptian president Hosni Mubarak lobbied heavily with U.S. president GEORGE H. W. BUSH on behalf of his countryman, who at the same time was enthusiastically supported by FRANCE. Meantime, most of the Third World found little to protest, and CHINA and the Soviet Union decided to go along with the nomination. Thus, although 14 sound candidates were presented to the SECURITY COUNCIL at a closed-door session on November 21, 1991, Boutros-Ghali won nomination on the first ballot.

Within a few months of his assuming office in January 1992, Boutros-Ghali forwarded the concepts of "peace enforcement" and "PEACE-BUILDING" as distinct from "PEACEKEEPING." This shift in UN policy, interpreted as not requiring the consent of all parties to a conflict, even if the conflict was internal to a sovereign state, resulted in an expansion of UN peacekeeping operations, with the most notable, and difficult, taking place in SOMALIA and the FORMER YUGOSLAVIA. Indeed, in 1988, there were fewer than 10,000 UN peacekeepers on duty in world hot spots, costing the organization $364 million annually. By early 1992 the number had barely nudged up to 11,500. But by the summer of that year, UN troops around the world had risen to 44,000, and by early 1993 approached 80,000, with a total cost of $4 billion.

With the conclusion of the GULF WAR in mind, world leaders met in January 1992 in the first Heads of Government Council meeting to consider the future role of the United Nations in the post–COLD WAR environment. The leaders directed the new Secretary-General to prepare recommendations on ways of strengthening the United Nations and making it more efficient in "PREVENTIVE DIPLOMACY" and peacekeeping. The Council requested that the report be submitted in six months. In June, Boutros-Ghali published his recommendations. Entitled *AGENDA FOR PEACE*, the report outlined the most ambitious UN program of peacekeeping in the organization's history. According to the report, the United Nations needed to identify "at risk" states and act early to avoid the collapse of state SOVEREIGNTY and internal order. The Secretary-General proposed that military forces be placed at the disposal of the United Nations for rapid action in times of crisis.

Boutros-Ghali then became the prime mover in mobilizing the world community to deal with the collapse of order in the east African nation of Somalia. At his initiative, Security Council RESOLUTION 751 (April 1992) created UNOSOM I, a small, unarmed, peacekeeping force for Somalia. But the situation continued to deteriorate. In late November the Secretary-General wrote to President Bush seeking immediate American action to secure food supplies in Somalia and

Secretary-General Boutros Boutros-Ghali (UN PHOTO 186266/FABRIC RIBERE)

to restore order. On December 3 the Security Council—at U.S. urging—approved Resolution 794 invoking CHAPTER VII. Under its authorization, and at the conclusion of the president's term in December 1992, he inserted U.S. forces, allegedly to lead the UN contingent for a limited time. The Americans soon became enmeshed in a nasty civil conflict between rival warlords. On October 3, 1993, the new Clinton administration was confronted with tragic front-page news stories of 18 U.S. soldiers being trapped in a firefight and killed, and a lurid photograph of one of them being dragged through the streets of Mogadishu. American support for more vigorous UN peacekeeping efforts now waned, troops were home within the year, and criticism mounted that the United Nations was incapable of ordering the internal affairs of any country.

For Rwandans the shifting mood was particularly perilous, since a brutal, genocidal civil conflict had broken out between the rival Tutsi and Hutu tribes. Although the Clinton administration had originally supported the UNITED NATIONS ASSISTANCE MISSION FOR RWANDA (UNAMIR), the outbreak of massacres in April 1994 caused it to propose the cutting back of the number of peacekeepers in the region out of fear for their safety. Meantime, the degenerating situation in the FORMER YUGOSLAVIA increasingly appeared to be beyond UN remedy. The 1994 off-year congressional elections in the United States, bringing Republicans into a majority in both houses for the first time in almost half a century, now brought the Secretary-General, and his ideas about an invigorated United Nations, into direct conflict with the world's most powerful nation.

In response to growing criticism about UN bureaucratic wastefulness, Boutros-Ghali froze the UN BUDGET and took a number of other steps to allay concerns, particularly those being expressed in Washington. By 1993 U.S. arrears to the organization reached $1 billion. In hopes of ending the freeze on American contributions to the UN, Boutros-Ghali appointed Richard Thornburgh, a former U.S. attorney-general, UNDER SECRETARY-GENERAL for administration and management. He gave Thornburgh carte blanche to review all operations in the world body. The new appointee, in turn, asked the Ford Foundation to conduct an external review of the United Nations. It set up a commission headed by PAUL VOLCKER, a former chairman of the U.S. Federal Reserve, and Shiguro Ogata, the former deputy governor of the Japan Development Bank. Within a year both Thornburgh and the Volcker-Ogata Commission issued reports highlighting many of the same weaknesses in the United Nations. Both called for tighter quality control of the UN staff, and budgetary reforms. The Thornburgh Report also suggested the appointment of an inspector-general to root out fraud, waste, and abuse. Seeking greater efficiency, the Ford Foundation group called for a unified peacekeeping budget. When the Clinton administration signaled its support of both reports, Boutros-Ghali indicated he would take steps to implement many

of the recommendations. In 1994, Boutros-Ghali supported the creation of the OFFICE OF INTERNAL OVERSIGHT SERVICES (OIOS), headed by an under secretary-general. The new director of OIOS was given a five-year term and virtual independence from the Secretary-General with a mandate to conduct broad investigations and evaluations throughout the UNITED NATIONS SYSTEM. None of these moves, however, stopped the growing criticism from conservative U.S. senators, who saw the United Nations as inefficient, inept, yet bent on gaining too much power at the expense of U.S. SOVEREIGNTY. The Secretary-General and Senator Jesse Helms of North Carolina—new chair of the powerful Senate Foreign Relations Committee—now engaged in a public argument in the pages of the respected journal *Foreign Affairs*. In the spring of 1996 Boutros-Ghali penned a defense of his ideas regarding an active Secretary-General at the head of a more vigorous United Nations. Five months later, in the same journal, Helms used highly blunt language to lambaste the United Nations and excoriate its executive leader.

Although Boutros-Ghali had disavowed a second term when he entered office in 1992, a number of nations, including some of America's closest allies, strongly supported his continuing in 1997. But the political climate in Washington clearly made such continuance impossible. The Secretary-General, the object of unkind remarks during the American presidential campaign of 1996, had become the lightning rod in the United States for displeasure at all that seemed wrong with the United Nations. There was no way his nomination could avoid a U.S. VETO in the Security Council. Having entered office at a high point of optimism regarding the possibilities of the international organization, Boutros Boutros-Ghali, the victim of a spate of uncontrollable in-state collapses and the decline of UN financing, left office after one tumultuous term.

After leaving office, Boutros-Ghali served as a senior officer of several international entities. He was secretary-general of La Francophonie (1997–2002), an organization of French-speaking nations, president of the Institute for Mediterranean Political Studies (2002–06), and president of the Society for International Development. He also accepted the presidency of the Curatorium Administrative Council at the Hague Academy of International Law. The Curatorium hires the professors for the academy and sets its scientific research program. From 2003 to 2006 the former secretary-general served as the chairman of the South Centre, an organization of 46 developing nations that promote South-South cooperation.

See also AGENDA FOR DEVELOPMENT; ANNAN, KOFI; REFORM OF THE UNITED NATIONS; SECRETARIAT.

Further Reading: Boutros-Ghali, Boutros. *Unvanquished: A U.S.–U.N. Saga.* New York: Random House, 1999. Moore, John Allphin, Jr., and Jerry Pubantz. *To Create a New World?: American Presidents and the United Nations.* New York: Peter Lang Publishing, 1999.

Brahimi Report

On August 23, 2000, the Panel on United Nations Peace Operations published a 70-page report calling for dramatic REFORM of the UN's PEACEKEEPING missions, its DEPARTMENT OF PEACEKEEPING OPERATIONS (DPKO), the process by which the SECURITY COUNCIL and the SECRETARY-GENERAL implemented decisions to intervene in conflicts, and the funding MECHANISMS for peacekeeping efforts. The panel was chaired by Algerian ambassador and former foreign minister Lakhdar Brahimi, who had also served as UN SPECIAL REPRESENTATIVE to AFGHANISTAN. Secretary-General KOFI ANNAN appointed the panel on March 7, 2000. Made up of 10 experts on peace operations, including representatives from the UNITED STATES and the RUSSIAN FEDERATION, Brahimi's panel issued its report on the eve of the MILLENNIUM SUMMIT. The report's recommendations elicited the most earnest and sustained discussion among the attending heads of government.

Consisting of nearly 60 proposals, the report reflected Secretary-General Annan's desire to strengthen and make more effective UN peacekeeping. Pressured particularly by the United States, the Secretary-General asked Brahimi to prepare frank and specific recommendations that would narrow the gap between the UN's burgeoning peacekeeping responsibilities and its limited financial and organizational resources.

The Brahimi Report recommended formalizing the UN's peacekeeping activities and ending ad hoc deployments. One of the central recommendations was to create a new information-gathering and analysis office within the United Nations to assemble databases and act as a professional policy planning staff. The panel further recommended the establishment of an integrated task force for each mission, combining political analysis, military operations, civilian police, electoral assistance, aid to refugees, finance, logistics, public information, and streamlined procurement procedures. The panel also urged that definitions of self-defense be stretched to allow UN peacekeeping missions to take a more offensive posture in dangerous situations. It recommended that traditional UN "impartiality" between combatants in a conflict not be allowed to "amount to complicity with evil." According to the panel, the credibility of UN peacekeeping depended on being able "to distinguish victim from aggressor."

While it did not call for a standing UN army, the Brahimi Report advocated reform of the United Nations Standby Arrangements System (UNSAS) in order to ensure that the UN could fully deploy a peacekeeping force within 30 days of a Security Council decision to do so. In order to fund rapid deployment, the panel recommended that the Secretary-General be authorized to commit up to $50 million in advance of a contemplated Security Council decision to undertake a new operation.

The report encouraged "a substantial increase in resources for HEADQUARTERS support of peacekeeping operations," and called upon Annan to submit a financing proposal to the GENERAL ASSEMBLY, as well as a plan for implementation of the report's other recommendations. Annan welcomed the report's findings and directed DEPUTY SECRETARY-GENERAL LOUISE FRÉCHETTE to proceed with implementation. He requested that the General Assembly authorize expenditure of $22 million to carry out all of the recommendations. In January 2001 it granted a first installment of $9.5 million for this purpose. The General Assembly's willingness to fund the reforms was due in part to a fall review by the Security Council's Special Committee on Peacekeeping Operations that had endorsed them, a Security Council resolution on November 13 approving them, and Annan's subsequent steps toward implementation.

The General Assembly's action marked a victory for Annan and for the United States, which had sought significant reform before it would support any new operations or pay its assessments arrears. Initial reaction to the report among developing states had been cool, fearing the new rules for peacekeeping might amount to a form of UN "colonialism" at the behest of U.S. foreign policy and might take funds away from development. Among the PERMANENT MEMBERS OF THE SECURITY COUNCIL, concern was initially reflected in the demur from Chinese president Jiang Zemin and Russian president Vladimir Putin. But a vigorous public relations effort by Annan and Brahimi, combined with the promise of U.S. funding if the recommendations were accepted, dispelled the opposition.

Subsequent peacekeeping missions were comprehensive efforts at NATION-BUILDING, often initiated by the Security Council authorizing a major power or REGIONAL ORGANIZATION to lead the original intervention, and then sending in UN personnel and supervisors to repatriate refugees, administer local government, protect HUMAN RIGHTS, bring about reconciliation among warring groups, and assist with constitution-writing and elections. This approach was first attempted in the Balkans—BOSNIA and KOSOVO—and was replicated in TIMOR-LESTE, where Australia organized the intervention. In SIERRA LEONE, ECOWAS (ECONOMIC COMMUNITY OF WEST AFRICAN STATES) intervened with UN approval, and the AFRICAN UNION sent the initial forces into DARFUR, Sudan. At UN headquarters, Secretary-General Annan established a Lessons Learned Unit in DPKO to draw insights from both successful and failing interventions.

Further Reading: Report of the Panel on United Nations Peace Operations Web site: <www.un.org/peace/reports/peace_operations/>. Millennium Report of the Secretary-General Web site: <www.un.org/millennium/sg/report/>. Global Policy Forum "Peacekeeping" Web site: <http://globalpolicy.igc.org/security/peacekpg/reform/>.

Bretton Woods

The United Nations Monetary and Financial Conference convened in Bretton Woods, New Hampshire, from July 1 to 22, 1944. The conference drafted agreements establishing three institutions meant to create a postwar global free trade system: the INTERNATIONAL MONETARY FUND (IMF), the International Bank of Reconstruction and Development (IBRD)—better known as the WORLD BANK—and the GENERAL AGREEMENT ON TARIFFS AND TRADE (GATT). The last of these was supposed to be an "interim" agreement until an International Trade Organization (ITO)—which would provide a more ambitious regulatory framework for world trade—could be established. GATT, however, remained in place until January 1, 1995, when it was superseded by the WORLD TRADE ORGANIZATION (WTO).

Sponsored by the UNITED STATES, the Bretton Woods Conference and its ensuing agreements attempted to create a new international monetary and trade regime that was stable and predictable. Negotiators structured the IMF to limit the fluctuation of foreign currency exchange rates while using the World Bank to pump needed capital investment into nations devastated by the war. American planners hoped to avoid the economic nationalism of the interwar years by gradually removing protectionist barriers to free trade. Through "rounds" of negotiation members of GATT eliminated tariffs, quotas, and other impediments to international commerce. The success of the measures initiated at Bretton Woods depended, however, on the willingness of the United States, whose economy accounted in 1944 for more than half of world domestic product, to fund these institutions and to maintain monetary policies conducive to world economic growth.

The Bretton Woods meeting was held nearly in tandem with the DUMBARTON OAKS CONFERENCE, which prepared the draft CHARTER OF THE UNITED NATIONS. Each was undertaken by the United States to create a postwar international framework that would avoid the kind of financial and economic instability that had followed World War I. Soon after the Bretton Woods institutions came into being, Washington pegged the dollar to gold at $35 an ounce, enacted large foreign aid programs in order to pump liquidity into the international economic system, and made the largest subscription of funds of any IBRD member to the assets of the World Bank. IMF, GATT, and the World Bank, while independent institutions, are considered part of the UNITED NATIONS SYSTEM.

See also ACHESON, DEAN; CHIEF EXECUTIVES BOARD OF THE UNITED NATIONS SYSTEM; INTERNATIONAL LAW; NEW INTERNATIONAL ECONOMIC ORDER; PASVOLSKY, LEO.

Further Reading: Schild, Georg. *Bretton Woods and Dumbarton Oaks: American Economic and Political Postwar Planning in the Summer of 1944.* New York: St. Martin's, 1995. Schwartz, Herman M. *States versus Markets. History, Geography, and the Development of the International Political Economy.* New York: St. Martin's, 1994.

Bricker Amendment

During the post–World War II era a major American constitutional issue arose out of the potential impact of the United Nations CHARTER and the UN COVENANT on Human Rights upon U.S. federal-state relations. The problem first attracted notice in the Supreme Court case *Oyama v. California* (1948), in which the court held that a California law denying aliens ineligible to become citizens the right to own land was void because, among other reasons, it conflicted with Article 55 of the UN Charter. Under Article 55 the United States pledged itself to "promote . . . universal respect for, and observance of, HUMAN RIGHTS and fundamental freedoms for all without distinction as to race, sex, LANGUAGE, or religion." A California court subsequently ruled the state law invalid on this ground.

The decision initiated a widespread legal discussion over whether the UN Charter was a self-executing TREATY and capable, as the supreme law of the land, of setting aside state and federal statutes in areas of civil rights and property rights. One view held that the Charter was merely a vague DECLARATION of national intent, to be effective only when implemented by congressional statute. Others insisted that it was indeed a self-executing treaty and thus supreme law. The pending International Covenant on Human Rights would have gone further, essentially binding signatory states to an elaborate series of guarantees, in the form of an international bill of rights.

In response to widespread public agitation over the issue, Senator John Bricker (R-Ohio) in 1952 introduced a constitutional amendment to limit the scope of the federal treaty power. The Bricker Amendment sought to negate any treaty that conflicted with the U.S. Constitution, to demand appropriate enabling legislation to make a treaty valid as internal law, and to regulate all executive and other agreements with any foreign power or international organization.

Critics of the amendment insisted that it would interfere with the president's conduct of foreign affairs so decisively as to make an effective foreign policy impossible. Despite growing popularity, Bricker's initiative was confounded when President Eisenhower and Secretary of State John Foster Dulles announced their opposition to the proposal. Nevertheless, in February 1954 the Senate voted 60 to 31, one vote short of the required two-thirds constitutional majority, for a modified and weakened version of the Bricker Amendment. Subsequently, the issue rapidly lost its political appeal and became a dead issue.

Further Reading: Eisenhower, Dwight D. *The White House Years.* Vol. 1. *Mandate for Change, 1953–1956.* Garden City, N.Y.: Doubleday, 1963. Tannenbaum, Duane A. "The Bricker Amendment Controversy: Its Origins and Eisenhower's Role." *Diplomatic History* 9 (Winter 1985): 73–93.

— *E. M. Clauss*

Brundtland Commission *See* WORLD COMMISSION ON ENVIRONMENT AND DEVELOPMENT.

Brundtland, Gro Harlem (1939–)

The chairperson of the WORLD COMMISSION ON ENVIRON-MENT AND DEVELOPMENT (WCED) in the 1980s, Dr. Gro Harlem Brundtland gave birth to one of the United Nations's most enduring programmatic ideas, that of "SUSTAINABLE DEVELOPMENT." Brundtland, a medical doctor and former prime minister of Norway, led the effort to link DEVELOP-MENT and environmental protection on a global scale, and in compatible ways that would preserve the earth and the economic prospects of future generations. As a result of her efforts, she became one of the most visible WOMEN working within the UNITED NATIONS SYSTEM, becoming DIRECTOR-GENERAL of the WORLD HEALTH ORGANIZATION (WHO) in 1998.

Gro Harlem Brundtland was born in Oslo, Norway, in April 1939. After becoming a doctor and earning a Master of Public Health (MPH) she pursued advanced studies at Harvard University. When she returned to Norway she held a succession of public health positions. In 1974 she was appointed Norway's minister of the ENVIRONMENT. In 1981 she became the country's youngest and first female prime minister. She served in that post at different times for more than 10 years between 1981 and 1996.

Dr. Brundtland's public expressions of concern about global issues related to the environment led UN SECRETARY-GENERAL JAVIER PÉREZ DE CUÉLLAR to appoint her the chair of the WCED in 1983. In an effort to revitalize the program of action proposed by the 1972 UNITED NATIONS CONFER-ENCE ON THE HUMAN ENVIRONMENT (UNCHE), he urged Brundtland's commission to establish "a global agenda for change." The commission held nearly two years of public hearings and interviewed thousands of individuals and orga-nizations on the problems of environment and development. In 1987 it issued its final report, *Our Common Future,* which became the bedrock statement for sustainable development, the central doctrine around which all future UN efforts in the two fields would be built. The "Brundtland Commis-sion," as it became known, defined sustainable development as "development that meets the needs of the present without compromising the ability of future generations to meet their own needs." *Our Common Future* called upon governments to include environmental concerns in the process of devel-opment, and the document noted the intrinsic link between economic growth, and socioenvironmental factors such as health, population growth water and air purity, and natural beauty. The WCED recommended that the United Nations convene a global conference on sustainable development, which it did in Rio in 1992. Known as the Earth Summit, the meeting enshrined Brundtland's concept as the centerpiece for future UN development efforts.

After she stepped down as Norwegian prime minister in 1996 Brundtland sought, and achieved, appointment as direc-tor-general of WHO in May 1998. In so doing, she returned to her professional roots in public health. She restructured the organization to include "Sustainable Development and Healthy Environment" as one of WHO's primary "clusters" of activity, demonstrating the breadth to which the concept could be applied. She told the World Health Assembly in her 1998 acceptance speech that the organization needed "to unleash development and alleviate suffering." It should do this by "promoting sustainable and equitable health systems in all countries." Her leadership of WHO along these lines had the effect of expanding sustainable development from a concept focused solely on development and environment to one that included Sustainable Human Development in all of its dimensions.

Dr. Brundtland left the World Health Organization in 2003. The following year the British newspaper *Financial Times* named her the fourth most influential European of the previous quarter century, after Pope John Paul II, MIKHAIL GORBACHEV, and Margaret Thatcher. Often called *"Landsmo-deren"*—Mother of her Country—in her native Norway, Gro Harlem Brundtland was awarded an honorary doctorate in medicine from the University of Oslo in 2005. Following her service at WHO, she joined the Board of Directors of the UN Foundation, a philanthropic organization founded by Ted Turner to support UN activities.

See also COMMISSION ON SUSTAINABLE DEVELOPMENT, UNITED NATIONS CONFERENCE ON ENVIRONMENT AND DEVELOPMENT, UNITED NATIONS ENVIRONMENT PRO-GRAMME.

Further Reading: Brundtland, Gro Harlem. *Madam Prime Minister: A Life in Power and Politics.* New York: Farrar, Straus, and Giroux, 2002. Elliott, Lorraine. *The Global Poli-tics of the Environment.* New York: New York University Press, 1998. World Commission on Environment and Devel-opment. *Our Common Future.* New York: Oxford University Press, 1987.

budget of the United Nations

There are three major budgets for UN operations: the regular budget funded by assessment of contributions from member states, a budget for international tribunals, and a PEACEKEEP-ING budget. For the biennium of 2004–05 the regular budget of the United Nations was slightly more than $3.1 billion (the peacekeeping budget—the most expensive segment of UN expenditures—was about $5 billion).

Each of these budgets is approved by the General Assembly (GA) upon the recommendation of panels of experts that have reviewed proposals from the SECRETARY-GENERAL. In addition there are many voluntary program FUNDS to which states may make contributions. These funds provide resources for UN PROGRAMMES and special initiatives. Often "pledging conferences" and other solicitation techniques will be used to raise sufficient voluntary contributions. In the wider UNITED NATIONS SYSTEM, SPECIALIZED AGENCIES maintain separate budgets with some effort at system-wide coordination of budgetary and administrative policies.

Since its founding, the United Nations has employed "the capacity to pay" as its primary budgetary principle, with the consequence that rich industrialized states are charged significant percentages of UN expenses while new developing states are responsible for an insignificant proportion of the budget. Beyond a state's gross domestic product, its per capita income and level of debt are also factored into determining its assessment. The unwillingness of states large and small to pay their assessments, however, has left the world body regularly on the brink of financial collapse. At the time of the MILLENNIUM SUMMIT in 2000, unpaid assessments to the regular budget totaled in excess of $244 million, to tribunals $31 million, and to peacekeeping more than $1.3 billion. Within a year the deficit in the regular budget rose to $723 million with 103 members delinquent in their payments. By April 2006 the regular budget deficit was $1.2 bil-

lion, with U.S. arrears at $675 million, or about 56 percent. The total debt in April 2006 (covering the regular budget as well as peacekeeping, international tribunals, and the capital master plan) came to $3 billion, with the U.S. shortfall representing $1.4 billion of that. A significant part of Secretary-General KOFI ANNAN's REFORM program after 1997 was directed at restoring confidence by nonpaying states in the effectiveness of the United Nations in order to importune payment of arrearages, and to find cost savings through the results-based budgeting technique.

The GA's FIFTH COMMITTEE recommends the regular two-year budget to the plenary body. In its deliberations, the committee depends heavily on the oral and written reports of the ADVISORY COMMITTEE ON ADMINISTRATIVE AND BUDGETARY QUESTIONS (ACABQ), which is made up of 16 financial experts, and those of the 34-member Committee for Programme and Coordination. The Fifth Committee has the responsibility of recommending the SCALE OF ASSESSMENTS every three years, which establishes how much each state must pay to the organization. This is done on the recommendation of the COMMITTEE ON CONTRIBUTIONS, one of the two standing committees of the General Assembly. In December 2000, the Fifth Committee lowered the "ceiling" that any

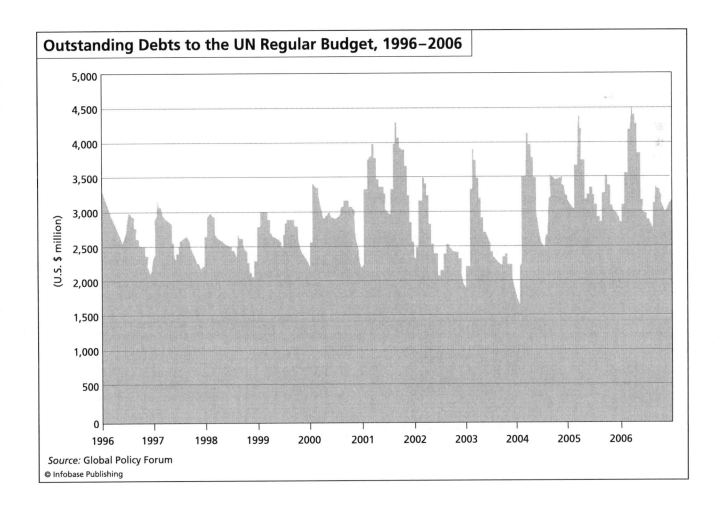

Outstanding Debts to the UN Regular Budget, 1996–2006

Source: Global Policy Forum

© Infobase Publishing

member was required to pay to the regular budget from 25 percent to 22 percent, and to 27 percent of the peacekeeping budget. As the largest contributor, only the UNITED STATES was affected by such a ceiling, although several other states then saw their assessments rise as a consequence of the U.S. reduction. The "floor," or lowest assessment assigned, was .001 percent and was applied to the poorest states in the United Nations.

The most problematic of the three UN budgets has been peacekeeping. With no direct authorization in the CHARTER for this activity, some states have refused to accept responsibility for such costs. Beginning with the creation of the UNITED NATIONS EMERGENCY FORCE (UNEF) during the 1956 SUEZ CRISIS, the world body has had difficulty obtaining the needed funds to carry out its assigned duties. During the 1960 Congolese civil war, the Soviet Union ceased making payments, generating the institution's first financial crisis, and requiring other states through voluntary contributions to make up the difference.

The United States contributed more than 30 percent of the total budget at its peak. The huge expansion of peacekeeping operations in the wake of the COLD WAR imposed costs far exceeding anticipated contributions, placing increased budgetary strains on the organization. As the UN's financial crisis worsened in recent years the organization was forced to move funds from one account to another in order to pay salaries, and it asked states that contributed peacekeeping troops to cover their own costs.

Growing dissatisfaction with UN activities and with the proportion of the budget paid by the United States led in the 1980s to American refusal to pay as much as UN officials argued it owed. By 1993 the United States had become the UN's largest debtor and Washington demanded institutional reform before it would pay arrearages. The U.S. debt to the United Nations reached more than $1.1 billion before a package of reforms and repayments was negotiated between Washington and UN HEADQUARTERS.

In October 2001 the United States made a lump payment fulfilling past commitments. However, strains between Washington and the United Nations intensified as a consequence of international disagreement over IRAQ policy and other matters, and, in the event, U.S. arrears mounted into the middle of the 21st century's first decade. The GEORGE W. BUSH administration also withheld funds from UN SPECIALIZED AGENCIES, among them the UN CHILDREN'S FUND, the WORLD HEALTH ORGANIZATION, and the UN POPULATION FUND, because it did not agree with these agencies' policies. In 2005, Washington blocked the routine approval of the biennial UN budget for 2006–07, demanding administrative reforms as the price for its approval of the budget. A compromise was reached that approved a budget of $3.79 billion, but limited the first portion of expenditures to $950 million for 2006. The rest could be released only on the request of the Secretary-General with his determination that sufficient progress on reform had been

made. Kofi Annan issued that request on June 20, 2006, to the Fifth Committee, which recommended a release of the funds. The United States, JAPAN, which makes the second largest contribution to the UN budget, and Australia disassociated themselves from that decision.

See also BOLTON, JOHN R.; BOUTROS-GHALI, BOUTROS; GOLDBERG RESERVATION; IMPORTANT QUESTION; PÉREZ DE CUÉLLAR, JAVIER; SECRETARIAT; SUSPENSION AND EXPULSION OF MEMBERS.

Further Reading: McDermott, Anthony. *The New Politics of Financing the UN.* Basingstoke, U.K.: Macmillan, 2000. Tessitore, John, and Susan Woolfson. *A Global Agenda: Issues before the 55th General Assembly of the United Nations.* 2000–01 edition. New York: Rowman and Littlefield, 2001. Fifth Committee Web site: www.un.org/ga/fifth/>. Global Policy Forum "UN Finance" Web site: <http://globalpolicy.igc.org/finance/tables/index.htm>.

budget process   *See* BUDGET OF THE UNITED NATIONS.

Bunche, Ralph (1903–1971)

Ralph Johnson Bunche was born on August 7, 1903 (some records list 1904), in Detroit, Michigan. In the 1930s he organized the first department of political science at any historically black university, at Howard University. In 1945 he became the first African American to head a division in the UNITED STATES Department of State. His work with the United Nations began that same year during the UN conference in San Francisco, where he drafted the sections of the CHARTER on decolonization and trusteeship issues. The next year, despite offers of a high position at the State Department, Bunche joined the permanent SECRETARIAT in New York when he accepted the call to direct the Trusteeship Division. In 1947 he became the principal secretary for the Commission for Palestine. After the assassination of Count FOLKE BERNADOTTE in Jerusalem in 1948, Bunche was entrusted by SECRETARY-GENERAL TRYGVE LIE with the position of chief mediator to negotiate a truce between Israel and its Arab adversaries (EGYPT, Jordan, LEBANON, and Syria). For his diligent diplomacy between February and May 1949 (on the island of Rhodes) that brought about an armistice between Israel and its Arab opponents he was awarded the Nobel Prize for Peace in December 1950.

Bunche worked under Secretaries-General DAG HAMMARSKJÖLD and U THANT, serving after 1958 as UNDER SECRETARY-GENERAL (USG) for Special Political Affairs. During the early years of his service, besides working with the UN program for the peaceful use of atomic energy, he was mainly occupied with bringing stability to war-ridden regions. Bunche established the guiding principles for PEACEKEEPING missions. He served as supervisor for the deployment of the

Ralph Bunche in Palestine (OFFICIAL UN PHOTO DEPARTMENT
OF PUBLIC INFORMATION)

UNITED NATIONS EMERGENCY FORCE (UNEF) to the Suez
Canal zone in December 1956. In 1960, he tried to negotiate a peaceful settlement in the CONGO and was responsible for the ill-fated UN peacekeeping effort ONUC (UNITED
NATIONS OPERATION IN THE CONGO) as SPECIAL REPRESEN-
TATIVE for the Secretary-General, overseeing both the military
and the civilian aspects of the undertaking. In 1964, Bunche
directed the UN mission to intervene between hostile Greek
and Turkish Cypriots and their respective countries (UNITED
NATIONS FORCE IN CYPRUS [UNFICYP]).

Despite growing health problems Bunche participated in
the Civil Rights movement in the United States, serving as a
board member of the National Association for the Advancement of Colored People (NAACP) for many years. Notes that
he kept during his career have been published, and they are
available to scholars and students. Ralph Bunche died on
December 9, 1971, in New York City. To honor his countless
achievements, a small park across from the UN HEADQUAR-
TERS has been dedicated to him.

See also ARAB-ISRAELI DISPUTE, CYPRUS DISPUTE, SUEZ
CRISIS.

Further Reading: Bunche, Ralph J. *An African American in
South Africa: The Travel Notes of Ralph J. Bunche, 28 Septem-
ber 1937–1 January 1938,* edited by Robert R. Edgar. Ath-
ens: Ohio University Press, 1992. Henry, Charles P. *Ralph J.
Bunche: Selected Speeches and Writings.* Ann Arbor: University
of Michigan Press, 1995. Rivlin, Benjamin, ed. *Ralph Bunche:
The Man and His Times.* New York: Holmes and Meier, 1990.
Urquhart, Brian. *Ralph Bunche: An American Odyssey.* New
York: W.W. Norton, 1993.

— *T. J. Weiler*

Bush, George Herbert Walker (1924–   )

The first U.S. president Bush held important diplomatic posts
prior to serving as president from 1989 to 1993. Among
those positions were his appointments as U.S. ambassador
to the United Nations (1971–73) and as chief of the U.S.
Liaison Office in the People's Republic of CHINA (1974–76;
there was no official U.S. ambassador to the PRC until President JIMMY CARTER appointed Leonard Woodcock in 1979).
Thus, unlike most presidents, Bush entered the White House
having accumulated direct experience in international diplomacy, including at the United Nations's HEADQUARTERS.

Bush was born June 12, 1924, in Milton, Massachusetts,
to Prescott Bush and Dorothy Walker Bush, and named for
his maternal grandfather George Herbert Walker. His father
was U.S. senator from Connecticut. He realized a privileged
childhood, being educated at Greenwich Country Day School
and Phillips Academy in Andover, Massachusetts. He joined
the U.S. Navy as a pilot in June 1942 and was eventually sent
into the Pacific theater where he saw extensive and dangerous duty during World War II. In September 1944 Bush's
aircraft was hit by enemy fire. He completed his mission,
then parachuted out, and after several hours was rescued
from his inflated raft. He received the Distinguished Flying
Cross for his efforts. He returned to the navy and took part
in operations in the Philippines. In 1945, at war's end, he
received an honorable discharge and entered Yale University,
where he was captain of the college baseball team. Before
entering Yale he married Barbara Pierce. After Yale, Bush
moved to Texas and engaged in the oil exploration business.
In 1964 he ran unsuccessfully for the U.S. Senate from Texas
as a Republican. However, he did win a seat to the House of
Representatives from Texas in 1966 and 1968. He contended
again for Senate in 1970, losing to Democrat Lloyd Bentsen.
President Richard Nixon appointed him ambassador to the
United Nations (where he served from 1971 to 1973) and
chairman of the Republican National Committee, a position
he held during the Watergate scandal (1973–74). During his
brief term in office (August 1974–January 1977), President
Gerald Ford picked Bush to represent the UNITED STATES
in Beijing and then brought him back to Washington to be
director of the Central Intelligence Agency (CIA).

When George Bush served as the U.S. permanent representative to the United Nations, he was known for his
affability and personal knowledge of all of his counterparts
at UN Headquarters. It was a difficult time for any American ambassador to serve in New York. A large anti-American majority existed in the GENERAL ASSEMBLY. He often
cast lone VETOES on the SECURITY COUNCIL. The most con-

tentious issue during his tenure was the matter of Chinese representation. Against rising opposition, the United States had maintained the UN seat for the nationalist Chinese government situated on Taiwan. But the Nixon administration changed policy in 1972, and Ambassador Bush was asked to seek "dual representation" for both the nationalists and the People's Republic of China (PRC) in the Assembly. The maneuver failed, and Bush was relegated to publicly escorting the Taiwanese delegate from the hall after the PRC was officially elected the sole representative of China.

Bush ran for the Republican nomination for president in 1980, losing to former California governor Ronald Reagan. Unexpectedly, Reagan chose his erstwhile rival (who during the 1980 primaries had called the Californian's tax and financial proposals "voo-doo economics") as his vice presidential running mate. The tandem won the election of 1980 and reelection in 1984. Bush was considered a complement to the conservative Reagan in part because of his international experience and particularly his high-level work at the United Nations, in China, and with the CIA. In 1988 Bush garnered the Republican nomination for president and defeated Democrat Michael Dukakis in the November election of that year. His one term (1989–93) was marked by noteworthy international events, including the conclusion of the COLD WAR and the breakup of the SOVIET UNION. Thus, his administration was faced with developing fresh policies to manage the final days of Russian-American competition, to ensure that the large stockpiles of nuclear WEAPONS in the former Soviet Union were under control or dismantled, and to deal with new independent states in Eastern Europe that had emerged from the now defunct USSR.

In spring 1989 China brutally suppressed huge liberal protests taking place in historic Tiananmen Square in Beijing. The president, who had represented Washington in China two decades earlier, determined to censure the Tiananmen repression while still maintaining normal diplomatic relations with a world power growing more important. Bush issued a public statement announcing the suspension of military sales to China and the cessation of military contacts. However, he did not end commercial links, he emphasized the normal diplomatic relationship between Washington and China, he used measured LANGUAGE at his press conference, and at the end of June he sent National Security Advisor Brent Scowcroft (accompanied by State Department official Lawrence Eagleburger) on a quiet trip to Beijing to record America's revulsion at the Tiananmen crackdown while assuring officials there of continuing diplomatic relations.

Although there was no international consensus backing the U.S. invasion of Panama in December 1989 to remove General Manuel Noriega from power, Bush's careful cultivation of the major powers, particularly the PERMANENT MEMBERS OF THE SECURITY COUNCIL redounded to his considerable advantage following IRAQ's invasion of Kuwait on August 2, 1990. The president immediately engaged

the United Nations to confront the crisis. On August 2 he authorized Ambassador Thomas Pickering to request an emergency meeting of the Security Council. Over the next three months the administration sought and obtained 10 SC RESOLUTIONS isolating Iraq and establishing the international legal ground for collective military action. In the event, Bush successfully maintained a consensus among the five permanent members of the Council. The Council condemned the invasion (SC Res. 660), declared null and void the annexation of Kuwait (SC Res. 662), imposed economic SANCTIONS on Iraq (SC Res. 661), set up a naval blockade (SC Res. 665), and, on November 29, 1990, adopted SC Res. 678, demanding that Iraq withdraw from Kuwait within 48 hours or face military retaliation, including "all necessary means . . . to restore peace and security in the area." The president then brought together a coalition of 35 nations (including NATO allies, Arab states, and others) to act under UN authority. In mid January 1991, both houses of the U.S. Congress approved military action as provided by UN Resolution 678. The coalition forces were quickly successful in removing Iraq from Kuwait and restoring the SOVEREIGNTY of the small state. On February 28, 1991, Bush announced the conclusion of hostilities, declaring that "No one country can claim this victory as its own. . . . This is a victory for the United Nations, for all mankind, and for what is right." When criticized for not continuing military operations on to Baghdad, Bush later said: "The coalition would instantly have collapsed, the Arabs deserting it in anger and other allies pulling out as well . . . unilaterally exceeding the United Nations' mandate would have destroyed the precedent of international response to AGGRESSION that we hoped to establish." When the war ended, the Security Council created a Sanctions Commission, an observation mission (UNIKOM), and a commission to monitor Baghdad's WEAPONS programs (UNSCOM) that fashioned the most rigorous monitoring and sanctions regime ever imposed on a NATION-STATE by the United Nations.

As the president pursued his broad international response to the Kuwait crisis, he addressed a joint session of Congress on the portentous date of September 11, 1990, saying that "out of these troubled times" we could visualize "a New World Order," by which he undoubtedly meant a world conforming to the collaborative principles originally expressed by the founders of the United Nations. His administration tried to use the momentum of cooperation to effect a breakthrough in the ARAB-ISRAELI DISPUTE (the Madrid Conference of October 1991), to address the sudden breakup of YUGOSLAVIA, to reverse the military coup in HAITI, and to contain the violence afflicting SOMALIA. For a moment in the early 1990s, both the United States and the United Nations were atypically upbeat about relations between Washington and New York.

Particularly in the case of Somalia, President Bush sought to serve UN purposes by affirmatively responding to a request from SECRETARY-GENERAL BOUTROS BOUTROS-GHALI for assistance. Over the serious objections of several of his advisers who were less enamored with the potential of the United Nations to resolve complex problems in conflict zones, Bush agreed to intervene militarily in Somalia, assuming Security Council authorization, which was forthcoming, in support of the UN's humanitarian mission there. He took this step in December 1992, just a month after losing the presidency to Governor BILL CLINTON of Arkansas. President Bush told the American people that he expected that American troops would already be withdrawing from Somalia when President-elect Clinton took office in January. He contemplated a hand-off of responsibilities to the United Nations once law, order, and effective food distribution in the country were achieved. The Somalia affair would linger long after Bush left office, but his intervention on behalf of the United Nations reflected his new confidence in the organization.

In the last week of 2004 President Bush undertook another global assignment at the request of his son, U.S. president GEORGE W. BUSH. He agreed to join now former president Bill Clinton in raising aid at home and abroad for the victims of the Indian Ocean tsunami. He traveled to the region with Clinton, who became the official representative of the United Nations for this effort. Bush visited sites of the devastation and called upon politicians and Asian leaders he had known for decades. The Bush-Clinton campaign produced several billion dollars in commitments.

See also GULF WAR.

Further Reading: Baker, James A. *The Politics of Diplomacy.* New York: Putnam, 1995. Bush, George, and Brent Scowcroft. *A World Transformed.* New York: Knopf, 1998. Moore, John Allphin, Jr., and Jerry Pubantz. *To Create a New World?: American Presidents and the United Nations.* New York: Peter Lang, 1999. Powell, Colin L., with Joseph E. Persico. *My American Journey.* New York: Random House, 1995. Pubantz, Jerry. "George Bush and the United Nations: A Prudent Journey from Realism to Moralism, 1971–1993." In *A Noble Calling. Character and the George H. W. Bush Presidency,* edited by William Levantrosser and Rosanna Perotti, 195–218. Westport, Conn.: Praeger, 2004.

Bush, George Walker (1946–)

During the U.S. presidency of the younger Bush (2001–09) UN–UNITED STATES relations slipped to a low point. America's unilateral response to the September 11, 2001, attacks was partly responsible for the disharmony, but early decisions by the new Bush administration to reject the KYOTO PROTOCOL, to "unsign" the INTERNATIONAL CRIMINAL COURT agreement, to withdraw from the 1972 Anti-Ballistic Missile TREATY and the International Land Mine Treaty, and to limit U.S. funding of the UNITED NATIONS POPULATION FUND (which the administration charged with providing abortions)

all were decisions taken separately from the president's determination to initiate a war on IRAQ in the spring of 2003 in the face of SECURITY COUNCIL opposition.

George W. Bush is the eldest son of former president GEORGE H. W. BUSH and Barbara Pierce Bush. He was born in New Haven, Connecticut, on July 6, 1946, and, since his parents moved to Texas soon after his birth, was raised in Midland and Houston. The young man was sent to school in New England, attending the same institutions as had his father—Phillips Academy in Andover, Massachusetts. and Yale University, graduating in 1968. During the Vietnam War he served in the Texas Air National Guard, leaving the guard early to enter Harvard Business School, where he earned a Masters of Business Administration in 1975. In 1977 he married Laura Welch. He then entered the oil business in Texas. In 1964 and 1970 he worked in his father's unsuccessful campaigns for senator from Texas, and, in 1978, ran for Congress, without success. In the late l980s, Bush bought a share of the Texas Rangers baseball team and served as managing general partner of the franchise until the mid 1990s. In 1994 he ran for governor of Texas and defeated incumbent Ann Richards. His reputation was enhanced with his landslide reelection victory in 1998, which propelled him into national presidential politics.

In 2000 Bush won the Republican nomination for the presidency and took part in one of the closest elections in American history. When the November 7 election ballots were counted nationwide, Bush's opponent, Vice President Albert Gore, had accumulated a significant edge over Bush of about 500,000 votes nationwide, but the vote in Florida remained too close to call. Without the Florida electoral vote in the count, Gore had 267 electoral votes and Bush 246. Whichever candidate won in Florida would add that state's 25 electoral votes and thus surpass the 270 necessary to gain a majority in the Electoral College. The vote in Florida showed Bush barely ahead, but was so close that Gore requested a recount in selected precincts. A hand count began, and Gore continued to narrow the margin. At this point both sides sought remedy in the courts. Eventually, the Florida State Supreme Court ruled that the recount should continue. The Bush campaign then appealed to the U.S. Supreme Court, which heard the case (*Bush v. Gore*) on December 11 and the next day issued a 5-4 decision voiding the state court directive, ending the recount, and guaranteeing Bush's election. Bush would become the second U.S. president to be the son of a former president (the first was John Quincy Adams). In 2004, Bush won reelection against Democrat John Kerry.

In addition to the several unilateral policies initiated by the Bush administration early in its first term, the conflict in Iraq caused the most querulous tension between the country and the United Nations. The crisis of September 11, 2001, seemed to mold the Bush policy toward Iraq. The 9/11 attacks elicited worldwide empathy. The Security Council and the GENERAL ASSEMBLY passed RESOLUTIONS within 48 hours denouncing the assault, holding that any act of international TERRORISM was a threat to international peace and security, and calling on all states to "prevent and suppress the financing of terrorist acts." Washington received wide-ranging multilateral support to remove the Taliban from power in AFGHANISTAN, curtail AL-QAEDA activities there, and seek the reconstruction of the country. Following the multilaterally supported incursion into Afghanistan in late 2001, the Bush administration switched its concentration to Iraq, insisting that the nation be attacked, even unilaterally should the UN Security Council refuse to accede to U.S. demands for military action. By the fall of 2002 there were clear divisions of opinion between the United States and the United Kingdom on the one hand, and the other PERMANENT MEMBERS OF THE SECURITY COUNCIL on the other. Led by FRANCE and joined by long-time U.S. ally GERMANY (at the time a member of the Security Council), these nations resisted the U.S. call for war and urged that UN arms inspectors be allowed to complete their work in Iraq.

The great power confrontation came to a head in the Security Council in November 2002. The United States acceded to a new resolution that would give the SADDAM HUSSEIN regime one more chance to account for suspected WEAPONS OF MASS DESTRUCTION. RESOLUTION 1441 found the Baghdad government in "material breach" of past UN resolutions, which is what the United States sought. From President Bush's perspective this meant that military action to enforce previous mandates from the Council would be legitimate. On the other hand, states opposed to military action provided in the resolution for another arms inspection team under Dr. HANS BLIX of Sweden. Until that team reported on compliance or non-compliance by Iraq with UN resolutions there could be no invasion of the country. France and the RUSSIAN FEDERATION argued that regardless of whether Blix found WEAPONS or not, another Council resolution would be needed to authorize an attack. When Blix gave his report in the spring, he noted that the Iraqi regime had not been fully forthcoming, but that there was no conclusive evidence that Saddam Hussein had such weapons. When the United States sought an authorizing resolution in the wake of the Blix report, France in particular indicated that it would VETO the proposal.

After making its case for war in a globally televised presentation by Secretary of State Colin Powell before the Security Council, the United States went to war in March 2003. SECRETARY-GENERAL KOFI ANNAN would later call the invasion illegal under the UN CHARTER.

Relations between Washington and the resistant European states became particularly confrontational once the United States launched the invasion. In addition, the United States had announced that it would henceforth pursue new and novel policies of preemptive war and unilateral diplomatic action, thus discarding more traditional multilateral approaches to world affairs usually associated with the United Nations. When inspectors found no weapons of mass destruction following American occupation of Iraq, and most pundits conceded that there had been no al-Qaeda–Iraqi collaboration in the 9/11 attacks (the two *causis belli* cited most often by administration officials to explain the war), disagreements with erstwhile allies deepened, and Secretary-General Annan opined that a crisis of confidence faced the United Nations.

Complicating matters further, President Bush picked controversial State Department official JOHN BOLTON in August 2005 to be the U.S. ambassador to the United Nations. Because Bolton, a vocal and hawkish critic of the United Nations, was unable to gain approval even in the Republican-controlled U.S. Senate, the president had to make a "recess" appointment (made during a congressional recess, and valid only until the next elected Congress assumed power). Friction between the United Nations and Washington did not abate.

Almost immediately upon his arrival in New York to take up his duties, Ambassador Bolton raised eyebrows by challenging the draft final document for the pending WORLD SUMMIT scheduled for September. His government sought the removal of any references to the MILLENNIUM DEVELOPMENT GOALS (MDGs) and targets. He proposed several hundred amendments to the laboriously negotiated draft. The United States also indicated only lukewarm support for Annan's REFORM proposals, which he had put forward in April titled *IN LARGER FREEDOM*. In particular, the U.S. government only supported the expansion of the Security Council by the addition of JAPAN as a permanent member, and the creation of a new HUMAN RIGHTS COUNCIL elected at-large by a two-thirds vote of the General Assembly. In the end, the United States allowed for references to the MDGs, but the outcome of the summit was disappointing. Many observers laid some of the responsibility for the summit's failure at the doorstep of Washington.

In December 2005, Bolton disparaged remarks made by Louise Arbour, UN HIGH COMMISSIONER FOR HUMAN RIGHTS, commenting on U.S. policy toward suspected terrorist detainees. Arbour had criticized the United States's "watering down the definition of torture." Bolton called the remarks "inappropriate and illegitimate." Secretary-General Annan vigorously defended Ms. Arbour, who, as a WAR CRIMES prosecutor, had indicted former Yugoslav president SLOBODAN MILOŠEVIĆ. In March 2006 the United States voted with three others in opposition (two nations abstaining) as the United Nations overwhelmingly approved a new Human Rights Council, but not one elected by the VOTING procedure sought by the Bush administration. In June 2006 Mark Malloch Brown, DEPUTY SECRETARY-GENERAL (DSG), gave a speech in New York saying that Washington had failed to stand up for the United Nations, did not acknowledge how closely the American government worked with the international organization, and allowed the UN's harshest critics in the United States to go unanswered by public officials. Part of Brown's distress grew out of the momentary budgetary crisis of the United Nations. The United States had blocked the passage of the regular biennial BUDGET the previous December, allowing only a portion of the allocated funds to be spent during the first half of 2006, pending expected reform. Ambassador Bolton reacted to the DSG angrily, calling the matter "very, very grave," and demanded that Secretary-General Annan repudiate Brown "personally and publicly." Annan turned back the entreaty, indicating that he agreed with the general thrust of Brown's remarks. Midway through President Bush's second term, UN-U.S. relations appeared as strained as ever.

Still, Condoleezza Rice, who replaced Colin Powell as the president's secretary of state in early 2005, made a good-will tour to Europe one of her first—and most visible—activities; as crises mounted, Washington began to evince an interest in multilateral negotiations and the administration sought to engage the United Nations; and within a month after the controversial appointment of Ambassador Bolton to the United Nations, the president surprised listeners with his speech to the UN World Summit in New York on September 14, 2005. Before a large crowd of wary diplomats, Mr. Bush (1) committed his nation to the Millennium Development Goals, (2) confirmed his approval of the 100 percent cancellation of debts for the world's most heavily indebted nations, (3) urged that international financial institutions provide new aid in the form of grants rather than loans, and (4) indicated that the United States was prepared to eliminate agricultural subsidies that had so exasperated developing nations (although as of the end of 2006 no such action had transpired).

Moreover, responding to IRAN's renewed nuclear development program in early 2006, the administration employed uncharacteristic, vigorous, multilateral diplomacy to engage the Russians and Chinese, together with the EU-3 (United Kingdom, France, and Germany), all of whom joined the United States in common resolve to urge the INTERNATIONAL ATOMIC ENERGY AGENCY (IAEA) to bring the issue before the Security Council. And when North Korea, developing its own NUCLEAR WEAPONS program, conducted a series of worrisome missile tests in July 2006, the president urged cautious and collaborative action from the Security Council, telling reporters that "diplomacy takes a while." (This multilateral diplomatic approach appeared to pay off by February 2007 when North Korea agreed to stop, seal, and disable its nuclear operations, and to allow IAEA inspectors back into the country.) Deputy Secretary-General Brown may have been correct in suggesting that the United States worked more closely with the United Nations than administration officials had publicly conceded, or the administration's moves in late 2006 may have signaled a revised approach to world affairs and the United Nations.

See also ARAB-ISRAELI DISPUTE, INDIA, HIV/AIDS, DISARMAMENT, COLLECTIVE SECURITY, DARFUR, QUARTET, SMART SANCTIONS.

Further Reading: Baker, James A., and Lee H. Hamilton. *The Iraq Study Group Report.* New York: Random House, 2006. CRS Report for Congress. "U.S. Use of Preemptive Military Force" (September 18, 2002), <http://fpc.state.gov/documents/organization/13841pdf>. Daalder, Ivo, and James Lindsay. *America Unbound: The Bush Revolution in Foreign Policy.* Washington, D.C.: Brookings, 2003. Haass, Richard N. *The Opportunity: America's Moment to Alter History's Course.* New York: Public Affairs, 2005. The National Commission on Terrorist Attacks upon the United States. *The 9/11 Commission Report.* New York: W.W. Norton, 2004. "The National Security Strategy of the United States of America" (September 2002), <www.whitehouse.gov/nsc/nss.pdf>.

Cairo Declaration

FRANKLIN D. ROOSEVELT, Winston CHURCHILL, and Chiang Kai-shek issued the Cairo Declaration at the Cairo Conference held from November 23 to 26 and December 3 to 7, 1943 (before and after the TEHERAN CONFERENCE). The Soviet Union, although not represented at Cairo, had been consulted before it was issued.

The "Three Great Allies" in the Asian war announced their intent to strip JAPAN of all islands taken in World War I, of all territories "stolen" from CHINA, such as Manchuria, Formosa, and the Pescadores, and all other lands "taken by violence and greed." In addition, Korea was to be liberated and "in due course" become free and independent. The purpose of this sweeping statement was to boost the morale of the faltering Chiang government and forestall any efforts at a separate peace with Japan. In addition, this was part of a larger strategy by Roosevelt to elevate China to a great power in the postwar world in order to play her assigned role as one of the "FOUR POLICEMEN" in the international security organization-to-be.

In order to head off an effort by the Republican Party to formulate a postwar foreign policy statement for the 1944 election, FDR used the MOSCOW FOREIGN MINISTERS CONFERENCE (October 1943) to introduce CORDELL HULL's Four-Power DECLARATION on a postwar world organization. China comprised a crucial component, not only to serve as the Asian "policeman" but also as an ally of the UNITED STATES in its efforts to establish a security system of international trusteeships for colonies and mandates in the region. The Cairo Declaration was central to this vision.

Further Reading: Dallek, Robert. *Franklin D. Roosevelt and American Foreign Policy, 1932–1945.* New York: Oxford University Press, 1979. Feis, Herbert. *Churchill. Roosevelt. Stalin; The War They Waged and the Peace They Sought.* Princeton, N.J.: Princeton University Press, 1957. Kimball, Warren F. *Forged in War: Roosevelt, Churchill, and the Second World War.* New York: William Morrow, 1997.

— *E. M. Clauss*

Cambodia

Present-day Cambodia came under Khmer rule in the early seventh century, following which it became the center of a vast empire stretching over much of Southeast Asia. In the 12th century Buddhism was introduced into the region. In 1863 FRANCE colonized the area, joining Cambodia, Laos, and Vietnam into a protectorate called French Indochina. After World War II, Cambodia, along with other countries of Indochina recently freed from Japanese influence, sought independence, which was granted by France in 1953. Cambodia became a member of the United Nations in 1955. During the French Indochina War, which persisted until the Geneva Accords of 1954, Prince Norodom Sihanouk ascended to power, and he did his utmost first to achieve independence and then to secure Cambodian neutrality from all parties to the ongoing conflict in Vietnam. In 1970, General Lon Nol, with the concurrence of the UNITED STATES, overthrew Prince Sihanouk in a coup. Five years later, as the United States retreated from Southeast Asia, the Khmer Rouge, a Communist guerrilla movement led by Pol Pot, ousted Lon Nol.

Regional alignments shaped the UN's relationship with Cambodia in the 1980s, while the end of the COLD WAR and increased international cooperation facilitated UN action in the early 1990s to resolve Cambodia's internal conflict. After signing a mutual assistance TREATY with the Soviet Union in November 1978, Vietnam invaded Cambodia in December and replaced the Beijing-backed Pol Pot government with the Heng Samrin–Hun Sen regime. The USSR subsequently protected its ally by vetoing UN SECURITY COUNCIL condemnation of the Vietnamese occupation of a sovereign country. UN recognition of Vietnam's client government in Cambodia was blocked, however, through lobbying by the Association of Southeast Asian Nations (ASEAN) even though this appeared to legitimize the autogenocide inflicted on the Cambodian people by the Pol Pot group after it came to power in 1975. ASEAN also guided RESOLUTIONS through the UN GENERAL ASSEMBLY that called on Vietnam to withdraw its troops and to permit the Cambodians to select their own government. After the three Cambodian factions opposing the Hun Sen regime formed the Coalition Government of Democratic Kampuchea (CGDK) in 1982 at the urging of ASEAN, the United States, and CHINA, the United Nations seated the delegation from this government-in-exile as the legal representative of Cambodia.

The United Nations was involved early in seeking a political settlement of the conflict that followed the installation of the Hun Sen government. An international conference on Kampuchea was convened in 1981 at the urging of the General Assembly but failed to achieve concrete results. SECRETARY-GENERAL JAVIER PÉREZ DE CUÉLLAR instructed Rafeeuddin Ahmed, his SPECIAL REPRESENTATIVE for humanitarian affairs in Southeast Asia, to offer the UN's GOOD OFFICES. By 1985, Ahmed's consultations produced the outline of a solution to the conflict. Yet a significant UN role only became possible in the late 1980s with the end of the cold war and increased cooperation among the PERMANENT MEMBERS OF THE SECURITY COUNCIL. By August 1990, the permanent members reached agreement on a framework for a political settlement, and by September, the Cambodian parties, which had met informally as early as 1988 at talks hosted by INDONESIA, accepted the framework. After a series of meetings to negotiate the details, the Agreement on a Comprehensive Political Settlement of the Cambodian Conflict was approved on October 23, 1991, at the reconvened Paris International Conference on Cambodia. The Security Council approved the documents of the Paris conference within days and in February 1992 authorized the UNITED NATIONS TRANSITIONAL AUTHORITY IN CAMBODIA (UNTAC)

to ensure implementation of the Paris agreements. As the transitional authority over Cambodia for 15 months, UNTAC took on an unprecedented set of responsibilities to institutionalize the reconciliation of the parties to the Cambodian conflict. It managed daily administration of Cambodian foreign and defense policy, provided domestic government services, and stationed more than 20,000 UN personnel in the country.

Prince Sihanouk was appointed leader of an interim council to run the country pending elections, which, under the tutelage of UNTAC, took place in May 1993. Although Hun Sen lost the election, he insisted on, and achieved, a power-sharing arrangement with his co-prime minister, Prince Norodom Ranariddh, Sihanouk's son. Differences among the various factions of Cambodia continued. In 1997, Hun Sen executed a coup, removing his opponents from the power-sharing arrangement. The United Nations then refused to seat Cambodia's delegation to the General Assembly. Intricate internal negotiations ensued and in July 1998, again with international monitors present, another, controversial, election was held, won by Hun Sen, who agreed to head a coalition government. Cambodia regained its seat in the United Nations and in 1999 was accepted as a member of the Association of Southeast Asian Nations.

Hun Sen retained his position as prime minister when his People's Party won 50 percent of the vote in the fairly peaceful election of July 2003, which was followed by almost a year of negotiations before yet another coalition government was formed. The elections at the turn of the century offered encouraging signs of political stability. Local elections were scheduled for 2007 and national elections for 2008.

In January 2001 Hun Sen's government and the United Nations negotiated an agreement, approved by Cambodia's Senate and National Assembly, to establish an international tribunal to try the Pol Pot group accountable for the 1.6 million Cambodians who were executed or who died from starvation and disease during the rule of the Khmer Rouge. (Pol Pot, however, would not be tried, since he died in April 1998.) Finally, in March 2006 SECRETARY-GENERAL KOFI ANNAN was able to submit a list of international judges to serve on the international court (called the Extraordinary Chambers in the Courts of Cambodia for the Prosecution of Crimes Committed during the Period of Democratic Kampuchea). In 2007, the tribunal brought charges against Kaing Guek Eav, commandant of Tuel Sleng prison where 14,000 people were tortured before execution, and Nuon Cher, the party's ideologue.

See also LAND MINES; LEAST DEVELOPED COUNTRIES; SOUTHEAST ASIA TREATY ORGANIZATION; UNITED NATIONS ADVANCE MISSION IN CAMBODIA; UNITED NATIONS OFFICE FOR PROJECT SERVICES; WALDHEIM, KURT.

Further Reading: *Agreements on a Comprehensive Political Settlement of the Cambodia Conflict, Paris, 23 October 1991.*

New York: United Nations Department of Public Information, 1992. Kiernan, Ben. *The Pol Pot Regime: Race, Power, Genocide in Cambodia under the Khmer Rouge, 1975–1979.* New Haven, Conn.: Yale University Press, 1996. Permanent Mission of the Kingdom of Cambodia Web site: www.un.int/ cambodia>. Romano, Cesare P. R., André Nollkaemper, and Jann K. Kleffner, eds. *Internationalized Criminal Courts: Sierra Leone, East Timor, Kosovo, and Cambodia.* New York: Oxford University Press, 2004.

— *G. S. Silliman*

Cardoso Report

Reflective of SECRETARY-GENERAL KOFI ANNAN's several REFORM efforts, the Cardoso Report dealt with issues of UN–Civil Society relationships. Annan first proposed an examination of the subject in September 2002. In early 2003 he appointed a Panel of Eminent Persons, headed by former Brazilian president Fernando Henrique Cardoso, "to review the relationship between the United Nations and civil society and offer practical recommendations for improved modalities and interaction" (UN Doc. A/57/387). The implication was that the panel would consider the UN's linkages with both NON-GOVERNMENTAL ORGANIZATIONS (NGOs) as well as with the more capaciously defined "civil society," which could include parliamentarians, think tanks, business firms, and more.

The panel issued its 83-page report on June 21, 2004 (UN Doc. A/58/817), acknowledging that components of civil society had been among the prime innovators and motivators in global relations and, in a veiled reference to the crisis the United Nations faced when the UNITED STATES decided to go to war against IRAQ without UN endorsement, argued that these participants could serve as "a protection against further erosion of multilateralism." Panelists noted that "global civil society now wields real power in the name of citizens," and that the world was witnessing a new phenomenon: "global public opinion—that is shaping the political agenda and generating a cosmopolitan set of norms and citizen demands that transcend national boundaries." Panel members suggested a "paradigm shift" in UN work, based on four principles: (1) the organization should be "outward-looking" and put global issues rather than the institution at the center of its work; (2) it should include more, not fewer, actors in its deliberations, (3) it must connect global concerns with local realities, and (4) the United Nations should accept a role in global governance, emphasizing "participatory democracy" and "accountability."

The report contained 30 discrete proposals calling on the Secretary-General to pursue sometimes imprecise improvements, such as "multi-constituency dialogues," "inclusion of all constituencies relevant to issues" before the UN, "networked governance," "multi-stakeholder advisory forums," and "multi-constituency processes." The report also urged the GENERAL ASSEMBLY to "permit the carefully planned participation of actors besides central Governments" and accept "high-quality independent input," and suggested that the SECRETARIAT should strengthen its relationship with "actors in the private sector." Proposal 4 advised specifically that the "global conference MECHANISM" (apparently meaning WORLD SUMMITS and CONFERENCES) be used more "sparingly." And Proposal 24 called on the Secretary-General to appoint an UNDER-SECRETARY GENERAL to head a new Office of Constituency Engagement and Partnerships; panelists suggested incorporating the GLOBAL COMPACT into this proposed office. Several NGOs, fearing the proposals' ill effect on authentic democracy, the possible enhanced influence of corporate businesses in international forums, and possibly apprehensive that the report could result in diluting their influence at the United Nations, issued critical statements following public release of the report. On September 17, 2004, the Secretary-General released a short response of his own, omitting some of the more controversial elements of the report but retaining the basic ideas.

Further Reading: Panel of Eminent Persons on United Nations–Civil Society Relations. *We the Peoples: Civil Society, the United Nations and Global Governance.* New York: United Nations, 2004, A/58/817. Full Cardoso Report at http://www.globalpolicy.org/reform/initiatives/panels/cardoso/0611report.pdf. Comments about the Cardoso Report: <http://www.globalpolicy.org/reform/initiatives/panels/cardoso/O8gpf.pdf#search='Cardoso%20Report>. Report of the Secretary General on Cardoso Follow-Up (September 17, 2004): http://www.globalpolicy.org/reform/initiatives/panels/cardoso/O9O4sgreport.pdf.

Caribbean Development Bank (CDB)   *See* REGIONAL DEVELOPMENT BANKS.

Carter, Jimmy (1924–)

The 39th U.S. president, Jimmy Carter began his single term (1977–81) as one of the more popular post–World War II presidents at the United Nations. His appointment of former civil rights leader Andrew Young as ambassador to the organization, and his early visits and speeches to the UN boosted his and his country's image among especially DEVELOPING COUNTRIES. He announced that HUMAN RIGHTS would be at the center of his foreign policy, and he was able to realize some historic successes in international policy, including shepherding EGYPT and Israel to the Camp David Accords, consummating the negotiations of the Panama Canal TREATIES and obtaining Senate ratification, achieving full diplomatic relations with the Peoples Republic of CHINA, and completing negotiation of the SALT II Nuclear Limitation Treaty with the SOVIET UNION (which was not ratified, partly as a consequence of the Soviet invasion of AFGHANISTAN). Long after he left the presidency, Carter received numerous awards recognizing his efforts to forward international peace. Among the many honors were the UNESCO Félix Houphouët-Boigny Peace Prize (1994), the United Nations Human Rights Award (1998), the UNICEF International Child Survival Award (1999), and, at the apex, the 2002 Nobel Peace Prize for his "efforts to find peaceful solutions to international conflicts, to advance democracy and human rights, and to promote economic and social DEVELOPMENT."

James Earl Carter, Jr. was born in Plains, Georgia, on October 1, 1924. He attended the Naval Academy in Annapolis, Maryland, from which he earned a Bachelor of Science degree in 1946, the same year he married Rosalynn Smith. Carter served on submarines with the navy, became a command officer under Admiral Hyman Rickover, and did some postgraduate study in nuclear physics for a brief time at Union College. However, when his father died in 1953, he resigned his commission to return to Plains to take over the family's peanut farming business. In the early 1960s he became active in Georgia politics and in 1970 was elected governor of the state, where he established a reputation as a "new" style southern governor, emphasizing responsive, pared down government, environmental awareness, and elimination of all vestiges of racial segregation. In late 1974 Carter began a long and successful campaign to capture the 1976 Democratic nomination for president. In the general election of that year—in the immediate aftermath of the Watergate scandal—he was able to defeat sitting president Gerald Ford by a slender electoral margin of 297 to 241 votes. While president, he presided over the congressional passage of extensive energy and civil service REFORM programs, and he achieved deregulation of the trucking and airline industries, expanded the national park system, created the Department of Education, and appointed African Americans, Hispanics, and WOMEN to federal government positions in record numbers. However, his efforts to address the problems of unemployment and, particularly inflation, were less successful.

The president, an acknowledged "idealist," determined to thrust human rights to the forefront of his foreign policy, a posture that irritated the Soviet Union, more used to the "détente" and "realist" formulations of the previous Nixon-Ford administration. In good faith demonstration of his commitment to human rights, Carter lifted travel prohibitions on American travelers to CUBA, North Korea, CAMBODIA, and Vietnam; he appointed Patricia Derian, a civil rights lawyer from Mississippi, as assistant secretary of state for human rights, and asked diplomat Warren Christopher to establish the "Christopher Group" in the State Department to ensure that human rights goals were met in the nation's foreign policies. He also signed the UN COVENANT ON CIVIL AND POLITICAL RIGHTS and the COVENANT ON ECONOMIC, SOCIAL, AND CULTURAL RIGHTS. Carter's most important gesture to

developing nations was likely his appointment of veteran civil rights activist and former congressman Andrew Young as his ambassador to the United Nations, an appointment that carried, by presidential determination, the prestige of a cabinet position. Young was the first African American to serve in this post (his immediate successor, Donald McHenry, was the second), a symbolic act that did not go unnoticed by the numerous delegates from AFRICA. The new president requested and was granted permission by SECRETARY-GENERAL KURT WALDHEIM, to address an off-cycle meeting of the United Nations on March 17, 1977, but two months into his term. In his address he promised to bring new emphasis to traditional American ideals in the country's dealings with the UN and the world, to gain congressional approval of UN COVENANTS on civil and political and economic, social, and cultural rights, to urge the Senate to ratify the genocide convention and the Treaty for the Elimination of All Forms of Racial Discrimination, to lift travel bans on Americans, to fully support UN SANCTIONS on South Africa and Rhodesia, and to do all possible to aid developing countries.

Carter's most widely lauded accomplishment in international relations was the achievement of a peace accord between EGYPT and Israel. The president, first at Camp David in Maryland, then via shuttle diplomacy in the MIDDLE EAST, coaxed the leaders of the two countries—President Anwar Sadat of Egypt and Prime Minister Menachem Begin of Israel—to sign, finally in 1979, two agreements: a peace treaty between the two governments and a "framework" for a comprehensive solution to the ARAB-ISRAELI DISPUTE. This so-called Camp David agreement resulted in (1) peace between Israel and Egypt, (2) recognition of Israel by the largest Arab nation, (3) placement of the "Palestinian" question into the diplomatic discourse between Israel and her neighbors, and (4) reassertion of the importance of UN RESOLUTIONS 242 and 338.

These achievements, however, tended to be overshadowed by inimical and insoluble problems that beset the last years of Carter's term. The inflation rate began to rise, eroding the president's popularity. A forceful domestic conservative opposition to Carter's liberal, idealistic foreign policy blossomed. Although the United States and the Soviet Union signed the laboriously negotiated Strategic Arms Limitation Treaty (SALT), the U.S. Senate balked at ratification and, following the Soviet invasion of Afghanistan in December 1979, the president, in response, removed the treaty from Senate consideration. The most debilitating challenge to the administration was in IRAN, where, on November 4, 1979, following an Islamic uprising against the American-supported shah, student radicals seized the U.S. embassy in Tehran and took and held 52 American hostages. A tense and long international crisis followed, punctuated by the failed attempt of Secretary-General Waldheim to obtain release of the hostages, and an abortive U.S. military mission in April 1980, authorized by the president, to free them.

Although domestic support of the president rose during the initial stages of the crisis, public confidence ebbed as the election campaign of 1980 proceeded. Carter lost that election to former California governor RONALD REAGAN, one of his most vociferous foreign policy critics. The hostages were finally released on January 21, 1981, the precise moment of Reagan's inauguration.

Following his political defeat, Carter assumed an active and public career as a writer (one of the most prolific of all former presidents), human rights advocate, international mediator, election monitor, and leader of Habitat for Humanity, building homes for the needy. He founded the Carter Center at his presidential library in Atlanta, which, in addition to being a standard research facility, became a conference center entertaining forums for issues related to democracy, human rights, and related topics. In October 1994, former president Carter headed a high-level delegation to HAITI to encourage the military junta in power there to honor the Governor's Island Agreement that was negotiated by the American administration under the auspices of the United Nations. The agreement called for the military leaders to cede power to the previously elected Haitian president and to leave the island. Carter's diplomacy backed by an imminent threat of an American invasion produced the desired result. Later, be undertook difficult diplomatic missions to North Korea and BOSNIA.

See also MEDIATION; CLINTON, WILLIAM JEFFERSON.

Further Reading: Bourne, Peter G. *Jimmy Carter: A Comprehensive Biography from Plains to Postpresidency.* New York: Scribner, 1997. Brinkley, Douglas. *The Unfinished Presidency: Jimmy Carter's Journey beyond the White House.* New York: Viking, 1998. Carter, Jimmy. *Keeping Faith: Memoirs of a President.* New York: Bantam, 1982. ———. *The Nobel Peace Prize Lecture.* New York: Simon and Schuster, 2002. Moore, John Allphin, Jr., and Jerry Pubantz. *To Create a New World?: American Presidents and the United Nations.* New York: Peter Lang, 1999.

caucus groups

Since the United Nations is the meeting site of sovereign nations, it is a place where the majority of business is conducted through informal negotiations in halls, lounges, and meeting rooms. National representatives informally discuss their concerns and work out the precise wording of resolutions and reports to be adopted by the bodies in the United Nations. Most of the preparatory negotiations occur in caucus groups organized by geographical proximity, national identification with internationally recognized political or economic issues, or shared interests. The intense talks outside of the formal sessions continue until agreement is reached on a single RESOLUTION on each topic, whose wording and actions are, if not acceptable to all, at least not so

offensive or objectionable to any single nation that it is compelled to vote no. Because the United Nations is a universal organization in which virtually every nation of the world is represented, a wide range of viewpoints must be reconciled and included during negotiation regarding any issue. Typically such reconciliation must be accomplished informally, as it would be too cumbersome to attempt to reach agreement and hear all nations in formal session.

In any negotiation in a large body the delegates separate into smaller groups of representatives who share similar concerns and viewpoints, and caucusing groups are simply these smaller groups. They perform in the United Nations the function provided by political parties in a legislative body. Such groups are formed, both formally and informally, on a number of commonalities, which vary with any particular issue. The most influential caucusing groups at the United Nations are the NON-ALIGNED MOVEMENT and the GROUP OF 77, which represent the developing nations and exert considerable influence because of the large number of such nations.

Additionally the United Nations recognizes several geographical area groups for purposes of organization of, and election to, various UN positions. Election to posts such as the SECURITY COUNCIL membership, seats on the ECONOMIC AND SOCIAL COUNCIL (ECOSOC), the GENERAL ASSEMBLY vice presidents, the chairs of the various committees, and even the SECRETARY-GENERAL and the SECRETARIAT's senior staff positions are apportioned according to geographical blocs. In practice this means that regional groups select the candidates for the various positions prior to election by the General Assembly or by particular committees. The recognized geographical blocs, assuring "equitable geographical representation" in the world body, are the African, Asian, Latin American and Caribbean, East European, and the West European and Other groups. The latter is so named to allow it to represent nations that share Western culture and levels of DEVELOPMENT despite being located in other parts of the world, such as Australia and New Zealand. In 2000, Israel was added to this group. It should be noted that these are geographical, not regional groups, since the Middle East is divided between Africa and Asia. In practice these groups are also the points at which diplomatic negotiations begin on any given issue. Each group agreeing on a common position presents it to the body at large. The organization of these groups varies, with some meeting frequently during sessions of the various UN bodies. Such groups are particularly important to small and mid-sized nations that find it difficult to exert influence individually and hence are more likely to agree on a common position representing the entire group.

There are also subgroups within geographical groups (such as the Nordic Group), and other caucusing groups that span the geographical regions, such as the Middle Eastern Group. In addition, a number of other less formally organized groups exist, such as the Islamic Group. Specific groupings often may emerge on any given issue, and several have assumed considerable importance on individual issues. These include the Group of Seven (G7)—now the GROUP OF EIGHT (G8)—on economic matters, the Nuclear Powers Group in DISARMAMENT matters, the Organization of Petroleum Exporting Countries (OPEC), the least developed countries, the Small Island Developing States, and many other special issue groups formed by nations that share a particular concern with and usually a similar viewpoint on any given issue. On one topic, there was even a bloc named "the Group of Like Minded States." While all nations are members of an officially recognized geographical group, most nations are also members of several different blocs, which at times overlap and vary with each issue under consideration.

See also NORTH-SOUTH RELATIONS.

— *K. J. Grieb*

Centre for Human Rights   *See* HUMAN RIGHTS.

"Chance for Peace" Speech   *See* ATOMS FOR PEACE PROPOSAL.

Chapter VI

Chapter VI of the United Nations CHARTER is entitled "Pacific Settlement of Disputes." Chapter VI comprises Articles 33 through 38 of the Charter, which describes MECHANISMS for noncoercive measures to settle disputes peacefully between nations. It provides rules for the implementation of one of the overriding aims of the United Nations as described in Article 1 (1): eliminating threats to global peace and ensuring the settlement or adjustment of potential conflicts that could develop into a threat to international peace and security. In this context, the United Nations acts as a facilitator to help states solve their disputes through the nonuse of force.

Acting under Chapter VI, the SECURITY COUNCIL can decide to investigate a dispute or situation that could lead to a dispute to ascertain if it is likely to develop into a threat to international peace and security (Article 34), or a member state may bring a case to the attention of the Council under Article 35 (1). According to Article 35 (2), a non-member—since it has not ratified the UN CHARTER—must subject itself first to the principles of a peaceful solution in order to bring a dispute before the world organization. Also, the SECRETARY-GENERAL can alert the Security Council to such a case under Article 99. The SECRETARIAT, although not mentioned in Chapter VI, implements Chapter VI decisions, usually with a mandate but no clear plan from the Security Council.

All measures under Chapter VI described below are not legally binding for the parties involved and can be discussed by both the Security Council and the GENERAL ASSEMBLY. Once the Council takes up the matter, however, Article 12

(1) decrees that the General Assembly shall not pass any recommendations regarding it. The term "peace" used throughout this chapter, unlike in Article 1 (2) of the Charter, is to be understood in the negative sense, that is, it describes the state of an absence of war or other use of military force between two nations or parties to a dispute. Chapters VI and VII do not address the goal of establishing good and amicable relations between nations, only the aim of preventing war. Also, although the friction normally has been of an international nature, in some instances—such as the situation in Rhodesia after 1966, KOSOVO in 1999, and DARFUR, Sudan, in 2006—the Security Council has dealt with problems that did not directly threaten international peace and security but in fact were internal to a state. In some cases, the threat was not even clearly defined or established, but recommendations regarding it were passed nonetheless.

Once the Council has established that a threat exists, the following options present themselves for action. First are the measures mentioned in Article 33 (1): negotiation, MEDIATION, CONCILIATION, ARBITRATION, and judicial decisions, as well as using regional institutions and other peaceful means for resolving the threat. The United Nations urges the parties to avail themselves of these options (Article 33 [2]), and encourages the parties to settle peacefully the dispute themselves by direct bilateral negotiations. Mediation would include a third party, such as the United Nations, to serve as a facilitator. A judicial resolution would require the parties to take the dispute to the INTERNATIONAL COURT OF JUSTICE. Second, according to Articles 36 (1) and 37 (2), respectively, the Council can make recommendations regarding the procedure or method of adjustments and terms of settlement for disputes. It can also, finally, make recommendations of a more general nature if the parties request it (Article 38).

During the COLD WAR, with the Security Council often locked in a superpower stalemate, Chapter VI provisions became the only measures that could be agreed upon. In most of these cases the Security Council or the General Assembly passed RESOLUTIONS providing compromises or principles for resolving a certain dispute. The parties, under the obligations of Article 33, were urged to come to a peaceful settlement. Chapter VI also became the authorization for UN PEACEKEEPING operations, thus creating what became known as CHAPTER VI ½ PROVISIONS. The end of the cold war did not lessen the Security Council's desire to use Chapter VI when dealing with matters of peace and security. While CHAPTER VII ENFORCEMENT MEASURES were mandated in the cases of the 1991 GULF WAR, Kosovo, and SOMALIA, several PERMANENT MEMBERS OF THE SECURITY COUNCIL (P5) afterward were reticent to employ Chapter VII powers. They found the termination of Chapter VII measures impossible if one of the states holding the VETO opposed their repeal. Consequently, following the diplomatic standoff between the UNITED STATES on the one hand and FRANCE, CHINA, and the RUSSIAN FEDERATION on the other over the U.S. invasion of IRAQ in 2003, several states insisted on the use of Chapter VI in ensuing conflicts. Thus, the Council only could find unanimity among the P5 on a cease-fire in the 2006 war between Israel and Hezbollah under the terms of Chapter VI.

Chapter VI decisions, unlike those taken under Chapter VII, do not become part of INTERNATIONAL LAW but are recommendations. In this respect, this part of the UN Charter provides much less power to UN organs than Chapter VII gives to the Security Council. The persuasive role of Chapter VI, therefore, is to be seen against the background of more forceful action pending if UN actions within this context are ineffective. Both parts of the Charter were drafted at the DUMBARTON OAKS negotiations in 1944 and show a compromise between granting more power to the United Nations than the world community had given to the LEAGUE OF NATIONS on the one hand and assuring a state's right to maintain its sovereign authority over its actions and territory on the other hand. Most of the resolutions passed under Chapter VI have had limited impact, unless enforced by other means, such as meaningful peacekeeping operations, or the threat of SANCTIONS. Thus, Chapter VI efforts have led to "gray areas" of UN action, somewhere between Chapter VI and VII and not clearly mandated.

See also APPEALS TO THE SECURITY COUNCIL, ARAB-ISRAELI DISPUTE, LEBANON.

Further Reading: Lepgold, Joseph, and Thomas G. Weiss, eds. *Collective Conflict Management and Changing World Politics.* Albany, N.Y.: State University of New York Press, 1998. Ratner, Steven R. "Image and Reality in the UN's Peaceful Settlement of Disputes." *European Journal of International Law* 6, no. 3 (1995): 426. Roberts, A., and B. Kingsbury, eds. *United Nations, Divided World: The UN's Roles in International Relations.* 2d ed. New York: Oxford University Press, 1994. Simma, Bruno, ed. *The Charter of the United Nations. A Commentary.* 2d ed. New York: Oxford University Press, 2002.

— *T. J. Weiler*

Chapter VI ½ provisions

Peacekeeping operations (PKOs) are not explicitly mentioned in the United Nations CHARTER. However, provisions regarding the SECURITY COUNCIL, the GENERAL ASSEMBLY, and the SECRETARY-GENERAL (SG) may be interpreted as a legal basis for the institution of PEACEKEEPING. It is widely believed that peacekeeping is in line with the spirit of CHAPTER VI, but also close to CHAPTER VII of the Charter. The term "Chapter VI ½" has, therefore, been used to describe the guiding principles for PKOs.

The evolution of peacekeeping missions and their rules can be classified in four stages: The first missions (so-called First-Generation PKOs) were conducted according to guiding principles that had been codified in the latter half of the 1950s by RALPH BUNCHE, who at that time served as UNDER

SECRETARY-GENERAL (USG) for Special Political Affairs. Until 1986, the person holding this position was also responsible for the general supervision of all such missions. Bunche first developed these principles in crafting a response to the SUEZ CRISIS in 1956. Then in the CONGO (1960) and in CYPRUS (1964) he refined the UN model for all future COLD WAR peacekeeping operations. PKOs were to be conducted along conflict lines between states to disengage the warring parties and prevent a renewed outbreak of hostilities. Three principles had to be adhered to: (1) The parties involved had to agree to the stationing of UN peacekeeping and to a cease-fire or truce between them. (2) The troops deployed had to be only lightly armed, if at all, and were only authorized to use their WEAPONS in self-defense. (3) The UN had to be strictly impartial.

Because of these restrictions, advanced military capabilities were deemed unnecessary. Unarmed observers were sent to oversee agreements and report on the situation, or a peacekeeping force, lightly armed for purposes of self-defense, was established to act as a buffer between front lines of an international dispute. Theirs was a moral rather than military authority. These rules, although they were not always observed strictly, guided PKOs until the end of the COLD WAR.

With the change of the global situation after the collapse of the Soviet bloc, "Second Generation" PKOs came into being. Although based on the same principles, PKOs now included the help of the UN in the transition period toward the establishment of a lasting peace. The tasks and responsibilities were diversified and included, inter alia, the supervision of elections and the rebuilding of countries. The missions also included civilian personnel to provide the capabilities necessary for these "PEACE-BUILDING" efforts. As had been the case with the UNITED NATIONS OPERATIONS IN THE CONGO (ONUC), a SPECIAL REPRESENTATIVE of the SECRETARY-GENERAL was appointed to oversee both parts of the operation. The control over the missions was shifted from the USG for Special Political Affairs to the executive office of the SG in 1986; in 1992, a separate DEPARTMENT OF PEACEKEEPING OPERATIONS (DPKO), headed by an Under Secretary-General for Peacekeeping, was created.

Shortly thereafter, the nature of some missions changed toward peace enforcement, "Third Generation" PKOs, in which the UN coerced the parties to come to a peaceful settlement. These were ordered by the Security Council under Chapter VII of the Charter, which gives the Council authority to use force even when the parties oppose UN intervention. The mission in SOMALIA (UNOSOM) was the first to be conducted under the new guidelines, which allowed for the disarming of warring factions and so-called mission-defense. That is, peacekeepers were authorized to use force in order to reach the established goal of the operation. The failure of the UN in Somalia discredited Third-Generation PKOs and induced greater caution in subsequent missions.

Nonetheless, peacekeeping operations in the new millennium could be classified as a Fourth Generation in the sense that better trained and equipped troops were called upon to conduct "robust" missions, thus combining aspects of Chapter VI and Chapter VII PKOs. Troops had to be well trained and equipped to be able to defend not only themselves but also serve as a shield for refugees or uphold HUMAN RIGHTS with force, should the necessity arise. The United Nations undertook the reconstruction of failed states and the fashioning of civil societies, a process that came to be known as NATION-BUILDING. Operations at the turn of the century in BOSNIA, Kosovo, and East Timor reflected this new strategy. Specifically, the BRAHIMI REPORT was established to guide new missions. At the direction of Secretary-General KOFI ANNAN, Lakhdar Brahimi, the SG's Special Representative to AFGHANISTAN, prepared and submitted in 2000 a set of recommendations for future operations. The report established three rules: (1) The "BLUE HELMETS" should not cede the initiative to an attacker, (2) the UN's impartiality should have its limits, and (3) the PKO should only be authorized after the necessary resources are available.

Further Reading: Benton, Barbara, ed. *Soldiers for Peace: Fifty Years of United Nations Peacekeeping.* New York: Facts On File, 1996. Durch, William J., ed. *The Evolution of UN Peacekeeping: Case Studies and Comparative Analysis.* New York: St. Martin's, 1993. Durch, William J. *Twenty-first Century Peace Operations.* Washington, D.C.: U.S. Institute of Peace and the Henry L. Stimson Center, 2006. United Nations. *The Blue Helmets: A Review of United Nations Peace-Keeping.* 3d ed. New York: United Nations Publications, 1996. ———. *UN Peacekeeping: 50 Years, 1948–1998.* New York: United Nations Publications, 1998.

— T. J. Weiler

Chapter VII

Chapter VII of the United Nations CHARTER is essential to the UN's functioning as an effective system of global COLLECTIVE SECURITY. Providing more far-reaching powers than those in the ill-fated COVENANT of the LEAGUE OF NATIONS, it establishes the UN's ability to take collective measures in order to uphold or restore international peace and security. Article 39 gives the SECURITY COUNCIL the authority under INTERNATIONAL LAW to "determine the existence of any threat to the peace, breach of the peace, or act of AGGRESSION," and to "decide what measures shall be taken" to halt the threat or punish the aggressor. In enabling the Security Council to take coercive measures to achieve these tasks, Chapter VII denotes the United Nations as the international guarantor of peace and security.

A number of conditions have to be satisfied before the Security Council can act under the provisions of Chapter VII: First, it must be established that either an act of aggression or a threat to or breach of the peace has occurred (Article 39). The Charter does not contain definitions of these terms, thus the Council itself is the sole defining power. Consequently, the classification of a certain case as a threat to international peace has been among the most complicated matters throughout UN history. The fact that decisions of the Security Council are subject only to very limited judicial review by the INTERNATIONAL COURT OF JUSTICE (ICJ) is evidence for the broad margin of power Chapter VII grants to the Security Council.

The Security Council also has considered the following factors in its deliberations on whether to invoke Chapter VII ENFORCEMENT MEASURES: the international value or right endangered in the particular case, the extent and immediacy to which this right or value is being threatened or violated, and the international, transboundary character of the threat. Due to Article 2 (7), which prohibits UN intervention in the internal affairs of states, "peace" in Chapter VII is understood as "international peace." For this reason, actions being contemplated by the Security Council must be weighed against the right of SOVEREIGNTY of those states such actions would affect. However, following the close of the COLD WAR, the balance tilted somewhat against the claims of sovereign independence, as the Council, citing Chapter VII, authorized intervention in SOMALIA, East Timor, and AFGHANISTAN.

While in theory a differentiation among the three violations of international order mentioned in Article 39 is required, by definition, the term "act of aggression" demands that one of the parties to a conflict be classified as an aggressor. Thus the Security Council has been hesitant to be precise in its statements about transgressions of the article. So far, only North Korea in 1950, Argentina in 1982, and IRAQ in 1990 have been identified as "aggressors," or rather invaders/attackers; in 1960, while an aggression was identified in the CONGO, Belgium was not mentioned as the perpetrator. As in CHAPTER VI, "peace" is understood to mean the absence of war, rather than harmonious relations between nations.

Chapter VII gives the Security Council four possible actions if it determines that a threat to international peace exists: Article 40 empowers it to take provisional measures to prevent an escalation or aggravation of the situation. Such actions may include calls for a cease-fire or armistice, withdrawal of troops, or similar actions. These recommendations are not binding, but if they are ignored, coercive nonmilitary or military actions may be taken. Article 41 (actions not involving military force) and Article 42 (military actions) describe a gradual increase in coerciveness. Article 41 enumerates, in a nonexclusive way, steps that do not involve the use of WEAPONS, such as the cessation of diplomatic relations and economic SANCTIONS up to a blockade. The latter has been instituted only in a few cases, as in the post–GULF WAR sanctions against Iraq. The effectiveness of sanctions in general remains in dispute, the case of South Africa often cited as perhaps the only successful operation of this kind. Should sanctions not be adequate, Article 42 provides for even harsher measures as it authorizes the United Nations to take military action. It is common practice to empower individual states or other organizations/regional groups to take such action, usually in the form of an ad hoc "coalition of the willing" (Art. 48; cf. also Chapter VIII) in order to carry out the mandate issued by the Security Council.

All member states are asked and, at least according to the letter of Articles 43 and 44, are obliged to contribute troops and equipment to UN-led operations. In practice, however, setting up the forces necessary to conduct such operations as authorized by the Council is problematic, as numerous problems with PEACEKEEPING operations have shown. Finally, intending to ensure the UN's ability for swift action, Articles 45–47 call for the establishment of a UN military force. The PERMANENT MEMBERS discussed in vain this possibility during the founding period of the United Nations. Due to member states' unwillingness to confer command authority and independent forces to the United Nations, and because of the emergence of COLD WAR politics in the world body, troops being sent to war by the United Nations remained at the end of the century but a theoretical possibility. While the Charter mandated a MILITARY STAFF COMMITTEE (Art. 47), the only military action ever undertaken under the UN FLAG (although under U.S. command) occurred in the KOREAN WAR. In contrast, the 1991 GULF WAR against Iraq was not, strictly speaking, a UN operation. It was conducted by a U.S.-led coalition of member states on the basis of Article 42, sentence 2, and Article 48.

All of the enforcement measures described above can be instituted only if none of the five permanent members use their VETO power, as all decisions under Chapter VII are substantive (Article 27). Between fall 2002 and August 2006 the UNITED STATES solicited a Chapter VII mandate on three occasions only to be rebuffed by other permanent members. The American government sought approval for its war against Iraq initiated in 2003, but all permanent members of the Security Council—with the exception of the United Kingdom—and most nonpermanent members resisted Washington's urgings; thus, the U.S. invasion was conducted without UN authorization. These states, among other considerations, worried that once Chapter VII enforcement measures were in place, it would be impossible to terminate the occupation of Iraq, because termination would require a new RESOLUTION, which likely would be vetoed by the United States. Consequently, when the U.S. administration later proposed Chapter VII resolutions against IRAN and its nuclear program and as authority for a cease-fire in the 2006 Israeli-Hezbollah war, members of the Council demurred. In the case of Iran they would only agree to a reference to Article 40 in that Chapter, which makes no mention of the use of force. In the conflict in LEBANON, the Council could only come to a consensus on a cease-fire under the provisions of Chapter VI.

The veto power vitiated Security Council response to international crises during the cold war, as the superpowers often were unable to come to an agreement. Even in the post–cold war world, the Security Council would be unable to offer protection against aggression or threats committed by any of the permanent members. Article 51, finally, clarifies that the right to individual or COLLECTIVE SELF-DEFENSE even outside of the UNITED NATIONS SYSTEM is left untouched by the provisions of Chapter VII. For example, Article 5 of the North Atlantic Treaty Organization (NATO) explicitly refers to this provision.

See also CHAPTER VI ½ PROVISIONS.

Further Reading: Freudenschuss, Helmut. "Article 39 of the UN Charter Revisited." *Austrian Journal of Public and International Law,* no. 46 (1993). Lepgold, Joseph, and Thomas G. Weiss, eds. *Collective Conflict Management and Changing World Politics.* Albany, N.Y.: State University of New York Press, 1998. Simma, Bruno, ed. *The Charter of the United Nations—A Commentary.* 2d ed. New York: Oxford University Press, 2002. Weiss, Thomas G., et al. *The United Nations and Changing World Politics; Part One: International Peace and Security.* Boulder, Colo.: Westview Press, 1997.

— *T. J. Weiler*

Charter of the United Nations

The UN Charter is the "constitution" of the United Nations. Member states agree to abide by its principles and its procedures, laid out in a preamble and 19 chapters containing 111 articles. The Charter was signed on June 26, 1945, in San Francisco, at the conclusion of the UN CONFERENCE ON INTERNATIONAL ORGANIZATION. It came into force on October 24, 1945.

Article 108, in Chapter XVIII, provides the method for amending the Charter, which has been employed on only a few occasions. For an AMENDMENT to be added, it must be adopted by a vote of two-thirds of the members of the GENERAL ASSEMBLY (GA) and then ratified according to the respective constitutional processes of two-thirds of the member states, including all of the PERMANENT MEMBERS OF THE SECURITY COUNCIL (P5). Amendments to the Charter as of 2008 included alterations to Articles 23, 27, and 61, adopted by the General Assembly on December 17, 1963, and coming into force on August 31, 1965. An additional change in Article 61 was adopted on December 20, 1971, and entered into force on September 24, 1973. Article 109 was amended by the General Assembly on December 20, 1965, and the amendment came into force June 12, 1968. The amendment to Article 23 enlarged the MEMBERSHIP of the SECURITY COUNCIL (SC) from 11 to 15, and changes in Article 27 altered VOTING requirements in the Security Council—from seven to nine votes to pass procedural and all other matters. The VETO for the five permanent members remained. The two revisions of Article 61 enlarged the membership of the ECONOMIC AND SOCIAL COUNCIL (ECOSOC) from 18 to 27, and then to 54. The change in Article 109 increased the number from seven to nine of Security Council votes necessary to call a General Conference for the purpose of reviewing the Charter. The two-thirds vote required of the General Assembly remained.

It is useful in analyzing the Charter to distinguish the word *charter* from *COVENANT*. The latter term, used for the foundation document of the LEAGUE OF NATIONS, carries a more metaphysical and spiritual meaning than does charter. A covenant is a voluntary agreement entered into by two or more parties to do or refrain from some action or actions. In law, a covenant is a promise or contract of legal validity. In theology, a covenant is a contract or commitment between God and human beings, such as the biblical covenant between God and Israel, or the covenant entered into between the 17th-century American Puritans and their God. The League Covenant was a traditional agreement among governments, called in the Covenant "The High Contracting Parties," whereas the Preamble of the UN Charter begins "We the peoples of the United Nations."

The word *charter* customarily denotes the granting or gaining of rights, powers, or functions. A charter may be bestowed by the sovereign body of a state to a lower political level, to a corporation, to a university, or so on. One of the most legendary of all charters was the Magna Carta, famous in British constitutional history, which, in 1215, provided protection of certain rights for landed Englishmen against monarchal interference. This example gives evidence of the Latin origin of the word. One approximate—and telling—synonym, according to the *Oxford English Dictionary*, is "written constitution." In the UN's case, in the Preamble and thus in essence—if not with juridical precision—the world's peoples granted themselves the rights, powers, and responsibilities contained in the Charter.

Comparing the League's Covenant and the UN's Charter draws attention to certain new, or elaborated, principles of INTERNATIONAL LAW introduced by the latter. For example, the Covenant essentially suggested a voluntary commitment not to resort to force, while the Charter, in Article 2, paragraph 4, confirms the nonresort to war as an established principle: "All members shall refrain in their international relations from the threat or use of force against the territorial integrity or political independence of any state, or any other manner inconsistent with the purposes of the United Nations." The Covenant's Preamble speaks of the dealings of "organized peoples with one another," as though there were "disorganized," or perhaps, "less civilized" peoples in the world. As Nagendra Singh, former president of the INTERNATIONAL COURT OF JUSTICE, has pointed out, the Charter disavows an international "class" system by provisions devoted to decolonization (especially Chapters XI, XII, and XIII), to the equal SOVEREIGNTY of states (Article 2), and by

its encouragement of universal membership (Chapter II). Of equal significance is the principle of obligatory registration of TREATIES at a single, universally visible place and with a single institution—the United Nations—as provided in Article 102. This article additionally directs the SECRETARIAT to accumulate and publicize all registered treaties.

However, two of the Charter's accentuated themes sometimes have seemed to operate at cross-purposes. First is the principle of the independence and sovereignty of equal member states (Article 2) and the concomitant principle of noninterference in the domestic or internal affairs of states, as explicated in Article 2, paragraph 7: "Nothing contained in the present Charter shall authorize the United Nations to intervene in matters which are essentially within the domestic JURISDICTION of any state or shall require the Members to submit such matters to settlement under the present Charter." But second is the promotion of universal respect for HUMAN RIGHTS and fundamental freedoms, as found in Article 1, paragraph 3, in Article 13, paragraph 1, and in Article 55, section C, which, in succession, promotes and encourages "respect for human rights," advocates "assisting in the realization of human rights," and calls on the United Nations to promote "universal respect for, and observance of, human rights." Of course, sovereignty and noninterference appear to denote the right of a NATION-STATE to enforce its own version of human rights. Yet the UNIVERSAL DECLARATION OF HUMAN RIGHTS and several provisions of the Charter seem to proclaim rights as universal rather than culturally or nationally determined. In 1999 SECRETARY-GENERAL KOFI ANNAN maintained that such human rights could not be abridged in the name of state sovereignty. By the conclusion of the 20th century the proposition that sovereignty and the principle of non-interference deny any other nation, group of nations, or the United Nations, the right—even duty—to interfere in a state's domestic affairs came under increased challenge as the world community found itself dealing with human tragedies in collapsing and dysfunctional states in the FORMER YUGOSLAVIA, INDONESIA, and areas of Africa. The Security Council, for example, authorized direct humanitarian intervention in SOMALIA, Rwanda, and East Timor, not always at the clear invitation of any central government. Moreover, the BRAHIMI REPORT, prepared by a special committee on PEACEKEEPING operations and available for international consideration at the MILLENNIUM SUMMIT of 2000, underscored Annan's view and recommended strengthening UN peacekeeping and a more robust and offensive posture in dangerous and out-of-control situations in disintegrating states.

The Charter's original authors may well not have foreseen these recent developments. The basic framework for the Charter derived from discussions among the main Allies during World War II. The idea for a new world organization began to take form once it was clear that the League of Nations had collapsed. U.S. president FRANKLIN ROOSEVELT used the words "United Nations" in early 1942 to refer to those countries aligned against the Axis powers. During the war U.S. secretary of state CORDELL HULL convened an Advisory Committee to deal with issues of a new international organization. Hull presented a completed working paper—called "Charter of the UN"—in August 1943. This was the first time the word "Charter" had been used in reference to the proposed new organization, and the document became the focus of negotiations and discussions from that time forward. The Moscow DECLARATION of October 30, 1943, issued by CHINA, the United Kingdom, the UNITED STATES, and the Soviet Union represented the first official statement from the Allies on the need for a new international organization. On November 5, 1943, the U.S. Senate adopted the Connally Resolution, 85 to 5, calling for establishment of an international authority after the war. During the summer of 1944, the same four countries that had issued the Moscow Declaration sent representatives to the six and a half week conference held at DUMBARTON OAKS in Washington, D.C., where preliminary proposals for a Charter were drafted. At the YALTA CONFERENCE in February 1945, Roosevelt, WINSTON CHURCHILL, and JOSEPH STALIN reached further agreement on Charter provisions. At the founding conference in San Francisco in June 1945, all nations that had adhered to the original January 1, 1942, DECLARATION BY UNITED NATIONS, or who had declared war on GERMANY and JAPAN by March 1, 1945—totaling 50 nations—were invited to help draft the finished Charter. According to Article 110, paragraph 3, the Charter was to enter into force once it had received ratification by the five permanent Security Council members (United States, UNITED KINGDOM, China, USSR, and FRANCE) and a majority of all other signatories. The United States was the first to deposit its instrument of ratification (August 8) and the Soviet Union, Ukraine, Byelorussia, and Poland the last, on October 24, 1945, making the latter date the official "UNITED NATIONS DAY."

The Preamble indicates that the Charter is an agreement not among "governments" or "states," but among the "peoples" of the world, a notion that caused considerable debate in San Francisco. Less deliberation was directed to the remaining paragraphs of the Preamble, dealing with saving the future world from the "scourge of war," emphasizing human rights and the legitimacy of treaties and international law, and promoting social progress and better standards of living.

Chapter I outlines the UN's "Purposes and Principles," including the maintenance of international peace and security, respect for equal rights and self-determination, the encouragement of rights and freedoms, and the principle of sovereign equality of all member states. It establishes a COLLECTIVE SECURITY system among its members, requiring them to "settle their international disputes by peaceful means."

Chapter II deals with membership, the qualification for which is to be a "peace-loving" state. ADMISSION requires

Security Council recommendation followed by General Assembly approval. It also allows for the SUSPENSION of the membership of a state against which the UN has taken some ENFORCEMENT MEASURES. Under the most dire circumstances, a state may be expelled by the General Assembly upon recommendation of the Security Council.

Chapter III lists the PRINCIPAL ORGANS and explicitly commands that there be no restriction on "the eligibility of men and women to participate" in any principal or subsidiary organ. The Charter creates five principal organs: the General Assembly, the Security Council, the Economic and Social Council, the TRUSTEESHIP COUNCIL, and the Secretariat.

Chapters IV and V detail provisions for the General Assembly and the Security Council, including voting procedures for both bodies and the jurisdiction of actions each can take. Membership in the General Assembly is completely equal, since each country, whatever its size, has one vote. While a majority vote effects most actions, the more important decisions made by the GA are made on "IMPORTANT QUESTIONS," which require a two-thirds vote of those members present and voting (Article 18). In the 15-member Security Council, nine votes are required to pass a procedural matter, while "all other matters" require that the five permanent members concur (the veto provision in Article 27).

Chapters VI and VII constitute the core precepts for the historic development of UN peacekeeping policies and outline the collective security measures that the United Nations may employ to restore peace. CHAPTER VI describes the procedures for dealing with the "Pacific Settlement of Disputes" and threats to the peace. It lists the traditional methods in international diplomacy that the parties should use to resolve their differences. They are negotiation, MEDIATION, CONCILIATION, ARBITRATION, and judicial decisions. CHAPTER VII emphasizes the role of the Security Council under international law to "determine the existence of any threat to the peace, breach of the peace, or act of AGGRESSION," and to "decide what measures shall be taken" to halt the threat or punish the aggressor. In enabling the Security Council to take coercive measures to achieve these tasks, Chapter VII installs the United Nations as the international guarantor of peace and security.

Chapters VIII and IX define and sanction REGIONAL ORGANIZATIONS to keep the peace and encourage economic and social cooperation. Article 57 encourages SPECIALIZED AGENCIES to develop a relationship with the United Nations and to expedite raising living standards, resolving economic and social problems, and enhancing human rights. These chapters are followed by the related Chapter X, which defines and sets the parameters for action of the Economic and Social Council.

Chapters XI and XII deal with non-self-governing territories (typically colonies). The first of these two chapters is a declaration of UN intent to promote decolonization and the progressive development of "free political institutions." Chapter XIII establishes the Trusteeship Council and defines its membership (those states administering trust territories, the remaining permanent members of the Security Council that do not administer any territories in the system, and sufficient member states elected by the General Assembly to assure an equal number of administering and non-administering governments on the Council).

Chapter XIV provides for the International Court of Justice, the judicial arm of the United Nations. By Article 92, the ICJ replaced the PERMANENT COURT OF INTERNATIONAL JUSTICE (PCIJ), became an integral part of the United Nations, and gained its own statute, annexed to the UN Charter and based on the statute of the PCIJ.

Chapter XV creates the Secretariat, to be headed by a SECRETARY-GENERAL appointed by the General Assembly upon the recommendation of the Security Council. In addition to being the chief administrative officer of the United Nations, the Secretary-General plays an important political role. Article 99 allows him to bring to the Security Council's attention any matter that he believes threatens peace and security. The Secretariat is designed to be the administrative arm of the United Nations. Its members are "international officers responsible only to the Organization" (Article 100).

Chapter XVI outlines miscellaneous provisions for UN members. Chapter XVII, with the title "Transitional Security Arrangements," sorted out specific matters that concluded World War II, and Chapter XVIII explicates the method of amending the Charter (see above) while the Charter concludes with Chapter XIX, which describes the time line and process of ratification (see above).

See also CHAPTER VI ½, *IN LARGER FREEDOM*, REFORM OF THE UNITED NATIONS, STRUCTURE OF THE UNITED NATIONS, UNITED NATIONS SYSTEM, UNITING FOR PEACE RESOLUTION.

Further Reading: Gross, Leo. "The Development of International Law through the United Nations." *The United Nations; Past, Present, and Future.* Edited by James Barros. New York: The Free Press, 1972. Nicholas, H. G. *The United Nations as a Political Institution.* 5th ed. Oxford: Oxford University Press, 1975. Russell, Ruth B. *A History of the United Nations Charter: The Role of the United States, 1940–1945.* Washington, D.C.: Brookings Institution, 1958. Schlesinger, Stephen C. *Act of Creation: The Founding of the United Nations.* Boulder, Colo.: Westview Press, 2003. Simma, Bruno. *The Charter of the United Nations: A Commentary.* 2nd Ed. Oxford: Oxford University Press, 2002. Singh, Nagendra. "The UN and the Development of International Law." *United Nations, Divided World; The UN's Roles in International Relations.* 2d ed. Edited by Adam Roberts and Benedict Kingsbury. Oxford: Clarendon Press, 1993.

Chechnya *See* RUSSIAN FEDERATION.

chemical weapons (CW)

In April 1915, the German army first used chemical WEAPONS, in the form of chlorine gas. From then until the end of World War I, these WEAPONS OF MASS DESTRUCTION (WMD) killed or maimed tens of thousands of people. In what constituted the first arms race, each side developed methods of deployment and agents that even rendered gas masks worn by the enemy useless. At that time mostly chlorine and phosgene were used, both usually in gaseous form. Accordingly, chemical warfare was often called "Gas War." Most CW agents, however, were liquids or solids, like the so-called mustard gas, which was used later in World War I. Often, chemical weapons were used in their atomized form as aerosols, entering the body via the respiratory organs or penetrating the skin. Chemical weapons were not used during World War II, even though all sides possessed huge quantities of them.

With the onset of the COLD WAR, even more deadly agents were developed, mainly in the Warsaw PACT states. In 1969, the United Nations defined chemical warfare agents as "chemical substances, whether gaseous, liquid or solid, which might be employed because of their direct toxic effects on man, animals and plants." Not only the toxic chemicals but also the equipment for their dispersal was classified as a chemical weapon. In recent years, the Iraqi government used CW agents against the Iraqi Kurds (in Halabja in 1988) and during the IRAN-IRAQ WAR. Also, the chemical Sarin was used in a terrorist attack on the Tokyo subway in 1995.

On November 30, 1992, the GENERAL ASSEMBLY adopted the "Convention on the Prohibition of the Development, Production, Stockpiling and Use of Chemical Weapons and on their Destruction" (Res. 39), an accord submitted and recommended by the CONFERENCE ON DISARMAMENT. The Chemical Weapons Convention (CWC) was opened for signature in Paris on January 13, 1993. It entered into force on April 29, 1997, six months after Hungary became the 65th state to sign it. As of summer 2006, the CWC counted 178 states that had become or were in the process of becoming parties to the agreement.

The CWC regulates assistance to states that might be attacked with chemical agents and also regulates trade relationships among the parties in the field of chemicals and related equipment. The obligations imposed on signatory states are unprecedented in their scope. The CWC prohibits the development, acquisition, production, stockpiling, and use of chemical weapons. States are required to destroy all chemical weapons (including those left within the territory of another state) and production facilities that they may possess. The CONVENTION was the first international DISARMAMENT agreement with the purpose of eliminating an entire category of WMDs.

The ORGANISATION FOR THE PROHIBITION OF CHEMICAL WEAPONS (OPCW), headquartered in The Hague, was created to implement the CWC, including providing international verification and a forum for international cooperation in this field. The organization trains inspectors and promotes universal ACCESSION to the convention. The verification provisions of the CWC are far-reaching. They affect the military sector as well as the civilian chemical industry by imposing obligations and restrictions on the production, processing, and consumption of all chemicals that potentially could be used in weapons production.

Further Reading: *Chemical Disarmament: Basic Facts.* 1999 edition. The Hague: Organization for the Prohibition of Chemical Weapons, 2000. Moodie, Michael, and Javed Ali, eds. *Synthesis 2000: A Year in Review.* The Hague: Organization for the Prohibition of Chemical Weapons, 2001. Tucker, Jonathan B., ed. *Toxic Terror: Assessing Terrorist Use of Chemical and Biological Weapons.* Cambridge: MIT Press, 2000. ———. *The Chemical Weapons Convention: Implementation Challenges and Solutions.* Monterey, Calif.: Monterey Institute of International Studies Center for Nonproliferation Studies, 2001. OPCW Web site: <www.opcw.org>.

— *T. J. Weiler*

Chief Executives Board for Coordination (CEB)

The Chief Executives Board is the successor body to the Administrative Committee on Coordination (ACC). Renamed the CEB in 2002, it works to foster cooperation within the United Nations SYSTEM and tries to bring to the full UN harmonization on a range of management and substantive issues.

The UN ECONOMIC AND SOCIAL COUNCIL (ECOSOC) created the Administrative Committee on Coordination in 1946 to supervise implementation of recently signed agreements with SPECIALIZED AGENCIES being brought into the United Nations System under the CHARTER's Articles 57 and 63. Over the next 50 years the ACC was greatly expanded in MEMBERSHIP and purpose, becoming the primary organ for cooperation at the policy level among all UN bodies. By the end of the 20th century the committee included representation from 25 UN System organizations, FUNDS, and PROGRAMMES, as well as members from the BRETTON WOODS institutions, and all specialized agencies. Its metamorphosis led SECRETARY-GENERAL KOFI ANNAN to propose as part of his REFORM effort a review of the committee's STRUCTURE, subordinate bodies, and even its name.

The size of the membership and broad scope of the ACC's mandate produced an overly complex administrative structure. It had five major subsidiary committees. The Organizational Committee (OC) proposed the agenda and organized the meetings of the ACC. Each agency on the ACC has a representative on the OC. The Consultative Committee on Administrative Questions (CCAQ) advised the CEB on management and administrative policy questions, and worked to create systemwide policies on personnel, budgetary, and financial matters. The Inter-Agency Committee on WOMEN and Gender Equity (IACWGE) was a response to the 1995 FOURTH WORLD CONFERENCE ON WOMEN, held in Beijing, CHINA. Replacing an earlier Ad Hoc Inter-Agency Meeting on women, the IACWGE was meant to implement the Beijing Platform for Action and to bring about a gender perspective throughout the UN System. The INTER-AGENCY COMMITTEE ON SUSTAINABLE DEVELOPMENT (IACSD) advised the ACC on ways that the United Nations System might coordinate efforts to carry out the decisions of the UNITED NATIONS CONFERENCE ON ENVIRONMENT AND DEVELOPMENT (UNCED), including AGENDA 21 and the Plan of Action for the SUSTAINABLE DEVELOPMENT of small island developing states (SIDS). The Consultative Committee on Programme and Operational Questions (CCPOQ) was created in 1993, merging two earlier committees. It was an "inter-secretariat coordinating body" that sought to mobilize the complementary capabilities of the different UN agencies in order to accomplish the goals of all UN initiatives, particularly at the field level. In addition to all ACC members being represented on CCPOQ, so too were the UNITED NATIONS UNIVERSITY, the WORLD TOURISM ORGANIZATION, and the United Nations Staff College. In the 1990s each subsidiary committee of the then ACC developed its own set of subcommittees and ad hoc meetings. This trend made the ACC an example of the redundancy and bureaucratization in the United Nations that critics decried.

At the ACC's October 2000 meeting the committee accepted Secretary-General Annan's recommendation and created two High-Level Committees—one to oversee management functions (HLCM), and one to supervise programmatic work (HLCP). Their creation was part of a general review of the committee's structure in an effort to streamline the ACC's operation which in part led to the new name—Chief Executives Board.

In 2002 the new name became official. An immediate decision was taken to abolish all of the old ACC's subsidiary committees, and to reorganize all of the agencies reporting to the CEB under the two remaining High-Level Committees—the HLCP and HLCM. Several of the former subcommittees were renamed, others replaced. Not part of the UN's SECRETARIAT, the Chief Executives Board brings together leaders of all UN System secretariats under the chairmanship of the Secretary-General semi-annually for a two-day meeting. At its sessions it discusses coordinated efforts that can be taken to implement UN initiatives, WORLD CONFERENCE recommendations, and needed responses to new international challenges. In the spring the CEB meets at the headquarters of one of its member agencies, and in the fall at UN HEADQUARTERS in New York City. Biennially it holds a "retreat" for its membership. It issues the *Annual Overview Report,* highlighting the critical issues on which it believes the UN System should focus in the near term.

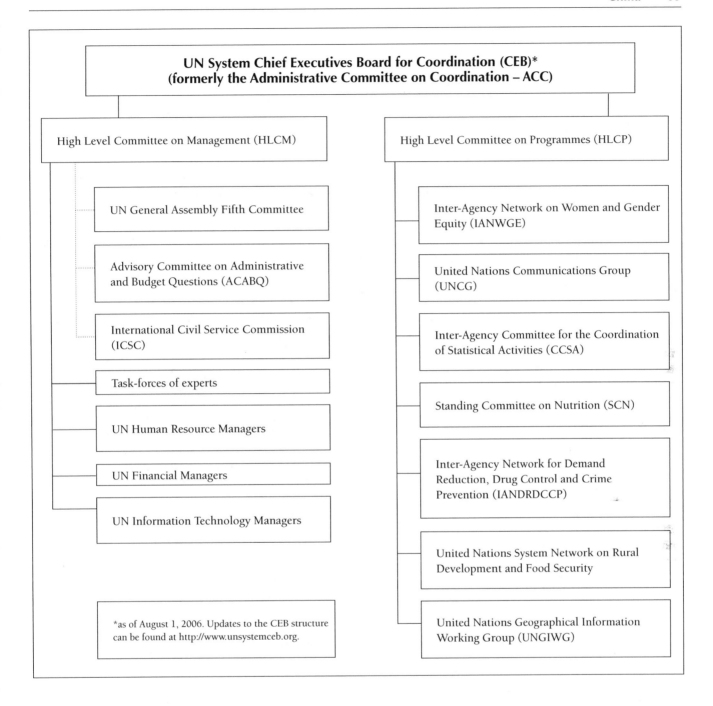

UN System Chief Executives Board for Coordination (CEB)*
(formerly the Administrative Committee on Coordination – ACC)

High Level Committee on Management (HLCM)

UN General Assembly Fifth Committee

Advisory Committee on Administrative and Budget Questions (ACABQ)

International Civil Service Commission (ICSC)

Task-forces of experts

UN Human Resource Managers

UN Financial Managers

UN Information Technology Managers

*as of August 1, 2006. Updates to the CEB structure can be found at http://www.unsystemceb.org.

High Level Committee on Programmes (HLCP)

Inter-Agency Network on Women and Gender Equity (IANWGE)

United Nations Communications Group (UNCG)

Inter-Agency Committee for the Coordination of Statistical Activities (CCSA)

Standing Committee on Nutrition (SCN)

Inter-Agency Network for Demand Reduction, Drug Control and Crime Prevention (IANDRDCCP)

United Nations System Network on Rural Development and Food Security

United Nations Geographical Information Working Group (UNGIWG)

The CEB's identification of the critical issues to be addressed by the UN System has great weight because it reflects the consensus of the heads of all important UN agencies. In 2006 the CEB included, in addition to the Secretary-General, the heads of the specialized agencies, funds, and programmes, the INTERNATIONAL ATOMIC ENERGY AGENCY (IAEA), and the WORLD TRADE ORGANIZATION (WTO).

Further Reading: CEB Web site: <www.unsystemceb.org/>. United Nations Handbook. Wellington, N.Z.: Ministry of Foreign Affairs and Trade, published annually.

China

China was one of the 26 countries that joined in the January 1, 1942, DECLARATION BY UNITED NATIONS to overcome the Axis powers. The country then joined with the UNITED STATES, the UNITED KINGDOM, and the Soviet Union in the MOSCOW DECLARATION of October 30, 1943—the first official statement on the necessity of creating a new international organization to replace the LEAGUE OF NATIONS. China participated with the same three countries in drafting specific proposals for the UN CHARTER at the DUMBARTON OAKS CONFERENCE of 1944, and, although not in attendance at the YALTA CONFERENCE of February 1945, achieved at that meeting the status of PERMANENT MEMBER OF THE SECURITY COUNCIL. For a nation that had suffered Japanese occupation of much of its territory from 1931 to the end of World War II, and repeated humiliations at the hands of other nations since the early 19th century, this surfacing international respectability appeared extraordinary. Yet this high point was followed immediately by a brutal internal civil war, ending in 1949 with Mao Zedong's Chinese Communist Party victorious and the rival Republic of China's leader Jiang Jieshi (Chiang Kai-shek)—who had participated in all the wartime negotiations—removed to the island of Taiwan (Formosa). From 1949 to 1971, Jiang's republic officially represented China at the United Nations and as a permanent member in the SECURITY COUNCIL. But a dramatic GENERAL ASSEMBLY vote in 1971 removed the republic and elevated Mao's People's Republic of China (PRC) to fill China's seat. For the remainder of the 20th century, the PRC conducted China's business in the United Nations and in the myriad global organizations it joined.

Active diplomacy and collaboration across international boundaries were recent modi operandi for a country that for centuries had seen itself as the "Middle Kingdom" and superior to all others. Ethnocentrism, certainly not unique to the Chinese, rested in the Celestial Empire's expansiveness and centrality, as well as in its unusually long and continuous history, unmatched by most other civilizations. By the end of the 18th century, Manchu China extended to Tibet, beyond Xinjiang to Turkestan, and included Mongolia, Taiwan, and tributary allies in Korea, northern Vietnam and Burma. China was at its greatest territorial extent. Between 1700 and 1800 the POPULATION doubled to about 300 million, making China from then until the opening of the 21st century the most populous country on earth.

But by the end of the 19th century China had suffered three humiliating losses in wars and a subsequent loss of sovereign control over "spheres of influence," territories within the country administered by outside nations. Western-educated Sun Zhongshan (Sun Yat-sen) instigated a nationwide revolution against the weakened Manchus, who were overthrown in 1911. Sun became the first president of the new Provisional Chinese Republic. But soon he resigned in favor of strongman Yuan Shikai, whose death in 1916 was followed by years of factional civil war among aspiring warlords. Sun's hopes to forge a republican solution to China's problems seemed stillborn. Moreover, during World War I, JAPAN had successfully extracted further concessions, and in 1919 anger mounted when Chinese learned that the TREATY of Versailles ending World War I had granted former German concessions in China to the Japanese. Generalissimo Jiang Jieshi, who guided Sun's Guomindang (Nationalist) Party following the latter's death in 1925, defeated remaining warlords. He then turned on his erstwhile allies in the Chinese Communist Party (founded by Mao Zedong in 1921) and

brought some unity to the country. But it was short-lived. In 1931 Japan invaded Manchuria and turned it into the puppet state of Manzhouguo (Manchukuo). (After the invasion Mao voiced his disdain for international organizations by referring to the League of Nations as "a League of Robbers by which the various imperialisms are dismembering China.") In a reborn but fragile united front with the Communists, Jiang tried to resist Japanese incursion. Then, in 1937, Tokyo began its full-scale AGGRESSION on the Chinese mainland. Japan occupied Manchuria and much of the coastal region of China for the duration of World War II.

The Communist-Guomindang front began to crumple during the war and the disintegration simply merged into a civil conflict that continued after World War II had ended. On October 1, 1949, in Beijing, victorious Mao Zedong, announcing that at last China had "stood up," proclaimed the People's Republic of China. Meantime, Jiang crossed to the island of Taiwan, where in his capital of Taipei, he headed what he and the United States—and the United Nations— were to consider, for the next two decades, the legitimate government of China.

Taipei joined with the United States and the West in the rivalry now called the COLD WAR, while the Soviet Union and its allies recognized the new government in Beijing and urged its seating in the United Nations. The outbreak of the KOREAN WAR solidified cold war divisions. Documents released in 2000 from Soviet archives show that Soviet leader JOSEPH STALIN approved North Korea's June 25, 1950, invasion of the South, emphasizing to North Korean leader KIM IL SUNG that the victory of the Chinese Communists the previous year demonstrated that Americans were weak and would not respond to such an invasion, and that Chinese troops would be made available to fight with the North. In October 1950, following General Douglas MacArthur's landing at Inchon, Mao enthusiastically agreed to intervene (but wanted prior Soviet assurance of air cover, which never came, and marked an initial strain in the Sino-Soviet alliance signed in February of that year). The upshot was that the PRC found itself technically at war with the United Nations, whose U.S.-dominated forces were the main defenders of the South. Sino-American hostility deepened, and Washington used all its political muscle to assure exclusion of Beijing from the United Nations.

Meantime China reabsorbed Tibet (1951), tried and sentenced "class enemies," and confiscated land from landowners to give to peasants. Cut off from the new international financial and trade regimes, China in the late 1950s experienced Mao's "Great Leap Forward," a self-generated economic growth plan that established rural communes in place of peasant ownership and called for a crash program for village industrialization, all directed from the central government. Consequences were disastrous. The country suffered from widespread famine and economic downturn. When INDONESIA's leader Sukarno removed that country from the

Seating of PRC delegation, November 15, 1971 (UNITED NATIONS)

United Nations in 1965, Mao called for an alternate "revolutionary United Nations" made up only of leftist countries. A border dispute with INDIA, Russia's friend, further isolated the regime. Mao attempted to reenergize revolutionary fervor by activating the Great Proletarian Cultural Revolution in 1966. Schools were closed down. Officially sanctioned and ideologically pure Red Guard units, made up of rowdy, faithful youth, roamed the country engaging in nasty purges of wrong ideas and impure customs, and challenged any remnant signs of bourgeois capitalism, including those allegedly within the entrenched party bureaucracy. Formerly powerful leaders were placed under house arrest. Others, like future leader Deng Xiaoping, were exiled to distant rural areas. China seemed to turn completely within itself, and to be highly combustible.

Then three important developments began to alter China's position with the wider world and hint at a long-term effect on the nation's internal life as well as on its external diplomacy. One was the growing estrangement with the Soviet Union, whose invasion of Czechoslovakia in 1968 finally convinced the Chinese that Moscow was more dangerous than the United States. The second was the changing nature of UN MEMBERSHIP; as many former colonial nations entered the organization, support for Taiwan became more tenuous, and support for seating Beijing grew. The third

important development was the departure of the revolutionary generation leadership, and particularly that of Mao, who died in 1976, just short of the age of 83.

U.S. president Richard Nixon sensed an opportunity to exploit the Sino-Soviet unfriendliness and draw China closer to the United States. By early 1971 the two countries were engaged in secret talks. In July 1971 Nixon sent Henry Kissinger, his national security adviser, on a trip to China. In February 1972, the president himself was in the country, where he met with Mao and signed the historic Shanghai Communiqué, recognizing Beijing's SOVEREIGNTY in China and disavowing a "two-China" policy. These events enveloped one of the more interesting moments in UN history, as the annual General Assembly vote on China's representation came up in October 1971. The U.S. Department of State, long publicly committed to Taiwan, was prepared to pursue its regular procedural tactic of making the issue of seating Beijing an IMPORTANT QUESTION, thus requiring a two-thirds vote. This strategy had until then restrained a United Nations increasingly sympathetic to the PRC. Now, however, with the highest U.S. officials unexpectedly linked with the mainland, the U.S. position seemed at least confused, and the Third World pro-PRC coalition of representatives was able to surmount the two-thirds barrier. On October 25 the General Assembly, in a dramatic late night ballot, removed Taiwan and seated Beijing as China's UN representative.

For the most part, the PRC's behavior as a new member of the United Nations revealed a traditional, pragmatic posture of attention first to national interests and then, usually fairly quietly, endorsement of nonthreatening consensus actions. The first VETO exercised by Beijing in the Security Council was against the ADMISSION of Bangladesh, formed out of East Pakistan after the India-Pakistan War of 1971. The veto underscored the Pakistan-China friendship and the recurrent Sino-Indian hostility. Also early, Beijing positioned itself to take a leadership role among the smaller Third World nations by supporting RESOLUTIONS and initiatives against the white minority governments in South Africa and Rhodesia (now Zimbabwe). Of the 21 vetoes China cast from 1971 to 1996, 19 had to do with nominations for SECRETARY-GENERAL. Beijing consistently supported Third World candidates. At the 1972 Stockholm conference that established the UNITED NATIONS ENVIRONMENT PROGRAMME (UNEP), China played a surprisingly active role, and, consistent with its courting of the developing world, was a crucial influence on having UNEP's headquarters placed in Nairobi, Kenya.

Following Mao's death in 1976, the once dishonored Deng Xiaoping emerged from intraparty rivalry to the top leadership position in the country (as deputy premier, chief of staff of the army, and member of the central committee of the party). He achieved full diplomatic relations with the United States in 1979 and engineered a remarkable reinterpretation of communist ideology, leading to sweeping economic changes. In 1978 the government announced the policy of the "Four Modernizations" (agriculture, industry, science and technology, and defense). The new policy encouraged foreign investment and technology transfer. In a drive to modernize, Western management and market practices replaced Maoist tenets. By breaking up rural communes and returning land to individuals under long leases, China realized extraordinary progress in agricultural production during the 1980s. In 1993, the party's central committee called for the conversion of state-owned enterprises into joint-stock companies and the eventual creation of a central bank and modern tax system.

Official Chinese estimates showed by 1994 an economic growth rate of 12 percent retreating to an estimated 7.9 percent by 2001, then ascending again to an annual rate of 11.3 percent during the second quarter of 2006. From 1978 to 1998, economic output quadrupled, and by then China had the world's second largest gross domestic product (GDP), an estimated $4.8 trillion in 1999, and up to $8.5 trillion by 2006 according to the WORLD BANK. By 2006, China had moved to modernize its financial institutions, including the sale of equity in China's largest state banks to foreign investors, refinements in foreign exchange and bond markets, and—in response to complaints from overseas, particularly in the United States—revaluing its currency in July 2005 and, one year later, raising interest rates and tightening credit to control lending and allow the Chinese currency (the yuan) to rise relative to major foreign currencies such as the dollar. (Although some critics in the West continued to argue that China had not gone far enough to situate the yuan fairly to other currencies.)

But internal problems remained. With decreasing public-sector support, large groups of Chinese, particularly in rural areas, found themselves unemployed. Economic REFORMS were not followed by loosening political control from the central party. In the spring of 1989 student demonstrations took place in Beijing to mourn the death of disgraced former reformist party secretary Hu Yaobang. The demonstrations quickly took on a life of their own and student leaders and others convened in Tiananmen Square to demand wide-ranging democratic reforms. Protests spread to other parts of the country. Deng and a handful of powerful leaders replaced wavering party secretary Zhao Ziyang with Jiang Zemin and ordered military repression of the demonstrations. Beginning with the crackdown on June 3–4, thousands of protesters and dissidents were arrested and an unknown number killed.

For the next decade, China tried to put the Tiananmen unpleasantness behind it. After an initial explosion of outrage around the world, followed by some SANCTIONS, China's international economic and political relations resumed unhampered. They were guided by Jiang Zemin, who became president in 1993 and dominant party leader upon the death of Deng in February 1997. On July 1, 1997, the United Kingdom returned Hong Kong to Chinese sovereignty, and on December 20, 1999, China regained administrative control of Macao, the oldest permanent European enclave in Asia. Responding to President BILL CLINTON's urgings, the U.S. Congress in 2000 granted China permanent most-favored-nation trading status, opening the way for Beijing's entry into the WORLD TRADE ORGANIZATION on December 11, 2001. Also in 2001 China was chosen to host the 2008 Olympic Games.

From within the UNITED NATIONS SYSTEM came further evidence of the nation's full integration into world affairs. In the 1980s Beijing joined almost all important international governmental organizations, including the WORLD BANK and the INTERNATIONAL MONETARY FUND. China began participating in the CONFERENCE ON DISARMAMENT in 1980, the COMMISSION ON HUMAN RIGHTS in 1982, and in late 1984 a Chinese national—jurist Ni Zhengyu—became a judge on the INTERNATIONAL COURT OF JUSTICE. China acceded to several human rights CONVENTIONS, including those on racial discrimination, APARTHEID, WOMEN, GENOCIDE, torture, refugees, and the child (but not the INTERNATIONAL COVENANT ON ECONOMIC, SOCIAL AND CULTURAL RIGHTS or the INTERNATIONAL COVENANT ON CIVIL AND POLITICAL RIGHTS). By the turn of the century, China was a signatory to several international environmental agreements, including the Antarctic Environmental PROTOCOL, the ANTARCTIC TREATY, the UN CONVENTION ON THE LAW OF THE SEA, and UN Conventions on Biological Diversity, CLIMATE CHANGE, DESERTIFICATION, Hazardous Wastes, the Ozone Layer, and more. In September 2002, China announced its approval of the KYOTO PROTOCOL, which it had signed in 1998. On the occasion of the 40th anniversary of the United Nations, in 1985, Zhao Ziyang became the first PRC prime minister to address the General Assembly. Prime Minister Li Peng participated in the first-ever Security Council summit in January 1992, the Earth Summit at Rio in 1992, and the first WORLD SUMMIT ON SOCIAL DEVELOPMENT at Copenhagen in 1995. President Jiang Zemin attended the 50th anniversary meeting in 1995 and addressed the UN's MILLENNIUM SUMMIT in New York in September 2000. In May 2006, China was elected to the new HUMAN RIGHTS COUNCIL, which had replaced the reproved COMMISSION ON HUMAN RIGHTS.

Scholars noted a subtle shift in China's UN policy from a highly visible attempt to assume a leadership role among Third World nations to a concentration on Chinese national interests. Core issues for China appeared to include (1) an emphasis on state sovereignty and noninterference from outside powers in the internal affairs of member states, (2) a determination to maintain, solidify, and/or realize Chinese control over Tibet, Hong Kong, and Taiwan, (3) national security, (4) participation in global economic growth, and (5) maintenance of great power status.

These core interests mixed subtly when China considered specific issues. Typically, Beijing argued that all UN activities, including PEACEKEEPING and HUMAN RIGHTS formulations, should strictly observe the principles of state sovereignty and noninterference. For China these principles were crucial in order to assure no interference in China's policies toward its own people or its control over Tibet and other regions. Thus, China was not sympathetic to notions of extending INTERNATIONAL LAW in ways that would result in outside intrusion into the internal affairs of states. Yet, within the Security Council, China demonstrated a cooperative stance in VOTING for the extension of the UN peacekeeping force in Cyprus (UNFICYP) in 1981, in agreeing in 1989 to dispatch Chinese military observers to serve in the UN TRUCE SUPERVISION ORGANIZATION (UNTSO) in the Middle East, in participating in the UN TRANSITIONAL GROUP (UNTAG) to help monitor the independence process in NAMIBIA, and in supporting the establishment of the UN TRANSITIONAL AUTHORITY IN CAMBODIA (UNTAC). And, by abstaining on Security Council RESOLUTION 827, it allowed the creation of the INTERNATIONAL TRIBUNAL FOR THE FORMER YUGOSLAVIA. China to all intents and purposes abandoned its treasured policy of the inviolability of state sovereignty. Also, China—as seen in its acceptance of various DECLARATIONS, such as that negotiated at the WORLD CONFERENCE ON HUMAN RIGHTS in Vienna (1993)—gradually accepted the principles of JUS COGENS and agreed that there is a common heritage of the world's peoples that can be conceptualized in an expanding international law.

The Gulf Crisis of 1990–91 was the most serious test for China's position on noninterference. Its solution was to abstain on UN SECURITY COUNCIL RESOLUTION 678, which authorized punitive action against IRAQ. In effect this meant an approval of Security Council action. Subsequently, China found useful the tool of abstention, which students of the Security Council have come to see as a practiced and positive behavior in diplomacy among the great powers. The United States lifted its post-Tiananmen economic sanctions on China in gratitude for Beijing's abstention/cooperation on Security Council resolutions dealing with Iraq in the early 1990s. Both nations achieved important national priorities diplomatically.

The PRC's original support of Third World issues became more rhetorical than substantive as the century moved on. Accordingly, while offering moral support for greater Third World representation on the Security Council, China became clearly comfortable with not diluting its veto power by expanding the number of permanent seats on the Council. Thus, the Chinese government openly opposed any immediate expansion of the Council when Secretary-General KOFI ANNAN made that proposal in the spring of 2006. In fact, China seemed to relish its status as the only non-Western country in the center of UN great power politics. That status, with the veto, proved useful in affording considerable leverage that could be used in China's interest.

China's shift in UN policy to a more concentrated concern with national interest could be seen as well in budgetary politics. In 1973, but two years a UN member, China thrilled the world (and embarrassed the United States) by requesting to have its assessment rate raised from 4 percent to 5.5 percent. Then, in 1978, two years after Mao's death, China abandoned its economic policy of self-reliance and requested aid from the UN DEVELOPMENT PROGRAMME (UNDP) and then asked that its SCALE OF ASSESSMENT be revised downward. Following its entry into the World Bank and the International Monetary Fund in 1980, China proceeded to obtain the largest number of multilateral aid projects, becoming the world's leading recipient of multilateral aid and largest borrower from the World Bank.

Resolution of two crisis events at the turn of the century suggested the long way Chinese relations with the outer world had progressed from the early 1970s. On May 7, 1999, U.S. aircraft mistakenly bombed the Chinese embassy in Belgrade while on a raid during the NATO war to rescue KOSOVO. And on March 31, 2001, PRC fighter planes intercepted a U.S. Navy E-P 3 surveillance aircraft in the South China Sea, forcing a landing on Hainan island. In each instance emotions on either side ran high. But quick and adroit diplomacy relieved tensions and the crises both waned. China's march to the WTO remained on track. During the summer of 2001, in a speech commemorating the 80th anniversary of the founding of the Chinese Communist Party, President Jiang Zemin made a proposal that capitalists be encouraged to join the party. In mid August, Jiang, anticipating the invitation to host the 2008 Olympics, gave an extraordinarily expansive interview to the New York Times, accompanied by a cover story entitled "Chinese President Expresses Optimism on Relations with U.S." Less than a month later, Jiang flew to North Korea, Beijing's communist ally in its war with UN forces in the early 1950s, and encouraged that secluded country to seek closer ties with South Korea and join in the Asia Pacific Economic Cooperation forum (APEC), which, coincidentally, included a number of nations, like the United States, considered in days past dangerous enemies of the Chinese.

In November 2002, the 16th Communist Party Congress chose Hu Jintao to replace Jiang Zemin as party secretary and in March 2003 Hu also became president. Although China voted with a unanimous Security Council in supporting Resolution 1441 in November 2002 insisting that IRAQ abide by mandated arms monitoring, she joined with other permanent SC members and GERMANY in resisting U.S. urgings that the Council endorse the American invasion of March 2003. With North Korea developing a NUCLEAR WEAPONS capability, China became a key partner in six-nation talks (the others being North Korea, South Korea, JAPAN, RUSSIAN FEDERATION, and the United States) in trying to defuse the crisis. Into the fall of 2006, North Korea remained unyielding to international pressure and in October actually completed a nuclear test. China joined the Security Council in sanctioning North Korea in SC Resolution 1718, passed unanimously in mid October. China then exerted uncommon pressure on her neighbor and erstwhile ally, resulting in Pyongyang's return to the stalled six-nation talks in Beijing at the end of October. In February 2007 North Korea agreed to dismantle its nuclear program and allow international inspectors to return. China also participated during the late summer 2006 with the other permanent SC members in developing compromise resolutions to constrain IRAN's nuclear program and to try to seek a cease-fire in LEBANON.

In SC Res 1696 (July 31, 2006) the Council by a 14–1 vote (Qatar in opposition) demanded a suspension of Iran's nuclear enrichment and reprocessing activities. The resolution, with China's support, was passed under Article 40 of CHAPTER VII, which provided for enforcement measures; Iran was given until the end of August to comply. On August 11, 2006, following intense negotiations in New York, China joined with a unanimous Security Council to pass Resolution 1701, calling for a cease-fire in the Israeli-Hezbollah war in Lebanon and providing for a beefed-up UNIFIL (UNITED NATIONS INTERIM FORCE IN LEBANON) of 15,000 to be bonded with a Lebanese force of equal number to move into the south and restore Lebanese sovereignty there. In each instance (Iran and Lebanon) the situation remained fluid and dangerously unstable. However, China was overtly engaged in seeking commonly agreed upon resolutions in the Security Council to address the issues.

This was not the case in the crisis concerning the DARFUR region of Sudan. A close economic partner of the Sudanese government, China counseled against excessive pressure on the regime. In 2007, it accepted a Security Council resolution creating a hybrid UN–AFRICAN UNION peacekeeping force to protect the civilian POPULATION, but opposed enhanced SANCTIONS on the central government.

There remained at the turn of the 21st century distinguished scholars and public officials who saw China as a future danger to international order. Others insisted that the current regime would collapse within a very short time. What seemed clear was that China, impacted by its UN experiences, had moved far beyond the isolation so embedded in its history.

See also AFGHANISTAN; "FOUR POLICEMEN" PROPOSAL; FOURTH WORLD CONFERENCE ON WOMEN; NATIONAL LIBERATION; NON-ALIGNED MOVEMENT; PÉREZ DE CUÉLLAR, JAVIER; STIMSON DOCTRINE; UNITED NATIONS CONFERENCE ON INTERNATIONAL ORGANIZATION; WALDHEIM, KURT; WORLD HEALTH ORGANIZATION.

Further Reading: Cohen, Warren I. *America's Response to China.* New York: Columbia University Press, 2000. Economy, Elizabeth, and Michel Oksenberg, eds. *China Joins the World: Progress and Prospects.* New York: Council on Foreign Relations Press, 1999. Fairbank, John King, and Merle Goldman. *China: A New History.* Cambridge: Belknap Press, 1998. "In Jiang's Words: 'I Hope the Western World Can Understand China Better.'" *New York Times*, August 10, 2001. Stoessinger, John G. *The United Nations and the Superpowers: China, Russia, and America.* 4th ed. New York: Random House, 1977. CIA World Factbook on China Web site: <www.cia.gov/cia/publications/factbook/geos/ch.html>. Permanent Mission of PRC to UN Web site: <www.china.un.org/eng/>

China Representation   *See* CHINA.

Churchill, Winston (1874–1965)
Winston Churchill served as British prime minister from 1940 to 1945 and again from 1951 to 1955. He had first gained the attention of the British public as a reporter covering foreign events. His capture and imprisonment by the Boers of South Africa, while he was reporting the British-Boer conflict, raised his visibility sufficiently to win election to Parliament in 1900 as a Conservative. He switched to the Liberal Party during World War I, and he served in several capacities in the government. For much of the interwar period he was out of politics, but earlier than others he began to warn of the dangers of Adolf Hitler. He returned to Parliament (again as a Conservative) as war broke out and replaced Neville Chamberlain as prime minister.

As the leader of one of the "Big Three" wartime allies—the UNITED STATES, the UNITED KINGDOM, and the Soviet Union—he played a central role in crafting the United Nations. Churchill developed what he perceived to be a "special relationship" with President FRANKLIN D. ROOSEVELT both before and during U.S. involvement in World War II. America's "nonbelligerent" relationship with war-beleaguered Britain reached a peak with the Atlantic Conference, when the two men met in August 1941 aboard the naval vessel *Prince of Wales* in Placentia Bay near the harbor of Argentia, Newfoundland. There, Churchill and Roosevelt discussed strategic issues and announced war aims and a joint vision of the postwar world. The most famous product of the meeting was the eight-point concluding statement called the ATLANTIC CHARTER. Churchill had brought to the meeting hopes for a closer U.S. alignment with the British war effort. In a noteworthy statement in the Atlantic Charter Roosevelt accepted Churchill's proposal of an "effective international organization" after the war.

When the United States entered the war in December 1941, Churchill journeyed to Washington to coordinate Anglo-American strategy in a more formal manner. At the suggestion of U.S. secretary of state CORDELL HULL, the two leaders signed a DECLARATION BY UNITED NATIONS and invited, first CHINA and the Soviet Union, and then 22 smaller nations to join them in this initiative. The DECLARATION created a wartime alliance against the Axis powers but failed to announce a postwar international organization as many had hoped. Neither Churchill nor Roosevelt were as yet committed to such a proposition, although key figures in both the British Foreign Office and the U.S. State Department were keen enthusiasts. The two leaders concentrated on winning the war in the desperate year of reverses, 1942.

When the tide of war turned more in favor of the Allies in late 1942 and early 1943, Churchill began to think of regional councils to stabilize the postwar world (and to protect the British Empire). Roosevelt, on the other hand, began to develop his concept of the "FOUR POLICEMEN"— the United States, the United Kingdom, the Soviet Union, and CHINA—to win the war and ensure the peace by way of a great power-dominated association of nations. Neither vision reflected the idealism of Woodrow Wilson's LEAGUE OF NATIONS.

The year 1943 was not only the turning point of Allied fortunes of war but also the embryonic phase of the United Nations. In March, Churchill delivered an important radio address and at the same time sent an aide-memoire to Washington, each outlining his vision of the postwar world. Dismissive of China and suspicious of the Soviet Union, the prime minister expressed the hope that the three major powers (that is, minus China) would create some sort of vague umbrella organization after victory, with the focus on a Council of Europe and a Council of Asia to ensure regional stability. Churchill's initiative compelled Roosevelt to begin focusing his attention on postwar issues, and by the time of the QUADRANT CONFERENCE in Quebec in August, his advisers had devised a counterproposal to present to the British that combined elements of FDR's Four Policemen with Churchill's regional approach. Foreign Minister ANTHONY EDEN was especially receptive to the American proposal.

JOSEPH STALIN, however, was uninterested in any schemes that went beyond the wartime coalition against GERMANY. It was Churchill who suggested that the best approach to the Soviet leader was to present postwar plans as merely a continuation of wartime collaboration and to do so while the war was still going on. Attracted first by Churchill's regional approach and then Roosevelt's Four Policemen proposal, Stalin came to accept the concept of the United Nations at both the October 1943 MOSCOW CONFERENCE OF FOREIGN MINISTERS and the TEHERAN CONFERENCE in December.

During the course of 1944 it became apparent to Churchill, to Stalin (both realists), and, importantly, to the American people that Franklin Roosevelt's United Nations, dominated by the Four Policemen, reflected the realism of Theodore Roosevelt rather than the idealism of Woodrow Wilson. Nevertheless, the YALTA CONFERENCE in January 1945 revealed a surprising divergence of opinion between the Anglo-American powers. Churchill agreed with Stalin that the Big Four should be granted an absolute VETO power over the discussion of disputes presented to the SECURITY COUNCIL. U.S. secretary of state EDWARD STETTINIUS and British foreign secretary Anthony Eden spent the first evening of

the conference attempting to change Churchill's mind. The prime minister finally accepted Eden's view that the small nations would refuse to participate in such an arrangement of raw power.

On the third day of the Yalta Conference, Churchill backed the American proposal that the Security Council must accept the principle of free discussion in order to affirm great power confidence in each other as well as in the sentiments of lesser nations. On February 12, 1945, Churchill, Roosevelt, and Stalin met for the last time and announced that all nations that had signed the United Nations Declaration would be invited to a conference at San Francisco on April 12, 1945, to create a new world organization.

But troubling Churchill was American insistence on a role for the United Nations in the self-determination of colonial peoples. Ever an advocate of the civilizing role that Britain had played in the reaches of its empire, Churchill was concerned about the threat to British national interest if the United Nations promoted decolonization. As early as 1943, Roosevelt approved a State Department draft adding an "agency for trusteeship responsibilities" to the contemplated UN CHARTER. British objections, however, postponed final acceptance of the UN's TRUSTEESHIP COUNCIL until the UNITED NATIONS CONFERENCE ON INTERNATIONAL ORGANIZATION in 1945. In the final negotiations Churchill's government accepted a UN commitment to "self-government," but not "independence" of colonial peoples. During the remainder of his time in office he rebuffed efforts by U.S. presidents Truman and DWIGHT EISENHOWER to soften his position on this issue.

Churchill was one of the finest orators of the 20th century. Among his most legendary speeches was his "Iron Curtain" address, delivered at Fulton, Missouri, on March 5, 1946, which heralded the onset of the COLD WAR. He was also an accomplished writer, whose publications, including multivolume historical works on World Wars I and II and on the history of English-speaking peoples won him wide commendation and, in 1953, the Nobel Prize for Literature.

See also CAIRO CONFERENCE, TRUSTEESHIP SYSTEM.

Further Reading: Divine, Robert. *Second Chance: The Triumph of Internationalism in America during World War II.* New York: Atheneum, 1967. Eubank, Keith. *Summit at Teheran.* New York: Morrow, 1985. Gilbert, Martin. *Churchill: A Life.* New York: Holt, 1991. Gilbert, Martin, and Winston S. Churchill. *Road to Victory. 1944–1945.* Vol. 7. New York: Houghton Mifflin, 1986.

— *E. M. Clauss*

climate change

Climate change refers to deviations in climate or weather over time, either in regions of the world or over the entire globe. Such changes may range over long eons or simply decades. The changes may be due to processes internal to the Earth, to extraterrestrial sources, or to human activities. In recent years scientists have noticed that the world's oceans and atmosphere have experienced rising temperatures. Many scientists believe that the main cause of the recent rise rests in human activities, particularly the accelerated burning of fossil fuels accompanying the escalation of land clearing, the spread of industrialization, expanded urbanization, and modern agricultural developments. These activities have resulted in pressing into the atmosphere increased amounts of carbon dioxide and other greenhouse gases.

Scientists first noticed the so-called greenhouse effect in the late 19th century. The greenhouse effect refers to the warming that is generated when greenhouse gases trap heat in the atmosphere. While this effect plays a key role in regulating the Earth's temperature, the discernible rise in recent years has caused some apprehension. This alarm has led to the use of the more unequivocal term "global warming" to refer to a disquieting upturn in temperature. For millions of years the shifting presence of carbon dioxide caused by geological and biological changes (along with occasional novel celestial events) has at certain times altered the Earth's climate, sometimes significantly. However, despite a few outspoken doubters, a good number of scientists came to believe that the consistent rise during the last century in the temperature of the Earth's oceans and near-surface atmosphere, particularly since about 1950, has been due to rising carbon dioxide levels resulting from human activities.

An official report from the British government, issued in late October 2006, seemed to confirm the direst assessments about global warming. The report, issued by senior government economist Sir Nicholas Stem, warned that without rapid and substantial public attention, global warming would reduce worldwide productivity substantially, erode food sources, and cause a large-scale refugee problem. According to the Stern Report, the level of greenhouse gases by 2006 was 54 percent higher than before the industrial revolution and could double by 2035 under existing circumstances. One consequence would be the rise of temperatures by more than 3.6 degrees Fahrenheit by the middle of the 21st century.

Another important study appeared in early February 2007, when the UN's INTERGOVERNMENTAL PANEL ON CLIMATE CHANGE (IPPC) issued its fourth report. The Panel announced that it was 90 percent certain that global warming was "very likely" caused by human activities. The panel's "best estimates" were that temperatures would rise 3.2 to 7.8 degrees by 2100 and that sea levels could rise by seven to 23 inches during the same period. For its scientifically persuasive work on climate change, the IPCC was awarded the 2007 Nobel Peace Prize.

At Rio de Janeiro in 1992, the UNITED NATIONS CONFERENCE ON ENVIRONMENT AND DEVELOPMENT (UNCED)—also known as the Earth Summit—produced the UNITED NATIONS FRAMEWORK CONVENTION ON CLIMATE CHANGE (UNFCCC), which was designed to reduce greenhouse gas emissions and restrain global warming. Opened for signature on May 9, 1992, the Framework entered into force March 21, 1994. Its proclaimed objective was to address the challenge of human generated global warming, that is: "to achieve stabilization of greenhouse gas concentrations in the atmosphere at a low enough level to prevent dangerous anthropogenic interference with the climate system." UNFCCC provided no enforcement MECHANISMS and set no mandatory greenhouse emission standards for participating nations. It did, however, contain provisions for future negotiated "PROTOCOLS" by which approving nations could establish mandatory emission limits. The KYOTO PROTOCOL of 1997 established specific targets for signatory nations to meet. Although not ratified by some industrial nations (including the UNITED STATES, which however remained a signatory) the protocol received sufficient endorsements to enter into force on February 16, 2005.

On November 6–17, 2006, a UN Climate Change Conference took place in Nairobi, Kenya, to consider further actions to curtail emissions for the period beyond 2012 (Kyoto's target year) to 2017. Some delegates at this meeting urged participants to continue the ongoing discussion regarding the prospect of industrialized countries providing substantial financial or technological assistance to poorer countries to help them reduce greenhouse emissions and deal with global warming.

See also ENVIRONMENT; MONTREAL PROTOCOL, UNITED NATIONS ENVIRONMENT PROGRAMME, WORLD METEOROLOGICAL ORGANIZATION.

Further Reading: Gore, Al. *An Inconvenient Truth: The Planetary Emergency of Global Warming and What We Can Do about It.* Emmaus, Pa.: Rodale Press, 2006. Intergovernmental Panel on Climate Change 2007 Report Web site: <http://www.ipcc.chl>. Lindzen, Richard S. "There Is No Consensus on Global Warming," *Wall Street Journal,* June 26, 2006, A14. Oreskes, Naomi. "Global Warming—Signed, Sealed and Delivered," *Los Angeles Times,* July 24, 2006, B11. Ruddiman, William F. *Earth's Climate: Past and Future.* New York: W.H. Freeman, 2001. The Stern Review on the Economics of Climate Change Website: <http://news.bbc.co.uk/2/shared/bsp/hi/pdfs/30_10_06_slides.pdf>.

Clinton, William Jefferson (Bill) (1946–   )

Bill Clinton, the 42nd U.S. president, was the first Democrat since FRANKLIN ROOSEVELT to serve two terms as chief executive and only the second president to be impeached by the House of Representatives. During his presidency (1993–2001), Clinton pursued an active foreign policy and proved to be a popular leader overseas and a promoter of expanded international trade. Clinton worked to make the APEC

(Asia-Pacific Economic Cooperation) Summit a significant annual meeting, he supported and achieved Senate approval of NAFTA (North American Free Trade Agreement) and the WORLD TRADE ORGANIZATION (WTO), normalized relations with Vietnam, used military force to resolve the civil war in the Balkans, achieved the "Good Friday" accord in Northern Ireland, and came tantalizingly close to fashioning a settlement of the Palestinian-Israeli conundrum between PLO leader YASSER ARAFAT and Israeli prime minister Ehud Barak. In his final year as president, Clinton attended the UN's MILLENNIUM SUMMIT in New York City, where he gave a spirited speech appealing for international cooperation. With his secretary of state, Madeleine Albright, he stayed to listen to IRAN's president Mohammad Khatami's speech before the UN summit, an action widely interpreted at the time as a diplomatic reaching-out to Iran. It was also at this meeting that Clinton became the only president ever to shake hands with Fidel Castro, at a luncheon co-hosted with SECRETARY-GENERAL (SG) KOFI ANNAN.

Former U.S. President Clinton addresses UN member states on tsunami recovery (UN PHOTO 82767/ESKINDER DEBEBE)

President Clinton was a chief patron of Annan's nomination in late 1996; in so doing he was able to attract UN detractors in the U.S. Senate, led by North Carolina senator Jesse Helms (a harsh critic of Secretary-General BOUTROS BOUTROS-GHALI), to support the new SG. Richard Holbrooke, Clinton's second ambassador to the UN (Ms. Albright was the first) later argued that the decision to deny Boutros-Ghali a second term and install Annan was a crucial moment for the UN's endurance as a viable institution.

William Jefferson Blythe IV was born in Hope, Arkansas, on August 19, 1946. His father died in an automobile accident before his birth and his mother later married Roger Clinton. The young boy afterward had his name changed to that of his stepfather. He attended public schools in Hot Springs, Arkansas, and then entered the Foreign Service School at Georgetown University. While a student at Georgetown he landed a job as assistant clerk for the Senate Foreign Relations Committee, in effect working for its chairman William Fulbright, the foreign policy–minded senator from Arkansas. Clinton garnered a coveted Rhodes Scholarship in 1968 following his graduation from Georgetown, allowing him to study and travel overseas. In 1973 he received a law degree from Yale University. Two years later he married Hillary Rodham, also a graduate of Yale Law School. Their daughter Chelsea was born in 1980. In 1976 Clinton ran successfully for attorney general of Arkansas, moving on to win election as governor in 1978. Two years later Arkansas voters turned him out of office but he regained the governorship in 1982, where he served until winning the 1992 presidential election, running against incumbent GEORGE H. W. BUSH and third party candidate Ross Perot. He won reelection in 1996.

Clinton had a majority Democratic Congress only for two years since Republicans won both houses in the 1994 off-year elections. In 1998, as a consequence of issues surrounding his infamous relationship with intern Monica Lewinsky (he was charged with making false statements to a grand jury), Clinton was impeached by the House of Representatives. In the trial before the Senate in early 1999 the president was acquitted of impeachable offenses.

Clinton entered office in 1993 with a large agenda. He had hoped to enact a universal health care system, but, confronted by myriad opponents while offering a complex and confusing proposal, he saw his plans stillborn. In 1993, while the Congress was still under control of Democrats, he pushed for an increase of income taxes for high income groups. This altered tax policy plus the rapid growth of the economy resulted in a balanced federal budget along with a steady increase in the nation's gross national product and a substantial increase in jobs. In 1996, in cooperation with the Republican majority in the Congress, he pressed successfully for radical reform of welfare policy, replacing the emphasis on "entitlement" with what the president called "opportunity." Welfare rolls declined significantly but some welfare advocates harshly criticized the new policy.

President Clinton deployed U.S. military forces on several occasions. In 1993 he inherited American participation in the UN authorized intervention in SOMALIA that had been initiated by the previous Bush administration. However, following the deaths of 18 U.S. marines in an operation to arrest the warlord Muhammad Aideed, who was wanted by the United Nations for the earlier killings of Pakistani peacekeepers, Clinton ordered all U.S. troops out of the country by April 1994. Also in 1994 he sent troops to HAITI to enforce the UN-US brokered Governor's Island Agreement to restore Jean-Bertrand Aristide as president. He ordered military strikes on IRAQ in response to violations of UN SANCTIONS, and, even without UN authorization, he committed troops to the FORMER YUGOSLAVIA to stop ethnic violence. In the mid 1990s he approved military bombing to end the Croat-Serb-BOSNIA conflict. He then brought the three factional leaders of the area to Dayton, Ohio, where, under his tutelage, they hammered out a peace agreement in 1995. Under the agreement, NATO forces would provide security in Bosnia, while political supervision of the country would be under the authority of a High Representative appointed by the UN SECURITY COUNCIL. In the spring of 1999 he authorized a vigorous NATO bombing campaign against the Serbs, who were ravaging KOSOVO; bombing persisted until Serb president SLOBODAN MILOŠEVIĆ gave in and accepted a UN-approved peace agreement. Of all Clinton's many foreign policy trials, he cited as his most agonizing personal regret his failure to act during the RWANDA genocide of 1994. He agreed with critics that delays in Washington and at the United Nations in publicly acknowledging the massacre and in acting quickly had led to an intolerable death toll.

Undoubtedly with the backdrop of the unpleasantness of Somalia, the indecision in Rwanda, and the apparent failure of the UN and/or Europe to find a peace solution to the Balkan crisis, the Clinton administration became not only more cautious in its use of the UN, which it saw as tentative, but more demanding of fundamental REFORM of the institution. Just days after the opening horrific events in Rwanda, the administration issued Presidential Decision Directive 25 (PDD-25), significantly curtailing the American commitment to UN NATION-BUILDING operations. The president's statement confirmed that it was no longer U.S. policy "to expand the number of UN peace operations, or U.S. involvement in [them]." The policy established 16 criteria that had to be met before the United States would vote for a new PEACEKEEPING operation or directly participate in one. PDD-25 also demanded financial reform of the United Nations. The United States proposed a cut in the U.S. assessment for peacekeeping to 25 percent of the UN BUDGET, and the reform of the UN's DEPARTMENT OF PEACEKEEPING OPERATIONS. In subsequent operations the United States favored the procedure of "subcontracting," consisting of the Security Council authorizing a state or group of states to act on behalf of the world community in the restoration of peace and sta-

bility, or, following an intervention not yet sanctioned by the United Nations, submitting a request to the Council for the equivalent of a post-dated authorization. President Clinton employed the stratagem in Haiti, Bosnia, and Kosovo. The administration thus developed a template for responding to "failed" states in the post–COLD WAR world that it then urged on the UN as the prototype for future peacekeeping and nation-building missions. In so doing, the administration embraced a model of more robust humanitarian intervention that served President Clinton (and the United Nations as well) in such disparate conflicts as Kosovo and East Timor (TIMOR-LESTE). Moreover, as the examples above in this paragraph suggest, the administration developed a willingness to act outside the framework of the United Nations when serious disintegration in failed states seemed obvious, imminent, and hazardous to HUMAN RIGHTS.

Clinton invited members of the Asia-Pacific Economic Cooperation group (APEC) to a "leaders' meeting" in 1993, elevating APEC to the status of a regular summit. The president's tireless efforts to establish the North American Free Trade Agreement and convert the GENERAL AGREEMENT ON TARIFFS AND TRADE into the World Trade Organization bore fruit. His administration's handling of the Mexico financial crisis of late 1994 offered evidence of Clinton's commitment to economic interdependence. The Mexico peso had plunged on financial markets and, together with Treasury Secretary Robert Rubin, the president, in the face of resistance from Republicans in the Congress, went to the INTERNATIONAL MONETARY FUND and cobbled together a $48 billion "stabilization FUND" to provide immediate relief. Mexico did stabilize and the loan was repaid. The president also extended Most-Favored-Nation status to CHINA and committed himself to bringing that country into the WTO, a commitment that was achieved shortly after he left office.

President Clinton's commitment to free trade policies was most severely tested in fall 1999, when large protests disrupted the third ministerial meeting of the World Trade Organization that had convened in Seattle, Washington. The thousands of angry critics who had gathered in the streets, demanded changes in WTO policies, which they saw as unfair to WOMEN, the poor, DEVELOPING COUNTRIES, and low-wage workers, and that they argued were deleterious to the ENVIRONMENT. Violence and vandalism broke out in the city. In this setting, the president fulfilled his promise to address the conference. He restated his commitment to free trade and GLOBALIZATION, but he also recommended that the WTO be more transparent and that it create a "safety net" for those most harmed by global trade and financial policies.

Perhaps the most unexpected foreign policy move of the Clinton years was the diplomatic recognition of Vietnam. The fact that Clinton had avoided military service in Southeast Asia as a youth made the exchange of diplomatic representatives—before the reelection campaign of 1996—all the more surprising.

Clinton showed a tenacious interest in reaching a peace agreement in two long simmering conflicts: in Northern Ireland, and in the MIDDLE EAST. He appointed former Senate Majority Leader George Mitchell as his envoy in the first of these, visited the country on several occasions, and was satisfied to see the "Good Friday" agreement negotiated by all parties on April 10, 1998. Early in his first term, Clinton had hosted PLO leader Yasser Arafat and Israeli prime minister Yitzhak Rabin as they shook hands on the White House lawn after agreeing to the Oslo Accords, considered at the time a serious breakthrough in the ARAB-ISRAELI DISPUTE. But Rabin would be assassinated by a Jewish zealot and the peace process would stall. Clinton returned to this problem with exceptional vigor as his presidency came to a close. During the summer of 2000 at Camp David, in the fall of that year at Sharm el-Sheik (with Secretary-General Annan playing a central role), and in December 2000 he came very close to bringing the Israeli and Palestinian sides to a compromise, comprehensive agreement. But Chairman Arafat's hesitation and Prime Minister Ehud Barak's tenuous hold on political power in Israel (Ariel Sharon would be elected prime minister in early 2001) resulted in another agonizing disappointment.

According to most surveys, Clinton left office with the highest approval rating (between 60 and 65 percent) of any former president since DWIGHT EISENHOWER. His popularity persevered, both at home and even around the world, as he settled into an active post-presidency, including founding the William J. Clinton Foundation, which, in turn, initiated the Clinton Global Initiative, a nonpartisan endeavor, bringing together a select group of thinkers, business people, and current and former heads of state to address methods to increase the benefits and reduce the burdens of global interdependence. On behalf of the United Nations, he undertook the leadership of the relief fund for Asian tsunami victims in 2004. Raising millions of dollars, Clinton traveled widely in the region and worked closely with heads of government. He also played a central role in another UN initiative, the campaign to provide low-cost anti-retroviral drugs to HIV/AIDS sufferers in AFRICA. He negotiated an agreement with the major pharmaceutical corporations for a dramatic reduction in price for several African nations.

Further Reading: Albright, Madeleine. *Madam Secretary.* New York: Hyperion, 2003. Christopher, Warren. *Chances of a Lifetime.* New York: Scribner, 2001. Clinton, William. *My Life.* New York: Knopf, 2004. Holbrooke, Richard. *To End a War.* New York: Random House, 1998. Hyland, William G. *Clinton's World: Remaking American Foreign Policy.* Westport, Conn.: Praeger, 1999. MacKinnon, Michael G. *The Evolution of U.S. Peacekeeping Policy under Clinton. A Fairweather Friend?* London: Frank Cass, 2000. Moore, John Allphin, Jr., and Jerry Pubantz. *To Create a New World?: American Presidents and the United Nations.* New York: Peter Lang, 1999.

White House. "Clinton Administration Policy on Reforming Multilateral Peace Operations (PDD 25) May 5, 1994," <http://www.fas.org/irp/offdocs/pdd25.htm>. Clinton Global Initiative Web site: <www.clintonglobalinitiative.org/home. nsf/pt_our_mission>.

cold war

The "cold war" refers to the U.S.–USSR rivalry that emerged following the close of World War II to about 1991. The two superpowers, as they became known, engaged in a global competition with political, military, economic, ideological, and diplomatic dimensions, but avoided a "hot" or shooting war. Each side attracted allies, and the contest came to be seen as a struggle between the "West" (the UNITED STATES and its allies) and the East (the Soviet Union and its allies). Other nations, declining to join either side, began calling themselves "non-aligned" in the cold war. As it shaped the global environment into a sharply divided "bipolar" arrangement, the cold war greatly influenced the work and development of the United Nations. It differed sharply from earlier great power conflicts in its intense ideological struggle between communism on the one side and democracy and capitalism on the other, and further manifested itself in a conventional arms race as well as massive stockpiling of WEAPONS OF MASS DESTRUCTION (nuclear, biological, and CHEMICAL WEAPONS) by both sides; rivalry also was waged in the United Nations.

The United States declared its plan to "contain" communism until it would be forced to collapse or change, a policy recommended by diplomat George Kennan and first launched by President Harry S. Truman. Containment became the main aim of both the Truman Doctrine (1947) and the rebuilding of former World War II foes by way of the Marshall Plan (1947), and it found expression in military alliances, such as the North Atlantic Treaty Organization (NATO) initiated in 1949. The United States blocked the ADMISSION of pro-Soviet applicants to the United Nations, such as Albania, Bulgaria, Hungary, and Romania, and insisted that the Republic of CHINA, seated in Taiwan—not the communist regime in Beijing—was the "legitimate" representative of the Chinese people at the UN. Meantime, the USSR objected to the admission of pro-Western countries such as Austria, Italy, Ireland, and JAPAN. This deadlock was broken in 1955, when several NATION-STATES from each rival bloc were admitted to the organization. However, mainland China did not achieve admittance until 16 years later.

The cold war rivalry dominated the functioning of the SECURITY COUNCIL most intensely, beginning with its first session in 1946, which was called to address the failure of the USSR to remove its troops from northern IRAN. During World War II both GREAT BRITAIN and the Soviet Union had stationed troops in Iran to guard against a Nazi seizure of oil resources located there; British troops had withdrawn from

Nikita Khrushchev addresses the United Nations, 1959 (UNITED NATIONS)

established the UNITED NATIONS TEMPORARY COMMISSION ON KOREA (UNTCOK). When, in June 1950, North Korean troops invaded the South, the Security Council, with staunch U.S. encouragement, recommended that member states furnish assistance to repel the attack. The UNITED NATIONS COMMAND IN KOREA (UNC) carried the UN FLAG although it was not a UN peacekeeping operation under the SECRETARY-GENERAL, but, in fact, a unified force under American command. The Soviet Union, which had been absent from Security Council meetings in protest of the seating of the Republic of China in the United Nations instead of the government in Beijing, declared the Council's action illegal because it was adopted without the presence of two PERMANENT MEMBERS (the USSR and China). Moscow refused to provide any assessed funding for the operation, and, by all accounts, supported the North Koreans during the conflict. UN peacekeeping became, in the eyes of the Russians at least, U.S. warfare against an ally, and a demonstration of the unwelcome control of the organization by a cold war enemy. Troops from the People's Republic of China also entered the war as allies of the North Koreans, and Americans (under a UN flag) found themselves in direct combat with these Chinese forces. Thus the KOREAN WAR came to be seen as a "hot" war within the larger context of the global cold war. Fighting ended with an armistice in 1953, but the country remained—into the 21st century, long after the end of the cold war—the last divided country dating from the end of World War II.

In 1960 U.S. spy planes (a U-2 surveillance craft piloted by Francis Gary Powers and an RB-47 lost over the Arctic) were shot down over Soviet territory, sending the cold war into a deep freeze. Each side proceeded to use the United Nations for bombastic speeches about the perfidy of its opponent. Soviet leader NIKITA KHRUSHCHEV showed up at the General Assembly annual meeting in 1960 where he banged his shoe on a desk to protest Western treachery, while in the Security Council U.S. ambassador Henry Cabot Lodge accused the Russians of planting secret microphones in the U.S. embassy in Moscow. Television viewers were entranced. Nonaligned nations decried the inability of the United Nations to meet their needs or temper the contest between Moscow and Washington.

The CONGO crisis of the early 1960s further underscored the challenge of the cold war to the United Nations. When the Congo in 1960 became independent from Belgium, a complicated civil war broke out, with one side being supported by the Soviet Union, one side by Washington, and a third side trying to secede. In the confusion Secretary-General DAG HAMMARSKJÖLD tried to insert a UN presence to bring the disorder to an end. Believing the Secretary-General to be carrying out the wishes of the United States and its cold war partners in the West, the Soviet Union demanded a reorganization of the office of Secretary-General, replacing the single secretary with a

the country, complying with an agreement with Soviet leader JOSEPH STALIN, who, nonetheless, subsequently refused to pull out Red Army forces occupying northern Iran. The Security Council struggled to find a viable role in mediating the conflict consistent with its charge in the CHARTER to "maintain international peace and security, and to that end, to take effective collective measures for the prevention and removal of threats to the peace" (Article 1). But since the cold war had "divided" the UN members into competitive "East" and "West" camps, authentic collective action became difficult, if not impossible. Because of the ideological divide and the superpower VETO, the Security Council did not take up matters such as the French or American conflict in Vietnam, or the Soviet dispatch of troops and tanks to Hungary (1956) and Czechoslovakia (1968) to suppress anticommunist movements. Nor did the Soviets or Americans participate with significant troop deployments to UN PEACEKEEPING operations (PKO).

An early indication of the cold war's impact on the United Nations occurred with reference to Korea. The GENERAL ASSEMBLY first considered the question of Korea at its session in 1947, with unsuccessful efforts to reestablish a unified country via elections. By 1948 two separate countries came into being, divided at the 38th parallel. The General Assembly called for the withdrawal of all foreign troops and troika, whereby there would be a three-person executive with equal representation from the Western bloc, the Eastern bloc, and the neutral countries in the United Nations. Deflecting the Soviet challenge, Hammarskjöld persisted in his efforts, in the event dying in a plane crash in a remote part of Northern Rhodesia (now Zambia). The Congo dissolution persisted into the middle of the decade, after which the country was kept together, but was left under the rule of a dictatorship. The center of Africa continued to be a place where cold war differences disrupted any UN attempts at resolution. UN efforts in the Congo and elsewhere raised serious questions about the efficacy of UN peacekeeping, particularly in the era of cold war tension.

Perhaps the most dangerous encounter between the superpower rivals occurred during the CUBAN MISSILE CRISIS in 1962. In October of that year, U.S. intelligence discovered that the Soviet Union was placing intermediate range nuclear weapons in CUBA. The Kennedy administration challenged the Soviets to remove the WEAPONS under clear threat of military action against Cuba, and of necessity, against the Soviet Union. Adlai Stevenson, the U.S. ambassador to the United Nations, argued with vigor the American position in the Security Council and worked in private with Secretary-General U THANT, in an effort to craft a liaison role for the Secretary-General in ending the crisis. Soviet leader Nikita Khrushchev also suggested using the Secretary-General as intermediary. The American administration, imposing a naval quarantine on Cuba, hoped to incorporate the United Nations into its efforts to avoid war while assuring the removal of the missiles. Meanwhile urgent secret negotiations transpired in New York and Washington to defuse this most serious challenge of a possible nuclear exchange in the cold war's history. By the end of October, the Russians agreed to remove the weapons, and the United States, in response, was poised to dismantle its own nuclear weapons in Turkey. The incident seemed to have a deep impact on the rival leaders in the cold war—President JOHN KENNEDY and Soviet leader Khrushchev—who, in mid-1963, agreed to sign a nuclear test ban TREATY.

Following the Cuban missile crisis, relations between the cold war adversaries never reached such dire peril again, but within the United Nations the competition continued to have an effect. Each side was interested in using the United Nations to criticize the other in its foreign adventures—the United States in Vietnam, the Soviets in AFGHANISTAN. The United Nations had virtually no impact on the American involvement in Southeast Asia, but the United States and its allies were able to gain RESOLUTIONS in the General Assembly criticizing the Russian involvement in Afghanistan. Earlier, in 1971, the United States witnessed an embarrassing reversal of its cold war China policy when, by an overwhelming vote in the General Assembly, the government of Beijing replaced the Republic of China in the organization, becoming an official permanent member of the Security Council.

At the United Nations, in December 1988, Soviet leader MIKHAIL GORBACHEV made an important gesture toward bringing the cold war to an end. After a genial meeting on Governor's Island in New York with outgoing President RONALD REAGAN, the Soviet president addressed the full General Assembly, insisting that it was now "high time to make use of the opportunities provided by this universal organization." By the time of the crisis engendered by the Iraqi invasion of Kuwait in 1990 and the GULF WAR in 1991, Gorbachev's anticipation of an effective United Nations seemed prescient as Moscow and Washington cooperated within the Security Council in ways that would have astonished earlier diplomats in both countries. Evidence of the end of the cold war was visible early in 1991, before the Soviet Union's demise that year, when the Russian delegation did not veto a British and American resolution before the Security Council authorizing the use of "any means necessary" (Res. 678) against IRAQ to restore the SOVEREIGNTY of Kuwait. Iraq had been a Soviet ally. The Russians also joined a UN-sponsored multilateral peacekeeping operation in BOSNIA in 1995, and helped end the NATO bombing of Yugoslavia in 1999 by convincing the government led by SLOBODAN MILOŠEVIĆ to withdraw his forces from KOSOVO.

Upon the collapse of the Berlin Wall (1989) and the dissolution of the Soviet Union (1991), the cold war was declared over, and shock waves rippled through the international system and within the United Nations. The disintegration of two communist states, the USSR and Yugoslavia, in 1991, contributed to the swelling MEMBERSHIP of the United Nations. With the end of the cold war, peacekeeping and peace-making became central concerns of the United Nations, as demand for UN intervention in conflicts continued to rise. The September 2000 summit of 150 heads of state at UN HEADQUARTERS in New York (the MILLENNIUM SUMMIT) affirmed the importance of peacekeeping operations, now no longer blocked by issues of superpower proxies and rivalry. The importance of arms control and weapons proliferation also moved to the forefront of the United Nations' agenda with the COMPREHENSIVE TEST BAN TREATY (CTBT) signed by the American and Russian governments in 1996, and the NON-PROLIFERATION TREATY's (NPT) extension in 1995.

See also DISARMAMENT, UNITING FOR PEACE RESOLUTION.

Further Reading: English, Robert D. *Russia and the Idea of the West: Gorbachev, Intellectuals, and the End of the Cold War.* New York: Columbia University Press, 2000. Gaddis, John Lewis. *The Cold War: A New History.* New York: Penguin, 2005. Gaddis, John Lewis. *We Now Know, Rethinking Cold War History.* Oxford: Clarendon Press, 1998. Mingst, Karen, and Margaret Karns. *The United Nations in the Post–Cold War Era, Dilemmas in World Politics.* Boulder, Colo.: Westview Press, 2000. Moore, John Allphin, Jr., and Jerry Pubantz. *To Create a New World?: American Presidents and the United*

Nations. New York: Peter Lang Publishers, 1999. Muldoon, James P., JoAnn Fagot Aviel, Richard Reitano, and Earl Sullivan. *Multilateral Diplomacy and the United Nations Today.* 2nd ed. Boulder, Colo.: Westview Press, 2005.

— *D. M. Schlagheck*

collective security

Collective security refers to agreements and actions among several states uniting them against an aggressor. Collective security guarantees each state's security; an attack on one means an attack on all; and all nations party to the agreement agree to resist any AGGRESSION. It works on the assumption that no state would use force against any member of the collective security system, as any aggression would be met by overwhelming international force and therefore would be fruitless.

The United Nations is a "universal" collective security system, having all of the world's NATION-STATES as its members. However, throughout its history the UN has found it difficult to fulfill its collective security obligations. There are several reasons. First, member states have never met their obligations under Article 43 of the CHARTER "to make available to the SECURITY COUNCIL . . . in accordance with a special agreement or agreements, armed forces . . . for the purpose of maintaining international peace and security." Thus, the Security Council has had to depend on voluntary contributions of personnel, supplies, and funds in order to undertake COLLECTIVE SELF-DEFENSE efforts. Furthermore, all actions authorized by the United Nations in this respect are subject to the VETO power created in Article 27. The practical consequence of the veto is that no action can be taken against any of the PERMANENT MEMBERS OF THE SECURITY COUNCIL. During the COLD WAR this limitation meant that the concept of collective security had to be exercised through PREVENTIVE DIPLOMACY, PEACEKEEPING, pacific settlement methods authorized by CHAPTER VI of the charter, and CHAPTER VI ½ PROVISIONS.

With the end of the cold war during the last decade of the 20th century, the United Nations faced both the opportunity and the challenge of meeting threats to collective security through the original provisions laid down in the Charter for this purpose. The collective action taken against IRAQ in 1991 marked the first use of CHAPTER VII's ENFORCEMENT MEASURES since the "police action" in the KOREAN WAR (1950–53) and went much further than any previous peacekeeping effort. The rapid success of the war to liberate Kuwait from Iraqi control encouraged Council members to make more frequent use of their enforcement powers. In 1992 the Security Council authorized intervention in SOMALIA, and in 1999 it called upon a coalition of states led by Australia to intervene in East Timor and restore order. Following the terrorist attack on U.S. sites on September 11, 2001, the Council declared TERRORISM a threat to interna-

tional peace and security, and required all members to take collective measures against terrorist organizations.

See also FOURTEEN POINTS; GULF WAR; HAMMARSKJÖLD, DAG; LEAGUE OF NATIONS; REFORM OF THE UNITED NATIONS.

Further Reading: Freudenschuss, Helmut. "Between Unilateralism and Collective Security: Authorizations of the Use of Force by the UN Security Council," *European Journal of International Law* 5, no. 4 (1994): 492–531. Lepgold, Joseph, and Thomas G. Weiss, eds. *Collective Conflict Management and Changing World Politics.* Albany: State University of New York Press, 1998. Weiss, Thomas G., ed. *Collective Security in a Changing World.* Lynne Rienner, 1994.

— *T. J. Weiler*

collective self-defense

Article 51 of the UN CHARTER grants member states "the inherent right of individual or collective self-defense" against an armed attack until the SECURITY COUNCIL can undertake ENFORCEMENT MEASURES against the aggressor. Given that the maintenance of peace and security is one of the main functions of the United Nations, it may also exercise collective self-defense by acting militarily under CHAPTER VII. Additionally, a group of countries acting together in an alliance or through a REGIONAL ORGANIZATION may also undertake collective self-defense activities. However, the charter requires that they must report their action immediately to the Security Council.

The ability to act on a regional basis to deter AGGRESSION was important to the UNITED STATES and to other members of the ORGANIZATION OF AMERICAN STATES at the time of the 1945 San Francisco Conference. Many of the founding member states worried that the delegation of enforcement powers to the Security Council would limit the formation of regional alliances. Article 51's recognition of the right to collective self-defense and the Charter's Chapter VIII provisions on regional organizations provided a compromise on the issue.

The United Nations lacks a standing military force, and therefore in order to act decisively against aggression it must rely on coalitions of member states to carry out collective enforcement. This was the case in both the KOREAN WAR and the 1991 GULF WAR against IRAQ. Military operations in these cases were authorized by Security Council RESOLUTIONS that called upon member states to defend the international community by any necessary means against an identified aggressor. States, according to the Charter, are obliged to place forces at the disposal of the United Nations for the purposes of collective self-defense. However, none have done so on a standing basis, forcing the UN to seek voluntary troop commitments on an ad hoc basis in order to carry out its mandates.

See also COLLECTIVE SECURITY, MILITARY STAFF COMMITTEE, SOUTHEAST ASIA TREATY ORGANIZATION.

Further Reading: Gottlieb, Gidon. *Nation against State.* New York: Council on Foreign Relations, 1994. Lepgold, Joseph, and Thomas G. Weiss, eds. *Collective Management and Changing World Politics.* Albany: State University of New York Press, 1988.

— *T. J. Weiler*

Commission for Social Development (CSocD)

The Commission for Social Development is one of nine functional commissions of the ECONOMIC AND SOCIAL COUNCIL (ECOSOC). As the new millennium began, the commission was the main intergovernmental body of the United Nations focused on social concerns and their relationship to development. Its duties include advising governments and ECOSOC on the enhancement of national social policies, with a special emphasis on dependent groups such as the elderly, youth, the disabled, minorities, and INDIGENOUS PEOPLES.

Created in 1946 as the Social Commission, it received its current name in 1966. During its lengthy history its mandate and MEMBERSHIP have expanded. Originally consisting of 18 members, the commission grew to 21 in 1961, 32 in 1966, and 46 in 1996 with each member state elected to a four-year term. In order to assure appropriate geographical representation 12 Commission seats are allocated to Africa, 10 to Asia, five to Eastern European nations, nine to LATIN AMERICA and the Caribbean, and 10 to Western European and Other states. The commission meets annually in New York City, where since 1996 it has had responsibility for reviewing progress on the implementation of the 1995 Copenhagen DECLARATION on Social Development and the agreements made at the follow-up Copenhagen +5 Social Summit held in Geneva in 2000. The Commission also reviews the work of the UNITED NATIONS RESEARCH INSTITUTE FOR SOCIAL DEVELOPMENT (UNRISD) and nominates new members to UNRISD for election by ECOSOC.

Each year following the 1995 WORLD SUMMIT FOR SOCIAL DEVELOPMENT CSocD established a thematic agenda for its work based on the Copenhagen Programme for Action—the eradication of poverty (1996), productive employment (1997), promotion of social integration (1998), social services (1999), contributions made by the commission (2000), social protection and vulnerability during globalization, the role of volunteerism (2001), and the integration of social and economic policy (2002). At its 39th session in February 2001, the commission agreed on a multiyear program of work through 2006, continuing its thematic approach. The ensuing themes included: national and international cooperation for social development (2003), improving public sector effectiveness (2004), review of further implementation of the outcome of the Social Summit and the 24th special session

of the GENERAL ASSEMBLY (2005), and review of the first UN Decade for the Eradication of Poverty (2006).

During its 54th session the UN GENERAL ASSEMBLY decided that the commission would serve as the preparatory committee for the Second World Conference on Ageing, held in Madrid, April 8–12, 2002. The meeting was scheduled to correspond with the 20th anniversary of the first WORLD CONFERENCE on the topic that convened in Vienna. CSocD worked closely with the UN SECRETARY-GENERAL's Technical Committee of Experts in preparation for the conference. It set as its goal for the conference a revision of the 1982 International Plan of Action on Ageing; a revision that would take into account the growing number of ageing people in the developing countries and the incapacity of governments in these countries both to sustain national development and to provide for the well-being of this sector of the population.

See also DEPARTMENT OF ECONOMIC AND SOCIAL AFFAIRS.

Further Reading: New Zealand Ministry of Foreign Affairs. *United Nations Handbook.* Wellington, N.Z.: Ministry of Foreign Affairs, published annually. CSocD Web site: <www.un.org/esa/socdev/csd/>.

Commission on Human Rights (CHR)

On March 15, 2006, the GENERAL ASSEMBLY created the HUMAN RIGHTS COUNCIL to replace the controversial UN Commission on Human Rights, which concluded its final session on March 27, 2006. The UNCHR had had a long history dating from the very origins of the United Nations.

In 1946 the ECONOMIC AND SOCIAL COUNCIL (ECOSOC) created the UN Commission on Human Rights as one of its functional commissions. Chaired by ELEANOR ROOSEVELT, the commission realized its first major achievement with its composition of, and its subsequent securing of, international acceptance for the UNIVERSAL DECLARATION OF HUMAN RIGHTS, approved by the General Assembly on December 10, 1948.

The commission, made up of 53 members elected by ECOSOC for three-year terms on the basis of equitable geographical representation, met (until its termination) for about six weeks every March and April in GENEVA. Some 3000 delegates from member and OBSERVER delegations usually attended the commission's meetings in its latter stages. During regular annual sessions the commission tended to adopt about 100 or so RESOLUTIONS, decisions, and statements on issues related to HUMAN RIGHTS. A subcommission on the promotion and protection of human rights and a number of working groups supported the work of the commission.

With the Universal Declaration and other international instruments as guidelines, the commission was charged with reviewing the state of human rights around the world, receiving reports of violations of rights, and discussing ways to assure and protect them. The commission's mandate allowed it to appoint SPECIAL RAPPORTEURS to investigate and report back to the commission on specific human rights problems in identifiable countries. Working groups from the CHR drafted COVENANTS, CONVENTIONS, and DECLARATIONS for General Assembly approval and for ratification by UN member states. Among the most important of these were the INTERNATIONAL COVENANT ON CIVIL AND POLITICAL RIGHTS (and its first and second Optional PROTOCOLS) and the INTERNATIONAL COVENANT ON ECONOMIC, SOCIAL, AND CULTURAL RIGHTS, which together with the Universal Declaration make up the International Bill of Human Rights. Other international instruments initiated by the commission included the CONVENTION AGAINST TORTURE AND OTHER CRUEL, INHUMAN OR DEGRADING TREATMENT OR PUNISHMENT (1984), and the Convention on the Rights of the Child (1989).

In a surprising development in 2001, the UNITED STATES, for the first time in the history of the CHR, was not elected to MEMBERSHIP on the commission. This seemed a setback for Washington, which found itself suffering international criticism for lack of attention to the commission's work. At the same time, the CHR came to be increasingly disparaged for maintaining a membership of nations that were violators of the very rights it was supposed to be monitoring. Led by critics from the West (particularly the United States), joined by SECRETARY-GENERAL KOFI ANNAN, a REFORM effort was initiated that resulted in replacing the CHR with a more compelling and representative new HUMAN RIGHTS COUNCIL, which became a subsidiary body of the United Nations (CHR was independent) and whose membership was 47 (down from 53 for the CHR), chosen from regions, but, unlike with the CHR, approved by a majority vote of the General Assembly, such vote taken by secret ballot.

See also AFGHANISTAN, COMMITTEE OF 24, INQUIRY, INTERNATIONAL LAW, UNITED NATIONS CONFERENCE ON INTERNATIONAL ORGANIZATION.

Further Reading: Annan, Kofi. Report of the Secretary-General: *In Larger Freedom: Towards Development, Security and Human Rights for All.* March 21, 2005, A/59/2005. United Nations. *The United Nations and Human Rights: 1945–1995.* New York: United Nations, 1995. CHR concluding Web site: <www.ohchr.org/english/bodies/chr/index.htm>.

Commission on Human Settlements (HABITAT)

The Commission on Human Settlements replaced the Committee on Housing, Building and Planning in 1977. It was created by the UN GENERAL ASSEMBLY. Its MEMBERSHIP is representative of equitable geographical distribution, with its 58 members elected from Africa (16 members), Asia (13),

Eastern Europe (six), LATIN AMERICA and the Caribbean (10), and Western European and Other States (13). Members serve four-year terms and have primary responsibility for policy guidance of the UNITED NATIONS CENTRE FOR HUMAN SETTLEMENTS (UNCHS). The commission meets every two years.

Commission on Narcotic Drugs (CND)

The ECONOMIC AND SOCIAL COUNCIL (ECOSOC) created the Commission on Narcotic Drugs in 1946 by way of RESOLUTION 9 (I). One of ECOSOC's first functional commissions, CND was authorized to advise the Council on issues related to narcotic drugs and to prepare and draft appropriate agreements. CND is the main UN policy-making body for all drug-related matters, including analyses of drug abuse globally and efforts to enhance international drug control. The commission supervises application of international treaties and CONVENTIONS related to narcotic drugs and works to effect cooperation in drug-related law enforcement efforts at regional levels. Pursuing the latter goal, the CND has created subsidiary bodies, including the Subcommission on Illicit Drug Traffic Enforcement Agencies (HONLEA). It also directs the activities of the UN INTERNATIONAL DRUG CONTROL PROGRAMME (UNDCP), founded in 1991.

Membership of CND initially was 15 but, by 2001, had expanded to 53 by ECOSOC resolution. Members are elected every two years by ECOSOC for staggered four-year terms from among UN member states, members of SPECIALIZED AGENCIES, and parties to the Single Convention on Narcotic Drugs (1961). In electing the members, ECOSOC takes into account a concern for adequate representation from countries directly affected by illicit drug production, trafficking, and addiction. CND's headquarters is in Vienna. It meets annually.

See also OFFICE FOR DRUG CONTROL AND CRIME PREVENTION.

Further Reading: UNDCP Web site: <www.unodc.org/unodc/en/cnd.html>.

Commission on Population and Development *See* INTERNATIONAL CONFERENCE ON POPULATION AND DEVELOPMENT.

Commission on Sustainable Development (CSD)

The United Nations GENERAL ASSEMBLY (GA) authorized the creation of the commission in 1992 (Res. 191). The Assembly made the commission one of the nine permanent commissions reporting to the ECONOMIC AND SOCIAL COUNCIL (ECOSOC) and, by way of ECOSOC, to the GA

SECOND COMMITTEE. In so doing, the Assembly fulfilled the most important structural recommendation to come out of the UNITED NATIONS CONFERENCE ON ENVIRONMENT AND DEVELOPMENT (UNCED) that convened in Rio de Janeiro in 1992. The conference, also known as the Earth Summit, recommended the creation of the commission to monitor global progress on one of the summit's approved programs, AGENDA 21. The purpose of the agenda was to promote DEVELOPMENT in the LESS DEVELOPED COUNTRIES (LDCs) in ways that sustained environmental resources for their needed use by future generations. The UNCED sought ways to harmonize economic development with global environmental concerns. The commission was also directed to encourage NON-GOVERNMENTAL ORGANIZATIONS (NGOs), business, industry, and governments to implement Agenda 21. Given the nature of its work, the commission collaborates with the UNITED NATIONS CONFERENCE ON TRADE AND DEVELOPMENT (UNCTAD), the WORLD TRADE ORGANIZATION (WTO), the UNITED NATIONS ENVIRONMENT PROGRAMME (UNEP), and other UN bodies involved with environmental or development issues.

The Commission on Sustainable Development comprises 53 member governments elected to three-year terms by ECOSOC. One-third of the body is elected annually, and members may be reelected. The size of the commission constituted a matter of debate between the developed states of the North and the developing countries of the south. The former pushed for a small efficient commission in which the developed states would not be outvoted, while the LDCs wanted a large body with geographical representation. With a MEMBERSHIP of 53 the CSD has one fewer participant than ECOSOC and allows for extensive participation from the South. Membership is regionally allocated with 13 seats assigned to elected African states, 11 seats for Asian governments, 6 to Eastern Europe, 10 to LATIN AMERICA and the Caribbean, and 13 for the Western European and Others caucus. The 47th session of the General Assembly also directed that non-governmental organizations, other UN bodies, and intergovernmental economic organizations, both on global and regional levels, participate in the work of the commission. NGOs are authorized to submit written reports, address the commission with the permission of the chairman, and conduct "consultations" with members at the invitation of the chair or the United Nations SECRETARY-GENERAL. More than 1,000 NGOs are accredited to CSD.

The commission meets annually in New York City in two-year cycles, each cycle addressing a thematic issue. Each year the Commission reviews national reports from member states on meeting the targets of Agenda 21. These reports are submitted voluntarily and sporadically. Some participants at the Earth Summit had hoped to make such reporting mandatory, but opposition from developing states, worried about possible international pressure to alter their development programs, vetoed the requirement.

In all of its work, CSD has faced two overriding dilemmas: the apparent conflict between environmental protection and economic development, and the intrusiveness of international efforts to preserve the ENVIRONMENT on the one hand and the inviolability of SOVEREIGNTY on the other. Environmental issues are inherently global concerns. National borders do not restrict the deleterious effects of bad environmental practices from migrating. Furthermore, any efforts to limit these effects require the international community to focus on internal practices of NATION-STATES. Consequently, sovereignty, the bedrock principle of the international system, must give way to some extent if the environment is to be protected. Environmental protection can also run contrary to development strategies put in place by developing states. These strategies may cause environmental problems, or the effort to accommodate them to environmentally friendly techniques may be too costly. Thus, developing nations often see the demand that states alter their development programs to meet international environmental standards as unwarranted and counterproductive intrusion in their internal affairs.

Faced with these countervailing pressures, the Commission on Sustainable Development has had limited success in implementing Agenda 21 objectives. It has established two working groups that meet frequently to review each of the areas given priority by that document, however. In addition, there have been intersessional meetings sponsored by member states on a variety of topics before the commission. These meetings, held around the world, have considered issues related to health, the transfer of technology, water and environmental sanitation, chemical safety, finance, and sustainable consumption, among other items suggested by Agenda 21.

Between 1994 and 1996 the CSD reviewed each area identified by Agenda 21, including DESERTIFICATION, health, toxic chemicals and hazardous waste, biodiversity, human settlements, the atmosphere, and oceans and seas. It has held sessions on the overlapping issues of trade and the environment, poverty, demographic pressures on the environment, financial resources and MECHANISMS, and the transfer of environmentally sound technology to the underdeveloped world. In 1997 the Earth+5 SPECIAL SESSION OF THE GENERAL ASSEMBLY directed CSD to monitor carefully a few major identified provisions of Agenda 21. The 15th session of the CSD in spring 2007 continued to focus on the thematic issues introduced in 2006, including energy for SUSTAINABLE DEVELOPMENT, industrial development, air pollution, and CLIMATE CHANGE. The commission also has prepared reports and agenda for other UN activities in environment and development. In 1999 it prepared the plan for the General Assembly's review of SUSTAINABLE DEVELOPMENT of small island DEVELOPING COUNTRIES.

Earth+5 directed the commission to begin work on the identification of "Indicators of Sustainable Development" that could be used to measure progress toward the goals of the RIO DECLARATION. Three types of indicators were agreed to. The commission identified "Driving Force" indicators that it defined as "human activities, processes and patterns that impact on sustainable development." They included unemployment rates, adult literacy rates, POPULATION growth rates, annual energy consumption, per capita gross domestic product (GDP), emission of greenhouse gases, and the generation rate of hazardous wastes. The commission additionally identified "State" indicators as measures of the status of sustainable development within individual nations. They included population density, poverty indices, life expectancy, average rainfall, changes in land conditions, energy reserves, debt as a ratio of gross national product, the nutritional status of children, arable land per capita, and the percentage of the population in urban areas. Finally, CSD established "Response" indicators that measured the range of policy options a state had to use in meeting its current sustainable development challenges. Among them were GDP spent on education, immunization against childhood diseases, national health care expenditures as a ratio of GDP, infrastructure expenditures per capita, waste water treatment coverage, and environmental protection expenditures as a percent of GDP.

Further Reading: Elliott, Lorraine. *The Global Politics of the Environment.* New York: New York University Press, 1998. Mensah, Chris. "The United Nations Commission on Sustainable Development." In *Greening International Institutions.* Edited by Jacob Werkman. London: Earthscan Publications, 1996. Sands, Philippe, ed. *Greening International Law.* New York: The New Press, 1994. Commission on Sustainable Development Web site: <www.un.org/esa/sustdev/csd/aboutCsd.htm>.

Commission on the Status of Women (CSW)

By RESOLUTION 11 (II) of June 21, 1946, the ECONOMIC AND SOCIAL COUNCIL (ECOSOC) created the Commission on the Status of Women, making it one of the first functional commissions of ECOSOC. Committed to the principle that WOMEN and men should have equal rights, CSW forwards recommendations and reports to the Council promoting women's civil and social rights, emphasizing gender equity in politics, education, and economics. Additionally, the commission alerts ECOSOC to pressing challenges for women that may require prompt attention, and drafts treaties, CONVENTIONS, and other instruments designed to elevate the status of women.

ECOSOC has periodically expanded CSW's mandate. Beyond defining women's rights, the commission also studies the underlying causes of gender discrimination and makes recommendations for remedying them. In 1993 the GENERAL ASSEMBLY adopted a DECLARATION ON THE ELIMINATION OF VIOLENCE AGAINST WOMEN that had been recommended by the commission.

The CSW has prepared several WORLD CONFERENCES ON WOMEN. After the fourth of these, the 1995 WORLD CONFERENCE on Women in Beijing, the General Assembly authorized the commission to review progress in the areas of concern articulated in the Beijing Platform for Action. The commission has worked to eliminate gender discrimination and violence against women, to advance the status of women, including the achievement of a 50 percent gender balance at the highest professional levels in the UN SECRETARIAT, as well as to continue the promotion of political, social, and economic rights for women.

Beginning with 15 members, the commission expanded its MEMBERSHIP to 45 by 2001. As of 2006, membership was accorded on a geographic basis: 13 from Africa, 11 from Asia, 4 from Eastern Europe, 9 from LATIN AMERICA and the Caribbean, and 8 from Western Europe and Other States. ECOSOC elects CSW's members for four-year terms from a pool appointed by UN member governments. The commission usually meets once a year for about eight days. Its officers—a chairperson and four vice chairs—are chosen by its members, and its headquarters is in Vienna.

See also APPENDIX G, BEIJING +10, CONVENTION ON THE ELIMINATION OF DISCRIMINATION AGAINST WOMEN, HUMAN RIGHTS.

Further Reading: Jain, Devaki. *Women, Development, and the UN: A Sixty-Year Quest for Equality and Justice.* Bloomington: Indiana University Press, 2005. United Nations. *The United Nations and the Advancement of Women, 1945–1996.* New York: United Nations Department of Public Information, 1996. CSW Web site: <www.un.org/womenwatch/daw/csw>.

Committee of International Development Institutions on the Environment (CIDIE)

The Committee coordinated the work of international organizations involved in environmental affairs with the activities of the WORLD BANK and other development agencies. The United Nations does not have direct control over the affiliated bodies of the World Bank Group, and, therefore, must negotiate cooperative policies with those entities. On February 1, 1980, the Bank and several UN bodies signed the "Declaration of Environment Policies and Procedures Relating to Economic Development" in recognition of the critical impact that development projects have on the ENVIRONMENT. The signatories established CIDIE at that time to carry out the objectives of the DECLARATION.

In particular, the committee sought to resolve the competing interests between development in LESS DEVELOPED COUNTRIES and the global environmental initiatives launched at the 1972 UNITED NATIONS CONFERENCE ON THE HUMAN ENVIRONMENT in Stockholm. It also attempted to improve the work of the different intergovernmental organizations focused on environmental matters. Despite its purposes, the committee had only limited success because economic incentives in development programs generally override environmental concerns. The MEMBERSHIP of the committee included the UNITED NATIONS ENVIRONMENT PROGRAMME (UNEP), the World Bank, the African Development Bank, the Arab Bank for Economic Development in Africa, the Asian Development Bank, the Caribbean Development Bank, the Inter-American Development Bank, the Commission of the European Community, the ORGANIZATION OF AMERICAN STATES, the European Investment Bank, and the UNITED NATIONS DEVELOPMENT PROGRAMME (UNDP).

See also REGIONAL DEVELOPMENT BANKS.

Further Reading: Caldwell, Lynton Keith. *International Environmental Policy, Emergence and Dimensions.* Durham, N.C.: Duke University Policy Studies, 1984. Elliott, Lorraine. *The Global Politics of the Environment.* New York: New York University Press, 1998. Sands, Philippe, ed. *Greening International Law.* New York: The New Press, 1994.

Committee of 24

The UN GENERAL ASSEMBLY in 1960 adopted the DECLARATION ON THE GRANTING OF INDEPENDENCE TO COLONIAL COUNTRIES AND PEOPLES, urging a faster pace in the process of decolonization. While one of the principal organs of the United Nations—the TRUSTEESHIP COUNCIL—was created to preside over the self-determination of NON-SELF-GOVERNING TERRITORIES, relatively few territories were under the Council's JURISDICTION, and half of the Council's members were administering powers. The Asian and African states that had only recently become members of the United Nations believed that neither the Council nor the United Nations as a whole was doing enough to encourage independence. In the effort to realize the goals of the DECLARATION, the General Assembly established the Special Committee on the Implementation of the Declaration on Decolonization. The original MEMBERSHIP in 1961 included 17 members, largely from the developing world. The committee was enlarged to 24 in 1962 (Res. 1810), and thus became known as the Committee of 24. The total membership has varied from 23 to 25 during the committee's life, but it has retained the same name.

The committee became the primary voice in the UN STRUCTURE for the end to colonialism. The stridency of its debates, public pronouncements, and agenda drove all colonial and administering powers from its membership by 1971. The committee established two subcommittees to focus attention on particular colonial holdings and to receive petitions from inhabitants in non-self-governing territories. Those petitions were used to shed light on what the committee saw as violations of indigenous populations' rights. It was particularly harsh in its criticism of Portuguese colonial

policy in Africa, and South African control of NAMIBIA. In the latter case the committee regularly called for economic SANCTIONS against South Africa. It was also at the forefront of UN efforts to sanction the breakaway state of Rhodesia under Ian Smith's APARTHEID regime. In addition to receiving and debating petitions, the committee created visiting missions to colonial territories and held local forums for the inhabitants to express their sentiments. On a very constructive note, the Committee of 24 sponsored talks between the United Kingdom and Argentina over the Falkland (Malvinas) Islands from 1965 to 1982.

As the number of colonial possessions declined, the impact on UN policies by the Committee of 24 shifted from mobilizing decolonization efforts to spurring HUMAN RIGHTS protections both in the remaining non-self-governing territories and in the developing world. In 1947 the UN COMMISSION ON HUMAN RIGHTS (CHR) concluded that "it had no power to take any action in regard to any complaints concerning human rights" by individuals against their own governments. This was known as the doctrine of impotency and was quickly endorsed by the ECONOMIC AND SOCIAL COUNCIL (ECOSOC). In 1965 the Committee of 24 urged ECOSOC to look at the violations of human rights in southern Africa that had been submitted to the committee by petitioners. ECOSOC, influenced by the new African and Asian voices in the United Nations, directed the Human Rights Commission, as a matter of importance and urgency, to take up these allegations, which it did. Since then, both ECOSOC and CHR asserted the authority of UN bodies to protect individual rights. The Committee of 24 was also instrumental in the 1970s in getting the Human Rights Commission to take special notice of conditions in Western Sahara. In that case, the committee, the CHR, and the INTERNATIONAL COURT OF JUSTICE all concluded that people had an inherent human right to self-determination. The human rights focus of the committee continued in 2006 under the leadership of its chairman, Julian R. Hunte from Saint Lucia. At the time 16 non-self-governing territories remained (Western Sahara, American Samoa, Guam, New Caledonia, Pitcairn, Tokelau, Anguilla, Bermuda, British Virgin Islands, Cayman Islands, Falkland Islands (Malvinas), Gibraltar, Montserrat, Saint Helena, Turks and Caicos Islands, and the UNITED STATES Virgin Islands) under the supervision of FRANCE, New Zealand, the United Kingdom, and the United States as administering powers.

Further Reading: Baehr, Peter R., and Leon Gordenker. *The United Nations at the End of the 1990s.* 3rd ed. New York: St. Martin's, 1999. *United Nations Handbook.* Wellington, N.Z.: Ministry of External Affairs, published annually.

Committee of 24 at the World Bank and International Monetary Fund   *See* GROUP OF 77.

Committee on Contributions

One of two STANDING COMMITTEES OF THE GENERAL ASSEMBLY (GA), the Committee on Contributions recommends to the Assembly the SCALE OF ASSESSMENTS that determines the amount each member state must contribute to the regular BUDGET of the United Nations. The 18-member committee is made up of financial experts who work closely with the GA's FIFTH COMMITTEE and the ADVISORY COMMITTEE ON ADMINISTRATIVE AND BUDGETARY QUESTIONS to determine the budgetary needs of the organization. It determines each country's contribution on the "capacity to pay" principle—as determined by measuring a state's total national income in comparison to other states. The Committee on Contributions also takes into consideration low per capita income, giving affected states relief up to 85 percent of their assessment. A state's level of debt is factored into the determination. The committee also makes recommendations on the application of Article 19 of the CHARTER, which allows for the removal of a state's right to vote in the GENERAL ASSEMBLY if it is in arrears equaling a full two years of assessed contributions. As of May, 2006, nine nations were in violation of Article 19: Central African Republic, Comoros, Georgia, Guinea-Bissau, Liberia, Niger, São Tomé and Príncipe, SOMALIA, and Tajikistan. The General Assembly, however, decided that these states could continue to cast their votes until the end of the Assembly's 60th session.

See also COMMITTEE SYSTEM OF THE GENERAL ASSEMBLY.

Committee on Non-Governmental Organizations

According to Article 71 of the UN CHARTER, the ECONOMIC AND SOCIAL COUNCIL (ECOSOC) may grant CONSULTATIVE STATUS to NON-GOVERNMENTAL ORGANIZATIONS (NGOs) whose concerns fall within the COMPETENCE of ECOSOC and its subsidiary bodies. Although the DEPARTMENT OF ECONOMIC AND SOCIAL AFFAIRS (DESA) at UN HEADQUARTERS processes requests for consultative status, applicant organizations must complete a questionnaire that is then presented to the Committee on Non-governmental Organizations. ECOSOC RESOLUTION 1996/31 established the principles required for gaining consultative status and provided guidance for the Committee on NGOs.

The members of the committee are elected by ECOSOC on the basis of equitable geographic representation. In 2006 it had 19 members. The committee selects its own officers. It carries a mandate to monitor the growing relationship between NGOs and the United Nations. It consults with NGOs and issues reports to ECOSOC regarding those consultations. The committee is also expected to confer with the SECRETARY-GENERAL on matters arising under Article 71 of the Charter, and it may receive referrals from ECOSOC for consideration and recommendations on matters regarding NGOs. The committee considers applications for consultative status at its annual meeting before the substantive sessions of ECOSOC. Every fourth year organizations with consultative status must submit to the committee a report on their activities with specific explanation of their support of UN activities. On the basis of these reports, the committee may recommend reclassification in the status of an NGO.

See also CONFERENCE OF NON-GOVERNMENTAL ORGANIZATIONS IN CONSULTATIVE RELATIONSHIP WITH THE UNITED NATIONS.

Further Reading: Committee on Non-Governmental Organizations Web site: <www.un.org/esa/coordination/ngo/committee.htm>. Willetts, Peter, ed. *The Conscience of the World: The Influence of Non-governmental Organizations in the UN System*. Washington, D.C.: Brookings Institution, 1996.

Committee on the Elimination of Racial Discrimination (CERD)

The 1965 International Convention on the Elimination of all Forms of Racial Discrimination created the Committee on the Elimination of Racial Discrimination (Articles 8 and 9). Made up of 18 experts "of high moral standing and acknowledged impartiality," CERD receives reports from its member states on the status of racial discrimination and efforts to abolish it within their countries. The committee meets twice a year, usually in Geneva. Under the convention's OPTIONAL CLAUSE (Article 14), private citizens of CONVENTION signatories may submit complaints about government policies and incidents of racial discrimination. States may also submit complaints about other convention members. The committee then may conduct investigations and discuss the complaints, bringing pressure on states to correct any violations of the TREATY. The Optional Clause entered into effect in 1982. CERD reports on its work to the UN GENERAL ASSEMBLY annually.

Further Reading: Committee on the Elimination of Racial Discrimination Web site: <www.ohchr.org/english/bodies/cerd/>.

Committee on the Elimination of Discrimination Against Women (CEDAW) *See* CONVENTION ON THE ELIMINATION OF DISCRIMINATION AGAINST WOMEN.

Committee on the Peaceful Uses of Outer Space (COPUOS)

In 1958, following the Soviet Union's successful launching of *Sputnik*, the first artificial space satellite, the GENERAL ASSEMBLY established an ad hoc Committee on the Peaceful Uses of Outer Space. The 18-member committee was charged with considering how the United Nations and its SPECIALIZED

AGENCIES, plus other international bodies, might provide help and guidance in promoting international cooperation, legal advice, and organizational arrangements to assure the peaceful uses of outer space in what was seen to be a future of space exploration. In Resolution 1472 (XIV) of 1959, the General Assembly made the committee a permanent body, with headquarters in Vienna and a membership of 24.

By instruction from the General Assembly (Res. 1721 of 1961), COPUOS was expected to maintain close contact with governments and NON-GOVERNMENTAL ORGANIZATIONS active in outer space, encourage full exchange of information and research about outer space activities, support the study of methods to assure cooperation in outer space, and play a role in the development of international space law. By the same RESOLUTION, the SECRETARY-GENERAL was authorized to maintain a public registry of space launchings.

Membership in COPUOS grew to 67 by 2006. Also, several international organizations and non-governmental organizations gained OBSERVER STATUS. The committee has two standing subcommittees of the whole—the Scientific and Technical Subcommittee and the Legal Subcommittee. The former of these subcommittees discusses topics such as remote sensing by satellite, nuclear power in outer space, the challenge of space debris, environmental concerns relating to space exploration, and space and planetary exploration. The Legal Subcommittee is interested in the legal definition of space and its boundaries, and reviews the status and effectiveness of international agreements, treaties, and CONVENTIONS governing outer space. As of 2006, due to the work of the committee and its Legal Subcommittee, there were in force five international instruments that were part of INTERNATIONAL LAW: the Treaty on Principles Governing the Activities of States in the Exploration and Use of Outer Space, including the Moon and Other Celestial Bodies (the "Outer Space Treaty" of 1966), the Agreement on the Rescue of Astronauts, the Return of Astronauts and the Return of Objects Launched into Outer Space (the "Rescue Agreement" of 1967), the Convention on International Liability for Damage Caused by Space Objects (the "Liability Convention" of 1971), the Convention on Registration of Objects Launched into Outer Space (the "Registration Convention" of 1974), and the Agreement Governing Activities of States on the Moon and Other Celestial Bodies (the "MOON AGREEMENT" of 1979).

Also, over the years COPUOS has embraced an array of principles to guide the international community in its conduct toward outer space. These principles complement the international agreements listed above. They address such matters as respect for state SOVEREIGNTY and equitable dissemination of information during direct television broadcasting and remote sensing activities from outer space, guidelines for the safe use of nuclear power in space and for notification of malfunctions during reentry of radioactive material, and cooperation in space exploration.

COPUOS and its subcommittees meet annually, often in the late spring. Both work on the basis of consensus, both receive reports from member states and queries from the General Assembly, and the full body makes recommendations to the General Assembly. Annual reports from the committee and its subcommittees detail their work. In Vienna, the UN Office for Outer Space Affairs serves as the SECRETARIAT for the committee.

Further Reading: COPUOS Web site: <www.unoosa.org/oosa/COPUOS/copuos.html>.

Committee on Torture (CAT) *See* CONVENTION AGAINST TORTURE AND OTHER CRUEL, INHUMAN OR DEGRADING TREATMENT OR PUNISHMENT.

Committee System of the General Assembly

The GENERAL ASSEMBLY (GA), one of the PRINCIPAL ORGANS OF THE United Nations, has a committee system that allows most agenda items to be considered initially by one of its six main committees. All UN members are represented on each of the committees, and all member states have an equal vote on each committee. Committee decisions are made by a majority of those present and VOTING. At the beginning of the annual session, the GA president, with the formal approval of the Assembly, assigns agenda items to the committees. Normally, the General Assembly considers only RESOLUTIONS passed by its committees, although a few items are placed directly on its agenda without committee referral.

In the committees diplomats negotiate intensely to arrive at a consensus on agenda items, usually recommending one resolution on each topic. Members of each delegation consult each other regularly in order to assure that the content of each committee resolution is acceptable to their government. The primary GA debate on international issues occurs in committee. Since all states participate in committee work, consensus resolutions from committees tend to pass with ease through the full General Assembly.

The main committees of the General Assembly, each with its own topical specialization, are: FIRST COMMITTEE (DISARMAMENT and International Security), SECOND COMMITTEE (Economic and Financial), THIRD COMMITTEE (Social, Humanitarian, and Cultural), FOURTH COMMITTEE (Special Political and Decolonization), FIFTH COMMITTEE (Administrative and Budgetary), and SIXTH COMMITTEE (Legal). Designated the Political and Security Committee under its original mandate, the First Committee deals almost exclusively with disarmament affairs. GA member states decided that this topic was so central to the international system that it required its own committee. A separate Special Political Committee formerly considered all other political questions, but it was merged in the 1990s with the TRUSTEESHIP committee, creating a new mandate for the Fourth Committee. Developing countries consider the Second Committee one of the most pivotal bodies in the United Nations, since it addresses questions of DEVELOPMENT and international trade and finance. Topics before the Third Committee each year include, among other issues, HUMAN RIGHTS, the impediments to WOMEN, INDIGENOUS PEOPLES, children, and minorities, drug trafficking and other social problems, and refugees and trans-boundary migration. The Fifth Committee reviews the proposed UN BUDGETs and SCALE OF ASSESSMENTS sent to it by the ADVISORY COMMITTEE ON ADMINISTRATIVE AND BUDGETARY QUESTIONS (ACABQ), and forwards its recommendations to the General Assembly. The Sixth Committee deals with the intricacies of INTERNATIONAL LAW, negotiating the texts of treaties and the meaning of legal concepts, as well as reviewing the work of UN judicial and legal bodies.

The General Assembly is empowered to establish other committees and working groups to deal with specific issues or to handle procedural matters. Each session, the GA creates several ad hoc and subsidiary committees in order to assure that important and controversial questions are negotiated before being brought to the full Assembly for a final vote. In 2006, there were in excess of 40 such bodies. The Assembly has two permanent PROCEDURAL COMMITTEES: the GENERAL COMMITTEE, made up of the president of the General Assembly and its 21 vice presidents, and the CREDENTIALS COMMITTEE, which is responsible for accrediting delegations to the UN.

See also IMPORTANT QUESTION, STRUCTURE OF THE UNITED NATIONS.

Further Reading: Mingst, Karen A., and Margaret P. Karns. *The United Nations in the Post–Cold War Era.* Boulder, Colo.: Westview, 1995. Moore, John Allphin, Jr., and Jerry Pubantz. *The New United Nations: International Organization in the Twenty-first Century.* Upper Saddle River, N.J.: Prentice Hall, 2006. Muldoon, James P., Jr., JoAnn Fagot Aviel, Richard Reitano, and Earl Sullivan, eds. *Multilateral Diplomacy and the United Nations Today.* Boulder, Colo.: Westview, 1999. Peterson, M. J. *The General Assembly in World Politics.* Boston: Allen and Unwin, 1986. GA Web site: <www.un.org/ga/>.

— *K. J. Grieb*

competence of United Nations organs

Lawful competence of a political organization is the grant of responsibility for designated functions, usually by some authoritative source such as a constitution or decree. The organization itself must be seen as "legitimate" by those persons and entities subject to its decisions. In the case of an international organization, competence arises from the organization having an "international legal personality" and being authorized by its founding document to do certain

things, such as make TREATIES, adjudicate disputes, and allocate funds for approved activities. Closely intertwined with the concept of JURISDICTION, competence is not synonymous with it. The latter describes the legal authority upon which the organization, or a component of it, asserts a legitimate right to consider and act within a particular area of the organization's mission. It is a state of being, while jurisdiction describes a range of meaningful control, which may be large or small, over people, territory, and human behavior as the body exercises its competence.

In the 1949 *Reparations for Injuries Suffered in the Service of the United Nations* case, the INTERNATIONAL COURT OF JUSTICE (ICJ) decided that the states that created the United Nations, "by entrusting certain functions to it, with the attendant duties and responsibilities, . . . clothed it with the competence required to enable those functions to be effectively discharged." The Court concluded that the United Nations had an "objective international personality" that gave it a competence in international affairs going beyond a legitimacy solely among the states that founded it. In other words, the ICJ held that the United Nations was an independent actor in international relations with expressed and implied powers.

Within the United Nations different organs are competent to undertake certain specified actions. The CHARTER grants the broadest competence to the GENERAL ASSEMBLY. It may "discuss any questions or any matters within the scope of the . . . Charter or relating to the powers and functions of any organs" of the United Nations. All other bodies report to it. It may also pass RESOLUTIONS and convene international meetings. The SECURITY COUNCIL is competent under the Charter to deal with all threats to international peace, even to the exclusion of all other UN organs. Administrative competence is lodged in the SECRETARIAT. The International Court of Justice is the "judicial" organ of the United Nations, and draws its competence to define INTERNATIONAL LAW through rulings on cases brought before it, not only from the Charter but also from a separate statute to which all UN members are parties.

Comprehensive Nuclear Test Ban Treaty (CTBT)

The Comprehensive Nuclear Test Ban Treaty was negotiated in Geneva at the CONFERENCE ON DISARMAMENT (CD) and adopted by the UN GENERAL ASSEMBLY on September 10, 1996. The idea for a comprehensive nuclear test ban was first suggested by Prime Minister Jahwaharlal Nehru to the Indian parliament as a "standstill agreement" on nuclear explosions. The CTBT's ultimate journey to the General Assembly resulted because INDIA, along with IRAN, blocked a consensus regarding test bans in the Conference on Disarmament. The purpose of the TREATY was to stop nuclear testing in all environments and, as such, represented the definitive treaty in a series of accords dating back to the Partial Test Ban Treaty of 1963, and including the Threshold Test Ban Treaty concluded bilaterally between the UNITED STATES and the Soviet Union in 1974. At the 1995 NUCLEAR NON-PRO-LIFERATION TREATY Review and Extension Conference, the five NUCLEAR WEAPONS States—CHINA, FRANCE, Russia, the UNITED KINGDOM, and the United States (NWS)—agreed to conclude a CTBT by 1996. This decision both facilitated the indefinite extension of the Non-Proliferation Treaty (NPT) and coordinated the Nuclear Weapons States' stances on a test ban treaty.

The CTBT provided for a comprehensive verification system. It included as well a network of both land- and sea-based sensor stations, using four different technologies, called the International Monitoring System (IMS). The purpose of the IMS was to detect "anomalous events" world-wide. The treaty established a Comprehensive Test Ban Treaty Organization (CTBTO) with 51 seats on an executive council, apportioned geographically, whose functions included considering data from the IMS and implementing the treaty's provisions in conjunction with national authorities and a technical staff. The detection of any anomalous event within the territory of a state party to the treaty would require an effort to determine the exact nature of the occurrence, perhaps to distinguish it from a mine explosion, earthquake, or other natural or man-made event. An unexplained incident could trigger a request for an on-site inspection, which could be initiated within 72 hours with an affirmative vote of at least 30 of the executive council members. Other provisions of the treaty included standard administrative and withdrawal procedures. But the topic of greatest concern and controversy was the entry-into-force provision. According to Article XIV of the CTBT, all of the 44 states that participated in the work of the 1996 session of the Conference on Disarmament and that appeared in the 1996 INTERNATIONAL ATOMIC ENERGY AGENCY's April 1996 edition of *Nuclear Powers of the World* were required to sign and ratify the treaty before it could enter into force. India and Pakistan were among that group and, as of the turn of the century, remained vocal critics of the treaty. Moreover, the U.S. Senate rejected the treaty for consent to ratification on October 13, 1999. As of mid 2006 the treaty had been signed by 176 states and ratified by 132. However, India, Pakistan, and the Democratic Republic of Korea (North Korea) had not signed and CHINA, Colombia, EGYPT, India, Iran, Israel, and the United States had not ratified. Moreover, only 34 of the 44 necessary states (the so-called Annex 2 countries) had ratified, so the actual entry into force of the CTBT was subject to an uncertain future. Although work to establish the IMS stations and the CTBTO continued to take place, no inspections were supposed to occur until the treaty entered into force.

See also COLD WAR, DISARMAMENT, WEAPONS OF MASS DESTRUCTION.

Further Reading: Ghose, Arundhati. "Negotiating the CTBT: India's Security Concerns and Nuclear Disarmament." *Journal of International Affairs* (Summer 1997). Hawkins, Wohlety K. "Visual Inspection for CTBT Verification." *Los Alamos Lab Report* 15244-MS, Spring 1997. York, Herbert F. *The CTBT and Beyond.* New York: United Nations Department of Public Information, 1994.

— *S. L. Williams*

Comprehensive Test Ban Treaty Organization (CTBTO) *See* COMPREHENSIVE NUCLEAR TEST BAN TREATY.

compulsory jurisdiction

Because NATION-STATES are sovereign, they are not required to submit legal disputes with other states to any court, panel, or tribunal. However, they may agree to do so as part of a TREATY or the PROTOCOL to a multilateral CONVENTION. Even in these circumstances, a state may decline to be sued or to accept the judgment made by the judicial body that heard the case. Despite these limitations on judicial resolution of international disputes, since the founding of the United Nations many agreements have included compulsory jurisdiction provisions. The most famous is OPTIONAL CLAUSE 36 (paragraphs 2 and 3) in the STATUTE OF THE INTERNATIONAL COURT OF JUSTICE. Countries that have signed the Optional Clause agree to adjudicate before the INTERNATIONAL COURT OF JUSTICE (ICJ) legal disputes concerning: (1) the interpretation of a treaty, (2) any question of INTERNATIONAL LAW, (3) the existence of any fact which may constitute a breach of an international obligation, or (4) the nature and extent of a reparation for such a breach. However, states may withdraw their consent to the Optional Clause, as the UNITED STATES did in the 1984 case of *Nicaragua v. U.S.A.*, refusing for two years to accept prior compulsory jurisdiction of the International Court in matters relating to Central America.

Some tribunals created by international conventions have grappled with the question of when a state may withdraw its consent to the agreement's compulsory jurisdiction requirements. In 1999 the Inter-American Court of HUMAN RIGHTS held that if a signatory of the 1969 American Convention on Human Rights had agreed to compulsory jurisdiction, its only option for withdrawing its consent was through the process of denouncing the convention itself. If this principle were to apply universally, it would undermine the principle of SOVEREIGNTY central to the "Westphalian" system of independent states. This problem was addressed in another 1999 case involving the LAW OF THE SEA Convention (LOS). Under its terms, states agree to the compulsory jurisdiction of LOS ARBITRATION procedures. But the convention's provisions overlap with many other international agreements and regional treaties. When a case was brought before the LOS Arbitral Tribunal on a matter also covered by a regional agreement that did not have a compulsory jurisdiction provision, the tribunal held that it did not have JURISDICTION, severely limiting the enforcement MECHANISMS of the Law of the Sea regime. As these cases demonstrated, the evolution of the compulsory jurisdiction principle at the turn of the century was closely intertwined with broader conceptions of the international system as either a collection of independent nation-states or an emerging international civil society in which sovereignty could be limited by international agreement.

Further Reading: Oxman, Bernard H. "Complementary Agreements and Compulsory Jurisdiction." *American Journal of International Law* 95, no. 2 (April 2001): 277–312.

conciliation

In international affairs conciliation refers to the process of seeking agreement between or among parties without recourse to ARBITRATION. Conciliation may be accomplished by having a dispute examined in depth by an impartial INQUIRY or "conciliation commission," leading to a nonbinding resolution. The General Act on the pacific settlement of International Disputes in 1928 provided elaborate measures for international conciliation efforts, but these techniques enjoyed a short period of notoriety during the interwar years. Nonetheless, some treaties still provide for well-defined conciliation practices, as does the LAW OF THE SEA (1982). Also, since 1975, the European Union has used a joint "conciliation committee" to resolve disagreements between the EU's Council of Ministers and the European Parliament.

See also CHAPTER VI, CONFLICT RESOLUTION, GOOD OFFICES, MEDIATION.

Conference of Non-Governmental Organizations in Consultative Relationship with the United Nations (CONGO)

The Conference of Non-Governmental Organizations is an independent, not-for-profit association of NON-GOVERNMENTAL ORGANIZATIONS (NGOs) dedicated to facilitating the participation of NGOs in UN activities. CONGO is active at UN HEADQUARTERS in New York and Geneva as well as elsewhere around the world. Founded in 1948, CONGO has mobilized NGOs in a number of efforts, including worldwide forums on HUMAN RIGHTS. Although not taking positions on substantive matters, it does represent the interests of its member NGOs in seeking influence on UN debates and decisions. Its MEMBERSHIP comprises national, regional, and international non-governmental organizations who are in CONSULTATIVE STATUS with the UN ECONOMIC AND SOCIAL COUNCIL (ECOSOC). CONGO associate membership is open to NGOs not holding consultative status. Annually the

executive committee of CONGO and the UN DEPARTMENT OF PUBLIC INFORMATION stage the world's largest NGO conference, attracting more than 2,000 participants to New York to discuss thematic issues such as the status of WOMEN, drug trafficking, social DEVELOPMENT, DISARMAMENT, and freedom of religion.

See also COMMITTEE ON NON-GOVERNMENTAL ORGANIZATIONS.

Further Reading: Congo Web site: <www.ngocongo.org/ngowhow/rbvoice.htm>.

Conference of the Committee on Disarmament (CCD) *See* CONFERENCE ON DISARMAMENT.

Conference on Disarmament (CD)

Located in Geneva, Switzerland, the Conference on Disarmament is the world's principal multilateral DISARMAMENT negotiating forum. While the United Nations provides conference services for the CD and the GENERAL ASSEMBLY makes recommendations that may become part of the CD's focus, the CD has its own rules, procedures, work program, and dynamics. Principal among its negotiating rules is a policy of consensus. Established in 1978 by consultations among members of its predecessor body, the CONFERENCE OF THE COMMITTEE ON DISARMAMENT (CCD, 1969), at the first UN Special Session on Disarmament, the CD was called the Committee on Disarmament until 1983. The EIGHTEEN NATION DISARMAMENT COMMITTEE (ENDC, 1962) and the Ten Nations Disarmament Committee (1960) were also predecessor bodies. By 1996, the CD had expanded from its original 38 member states to 61. At the turn of the century there were 66 members, lowered to 65 when Yugoslavia was deleted as a member in 2003 (states seceding from the FORMER YUGOSLAVIA were allowed to participate within the CD). Its set agenda, known as "the Decalogue," establishes 10 broad areas of disarmament for annual review. When the CD wishes to negotiate a specific topic, as it did successfully with the CHEMICAL WEAPONS CONVENTION (CWC, 1992) and the COMPREHENSIVE NUCLEAR TEST BAN TREATY (CTBT, 1996), it creates an ad hoc committee with a negotiating mandate to establish the TREATY's exact provisions. Reflecting a COLD WAR legacy, three groups act as informal negotiating parties within the CD. They are the East, West, and the non-aligned blocs. CHINA serves as a "group of one."

Several events in the mid-1990s affected the status and effectiveness of the CD. Perhaps most importantly, the CONVENTION ON THE PROHIBITION OF THE USE STOCKPILING, PRODUCTION, AND TRANSFER OF ANTI-PERSONNEL MINES AND THEIR DESTRUCTION (1997) was debated, negotiated, and adopted for ratification outside the CD in a "fast track" set of negotiations known as "The Ottawa Process." Moreover, in 1996 the UN General Assembly gave final approval to the Comprehensive Nuclear Test Ban Treaty when India refused to join the consensus for the treaty at the CD. Finally, in the years following the decision of the 1995 Review and Extension Conference of the NUCLEAR NON-PROLIFERATION TREATY (NPT) to extend the treaty's terms indefinitely, the CD was unable to achieve a consensus on a treaty banning the production of fissile materials; the Western Group refused a demand from the non-aligned Group of 21 within the CD to establish an ad hoc committee to discuss the abolition of nuclear weapons; and the UNITED STATES, GREAT BRITAIN, and FRANCE resisted one on the prevention of an arms race in outer space. The stalemate inside the CD and events outside the CD, including INDIA's and Pakistan's testing of nuclear weapons and the success of the Ottawa Process, led to widespread speculation among experts about the need either to maintain the status quo at the CD, to change the CD's rules and procedures, or to endorse the establishment of alternative negotiating fora to address a range of disarmament questions. At the turn of the century the CD was hampered by lack of consensus on a new negotiating mandate. In a bid to break the deadlock the Swedish-sponsored Weapons of Mass Destruction Commission recommended a change in the CD's VOTING requirements to allow for something less than complete agreement in order to pass proposals. Despite the differences on the committee, by 2006 two treaties were under discussion at the CD: a fissile material cutoff treaty (FMCT) and a prevention of an arms race in outer space (PAROS).

See also UNITED NATIONS INSTITUTE FOR DISARMAMENT RESEARCH, WEAPONS OF MASS DESTRUCTION.

Further Reading: Carle, Christophe, and Patricia Lewis. "Arms Control and Disarmament Mechanisms." *First Conference of the PfP Consortium of Defence Academies and Security Study Institutes,* Kongresshaus Zurich, Switzerland, October 18–21, 1998. Cordon, Pierce. "The Future of the Conference on Disarmament and Multilateral Arms Control." *Center for Nonproliferation Studies; China–US Conference on Arms Control, Disarmament, and Nonproliferation,* September 24–25, 1998. Conference on Disarmament, CD/8/Rev.8, August 17, 1999. Johnson, Rebecca. "CD Writes Off 1999 with Hopes for 2000." *Disarmament Diplomacy,* Issue no. 39. Sethi, Manpreet. "Conference on Disarmament: Groping Its Way Around." *Strategic Analysis* 23, no. 8 (November 1999). United Nations Institute for Disarmament Research. "Electronic Conference on the Future of the Conference on Disarmament and Its Agenda," January 13–27, 1998.

— *S. L. Williams*

conflict diamonds

Conflict diamonds (sometimes called "blood diamonds" or "war diamonds") are diamonds sold covertly and held by factions or militias fighting against recognized governments. Typically, conflict diamonds have been used to fund insurgent or invading forces involved in civil wars in highly fragmented African countries such as ANGOLA and SIERRA LEONE. The UN has struggled with attempts to create certification procedures to bring under control the dissemination of illicit diamonds. The World Diamond Council meeting at Antwerp in July 2000 adopted a RESOLUTION to bolster the diamond industry's capability to impede the sale and distribution of conflict diamonds. On December, 2000, the GENERAL ASSEMBLY, by unanimous vote, passed a resolution addressing the role of diamonds in intensifying conflict (A/RES-55/56) and calling for establishment of a method to allow certification that diamonds had not been sold for financing civil wars. In 2002, the UN approved the so-called Kimberley Process Certification Scheme (KPCS) to assure buyers that they were not purchasing conflict diamonds. Countries taking part in KPCS provide 9 percent of the world's trade in rough diamonds. The Kimberley Process derived from a conference of diamond producing states meeting in Kimberley, South Africa, in May 2000. Relevant nations approved the process by November 2002. Participants promise to ensure that (1) any diamond originating in the participating country will not fund any entity trying to overthrow a UN-recognized government, (2) a Kimberley Process certificate accompanies all diamond exports, and (3) no diamond is exported to nor imported from a nonmember of the Kimberley Process.

See also AFRICAN UNION, SANCTIONS.

Further Reading: Smilie, Ian, Lansana Gberie, and Ralph Hazleton. *The Heart of the Matter: Sierra Leone, Diamonds & Human Security.* Canada: Partnership Africa, January 2000. Tamm, Ingrid J. *Diamonds in Peace and War: Severing the Conflict-Diamond Connection.* Cambridge, Mass.: World Peace Foundation, 2002. UN Department of Public Information Conflict Diamonds Web site: <www.un.org/peace/africa/Diamond.html>.

conflict resolution

Unlike MEDIATION and CONCILIATION, with which it is sometimes compared, conflict resolution relies more on "academic" or even "social psychology" techniques. It depends less on an outside agent and suggests an approach and analysis of the causes and possible solutions to conflict as much as the final resolution itself. Implied in conflict resolution is that for a settlement of a conflict to be successful, the parties to the disagreement must redefine their relationship so as to perceive a way they can avoid conflict and deal reasonably with one another. Thus, conflict resolution requires that adversaries maintain contact, ongoing discussion, and even joint activities to resolve their differences. As an example, some Palestinian and Israeli groups in the Middle East have attempted to initiate formal associations to practice conflict resolution.

The United Nations has promoted conflict resolution as a necessary ingredient in trying to mitigate intrastate violence in unstable nations (such as in the FORMER YUGOSLAVIA, AFGHANISTAN, INDONESIA, and elsewhere) where ethnic, religious, and national rivalries have brought novel challenges to the maintenance of civil societies. In his *AGENDA FOR PEACE*, SECRETARY-GENERAL BOUTROS BOUTROS-GHALI called for "peace-building" in which the United Nations would play a critical role in the establishment of "social peace" among warring groups. The key problem seems to be that for conflict resolution to work, the parties to a dispute must demonstrate a committed resourcefulness and agree to enter into the process. Most critics see this as unlikely and thus deem conflict resolution as more an ideal to be sought after than a practical modus operandi.

See also ECONOMIC COMMUNITY OF WEST AFRICAN STATES.

Congo

The Congo is located in the heart of central Africa, containing a POPULATION of over 60 million in 2006, and comprising a territory larger than the state of Alaska. During the 19th-century European imperial scramble in Africa, King Leopold II of Belgium established the Congo Free State (in 1885) as a personal possession. Belgium ruled the country until granting independence on June 30, 1960, when the United Nations first became concerned with the area.

There have been two periods of United Nations involvement in the Congo. The first period (1960–64) followed Congo's independence from Belgium. On July 4, the Armée Nationale Congolaise (ANC) mutinied against its Belgian officers and began attacking European civilians. Against the wishes of the Congo government, Belgium sent 10,000 paratroopers to restore order. On July 10, Congolese prime minister Patrice Lumumba asked UN Secretary-General DAG HAMMARSKJÖLD for technical assistance to help restore order. On July 11, President Moise Tshombe of the mineral-rich Katanga province declared independence. With heavy fighting between Belgian and Congolese troops, both Lumumba and the Belgians requested the dispatch of UN troops to restore order on July 12. For the first time, the SECRETARY-GENERAL invoked Article 99 of the CHARTER to bring to the SECURITY COUNCIL's (SC) attention the Congo situation. Security Council RESOLUTIONS 4387 and 4405 urged the withdrawal of Belgian troops and established the UNITED NATIONS OPERATION IN THE CONGO (ONUC) to promote order. The SC passed Resolution 4426 in August in response to Katanga's refusal to allow ONUC troops to enter the province.

The UN became more involved in the civil war after a constitutional crisis emerged in late 1960 and Lumumba was murdered. On February 15, 1961, Hammarskjöld declared that ONUC could act to investigate the assassination, protect civilians, prevent clashes between armed units, reorganize the ANC, and remove Belgians from Katanga. On February 21, the SC authorized the use of force, if necessary, to prevent civil war in the Congo (Res. 4741). After abortive UN attempts to expel Belgian political and military advisers and mercenaries from Katanga in August–September 1961, most Belgian troops left the Congo. In response to an increasingly radical and violent secessionist movement, the Security Council extended ONUC's authorization to use force to detain and apprehend mercenaries and confiscate their arms (Res. 5002). In December 1961, the Katangans attacked the Elisabethville airport and ONUC retaliated, killing 50 civilians. Some member states criticized ONUC's use of force as beyond its mandate. After Hammarskjöld's death in a plane crash near Ndola, Rhodesia, Acting Secretary-General U THANT continued to mediate peace talks between the Congolese government and Katanga throughout 1962. In response to a UN budgetary crisis in 1963, the Congo government sought bilateral military aid from Belgium, Israel, Italy, and the UNITED STATES to counter the rebellion. On June 30, 1964, ONUC forces left Congo.

From 1960 to 1964, more than 93,000 troops served in ONUC, with 20,000 present at any one time; the total cost of military operations was $402 million. The Congo mission raised constitutional questions about PEACEKEEPING and military enforcement under CHAPTERS VI and VII of the UN Charter and helped to define the role of the Secretary-General regarding peace and security issues.

The second period of UN involvement in the Congo was precipitated by the 1994 Rwandan GENOCIDE and the consequent exodus of one million primarily Hutu ethnic refugees into eastern Congo (then called Zaire). This period of UN activity extended into the first decade of the 21st century. By 1997, the refugee camps had become a staging ground for Hutu extremists who had committed the genocide to attack Rwanda and Uganda. Zaire's long-time dictator Mobutu Sese Seko was unable to control the camps and faced rebel movements in eastern Zaire. In a move orchestrated by Rwandan president Paul Kagame and supported by Angolan and Ugandan troops, Laurent Kabila's Alliance of Democratic Forces for the Liberation of Congo (ADFL) overthrew President Mobutu in May 1997. In the process, ADFL forces attacked the refugee camps and killed more than 200,000 people. In April 1997, the UN COMMISSION ON HUMAN RIGHTS (CHR), with the support of the Security Council, established a mission headed by Roberto Garreton (Chile) to investigate alleged HUMAN RIGHTS abuses in the Democratic Republic of Congo (DRC; formerly Zaire). For almost a year, UN officials were detained, threatened, and denied access to the sites where refugees were massacred. On April 17, 1998, Secretary-General KOFI ANNAN announced the permanent withdrawal of the UN investigators because of the lack of cooperation from the Kabila government.

In August 1998, fighting broke out between the Kabila government and the insurgent Congolese Rally for Democracy (RCD), which was supported by Uganda and Rwanda. Past allies of Kabila, Rwanda and Uganda were disappointed that the new president had not secured the borders of eastern Congo. ANGOLA, Zimbabwe, and NAMIBIA sent troops to aid Kabila, and Chad and Sudan sent military advisers. In May 1999, the RCD broke into two factions, one backed by Rwanda (RCD-Goma) and the other supported by Uganda (RCD-Kisangani). The Movement for the Liberation of the Congo (MLC), a rebel movement backed by Uganda, also became involved in the conflict.

In April 1999, the Secretary-General appointed Moustapha Niasse of Senegal as UN SPECIAL ENVOY to assist in peace negotiations. In Resolution 1234 (1999), the Security Council supported the appointment of the special envoy, called for an immediate cease-fire, and condemned the presence of foreign state intervention in the DRC. On July 10, 1999, in Lusaka, Zambia, the DRC, Angola, Namibia, Rwanda, Uganda, and Zimbabwe signed a cease-fire agreement; the MLC and both RCD factions signed the agreement in early August. The Lusaka Agreement called for an inter-Congolese dialogue on the country's future, normalization of the DRC border, militia DISARMAMENT, and the establishment of a Joint Military Commission (JMC) of two representatives from each party under a neutral chairman. In Resolution 1258 (1999), the Security Council welcomed the Lusaka Agreement and authorized the deployment of 90 UN liaison personnel to the capitals of signatory states and the JMC provisional HEADQUARTERS. After a recommendation by the Secretary-General, the SC extended the mandate of the UN liaison personnel until January 15, 2000 (Res. 1973) and then in Resolution 1979 decided that these personnel would constitute the UNITED NATIONS ORGANIZATION MISSION IN THE DRC (MONUC). In February 2000, the council extended the mandate of MONUC until August 31, 2000, and authorized the expansion of the mission to 5,537 military personnel. When deployed, the mission would work with the JMC to monitor the cease-fire, facilitate humanitarian assistance, verify the disengagement of the contending parties' forces, and protect civilians (Security Council Res. 1291).

Despite the Lusaka Agreement, fighting continued between the parties. After another cease-fire was signed on April 8, 2000, JMC officials and the leaders of the signatory states urged the SC to deploy the MONUC peacekeepers. In an April 18 report, the Secretary-General expressed his concerns for human rights violations, the limited progress on the inter-Congolese dialogue, and the uncertain environment in which to deploy UN troops. On May 4–8, 2000, seven council members visited the region and met with the leaders of the involved parties to discuss the peace process. In spring 2000, fighting also erupted between Ugandan and Rwandan forces near Kisangani, killing more than 200 Congolese and injuring 1,000. In response, the SC called for the immediate withdrawal of Rwandan and Ugandan forces from Congo (Res. 1304).

On June 12, 2000, the Secretary-General reported that only 200 MONUC observers had been sent to the DRC. Plans to deploy additional troops were postponed indefinitely in July after Kabila refused to allow MONUC into some parts of the country. In response to Kabila's lack of cooperation with the UN and the JMC, the South African Development Community threatened SANCTIONS against the DRC on August 15, 2000. Kabila continued to insist that peacekeepers could not be deployed until Rwanda and Uganda withdrew from the DRC. On August 18, Secretary-General Annan sent former Nigerian ruler Abdulsalami Abubakar to the DRC to discuss Kabila's failure to provide for MONUC's security and his continued propaganda campaign against MONUC. Though he initially signaled his willingness to allow peacekeepers in all areas of the DRC, Kabila appeared to change his mind on August 25.

Member states were leery of committing troops to MONUC, especially in light of Kabila's animosity toward the UN and his refusal to participate in the inter-Congolese dialogue. In order to give the Security Council and the Secretary-General time to reconsider the mission, the Council passed Resolution 1316 (2000), which extended the mandate of MONUC until October 15, 2000. As of January 2004, at least 2.5 million Congolese had died of disease, malnutrition, and violence in the civil war.

When President Kabila was assassinated by a bodyguard in January 2001 the country faced further uncertainty. Parliament chose Joseph Kabila, the slain leader's son, as transitional president. Unsteady peace negotiations continued with UN encouragement until in 2003 the country signed a series of peace accords with Rwanda, Uganda, and two rebel militias. Over the next three years the UN mission worked assiduously to repatriate foreign fighters. Nonetheless, in 2006 nearly 9,000 foreign combatants remained on Congolese territory, raising the prospect of violence that could shatter the fragile peace agreements. In several incidents UN peacekeepers came under attack. The most serious confrontations occurred around the city of Bunia in the Ituri District. A brutal ethnic massacre of nearly 100 men and boys in 2004 triggered an assault by MONUC, using both infantry and helicopter gunships. Several of the rebel commanders were arrested, and one of them, Thomas Lubanga, was turned over to the INTERNATIONAL CRIMINAL COURT, becoming the tribunal's first-ever defendant.

On July 30, 2006, the Congo held the largest election the United Nations had ever tried to organize. With more than 26 million voters and some 50,000 polling stations, Congolese in large numbers trekked over paveless roads to vote while the UN deployed its largest peacekeeping force— 17,000 troops—to ensure order, and a consortium of UN agencies, European aid groups, and independent institutions, such as the CARTER Center, worked as well to make sure that voters could choose freely among the 9,700 candidates running for 500 National Assembly seats and the 33 contestants competing to be president. The election was touted as the first democratic election in the country for over 40 years. President Kabila garnered the most votes, but he was short of a needed majority to be elected outright. A run-off took place on October 30, and, after weeks of counting, officials determined that Kabila had defeated his closest rival, Vice President Jean-Pierre Bemba. Still, international observers worried that disappointed Congolese might not accept the electoral verdict and that violence would resume in this war-weary country. Despite progress, Africa's first war, as the conflict was termed, challenged the UN's ability to promote peace, defend state SOVEREIGNTY, and protect human rights.

Further Reading: Boulden, Jane. *The United Nations Experience in Congo, Somalia, and Bosnia.* Westport, Conn.: Praeger, 2001. Dayal, R. *Mission for Hammarskjöld: The Congo Crisis.* London: Oxford University Press, 1976. Lefever, Ernest. *Crisis in the Congo.* Washington, D.C.: Brookings Institution, 1965. MONUC Web site: <www.monuc.org/home.aspx?langen=>. Shearer, David. "Africa's Great War." *Survival* 41, no. 2 (1999): 89–106.

— *A. S. Patterson*

Congolese Civil War   *See* CONGO.

consultative status

Article 71 of the UN CHARTER allows the ECONOMIC AND SOCIAL COUNCIL (ECOSOC) to "make suitable arrangements for consultation with NON-GOVERNMENTAL ORGANIZATIONS (NGOs) which are concerned with matters within its COMPETENCE." Under this authority, as of mid-2006, over 2,700 NGOs had been admitted to consultative status with ECOSOC and an additional 400 to the same status with ECOSOC's COMMISSION ON SUSTAINABLE DEVELOPMENT. The growth in the number and diversity of non-governmental organizations formally affiliated with the United Nations reflected the growth in INTERNATIONAL CIVIL SOCIETY and the UN's effort to develop ties with additional entities beyond the NATION-STATES that make up its MEMBERSHIP.

Three categories of consultative status exist: General, Special, and Roster. These classifications were established in 1996 by the adoption of ECOSOC Resolution 31. The RESOLUTION considerably expanded the privileges that NGOs traditionally had maintained under the original system created shortly after the United Nations was founded. According to the resolution, organizations in the General Category must "be concerned with most of the activities of the ECOSOC and its subsidiary bodies." They receive the provisional agenda of the council and of its commissions and may propose items to be added. They may designate representatives who sit as observers at council meetings and may submit written statements to both the council and subsidiary bodies. Reflecting a democratization of UN procedures, non-governmental organizations accredited in the General Category may address the Council on subjects of interest. "Special" NGOs, while unable to address ECOSOC, may speak at commission meetings and may circulate written materials. NGOs may be placed in this category if they have a COMPETENCE or are concerned with "only a few of the fields of activity covered by the ECOSOC." NGOs with a very narrow or technical focus are placed on the "Roster," and have limited rights. But they are invited, along with General and Special NGOs, to send delegates to UN conferences and to appoint representatives to UN bodies.

While Article 71 links non-governmental organizations only to the Economic and Social Council, the United Nations has encouraged an expansion in NGO participation with all UN agencies. At WORLD CONFERENCES, they are urged to hold companion forums. They are also included in the implementation work of program agencies, such as the JOINT UNITED NATIONS PROGRAMME ON HIV/AIDS (UNAIDS). Those NGOs with an information distribution capability are also associated with the UN DEPARTMENT OF PUBLIC INFORMATION. Most SPECIALIZED AGENCIES have followed the pattern established by ECOSOC and have created consultative status for relevant private groups. Among the agencies to have done so are the INTERNATIONAL LABOUR ORGANIZATION, the UNITED NATIONS CONFERENCE ON TRADE AND DEVELOPMENT, the WORLD INTELLECTUAL PROPERTY ORGANIZATION, the INTERNATIONAL TELECOMMUNICATION UNION, the WORLD HEALTH ORGANIZATION, the FOOD AND AGRICULTURE ORGANIZATION, and the INTERNATIONAL MARITIME ORGANIZATION.

In 1999 UN SECRETARY-GENERAL KOFI ANNAN launched an initiative to bring private enterprises into a special relationship with the United Nations through the GLOBAL COMPACT. Corporations could commit to 10 principles established in important UN CONVENTIONS, and in so doing be given recognition and involvement in the work of the world body. Annan established a special bureau in his office for this liaison relationship, and a 17-member advisory board. Six sponsoring organizations supported the work of the new office: the UNITED NATIONS ENVIRONMENT PROGRAMME, the UNITED NATIONS DEVELOPMENT PROGRAMME, the ILO, the UN OFFICE ON DRUGS AND CRIME, the UNITED NATIONS INDUSTRIAL DEVELOPMENT ORGANIZATION, and the UNITED NATIONS HIGH COMMISSIONER FOR HUMAN RIGHTS.

See also BEIJING+5, CARDOSO REPORT, COMMITTEE ON NON-GOVERNMENTAL ORGANIZATIONS, DEPARTMENT OF ECONOMIC AND SOCIAL AFFAIRS, INDIGENOUS PEOPLES, INTERNATIONAL CIVIL SOCIETY, THEMATIC DIPLOMACY, UNITED NATIONS ASSOCIATION.

Further Reading: Weiss, Thomas, and Leon Gordenker, eds. *NGOs, the UN, and Global Governance.* Boulder, Colo.:

Lynne Rienner, 1996. Willetts, Peter, ed. *The Conscience of the World: The Influence of Non-governmental Organizations in the UN System.* Washington, D.C.: Brookings Institution, 1996. NGOs and ECOSOC Web site: <www.un.org/esa/coordination/ngo/>.

Contact Group for Namibia   *See* NAMIBIA.

convention

In the language of international affairs, *convention* is a term for an international agreement, bilateral or multilateral. Conventions may be open or closed for other states that have not participated in their preparation. There are several examples of conventions negotiated under the auspices of some entity in the UNITED NATIONS SYSTEM, such as the CONVENTION ON THE ELIMINATION OF ALL FORMS OF DISCRIMINATION AGAINST WOMEN, the Convention on the LAW OF THE SEA, and the CONVENTION AGAINST TORTURE.

Convention Against Torture and Other Cruel, Inhuman or Degrading Treatment or Punishment

The UN Convention against Torture, which was adopted and opened for signature, ratification, or ACCESSION by the GENERAL ASSEMBLY on December 10, 1984, codified the process of combating the practice of torture. The CONVENTION entered into force on June 26, 1987, after the 20th instrument of ratification was deposited with the SECRETARIAT in accordance with Article 27(1) of the convention. As of 2006, 141 nations had ratified the convention, 10 others had signed but not yet ratified it. The convention defined torture as "the deliberate infliction of severe physical or mental pain or suffering by public officials in order to intimidate, punish or obtain a confession or information from the victim." It required member states to take effective legal and other measures to prevent the practice.

To monitor compliance and implementation of the convention, the Committee on Torture was established. The committee met for the first time in April 1988 in Geneva and subsequently carried out intensive activities. The committee consists of 10 experts of high moral standing and recognized COMPETENCE in the field of HUMAN RIGHTS, who are elected by secret ballot by the state parties. The convention sets out a number of obligations designed to strengthen the sphere of protection of human rights and fundamental freedoms, while conferring upon the Committee on Torture broad powers of examination and investigation. The committee may invite SPECIALIZED AGENCIES, United Nations bodies concerned, REGIONAL ORGANIZATIONS, and NON-GOVERNMENTAL ORGANIZATIONS in CONSULTATIVE STATUS with the ECONOMIC AND SOCIAL COUNCIL to submit information, documentation, and written statements, as appropriate, relevant to the committee's activities. It submits an annual report on its activities to the state parties and to the UN General Assembly.

The work of the committee has been debilitated by the refusal of many parties to ratify the convention in full. By 2006 most ratifying states had done so only with reservations as provided under Article 22 or 28.

See also INTERNATIONAL DAY IN SUPPORT OF VICTIMS OF TORTURE, WAR CRIMES TRIBUNALS.

Further Reading: Burgers, Herman, and Hans Danelius. *United Nations Convention against Torture: A Handbook on the Convention against Torture and Other Cruel, Inhuman, or Degrading Treatment or Punishment.* The Hague: Kluwer Academic Publishers, 1988. Convention on Torture Web site: <www.ohchr.org/english/law/cat.htm>.

Convention on Biological Diversity (CBD)   *See* UNITED NATIONS CONFERENCE ON ENVIRONMENT AND DEVELOPMENT (UNCED).

Convention on International Trade in Endangered Species of Wild Fauna and Flora (CITES)

On March 3, 1973, 80 nations meeting in Washington, D.C., agreed on the text of the Convention on International Trade in Endangered Species of Wild Fauna and Flora. The CONVENTION, drafted 10 years earlier at a meeting of the World Conservation Union, entered into force on July 1, 1975. As of 2006 CITES counted 169 parties (although not all had fully ratified) and accorded protection to more than 30,000 species. The convention is an international agreement intended to assure the survival of specimens of wild animals and plants that constitute a growing part of international trade. That trade, estimated to be in the billions of dollars annually, ranges widely from live plants and animals to a variety of wildlife by-products such as food, leather goods, musical instruments, curios, medicine, and more. CITES underscores a concern with resisting habitat loss and protecting species from extinction. Since it came into force in 1975 no species listed under its provisions has become extinct as the result of trade practices.

CITES is administered by its own SECRETARIAT, which acts in an advisory role, is the repository for reports dealing with issues covered by the convention, distributes information relevant to the parties to the convention, and arranges meetings of the Conference of the Parties and the permanent committees of the conference. The Conference of the Parties, made up of all member states to the convention, meets every two or three years for about two weeks to review the implementation of the convention. These meetings are also attended by observers and by representatives of relevant UN agencies, who can participate in the meetings at the discretion of the member parties. The conference has established four permanent committees: a Standing Committee, an Animals Committee, a Plant Committee, and a Nomenclature Committee. The Standing Committee comprises VOTING representatives from member countries apportioned according to geographic region (Africa, Asia, Europe, North America, Central and South America and the Caribbean, and Oceania), with the number of committee members determined according to the number of participating parties in each region. The Standing Committee elects its chairperson and vice chair, meets once a year, provides policy guidance to the secretariat, oversees the secretariat's BUDGET, drafts RESOLUTIONS, and coordinates the efforts of the other committees and working groups. The Animals and Plants committees, composed of experts from the six geographic regions who are elected at meetings of the conference, provide knowledge and technical assistance regarding species. The Nomenclature Committee, made up of volunteers appointed by the conference, works to standardize the classification and standard naming of species and regularly reviews the convention's appendices to maintain correct use of zoological and botanical designations.

See also UNITED NATIONS ENVIRONMENT PROGRAMME.

Further Reading: Rosser, Alison, Mandy Haywood, and Donna Harris. *CITES: A Conservation Tool.* Cambridge: IUCN Species Survival Commission, 2001. CITES Web site: <www.cites.org>.

Convention on the Conservation of Migratory Species of Wild Animals (CMS)

Known as the Bonn Convention, or by its shortened title of Convention on Migratory Species, the Convention on the Conservation of Migratory Species of Wild Animals entered into force on November 1, 1983. As of 2006 MEMBERSHIP was 98 NATION-STATES from Africa, Central and South America, Asia, Europe, and Oceania. Three of the largest nations in the world—the RUSSIAN FEDERATION, CHINA, and the UNITED STATES—were, as of 2006, "non-parties in participation." That is, they had not ratified the CONVENTION but were abiding by its provisions. Members of CMS aspire to conserve migratory species and their sensitive habitats. CMS is guided by a list of endangered migratory species listed in the convention's Appendix I (51 in 2006, down from 85 in 2001). It seeks to achieve international agreements to promote conservation and reasonable management practices for the protection of migratory species listed in Appendix II and it encourages cooperation in research and dissemination of information on endangered species and protections for migratory wildlife.

A number of agreements have been composed under the auspices of CMS. They intend to conserve specific species, including bats in Europe, cetaceans in the Mediterranean and Black Seas, small cetaceans in the Baltic and North Seas, seals in the Wadden Sea, migratory waterbirds in Africa and Eurasia, the Siberian crane, the slender-billed curlew, and marine turtles.

Administrative support for the convention comes from a SECRETARIAT authorized by the UNITED NATIONS ENVIRONMENT PROGRAMME (UNEP). The Conference of the Parties, which holds periodic meetings, is the decision-making body for CMS. Between regular meetings of the conference a Standing Committee administers CMS's affairs. Member states appoint experts to a Scientific Council that provides technical and scientific advice to CMS bodies.

Further Reading: CMS Web site: <www.cms.int/>.

Convention on the Elimination of All Forms of Discrimination against Women (CEDAW)

During the UNITED NATIONS DECADE FOR WOMEN (1976 to 1985), the United Nations recognized WOMEN as important players in society. To endorse that view, the members of the HUMAN RIGHTS COMMISSION promoted a broad CONVENTION on the rights of women. In 1979 the GENERAL ASSEMBLY passed the United Nations Convention on the Elimination of All Forms of Discrimination Against Women. The convention extended the earlier 1952 CONVENTION ON THE POLITICAL RIGHTS OF WOMEN by prohibiting any distinction, exclusion, or restriction made or the basis of sex that impeded HUMAN RIGHTS and fundamental freedoms for women.

The process of ratification and implementation is monitored by the Committee on the Elimination of Discrimination Against Women (also known as CEDAW), which holds regular meetings to review reports from member states. U.S. president BILL CLINTON's administration supported CEDAW, but the U.S. Senate failed to ratify the convention. Supporters claimed that the convention would help protect women from many abuses, such as domestic violence, political oppression, and being sold into sexual slavery. Critics of the convention argued that it forced societies to adapt to UN notions of gender roles. Women's groups in the UNITED STATES such as NOW (National Organization of Women) favored the convention and pressed Congress to ratify it, but the United States remained the only developed country not to have ratified by 2006, by which time 183 countries had ratified or acceded to the convention.

In the fall of 1999, an additional Optional PROTOCOL was added to the convention. The Optional Protocol acknowledged the right to submit petitions to the United Nations and provided for individual complaint procedures. States that recognized the Optional Protocol accepted the COMPETENCE of the CEDAW Committee to consider petitions from individual women or groups of women who had exhausted all other national channels. The committee could conduct inquiries into grave or systematic violations of the convention. The Protocol, which was opened for signature and ratification, had an "opt-out clause," allowing states upon ratification or ACCESSION to declare that they did not accept the INQUIRY procedure. As of summer 2006, the Optional Protocol had been signed by 78 states. The Optional Protocol officially entered into force on December 22, 2000.

See also COMMISSION ON THE STATUS OF WOMEN, MILLENNIUM SUMMIT.

Further Reading: Byrnes, Andrew. "The Other Human Rights Body: The Work of the Committee on the Elimination of Discrimination Against Women." *Yale Journal of International Law*, no. 14 (Winter 1989): 1–67. Cooper, Mary H. "Women and Human Rights." *Congressional Quarterly* 9, no. 16 (April 30, 1999): 353. UN Women Watch Web site: <www.un.org/womenwatch/daw/cedaw/>.

— *K. J. Vogel*

Convention on the Elimination of All Forms of Racial Discrimination   *See* HUMAN RIGHTS, WORLD CONFERENCES TO COMBAT RACISM AND RACIAL DISCRIMINATION.

Convention on the Political Rights of Women

In July of 1954, the Convention on the Political Rights of Women entered into force. Considered at the time as a landmark effort in the push for political equality, the CONVENTION called for member states to allow WOMEN to vote and to hold public office on equal terms with men and without any discrimination. The convention, however, did not deal with broader concerns of discrimination, such as denial of equal pay for equal work or issues of violence against women. Negotiated in 1952, the convention did not provide any guidelines for enforcement and did not recognize the role of women in DEVELOPMENT, POPULATION policy, or food issues.

During the UNITED NATIONS DECADE FOR WOMEN (1976 to 1985), awareness of the key role of women in society grew, and UN participants, particularly those serving on the HUMAN RIGHTS COMMISSION, urged establishing a broader convention to deal with gender discrimination. In 1979, the GENERAL ASSEMBLY passed the UN CONVENTION ON THE ELIMINATION OF ALL FORMS OF DISCRIMINATION AGAINST WOMEN (CEDAW). This convention, generally characterized as an international bill of rights for women, prohibited any distinction, exclusion, or restriction made on the basis of sex that impeded HUMAN RIGHTS and fundamental freedoms for women.

See also COMMISSION ON THE STATUS OF WOMEN.

Further Reading: Cooper, Mary H. "Women and Human Rights." *Congressional Quarterly* 9, no. 16 (April 30, 1999): 353. UN Women/Watch Web site: <www.un.org/womenwatch/daw/cedaw>. UN High Commissioner for Human Rights Web site: <www.unhchr.ch/html/menu3/b/22.htm>.

— *K. J. Vogel*

Convention on the Prevention and Punishment of the Crime of Genocide (UNCG)

The UN GENERAL ASSEMBLY unanimously adopted the Convention on the Prevention and Punishment of the Crime of Genocide on December 9, 1948, opening it for signature, ratification, or ACCESSION. The CONVENTION entered into force on January 12, 1951, in accordance with Article 13. As of summer 2006, there were 41 signatories and 138 parties to the convention.

The term "genocide" derives from the combination of the Greek word for group or tribe—"genos"—and the Latin for killing—"cide." It was first used in 1944, when the jurist Raphael Lemkin published *Axis Rule in Occupied Europe,* in which he detailed the extermination policies pursued by the Third Reich and its allies. He called for the international prohibition of the "practice of extermination of nations and ethnic groups." Lemkin was instrumental in lobbying UN officials and representatives to secure the passage of a RESOLUTION by the General Assembly affirming that "genocide is a crime under INTERNATIONAL LAW which the civilized world condemns, and for the commission of which principals and accomplices are punishable." The matter was referred for consideration to the ECONOMIC AND SOCIAL COUNCIL, its deliberations culminating with the signing of the 1948 United Nations Convention on Genocide (UNCG).

The convention's definition of genocide as acts committed with intent to destroy—in whole or in part—a national, ethnic, racial, or religious group was intended in large part to prevent the systematic destruction of specific peoples, particularly as was the case with Jews and other groups in the Holocaust. As such, many experts, legal and academic, considered the criteria for genocide deficient in that the criteria were too narrow. For instance, it excluded the physical destruction of certain subgroups that regularly have been the victims of extensive killing programs. But vagueness of definition was to be expected in any legal instrument that was the outcome of negotiations among parties holding conflicting views as to the proper scope of the definition.

Because the Holocaust was so central to the conception of the UNCG, its application to other situations after 1948 was problematic. Situations such as the massacre of Armenians by the Turks during World War I, the destruction of the intelligentsia and others by the Khmer Rouge in CAMBODIA from 1975 to 1978, and the Ukrainian famine of the 1930s share some elements with the Nazi genocidal program. However, there were also important differences that raised questions about the applicability of the criteria specified by Article II of the UNCG. The slaughter of 800,000 Tutsis during the 1994 RWANDA CRISIS renewed interest in a broad definition of genocide. In the FORMER YUGOSLAVIA, as well, the international community sought the arrest and punishment of Serbian, Croatian, and Bosnian leaders for genocidal crimes. Most important among those detained was SLOBODAN MILOŠEVIĆ, former president of Yugoslavia, who was arrested and turned over to the INTERNATIONAL CRIMINAL TRIBUNAL FOR YUGOSLAVIA in the summer of 2001.

See also DARFUR, HUMAN RIGHTS, INTERNATIONAL COVENANT ON CIVIL AND POLITICAL RIGHTS, INTERNATIONAL CRIMINAL COURT.

Further Reading: Kuper, Leo. *Genocide: Its Political Use in the Twentieth Century.* Harmondsworth: Penguin Books, 1981. LeBor, Adam. *"Complicity With Evil": The United Nations in the Age of Modern Genocide.* New Haven, Conn.: Yale University Press, 2006. Minow, Martha. *Between Vengeance and Forgiveness: Facing History after Genocide and Mass Violence.* Boston: Beacon Press, 1998. Power, Samantha. *"A Problem from Hell": America and the Age of Genocide.* New York: Basic Books, 2002. Office of the High Commissioner for Human Rights. *Basic Human Rights Instruments.* Geneva: United Nations, 1998. United Nations *Manual on Human Rights Reporting under Six Major International Human Rights Instruments.* Geneva: United Nations, 1997. United Nations Department of Public Information. *Report of the Independent Inquiry into the Actions of the United Nations during the 1994 Genocide in Rwanda.* New York: United Nations Department of Public Information, 1999.

— *I. Kebreau*

Convention on the Prohibition of the Development, Production, and Stockpiling of Bacteriological (Biological) and Toxin Weapons and on their Destruction   *See* BIOLOGICAL WEAPONS.

Convention on the Prohibition of the Development, Production, Stockpiling and Use of Chemical Weapons (CWC)   *See* CHEMICAL WEAPONS.

Convention on the Prohibition of the Use, Stockpiling, Production and Transfer of Anti-Personnel Mines and Their Destruction

The Convention on the Prohibition of the Use, Stockpiling, Production and Transfer of Anti-Personnel Mines and Their Destruction is also known as the Ottawa Convention or the Landmines Treaty. The CONVENTION was opened for signa-

ture in Ottawa, Canada, on December 3, 1997. Under Article 15, the TREATY remained open for signature until its entry into force, which was March 1, 1999. After that date states could no longer sign it; rather, they could join the convention without signature through a one-step procedure known as ACCESSION. As of summer 2006, 154 states had signed or acceded to the convention, and 111 of those had ratified the agreement. Among the states notably absent from the list of signatories were CHINA, the UNITED STATES, INDIA, and the RUSSIAN FEDERATION.

The 1997 convention prohibited in all circumstances any use of anti-personnel LAND MINES. It also required the destruction of stockpiles within four years of the treaty's entry into force, and that mines already in the ground be destroyed within 10 years.

In October 1996, Canada's foreign minister Lloyd Axworthy initiated the Ottawa Process. This process consisted of conferences in Vienna, Brussels, and Oslo involving like-minded international actors determined to ban land mines. The Ottawa Treaty was drafted in Oslo and the process returned to Canada in December 1997 for the signing ceremony.

A coalition of state and non-state actors championed the Ottawa Process/Treaty, with Canada and Belgium leading the effort to establish a land mine ban. NON-GOVERNMENTAL ORGANIZATIONS (NGOs) such as the International Committee of the Red Cross (ICRC), Medecins sans Frontihres (MSF), and the International Campaign to Ban Landmines (ICBL) also advocated on behalf of the process/treaty. This last group was awarded the Nobel Peace Prize for its work.

The UN's role in the Ottawa Treaty was contradictory, yet notable. The UN had been involved in the movement to ban land mines since the 1970s. In 1980, it negotiated the Convention on Certain Conventional Weapons (CCW). The General Assembly, however, had established the UN's CONFERENCE ON DISARMAMENT (CD) in 1978 as the only global arms control negotiating forum. Frustration with the slow peace of the CD led several states to pursue negotiations on the Ottawa Treaty outside of the UN STRUCTURE. Paradoxically, the United Nations then circumvented its own negotiating forum by joining the Ottawa Treaty process. The UN acted as a policy partner with the NGOs. One example of such cooperation was the Survey Action Center. This represented the combined efforts of the UN Mine Action Service and NGOs such as Landmine Survivors Network and Norwegian Peoples' Aid. The Survey Action Center monitored standards and facilitated the international coordination of resources and expert personnel for the completion of the Global Landmine Survey in the most mine-affected countries.

See also UNITED NATIONS OFFICE OF PROJECT SERVICES, WEAPONS.

Further Reading: Short, N. "The Role of NGOs in the Ottawa Process to Ban Landmines." *International Negotiation*

4, no. 3 (1999): 481–500. Sundararaman, S. "The Landmines Question: An Overview of the Ottawa Process." *Strategic Analysis* 22, no. 1 (April 1998): 17–33. Thakur, R, and W. Maley. "The Ottawa Convention on Landmines: A Landmark Humanitarian Treaty in Arms Control?" *Global Governance: A Review of Multilateralism and International Organizations.* 5, no. 3 (July–September 1999): 273–302. International Campaign to Ban Landmines Web site: <www.icbl.org>.

— *S. F. McMahon*

Convention Relating to the Status of Refugees (Refugee Convention)

The basis for the right of return for refugees under INTERNATIONAL LAW is found in the Convention Relating to the Status of Refugees (1951) and its PROTOCOL of 1967. The CONVENTION, adopted by the GENERAL ASSEMBLY on December 14, 1950, was subsequently adopted by the UN Conference of Plenipotentiaries on the Status of Refugees and Stateless Persons at a meeting in Geneva in July 1951. The convention entered into force on April 22, 1954, and by 2006 there were 145 state parties to either or both the convention and the protocol.

According to international refugee law and international HUMAN RIGHTS law, the right of return is fundamental, although instruments of law usually emphasize voluntary repatriation. The issue of refugee repatriation grew out of the large displacement of persons during World War II. The concern continued to face the international community as the 20th century proceeded. The Refugee convention uses the concept of "country" rather than "nation" or "state" as the locale for return, since the former is more inclusive and considers ties and associations that an individual may have with a territory. Thus the convention recognizes the right of a stateless person to return to a country of "former habitual residence," suggesting that nationality is not necessarily an unquestionable standard to verify the right of repatriation. Refugee law, according to the convention as well as other international instruments, does not clearly obligate a state to bestow nationality, so, a returnee could be considered a resident and not a citizen. International protection ceases once a refugee has "re-availed himself of the protection of the country of his nationality," has "voluntarily re-acquired it," or when the circumstances that caused the refugee status in the first place no longer exist. Also a key provision of refugee law is the principle of "non-refoulment," which prohibits the forceful expulsion or forceful return of persons to a country where they would have reason to fear persecution.

See also UN HIGH COMMISSIONER FOR REFUGEES, UN RELIEF AND WORKS AGENCY FOR PALESTINE REFUGEES IN THE NEAR EAST, WORLD REFUGEE DAY.

Further Reading: Nicholson, Frances, and Patrick Twomey, eds. *Refugee Rights and Realities: Evolving International Con-* *cepts and Regimes.* Cambridge: Cambridge University Press, 1999. United Nations High Commissioner for Refugees. *Collection of International Instruments and Other Legal Texts Concerning Refugees and Displaced Persons.* Geneva: United Nations High Commissioner for Refugees, 1995. ———. *State of the World's Refugees.* New York: United Nations, issued every two years.

Convention to Combat Desertification (CCD and UNCCD)

In June 1992, the UNITED NATIONS CONFERENCE ON ENVIRONMENT AND DEVELOPMENT (UNCED or the Earth Summit) recommended the establishment of an Intergovernmental Negotiating Committee on Desertification (INCD), which drafted the Convention to Combat Desertification in Those Countries Experiencing Serious Drought and/or Desertification, Particularly in Africa. The committee approved the CONVENTION on June 17, 1994. It was opened for signature in Paris on October 14–15, 1994, and entered into force on December 26, 1996, 90 days after the 50th country had ratified it (there were 178 parties to the convention by 2006). In the meantime, many of the convention's provisions were carried out voluntarily on the basis of a Committee RESOLUTION calling for urgent action in Africa.

The convention offered new hope in the struggle against DESERTIFICATION. It was to be implemented through action programs addressing the underlying causes of desertification and drought and identifying measures to prevent and reverse these causes on the national level. Regional and subregional programs were also supposed to complement national programs, particularly where transboundary resources such as lakes and rivers were involved. Action programs were detailed in the four regional implementation annexes to the convention: Africa, Asia, LATIN AMERICA and the Caribbean, and the Northern Mediterranean.

The convention established a number of institutions and procedures for guiding international action. The Conference of the Parties (COP) oversees the implementation of the convention. The COP held its first session in October 1997 in Rome and meets once a year. While only national governments that ratify the convention are members of the COP, other bodies and organizations also participate. The convention made special provision for national and international agencies and qualified NGOs (NON-GOVERNMENTAL ORGANIZATIONS) to attend the COP's meetings and to contribute to its work. One of the COP's main functions is to review reports submitted by the member states detailing how they are carrying out their commitments. The COP makes recommendations on the basis of these reports. It also has the power to make AMENDMENTS to the convention or to launch negotiations for new annexes, such as additional regional implementation annexes. In this way, the COP guides the convention as global circumstances and national needs change. To assist the COP, the convention provided for several other supporting bodies and allowed the COP to establish additional ones if necessary.

The COP is supported by a SECRETARIAT. Like other convention secretariats, the CCD secretariat arranges COP meetings, prepares documents, provides coordination with other relevant bodies, compiles and transmits information, and facilitates consultations. Affected developing countries are also able to rely on the secretariat for information or advice on, for example, organizing their national consultation process.

The Committee on Science and Technology advises the COP on scientific and technological matters. It identifies priorities for research and recommends ways of strengthening cooperation among researchers. It also advises on such issues as joint research programs for new technologies. The COP may set up ad hoc panels to assist with specialized issues. The panels draw their members from a roster of government-nominated experts.

A Global Mechanism helps the COP promote funding for convention-related activities and programs. This MECHANISM does not raise or administer funds. Instead, it encourages and assists donors, recipients, development banks, non-governmental organizations, and others to mobilize funds and to channel them to where they are most needed. It seeks to promote greater coordination among existing sources of funding and greater efficiency and effectiveness in the use of funds.

The convention radically departed from the traditional approaches to desertification in its strong emphasis on a "bottom-up" approach with strong local participation in decision making. Traditionally, local communities have been relatively passive participants in development projects. The convention put them on an equal footing with other actors in the development process. Communities and their leaders, as well as non-governmental organizations, experts, and government officials, work closely together to formulate action programs.

NGOs have not only played a prominent role in the convention process, but they continue to raise public awareness of the convention and to lobby parliamentarians for its speedy ratification. For their part, international and REGIONAL ORGANIZATIONS provide crucial information, expertise, contacts, and research and managerial capabilities in the fight against desertification.

See also ENVIRONMENT, WORLD METEOROLOGICAL ORGANIZATION.

Further Reading: Scherl, Lea M. *Relationships and Partnerships among Governments, NGOs, CBOs and Indigenous Groups in the Context of the Convention to Combat Desertification and Drought.* Nairobi, Kenya: Environment Liaison Centre International, 1996. Convention to Combat Desertification Web site: <www.unccd.int/convention/menu.php>.

— *I. Kebreau*

covenant

A covenant is a voluntary agreement entered into by two or more parties to do or refrain from some action or actions. In law, a covenant is a contract or a promise—rather like a sacred promise—of legal weight. In the Bible, and in theology more generally, a covenant is a contract or engagement between God and human beings. For example, the "covenant" between God and Israel is fundamental to Jewish religious tradition, and the original 17th-century Puritan settlers in America "covenanted" together to create their civil and religious societies. Thus covenant takes on a more metaphysical and spiritual meaning than CHARTER or TREATY, which are more clearly secular documents. The LEAGUE OF NATIONS originated in a covenant, the United Nations in a charter. The League Covenant was a traditional agreement among governments, called in the Covenant "The High Contracting Parties." The preamble of the UN Charter begins, "We the peoples of the United Nations."

See also PACT, *and for examples of covenants* BRICKER AMENDMENT, INTERNATIONAL COVENANT ON CIVIL AND POLITICAL RIGHTS, INTERNATIONAL COVENANT ON ECONOMIC, SOCIAL, AND CULTURAL RIGHTS.

Credentials Committee of the General Assembly

The Credentials Committee is one of two PROCEDURAL COMMITTEES of the UN GENERAL ASSEMBLY (GA). Its nine members are appointed at the beginning of the Assembly's annual session on the recommendation of the GA president. The committee has the responsibility of recommending to the Assembly the seating of delegations and representatives. A routine task normally, the acceptance or rejection of a national delegation's credentials has been used to exclude or seat a controversial government. While the UN CHARTER allows for the SUSPENSION OR EXPULSION of a member, the UN MEMBERSHIP has been unwilling to take either drastic action. Instead, on occasion it has informally "suspended" the participation of states that it believes have violated UN principles by challenging the credentials of the representatives sent to New York. This was done to the South African delegation in 1974 and the Israeli delegation in 1982, effectively excluding them from participation in GA debate and VOTING. At the close of the century, the Credentials Committee also effectively had denied recognition to the Taliban government of AFGHANISTAN by continuing to seat the previous interim Afghan government's representatives. Following the defeat of the Taliban in 2001, the Kabul government of Hamed Karzai was returned to the UN as the official representative of the country.

See also COMMITTEE SYSTEM OF THE GENERAL ASSEMBLY.

Cuba

Cuba joined the United Nations as one of the body's original members on October 24, 1945. Its representatives were active in the first decade of the UN's development and operations. It supported failed efforts to limit the authority of the PERMANENT MEMBERS OF THE SECURITY COUNCIL and supported attempts to gain guaranteed regional representation within the SECURITY COUNCIL for the Latin American states.

Cuba gained notoriety for the loyalty that it offered to the UNITED STATES during the early COLD WAR. Its positions were especially anticommunist. For example, during cease-fire negotiations at the end of the KOREAN WAR, Cuba was one of only two delegations to vote against the participation of Mao Zedong's People's Republic of CHINA. Its cold war allegiance to the United States within the United Nations was an extension of the Batista dictatorship's foreign policy. When the Cuban Revolution forced Fulgencio Batista from power in 1959, Cuba transformed itself into an antagonist of the United States.

The transformation began with Fidel Castro's speech before a SPECIAL SESSION OF THE GENERAL ASSEMBLY in September 1960. Attacking American imperialism and asserting Cuban independence, the leader's speech accelerated the deterioration of Cuban-American relations. As the years passed, the United Nations became a forum for the new rivalry.

The abortive April 1961 Bay of Pigs invasion of the island became the first serious crisis between the American government and Cuba after its revolutionary shift. The United States, having sponsored the invasion, faced condemnation within the GENERAL ASSEMBLY. Washington's representatives, who argued that the ORGANIZATION OF AMERICAN STATES (OAS), as a recognized regional authority, held JURISDICTION over the matter, headed off all challenges with the threat of a VETO in the Security Council. A RESOLUTION did pass the Assembly, but its language merely urged all states to seek peaceful settlement of their differences.

In 1962, the United States imposed an economic embargo that blocked all U.S. trade with Cuba, and pressured its allies in LATIN AMERICA and Europe to follow suit. The Cuban government initially sought UN condemnation of the American action, but was unsuccessful. Thirty years later, the General Assembly did approve a resolution that called for the end of the embargo that, nonetheless, still remained in force in 2006.

Cuban-American relations at the United Nations worsened again during the missile crisis in October 1962. The crisis arose when U.S. intelligence discovered Soviet missile sites on the island. Cuba first inserted itself into the center of this superpower confrontation when Fidel Castro wrote to SECRETARY-GENERAL U THANT asserting Cuba's ability, willingness, and right to defend its territory from American AGGRESSION, referencing the downing of a U-2 spy plane over the island on October 27th. As tension mounted, however, Soviet and American representatives worked directly to defuse the crisis without any Cuban involvement.

In the years that followed, Cuba used the United Nations as a venue for two projects. First, through its representa-tives' votes, it demonstrated its support for the Soviet Union, which became the revolutionary regime's financial and military prop for two decades. Second, upon gaining membership in the GROUP OF 77 in 1971, it worked to forge alliances with its members, and more generally with the nations of the NON-ALIGNED MOVEMENT, particularly in the UN CONFERENCE ON TRADE AND DEVELOPMENT (UNCTAD).

Pursuing these two strands in its UN policy often proved counterproductive. Cuban support within the United Nations for the Soviet Union's invasions of Czechoslovakia in 1968 and of AFGHANISTAN in 1979 went against the sentiments of the majority of nonaligned states and reinforced efforts made by the United States and its allies to depict Cuba as a mere Soviet satellite. Also within the United Nations the Cuban delegation offered support for most NATIONAL LIBERATION movements, including those involving Vietnam, the African National Congress in South Africa, and the independence movement in Puerto Rico. Cuba's military assistance for resistance and liberation movements in Africa and the Americas strained its relations with other nations within the United Nations.

During the last two decades of the 20th century Cuba found its policies challenged in the United Nations by significant numbers of former supporters. In 1980, facing threats from the Bahamas and other English-speaking Caribbean nations, it apologized for its sinking of a Bahamian coast guard vessel in order to head off a Security Council resolution that would have sanctioned its actions. The UN COMMISSION ON HUMAN RIGHTS (CHR), under pressure from the United States, annually challenged Cuba for its treatment of political dissidents. In 1988, the CHR accepted an invitation from the Cuban government to investigate HUMAN RIGHTS conditions there. Cuban military involvement in ANGOLA complicated UN efforts to end that country's civil war. Security Council resolutions had sanctioned South Africa for its intervention in Angola. In 1984, the Cuban government agreed to withdraw its troops and civilian advisers once South Africa accepted the UN mandate. A UN settlement moved Angola toward peace after 1988. UN monitors reported the final withdrawal of all Cuban forces in 1991.

The collapse of the Soviet Union and the curtailment of its economic and military assistance led Cuba to adopt a more pragmatic approach within the United Nations. It obtained, despite U.S. opposition, financial and programmatic support from the UN DEVELOPMENT PROGRAMME (UNDP), the UN EDUCATIONAL, SCIENTIFIC AND CULTURAL ORGANIZATION (UNESCO), and the UN CHILDREN'S FUND (UNICEF). It also scaled back its public and private support for radical and revolutionary groups in the Americas and in Africa. However, the United Nations remained a forum for the continuing conflict between the United States and Cuba. The General Assembly endorsed the Cuban position in 1992 and again in 1997 with resolutions that condemned the U.S. trade embargo. In reaction, Washington continued to bring pressure against the Castro regime in the world body. Castro returned to the United Nations in 1995 to offer an address during the body's 50th anniversary. In 1996, U.S. efforts led to a UN investigation of the downing of a civilian aircraft flown from Miami over international waters. In 1999 Pope John Paul II visited a welcoming Cuba where he publicly urged the Castro regime to consent to genuine religious liberty and other freedoms. Castro attended the UN's MILLENNIUM SUMMIT in 2000 and, some years later, in July 2006, the rare-traveled Cuban president was a guest at a meeting in Argentina of South America's customs union MERCOSUR (Mercado Común del Sur) where his presence attracted considerable media attention. One month later, as he was turning 80, Castro underwent major surgery, during which he turned authority over to his brother Raul Castro. In February 2008 Castro announced his official retirement and his brother, Raul, was chosen to succeed him.

See also APPEAL TO THE SECURITY COUNCIL; CARTER, JIMMY; CUBAN MISSILE CRISIS; DEVELOPING COUNTRIES; KENNEDY, JOHN F.; KHRUSHCHEV, NIKITA; NAMIBIA; NUCLEAR NON-PROLIFERATION TREATY; NUCLEAR-WEAPONS-FREE ZONES; TREATY OF TLATLELOCO; UNITED NATIONS ANGOLA VERIFICATION MISSION; UN SECURITY COUNCIL RESOLUTION 678; WORLD SUMMIT ON THE INFORMATION SOCIETY.

Further Reading: Dominguez, Jorge I. *To Make a World Safe for Revolution: Cuba's Foreign Policy.* Cambridge, Mass.: Harvard University Press, 1989. Erisman, H. Michael. *Cuba's Foreign Relations in a Post-Soviet World.* Gainesville: University of Florida Press, 2000. Sadri, Houman A. *Revolutionary States, Leaders, and Foreign Relations: A Comparative Study of China, Cuba, and Iran.* Westport, Conn.: Praeger Publishers, 1977.

— D. K. Lewis

Cuban missile crisis

On October 15, 1962, American reconnaissance planes flying over CUBA discovered Soviet missile sites under construction. The U.S. administration of President JOHN F. KENNEDY decided to force the removal of these sites. What ensued were 13 days in which the world stood on the brink of nuclear war. President Kennedy estimated that the chances for war were "somewhere between one in three and fifty-fifty." During the crisis neither side made much use of the United Nations, except to utilize the SECURITY COUNCIL for propaganda statements meant to sway world public opinion. Only U.S. PERMANENT REPRESENTATIVE to the UN Adlai E. Stevenson made the case that diplomacy through the world body should be employed before resorting to the threat of force.

Soviet premier NIKITA KHRUSHCHEV had decided to place nuclear missiles in Cuba for strategic reasons. The Soviet Union lagged behind the UNITED STATES in NUCLEAR WEAPON warheads and sought to minimize this disparity. It sought to do so by placing missiles in Cuba with the range to hit almost anywhere in the United States. Prior to October 1962 its missiles had limited range and much of the United States was beyond their reach. Khrushchev also was annoyed that the United States had placed Jupiter missiles on the soil of geographically close Soviet rival Turkey. The Soviet leader reportedly considered deployment of Soviet missiles in Cuba to be, for Americans, a "taste of their own medicine." The Cubans, led by Fidel Castro, sought to use the missiles as a way to defend against another American invasion. In 1961 the United States had armed anti-Castro Cubans in an abortive effort to overthrow the regime. An American-sponsored invasion in April at the Bay of Pigs had been repelled by Cuban forces. By fall 1962, Castro, certain that the United States was planning another incursion, wanted to avoid a repetition of 1961 and considered the missiles to be the ultimate defense for his country.

Following the discovery of the missiles, Kennedy convened his National Security Council's Executive Committee (EXCOMM) to consider responses. EXCOMM debated the merits of an air strike as well as a blockade around the island. While most members of EXCOMM initially favored an air strike, the president's brother (and U.S. attorney-general) Robert Kennedy, declaring that "I will not have my brother be another Tojo," advocated instead a naval blockade of the island. Concerned that a blockade was an act of war, President Kennedy chose to call the action a "quarantine" and announced that Soviet ships headed to Cuba would be subject to American inspection. In the end, Khrushchev ordered Soviet ships not to run the blockade, occasioning U.S. secretary of state Dean Rusk to declare that "we stood eyeball to eyeball and the other guy blinked."

During the crisis Khrushchev floated the idea of using UN SECRETARY-GENERAL U THANT as an intermediary, but the Kennedy administration demurred. The most important diplomatic exchanges were kept directly between Moscow and Washington. At UN HEADQUARTERS the United States requested a session of the Security Council. During that televised meeting, Stevenson used surveillance photographs to make the U.S. case. In the most dramatic moment of the debate Stevenson asked Soviet ambassador Valery Zorin repeatedly whether there were offensive missiles in Cuba. Zorin gave no reply. At one point in a tense confrontation, Stevenson turned to Zorin and said that he "was prepared to wait until hell freezes over for your reply." Beyond the drama, negotiations in New York were limited to out-of-view discussions.

As the crisis unfolded, Khrushchev offered two different proposals. On October 25 he offered to remove the missiles if Kennedy would make a "no-invasion" pledge regarding Cuba. The next day Khrushchev added a second demand—the removal of American missiles in Turkey. According to popular history, Robert Kennedy suggested

Meeting of the Security Council during the Cuban missile crisis, 1962 (UNITED NATIONS)

accepting the first proposal while ignoring the second. The president directed Stevenson to explore with Secretary-General Thant the possibility of the United Nations providing observation teams to oversee any missile withdrawal. He also let his UN ambassador suggest that if an exchange of missile sites in Turkey for those in Cuba became necessary, then the proposal to do so would best come from Thant. As it happened, Robert Kennedy met on October 27 with Soviet ambassador to the United States Anatoly Dobrynin and agreed to both conditions, but insisted that the Soviets keep the second condition confidential. Kennedy dropped the idea of UN observation teams as well, depending on Central Intelligence Agency overflights to verify the dismantling of the missiles. On October 28 both sides announced that the crisis had been defused; the missiles would be withdrawn and the United States would make clear it had no intention of invading Cuba in the future. As a result of the crisis, the two countries agreed to the installation of a "hot line" telephone connection so that in the future negotiations could be initiated instantly, before an awkward situation became a crisis.

See also COLD WAR, LATIN AMERICA.

Further Reading: Allison, Graham T. *The Essence of Decision: Explaining the Cuban Missile Crisis.* New York: Addison, Wesley, Longman, 1999. Allyn, Bruce J., Georgy Shakhnazarov, David A. Welch, and James G. Blight, eds. *Back to the Brink: Proceedings of the Moscow Conference on the Cuban Missile Crisis, January 27–28, 1989.* Lanham, Md.: University Press of America, 1992. Garthoff, Raymond L. *Reflections on the Cuban Missile Crisis.* Washington, D.C.: Brookings Institution, 1990. Kennedy, Robert. F. *Thirteen Days: A Memoir of the Cuban Missile Crisis.* New York: W.W. Norton and Company, 1999. May, Ernest R., and Philip D. Zelikow, eds. *The Kennedy Tapes: Inside the White House during the Cuban Missile Crisis.* Cambridge, Mass.: Harvard University Press, 1998. Nathan, James A., ed. *The Cuban Missile Crisis Revisited.* New York: St. Martin's, 1993.

— *D. J. Becker*

Cyprus dispute

Controlled by the Turkish Ottoman Empire from the 16th century, Cyprus, the third largest island of the Mediterranean Sea, was annexed by GREAT BRITAIN during World War I. For centuries, the majority ethnic Greek population considered Greece the mother country of Cyprus. The country became independent in 1960, and full rights were promised to its minority Turkish population. In 1964 communal clashes occurred between Greek and Turkish Cypriots, and a temporary UN PEACEKEEPING force was sent to the island to help end the dispute. From 1964 to 1974 the United Nations pursued a single-state solution based on the agreements among the United Kingdom, Greece, and Turkey that granted independence to the island.

In 1974 Archbishop Makarios, the Cypriot president, was overthrown by a military coup apparently seeking merger with Greece. Turkey responded with an invasion to protect the Turkish minority. From 1974 until the early 21st century, the UNITED NATIONS FORCE IN CYPRUS (UNFICYP) sought a bi-zonal solution, supervising and maintaining a buffer zone between the Greek Cypriot National Guard and Turkish forces. Makarios eventually returned to power in late 1974, but Turkish troops remained in the north, controlling about 40 percent of the country, and in 1983 proclaimed a separate "Turkish" Republic. The UN SECURITY COUNCIL declared this action invalid, and the SECRETARY-GENERAL and his special adviser on the island continued to try to draw the opposing forces into direct discussions to end the long stalemate and initiate meaningful negotiations leading to a comprehensive settlement. The lengthy presence of UNFICYP, separating the two communities, had the ironic consequence of lessening incentives for reunification.

In 1998 the Cyprus situation was impacted by the European Union's (EU) decision to invite Cyprus to apply for MEMBERSHIP. The treaty signed with the EU in April 2003 concerned only the Greek portion of the island. That same month, Turkish Cyprus opened its border while Greek Cyprus ended trade SANCTIONS, causing hopes to rise for reunification. However, a 2004 referendum on reunification was overwhelmingly rejected by the Greek POPULATION (although approved by the Turkish minority).

Attempting to resuscitate progress toward reunification, UNDER SECRETARY-GENERAL for Political Affairs Ibrahim Gambari traveled to Cyprus in July 2006. He convened the first meeting between Greek Cypriot leader Tassos Papadopoulos and Turkish Cypriot leader Mehmet Ali Talat since April 2002. The two leaders signed a set of principles committing their communities to reunify the island on the basis of past Security Council RESOLUTIONS and to begin bi-communal discussions on day-to-day issues.

See also BUNCHE, RALPH; DEPARTMENT OF PEACEKEEPING OPERATIONS.

Further Reading: Ker-Lindsay, James. *EU Accession and UN Peacemaking in Cyprus.* New York: Palgrave Macmillan, 2005. Richmond, Oliver P. *Mediating in Cyprus. The Cypriot Communities and the United Nations.* London: Frank Cass, 1998. UNFICYP Web site: <www.un.org/Depts/DPKO/Missions/unficyp/body_unficyp.htm>.

D

Dag Hammarskjöld Library

Located on the southwest corner of UN HEADQUARTERS in New York City, the UN's main library, a gift of the Ford Foundation, is dedicated to the memory of the second SEC-RETARY-GENERAL, Dag HAMMARSKJÖLD, who died in Africa in 1961 while on a PEACEKEEPING mission to the CONGO.

The library was an addition to the larger project for the headquarters that included the GENERAL ASSEMBLY building, the conference building, and the 39-story SECRETARIAT building. The lead architect for the entire enterprise, Wallace K. Harrison, of New York, was the chief designer of the library, which opened officially in 1962, one year after the death of Hammarskjöld. Built of marble, the library has an expansive view north of UN headquarters and adjacent buildings and open spaces. It is not open to the public but is mandated to serve the information needs of UN permanent mission staffs and the Secretariat. It is also accessible to scholars to provide materials not available at other depository libraries. The library is open Monday through Friday, 9 A.M. to 5:30 P.M. except when the General Assembly is in session, when the hours of operation are extended to 6 P.M. during the work week.

The library contains about 400,000 volumes, as well as a newspaper collection, a microfilm laboratory, tape recording services, an extensive photography library, reading rooms, and an auditorium. The collection includes the official records of the principal organs of the United Nations and selected documents issued by SPECIALIZED AGENCIES. The library also maintain the Woodrow Wilson Collection, consisting of 8,600 volumes of LEAGUE OF NATIONS' documents and 6,500 books on the organization. An Oral History Collection is also part of the library's holdings. Interviews with important individuals in the history of the United Nations are preserved in both transcript and audio formats. By its mandate, the library maintains bibliographic control over the documentation of the United Nations. It provides, through the United Nations Bibliographic Information System (UNBIS), indexing for UN documents and publications issued in New York, Geneva, and Vienna, as well as documents released by regional commissions and other UN bodies. In 2003, the UN established a Steering Committee for the Modernization and Integrated Management of United Nations Libraries. Secretary-General KOFI ANNAN reported to the General Assembly on behalf of the Steering Committee in April 2005. The Steering Committee recommended that the Dag Hammarskjöld Library and other UN libraries shift their focus from acquisition of materials to access of the existing collections. This would include greater use of the Internet and online materials. The committee also recommended the use of systems that provide access to multiple types of information held in different UN locations. Given the new information technologies, the committee suggested that the Dag Hammarskjöld Library's system of 400 depository libraries around the world, which shelve paper copies of most important UN documents, should be reconsidered. Electronic access may allow a reduction in these facilities.

See also DEPARTMENT OF PUBLIC INFORMATION.

Further Reading: Hammarskjöld Library Web site: <www.un.org/Depts/dhl/services.htm>.

Darfur

The Darfur region of western Sudan has drawn international attention since fighting broke out between rebel groups and the Sudanese government in February 2003. The area was an independent Islamic sultanate until it was annexed to Sudan by the British in 1916. In 1994, the region, which is the size of FRANCE, was divided into three states—North, South, and West Darfur. Long neglected by the central government in Khartoum, Darfur found itself marginalized, and in 2003 a locally inspired militia, the Sudanese Liberation Movement (SLM), began attacks on government targets. Soon after, another rebel group, the Justice and Equality Movement (JEM), joined the SLM against the government. The government responded by organizing and supporting another local militia known as the janjaweed (although the government denies it provided support). Both sides in the fighting were accused of atrocities, but the government/janjaweed side was singled out by the international community, in particular for targeting civilians. Brutal attacks on the POPULATION resulted in over 200,000 casualties by 2006 and over two million displaced people. International efforts to end the crisis proved unsuccessful.

Sudan has been plagued by conflict for most of its independent existence. A 17-year rebellion against the government by southern rebels opposed to what they saw as Arab/Muslim dominance ended in 1972, but reignited after the government of Jaafar al-Nimeiri decided to impose Islamic law in 1983. In response, the Sudan Peoples Liberation Army took up arms against the government and quickly seized control of much of the south of the country. Largely a battle between the Arab/Muslim north and the African Christian/animist south, the fighting continued until peace talks led to the signing of the Comprehensive Peace Agreement (CPA) ending the north-south civil war in January 2005.

Although it dealt with a different rebellion, the CPA had an impact on the fighting in Darfur. As talks progressed toward the CPA (designed to promote power and revenue sharing), rebels in Darfur were inspired to press their own demands against the central government. Moreover, the desire to reach an agreement to end the north-south conflict may have hampered efforts to end the crisis in Darfur. Unwilling to undertake any action that might pressure the Sudanese government and cause it to back out of the negotiations, the international community was slow to take concrete action to stop the killing.

The fighting in Darfur is often portrayed as an Arab versus African conflict, but the reality is more complex; intermarriage has blurred ethnic distinctions and both parties to the conflict are Muslim. Like many ethnic/communal conflicts it was triggered by competition for scarce resources, in this case farmers and herders vying for shrinking land area. Drought exacerbated this crisis and combined with the government's long history of neglecting the region, encouraged rebel activity. The government responded in brutal fashion, unleashing the janjaweed militia, and before long the combination of Sudanese government air attacks followed by mounted assaults by the janjaweed (loosely translated, the term means "evil horsemen") began to take a devastating toll on the civilian population. It was not until March 2004, when the UN HUMAN RIGHTS coordinator for Sudan described the situation as the "world's worst humanitarian crisis," that the international community began to take notice. Humanitarian aid flowed into the region but the fighting made its distribution difficult and the government was accused of intimidating aid workers. In April 2004, the first cease-fire agreement between the government and the rebels resulted in agreement to allow AFRICAN UNION observers to be deployed. An initial force of 3,200 troops was committed with the number rising eventually to 7,000. The mandate was for the troops to monitor the cease-fire but did not extend to the protection of civilians except in cases of imminent danger. The cease-fire lasted barely six weeks before both sides accused the other of attacks. The first of several UN RESOLUTIONS was passed on July 30, 2004, and gave the Sudanese government 30 days to disarm the janjaweed and threatened SANCTIONS for failure to comply. In July 2004, the United States Congress passed a resolution calling the situation in Darfur GENOCIDE. In September, SECURITY COUNCIL Resolution 1564 called for the establishment of a commission of INQUIRY to determine whether genocide had occurred and threatened sanctions against the government of Sudan if it did not stop the violence. SECRETARY-GENERAL KOFI ANNAN commissioned a report on the question of genocide that sought to investigate reports of human rights violations, determine whether genocide had occurred, identify the perpetrators, and suggest ways to hold those responsible accountable. The report, issued in February 2005, concluded that the Sudanese government and the janjaweed, as well as the rebels, were responsible for serious violations of international and humanitarian law but found that the government had not pursued a policy of genocide, citing the absence of intent to annihilate a group on racial, ethnic, national, or religious grounds. The report did find evidence of war crimes and crimes against humanity and strongly recommended that violators be referred to the INTERNATIONAL CRIMINAL COURT. On March 29, 2005, the Security Council, under Resolution 1591, imposed an arms embargo on the government of Sudan and a travel ban and asset freeze on those accused of crimes in Darfur, and two days later under Resolution 1593 approved the referral of war crimes cases to the International Criminal Court.

Nevertheless, the catastrophe in Darfur continued unabated and spilled over into neighboring Chad when President Idriss Deby accused Sudan of backing rebels who attacked the capital, N'djamena, in April 2006. Inadequate funding and logistical problems rendered the African Union Mission in Darfur (AMIS) ineffective. Moreover, the 7,000 AU troops were simply inadequate to patrol such a large area. In May 2006, the Darfur Peace Agreement (DPA) was brokered by the African Union. Indicative of the splintering of the rebel forces, one faction of the Sudan Liberation Army (SLA) signed the agreement but another SLA faction and the JEM both refused to sign. Despite the peace agreement, by late August 2006, the UN emergency relief coordinator, Jan Egeland, said that insecurity in Darfur was at its highest level since 2004 and that humanitarian aid efforts were seriously jeopardized. Fatalities among aid workers between May and July 2006 were the highest since the start of the conflict in 2003.

Against this backdrop the UN Security Council passed Resolution 1706 on August 31, 2006, calling for the expansion of the mandate of the UN Mission in Sudan (UNMIS), established in conjunction with the CPA signed in January 2005. The resolution called for the expansion of UNMIS by up to 17,300 military personnel and up to 3,300 civilian police. The force would replace or absorb the AU mission, whose mandate extended only until the end of September 2006. Among the governments criticizing inaction by the United Nations was the U.S. administration of President GEORGE W. BUSH. The government of Sudan strenuously rejected the Security Council resolution, claiming it violated Sudan's SOVEREIGNTY, and said that instead it would send its own troops to battle those rebels who refused to sign the DPA. Shortly after Resolution 1706 passed, the UN HIGH COMMISSIONER FOR REFUGEES warned that the situation in Darfur was worsening and threatening to spark another round of civilian displacement and wider instability. Human Rights Watch reported in early September that the government had begun bombing villages in rebel areas of North Darfur, indicating that the government was following through on its intention to resolve the conflict militarily. Meanwhile, the stakes in this conflict, already unacceptably high for the civilian population, were also mounting for Security Council credibility.

In response to the mounting evidence of genocide and other war crimes by the janjaweed militia with the complicity of the Sudanese government, and the intransigence of Khartoum on accepting a UN peacekeeping force in the area, Security Council members referred suspected human rights abuses to the International Criminal Court. On February 27, 2007, Court Prosecutor Luis Moreno-Ocampo lodged 51 counts of war crimes and crimes against humanity against the former Sudanese state interior minister Ahmed Muhammad Harun and janjaweed leader Ali Muhammed Ali Abd-al-Rahman. The Sudanese government immediately rejected the ICC's indictments and JURISDICTION, and refused to turn over the suspects.

High on the priority list for the new UN Secretary-General, BAN KI-MOON, in January 2007 was the achievement of a peacekeeping operation in Sudan. Finally, in June the Sudanese government gave its approval to a joint AU-UN force, but insisted that the majority of peacekeepers be Africans. Ban Ki-Moon hoped to have a force of 26,000 peacekeepers in place by the end of the year.

See also BRAHIMI REPORT, CHAPTER VI, WAR CRIMES TRIBUNALS.

Further Reading: Flint, Julie, and Alex de Waal. *Darfur: A Short History of a Long War.* New York: Zed Books, 2006. International Crisis Group Policy Briefing. "Darfur's Fragile Peace Agreement," 20 June 2006, available at <www.crisisgroup.org/home/index>. Prunier, Gérard. *Darfur: The Ambiguous Genocide.* Ithaca, N.Y.: Cornell University Press, 2005. ———. "The Politics of Death in Darfur." *Current History* 105, no. 691 (May 2006): 195–203. Straus, Scott. "Darfur and the Genocide Debate." *Foreign Affairs* 84, no. 1 (January–February 2005): 123–33.

— *R. J. Griffiths*

Dayton Peace Accords

The death in 1980 of Marshall Josip Broz Tito, the post–World War II leader of the FORMER YUGOSLAVIA, foreshadowed a fractured future for the Balkan country, one in which BOSNIA and Herzegovina—one of the six original republics of the Socialist Federal Republic of Yugoslavia—would suffer miserably until the Dayton accords of 1995 formally ended a three-pronged civil war.

A disappointing economy and the end of the COLD WAR brought a splintering of Yugoslavia. DECLARATIONS of independence by Slovenia and Croatia in 1991 and Bosnia and Herzegovina in 1992 initiated a civil war, when the dominant Yugoslav republic Serbia attempted to thwart the secessions. As early as 1991 the UN SECURITY COUNCIL imposed an arms embargo on Yugoslavia and in early 1992 established the UNITED NATIONS PROTECTION FORCE (UNPROFOR), authorized by mid-year to protect the delivery of humanitarian aid in Bosnia. All three of the newly declared NATION-STATES were admitted to the United Nations in 1992. But, unlike the other seceding states, Bosnia and Herzegovina was not composed of a homogenous ethnic population. A plurality (44 percent) was Muslim, 31 percent Serb, and 17 percent Croat. Croatian president Franjo Tudjman and Serbian strongman SLOBODAN MILOŠEVIĆ set out to partition the area between themselves, all to the disadvantage of the Muslim population, led by Bosnian president Alija Izetbegović.

The siege of Sarajevo, Bosnia's capital, and the practice of "ethnic cleansing," carried out by Bosnian Serbs, shocked the world. By the middle of 1992, Serbs controlled more than 60 percent of the country, and the number of refugees and displaced persons mounted to more than 2 million, the largest refugee crisis in Europe since World War II. In May 1993, the Security Council declared Sarajevo and other Bosnian towns as "safe areas," but the devastating war continued. In August 1995 the North Atlantic Treaty Organization (NATO) intervened militarily following Bosnian Serb attacks on civilians in the UN enclaves at Srebrenica and Goradze—where they took UN peacekeepers hostage and systematically murdered civilian men and boys—after a brutal mortar attack on the marketplace in Sarajevo. NATO bombed Serb positions around the capital. A joint Bosnian Muslim and Croat military offensive followed NATO action and diminished Serbian areas of control.

In October, faced with military defeat, the government in Belgrade agreed to a U.S.–initiated peace conference in Dayton, Ohio, at Wright-Patterson Air Force Base. The following month, the three presidents—Izetbegović, Tudjman, and Milošević—agreed to end the fighting, to respect each other's SOVEREIGNTY and independence, and to accept a Muslim-Croat federation and a separate Serb entity (Republika Srpska) within the larger federation of Bosnia. Additional provisions of the accord, formally known as the General Framework Agreement for Peace in Bosnia and Herzegovina and officially signed in Paris on December 14, 1995, included promises by all sides to allow displaced persons to return to their homes, release all persons still detained, cooperate with the work of the INTERNATIONAL CRIMINAL TRIBUNAL FOR THE FORMER YUGOSLAVIA (ICTY), allow working journalists to perform their professional functions, resume commercial air travel between Bosnia and Herzegovina and the Federal Republic of Yugoslavia, and continue discussions toward the establishment of full diplomatic relations between Sarajevo and Belgrade at meetings of the Ministerial Contact Group (formed in 1994 by FRANCE, GERMANY, the RUSSIAN FEDERATION, the UNITED KINGDOM, and the UNITED STATES). NATO troops numbering 60,000 were to supervise the implementation of the agreement. Fighting abated, and in elections in September 1996, Izetbegović was chosen president of the new country. The same year, by act of the Security Council, the United Nations International Police Task Force became part of a larger UNITED NATIONS MISSION IN BOSNIA AND HERZEGOVINA (UNMIBH), which attempted to implement the Dayton accords, supervising the demilitarization of the region and organizing and administering elections. UNMIBH completed its mandate and terminated its activities on December 31, 2002.

The Dayton Accords placed primary responsibility for implementation of its terms in the hands of a High Representative. By 2006 five individuals had held the post: Carl Bildt (Sweden; December 1995–June 1997), Carlos Westendorp (Spain; June 1997–July 1999), Wolfgang Petritsch (Austria; August 1999–May 2002), Paddy Ashdown (United Kingdom; May 2002–January 2006), and Christian Schwarz-Schilling (Germany; took office on February 2006). The Office of High Representative (OHR) faced serious problems in Bosnia and Herzegovina after the turn of the century, including resettling refugees—by late summer 2000, UN officials reported that a record 25,000 refugees had returned to their homes since the start of that year—rebuilding the economy, establishing a working government, locating indicted war criminals who were still at large, and dealing with the fact of a rump Serbian entity within the country. Still, after Dayton there was, as of 2006, no further outbreak of ruinous civil war in the country. The government was also engaged in negotiations with the European Union on the possibility of MEMBERSHIP in the regional bloc, and with NATO on possible inclusion in the alliance's Partnership for Peace program, leading to full NATO membership. Progress in negotiations with NATO turned on continuing cooperation with the International Criminal Tribunal in The Hague. In particular, it required further efforts by the Republika Srpska to apprehend key war criminal indictees. Ten suspects were turned over to the ICTY in 2005, but the two most important indicted individuals, Ratko Mladić and Radovan Karadšić, remained at large.

See also INTERNATIONAL CRIMINAL COURT.

Further Reading: Holbrooke, Richard. *To End a War.* New York: Random House, 1998. General Framework Agreement for Peace in Bosnia and Herzegovina, signed in Paris, December 14, 1995: <www.ohr.int/dpa/default.asp?content_id=379>. Office of the High Representative in Bosnia and Herzegovina: <http://www.ohr.int/>.

Decade for Women   *See* UNITED NATIONS DECADE FOR WOMEN.

declaration

In the UNITED NATIONS SYSTEM, *declaration* is a term applied to legal statements made by governments or groups of governments. In the United Nations it typically refers to unanimously agreed upon statements, in contrast to RESOLUTIONS, which are adopted usually by a majority of votes. That is, a declaration is rather like a public proclamation, much in the manner of the U.S. Declaration of Independence (1776), or FRANCE's Declaration of the Rights of Man and the Citizen (1789). Nearly all UN-sponsored WORLD CONFERENCES conclude with the publication of a declaration of agreed principles, such as the RIO DECLARATION issued at the conclusion of the Earth Summit in 1992.

Declaration by United Nations

The UNITED STATES, the UNITED KINGDOM, CHINA, and the Soviet Union signed the DECLARATION by United Nations in Washington on January 1, 1942. The next day 22 other nations at war with the Axis powers signed the declaration. The decision to put the "Big Four" ahead of the lesser states in the signatory process reflected President FRANK-

LIN ROOSEVELT's belief that the great powers would have a unique responsibility for the war effort and the postwar peace. This principle guided future U.S. planning for the United Nations organization. Secretary of state CORDELL HULL and his aides in the U.S. State Department initially had suggested this statement, and when British prime minister WINSTON CHURCHILL arrived in Washington in late December, he and Roosevelt immediately agreed, making numerous changes in the draft. Hull insisted that Russia and China be invited to serve as joint sponsors with the United States and Great Britain. Roosevelt himself thought of the name "United Nations."

The declaration created a wartime alliance of "United Nations," each promising to wage war against the Axis powers with all of its resources and not to sign a separate peace. The signatories accepted the principles of the ATLANTIC CHARTER as a "common program of purposes," and promised "to defend life, liberty, independence and religious freedom, and to preserve HUMAN RIGHTS and justice in their own lands as well as in other lands." Many supporters of the subsequent 1945 United Nations CHARTER were later disappointed when this LANGUAGE was left out of the founding document. The formal expression of the world community's commitment to these values would be left to the promulgation of the UNIVERSAL DECLARATION OF HUMAN RIGHTS. A final clause in the declaration permitted other countries that entered the war in the future to join the United Nations. Eventually eight other nations signed the document.

Despite the jubilation of internationalists over the declaration by United Nations, there was also disappointment at the neglect to mention a postwar international organization. Roosevelt remained cool to the idea of such an organization. He made reference only to his hopes for a just postwar peace based on the Four Freedoms and the Atlantic Charter. Nevertheless, the declaration introduced the term "United Nations" to the American public and it slowly came to represent a conception of world organization.

See also ARTICLE 3 OF THE UNITED NATIONS CHARTER (Appendix A).

Further Reading: Divine, Robert A. *Second Chance: The Triumph of Internationalism in America during World War II.* New York: Atheneum, 1967. Kimball, Warren F. *The Juggler: Franklin Roosevelt as Wartime Statesman.* Princeton, N.J.: Princeton University Press, 1991. Sherwood, Robert. *Roosevelt and Hopkins: An Intimate Portrait.* New York: Harper, 1948.

— *E. M. Clauss*

Declaration on the Elimination of Violence against Women

On December 20, 1993, the GENERAL ASSEMBLY adopted the Declaration on the Elimination of Violence against Women.

The DECLARATION defined "violence against women" as any act of gender-specific brutality that causes, or is likely to result in physical, sexual, or psychological injury or torment. Threats, coercion, or arbitrary denial of freedom in private or public qualified as a violation of the declaration. Particular, but not exclusive, areas denoting violence included: physical, sexual, or psychological violence within the family, the general community, or that carried out by a state.

The declaration also provided a mandate for a SPECIAL RAPPORTEUR on violence against WOMEN. In 1994, the Office of the UN HIGH COMMISSIONER FOR HUMAN RIGHTS appointed Ms. Radhika Coomaraswamy of Sri Lanka to the post and authorized her to collect and analyze data and make recommendations regarding the causes for and the elimination of violence against women. At the 57th session of the COMMISSION ON HUMAN RIGHTS in April 2001, the Special Rapporteur submitted her first report, focusing on violence against women perpetrated and/or condoned by the state during times of armed conflict. She also presented a report of her fall 2000 mission to Bangladesh, Nepal, and India to investigate the issue of trafficking of women and girls, and a further report detailing country-by-country reviews of allegations and appeals that had been forwarded to specific governments, and the replies of those governments. In January 2003 the special rapporteur submitted a follow-up report that noted the impact of judicial tribunals on violence against women. She expressed her concern that neither the INTERNATIONAL CRIMINAL COURT nor the existing WAR CRIMES TRIBUNALS provided sufficient protections for the rights of female victims. Ms. Coomaraswamy was succeeded by Dr. Yakin Ertürk of Turkey in August 2003.

The UN effort to meet the mandates of the declaration has included activities by nearly all of the organization's offices, agencies and PROGRAMMES. The SECRETARIAT's Division for the Advancement of Women (DAW) has provided much of the leadership. In May 2005, working with the UN OFFICE ON DRUGS AND CRIME, DAW produced a lengthy list of "good practices" for eliminating violence against women. The report of a group of experts assembled by DAW came in response to a request from the General Assembly in 2003. DAW recommended that states end the impunity that often exists in national judicial systems for violence against women, that women themselves be empowered within their political systems, that alternative dispute resolution processes be implemented in societies so as to assure "restorative justice," and that male control over female sexuality be delegitimatized in states by criminalizing such practices as marital rape and honor killing. The panel also called for compensation to women who had been subjected to violence.

See also COMMISSION ON THE STATUS OF WOMEN, CONVENTION ON THE ELIMINATION OF ALL FORMS OF DISCRIMINATION AGAINST WOMEN, INTERNATIONAL DAY FOR THE ELIMINATION OF VIOLENCE AGAINST WOMEN, WORLD CONFERENCES ON WOMEN.

Further Reading: Bunch, Charlotte, and Niamh Reilly. *Demanding Accountability: The Global Campaign and Vienna Tribunal for Women's Human Rights.* New Brunswick, N.J.: Center for Women's Global Leadership, 1994. Reilly, Niamh, ed. *Testimonies of the Global Tribunal on Violations of Women's Human Rights at the United Nations World Conference on Human Rights, Vienna, June 1993.* New Brunswick, N.J.: Center for Women's Global Leadership, 1994. *Report of the United Nations Development Fund for Women on the Elimination of Violence against Women.* Economic and Social Council, E/CN.6/2006/l0, December 20, 2005. Spindel, Cheywa, Elisa Levy, and Melissa Connor. *With an End in Sight: Strategies from the UNIFEM Trust Fund to Eliminate Violence against Women.* New York: United Nations Development Fund for Women, 2000. Declaration Web site: <www.unhchr.ch/huridocda/huridoca.nsf/(Symbol)/A.RES.48.104.En?Opendocument>. UN Secretariat Division for the Advancement of Women Web site: <www.un.org/womenwatch/daw/.>.

Declaration on the Granting of Independence to Colonial Countries and Peoples

On December 14, 1960, the UN GENERAL ASSEMBLY adopted the Declaration on the Granting of Independence to Colonial Countries and Peoples, urging a faster pace in the process of decolonization. The Asian and African states that had only recently become members of the United Nations believed that neither the TRUSTEESHIP COUNCIL nor the United Nations as a whole was doing enough to encourage independence. Their impatience with the colonial powers was reflected in the declaration's demand that independence be granted even where there was an "inadequacy of political, economic, social or educational preparedness." The emerging majority in the General Assembly from the newly independent states of the developing world used the DECLARATION to reenforce the principle of self-determination as a central tenet of the UN CHARTER. The text of the declaration follows.

The General Assembly,

Mindful of the determination proclaimed by the peoples of the world in the Charter of the United Nations to reaffirm faith in fundamental HUMAN RIGHTS, in the dignity and worth of the human person, in the equal rights of men and WOMEN and of nations large and small and to promote social progress and better standards of life in larger freedom,

Conscious of the need for the creation of conditions of stability and well-being and peaceful and friendly relations based on respect for the principles of equal rights and self-determination of all peoples, and of universal respect for, and observance of, human rights and fundamental freedoms for all without distinction as to race, sex, language or religion,

Recognizing the passionate yearning for freedom in all dependent peoples and the decisive role of such peoples in the attainment of their independence,

Aware of the increasing conflicts resulting from the denial of or impediments in the way of the freedom of such peoples, which constitute a serious threat to world peace,

Considering the important role of the United Nations in assisting the movement for independence in Trust and NON-SELF-GOVERNING TERRITORIES,

Recognizing that the peoples of the world ardently desire the end of colonialism in all its manifestations,

Convinced that the continued existence of colonialism prevents the development of international economic cooperation, impedes the social, cultural and economic DEVELOPMENT of dependent peoples and militates against the United Nations ideal of universal peace,

Affirming that peoples may, for their own ends, freely dispose of their natural wealth and resources without prejudice to any obligations arising out of international economic cooperation, based upon the principle of mutual benefit, and INTERNATIONAL LAW,

Believing that the process of liberation is irresistible and irreversible and that, in order to avoid serious crises, an end must be put to colonialism and all practices of segregation and discrimination associated therewith,

Welcoming the emergence in recent years of a large number of dependent territories into freedom and independence, and recognizing the increasingly powerful trends towards freedom in such territories which have not yet attained independence,

Convinced that all peoples have an inalienable right to complete freedom, the exercise of their SOVEREIGNTY and the integrity of their national territory,

Solemnly proclaims the necessity of bringing to a speedy and unconditional end colonialism in all its forms and manifestations;

And to this end

Declares that:

1. The subjection of peoples to alien subjugation, domination and exploitation constitutes a denial of fundamental human rights, is contrary to the Charter of the United Nations and is an impediment to the promotion of world peace and cooperation.

2. All peoples have the right to self-determination; by virtue of that right they freely determine their political status and freely pursue their economic, social and cultural development.

3. Inadequacy of political, economic, social or educational preparedness should never serve as a pretext for delaying independence.

4. All armed action or repressive measures of all kinds directed against dependent peoples shall cease in order to enable them to exercise peacefully and freely their

right to complete independence, and the integrity of their national territory shall be respected.

5. Immediate steps shall be taken, in Trust and Non-Self-Governing Territories or all other territories which have not yet attained independence, to transfer all powers to the peoples of those territories, without any conditions or reservations, in accordance with their freely expressed will and desire, without any distinction as to race, creed or colour, in order to enable them to enjoy complete independence and freedom.

6. Any attempt aimed at the partial or total disruption of the national unity and the territorial integrity of a country is incompatible with the purposes and principles of the Charter of the United Nations.

7. All States shall observe faithfully and strictly the provisions of the Charter of the United Nations, the UNIVERSAL DECLARATION OF HUMAN RIGHTS and the present Declaration on the basis of equality, non-interference in the internal affairs of all States, and respect for the sovereign rights of all peoples and their territorial integrity.

Declaration on the Right to Development

Adopted by the GENERAL ASSEMBLY in RESOLUTION 128 of December 4, 1986, the Declaration on the Right to Development proclaimed DEVELOPMENT "an inalienable HUMAN RIGHT by virtue of which each person and all peoples are entitled to participate in, contribute to and enjoy economic, social, cultural and political development in which all human rights and fundamental freedoms can be fully realized." The Assembly's action came five years after the adoption of the African Charter of Human and Peoples' Rights, also known as the Banjul Charter, which was the first international document to assert the right. Several WORLD CONFERENCES subsequently reaffirmed the principle in their final documents. Among them the RIO DECLARATION (Principle 3) of the 1992 Earth Summit, the 1993 Vienna DECLARATION and Programme of Action at the WORLD CONFERENCE ON HUMAN RIGHTS, the Declaration of the Third UN CONFERENCE ON THE LEAST DEVELOPED COUNTRIES in 2001, and the 2005 WORLD SUMMIT Outcome were the most important.

Ten years after its promulgation, the General Assembly, believing that little progress had been made to implement the principles contained in the declaration, passed Resolution 184 in 1996. The Assembly called upon the UN HIGH COMMISSIONER FOR HUMAN RIGHTS (UNHCHR) to promote the right, and also urged the COMMISSION ON HUMAN RIGHTS, the Centre for Human Rights, and the REGIONAL ECONOMIC COMMISSIONS to do the same. The Commission on Human Rights subsequently created the open-ended Working Group on the Right to Development, which held its seventh session in January 2006. The Working Group was charged with monitoring progress on the implementation of the right, and reviewing reports submitted by states and international and

NON-GOVERNMENTAL ORGANIZATIONS. In its December 2005 report to the ECONOMIC AND SOCIAL COUNCIL, UNHCHR noted its efforts to sustain the Working Group, its negotiations with the WORLD TRADE ORGANIZATION to promoted development from a "rights-based" approach, and its promotion of democracy, good governance, and WOMEN's empowerment as essential components of the right to development.

See also APPENDIX G, SECOND COMMITTEE OF THE GENERAL ASSEMBLY.

Declaration on the Rights of the Child

On November 20, 1959, the UN GENERAL ASSEMBLY adopted 10 principles, dedicated to the well-being of every child "without distinction or discrimination." The Assembly's DECLARATION was unusually specific concerning the policies NATION-STATES should implement on behalf of their young people. In subsequent years the United Nations regularly focused world attention on the plight of children in many parts of the world. It declared 1979 the International Year of the Child, directed the UNITED NATIONS CHILDREN'S FUND (UNICEF), the institution's lead agency on children's issues, to prepare a CONVENTION on the Rights of the Child, and urged relevant SPECIALIZED AGENCIES to develop assistance programs for children. The text of the declaration follows.

Principle 1
The child shall enjoy all the rights set forth in this Declaration. Every child, without any exception whatsoever, shall be entitled to these rights, without distinction or discrimination on account of race, colour, sex, LANGUAGE, religion, political or other opinion, national or social origin, property, birth or other status, whether of himself or of his family.

Principle 2
The child shall enjoy special protection, and shall be given opportunities and facilities, by law and by other means, to enable him to develop physically, mentally, morally, spiritually and socially in a healthy and normal manner and in conditions of freedom and dignity. In the enactment of laws for this purpose, the best interests of the child shall be the paramount considerations.

Principle 3
The child shall be entitled from his birth to a name and a nationality.

Principle 4
The child shall enjoy the benefits of social security. He shall be entitled to grow and develop in health; to this end, special care and protection shall be provided both to him and to his mother, including adequate pre-natal and post-natal care. The child shall have the right to adequate nutrition, housing, recreation and medical services.

Principle 5

The child who is physically, mentally or socially handicapped shall be given the special treatment, education and care required by his particular condition.

Principle 6

The child, for the full and harmonious development of his personality, needs love and understanding. He shall, wherever possible, grow up in the care and under the responsibility of his parents, and, in any case, in an atmosphere of affection and of moral and material security; a child of tender years shall not, save in exceptional circumstances, be separated from his mother. Society and the public authorities shall have the duty to extend particular care to children without a family and to those without adequate means of support. Payment of State and other assistance towards the maintenance of children of large families is desirable.

Principle 7

The child is entitled to receive education, which shall be free and compulsory, at least in the elementary stages. He shall be given an education which will promote his general culture, and enable him, on a basis of equal opportunity, to develop his abilities, his individual judgement, and his sense of moral and social responsibility, and to become a useful member of society.

The best interests of the child shall be the guiding principle of those responsible for his education and guidance; that responsibility lies in the first place with his parents.

The child shall have full opportunity for play and recreation, which should be directed to the same purposes as education; society and the public authorities shall endeavour to promote the enjoyment of this right.

Principle 8

The child shall in all circumstances be among the first to receive protection and relief.

Principle 9

The child shall be protected against all forms of neglect, cruelty and exploitation. He shall not be the subject of traffic, in any form.

The child shall not be admitted to employment before an appropriate minimum age; he shall in no case be caused or permitted to engage in any occupation or employment which would prejudice his health or education, or interfere with his physical, mental or moral development.

Principle 10

The child shall be protected from practices which may foster racial, religious and any other form of discrimination. He shall be brought up in a spirit of understanding, tolerance, friendship among peoples, peace and universal brotherhood, and in full consciousness that his energy and talents should be devoted to the service of his fellow men.

The declaration initiated a 30-year process that culminated in the convocation of a WORLD SUMMIT on Children and the adoption of the Convention on the Rights of the Child in 1990 and the subsequent adoption at the 2000 MILLENNIUM SUMMIT of several MILLENNIUM DEVELOPMENT GOALS (MDGs) dedicated to improving children's living conditions in the developing world. MDG #2 called for the achievement of universal primary education for all children by 2015. By that same year the world community hoped to reduce mortality for children under the age of five by two-thirds (MDG #4). In 2002 the General Assembly convened a SPECIAL SESSION on Children, attended by more than 7,000 participants, to review progress made since the initial declaration. The session adopted 21 specific goals and targets to aid children over the succeeding decade.

Further Reading: UN Department of Public Information. *Basic Facts about the United Nations.* New York: United Nations, 2004. Web site for UN activities related to children: <www.un.org/issues/m-child.html>.

decolonization   *See* NATIONAL LIBERATION.

democratization

Although the UN CHARTER references HUMAN RIGHTS, equality, individual rights for both men and WOMEN, popular participation in society, and other characteristics common to democratic life, the document does not include the word "democracy." Other early UN documents are also laconic on the role of the world body in the promotion of democratic political systems. For example, the UNIVERSAL DECLARATION OF HUMAN RIGHTS only once mentions "democratic society," and then as an allusion to the types of political rights citizens should have in their national political systems. Democracy, of course, is not precisely synonymous with "human rights" or "equality." Most simply, it refers to rule by a majority (50 percent plus one) of a given population. Thus, majority rule could be repressive to a minority or to an individual, as several classic political philosophers have pointed out. Nonetheless, in the modern world, democracy is typically associated with a society that meets certain qualifications, including the assurance of human rights, regular and competitive elections, sensible administration of justice, and more.

As a universal international organization made up of all "peace-loving nations," the United Nations during its first 40 years of existence had a MEMBERSHIP of NATION-STATES with diverse political ideologies. The COLD WAR, which immersed the world body in the struggle between socialist and Western capitalist systems, and the addition of many nondemocratic regimes from the developing world eliminated any possibility of the UN promoting a particular form of governance.

However, the end of the cold war in the 1980s and the subsequent "third wave" of democratic revolutions in the 20th century meant that UN membership shifted dramatically in its composition, and by 1990 democratic governments held a majority in the United Nations. This development came at a time when the UN SECURITY COUNCIL was expanding significantly UN PEACEKEEPING missions in conflict areas. These new missions moved beyond separating combatants and monitoring truces—as earlier peacekeeping had been limited to—with the goal of reconstructing domestic governments and civil societies. With the first efforts at "NATION-BUILDING" being undertaken during SECRETARY-GENERAL JAVIER PÉREZ DE CUÉLLAR's tenure, the United Nations sought to introduce democratic practices. These included regular elections, human rights protections, transparent government and accountability, the rule of law, established court systems, popular participation, training for national and local legislators and executives, and the creation of civil society organizations such as media uncontrolled by government, political parties, and private interest groups. The Western democratic model became the initial template for UN democratization efforts, as the GENERAL ASSEMBLY passed several "election resolutions" (Res. 43/157, December 8, 1988; Res. 44/146, December 15, 1989; Res. 52/129, December 12, 1997) and "democracy resolutions" (Res. 50/133, December 20, 1995; Res. 51/31, December 6, 1996, Res. 52/18, November 21, 1997) between 1988 and 1998.

The first UN democratization mission in a post-conflict setting was initiated in NAMIBIA in 1989. The former mandate territory controlled by South AFRICA gained the right to SELF-DETERMINATION as the region became a zone of decreasing competition between the superpowers. Under authorizing RESOLUTIONS from the Security Council the United Nations took full administrative control of Namibia for the purpose of orchestrating a constitutional assembly, presiding over elections, and transferring power to an independent government. The Council established the United Nations Transition Assistance Group (UNTAG) to supervise the process. On March 21, 1990, Namibia achieved full independence as a democratic state.

The democratization process was replicated in two Latin American states—EL SALVADOR and GUATEMALA—in the early 1990s. Unlike Namibia, these two countries had long-standing histories as sovereign nation-states. However, each had experienced violent civil wars. In both cases UN missions facilitated the reintegration of guerrilla forces into the democratic process. The United Nations assisted with elections and civil society formation in order that forces previously opposed to the established government could express their opposition in democratic ways, rather than returning to violent methods.

During Secretary-General Pérez de Cuéllar's term, the most difficult democratization experiment came in CAMBODIA. The nation had been wracked with internal conflict, totalitarian dictatorship, and foreign intervention at one time or another since the end of the Vietnam War in the 1970s. In August 1990, the Security Council created the UNITED NATIONS TRANSITIONAL AUTHORITY IN CAMBODIA (UNTAC). In addition to seeking the reconciliation of the warring parties, UNTAC managed the daily administration of the Cambodian government, provided domestic social services, and administered the first round of elections in 1993. UN diplomats hammered together a power-sharing government, but, unfortunately it did not last. The leadership was ousted in a coup in 1997, and over the next nine years new elections were administered by the UN on several occasions, and UN agencies sought to address human rights violations past and present.

Pérez de Cuéllar's successor as Secretary-General, BOUTROS BOUTROS-GHALI, made the democratization of "states at risk" a hallmark of his tenure. In June 1992, Boutros-Ghali outlined an ambitious program for UN-sponsored democratic nation-building in a report entitled *An AGENDA FOR PEACE*, followed four years later by *An Agenda for Democratization*. The first of these reports came at the request of the UN Security Council. In the wake of the successful GULF WAR, the PERMANENT MEMBERS convened the first-ever heads of government Council meeting, and asked Boutros-Ghali to draft recommendations on ways the UN could address the new challenges wrought by ethnic, religious, and sectarian conflicts arising from the new post–cold war circumstances. The Secretary-General argued for policies that promoted democracy at both the national and the international levels. Not only would world peace be enhanced by instilling democracy in weak states and former autocratic societies, but a culture of democracy needed to be developed internationally.

The UN's democratic nation-building initiatives necessarily involve subsidiary bodies and SPECIALIZED AGENCIES. With the growing acceptance of democratization as the primary strategy for nation-building in conflict zones or weak states, the General Assembly created the Electoral Assistance Division (EAD) in the UN SECRETARIAT in 1992 to assist with national and municipal elections. Later made part of the Department of Political Affairs, EAD received requests for electoral assistance from more than 140 countries by 2005, and provided help in 91 cases, including troubled places such as MOZAMBIQUE, BOSNIA, Palestine, and ANGOLA. Its most serious challenge may have been in 2006 in CONGO, where it worked with the existing peacekeeping mission to hold the first legitimate, free, and fair elections in 40 years. The elections occurred even as the eastern part of the country remained in rebellion.

The division coordinates its activities with the other agencies and NON-GOVERNMENTAL ORGANIZATIONS operating in the country. The United Nations also encourages REGIONAL ECONOMIC COMMISIONS and REGIONAL ORGANIZATIONS to assist in sustaining stable democracies. Also central to the UN democracy promotion is the UN HIGH COMMISSIONER FOR HUMAN RIGHTS in Geneva.

Additionally, the UN DEVELOPMENT PROGRAMME (UNDP) and the WORLD BANK direct resources toward improved governance STRUCTURES in poor countries. By 2000, one-third of the UNDP BUDGET went toward democracy promotion. These funds are administered through the Division of Management, Development, and Governance, which spends close to $1 billion annually on democratic governance projects. In recent years these projects have included national elections in SIERRA LEONE, public participation in Nigeria, and the creation of a judicial commission in AFGHANISTAN to restore the country's judicial system.

The Department of Political Affairs (DPA), in addition to housing the elections unit, holds international conferences on a regular basis for new and restored democracies (ICNRD). By 2006, DPA had convened six of these meetings on a regional basis. The latest conference met in Doha, Qatar, the first Arab state to host an ICNRD, from October 30 to November 2 of that year. The first such conference, held in 1988, adopted the Manila DECLARATION, which linked democratization with the maintenance of international peace and DEVELOPMENT. This theme became increasingly central to UN democracy promotion initiatives. Seeing the Western conception of democracy as too limited, because it emphasized procedural and representational aspects of democracy almost to the exclusion of other necessary factors, future ICNRDs endorsed a comprehensive approach that included economic and social transformation as well. The fourth conference, which convened in December 2000, in Cotonou, Benin, attracted 110 government delegations, demonstrating the widening global trend to promote democratization. An innovation at the fifth conference, held in Ulaanbaatar, Mongolia, was the convening of a simultaneous Parliamentary Forum, attended by 120 participants from 47 countries. A civil society forum also materialized with 240 participants from 64 nations.

These conferences were important to the evolution in the understanding of democratization by UN authorities. Going beyond Lockean conceptions that defined democracy largely in terms of how political systems are structured and work, and how citizens are associated with the state, the UN definition incorporated an international component that allowed intervention within the state to protect democratic rights and an assertion that economic development, social equality, and groups must be promoted in order to assure democratic stability.

KOFI ANNAN, the UN's seventh Secretary-General, was a strong advocate of this approach to democratization. Agreeing with students of 18th century-German philosopher Immanuel Kant that democratic states do not go to war with each other, Annan strongly endorsed the promotion of democracy as an important element in securing international peace. The Secretary-General also promoted the concept of "personal sovereignty," which he argued required intervention in nondemocratic states that do not protect the rights of their citizens. Defending the new era of nation-building, he made the case that "surely no legal principle—not even [state] sovereignty—can ever shield crimes against humanity." There is a "moral duty" for the United Nations to intervene on behalf of the individual. At the time of the Millennium Summit in 2000 the Secretary-General asserted that "Even though the United Nations is an organization of states . . . the Charter is written in the name of 'We the peoples.' It reaffirms the dignity and worth of the human person, respect for human rights and the equal rights of men and women, and a commitment to social progress . . . in freedom from want and fear alike." In his UN REFORM report of April, 2005, entitled *IN LARGER FREEDOM,* Annan noted that the promotion of democracy is essential to the world's security agenda and to social and economic development.

Given democracy promotion's importance, Annan contended the United Nations should not limit its role to norm creation, or to providing legitimacy for international missions intruding in nondemocratic states. In his report, he called for practical steps that would speed the process of democratization. He proposed the establishment of a Democracy FUND to assist countries making the transition to democratic politics. He also recommended a number of reforms that would coordinate better UN agencies and programs working on democratization, particularly the efforts of UNDP, EAD. and DPA.

The Millennium Summit proved a watershed in the UN's redefinition of democracy promotion. The summit's declaration endorsed a combination of development, human rights, and democratization targets. Member governments proclaimed "We shall spare no effort to promote democracy and strengthen the rule of law, as well as respect . . . all internationally recognized human rights and fundamental freedoms, . . . to strengthen the capacity of all our countries to implement the principles and practices of democracy and respect for human rights, including minority rights . . . [and] to work collectively for more inclusive political processes, allowing genuine participation by all citizens in all our countries."

The late SERGIO VIEIRO DE MELLO, former UN High Commissioner for Human Rights, described the UN effort to create "holistic democracy" to the COMMISSION ON HUMAN RIGHTS in April 2003. He defined democracy as "normatively grounded," and inclusive of both procedural and substantive rights. According to Vieiro de Mello, democracy in UN parlance is encapsulated in the Universal Declaration of Human Rights (1948), and the International Covenants on Political and Civil Rights and on Economic, Social and Cultural Rights (1966), and thus encompasses "formal institutions and informal processes, majorities and minorities, males and females, governments and civil society, the political and economic, the national and international . . . the interdependence of human rights and the rights they defend . . . the principle and right of self-determination . . . as well as the rights to an adequate standard of living and to education."

See also THEMATIC DIPLOMACY, UNITED NATIONS CONFERENCES ON THE LEAST DEVELOPED COUNTRIES, UNITED NATIONS INTERIM ADMINISTRATION MISSION FOR KOSOVO.

Further Reading: Annan, Kofi A. "Democracy as an International Issue." *Global Governance* 8, no. 2 (April–June 2002): 135–42. Boutros-Ghali, Boutros. *An Agenda for Democratization.* New York: United Nations, 1996. Brown, Mark Malloch. "Democratic Governance: Toward a Framework for Sustainable Peace." *Global Governance* 9, no. 2 (April–June 2003): 141–46. Dobbins, James, Seth G. Jones, Keith Crane, Andrew Rathmell, Brett Steele, and Richard Teltschik. *The UN's Role in Nation-Building: From the Congo to Iraq.* Santa Monica, Calif.: RAND Corporation, 2004. Fox, Gregory H., and Brad R. Roth, eds. *Democratic Governance and International Law.* Cambridge: Cambridge University Press, 2000. Joyner, Christopher C. "The United Nations: Strengthening an International Norm." In *Exporting Democracy: Rhetoric vs. Reality,* edited by Peter J. Schraeder, 147–72. Boulder, Colo.: Lynne Rienner, 2002. Newman, Edward, and Ronald Rich. *The UN Role in Promoting Democracy: Between Ideals and Reality.* Tokyo: United Nations University Press, 2004. Report of the High Commissioner for Human Rights. "Civil and Political Rights: Continuing Dialogue on Measures to Promote and Consolidate Democracy," Commission on Human Rights, E/CN.4/2003/59.

Department for Disarmament Affairs (DDA)

After a hiatus of six years the Department for Disarmament Affairs was reestablished in 1998 on the recommendation of the GENERAL ASSEMBLY (GA) as one of the UN SECRETARIAT's major departments. It had earlier existed (1982-92) as a product of the Assembly's Second SPECIAL SESSION ON DISARMAMENT. Headed by UNDER SECRETARY-GENERAL Nobuaki Tanaka from JAPAN, in 2006 DDA had five branches: WEAPONS OF MASS DESTRUCTION (WMD), Conventional Arms including Practical DISARMAMENT Measures (CAB), Regional Disarmament (RDB), Monitoring, Database and Information (MDI), and CONFERENCE ON DISARMAMENT (CD). Secretariat and Conference Support are located in Geneva. With the overall goal of promoting global norms of disarmament, DDA branches provide informational and administrative assistance to the GA's FIRST COMMITTEE, the Conference on Disarmament, the DISARMAMENT COMMISSION, the UN Standing Advisory Committee on Security Questions in Central AFRICA, the SECRETARY-GENERAL's Advisory Board on Disarmament Matters, and other UN disarmament bodies and conferences. The department also promotes public edu-

cation on disarmament issues by publishing the *Disarmament Yearbook, Disarmament Notes,* and a quarterly *DDA Update,* and by working closely with UNIDIR (UNITED NATIONS INSTITUTE FOR DISARMAMENT RESEARCH).

Following its reestablishment, the Department for Disarmament Affairs emphasized certain issues for international negotiation and public debate. Among them were transparency and openness in military affairs, confidence-building measures, disarmament verification, regional disarmament, curbs on the flow of small arms and arms trafficking, and containing the proliferation of WEAPONS OF MASS DESTRUCTION. This last topic led DDA to work closely with the ORGANISATION FOR THE PROHIBITION OF CHEMICAL WEAPONS, the INTERNATIONAL ATOMIC ENERGY AGENCY, and the Preparatory Committee of the COMPREHENSIVE TEST BAN TREATY Organization. Its efforts to slow regional arms buildups were bolstered by the creation of UN Regional Centres for Peace and Disarmament in Africa, Asia and the Pacific, and LATIN AMERICA, which DDA oversaw and coordinated.

At the turn of the century DDA had identified three "emerging" issues it intended to address in its work: Disarmament and DEVELOPMENT, Gender Perspectives on Disarmament, and Disarmament Education. As part of SECRETARY-GENERAL KOFI ANNAN's Steering Group on Disarmament and Development, DDA assisted in the preparation of the Secretary-General's report on the subject and coordinated its activities with other agencies involved in aspects of the issue. Given that gender and disarmament linkages were not readily apparent, DDA launched a series of research projects including "Gender Perspectives on Weapons of Mass Destruction," "Gender Perspectives on Small Arms," and "Gender Perspectives on LAND MINES." Finally, it provided administrative support for a GA-authorized "United Nations Study on Disarmament and Non-Proliferation Education." To be carried out by a panel of 10 governmental experts from Egypt, Hungary, INDIA, JAPAN, Mexico, New Zealand, Peru, Poland, Senegal, and Sweden, the study was scheduled to be the basis of a report by Secretary-General Annan to the General Assembly in 2002. The first two working sessions of the 10-member group were organized by DDA in August 2001.

An important assignment for the department is the maintenance of the Register of Conventional Arms. Each year governments report on arms transfers to other states. This responsibility has become more important as the world has become increasingly concerned about the movement of small arms and light weapons (SALW). Particularly with the failure of the UN Review Conference on the illicit trade in these WEAPONS, held in June 2006, the monitoring of arms flows by the department took on new urgency.

Further Reading: DDA Web site: <http://disarmament.un.org/dda.htm>. *Disarmament Notes* Web site: <http://disarmament.un.org/ddanotes/ddanotes1.pdf>.

Department of Economic and Social Affairs (DESA)

One of the departments of the UN SECRETARIAT, DESA provides administrative services for the many commissions and committees of the ECONOMIC AND SOCIAL COUNCIL (ECOSOC). Created as a consolidation of three former departments, DESA is directed by an UNDER SECRETARY-GENERAL—in 2006, Mr. José Antonio Ocampo of Colombia—who also chairs the Secretariat's Executive Committee on Economic and Social Affairs, which brings together 18 UN agencies working in the field. In addition to its administrative services the department has a number of normative, policy analysis, and advisory duties that its carries out in its 11 divisions.

Central to the work of the department since 2000 has been the promotion of the MILLENNIUM DEVELOPMENT GOALS set at that year's MILLENNIUM SUMMIT. World leaders established several social and economic goals—eradicating extreme poverty and hunger, achieving universal primary education, promoting gender equality and empowering WOMEN, reducing child mortality, improving maternal health, and combating HIV/AIDS—through a set of measurable targets to be achieved by the year 2015. DESA has directed much of the effort to cut in half the proportion of those who earn less than a dollar a day; to achieve universal primary education; to eliminate gender disparity in education; and to reduce child mortality.

Entering the new millennium, the Department of Economic and Social Affairs sought to promote SUSTAINABLE DEVELOPMENT, with a particular emphasis on Africa, small island developing states, and North-South cooperation. As the focal point for UN SECRETARY-GENERAL KOFI ANNAN's promotion of DEVELOPMENT in Africa, DESA housed the Office of the Special Coordinator for Africa and the LEAST DEVELOPED COUNTRIES (OSCAL) until it was merged into the Office of the Special Adviser on Africa in 2003. DESA emphasizes gender-related issues, ENVIRONMENT, population effects, and social dimensions of development. In all of these areas the department works to translate the Plans of Action and Final DECLARATIONS of recent WORLD CONFERENCES into practical steps that governments could take to meet conference goals. This requires working closely with SPECIALIZED AGENCIES and bodies created by UN conferences, as well as with the Second and THIRD COMMITTEES OF THE GENERAL ASSEMBLY, and ECOSOC and its commissions.

Particularly under Annan's REFORM program, DESA has developed extensive coordination and support functions. As the lead agency of one of Annan's four thematic executive committees, the Executive Committee on Economic and Social Affairs, DESA promotes coherence and efficiency in the work of the committee's members. The 2005 WORLD SUMMIT called for greater coherence in the UN SYSTEM. To this end DESA organized the executive committee into 11 thematic clusters bringing together program directors with thematically similar missions. The Executive Committee

membership includes the United Nations OFFICE FOR DRUGS AND CRIME (UNODC), the UNITED NATIONS DEVELOPMENT PROGRAMME (UNDP), the UN regional economic commissions, HABITAT, the UNITED NATIONS CONFERENCE ON TRADE AND DEVELOPMENT (UNCTAD), UNITED NATIONS UNIVERSITY (UNU), the UNITED NATIONS RESEARCH INSTITUTE FOR SOCIAL DEVELOPMENT (UNRISD), the United Nations INTERNATIONAL RESEARCH AND TRAINING INSTITUTE FOR THE ADVANCEMENT OF WOMEN (INSTRAW), the UNITED NATIONS ENVIRONMENT PROGRAMME (UNEP), the Office of the Special Adviser on Africa (OSAA), the UNITED NATIONS INSTITUTE FOR TRAINING AND RESEARCH (UNITAR), the Office of the High Representative for the Least Developed Countries, Landlocked Developing Countries, and Small Island Developing States (OHRLLS), and the Office of the UN HIGH COMMISSIONER FOR HUMAN RIGHTS (UNHCHR). Additionally, DESA's Division for Public Economics and Public Administration manages the UN's Programme in Public Administration and Finance. Its Division for Social Policy and Development provides guidance to ECOSOC's COMMISSION FOR SOCIAL DEVELOPMENT (CSocD). By 2001, the division had also convened four sessions of the World Youth Forum to enhance ties between youth NON-GOVERNMENTAL ORGANIZATIONS (NGOs) and youth-related UN bodies. Its Population Division provides the secretariat for the COMMISSION ON POPULATION AND DEVELOPMENT, undertaking research studies and preparing public reports on the topic. Its Division for the Advancement of WOMEN (DAW) provides administrative support for the COMMITTEE ON THE ELIMINATION OF DISCRIMINATION AGAINST WOMEN (CEDAW); its Division for Sustainable Development provides the secretariat for the COMMISSION ON SUSTAINABLE DEVELOPMENT (CSD), and supplies data and policy recommendations to CSD; and its Division for ECOSOC Support and Coordination provides system-wide guidance on ECOSOC activities, oversight and coordination of subsidiary bodies, and support for the NGOs that have CONSULTATIVE STATUS with the Council.

DESA has an independent research and policy analysis function that provides extensive data and reports to the world community, assisting governments and NGOs engaged in the development process. Among its more important publications is the United Nations *WORLD ECONOMIC AND SOCIAL SURVEY,* published annually by its Division for Development Policy Analysis. The *Survey* analyzes topical global economic issues and provides UN forecasts on the world economy and world trade. DESA's Statistical Division publishes the *Statistical Yearbook,* the *World Statistics Pocketbook,* and statistical publications on international merchandise trade, national accounts, demography, gender, population, energy, environment, human settlements, disability, social indicators, and industry. The division also monitors progress on achieving the MILLENNIUM DEVELOPMENT GOALS. Additionally, DESA maintains major databases, such as its Population Division's

World Population Projections to 2150, the *Global Review and Inventory of Population Policies* (GRIPP), and the *Population Information Network* (POPIN).

See also INTER-AGENCY COMMITTEE ON SUSTAINABLE DEVELOPMENT.

Further Reading: United Nations Department of Public Information. *Basic Facts about the United Nations.* New York: United Nations Department of Public Information, 2004. DESA Web site: <www.un.org/esa/desa>.

Department of General Assembly Affairs and Conference Services (DGAACS)   *See* SECRETARIAT.

Department of Management (DM)   *See* SECRETARIAT.

Department of Peacekeeping Operations (DPKO)

The Department of Peacekeeping Operations was created in 1992 as an integral part of the Executive Office of the UN SECRETARY-GENERAL. Prior to 1992 the UNDER SECRETARY-GENERAL (USG) for Special Political Affairs controlled missions authorized by the SECURITY COUNCIL or GENERAL ASSEMBLY. The department has administrative, managerial, planning, and preparation responsibilities for PEACEKEEPING missions. It is headed by the Under Secretary-General for Peacekeeping—in 2006, USG Jean-Marie Guéhenno of FRANCE—and has divisions for operations, planning and support, training and evaluation, and assessment of past operations. This last division was established in April 1995 as the Lessons Learned Unit, established in April 1995 by UN Secretary-General KOFI ANNAN, himself a former USG for Peacekeeping; then in 2001 merged with the department's Policy and Analysis Unit and renamed the Peacekeeping Best Practices Unit (PBPU). Among its other activities, PBPU sponsors seminars on PEACE-BUILDING, reconstruction, and CONFLICT RESOLUTION. The Training and Evaluation Office was established by the General Assembly to coordinate and standardize training for national peacekeeping units. It provides courses, publications, and training exercises for those member states that contribute forces to peacekeeping operations.

The end of the COLD WAR occasioned a significant increase in peacekeeping operations. Following apparent peacekeeping successes in ANGOLA and NAMIBIA, confidence emerged that the United Nations could intervene effectively in disintegrating states, not only to restore peace but to undertake state-building. Failures, however, in SOMALIA and Rwanda, induced strong pressures for an evaluation of DPKO operations and the UN peacekeeping function in general. The department struggled with inadequate resources trying to meet new mandates that went far beyond the original idea of peacekeeping. The UNITED STATES, in particular, urged an overhaul of DPKO, including the creation of a rapidly deployable headquarters team, the maintenance of a database of available forces, and a modest airlift capability. An initial response to these recommendations was the creation of the Lessons Learned Unit, with the mandate to study past peacekeeping operations, discover the strengths and weaknesses of those efforts, and make recommendations for administrative improvement.

In March 2000, Secretary Annan appointed a panel of experts to study the new challenges facing UN peacekeeping. He hoped the experts would complement the work of the Lessons Learned Unit. The panel's report, issued just before the September 2000 meeting of the MILLENNIUM SUMMIT, recommended formalizing the UN's peacekeeping activities, ending ad hoc deployments, and creating a new information-gathering and analysis office within the United Nations to act as a professional policy planning staff for DPKO.

In the new millennium the Department saw its BUDGET grow to more than $4 billion annually ($5.03 billion for July 2005 through June 2006) as force sizes and the functions of peacekeeping operations expanded. To assist with costs and to gain more flexibility in response to different crises, DPKO worked closely with REGIONAL ORGANIZATIONS. In Africa, the department worked with the ECONOMIC COMMUNITY OF WEST AFRICAN STATES (ECOWAS) to deal with conflict in Liberia, SIERRA LEONE, and Côte d'Ivoire. The AFRICAN UNION assisted in Sudan. It has also worked with the ORGANIZATION OF AMERICAN STATES in HAITI and the European Union in the FORMER YUGOSLAVIA.

Past and present second-generation peacekeeping and peace-building operations include:

AFRICA			
Angola	UN ANGOLA VERIFICATION MISSION (UNAVEM I)		December 1988–May 1991
	UN Angola Verification Mission (UNAVEM II)		May 1991–February 1995
	UN Angola Verification Mission (UNAVEM III)		February 1995–June 1997
	UN Observer Mission in Angola (MONUA)		June 1997–February 1999
	UN Office in Angola (UNOA)		October 1999–August 2002
	UN Mission in Angola (UNMA)		August 2002–February 2003

(continues)

Africa (*continued*)

Burundi	United Nations Operation in Burundi (UNOB)	June 2004–
Central African Republic	UN Mission in the Central African Republic (MINURCA)	April 1998–February 2000
	UN Office in the Central African Africa (BONUCA)	February 2000–
Chad/Libya	UN Aouzou Strip Observer Group (UNASOG)	May 1994–June 1994
CONGO	UN Operation in the Congo (ONUC)	July 1960–June 1964
Côte d'Ivoire	UN Operation in Côte d'Ivoire (UNOCI)	April 2004–
Democratic Republic of the Congo	UN ORGANIZATION MISSION IN THE DEMOCRATIC REPUBLIC OF THE CONGO (MONUC)	December 1999–
Ethiopia/Eritrea	UN Mission in Ethiopia and Eritrea (UNMEE)	July 2000–
Great Lakes Region	Office of the Special REPRESENTATIVE OF THE SECRETARY-GENERAL for the Great Lakes Region	December 1997–
Guinea-Bissau	UN Peace-building Support Office in Guinea-Bissau (UNOGBIS)	March 1999–
Liberia	Observer Mission in Liberia (UNOMIL)	September 1993–September 1997
	UN Peace-building Support Office in Liberia (UNOL)	November 1997–September 2003
	UN MISSION IN LIBERIA (UNMIL)	September 2003–
MOZAMBIQUE	UN Operation in Mozambique (ONUMOZ)	December 1992–December 1994
Namibia	UN TRANSITION ASSISTANCE GROUP (UNTAG)	April 1989–March 1990
Rwanda	UN ASSISTANCE MISSION FOR RWANDA (UNAMIR)	October 1993–March 1996
Rwanda/Uganda	UN Observer Mission for Uganda-Rwanda (UNOMUR)	June 1993–September 1994
Sierra Leone	UN Observer Mission in Sierra Leone (UNOMSIL)	July 1998–October 1999
	UN Mission in Sierra Leone (UNAMSIL)	October 1999–December 2005
	UN Integrated Office in Sierra Leone (UNIOSIL)	January 2006–
SOMALIA	UN OPERATIONS IN SOMALIA (UNOSOM I)	April 1992–March 1993
	UN Operations in Somalia (UNOSOM II)	March 1993–March 1995
	UN Political Office for Somalia (UNPOS)	April 1995–
Sudan	UN Advance Mission in the Sudan (UNAMIS)	June 2004–March 2005
	UN Mission in the Sudan (UNMIS)	March 2005–
West Africa	Office of the Special Representative of the Secretary-General for West Africa (UNOWA)	November 2001–
Western Sahara	UN Mission for the Referendum in Western Sahara (MINURSO)	April 1991–

LATIN AMERICA and the Caribbean

Central America	UN OBSERVER GROUP IN CENTRAL AMERICA (ONUCA)	November 1989–January 1992
Dominican Republic	Mission of the SPECIAL REPRESENTATIVE OF THE SECRETARY-GENERAL in the Dominican Republic (DOMREP)	May 1965–October 1966
EL SALVADOR	UN OBSERVER MISSION IN EL SALVADOR (ONUSAL)	July 1991–April 1995
GUATEMALA	UN VERIFICATION MISSION IN GUATEMALA (MINUGUA)	January 1997–May 1997
HAITI	UN Mission in Haiti (UNMIH)	September 1993–June 1996
	UN Support Mission in Haiti (UNSMIH)	July 1996–July 1997
	UN Transition Mission in Haiti (UNTMIH)	August–November 1997
	UN CIVILIAN POLICE MISSION IN HAITI (MIPONUH)	December 1997–March 2000
	International Civilian Support Mission in Haiti (MICAH)	March 2000–February 2001
	UN Stabilization Mission in Haiti (MINUSTAH)	April 2004–

ASIA

AFGHANISTAN/ PAKISTAN	UN GOOD OFFICES Mission in Afghanistan and Pakistan (UNGOMAP)	March 1988–March 1990
	UN SPECIAL MISSION TO AFGHANISTAN (UNSMA)	December 1993–December 2002
	UN Assistance Mission in Afghanistan (UNAMA)	March 2002–
CAMBODIA	UN Advance Mission in Cambodia (UNAMIC)	October 1991–March 1992
	UN TRANSITION AUTHORITY IN CAMBODIA (UNTAC)	March 1992–September 1993
TIMOR-LESTE	UN Mission in East Timor (UNAMET)	June 1999–October 1999
	UN TRANSITIONAL ADMINISTRATION IN EAST TIMOR (UNTAET)	October 1999–May 2002
	UN Mission in Support of East Timor (UMISET)	May 2002–May 2005
	UN Office in Timor-Leste (UNITOL)	May 2005–August 2006
Georgia	UN Observer Mission in Georgia (UNOMIG)	August 1993–
INDIA/Pakistan	UN INDIA-PAKISTAN OBSERVATION MISSION (UNIPOM)	September 1965–March 1996
	UN MILITARY OBSERVER GROUP IN INDIA AND PAKISTAN (UNMOGIP)	January 1949–

Asia (*continued*)

Tajikistan	UN Mission of Observers in Tajikistan (UNMOT)	December 1994–May 2000
	UN Tajikistan Office of Peace-building (UNTOP)	June 2000–June 2006
West New Guinea	UN SECURITY FORCE (UNSF)	October 1962–April 1963

EUROPE

BOSNIA and Herzegovina	UN MISSION IN BOSNIA AND HERZEGOVINA (UNMIBH)	December 1995–December 2002
	UN Mission of Observers in Prevlaka (UNMOP)	January 1996–December 2002
Croatia	UN Confidence Restoration Operation (UNCRO)	March 1995–January 1996
	UN Transitional Authority in Eastern Slavonia, Baranja, and Western Sirmium (UNTAES)	January 1996–January 1998
	UN Civilian Police Support Group (UNPSG)	January 1998–October 1998
Cyprus	UN PEACEKEEPING FORCE IN CYPRUS (UNFICYP)	March 1964–
Former Yugoslav Republic of Macedonia	UN PREVENTIVE DEPLOYMENT FORCE IN THE FORMER YUGOSLAV REPUBLIC OF MACEDONIA (UNPREDEP)	March 1995–February 1999
FORMER YUGOSLAVIA	UN PROTECTION FORCE (UNPROFOR)	February 1992–March 1995
	UN INTERIM ADMINISTRATION MISSION IN KOSOVO (UNMIK)	June 1999–
Georgia	UN Observer Mission in Georgia (UNOMIG)	August 1993–

MIDDLE EAST

Golan Heights	UN Disengagement Observer Force (UNDOF)	June 1974–
IRAN/Iraq	UN Iran-Iraq Military Observer Group (UNIIMOG)	August 1988–February 1991
IRAQ	UN Assistance Mission in Iraq (UNAMI)	August 2003–
Iraq/Kuwait	UN IRAQ-KUWAIT OBSERVATION MISSION (UNIKOM)	April 1991–
LEBANON	UN Observer Group in Lebanon (UNOGIL)	June 1958–December 1958
	UN INTERIM FORCE IN LEBANON (UNIFIL)	March 1978–
Middle East	UN EMERGENCY FORCE (UNEF I)	November 1956–June 1967
	UN Emergency Force (UNEF II)	October 1973–July 1979
Yemen	UN YEMEN OBSERVATION MISSION (UNYOM)	July 1963–September 1964

Possibly the most serious challenge to DPKO raised by the large number of NATION-BUILDING operations around the world was guaranteeing professional and effective service by its personnel. In 2004 three current and former peacekeepers published *Emergency Sex and Other Desperate Measures: A True Story from Hell on Earth,* detailing their demoralizing and even sordid experiences in UN operations around the world. The volume depicted excessive alcohol use and inappropriate sexual behavior by peacekeepers. About the same time the world's media reported on cases where peacekeepers were trading food and other necessitates of life for sex with local WOMEN. More seriously, there were charges of rape lodged against UN personnel. SECRETARY-GENERAL KOFI ANNAN announced a "zero-tolerance" policy for such practices, and promised to establish new disciplinary procedures to punish anyone violating UN strictures.

In 2005 the Department of Peacekeeping Operations launched a number of initiatives to give meaning to Annan's policy statements. DPKO established Conduct and Discipline Units at UN HEADQUARTERS and in the eight largest peacekeeping missions. It also created a victim's assistance program. Training programs for personnel were greatly enhanced. New communications programs that conveyed the "duty of the peacekeeper" were put in place, and senior UN administrators made trips to UN operations to convey the zero-tolerance message. On a positive note, efforts were made to improve the living conditions and social services for peacekeepers. Finally, the United Nations moved to strengthen agreements with contributing countries to assure that their nationals would be prosecuted if charged with important infractions. DPKO established a database to record misconduct cases. The OFFICE OF INTERNAL OVERSIGHT SERVICES (OIOS) undertook responsibility for investigating charges of abuse and sexual exploitation.

See also BRAHIMI REPORT, SECRETARIAT.

Further Reading: Report of the Panel on United Nations Peace Operations Web site: <www.un.org/peace/reports/peace_operations/>. *United Nations Peace Operations: Year in Review 2005.* New York: United Nations Department of Public Information, 2006. DPKO Web site: <www.un.org/Depts/dpko/dpko/index.asp>.

Department of Political Affairs *See* SECRETARIAT.

Department of Public Information (DPI)

The GENERAL ASSEMBLY created the Department of Public Information in 1946. It is a department within the United Nations's administrative organ, the SECRETARIAT. The mandate of DPI is to enlist public support for the United Nations by building awareness and understanding of the purpose and activities of the organization among the peoples of the world. The department functions as the catalyst for information related to the United Nations and its system. It assists all the other UN departments, commissions, committees, programs, and SPECIALIZED AGENCIES in gathering, coordinating, preparing, and disseminating information in the form of teaching guides, exhibits, documentary films, reports, press releases, topical promotional campaigns, and newsletters, such as *African Recovery*. The information includes photographs, maps, and regional statistics collected by the economic and social commissions of the United Nations.

The Department of Public Information disseminates information through its Media Division, which uses a wide variety of channels, such as online, print, television, and radio. DPI has information centers in more than 130 countries, including 50 in Africa, 35 in Asia and Oceania, and 15 in Europe, and a regional center in Brussels, Belgium. The UN-guided tours began with the opening of UN HEADQUARTERS in 1952 and are now also conducted at the UN offices in Geneva and Vienna. Some 300 depository libraries throughout the world make UN documents accessible locally to researchers, students, and parliamentarians. Furthermore, since the launching of the UN web site in 1997, an increasing number of documents have been made available directly on the Internet. The Public Inquiries Unit provides information over the phone or by e-mail free of charge. Media accreditation and press kits ensure that the world press has the opportunity to cover UN events. The Office of the Spokesman of the SECRETARY-GENERAL briefs international journalists and press officers of the member states on a daily basis and coordinates the media-related activities of the Secretary-General, such as press conferences and interviews. Besides enlisting the press to help disseminate UN information, DPI coordinates the relationship of NON-GOVERNMENTAL ORGANIZATIONS (NGOs) with the United Nations. The NGOs, in exchange for varying degrees of CONSULTATIVE STATUS with the ECONOMIC AND SOCIAL COUNCIL, disseminate UN-related information to their members. An elected 18-member DPI/NGO Executive Committee acts in an advisory and liaison capacity to represent the interests of the more than 1500 NGOs that work with DPI. Annually the department stages the largest NGO conference convened by the United Nations. In 2002 the conference attracted more than 2,000 representatives from 760 NGOs in 70 countries.

In addition to its Media Division, DPI has a Division of Promotion and Public Services, and a Division for Library and Publications. The latter is responsible for the DAG HAMMARSKJÖLD LIBRARY, which is the documentation, research, and reference facility of the UN. The Promotion and Public Services Division conducts public awareness campaigns and conferences.

The UNDER SECRETARY-GENERAL (USG) for Communication and Public Information coordinates the work of DPI

with other UN bodies and programs. On May 31, 2002, Secretary-General KOFI ANNAN elevated the interim department head, Shashi Tharoor of INDIA, to the USG position.

The department translates its message into a variety of LANGUAGES. All UN documents are written in the two working languages of the United Nations—French and English—and many documents are translated into the other four official languages: Arabic, Chinese, Russian, and Spanish. UN radio broadcasts are prepared in 18 languages, public tours are conducted in approximately 30 languages, and the information centers provide the translation of UN documents into local languages.

See also STRUCTURE OF THE UNITED NATIONS.

Further Reading: United Nations Department of Public Information. *Basic Facts about the United Nations.* New York: United Nations Department of Public Information, published periodically. Department of Public News Web site: <www.un.org/News>.

— *A. S. Hansen*

Deputy Secretary-General (DSG)

On March 2, 1998, LOUISE FRÉCHETTE became the United Nations's first Deputy Secretary-General (DSG). The GENERAL ASSEMBLY had authorized SECRETARY-GENERAL KOFI ANNAN's creation of the post under Article 101 of the CHARTER the previous December (Res. 12). The Assembly's action was part of the general REFORM OF THE UNITED NATIONS first proposed by Annan in September 1997.

The duties of the Deputy Secretary-General are to assist the Secretary-General (SG) in managing the SECRETARIAT, act for the SG at United Nations HEADQUARTERS when he or she is not there, enhance coherence and cooperation among UN bodies, provide leadership in economic and social activities of the UN, represent the Secretary-General at conferences and official functions, and "undertake such assignments as may be determined by the Secretary-General." The Deputy Secretary-General serves only during the term of the Secretary-General who appointed him or her.

As the first occupant of the office, Fréchette defined by her actions and assigned duties the initial parameters of the position. Annan's reform proposal, *RENEWING THE UNITED NATIONS,* called for the Deputy Secretary-General to be his senior adviser who would oversee day-to-day operations at UN HEADQUARTERS. Responding largely to demands from the UNITED STATES for greater efficiency and accountability, the Secretary-General established a cabinet of his most senior staff. Fréchette served on this SENIOR MANAGEMENT GROUP and other secretariat committees. She was given responsibility for implementing the rest of the UN reforms approved by the General Assembly, including chairing the Steering Committee on Reform and Management Policy. In addition to her responsibilities for reform, she focused atten-

Portrait of Deputy Secretary-General Mark Malloch Brown (UN PHOTO 118256/MARK GARTEN)

tion on UN social, economic, and development activities. She was also given a major role in Annan's efforts to develop cooperation between the United Nations and "civil society," including partnerships with NON-GOVERNMENTAL ORGANIZATIONS and private businesses. She was appointed chair of the Advisory Board of the United Nations Fund for International Partnerships (UNFIP). Among the special assignments given to Fréchette was implementation of the BRAHIMI REPORT. Named for the chairman of the Panel on United Nations Peace Operations, the report recommended structural reforms of UN PEACEKEEPING, requiring the acquisition and expenditure of $22 million over several years.

Fréchette, much experienced in UN affairs after lengthy service in the Canadian External Affairs Department and as Canada's PERMANENT REPRESENTATIVE to the United Nations, quickly acquired a moderate public presence that was not required by the position. She regularly spoke in favor of creating a "new" United Nations, that is, an institution increasingly focused on "human beings, respect for their rights, and the satisfaction of their basic needs." As the first Deputy Secretary-General, she gave the post a legitimacy that made the DSG more than just another senior member of the UN Secretariat. On the other hand, she was largely self-effacing, working behind the scenes to support the Secretary-

General, and to encourage effective coordination within the organization.

Following Fréchette's resignation in 2006, Secretary-General Annan appointed Mark Malloch Brown (UNITED KINGDOM) as her replacement. Malloch Brown almost immediately staked out controversial positions. In the midst of the tensions at UN Headquarters surrounding the U.S. invasion of IRAQ, the DSG criticized Washington's policies and public attitude toward the United Nations. He suggested that the American approach was counterproductive to its interests. Malloch Brown's comments generated a strong reaction from U.S. Ambassador JOHN BOLTON who complained to the Secretary-General. Annan, however, fully backed his subordinate.

When BAN KI-MOON became Secretary-General in 2007, he replaced Malloch Brown with Dr. Asha-Rose Migird of Tanzania. She had previously served as Tanzania's foreign minister.

See also PRINCIPAL ORGANS OF THE UNITED NATIONS, STRUCTURE OF THE UNITED NATIONS.

Desert Shield   *See* GULF WAR.

Desert Storm   *See* GULF WAR.

desertification

As defined in chapter 12 of the 1992 Earth Summit's AGENDA 21, "desertification is land degradation in arid, semi-arid and dry sub-humid areas resulting from various factors, including climatic variations and human activities." By the close of the 1990s, Asia possessed the largest land area affected by desertification. In the areas of Asia suffering from desertification 71 percent was moderately to severely degraded. For LATIN AMERICA, this proportion was 75 percent. In Africa, two-thirds of which was desert or drylands, 73 percent of the agricultural drylands were moderately to severely degraded. Africa was under the greatest desertification threat, with a rate of disappearance of forest cover of 1.4 to 1.9 million square miles per year depleting both surface and groundwater resources, and with half the continent's farmland suffering from soil degradation and erosion. By 2004 desertification threatened the well-being of 1 billion people in 100 countries.

More than 23 million people were at risk of famine as a consequence of the continuing drought in the Horn of Africa, Kenya, Tanzania, and ANGOLA. Half of the population of Tajikistan faced severe food access problems due to severe drought and inadequate irrigation systems. CHINA was losing 984 square miles of land every year to desertification and 2 percent of its territory was already desert. Dust from desertification-affected areas of INDIA and Pakistan covered much of East Asia, reaching as far as JAPAN. Water scarcity and land degradation increased in southern European countries.

The attention of the international community shifted at the millennium from the climatic factors of desertification to its human causes. Desertification was also linked to the security concerns of many DEVELOPING COUNTRIES. Soil erosion and water scarcity clearly led to urban migration, overpopulation, poverty, and instability. It also produced famine, leading to the displacement of civilians, which, in turn, threatened the stability of entire regions. As neighboring countries not experiencing desertification become hosts to migrating refugees, the difficulty of feeding several million more people each year put food security ahead of military security as the principal preoccupation of many governments. Thus, the issue of combating desertification was at the forefront among the agendas of many nations and international organizations, including the United Nations.

The United Nations Sudano-Sahelian Office (UNSO) opened in 1973 to address the problem of desertification in West Africa. However, the effort remained largely regional in character for the rest of the decade. The United Nations Committee on Desertification (UNCOD) took the first major step on the international level in 1977 by approving a Plan of Action to Combat Desertification (PACD). The plan was modified and expanded at the 1992 UNITED NATIONS CONFERENCE ON ENVIRONMENT AND DEVELOPMENT (UNCED) in Rio de Janeiro, Brazil (the Earth Summit). One hundred heads of state met in Rio de Janeiro, endorsed the RIO DECLARATION and the STATEMENT OF FOREST PRINCIPLES, and adopted AGENDA 21, a 300-page plan for achieving SUSTAINABLE DEVELOPMENT in the 21st century. The conference gave the UNITED NATIONS DEVELOPMENT PROGRAMME (UNDP) the lead role in working on desertification and drought. UNDP subsequently established the Drylands Development Centre in Nairobi, Kenya, to develop programs for people living in dryland areas. An Intergovernmental Negotiating Committee on Desertification (INCD), initiated by UNCED, created the CONVENTION TO COMBAT DESERTIFICATION in those countries experiencing serious drought and/or desertification, particularly in Africa (UNCCD or CCD), which entered into force on December 26, 1996. Its CHARTER created four regional annexes in Africa, Asia, LATIN AMERICA and the Caribbean, and the Northern Mediterranean, and the document provided for the implementation of action programs on national, regional, and subregional levels. Within 10 years of its formulation the convention had garnered more than 185 signatories.

The Committee on Desertification identified four different levels of drought: meteorological (or climatological), agricultural, hydrological, and socioeconomic. The work of UNCCD concentrated predominantly on socioeconomic aspects of desertification because this final category of drought encompassed all other categories. This approach emphasized that the most constructive action to combat desertification needed to be done on a local level. The CONVENTION provided for research and education efforts on both global and regional levels. The 2000 meeting of the convention's conference of parties (COP) in Bonn, Germany, emphasized full involvement of civil society and science as essential for success in combating desertification worldwide.

At the turn of the century the problem of desertification was so overwhelming that other UN bodies and agencies joined the UNITED NATIONS ENVIRONMENT PROGRAMME (UNEP) and the CCD organization in their efforts to combat the growing crisis. The General Assembly designated June 17 as "WORLD DAY TO COMBAT DESERTIFICATION AND DROUGHT" and 2006 as the International Year of Deserts and Desertification. The FOOD AND AGRICULTURE ORGANIZATION (FAO) created and enabled databases containing information about desertification and related subjects. Organizations involved in combating the effects of desertification included the UNITED NATIONS CHILDREN'S FUND (UNICEF), the WORLD FOOD PROGRAMME (WFP), and the UNITED NATIONS HIGH COMMISSIONER FOR REFUGEES (UNHCR). The WORLD HEALTH ORGANIZATION (WHO) focused on the impact of desertification and droughts on human health and devised health policies that would minimize their devastating effects. These many activities, however, required extensive funding, which proved difficult to raise. Under the desertification convention the guiding committee was charged with setting up its own financing STRUCTURE. The INTERNATIONAL FUND FOR AGRICULTURAL DEVELOPMENT (IFAD) took on the task of raising the resources, but the results were disappointing. In August 2002 the convention's executive secretary asked the WORLD SUMMIT ON SOCIAL DEVELOPMENT to recommend the GLOBAL ENVIRONMENT FACILITY (GEF) of the WORLD BANK to take over the funding MECHANISM. Subsequently, the GEF Council approved desertification as a central area of its work and invested $63 million by 2004 to reverse the phenomenon.

See also ENVIRONMENT, REGIONAL DEVELOPMENT BANKS, SECOND COMMITTEE OF THE GENERAL ASSEMBLY, WORLD METEOROLOGICAL ORGANIZATION.

Further Reading: Biswas, Margaret R., and Asit K. Biswas. *Desertification: Associated Case Studies Prepared for the United Nations Conference on Desertification.* New York: Pergammon Press, 1980. Minguet, Monique. *Desertification: Natural Background and Human Mismanagement.* Spring Study Edition. New York: Springer-Verlag, 1994. Mouat, David A., and Charles F. Hutchinson, eds. *Desertification in Developing Counties: International Symposium and Workshop on Desertification in Developing Countries.* The Hague: Kluwer Academic Publishers, 1996. Scherl, Lea M. *Relationships and Partnerships among Governments, NGOs, CBOs and Indigenous Groups in the Context of the Convention to Combat Desertification and Drought.* Nairobi, Kenya: Environment Liaison Centre International, 1996.

— *I. Kebreau*

developing countries

"Developing countries" is a term denoting all NATION-STATES that are not highly industrialized. There is no official definition for the term, although it is used frequently in international affairs and at the United Nations. The designation is inclusive of LEAST DEVELOPED COUNTRIES and middle-income countries. The WORLD BANK has determined that the base line between middle-income countries and high-income countries is $6,000 per capita in 1987 dollars. Nations with a per capita income below that line are considered developing countries. Some commentators refer to these states as Third World countries, a term dating from the COLD WAR, or as nations of the global South, since the majority of developing countries are located in the Southern Hemisphere. The people and governments of these nations, however, prefer the term "developing countries," which they consider a more positive term, since it implies that they are in the process of improvement. These poorer nations are also sometimes referred to as LESS DEVELOPED COUNTRIES.

Developing countries, despite their vast differences, share many common characteristics, problems, and interests. These states include the vast majority of the planet's POPULATION. All developing nations share the goal of achieving a higher level of production and a higher standard of living. Most developing nations formerly were colonies, and became independent during the latter half of the 20th century. Often the United Nations played an important role in their emergence as independent nations, since the United Nations emphasized decolonization during its initial years, stressing the right of all peoples to SELF-DETERMINATION. Most of these nations are in their second or third generation of independence, and are still in the process of building sound political institutions. For the most part developing nations can do little to provide citizens with essential services, since their governments have a limited income. Developing nations are characterized by low income per capita, low productivity, limited infrastructure, limited social services, and predominantly agricultural economies where farming is typically done by primitive, labor-intensive methods.

Promoting DEVELOPMENT in all nations that are not yet industrialized is one of the central purposes of the United Nations, and developing nations tend to regard this as the most important goal of the UN, citing the opening paragraph of its CHARTER, which refers to the promotion of "social progress and better standards of life." Within the UNITED NATIONS SYSTEM, these nations are represented by the NON-ALIGNED MOVEMENT (NAM) and the GROUP OF 77, the largest CAUCUS GROUPS in the UN. These caucus groups have effectively pressed the United Nations to give precedence to development issues.

In 1986, the GENERAL ASSEMBLY adopted the DECLARATION ON THE RIGHT TO DEVELOPMENT, proclaiming development more than a mere aspiration of poor nations. The consequent *right* to development has been reaffirmed since

that time in numerous statements, including at the Vienna Conference of 1993 that reviewed HUMAN RIGHTS, and in the MILLENNIUM DECLARATION (2000) and the RESOLUTION establishing the HUMAN RIGHTS COUNCIL (2006), which lists the enforcement of that right among the new council's mandates. The MILLENNIUM DEVELOPMENT GOALS approved unanimously at the MILLENNIUM SUMMIT in September 2000 established specific development targets to be achieved in developing countries by 2015.

Developing nations receive special consideration in trade negotiations and in the granting of financing from World Bank loans and bilateral foreign aid. World trade agreements guarantee developing countries "special and differential treatment," meaning that they are granted a longer period to adjust their economies to global trade rules. They are also eligible for non-reciprocity in trade agreements with industrialized countries, since they are not expected to make matching offers of trade concessions from industrialized countries.

See also AGENDA FOR DEVELOPMENT, COMMISSION ON SUSTAINABLE DEVELOPMENT, ENVIRONMENT, KYOTO PROTOCOL, SUSTAINABLE DEVELOPMENT, UNITED NATIONS CONFERENCE ON ENVIRONMENT AND SUSTAINABLE DEVELOPMENT, UNITED NATIONS CONFERENCE ON TRADE AND DEVELOPMENT, WORLD TRADE ORGANIZATION.

Further Reading: Jolly, Richard, Louis Emmerij, Dharam Ghai, and Frederick Lapeyre. *UN Contributions to Development Thinking and Practice.* Bloomington: Indiana University Press, 2004. Toye, John, and Richard Toye. *The UN and the Global Political Economy: Trade, Finance, and Development.* Bloomington: Indiana University Press, 2004. United Nations Department of Economic and Social Affairs. *The Millennium Development Goals Report.* New York: United Nations, annually since 2001. World Bank. *World Development Report 2003: Sustainable Development in a Dynamic World: Transforming Institutions, Growth, and Quality of Life.* New York: Oxford University Press, 2002.

— *K. J. Grieb*

development

The precept that the maintenance of international peace and security depends in part on the amelioration of economic and social problems in poor societies found broad acceptance at the founding conference of the United Nations in San Francisco in 1945. Led by the UNITED STATES delegation and supported by countries in LATIN AMERICA, the Middle East, Asia, and Africa, the framers of the UN CHARTER included binding commitments in the document to provide "higher standards of living, full employment, and conditions of economic and social progress and development . . . [and] solutions of international economic, social, health, and related problems" (Article 55). The Charter's opening article established as one of the purposes of the world body "to achieve international co-operation in solving international problems of an economic, social, cultural, and humanitarian character."

The steady increase in UN MEMBERSHIP after 1955, coming largely from postcolonial parts of the world and made up of weak, poor, DEVELOPING COUNTRIES, reinforced the demands on the world body to address economic development issues. The new members also demonstrated by their presence and their agenda that serious divisions existed between the "NORTH" and the "SOUTH" in terms of economic well-being and approaches to closing the gap between the "have" and "have-not" nations. While COLD WAR tensions between East and West overshadowed the significance of these differences prior to the 1980s, with the closing of that era in international politics the connection between development and international peace came into new relief. Particularly in Africa, where poverty and social deprivation were intermixed with ethnic, religious, and political conflict, the link between economic improvement and stability became clear. At the MILLENNIUM SUMMIT in 2000 world leaders outlined a set of development goals and targets, nearly all of which were directed at improving living standards in the developing countries. By the new millennium nearly all UN PEACEKEEPING and NATION-BUILDING missions were located in the poorest parts of the world, demonstrating the wisdom of the framers that peace was not possible without economic and social improvement.

While governments in 1945 understood the importance of economic development to international peace, the effort to promote it was not a priority in the early years of the United Nations. The crises of the burgeoning cold war, DISARMAMENT, and regional disputes took precedence. Even if the UN had wished to encourage economic development, the organization lacked the financial resources to invest in the poorest states. UN initiatives would require the commitment of the wealthiest members to provide the needed funds.

In the spring of 1949, U.S. president Harry Truman proposed to the Congress the POINT FOUR PROGRAM, a foreign aid package to be administered by the United Nations. The president rationalized the assistance as a weapon against the spreading threat of communism in poor countries. He argued that the funds would bolster Western-oriented and new NATIONAL LIBERATION governments against subversive movements. Congress provided the funds, and by 1950 the UN ECONOMIC AND SOCIAL COUNCIL (ECOSOC) had established the EXPANDED PROGRAM OF TECHNICAL ASSISTANCE (EPTA) that sought additional funds from other members. Its $20 million BUDGET—60 percent provided by the United States—made EPTA the largest UN program at the time.

EPTA focused primarily on providing technical assistance and experts rather than transferring financial capital to the developing world. To encourage the latter the UN GENERAL ASSEMBLY established the SPECIAL UNITED NATIONS FUND FOR ECONOMIC DEVELOPMENT (SUNFED) in hopes of trans-

ferring $250 million from the developed to the developing world. The response was tepid, in part because the major powers wanted to control their foreign aid contributions through bilateral arrangements. The United States and Soviet Union saw foreign assistance as an important instrument in their competition for influence in the Third World. In 1965 SUNFED and EPTA were merged into a single UN agency, the UNITED NATIONS DEVELOPMENT PROGRAMME (UNDP). Over the next 40 years UNDP became the world's largest multilateral economic development agency, coordinating nearly all UN efforts in this field.

While UNDP is an Assembly-created body, it also reports to and works closely with the Economic and Social Council. As a PRINCIPAL ORGAN OF THE UNITED NATIONS, ECOSOC traditionally has had primary responsibility for the many policy aspects of development, which are addressed through its functional commissions. The Council also begins each annual session with what is called a High-Level Segment, which is a meeting of the Council's members and key UN officials to define the important economic and social themes for the Council's subsequent work. One of the Council's subordinate bodies, the Committee for Development Planning was established in 1965. The committee was given new importance in 1998. Renamed the Committee for Development Policy (CDP) and made up of 24 development experts serving in a personal capacity, the committee examines various topics assigned by ECOSOC. CDP has addressed aid effectiveness, the connections between development and good governance, and new financial MECHANISMS to assist development. Importantly the CDP every three years reviews the list of LEAST DEVELOPED COUNTRIES (LDCs) in order to advise ECOSOC on which nations should be added to or removed from the designation.

Beginning in 1961 the General Assembly launched four consecutive DEVELOPMENT DECADES to give visibility to UN efforts to assist the least developed countries. During the Second and Third Decades (1971–90) the General Assembly majority promoted the agenda of the NEW INTERNATIONAL ECONOMIC ORDER (NIEO), which urged an annual transfer of 1 percent of GDP from the developed world to poor nations. The momentum created by the Development Decades contributed to the creation of several UN bodies and programs, including UNDP in 1965. Also created during the First Decade was the UNITED NATIONS INDUSTRIAL DEVELOPMENT ORGANIZATION (UNIDO) in 1967. In the early years UNIDO emphasized industrialization. This gave way in the wake of the 1992 UNITED NATIONS CONFERENCE ON ENVIRONMENT AND DEVELOPMENT to the pursuit of SUSTAINABLE DEVELOPMENT. In the Third Development Decade, the United Nations adopted the SUBSTANTIAL NEW PROGRAMME OF ACTION for least developed countries and the New Industrial Development Strategy.

The Development Decades never fully met their goals. The broad exhortation to provide development aid to LDCs did not produce significant increases in giving by developed nations. Consequently, at the conclusion of the Fourth Development Decade a new approach was attempted in the MILLENNIUM DEVELOPMENT GOALS (MDGs) agreed to by all member states in September 2000. The MDGs set specific targets, such as halving the proportion of people whose income is less that $1 a day and who do not have sustainable access to drinking water. Most of the goals set 2015 as the deadline for their achievement. MDG #8 called for a new global partnership for development that met the special needs of the least developed countries.

The fact that the MDGs reflected a consensus of the world's leaders and spoke of partnership marked a new era in UN development history. Much of the previous four decades had been characterized by contrasting views between states of the North and developing countries over how development could best be achieved. Generally, industrialized nations promoted the global free market and access to that market through the BRETTON WOODS institutions (WORLD BANK, INTERNATIONAL MONETARY FUND, WORLD TRADE ORGANIZATION) as the best route for sustainable economic growth. Developing nations often argued that the world trading system was inherently unfair, serving the economic interests of the developed world at the continuing expense of the LDCs. The less developed countries pressed their case within UN bodies, beginning with the UNITED NATIONS CONFERENCE ON TRADE AND DEVELOPMENT (UNCTAD) in 1964. Within UNCTAD, the GROUP OF 77 and the NON-ALIGNED MOVEMENT, both CAUCUSES of underdeveloped states, pressed for a New International Economic Order. Arguing the existing system produced dependency on the economies of the North, raised unsustainable levels of debt, and made the creation of domestic industries nearly impossible, advocates of the NIEO sought more favorable terms of trade for primary commodities, a global redistribution of wealth, a Code of Conduct for Transnational Corporations, and a charter of the economic rights and duties of states.

In 1974 the General Assembly approved the NIEO, adding to the already existing demands the transfer of technology to developing countries and more liberal aid policies on the part of donor nations. Despite UN approval, the NIEO accomplished little. Without the developed nations' endorsement, no change in the international trading system was possible. By the 1980s the NIEO agenda was politically dead, superseded by a new concern for the growing debt levels in the LDCs and for the impact of GLOBALIZATION on developing countries. With the collapse of socialist economies during that decade, it became incumbent for poor nations to find ways to benefit from globalized capitalist trade. Many national economies turned to enticing foreign direct investment and to export-oriented economic policies. Developing nations modified their objectives considerably and adopted more pragmatic goals. The most radical ideas—the development of an entire new trading system and a global redis-

tribution of wealth—were abandoned, and replaced with calls for debt reduction and debt forgiveness. LDC objectives continued to include special trade privileges, such as tariff exemptions, protection for infant industries in developing nations, commodity price supports, development assistance, export diversification, and guaranteed access to the markets of industrialized countries.

The shift in LDC strategy meant that commissions and bodies of the United Nations that traditionally had been the center of the developing world's attention for development assistance became less important. Developing states brought pressure instead on the International Monetary Fund, World Bank, and World Trade Organization to adjust their policies in order to take into account the development needs of poor countries. They demanded debt relief in return for a reduction in the requested amount of direct aid from 1 percent of the donor nations' gross domestic product annually to .7 percent. Also, through a series of multilateral trade negotiations the LDCs particularly sought a cut in domestic agricultural subsidies in developed countries, making the LDCs' farm exports more competitive. Unable to achieve subsidy concessions from the major economies, especially from the United States and the European Union, nearly two dozen delegations from the South walked out of the 2003 negotiations in Cancún, Mexico. Ongoing talks to consummate the "Doha" (Qatar) round of trade talks had proved futile by 2006.

The changing fortunes of the capitalist and socialist economic systems were not the only challenges faced by poor countries seeking economic improvement in the last third of the 20th century. The new phenomenon of environmentalism also raised concerns for developing countries. Calls to protect the Earth, and its water, atmosphere, and biological diversity appeared to limit the options states would have for developing their economies within their sovereign borders. To address this dilemma the United Nations convened the 1972 UN CONFERENCE ON THE HUMAN ENVIRONMENT in Stockholm, Sweden. At the meeting the gulf between industrialized and developing countries became readily apparent. Conservation of the ENVIRONMENT seemed at odds with the RIGHT TO DEVELOPMENT carried out freely by sovereign governments in the developing world. Using their VOTING power in the UN General Assembly, these states asserted this right in a formal DECLARATION in 1986.

Seeking a resolution between the competing demands of environmental protection and economic development, the General Assembly appointed the WORLD COMMISSION ON ENVIRONMENT AND DEVELOPMENT (WCED), which issued its report in 1987. OUR COMMON FUTURE introduced a new formulation known as sustainable development, defined as "development that meets the needs of the present without compromising the ability of future generations to meet their own needs." Based on this concept, the United Nations convened the EARTH SUMMIT in 1992 that made more than a thousand recommendations on methods to achieve development of this kind. It also established the COMMISSION ON SUSTAINABLE DEVELOPMENT to promote development in less developed countries in ways that conserved the LDCs' natural resources.

Sustainable development became the mantra of all following UN efforts related to economic improvement in the developing world. The MILLENNIUM SUMMIT in 2000, which promulgated the Millennium Development Goals, connected the pursuit of development with the protection of the global commons and the maintenance of peace and security. SECRETARY-GENERAL KOFI ANNAN explicitly described the connection between development and international security in his 2005 report *IN LARGER FREEDOM*, which served as the basis for the 2005 WORLD SUMMIT's agenda. In his analysis peace was dependent on the harmonization of three phenomena: sustainable development, international security, and HUMAN RIGHTS protection. He argued that none of these could be achieved without fulfillment of the other two. Development, which had been an important but secondary pursuit for the United Nations in 1945, was now central to the organization's work and a fundamental building block of world peace.

See also UNITED NATIONS CONFERENCE ON LEAST DEVELOPED COUNTRIES.

Further Reading: Fraser, Arvonne, and Irene Tinker, eds. *Developing Power: How Women Transformed International Development.* New York: The Feminist Press at the City University of New York, 2004. Grady, Patrick, and Kathleen Macmillan. *Seattle and Beyond: The WTO Millennium Round.* Ottawa, Canada: Global Economics, 1999. Jain, Devaki. *Women, Development, and the UN: A Sixty-Year Quest for Equality and Justice.* Bloomington: Indiana University Press, 2005. Moore, John Allphin, Jr., and Jerry Pubantz. *The New United Nations: International Organization in the Twenty-first Century.* Upper Saddle River, N.J.: Prentice Hall, 2006. United Nations Conference on Trade and Development. *The Least Developed Countries Report 2006: Developing Productive Capacities.* New York: UNCTAD, 2006. United Nations Development Programme. *Human Development Report 2005: International Cooperation at a Crossroads: Aid, Trade and Security in an Unequal World.* New York: UNDP, 2005. World Bank. *World Development Report 2003: Sustainable Development in a Dynamic World: Transforming Institutions, Growth, and Quality of Life.* New York: Oxford University Press, 2002. United Nations Development Programme Web site: <www.undp.org>.

development account

UN SECRETARY-GENERAL KOFI ANNAN proposed the creation of a Development Account as part of his 1997 REFORM proposals for the world organization. In *RENEWING THE UNITED NATIONS,* Annan suggested that the account should be funded with savings from the implementation of contemplated cost-cutting measures in the administration of the United Nations. The GENERAL ASSEMBLY created the Development Account in October 1999 and directed that its resources be used for "supplementary DEVELOPMENT activities." By 2001 more than $30 million had been generated by streamlining the SECRETARIAT and its activities, better coordination of entities in the UNITED NATIONS SYSTEM, and the expanded use of electronic information technologies. The UNDER SECRETARY-GENERAL for Economic and Social Affairs serves as the program manager for the account.

Projects funded by the account are approved by the General Assembly. During its first two years of operation the account supported more than 20 projects focused on capacity-building through regional cooperation of developing states. They included the promotion of electronic commerce, the creation of the United Nations Public Administration Network (UNPAN), and the convocation of several international workshops on aspects of capacity-building. In 2001 the UN DEPARTMENT OF ECONOMIC AND SOCIAL AFFAIRS announced that the next set of projects would focus on "capacity-building for managing globalization." By 2006, 97 projects worth $67 million had been approved by the General Assembly. In addition to capacity-building, projects focused on the advancement of WOMEN, drug and crime prevention, governance, ENVIRONMENT, debt, human settlements, and countries with special needs. Among the agencies spending Development Account funds have been the UNITED NATIONS CONFERENCE ON TRADE AND DEVELOPMENT (UNCTAD), the UNITED NATIONS ENVIRONMENT PROGRAMME (UNEP), HABITAT, and the REGIONAL ECONOMIC COMMISSIONS.

Further Reading: Development Account Web site: www.un.org/esa/devaccount/.

Development Decades

Beginning in 1961 the UN GENERAL ASSEMBLY established four consecutive Development Decades in order to bring attention to the plight of DEVELOPING COUNTRIES. Originally conceptualized as an economic planning rubric, the Development Decades' greatest service was to give visibility to UN efforts to assist the LEAST DEVELOPED COUNTRIES and to inspire international campaigns meant to pressure rich nations into increasing foreign assistance. Particularly during the Second and Third Decades (1971–90) there was a concerted effort by the General Assembly majority to promote the agenda of the NEW INTERNATIONAL ECONOMIC ORDER (NIEO). Central to the urgings of the developing SOUTH was an annual transfer of 1 percent of GDP from the developed world to the Third World. At first they sought that aid in the form of multilateral grants, but by the 1980s they stressed debt relief.

The NIEO described the principal problems facing the LESS DEVELOPED COUNTRIES (LDC) and concluded that only a drastic revision of global trading rules and processes could improve their lot. Beginning with the premise that the existing system had been developed by the major industrialized states before most of the developing nations achieved their independence, and, therefore, unfairly discriminated against LDC, the NIEO called for the replacement of the BRETTON WOODS system with a new set of rules to assure that the voices of developing nations were heard. Much of the developing states' efforts to replace the international trade system came in the UNITED NATIONS CONFERENCE ON TRADE AND DEVELOPMENT (UNCTAD), which convened for its first session in 1964 during the First Development Decade, and then met every four years through the end of the century.

The momentum created by the Development Decades contributed to the creation of several UN bodies and programs. During the First Decade two pivotal organizations were established: the UNITED NATIONS DEVELOPMENT PROGRAMME (UNDP) in 1965 and the UNITED NATIONS INDUSTRIAL DEVELOPMENT ORGANIZATION in 1967. In the early years of these organizations both emphasized industrialization. This gave way in the wake of the 1992 UNITED NATIONS CONFERENCE ON ENVIRONMENT AND DEVELOPMENT to the pursuit of SUSTAINABLE DEVELOPMENT. In the Third Development Decade, the United Nations adopted the SUBSTANTIAL NEW PROGRAMME OF ACTION for least developed countries and the New Industrial Development Strategy. As part of the effort to keep the Development Decades at the forefront of world attention the United Nations also launched a number of new publications through the DEPARTMENT OF PUBLIC INFORMATION and UNDP. Of particular note were *Development Forum* and *Development Update*.

The Development Decades never fully met their goals. The broad exhortation to provide DEVELOPMENT aid to LDCs did not produce significant increases in giving by developed nations. In 2000 the United Nations took a new approach with the approval of the MILLENNIUM DEVELOPMENT GOALS (MDGs). The MDGs set specific targets, such as halving the proportion of people whose income is less that $1 a day and who do not have sustainable access to drinking water. Most of the goals set 2015 as the deadline for their achievement. MDG #8 called for a new global partnership for development that met the special needs of the least developed countries.

Further Reading: United Nations Department of Public Information. *Everyone's United Nations; A Handbook on the Work of the United Nations.* New York: United Nations Department of Public Information, 1986. Riggs, Robert E., and Jack C. Plano. *The United Nations: International Organization and World Politics.* Pacific Grove, Calif.: Brooks/Cole Publishing Co., 1988.

director-general

A necessary concomitant of emerging intergovernmental organizations (IGOs) in the 19th and early 20th centuries was the development of permanent SECRETARIATs to implement the policies of these organizations, to maintain their international HEADQUARTERS, and to prepare meetings, BUDGETS, and agenda. The chief administrator was known by different titles, including executive secretary or executive director. The most common appellation, however, was director-general. This administrator was considered to be the servant of the organization and not of his or her national state, was paid out of the agency's regular budget, and was expected to maintain impartiality in the administration of the organization. During early planning for the United Nations, many draft CHARTER proposals included the post of director-general as head of the organization, in part to dissociate the new body from the out-of-favor LEAGUE OF NATIONS that was administered by a SECRETARY-GENERAL. Those who argued for the title suggested that "Director-General" conveyed a dynamic political leadership role not evident in "Secretary-General," such as that played by the director-general of the International Labour Office after World War I.

The appointment of a director-general to head an IGO continues to be a normal practice in the SPECIALIZED AGENCIES of the United Nations. Since specialized agencies are autonomous organs of the world body, directors-general are not accountable to the UN Secretariat, but to their individual agency organs as defined in the organizations' constitutional documents. Usually elected by the agency's plenary body, the director-general has extensive latitude in the appointment, supervision, and activities of the body's bureaucracy. The director-general also maintains the diplomatic immunities and benefits that are accorded to international civil servants under INTERNATIONAL LAW. Some of the most important of the UN specialized agencies are headed by directors-general, including the WORLD TRADE ORGANIZATION (WTO), the WORLD HEALTH ORGANIZATION (WHO), the INTERNATIONAL ATOMIC ENERGY AGENCY (IAEA), the FOOD AND AGRICULTURE ORGANIZATION (FAO), the ORGANISATION FOR THE PROHIBITION OF CHEMICAL WEAPONS (OPCW), and the UNITED NATIONS EDUCATIONAL, SCIENTIFIC AND CULTURAL ORGANIZATION (UNESCO).

While an agency's director-general is independent of UN Secretariat control, in 1946 the United Nations established the ADMINISTRATIVE COMMITTEE ON COORDINATION (ACC). Renamed the UN System CHIEF EXECUTIVES BOARD FOR COORDINATION (CEB) in 2002, it is chaired by the UN Secretary-General and made up of executive leaders from the specialized agencies. The CEB has subsidiary committees on which many of the directors-general or their representatives serve. Through this body, which meets semi-annually, the UN Secretariat tries to bring about a coordinated effort to implement UN initiatives, WORLD CONFERENCE recommendations, and agency responses to new international challenges. Directors-general's discretion is also limited by the relationship agreements between their agencies and the United Nations, which contain specific provisions on terms of employment and service, headquarters agreements, and stipulations on the privileges and immunities of the agencies' civil servants. A "Common System" for budget, staffing, and personnel policy has emerged that restricts the discretion of a director-general when hiring, removing, promoting, and disciplining agency personnel. Employees are also protected through a system of ADMINISTRATIVE TRIBUNALS.

disarmament

Disarmament, a major focus of the United Nations from the beginning, by definition refers to the actual destruction, removal, or deactivation of existing WEAPONS. Agreements achieving this ultimate end were very difficult and very few until the end of the COLD WAR allowed the two former antagonists—the UNITED STATES and the Soviet Union—seriously to engage in deep and mutual disarmament, starting with the Intermediate Nuclear Forces Agreement of 1987. Negotiations, however, within and without the UNITED NATIONS SYSTEM, have also taken place to effect arms *control* regimes, arms *limitation* agreements (which sometimes simply limited the *growth* in armaments), non-proliferation of existing weapons and weapons technologies, and weapons-free areas. Often these efforts have been subsumed under the general category of "disarmament."

The UN effort has been a continuation of pre–World War II diplomacy that sought to reduce the threat of war by reducing the modern weapons possessed by states. The COVENANT of the LEAGUE OF NATIONS had committed the organization to the pursuit of world disarmament. In the 1920s efforts were also made by the United States and other major powers to negotiate limits on armed forces, most notably to seek naval disarmament. The rise of military dictatorships in Europe and Asia only reenforced the belief that the reduction of armaments was crucial to the maintenance of peace and to the replacement of the use of force with the rule of law.

In 1945 the new UN CHARTER committed the United Nations to global efforts to achieve disarmament. Article 11 authorized the GENERAL ASSEMBLY (GA) to "consider the general principles . . . governing disarmament." Article 26 charged the SECURITY COUNCIL (SC) with the responsibility for "formulating . . . a system for the regulation of armaments." The American use of nuclear weapons against JAPAN in August 1945, only four months after the Charter signing in San Francisco, generated strong interest in a UN initiative to pursue nuclear disarmament and to promote nuclear energy for peaceful purposes. As the wartime amity between the United States and the Soviet Union faded, and the prospects of a superpower nuclear arms race emerged, the United Nations seemed the suitable venue for working out what U.S.

president Harry S. Truman called "a satisfactory arrangement for the control of this discovery."

The establishment in 1946 of the ATOMIC ENERGY COMMISSION (UNAEC) initiated a permanent UN effort to limit the growth of nuclear arsenals. At its inaugural meeting in June the United States proposed the international control of all nuclear materials, uranium mines, and processing facilities. Known as the BARUCH PLAN—it was named for Bernard Baruch, the U.S. representative to the UNAEC who presented the U.S. proposal—the contemplated UN authority would have the power to impose SANCTIONS and fines on offending states, and would operate independent of the VETO power in the Security Council. The USSR immediately rejected the proposal as an effort by the United States to maintain its monopoly on nuclear weapons. Soviet delegate Andrei Gromyko proposed the alternative of a moratorium on atomic development prior to any plan for nuclear internationalization. Americans saw this as a ploy by the Soviets to limit U.S. defense efforts while pursuing a nuclear buildup undetected by international inspections.

Negotiations in the Atomic Energy Commission in the summer of 1946 foreshadowed the general pattern of UN nuclear disarmament efforts during the cold war. The deadlock produced by the competing interests of the United States and the Soviet Union undermined the possibility of fruitful negotiations. It also demonstrated the central role of the superpowers to any disarmament arrangement, and therefore the limited peripheral roles non-nuclear member states could play in promoting disarmament and arms control. In 1952 the Atomic Energy Commission and the UN's Commission on Conventional Armaments were merged into the UN DISARMAMENT COMMISSION, but this forum served as little more than a setting for Soviet and American propaganda bombasts, the former power calling for "general and complete disarmament," the latter insisting on verifiable and intrusive inspection under any disarmament plan—with neither state expecting its proposals to be accepted by the other side.

The UN's impact on disarmament in the 1950s was negligible. Serious discussions within the Disarmament Commission occurred only in the Subcommittee on Disarmament, created in 1954 and made up of the United States, the Soviet Union, the United Kingdom, FRANCE, and Canada. These states conducted their talks in secret. Otherwise, the commission was reduced to debating proposals by non-nuclear and non-aligned states. To be sure, the growing number of new UN members from the Third World and the desire to maintain influence in these countries led the superpowers to make organizational concessions to the UN MEMBERSHIP, but substantive issues were monopolized by the nuclear powers. In August 1959 the subcommittee was enlarged, becoming the Ten Nation Disarmament Committee with the addition of Bulgaria, Czechoslovakia, Poland, and Romania from the Warsaw PACT, and Italy from the North Atlantic Treaty Organization. Eight non-aligned nations were added in 1961, creating the

EIGHTEEN NATION DISARMAMENT COMMITTEE (ENDC). The only serious negotiations, however, were conducted in bilateral contacts between Washington and Moscow.

As a product of U.S.–USSR talks a number of agreements were reached in the 1960s and early 1970s. Following the dangerous confrontation in the CUBAN MISSILE CRISIS, the two sides agreed to the 1963 Partial Test Ban TREATY and a communications hotline between the two capitals to assure no misunderstandings on the deployment or use of weapons and personnel. In 1972 they reached agreement on the Anti-Ballistic Missile Treaty.

In the nuclear field UN negotiations were relegated to what were then seen as peripheral matters. Two topics dominated UN diplomacy: NUCLEAR-WEAPONS-FREE ZONES (NFZ) and nuclear non-proliferation. The ANTARCTIC TREATY of 1959 was the first agreement to ban nuclear weapons on a regional basis. Sponsored by the nuclear weapons states, the treaty prohibited weapons or weapons testing on the Antarctic continent. Signatories pledged to

Poster for Second Special Session on Disarmament, 1982 (UN PHOTO)

demilitarize Antarctica. Recognizing the fragile ENVIRONMENT of the region, the treaty also banned the dumping of radioactive wastes. Verification provisions included required inspections. This was followed in 1976 by the TREATY OF TLATLELOCO, negotiated among Latin American nations, prohibiting nuclear weapons in Central and South America and the Caribbean. In later decades NFZ accords were reached in Africa (TREATY OF PELINDABA, 1996), Southeast Asia (TREATY OF BANGKOK, 1995), and the South Pacific (TREATY OF RAROTONGA, 1985). Obstacles to equivalent agreements in the Middle East and on the broader Asian continent, however, proved more intractable. Conflicts between Israel and Arab states made a Middle East Nuclear-Weapons-Free Zone unattainable. In Asia, due to the presence of INDIA and PAKISTAN—two states with a history of deep mutual hostility and divided by ongoing tension in the disputed Kashmir province, and each possessing a nuclear arsenal—an NFZ treaty was not a possibility.

The UN's single greatest achievement in restraining the nuclear arms race was the NUCLEAR NON-PROLIFERATION TREATY (NPT, opened for signature on July 1, 1968) that entered into force in 1970. The PACT was the direct result of multilateral negotiations on a joint draft submitted by the United States and the Soviet Union to the ENDC on August 24, 1967. The NPT's intention was to halt and then reverse the spread of independent control over nuclear weapons. It established in Article IX that only states that had acquired nuclear weapons by January 1, 1967, qualified as Nuclear Weapons States (NWS). All others were considered Non-Nuclear Weapons States (NNWS) and any such state adhering to the NPT was obligated to subject its entire peaceful nuclear program to the INTERNATIONAL ATOMIC ENERGY AGENCY (IAEA) material accountancy safeguards, and to pledge only to acquire nuclear materials and equipment for peaceful purposes. Conversely the NWS, which happened to be the five PERMANENT MEMBERS OF THE SECURITY COUNCIL, pledged not to transfer nuclear weapons to any NNWS or to assist it in manufacturing or acquiring nuclear weapons (Article I); to share the benefits of the "Peaceful Atom" with any NNWS party to the treaty (Articles IV and V); and to pledge to make a "good faith" effort to end the arms race at an "early date" (Article VI).

The treaty called for five-year review conferences (Article VIII) and for a conference 25 years from entry into force for the parties to the treaty to determine whether it should be extended indefinitely or for a defined period (Article X). That conference, held at the UN HEADQUARTERS in 1995, reached a consensus that a majority of the parties wished to extend the NPT indefinitely. The parties also agreed to an "enhanced" review process to hold all parties "accountable" for their NPT obligations, and the NWS further committed to achieve a COMPREHENSIVE NUCLEAR TEST BAN TREATY (CTBT). The CTBT was opened for signature on September 24, 1996. During the 1990s adherence to the

NPT accelerated as long-time holdouts like France (1992), CHINA (1992), and South Africa (1991) signed and ratified the treaty. By 2006, only four states stood outside the treaty's framework: CUBA, India, Pakistan, and Israel.

Following the adoption of the Nuclear Non-Proliferation Treaty, the General Assembly expanded the ENDC to include all UN members, changing the name to the Conference of the Committee on Disarmament (CCD). The CCD, in turn, was replaced by the CONFERENCE ON DISARMAMENT (CD) in 1978. Located in Geneva, the Conference on Disarmament became the world's principal multilateral disarmament negotiating forum. While the General Assembly, as of 2006, had convened three SPECIAL SESSIONS on disarmament since 1978, and had maintained its FIRST COMMITTEE as a forum for disarmament issues, it was the Conference on Disarmament that served as the UN's initiating body for disarmament agreements. The UN SECRETARIAT's DEPARTMENT FOR DISARMAMENT AFFAIRS (DDA) provided administrative services for the CD, and the General Assembly made recommendations that became part of the CD's agenda.

Several events in the mid-1990s, however, affected the status and effectiveness of the CD. Perhaps most importantly, the CONVENTION ON THE PROHIBITION OF THE USE, STOCKPILING, PRODUCTION AND TRANSFER OF ANTI-PERSONNEL MINES AND THEIR DESTRUCTION (1997) was debated, negotiated, and adopted for ratification outside the conference in a "fast track" set of negotiations known as "The Ottawa Process." Moreover, in 1996 the General Assembly gave final approval to the Comprehensive Nuclear Test Ban Treaty when India refused to join the consensus for the Treaty at the CD. The stalemate inside the CD led to widespread speculation among experts about the need to change the CD's rules and procedures or to endorse the establishment of alternative negotiating forums to address the range of disarmament questions.

The International Atomic Energy Agency, charged with verifying that national nuclear energy programs are not being subverted for military use, approved a Model PROTOCOL to the NPT in May 1997. If a nation accepts the protocol, the IAEA gains access to all aspects of the country's fuel cycle-related research, all buildings on a nuclear energy site, and documentation of any export of nuclear-related technologies. The IAEA's Board of Governors thought the protocol essential given the growing danger of nuclear proliferation at the turn of the century. Secretary-General KOFI ANNAN opined in the spring of 2006 that urgent steps were needed to discourage many states from joining the nuclear club. In May in a speech at the University of Tokyo he observed that there was a growing perception that the possession of WEAPONS OF MASS DESTRUCTION, particularly nuclear weapons, offered the best protection against being attacked by another power.

By 2004, IRAN and North Korea seemed poised to join the nuclear club. While Iran signed the Additional Protocol on November 26, 2003, giving the IAEA the right to make unannounced inspections and to access sensitive Iranian information concerning the country's nuclear program, the Iranian government claimed sovereign authority to continue its nuclear research program. However, the United States and several European nations asserted Tehran was seeking a nuclear weapons capability. Negotiations between Iran and three European governments—GREAT BRITAIN, France, and GERMANY—were unable to persuade Tehran to halt uranium enrichment. The IAEA referred the Iranian case to the Security Council at the end of March 2006. In August the Council demanded that Iran terminate its enrichment program by the end of the month or face mandatory sanctions.

In 2002 North Korean officials admitted that the country was developing a nuclear weapons system in secret. The government barred inspectors from the IAEA in violation of its commitments under the agency's safeguards program. The agency referred the North Korean case to the Security Council in February 2003. "Six-party talks" were undertaken that included the United States, North Korea, CHINA, RUSSIAN FEDERATION, South Korea, and Japan. However, in the face of general international condemnation, the North Korean government carried out missile tests in July 2006, leading to a Security Council RESOLUTION demanding that the country suspend its missile program. To the consternation of the United States and Japan, however, the Council dropped any reference to CHAPTER VII of the Charter, which would have given the Security Council strong powers to act against the government in Pyongyang.

The Security Council did employ Chapter VII on April 28, 2004, requiring member states to establish "domestic controls to prevent the proliferation of nuclear, chemical, or BIOLOGICAL WEAPONS and their means of delivery" (Res. 1540). Unlike past tradition of enhancing arms control through multilateral treaties, the Security Council used its power to impose mandatory requirements on all governments. Resolution 1540 established a Security Council Committee of the Whole to monitor progress by states obligated under its terms to alter their domestic laws and regulations.

The passage of Resolution 1540 marked a concern for an emerging potential of new nuclear proliferation among terrorist groups. The terrorist attacks of September 11, 2001, the war in IRAQ, the disparate investigations in many countries of non-state groups that governments suspected of planning further TERRORISM raised fears that nuclear weapons might be used. At the suggestion of UN officials in 2002, the Swedish government established a commission to investigate ways to slow proliferation. Sweden appointed HANS BLIX, former chief weapons inspector in Iraq, to chair the commission. Blix presented Secretary-General Annan with the commission's recommendations on June 1, 2006. Among other proposals the group suggested the convocation of a World Summit on disarmament and a revision of VOTING rules in the Conference on Disarmament to allow something less than unanimity to move international disarmament efforts forward. The call for an international conference was particularly welcomed by Annan since the WORLD SUMMIT of 2005 had failed to address nuclear proliferation, much to Annan's consternation.

Beyond nuclear weapons, the Conference on Disarmament categorizes chemical and biological agents as weapons of mass destruction. While nuclear disarmament efforts have overshadowed UN attempts to limit other arsenals, the United Nations has pursued arms reductions in each of these areas. In 1969, the United Nations defined CHEMICAL WEAPONS as "chemical substances, whether gaseous, liquid or solid, which might be employed because of their direct toxic effects on man, animals and plants." Not only the toxic chemicals but also the equipment for their dispersal was classified as a chemical weapon. On November 30, 1992, the General Assembly adopted the Convention on the Prohibition of the Development, Production, Stockpiling and Use of Chemical Weapons and on Their Destruction (CWC). As of August 2006, 178 states had become or were in the process of becoming parties to the CONVENTION. It was the first international disarmament agreement with the goal of eliminating an entire category of WMDs. To enforce its provisions the convention established the ORGANISATION FOR THE PROHIBITION OF CHEMICAL WEAPONS (OPCW) with the authority to conduct surprise inspections. The dual use nature of chemicals and the ease of their production, however, made the exclusion of chemical weapons from the world's arsenals nearly impossible.

Biological weapons (BW) are living organisms, most commonly bacteria and viruses, deliberately disseminated to cause death or disease in humans, animals, or plants. Biological weapons are considered weapons of mass destruction because they have the potential to destroy life equaled only by nuclear weapons. The 1925 Geneva PROTOCOL prohibited the use of biological weapons in warfare. The 1972 Convention on the Prohibition of the Development, Production and Stockpiling of Bacteriological (Biological) and Toxin Weapons and on Their Destruction (BWC) went further by prohibiting their development and possession. The UN SECRETARY-GENERAL has the authority under the treaty to investigate the alleged use of biological weapons, ascertain facts regarding such alleged use, and report the findings to member states. A number of countries violated their obligations under the BWC by initiating or continuing to develop and produce biological weapons following its entry into force. The Soviet Union maintained a secret BW program; South Africa produced biological weapons in the 1980s and 1990s; and IRAQ, while a signatory of the BWC, developed an offensive biological program in the 1980s.

The expanded use of conventional weapons such as LAND MINES and small arms in the post–cold war context of sectarian violence caused heightened concern among UN member states in the 1990s. In 1997 the United Nations opened for signature the Landmines Convention. It prohibited in all circumstances any use of antipersonnel land mines. It also required the destruction of stockpiles within four years of the treaty's entry into force and mandated that mines already in the ground be destroyed within 10 years. As of July 2005, 145 states had signed or acceded to the convention. Among the states notably absent from the list of signatories were the United States, Israel, and the Russian Federation, although the U.S. government announced in February 2004 that it would end the production and use of "persistent" land mines after 2010. Washington promised to produce only land mines that rendered themselves inert within days of their deployment and ones that were detectable by metal detectors.

The United Nations had been involved in the movement to ban land mines since the 1970s. In 1980, it negotiated the Convention on Certain Conventional Weapons (CCW). Frustration, however, with the slow pace of developing a specific land mine agreement in the Conference on Disarmament led several states to pursue negotiations outside the UN STRUCTURE. Beginning in October 1996, a coalition of states and non-state actors championed the Ottawa Process, with Canada and Belgium leading the effort to establish a land mine ban. NON-GOVERNMENTAL ORGANIZATIONS (NGOs) such as the International Committee of the Red Cross (ICRC), Medecins sans Frontières (MSF—"Doctors without Borders"), and the International Campaign to Ban Landmines (ICBL) also advocated on behalf of a treaty. Following conferences in Vienna, Brussels, and Oslo, the process returned to Canada in December 1997 for the signing ceremony. In the negotiations the United Nations acted as a policy partner with the NGOs. One example of such cooperation was the work of the Survey Action Center. It monitored standards and facilitated the international coordination of resources and expert personnel for the completion of the Global Landmine Survey in the most mine-affected countries. That data was then used to urge completion of the treaty.

Conflicts in the post–cold war era have been fought almost exclusively with light or small arms. Clandestine arms brokers found these types of weapons the easiest to sell and deploy, exacerbating international efforts to limit their numbers. The disintegration of states and the weakening of central control over national arsenals also produced a huge dispersion of these armaments. In 2001 the United Nations convened a WORLD CONFERENCE to address this type of weapon, but participating states could not arrive at a consensus on how to cut small arms quantities or how to regulate their movement. A review conference occurred in New York City, June 26 through July 7, 2006, but the participants were even unable to agree on a final statement from the meeting. At best, there seemed to be a growing sentiment for "practical disarmament measures" (PDMs) that would lead to the destruction of small arms and light weapons (SALW).

See also ACHESON-LILIENTHAL REPORT; ATOMS FOR PEACE PROPOSAL; COMMITTEE ON THE PEACEFUL USES OF OUTER SPACE; HAMMARSKJÖLD, DAG; *JUS COGENS*; MOON

AGREEMENT, UNITED NATIONS INSTITUTE FOR DISARMAMENT RESEARCH.

Further Reading: *Chemical Disarmament: Basic Facts.* 1999 edition. The Hague: Organization for the Prohibition of Chemical Weapons, 2000. Cirincione, Joseph, ed. *Repairing the Regime: Preventing the Spread of Weapons of Mass Destruction.* New York: Routledge, 2000. Lederberg, Joshua, ed. *Biological Weapons: Limiting the Threat.* Cambridge, Mass.: MIT Press, 1999. *Portfolio of Mine Action Projects, 2006.* 9th ed. New York: United Nations Mine Action Service, 2006. United Nations Department of Public Information. *The United Nations and Nuclear Non-Proliferation.* Volume 3 of the United Nations Bluebook Series. New York: United Nations Department of Public Information, 1995. *United Nations Treaty Series.* New York: United Nations, updated regularly. United Nations. *Verification and the United Nations: The Role of the Organization in Multilateral Arms Limitation and Disarmament Agreements.* New York: United Nations, 1991. Weapons of Mass Destruction Commission. *Weapons of Terror: Freeing the World of Nuclear, Biological and Chemical Arms.* Stockholm: Weapons of Mass Destruction Commission, 2006. United Nations Disarmament Treaty Web site: <domino.un.org/TreatyStatus.nsf>. UNIDIR Web site: <www.unog.ch/unidir>. DDA Web site: <http://disarmament.un.org/dda.htm>. Disarmament Commission Web site: <http://disarmament.un.org/undiscom. htm>. Advisory Board on Disarmament Web site: <http://disarmament.un.org/advisoryboard/index.html>.

Disarmament and International Security Committee   *See* FIRST COMMITTEE.

Disarmament Commission (UNDC)

In 1952 the ATOMIC ENERGY COMMISSION and the Commission on Conventional Armaments were merged into the UN Disarmament Commission. But this forum served as little more than a setting for Soviet and American propaganda, the former power calling for "general and complete DISARMAMENT," the latter insisting on verifiable and intrusive inspection under any disarmament plan. Serious discussions within the Disarmament Commission occurred only in the Subcommittee on Disarmament, created in 1954 and made up of the UNITED STATES, the Soviet Union, the UNITED KINGDOM, FRANCE, and Canada. These states conducted their talks in secret. Otherwise, the commission was reduced to debating proposals by non-nuclear and non-aligned states.

In August 1959 the commission's subcommittee was enlarged, becoming the Ten Nation Disarmament Committee, and then in 1961 the EIGHTEEN NATION DISARMAMENT COMMITTEE (ENDC). The ENDC was largely an independent venue for negotiations on a number of disarmament

and arms control issues. Most important, it served as the institutional setting for the negotiation of the 1968 NUCLEAR NON-PROLIFERATION TREATY.

The SPECIAL SESSION OF THE GENERAL ASSEMBLY on Disarmament (SSOD-I) in 1978 attempted to revive the Disarmament Commission as "a deliberative body, a subsidiary body of the GENERAL ASSEMBLY, the function of which [is] to consider and make recommendations in the field of disarmament." All UN member states are represented on the commission. Without a clear focus to its agenda, however, the commission has been eclipsed both by the FIRST COMMITTEE OF THE GENERAL ASSEMBLY and the CONFERENCE ON DISARMAMENT in Geneva. The commission normally meets for three weeks annually in May and June, and is provided SECRETARIAT services by the DEPARTMENT FOR DISARMAMENT AFFAIRS.

The commission, like the Conference on Disarmament, was plagued with organizational difficulties at the turn of the century. No consensus could be reached on the important topics to be pursued nor the best measures for promoting disarmament. The UNDC did not meet at all in 2002. The commission met in spring 2006 with an agreed agenda for the first time in two years. Participating states agreed to discuss "recommendations for achieving the objective of nuclear disarmament and non-proliferation of NUCLEAR WEAPONS" and "practical confidence-building measures in the field of conventional WEAPONS," but there was little prospect for progress on these issues in the foreseeable future.

Further Reading: United Nations. *Compilation of All Texts of Principles, Guidelines or Recommendations on Subject Items Adopted Unanimously by the Disarmament Commission.* New York: United Nations, 1999. Disarmament Commission Web site: <http://disarmament.un.org/undiscom.htm>.

dispute settlement   *See* CHAPTER VI.

domestic jurisdiction clause

Article 2, Paragraph 7 of the UN CHARTER reads in part: "Nothing contained in the present Charter shall authorize the United Nations to intervene in matters which are essentially within the domestic jurisdiction of any state." This so-called Domestic JURISDICTION of states provision was first introduced in 1919 in the COVENANT of the LEAGUE OF NATIONS in Article 15, Paragraph 8. By the same UN Charter clause, the only exception to the principle occurs when there are breaches of peace and acts of AGGRESSION. At that point, CHAPTER VII of the charter becomes operative, and the SECURITY COUNCIL may apply mandatory ENFORCEMENT MEASURES, including intervention with military force. An assertion of the principle of state SOVEREIGNTY, the domestic jurisdiction clause came under challenge at the close of the century as the United Nations increasingly defended the HUMAN RIGHTS of men and WOMEN against violations by their own governments, pursued NATION-BUILDING in disintegrating states, and established WAR CRIMES TRIBUNALS to try NATION-STATE leaders charged with crimes against humanity and GENOCIDE inside their countries' borders. At the time of the MILLENNIUM SUMMIT in 2000 SECRETARY-GENERAL KOFI ANNAN argued for a limitation on state sovereignty when it violates the "personal sovereignty" of its citizens or cannot protect them or their rights from internal violence. Particularly in AFRICA the United Nations during the early years of the new millennium asserted a "RESPONSIBILITY TO PROTECT" individuals from their governments even if that required uninvited international intervention.

See also CHAPTER VI ½, INTERNATIONAL LAW, PEACE-KEEPING.

Further Reading: Simma, Bruno, ed. *The Charter of the United Nations; A Commentary.* 2nd ed. New York: Oxford University Press, 2002.

double veto

Matters considered by the SECURITY COUNCIL are defined in the UN CHARTER as "procedural" or "non-procedural." The latter, often referred to as "substantive questions," are subject to the VETO by any of the Council's PERMANENT MEMBERS. Procedural matters are not, and are decided by a simple majority vote of the Council MEMBERSHIP. According to the Statement of the Sponsoring Powers at the 1945 San Francisco Conference, certain items are clearly procedural in nature. However, when a dispute arises about the procedural or substantive character of a particular question before the Security Council, that matter itself is considered a substantive question, and, therefore, subject to the veto. This creates the possibility of a "double veto" by the UNITED STATES, CHINA, the United Kingdom, FRANCE, or the RUSSIAN FEDERATION. Theoretically, each can keep the council from even taking up a matter that it finds objectionable.

The Soviet Union used the double veto successfully three times in the late 1940s. However, in 1950 when the Republic of China attempted the stratagem to keep supporters of the People's Republic of China from addressing the Security Council, the council president summarily ruled that the matter was a procedural question. The Chinese representative was unable to muster the necessary seven votes to overrule the chair, and the decision stood. The device of a ruling from the chair was used several times after the 1950 experience, greatly limiting the use of the double veto to thwart council action.

drug control *See* COMMISSION ON NARCOTIC DRUGS, OFFICE ON DRUGS AND CRIME.

Dumbarton Oaks Conference

The Dumbarton Oaks Conference convened in Washington, D.C., from August 21 to October 7, 1944. Representatives from CHINA, the Soviet Union, the UNITED KINGDOM, and the UNITED STATES participated in the conference. The aim of the negotiations was to establish a postwar international institution. The conference gave rise to the Dumbarton Oaks Proposals for the Establishment of a General International Organization.

The Dumbarton Oaks Proposals are important for three reasons. First, the proposals outlined the STRUCTURE of the evolving international organization. Chapter IV of the proposals established the GENERAL ASSEMBLY, SECURITY COUNCIL, INTERNATIONAL COURT OF JUSTICE, and SECRETARIAT as the principal organs of the United Nations. Second, the proposals assigned different responsibilities to each of these organs. Most important, Chapter VI conferred responsibility for international peace and security on the proposed Security Council, while Chapter V indicated that the General Assembly should be more involved in the economic and social spheres and supervise the operations of the organization. This division of labor is reflected in CHAPTER V, Article 24 of the UN CHARTER, where "primary responsibility for the maintenance of international peace and security" is conferred on the Security Council. Third, the proposals articulated the idea that the PERMANENT MEMBERS OF THE SECURITY COUNCIL—China, FRANCE, the United Kingdom, the United States, and the USSR—should be able to VETO any substantive (non-procedural) matters before the body. The Dumbarton Oaks Proposals, like the UN Charter, did not use the term "veto." Rather, Chapter VI, Section C3 stated that an affirmative vote of the Council required the "concurring votes of the permanent members." A negative vote by any of the permanent members meant the failure of the proposed RESOLUTION. It is arguable whether the Dumbarton Oaks Conference settled the issue of the veto, since the subsequent YALTA CONFERENCE in February 1945 took up the matter again among the three wartime allied leaders: FRANKLIN DELANO ROOSEVELT, WINSTON CHURCHILL, and JOSEPH STALIN. Ultimately, however, the permanent members did receive their vetoes in the adopted UN Charter.

The Yalta Conference resolved issues left outstanding from the Dumbarton Oaks Conference. Specifically, Soviet insistence that each of its 16 constituent republics be given VOTING rights was addressed. An arrangement that gave the Ukraine and Byelorussia special voting status was agreed to by the United States, the United Kingdom, and the Soviet Union.

At the UN founding conference in San Francisco in 1945 some changes were made to the Dumbarton Oaks Proposals. This was done to make the proposed international organization more acceptable to the wider range of participants. Arguably the most significant modification involved the establishment of the TRUSTEESHIP COUNCIL. Despite such changes, the proposals that originated at the Dumbarton Oaks Conference constituted the basis of the UN Charter.

See also CHAPTER VI; MOSCOW CONFERENCE OF FOR-EIGN MINISTERS; PEARSON, LESTER.

Further Reading: For the text of the Dumbarton Oaks Proposals, see *Postwar Foreign Policy Preparation, 1939–1945,* Department of State Publication 3580 (Washington, D.C.: U.S. Government Printing Office, 1949). Claude, Inis. *Swords into Plowshares: The Problems and Progress of International Organization.* 4th ed. New York: Random House, 1971. Krasno, J. "A Step Along an Evolutionary Path: The Founding of the United Nations." *Global Dialogue* 12, no. 2 (Spring 2000): 9–18.

— S. F. McMahon

E

Earth Summit *See* UNITED NATIONS CONFERENCE ON ENVIRONMENT AND DEVELOPMENT (UNCED).

East Timor dispute *See* TIMOR-LESTE.

Economic and Financial Committee *See* SECOND COMMITTEE OF THE GENERAL ASSEMBLY.

Economic and Social Affairs Executive Committee *See* DEPARTMENT OF ECONOMIC AND SOCIAL AFFAIRS, THEMATIC DIPLOMACY.

Economic and Social Commission for Asia and the Pacific (ESCAP) *See* REGIONAL ECONOMIC COMMISSIONS OF THE ECONOMIC AND SOCIAL COUNCIL.

Economic and Social Council (ECOSOC)

The Economic and Social Council is one of the six principal organs of the United Nations. It is charged with overseeing the considerable UN activities in the economic and social fields (UN CHARTER Chapter X, Articles 62–66). Perhaps because of the breadth of its functions and the fact that the GENERAL ASSEMBLY can take up any issue, the functions and role of ECOSOC are less clear than the other main organs, and member states have very different views about its role.

In essence, ECOSOC is the UN body most concerned with economic and social DEVELOPMENT. While industrialized nations regard development as secondary to the maintenance of international peace and security, developing nations regard it as the central purpose of the United Nations, believing that it constitutes a necessary precondition to the maintenance of international peace and security. Hence discussions of strengthening or reforming the United Nations often focus on the role and powers of ECOSOC. The importance of the Economic and Social Council is indicated by the fact that two of the only five AMENDMENTS to the UN CHARTER have dealt with the size of ECOSOC. In reaction to the expansion in UN MEMBERSHIP following decolonization, and to meet the desires of newly independent nations to be represented within the United Nations in proportion to their numbers, the Charter was amended twice to expand membership in ECOSOC. In 1965 membership rose from 18 to 27, and in 1971 to 54. This membership growth clearly reflected the priority developing nations placed on ECOSOC. Currently there are 54 nations represented on ECOSOC serving three-year terms, with one-third elected annually by the General Assembly, in accordance with a formula guaranteeing regional representation (14 seats are allocated to African states, 11 to Asian states, six to East European governments, and 13 to Western European

ECOSOC Chamber (UN/DPI BY RON DA SILVA)

and Other States). The work of the Council is guided by a five-member bureau that sets the agenda and coordinates Council activities with the SECRETARIAT.

The opening paragraph of the Charter, following the phrase "We the peoples of the United Nations," lists the UN's purposes: to preserve international peace and security, to reaffirm HUMAN RIGHTS, to preserve INTERNATIONAL LAW as the basis for international relations, and "to promote social progress and better standards of life." Industrialized nations have focused on the initial three purposes, regarding development as secondary. But developing nations have regarded the promotion of development as equal in priority to preserving international peace and security, contending that these are the two preeminent purposes of the United Nations. In fact, developing nations have always preferred that the United Nations concentrate on development. In their view, strengthening ECOSOC is one of the most effective ways to do this.

Despite ECOSOC's broad responsibilities, its powers are quite limited, and its decisions are considered recommendations to the General Assembly. The functions of ECOSOC are primarily designed to focus discussion on issues and thereby to direct attention to economic and social problems. Specifically, ECOSOC conducts studies, drafts TREATIES, calls conferences dealing with economic and social issues, and makes recommendations to the General Assembly. It is up to the

individual member states to decide how best to address these issues, in the General Assembly, at a summit conference, or by signing and ratifying a treaty. Yet the function of ECOSOC is highly important, since its studies and reports set the agenda, guide preparations, and identify the terms of discussion at conferences, in other bodies, and in international documents. Article 62 of the Charter states that ECOSOC is to deal with "international economic, social, cultural, educational, health, and related matters," defining a very comprehensive mandate. ECOSOC also coordinates the activities of the independent SPECIALIZED AGENCIES, and accredits the NON-GOVERNMENTAL ORGANIZATIONS that play an important role in ECOSOC and the specialized agencies.

In addition to recommending and initiating actions, ECOSOC monitors the actions of member states in implementing decisions by its commissions and in meeting commitments made through treaties. It assists nations in drafting the necessary legislation to implement internationally agreed upon standards required by these decisions and treaties. This role is viewed as part of the UN's mission of "harmonizing the actions of nations" (Article 1 [4] of the Charter). ECOSOC's primary means of exerting influence is through requiring and reviewing reports from member states, providing the governments of those nations with advice, and assessing their progress on the implementation of international agreements. The Economic and Social Council publicizes the progress or lack thereof of member states in living up to their commitments to the international community, thus relying on the moral force of disclosure to achieve its aims.

ECOSOC has created a broad range of both regional and functional commissions to address specific challenges in the economic and social realms. Regional commissions are designed to promote cooperation and coordination among geographically proximate governments regarding economic and social matters. There are also functional commissions dealing globally with specific topics, such as the COMMISSION ON HUMAN RIGHTS, the COMMISSION ON THE STATUS OF WOMEN, and the COMMISSION ON SOCIAL DEVELOPMENT, each the primary UN agency in its field. ECOSOC's commissions include among their functions making international rules, drafting treaties, and monitoring the measures to carry out agreements. ECOSOC and its commissions serve to promote agreements setting voluntary norms and minimum standards that become standards of behavior by which the efforts of each government are assessed. ECOSOC and its commissions also publish informational material and model legislation in various fields.

FUNCTIONAL COMMISSIONS OF THE ECONOMIC AND SOCIAL COUNCIL

Statistical Commission
Commission on Population and Development
Commission for Social Development
Commission on the Status of Women
Commission on Narcotic Drugs
Commission on Crime Prevention and Criminal Justice
Commission on Science and Technology for Development
Commission on Sustainable Development

REGIONAL COMMISSIONS OF THE ECONOMIC AND SOCIAL COUNCIL

Economic Commission for Africa (Addis Ababa, Ethiopia)
Economic and Social Commission for Asia and the Pacific (Bangkok, Thailand)
Economic Commission for Europe (Geneva, Switzerland)
Economic Commission for Latin America and the Caribbean (Santiago, Chile)
Economic and Social Commission for Western Asia (Beirut, LEBANON)

STANDING COMMITTEES OF THE ECONOMIC AND SOCIAL COUNCIL

Committee for Programme and Coordination
Commission on Human Settlements
Committee on Non-governmental Organizations
Committee on Negotiations with Inter-governmental Agencies

AD HOC BODIES

Ad hoc Open-ended Working Group on Informatics
Ad hoc Open-ended intergovernmental group of experts on energy and SUSTAINABLE DEVELOPMENT
Ad hoc Group of Experts on International Cooperation in Tax Matters
Ad hoc Advisory Groups on African Countries Emerging from Conflicts
Ad hoc Advisory Group on HAITI
Information and Communications Technologies Task Force
Public-Private Alliance for Rural Development
Committee on Negotiations with Intergovernmental Agencies

EXPERT BODIES

Committee of Experts on the Transport of Dangerous Goods and on the Globally Harmonized System of Classification and Labelling of Chemicals
United Nations Group of Experts on Geographical Names
Committee for Development Policy
United Nations Committee of Experts on Public Administration
Committee on Economic, Social and Cultural Rights
Permanent Forum on Indigenous Issues

OTHER RELATED BODIES

International Narcotics Control Board
Board of Trustees of the INTERNATIONAL RESEARCH AND TRAINING INSTITUTE FOR THE ADVANCEMENT OF WOMEN

FUNDS AND PROGRAMMES THAT SEND REPORTS TO ECOSOC

UNITED NATIONS CHILDREN'S FUND
UNITED NATIONS CONFERENCE ON TRADE AND DEVELOPMENT
UNITED NATIONS DEVELOPMENT FUND FOR WOMEN
United Nations Development Programme
United Nations Environment Programme
UNITED NATIONS HIGH COMMISSIONER FOR REFUGEES
UNITED NATIONS POPULATION FUND
UNITED NATIONS RELIEF AND WORKS AGENCY FOR PALESTINE REFUGEES IN THE NEAR EAST
OFFICE ON DRUGS AND CRIME
WORLD FOOD PROGRAMME
UN-HABITAT

Each July, ECOSOC convenes a month-long session at UN HEADQUARTERS in either New York City or Geneva. Known as the "High-Level Segment," this session concentrates on a specific theme of global significance. The participating governments then issue a DECLARATION that guides the work of ECOSOC's commissions for the following year. In 2002 the High-Level Segment endorsed the NEW PARTNERSHIP FOR AFRICA'S DEVELOPMENT (NEPAD). In 2003 and 2004 respectively the Council focused on integrated approaches to rural development in poor countries and poverty eradication in LEAST DEVELOPED COUNTRIES (LDCs). Much of the Council's work since the beginning of the century has been guided by the MILLENNIUM DEVELOPMENT GOALS (MDGs) established at the MILLENNIUM SUMMIT in 2000. In 2006 the session sought ways to produce full employment under desired conditions of sustainable development. The High-Level Segment's Declaration called upon all funds, programs and agencies of the UN SYSTEM to support efforts at achieving full employment goals.

See also STRUCTURE OF THE UNITED NATIONS.

Further Reading: Moore, John Allphin, Jr., and Jerry Pubantz. *The New United Nations: International Organization in the Twenty-first Century.* Upper Saddle River, N.J.: Prentice Hall, 2006. South Centre. *Enhancing the Role of the United Nations.* Geneva: South Centre, 1992. ———. *For a Strong and Democratic United Nations: A South Perspective on UN Reform.* London: Zed Books, 1995. ———. *The United Nations at a Critical Crossroads: Time for the South to Act.* Geneva: South Centre, 1993.

— *K. J. Grieb*

Economic Commission for Africa (ECA)

The ECONOMIC AND SOCIAL COUNCIL (ECOSOC) created the Economic Commission for Africa (ECA) in 1958 as one of the UN's REGIONAL ECONOMIC COMMISSIONS. As of 2006, ECA had 53 member states, and promoted economic and social DEVELOPMENT across the continent. The Commission works closely with the AFRICAN DEVELOPMENT BANK, the WORLD BANK Group, NON-GOVERNMENTAL ORGANIZATIONS, and other African REGIONAL ORGANIZATIONS, specifically the ECONOMIC COMMUNITY OF WEST AFRICAN STATES (ECOWAS), the African Institute for Economic Development and Planning, the AFRICAN UNION, the Southern Africa Development Community (SADC), the Inter-governmental Authority on Development (IGAD), the Central African Economic and Monetary Community (CEMAC), and the Common Market for Eastern and Southern Africa (COMESA). Since its establishment, the commission has had seven executive secretaries: Mekki Abbas (Sudan; 1959–61), Robert K. A. Gardiner (Ghana; 1961–75), Adebayo Adedeji (Nigeria; 1975–91), Issa Diallo (Guinea; 1991–92), Layashi Yaker (Algeria; 1992–95), Kingsley Amoako (Ghana; 1995–2005), and Abdoulie Janneh (Gambia; 2005–   ).

The commission has six program divisions covering the various aspects of development, including trade policy, gen-

der issues, and management concerns. Its primary goal is to make development progress through regional cooperation. Annually ECA convenes a conference of its members' finance ministers, and since 1999 has sponsored an African Development Forum. The May 2006 finance ministers' conference proposed a redirection to the work of the commission. Given that projections indicated the improbability of African states achieving the MILLENNIUM DEVELOPMENT GOALS (MDGs) by 2015 as mandated by the United Nations, the ministers urged the commission to narrow its priorities to those programs that could lay the basis for progress on the MDGs. The conference DECLARATION recommended ECA work more closely with the African Union and promote strongly the NEW PARTNERSHIP FOR AFRICA'S DEVELOPMENT (NEPAD). In the latter case, the Commission signed a framework agreement on collaboration with the NEPAD SECRETARIAT on July 31, 2006.

Further Reading: ECA Website: <http://www.uneca.org/>.

Economic Commission for Europe (ECE) *See* REGIONAL COMMISSIONS OF THE ECONOMIC AND SOCIAL COUNCIL.

Economic Commission for Latin America and the Caribbean (ECLAC)

Originally named the Economic Commission for Latin America (ECLA, CEPAL in Spanish), the organization was created by the UN ECONOMIC AND SOCIAL COUNCIL (ECOSOC) in 1948 to promote regional economic DEVELOPMENT. In order to gain approval for its establishment, the proposers of ECLA included in its initial membership nations with colonial territories in the region (FRANCE, GREAT BRITAIN, the Netherlands, and the UNITED STATES) as well as regional nations. In 1984, recognizing the inclusion of independent former colonies of Great Britain and the Netherlands, ECOSOC redesignated the organization as the Economic Commission for Latin America and the Caribbean. It became a leader in theory building, policy promotion, and gathering economic data for nations largely lacking the resources to engage in such activities themselves. Its economists came to occupy policy-making positions in most countries of the region.

The organization was profoundly influenced by the thought of its second Executive Secretary RAÚL PREBISCH, and the dominant thrust of its initial work involved promoting cooperation among the region's nations and encouraging the adoption of policies designed to modernize national economies through the policy of import substitution. It was anticipated that discouraging imports of manufactured goods through tariffs and targeted exchange rates would make the preexisting market for exports available for domestically produced consumer items and that the market would expand as workers in the new industries also became consumers. Successive ripple effects would render the process self-sustaining. The Latin American Free Trade Area (LAFTA) and the Central American Common Market were to implement the program regionally. The scenario did not materialize, although the level of industrialization did increase substantially. By the end of the 20th century, ECLAC had shifted its position away from protectionism and accepted the prevailing neoliberal doctrine of open markets.

ECLAC's HEADQUARTERS is in Santiago, Chile. The MEMBERSHIP in 2006 included 42 nations, encompassing all nations in Latin America and the Caribbean and also including Italy, Spain, and Portugal, and seven non-independent associate members from the Caribbean. The organization's Executive Secretary is appointed by the UN SECRETARY-GENERAL. In 1998 Secretary-General KOFI ANNAN appointed Josi Antonio Ocampo from Colombia to the post. Ocampo headed ECLA until his appointment as UNDER SECRETARY-GENERAL for Economic and Social Affairs in September 2003. He was succeeded by José Luis Machinea of Argentina. Meetings of ECLAC occur every two years with a Committee of the Whole meeting between sessions. The 28th through 31st sessions were held respectively in Mexico City (2000), Brazil (2002), San Juan (2004), and Montevideo (2006).

In 1995 ECLAC's executive secretary noted that the organization's work "had become part of the intellectual heritage of LATIN AMERICA;" that it had changed "the economic theories in vogue in the world . . . adapting them to the actual conditions of Latin America." The following year its member countries expanded ECLAC's mission to include provision of expert analysis of the development process. The UN's approval of the MILLENNIUM DEVELOPMENT GOALS (MDGs) in September 2000 also influenced ECLAC's subsequent work. Among the goals put forward by the MILLENNIUM SUMMIT, ECLAC made a special effort to incorporate in its work the commitment to halve the proportion of the world's people living in extreme poverty in the region and to make water and education accessible to all. Beyond the MDGs, the commission focused on the impact of globalization in the DEVELOPING COUNTRIES of the WESTERN HEMISPHERE.

In addition to the full commission sessions, ECLAC does much of this work through the Latin American and Caribbean Institute for Economic and Social Planning, and the Latin American Demographic Centre. These organs provide research, training, and policy advice to member states. The organization has also established the following subsidiary bodies: the Central American Economic Co-operation Committee, the Committee of High-Level Government Experts from developing member countries for analysis of the achievement of the International Development Strategy in the Latin American region, the Caribbean Development and Co-operation Committee, the Conference on the Integration of WOMEN into the Economic and Social Development of Latin America and the Caribbean, and the Regional Council for Planning.

See also REGIONAL DEVELOPMENT BANKS, REGIONAL COMMISSIONS OF THE ECONOMIC AND SOCIAL COUNCIL, SENIOR MANAGEMENT GROUP.

Further Reading: Cayuela, Jose. *ECLAC 40 Years (1948–1988)*. Santiago, Chile: Economic Commission for Latin America and the Caribbean, 1988. Rosenthal, Gert. "The United Nations and ECLAC at the Half-Century Mark." *CEPAL Review*, no. 57 (December 1995): 7–15. Santa Cruz, Hernan. "The Creation of the United Nations and ECLAC." *CEPAL Review*, no. 57 (December 1995): 17–33. ECLAC Web site: <www.eclac.cl/default.asp?idioma=IN>.

— *M. W. Bray*

Economic Commission for Western Asia (ECWA)   *See* REGIONAL COMMISSIONS OF THE ECONOMIC AND SOCIAL COUNCIL.

Economic Community of West African States (ECOWAS)

The Treaty of Lagos established the Economic Community of West African States in May 1975. The 15 original signatories included Benin, Côte d'Ivoire, Gambia, Ghana, Guinea, Guinea-Bissau, Liberia, Mali, Mauritania, Niger, Nigeria, Senegal, SIERRA LEONE, Togo, and Upper Volta (Burkina Faso). Cape Verde joined in 1977; Mauritania withdrew its MEMBERSHIP in 2001.

The main aim of ECOWAS is to promote regional cooperation "in all fields of economic activity, particularly industry, transport, telecommunications, energy, agriculture, natural resources, commerce, monetary and financial questions, social and cultural matters." During 1991 and 1992, member states revised the original TREATY to strengthen regional integration, in both the political and economic spheres. The revised treaty was signed in July 1993. Its main political goal has been the creation of a West African parliament to enhance regional governance, identity, and citizenship. Its main economic goal has been to create a common market and a single currency.

Institutions in ECOWAS include the Authority of Heads of States and Government that meets once a year; the Fund for Cooperation, Compensation and Development (Fund); the Executive Secretariat with representatives elected for four-year terms; the Council of Ministers with two representatives from each country; the Community Parliament; the Economic and Social Council; and the Community Court of Justice. The SECRETARIAT, located in Abuja, Nigeria, and the fund located in Lomé, Togo, are two of ECOWAS's most important governance and policy-making bodies.

There are five specialized commissions of the secretariat responsible for various sectoral activities in the region: (1) trade, customs, immigration, and monetary payments; (2)

transportation, telecommunications, and energy; (3) industry, agriculture, and natural resources; (4) social and cultural affairs; and (5) administration and finance. In the area of energy, ECOWAS has planned to establish regional centers to disseminate information on alternative and renewal energy resources. In agriculture, its goal of self-sufficiency by 2000 was not realized. However, regional centers were established to provide information on seed selection and livestock, and to increase overall agricultural productivity. In the social and cultural areas, there are organizations for health, trade unions, youth, universities, WOMEN, and annual sports events. In March 2001, ECOWAS met with a 17-member UN Inter-Agency Mission to West Africa to explore continued cooperation in the areas of good governance, national reconciliation, arms reduction, and human security, including HIV/AIDS, malaria, refugees, displaced persons, and war-affected children.

The Community's fund for Cooperation, Compensation, and Development has entered into a number of agreements to promote regional economic DEVELOPMENT, integration, and external investments to the region. In 1988, the fund signed an agreement with the African Development Bank and the ISLAMIC DEVELOPMENT BANK to cofinance projects both for regional and nonregional entrepreneurs and microenterprises. Private investment to the region is promoted through the private regional investment bank, Ecobank Transnational Inc., located in Lomé, Togo.

The Economic Community of West African States has tried to enhance both intraregional and international cooperation. In the 1990s ECOWAS and the United Nations cooperated on CONFLICT RESOLUTION and management in Liberia, Guinea-Bissau, and Sierra Leone. In August 1990, ECOWAS's Standing MEDIATION Committee established ECOMOG, a cease-fire monitoring group to oversee the implementation of the Abuja Agreement for Liberia. Subsequently, a joint UN-ECOWAS-Sierra Leone government coordination MECHANISM was established for conflict management in Sierra Leone. ECOWAS member states also agreed to a Moratorium on the Importation, Exportation, and Manufacture of Light WEAPONS in West Africa that became effective in November 1998, and the Mechanism for Conflict Prevention, Management, Resolution, PEACEKEEPING and Security in December 1999.

In the Liberian case, the community authorized ECOMOG to conduct military operations if necessary to restore order. The UN SECURITY COUNCIL endorsed the ECOWAS intervention. Leaders lauded the organization as an example of the emerging value of REGIONAL ORGANIZATIONS in the restoration of peace in "failed states." Based on the Liberian precedent, ECOWAS established a security mechanism in December 1999 in order to institutionalize this type of intervention to be among the purposes of the organization.

See also AFRICAN UNION, ECONOMIC COMMISSION FOR AFRICA.

Further Reading: Anda, Michael O. *International Relations in Contemporary Africa.* Lanham, Md.: University Press of America, 2000. Déme, Mourtada. *Law, Morality and International Armed Intervention: The United Nations and ECOWAS in Liberia.* New York: Routledge, 2005. Dutt, Sagarika. *Africa at the Millennium: An Agenda for Mature Development.* New York: Palgrave, 2000. Ezenwe, Uka. *ECOWAS and the Economic Integration of West Africa.* New York: St. Martin's, 1983. Senghor, Jeggan Colley. *ECOWAS: Perspectives on Treaty Revision and Reform.* Dakar: United Nations African Institute for Economic Development and Planning, 1999. Shaw, Timothy M., and Julius Emeka Okolo. *The Political Economy of Foreign Policy in ECOWAS.* New York: St. Martin's, 1994. ECOWAS Web site: <www.ecowas.int>.

— *M. S. Smith*

Eden, Anthony (1897–1977)

As British foreign secretary from 1941 to 1945, Eden was a supporter of a new postwar international organization and worked with U.S. secretary of state CORDELL HULL at the MOSCOW CONFERENCE OF FOREIGN MINISTERS in 1943 to persuade the Soviets to accept the general terms of the Four Power DECLARATION that had been drafted earlier at the Quebec Conference. It recognized the "necessity" of a postwar "international organization" to keep the peace. In Moscow, representatives of the great powers, including CHINA, committed themselves to forming a general international organization composed of "all peace-loving states . . . for the maintenance of international peace and security." Eden attended the founding San Francisco conference, expressing a strong desire to serve as the SECRETARY-GENERAL of the new United Nations.

In later years, however, Eden expressed skepticism about the efficacy of international organizations in thwarting AGGRESSION. As British prime minister (1955–57) he played a central role in attempting to bypass the United Nations in the ill-considered international crisis prompted by Egypt's GAMAL ABDUL NASSER's nationalization of the Suez Canal in 1956. Despite efforts to halt UN action against British, French, and Israeli military initiatives by the first Western use of the VETO power, pressure from the United Nations and the UNITED STATES forced the Western allies to yield their positions on the Suez Canal to the first United Nations PEACEKEEPING force in November 1956. Despite Eden's proposal that British and French troops make up the force, the UNITED NATIONS EMERGENCY FORCE (UNEF) consisted of troops from small neutral states, establishing the model for all future UN peacekeeping units during the COLD WAR.

The diplomatic fiasco of the SUEZ CRISIS led to Eden's resignation and retirement from public life in January 1957. He subsequently wrote several political memoirs and appeared in British documentaries of the war years. He died on January 14, 1977.

Further Reading: Boyle, Peter G., ed. *The Eden-Eisenhower Correspondence, 1955–1957.* Chapel Hill: University of North Carolina Press, 2005. Dutton, David. *Anthony Eden: A Life and Reputation.* New York: St. Martin's, 1997. Ostrower, Gary. *The United Nations and the United States.* New York: Twayne, 1998. Pearson, Jonathan. *Sir Anthony Eden and the Suez Crisis: Reluctant Gamble.* New York: Palgrave Macmillan, 2003. Thomas, Hugh. *Suez.* New York: Harper, 1967.

— *E. M. Clauss*

Egypt *See* ARAB-ISRAELI DISPUTE, SUEZ CRISIS.

Eighteen Nation Disarmament Committee (ENDC)

Created in 1961 as a replacement for the Ten Nation Disarmament Committee, the ENDC for the first time brought the voice of the non-aligned states into the UN DISARMAMENT debate, which to that point had been the sole preserve of the two superpowers and their closest allies. Ostensibly a subordinate committee to the United Nations DISARMAMENT COMMISSION, the ENDC was largely an independent venue for negotiations on a number of disarmament and arms control issues. Most important, it served as the institutional setting for the negotiation of the 1968 NUCLEAR NON-PROLIFERATION TREATY.

The UNITED STATES and the USSR had monopolized nuclear disarmament negotiations within the Disarmament Commission by relegating those talks to a subcommittee consisting of the two states and the United Kingdom. The subcommittee was expanded in 1959 with the addition of seven new members, but little changed, because care was taken to assure that each side could count on five votes on the committee. The additional members were Bulgaria, Czechoslovakia, Italy, Canada, Poland, Romania, and FRANCE. SECRETARY-GENERAL DAG HAMMARSKJÖLD, among others, complained on several occasions that the UN's responsibilities were being undermined by the East-West domination of arms control.

By 1961, however, the United States was interested in developing good relations with the newly independent states of the Third World. So too, NIKITA KHRUSHCHEV's government in Moscow sought to appeal to the nonaligned nations. Under pressure from those states and from the GENERAL ASSEMBLY, the U.S. and USSR agreed to expand the committee to 18 nations with the superpowers as the co-chairs. The new members were Brazil, Burma, Ethiopia, INDIA, Mexico, Nigeria, Sweden, and the United Arab Republic.

The lesser powers were concerned particularly with the problem of "horizontal" proliferation, the spread of nuclear WEAPONS to non-nuclear states. In 1959 the General Assembly passed Resolution 1380, proposed by Ireland, calling upon the Ten Nation Disarmament Committee to consider "the feasibility of an international agreement . . . whereby the Powers producing nuclear weapons would refrain from handing over control of such WEAPONS to any nation not possessing them, and whereby the Powers not possessing such weapons would refrain from manufacturing them." The ENDC became the new STRUCTURE through which the non-nuclear states initiated non-proliferation proposals. The idea of a "non-atomic club" gained credence, and that group helped clarify the necessary aspects of any successful non-proliferation TREATY.

On May 25, 1962, the ENDC co-chairs placed "Measures to Prevent Further Dissemination of Nuclear Weapons" on the committee's agenda. The eight nonaligned members outlined the main principles a non-proliferation treaty should have, among them an agreement that it should embody an acceptable balance of mutual responsibilities and obligations for nuclear and non-nuclear states. The ENDC negotiations reached a critical point in August 1967 when the Soviet Union and the United States tendered a joint draft treaty on non-proliferation. It prohibited the transfer of nuclear weapons to non-nuclear states and barred non-nuclear signatories from obtaining them by any means. Nonaligned states on the committee, however, balked at the one-sided nature of the proposal. It created, in their view, a world of nuclear "haves" and "have nots," without placing any restrictions on the arsenals of the nuclear powers. The nonaligned committee members, led by Brazil, emerged as representatives for the prevalent views of the General Assembly majority.

Brazil and other states argued that there was no "acceptable balance of responsibilities" in the draft between nuclear and non-nuclear states. Nothing in the draft committed the United States and the Soviet Union to decreasing "vertical" proliferation, that is, the size of their already existing stockpiles. Without revision, the smaller states made clear they would not accept the treaty. The superpowers had hoped to ignore the question of vertical proliferation, since this would call for extensive deprivation of their own freedom of action in the nuclear sphere. But the need for acceptance by the non-nuclear states of the draft in order to give it any value led to a major concession. Article Six of a revised treaty was added. It required the nuclear powers "to pursue negotiations in good faith on effective measures relating to cessation of the nuclear arms race at an early date and to nuclear disarmament." Article Six, imposed by the will of the ENDC's nonaligned states, laid the basis for the next stage in arms control negotiations, the Strategic Arms Limitation Talks between Washington and Moscow.

Further Reading: Bader, William. *The United States and the Spread of Nuclear Weapons.* New York: Pegasus, 1968. Beker, Avi. *Disarmament without Order.* Westport, Conn.: Greenwood, 1985. Larson, Thomas B. *Disarmament and Soviet Policy, 1964–1968.* Englewood Cliffs, N.J.: Prentice Hall, 1969. United Nations Department of Public Information.

The United Nations and Disarmament, 1945–1965. New York: United Nations Department of Public Information, 1967.

Eisenhower, Dwight D. (1890–1969)

Born in 1890 the third son of a poor Midwestern family, Dwight David Eisenhower rose to become commander in chief of allied forces in World War II and the 34th president of the UNITED STATES. His parents were pacifists, members of the Brethren of Christ, an offshoot of the Mennonite faith. Unable to afford college for their son, the Eisenhowers allowed him to apply to West Point Military Academy where the cost of his education would be paid by the government. Dwight ("Ike") Eisenhower graduated from the Academy in 1915 and married Mary Geneva ("Mamie") Doud the following year.

Eisenhower did not see action in World War I, but used the interwar years to make important connections within the military establishment. He honed his command and bureaucratic skills during this period. In 1942 he was given command, ahead of more senior officers, of the Anglo-American invasion of North Africa, and then of the 1943 assault on Sicily and the Italian mainland. As the mastermind of the D-day invasion that liberated FRANCE in 1944, Eisenhower became a household name around the world and a national hero at home.

His celebrity made Ike a popular choice for the presidency. Both political parties sought his candidacy. President Truman offered to support him in the 1948 elections if Eisenhower ran as a Democrat. But Eisenhower declined. After a brief stint as postwar army chief of staff, Eisenhower left the military and accepted the presidency of Columbia University. However, Truman recalled him to service in 1951 as the first Supreme Allied Commander of the new North Atlantic Treaty Organization (NATO).

It was during this period with the KOREAN WAR underway and the apparent rising threat of Soviet expansionism that Eisenhower decided to seek the Republican presidential nomination. He feared that the Republican Party was moving too far toward isolation under the leadership of the likely Republican candidate, Robert A. Taft. And he opposed the "big government" domestic policies put in place under FRANKLIN D. ROOSEVELT and Truman.

Elected in a landslide in 1952 and again in 1956, Eisenhower sought "a middle way." A pragmatic internationalist, the president held no overarching worldview in which the United Nations fit neatly. His primary foreign policy concerns were the challenge of Soviet communism and the defense of the "free world." Influenced by his Secretary of State John Foster Dulles, Eisenhower invoked the COLLECTIVE SELF-DEFENSE provisions of the UN CHARTER's Article 51 to create several military alliances around the world as part of the U.S. containment of Soviet Union. He also endorsed the development of the American nuclear arsenal as a deterrent to a

Soviet strategic threat, nuclear or conventional, to the United States or its European allies. This policy came at a time when the highest priority of the United Nations seemed to be DISARMAMENT and an end to the arms race.

President Eisenhower moved quickly to bring the war in Korea to an armistice. Eisenhower won the U.S. presidential election in part because of a widespread belief that a new administration was necessary to end the unpopular war. Keeping a campaign pledge, the president-elect flew to Korea in early December where he met with South Korean president Syngman Rhee and U.S. commander Mark Clark, making it clear that any escalation of the conflict would risk global war. The United States offered a mutual security PACT with South Korea if it would accept a UN-proposed armistice and leave Korean forces under the control of the UN command. During his first months in office Eisenhower subtly warned CHINA of the possibility of nuclear retaliation if it escalated the war. The North Korean government and the UN Command agreed to armistice terms in June 1953.

Having achieved a halt in the fighting on the Korean Peninsula, the president turned his attention to what he saw as the more serious challenge, the long-term Soviet strategic threat to Europe, America's allies around the world, and the U.S. mainland. In the confrontation between East and West, the United Nations, while a useful setting for diplomacy, for shaping public opinion, and for addressing important but peripheral issues of world affairs, appeared to be more an arena of superpower competition than an asset to U.S. policy. Particularly as the United States lost its traditional working majority among the UN MEMBERSHIP after the middle of the decade, the Eisenhower administration gave increasing weight to U.S. alliance relations, bilateral ties, unilateral foreign aid programs, and direct communications with the Soviet Union.

Part of the new president's reticence to lend more than lukewarm endorsement to the UN—despite his support in 1945 for the SAN FRANCISCO CONFERENCE, which he later called "hope's high point"—arose from the strong domestic opposition to the United Nations found particularly in his own Republican Party. The institution was under withering attack from well-known U.S. Senators Joseph McCarthy, William Knowland, and Robert Taft. They charged that the UN was a haven for communist spies and saboteurs. Beyond the perceived communist threat, isolationists worried that the United Nations could undermine U.S. SOVEREIGNTY. To forestall that possibility, Senator John W. Bricker introduced in the Senate a constitutional AMENDMENT limiting the authority of TREATIES to override federal and state law without specific congressional approval.

The administration opposed the BRICKER AMENDMENT, but believed it could only defeat its passage by being publicly vigilant about communist infiltration of UN HEADQUARTERS and denying any UN influence on U.S. policy. The first casualty was U.S. endorsement for any UN HUMAN RIGHTS conventions, for fear such treaties could be used by Bricker's supporters as examples of international agreements that could affect U.S. domestic law. Second, the administration pressured UN SECRETARY-GENERAL TRYGVE LIE to allow the imposition of a loyalty and security check program on American employees at the United Nations. The Secretary-General allowed the U.S. Federal Bureau of Investigation to set up an office at the UN and to question and fingerprint U.S. nationals who were supposedly international civil servants. Eisenhower's International Organizations Employees Loyalty Board reviewed more than 4,000 individuals, including the highest ranking American UN official, RALPH BUNCHE.

While President Eisenhower acknowledged that COLLECTIVE SECURITY was the optimal strategy for the preservation of world peace, as long as the Soviet VETO in the SECURITY COUNCIL blocked what Eisenhower thought were essential steps toward peace, he was willing to substitute regional alliances—creating military ties with 42 states by 1956—and unilateral initiatives for UN action like that which had occurred in Korea. This was a strategy that could garner support from a Congress skeptical about the value of the United Nations. In at least four crises—GUATEMALA (1954), Suez and Hungary (1956), and LEBANON (1958)—the administration sought other avenues than the UN to achieve American ends.

In 1950 Colonel Jacobo Arbenz Guzmán won the presidency of Guatemala. His economic, social REFORM, and nationalization policies brought the ire of the U.S. administration, which saw the Arbenz government as a channel for communist influence in Central America. The president decided to employ the Central Intelligence Agency (CIA) to subvert the regime by assisting anti-Arbenz rebels operating out of Honduras and Nicaragua. Eisenhower also imposed a naval blockade to bar possible Soviet military shipments to Guatemala. President Arbenz requested a meeting of the Security Council under Articles 34 and 35 of the UN CHARTER. Secretary-General DAG HAMMARSKJÖLD, GREAT BRITAIN, and France supported the request, but the United States argued that any hearing should first be before the ORGANIZATION OF AMERICAN STATES (OAS). With strong pressure on its allies, the United States was able to defeat a Soviet RESOLUTION on June 25, 1954, to put the matter on the Council agenda. The Arbenz government was overthrown a week later.

If the London and Paris governments were anxious to bring the Guatemalan matter to the Security Council, they were not interested in having the 1956 SUEZ CRISIS appear before the United Nations. On July 26 of that year EGYPT's president GAMAL ABDUL NASSER nationalized the Suez Canal, jeopardizing British and French access to Asia and Israel's economy and ties to Europe. The three powers secretly orchestrated an invasion of the canal zone in late October. The Eisenhower administration had tried to defuse the crisis during the summer. However, it did not see the United Nations as a viable forum in this instance, repeatedly turning down Hammarskjöld's offers of UN involvement. Instead, Washington first proposed, and then convened an international conference that called for international management of the canal under Egyptian sovereignty.

When U.S. diplomacy failed and the allies invaded Egypt, Eisenhower was incensed. The Suez crisis entangled two American concerns: its relationship with the newly liberated postcolonial states of AFRICA and Asia, of which Egypt was considered a leader, and the overarching threat of Soviet expansionism that could be encouraged if U.S. allies were forced to withdraw from the MIDDLE EAST, or if Israel suffered a perceived defeat at the hands of Soviet allies. As the West became more embroiled in the Suez confrontation, the Soviet Union decided to quell a revolt in Hungary by dispatching Soviet troops to the communist bloc nation. Unless he were willing to lead the Western allies into war with the USSR at that critical moment, Eisenhower had little choice but to seek a face-saving condemnation of the Soviet invasion in the Security Council. With two crises underway, it seemed the Council had become the center of world affairs. However, it served more as a site for East-West recrimination than as a decision-making body. In the end the United Nations was used only in the aftermath of the Suez crisis to provide a diplomatic avenue for British, French, and Israeli forces to withdraw once the United States decided the canal occupation could not be supported by Washington. These armies were replaced on the ground by the UN's first PEACEKEEPING force, the UNITED NATIONS EMERGENCY FORCE (UNEF), an international innovation with long-term significance for the world organization, but at the time a limited multilateral response meant to provide political cover for both sides in the confrontation.

In the eyes of the American administration, the denouement of the Suez crisis did not diminish the threat to U.S. interests in the Middle East either by Soviet leaders or, in the American view, by the Soviet surrogate, President Nasser. Eisenhower decided to commit the United States to defend its friends in the region from communist expansionism. Under the "Eisenhower Doctrine," the American government offered military aid and, if necessary, U.S. unilateral military support to friendly governments threatened by the Soviet Union or its regional allies. Under the Eisenhower Doctrine, the administration sent 14,000 marines to Lebanon in the summer of 1958 to protect the Maronite Christian regime of President Camille Chamoun. Following a bloody coup in Baghdad, IRAQ, Eisenhower became convinced that Lebanon, which was experiencing severe political unrest in the wake of Chamoun's decision to serve a second term as president in violation of the Lebanese constitution, was the victim of "indirect aggression" by Nasser. The Egyptian president was extremely popular in Lebanon, had formed the United Arab Republic that combined Egypt and Syria into one state, and had given speeches calling for the inclusion of Lebanon in the new union.

Eisenhower indicated that he had no wish for the U.S. forces to stay long. He hoped a UN force might take the Americans place once stability was restored. But no UN mission was sent, as Chamoun recanted his political plans and was succeeded in August 1958 by Faud Chebab as president. Domestic politics returned to normal in Lebanon and American forces were withdrawn.

The COLD WAR provided the policy lens through which the Eisenhower administration interpreted world affairs, including the nature, role, and value of the United Nations. On matters of war and peace, the president preferred direct U.S. action, and saw the UN as one of many forums in which the struggle with worldwide communism needed to be fought. In the United Nations the United States sought to keep a working majority in the GENERAL ASSEMBLY, and most importantly to keep Mao Zedong's communist government in mainland CHINA from being seated in place of the Republic of China that had held permanent representation on the Security Council since 1945. On the latter issue, the United States insisted that the UN treat the matter of Chinese representation as a "substantive" rather than a "procedural" question. This required a two-thirds vote to seat Mao's government. The Eisenhower strategy was successful throughout his term, and would keep the People's Republic of China out of the UN until 1971.

When Dwight Eisenhower was inaugurated in 1953, there were 56 members of the United Nations, most of them strong allies of the United States. Eisenhower was not interested in seeing Soviet puppet regimes from Eastern Europe added to the MEMBERSHIP. For their part, Soviet leaders were not willing to admit Western-oriented governments unless Warsaw PACT states were also admitted. Eisenhower finally relented in 1955 because of increasing pressure from third world nations that wanted entrance to the world body. The logjam was broken in December 1955 when both sides agreed to admit 16 nations, four from the Soviet bloc and 12 from Africa, Asia, and the Arab world. The first wave of new members was quickly followed by other successful applicants. By the time Eisenhower left office, African and Asian states were approaching a majority in the Assembly, and the United States could count on less than the majority necessary to pass or block important UN actions.

The Eisenhower administration's desire to make diplomatic inroads with the new nations of the SOUTH led it to give up its early objection to UN economic DEVELOPMENT programs and to suggest that an easing of the East-West confrontation might lead to military savings that could be transferred to development projects. The strongest advocate in the administration for this policy direction was Eisenhower's ambassador to the United Nations, Henry Cabot Lodge. The ambassador urged increased U.S. contributions to UN agencies, in particular to the SPECIAL UNITED NATIONS FUND FOR ECONOMIC DEVELOPMENT (SUNFED) created in 1957. Eisenhower promised to make a contribution to SUNFED equal to two-thirds of the sum given by all other nations. The president also supported new forms of aid, including food assistance. He strongly endorsed the creation of the FOOD AND AGRICULTURE ORGANIZATION (FAO).

President Eisenhower often linked U.S. promised development contributions to progress on disarmament. On April 16, 1953, the president delivered what came to be known as his "Chance for Peace" speech. In the wake of JOSEPH STALIN's death, Eisenhower argued that if the new Soviet leaders proved to be more responsible than their predecessor and were willing to forego subversion of free governments, then the two superpowers could move forward on the reduction of armaments under the aegis of the United Nations. He proposed that arms control should include bilateral reductions in forces and the prohibition of certain types of WEAPONS. Money saved from these initiatives could be placed in a UN FUND for aid and development in poorer parts of the world.

Following up on this proposal, Eisenhower addressed the UN General Assembly in December 1953. In his "ATOMS FOR PEACE PROPOSAL," he suggested that the nuclear powers transfer a percentage of their fissionable materials to an as yet uncreated UN agency. The proposed body would safeguard the plutonium and look for ways to use the material for peaceful purposes. The United States offered to put U.S. stockpiles under agency control at a five-to-one ratio to that contributed by the Soviet Union. Eisenhower's proposal, while it led to no transfer of nuclear materials to the UN, initiated negotiations that brought about the creation of the INTERNATIONAL ATOMIC ENERGY AGENCY in 1957.

Eisenhower's 1953 speeches seemed to highlight the important role the United Nations might play in the field of disarmament, but the administration's actions belied the rhetoric. Strategic NUCLEAR WEAPONS policy was too important to leave to multilateral negotiations. At most, the United Nations might provide the STRUCTURE behind which the superpowers secretly could negotiate minor and partial agreements. The UN ATOMIC ENERGY COMMISSION was replaced in 1952 by the DISARMAMENT COMMISSION, which in turn created a Subcommittee on Disarmament made up of the United States, the United Kingdom, France, Canada, and the USSR. Any Disarmament Commission negotiations of note took place in the subcommittee. Otherwise the UN's disarmament machinery served as a venue for propaganda.

The Soviet Union regularly called for general and complete disarmament while the United States insisted on intrusive inspections to verify any agreement. At the Geneva Summit of 1955 Eisenhower put forward his "OPEN SKIES" PROPOSAL. He suggested that each side provide complete blueprints to their military facilities. Then he proposed that each side conduct aerial surveillance of the other's installations as a practical step to assure there could be no surprise attack or secret development of nuclear superiority. The Soviets rejected the plan as nothing but a ruse for American spying. With no progress on substantive disarmament, the administration could only join the Soviets in supporting an enlargement of the Subcommittee to 10 members, five from each side of the ideological divide. The UN disarmament forum became emblematic of the cold war deadlock that persisted in all UN bodies during the Eisenhower years.

See also ACHESON-LILIENTHAL REPORT; CHURCHILL, WINSTON; QUANTICO MEETING.

Further Reading: Ambrose, Stephen. *Eisenhower: The President.* 2 vols. New York: Simon and Schuster, 1984. Eisenhower, Dwight D. "Chance for Peace" speech delivered before the American Society of Newspaper Editors, April 16, 1953. *Public Papers of the Presidents, 1953,* Washington: U.S. Government Printing Office, 179. Moore, John Allphin, Jr., and Jerry Pubantz. *To Create a New World?: American Presidents and the United Nations.* New York: Peter Lang Publishing, 1999. Pruden, Caroline. *Conditional Partners: Eisenhower, the United Nations, and the Search for a Permanent Peace.* Baton Rouge: Louisiana State University Press, 1998. Web site for Eisenhower's "Atoms for Peace" Speech: <www.iaea.org/About/history_speech.html>.

El Salvador

El Salvador entered the United Nations as an original member on October 24, 1945. Its participation within the organization during the UN's first decades of operations showed it to be a close ally of the UNITED STATES in the developing COLD WAR confrontations with the Soviet Union and its allies.

A brutal civil war in El Salvador escalated after 1981. The country's military, backed by the United States, worked to block an increasingly effective guerrilla movement. A military stalemate and the success of UN-brokered agreements elsewhere in Central America led to deeper UN involvement in the country. Working in concert with the Contadora Peace initiative launched in 1985, SECRETARY-GENERAL BOUTROS BOUTROS-GHALI backed the efforts of the "Friends of the Secretary General" to reach a negotiated settlement to the conflict. In 1989, Secretary-General JAVIER PÉREZ DE CUÉLLAR urged the presidents of the Central American countries to focus their efforts toward achieving a settlement. Working both directly and through representatives, the Secretary-General helped craft the San José HUMAN RIGHTS Accord in 1990 and gained acceptance from the Salvadoran government for UN observers in the country's transition from civil war to democratic elections.

Successful negotiations that ended the civil war then led to more direct UN involvement. In May 1991, a SECURITY COUNCIL RESOLUTION authorized the creation of the UN OBSERVER MISSION IN EL SALVADOR (ONUSAL). ONUSAL helped ensure the successful application of a peace agreement between the Salvadoran government and the Frente Faribundo Martí para la Liberación Nacional (FMLN). It

then stationed observers throughout the country to help certify a national election. Representatives signed a final version of the peace TREATY in 1992. This treaty granted a "Peace Commission" (the National Commission for Consolidation of Peace, or COPAZ) authority over the demilitarization of the guerrilla forces and their integration into Salvadoran society and political affairs. It also established a "Truth Commission" to investigate human rights violations connected with the civil war. The treaty gave ONUSAL a cooperative role in this process. The observer mission remained in place to monitor the 1994 elections and to facilitate continuing negotiations between the two sides in the conflict. It was replaced in April 1995 with the United Nations Mission in El Salvador (MINUSAL), a small civilian contingent to provide UN GOOD OFFICES to the parties.

The stability and regional stature of El Salvador was recognized in 2006 by the UN GENERAL ASSEMBLY's election of the government to one of the three Latin American seats on the newly established PEACEBUILDING COMMISSION. However, worries remained that the country might slide back into political turmoil following elections in 2004 that were marked by extreme polarization in the electorate. The UN SPECIAL RAPPORTEUR that year also reported serious incidents of violence against WOMEN.

See also BASEL CONVENTION ON THE CONTROL OF TRANS-BOUNDARY MOVEMENTS OF HAZARDOUS WASTES AND THEIR DISPOSAL, DEMOCRATIZATION, LATIN AMERICA.

Further Reading: Johnston, Ian. *Rights and Reconciliation: UN Strategies in El Salvador.* Boulder, Colo.: Lynn Rienner, 1995. Roberts, Adam, and Benedict Kingsbury, eds. *United Nations, Divided World: The UN's Roles in International Relations.* Oxford: Clarendon Press, 1993. Tulchin, Joseph, ed. *Is There a Transition to Democracy in El Salvador?* Boulder, Colo.: Lynn Rienner, 1992.

— D. K. Lewis

election assistance

Following the close of the COLD WAR in the 1980s the United Nations became a critical international actor in the promotion of democratic electoral procedures, both in states making the transition from authoritarian forms of government and in nations emerging from civil war or rebellion. During the tenure of SECRETARY-GENERAL JAVIER PÉREZ DE CUÉLLAR (1982–91) the UN also introduced democratic elections as a central component of NATION-BUILDING wherever new "robust" PEACEKEEPING operations were undertaken. Regular elections for national and local political posts were understood to be one of the essential ingredients, along with HUMAN RIGHTS protection, transparent government accountability, the rule of law, an established court system, popular political participation, political parties, and a vibrant civil society, in the DEMOCRATIZATION process pursued by Pérez

A voter in parliamentary elections approaches the entrance to a voting center watched by a United Nations Stabilization Mission in Haiti (MINUSTAH) member of the Brazilian Battalion, in Port-Au-Prince, Haiti. (UN PHOTO 116991/SOPHIA PARIS)

de Cuéllar and succeeding secretaries-general. One of the earliest and most successful efforts came in NAMIBIA. Under SECURITY COUNCIL authorization, the UN Transition Assistance Group (UNTAG) assisted with the establishment of an independent government following the withdrawal of South African forces in 1988. UNTAG educated and registered voters, administered elections for a constituent assembly, and monitored the Namibian government's first election, in which 96 percent of eligible voters participated. With varying levels of success, the United Nations later replicated the Namibian model of democratic elections in CAMBODIA, GUATEMALA, EL SALVADOR, and TIMOR-LESTE.

The GENERAL ASSEMBLY (GA) passed several "election RESOLUTIONS" during the last two decades of the 20th century, endorsing the Western model of democratic government. In Resolution 157 (1988), the Assembly declared "the authority to govern shall be based on the will of the people, expressed in periodic and genuine elections." According to the Assembly, this method of choosing a nation's leaders was mandated by the UNIVERSAL DECLARATION OF HUMAN

RIGHTS and the INTERNATIONAL COVENANT ON CIVIL AND POLITICAL RIGHTS. The following year Assembly members passed Resolution 146 asserting that determining the will of a people requires an electoral process that "provides an equal opportunity for all citizens to become candidates and put forward their political views." In Resolution 129 on December 12, 1997, the Assembly formally affirmed the role of the United Nations in electoral assistance, and called for an expansion of this activity through several UN agencies. The GA endorsement of international election monitoring, administration, and advice to governments was reinforced by a series of "democracy resolutions" (Res. 50/133, December 20, 1995; Res. 51/31, December 6, 1996; Res. 52/18, November 21, 1997) passed between 1988 and 1998 that defined democracy based on periodic and free elections as the only legitimate form of government.

Pérez de Cuéllar's successor as Secretary-General, BOUTROS BOUTROS-GHALI, outlined an ambitious program for UN-sponsored democratic nation-building in a report entitled *AN AGENDA FOR PEACE,* followed four years later by

An Agenda for Democratization. In both, the Secretary-General argued for policies that included democratic electoral processes. He contended that these were essential for the restoration of weak states and former autocratic societies.

The UN's democratic nation-building initiatives necessarily involved subsidiary bodies and SPECIALIZED AGENCIES. With the growing acceptance of democratization as the primary strategy for nation-building in conflict zones or weak states, the General Assembly created the Electoral Assistance Division (EAD) in the UN SECRETARIAT in 1992 to assist with national and municipal elections. Later made part of the Department of Political Affairs, EAD had by 2005 received requests for electoral assistance from more than 140 countries and provided help in 91 cases, including troubled places such as MOZAMBIQUE, BOSNIA, Palestine, and ANGOLA. Its most serious challenge may have been in 2006 in CONGO, where it worked with the existing peacekeeping mission to hold the first legitimate, free, and fair elections in 40 years. The elections occurred even as the eastern part of the country remained in rebellion.

The division coordinates its activities with the other agencies and NON-GOVERNMENTAL ORGANIZATIONS operating in the country. The United Nations as well encourages REGIONAL ECONOMIC COMMISIONS and REGIONAL ORGANIZATIONS to assist in sustaining stable democracies. Also central to the UN democracy promotion is the UN HIGH COMMISSIONER FOR HUMAN RIGHTS in GENEVA.

Additionally, the UN DEVELOPMENT PROGRAMME (UNDP) and the WORLD BANK direct resources toward improved governance STRUCTURES in poor countries. By 2000, one-third of the UNDP BUDGET went toward democracy promotion. These funds are administered through the Division of Management, Development, and Governance, which spends close to $1 billion annually on democratic governance projects. In recent years these projects have included national elections in SIERRA LEONE, public participation in Nigeria, and the creation of a judicial commission in AFGHANISTAN to restore the country's judicial system.

See also BRAHIMI REPORT, CHAPTER VI ½ PROVISIONS, DAYTON PEACE ACCORDS, HAITI, INDONESIA, INTERNATIONAL CIVILIAN MISSION IN HAITI, PEACEBUILDING COMMISSION, UNITED NATIONS ANGOLA VERIFICATION MISSION, UNITED NATIONS INTERIM ADMINISTRATION MISSION FOR KOSOVO, UNITED NATIONS MISSION IN BOSNIA AND HERZEGOVINA, UNITED NATIONS OBSERVER MISSION IN EL SALVADOR, UNITED NATIONS OBSERVER MISSION FOR THE VERIFICATION OF ELECTIONS IN NICARAGUA, UNITED NATIONS OPERATION IN MOZAMBIQUE, UNITED NATIONS TRANSITIONAL ADMINISTRATION IN EAST TIMOR, UNITED NATIONS TRANSITIONAL AUTHORITY IN CAMBODIA, UNITED NATIONS VOLUNTEERS.

Further Reading: Beigbeder, Yves. *International Monitoring of Plebiscites, Referenda, and National Elections: Self-Determination and Transition to Democracy.* Boston: M. Nijhoff, 1994. Bjornlund, Eric. *Beyond Free and Fair: Monitoring Elections and Building Democracy.* Washington, D.C.: Woodrow Wilson Center Press, 2004. Boutros-Ghali, Boutros. *An Agenda for Democratization.* New York: United Nations, 1996. Dobbins, James, Seth G. Jones, Keith Crane, Andrew Rathmell, Brett Steele, and Richard Teltschik. *The UN's Role in Nation-Building: From the Congo to Iraq.* Santa Monica, Calif.: RAND Corporation, 2004. Kumar, Krishna. *Postconflict Elections, Democratization, and International Assistance.* Boulder, Colo.: Lynne Rienner, 1998.

Election Assistance Division

The UN GENERAL ASSEMBLY created the Election Assistance Division (EAD) in the SECRETARIAT in 1992 to assist with national and municipal elections. Later made part of the Department of Political Affairs, EAD receives requests for electoral assistance from countries in the developing world, new and restored democracies, nations in transition from authoritarian forms of government, and NATION-BUILDING operations in formerly failed states. By 2005 EAD had provided help in 91 cases out of 140 requests. Among its most visible initiatives was electoral help in MOZAMBIQUE, BOSNIA, Palestine, ANGOLA, and CONGO. In this last case, the division worked with the existing PEACEKEEPING mission in 2006 to hold the first free elections in 40 years.

While the EAD asserts that "there is no single political system or electoral method equally suited to all nations," the division's endeavors are part of the UN's broad DEMOCRATIZATION program launched in the wake of the COLD WAR. EAD works closely with other UN agencies and outside organizations to encourage national political processes that conform closely to Western models of democratic governance, in particular the holding of periodic elections, the guarantee of equal political access, and the provision of fair participation by a government's opposition. Of particular importance have been EAD's efforts to achieve equal access to national media for all competing groups. It has also encouraged party pluralism as essential to giving voters a meaningful electoral choice. Some of the agency's most important work has been in small-scale projects such as election-monitoring. By the mid 1990s the Division had developed standard practices for monitoring that universally were considered noncontroversial. In part this is because EAD has used monitoring techniques that were first employed by the LEAGUE OF NATIONS when the earlier international organization supervised plebiscites in the 1920s, and because it has scrupulously acknowledged the independence and authority of existing national election institutions. Finally the Secretariat office has insisted that all elections and the campaigns leading up to them respect the provisions of HUMAN RIGHTS treaties and universal legal norms.

Within the UNITED NATIONS SYSTEM the division coordinates its activities with other UN bodies and SPECIALIZED AGENCIES. In particular, it works closely with the UNITED

NATIONS DEVELOPMENT PROGRAMME (UNDP), the OFFICE OF THE HIGH COMMISSIONER FOR HUMAN RIGHTS, the Centre for HUMAN RIGHTS and the UN VOLUNTEERS (UNV) to provide technical and observation assistance. EAD also works closely with non-UN intergovernmental and NON-GOVERNMENTAL ORGANIZATIONS operating in the country. In recent years these have included the European Union, the ORGANIZATION OF AFRICAN UNITY, the ORGANIZATION OF AMERICAN STATES, the INTER-PARLIAMENTARY UNION, the Organization for Security and Co-operation in Europe, the International Institute for Democracy and Electoral Assistance, the National Democratic Institute for International Affairs, and the CARTER Center.

See also ELECTION ASSISTANCE.

Further Reading: Fox, Gregory H. "The Right to Political Participation in International Law." *Democratic Governance and International Law,* edited by Gregory H. Fox and Brad R. Roth, 48–90. Cambridge: Cambridge University Press, 2000.

emergency special sessions of the General Assembly

Under the terms of the 1950 UNITING FOR PEACE RESOLUTION, when the UN SECURITY COUNCIL is unable to act on a threat to peace and security because of a lack of unanimity among the PERMANENT MEMBERS, nine members of the Council may request the convocation of an emergency SPECIAL SESSION of the GENERAL ASSEMBLY. The RESOLUTION urged states to keep representatives in New York City so that the session could be convened within 24 hours. The Assembly could then discuss the issue and make recommendations for restoring peace, including a recommendation that armed force be used. The UNITED STATES proposed the procedure during the KOREAN WAR when it appeared that VETOES by the Soviet Union would block effective action on the Korean peninsula and in subsequent COLD WAR conflicts. While the Soviet Union protested the constitutionality of the procedure—because the CHARTER prohibits Assembly consideration of any issue involving the maintenance of peace and security while the Security Council has it on its agenda—the USSR subsequently employed the Uniting for Peace Resolution to convene emergency special sessions in 1956 and 1967, respectively. FRANCE also objected to any ENFORCEMENT MEASURES or expenses associated with them undertaken by the United Nations as a product of General Assembly action. Paris argued that only the Security Council could authorize CHAPTER VII measures and require member states to honor or pay for them. Following the 1960 emergency session on the Congolese civil war, France and the

EMERGENCY SPECIAL SESSION	TOPIC	DATE OF THE SESSION
First	SUEZ CRISIS	November 1–10, 1956
Second	Hungarian Crisis	November 4–10, 1956
Third	Lebanon and Jordan	August 8–21, 1958
Fourth	CONGO Question	September 17–19, 1960
Fifth	MIDDLE EAST WAR OF 1967	June 17–September 18, 1967
Sixth	AFGHANISTAN	January 10–14, 1980
Seventh	Palestine	July 22–29, 1980; April 20–28, June 25–26, August 16–19, September 24, 1982
Eighth	NAMIBIA	September 3–14, 1981
Ninth	Occupied Arab Territories	January 29–February 5, 1982
Tenth	Occupied East Jerusalem and the Rest of the Occupied Palestinian Territories	April 24–25, July 15, and November 13, 1997; March 17, 1998; February 5, and 8–9, 1999; October 18–20, 2000; December 20, 2001; May 7 and August 5, 2002; September 19, October 20–21, and December 8, 2003; July 16, and 19–20, 2004

Soviet Union, using these arguments, refused to pay their assessments for the Congolese PEACEKEEPING operation, precipitating a financial crisis for the United Nations. The provision for emergency special sessions of the General Assembly amounted to an informal AMENDMENT of the Charter, reflecting a need to make the United Nations a viable guarantor of peace in the midst of cold war hostility between the USSR and the United States. Between 1956 and 2000, 10 emergency special sessions convened on the topics listed on the previous page.

enforcement measures

The United Nations CHARTER establishes a COLLECTIVE SECURITY system, and lodges in the SECURITY COUNCIL the authority to take any action that might be necessary to maintain international peace and security. All members are obligated to carry out the Council's decisions when it imposes military or nonmilitary measures to halt an aggressor or to restore international peace. This authority is granted under CHAPTER VII of the Charter (Articles 41 and 42). Among the nonmilitary measures the Council may take are economic SANCTIONS, the severance of diplomatic relations, and the full or partial disruption of communications between the states responsible for the breach of the peace and the outside world. If the Security Council believes these measures would be inadequate, it may enforce its decisions with military "air, land, and sea forces" of UN member states, and may also impose embargoes, blockades, or any other measures deemed necessary.

Generally the Security Council has sought to resolve international disputes by employing the more traditional diplomatic means of pacific settlement outlined in CHAPTER VI. During the COLD WAR, when a breach of the peace called for the use of Chapter VII, the Council's PERMANENT MEMBERS often deadlocked, sometimes leading to no action being taken, the use of the UNITING FOR PEACE RESOLUTION to allow the GENERAL ASSEMBLY to make a recommendation for action, or the ad hoc creation of PEACEKEEPING efforts—referred to as CHAPTER VI ½ PROVISIONS. When enforcement measures were used, they were applied in a graduated manner, beginning with less threatening sanctions. Economic and military sanctions were imposed against the APARTHEID regime in South Africa during the 1970s. They remained in place until the presidential election of Nelson Mandela in 1994. At later times, and for a variety of reasons, the Council imposed economic sanctions on SIERRA LEONE, IRAQ, FORMER YUGOSLAVIA, Libya, HAITI, Liberia, AFGHANISTAN, Ethiopia, Sudan, and Rwanda. The effectiveness of economic sanctions, however, was often hard to measure, and usually slow to materialize. Quite often they were insufficient to force compliance with Council mandates.

Only four times between 1945 and 2001 did the Council invoke Chapter VII to declare a threat to international peace and security, or to identify an act of AGGRESSION requiring UN members to act "by any means necessary" to restore the peace. In 1950, the Council called for the world community to repel North Korean aggression against South Korea. In 1991, the Security Council declared Iraq the aggressor and urged the liberation of Kuwait. In 1992, Council members found the instability in SOMALIA to be a threat to international peace and authorized intervention under U.S. leadership. Finally, following the September 11, 2001, terrorist attack on the World Trade Center in New York City, the UNITED STATES shepherded through the Council Resolution 1368, which declared the attacks a threat to international peace and expressed the Council's "readiness to take all necessary steps to respond to the terrorist attacks . . . and to combat all forms of TERRORISM." Based on this RESOLUTION and its inherent right to self-defense the United States mobilized a large coalition of states and launched military attacks on the suspected perpetrator, Osama bin Laden, his international network of operatives, and the Taliban government in Afghanistan that was accused of harboring him. The Resolution also required all member states to confiscate the assets of terrorist organizations, and to cooperate with the international community in the effort to end terrorism.

The end of the cold war occasioned a new interest among the permanent members of the Security Council in employing Chapter VII enforcement measures. They encouraged SECRETARY-GENERAL BOUTROS BOUTROS-GHALI to draft proposals on ways the Council, and the United Nations in general, might act more forcefully to maintain peace. In 1992 Boutros-Ghali submitted his report, An AGENDA FOR PEACE, in which he promoted "preventive diplomacy." He encouraged the Council to act early in order to assist "states at risk." He also urged member states to earmark military contingents for quick UN activation. While many of the Secretary-General's proposals were neglected, Council members did show an interest in authorizing particular states—such as the United States in the GULF WAR, and Australia in the East Timor secession crisis—or other organizations, for example, the North Atlantic Treaty Organization in BOSNIA, to take the lead in UN-sanctioned military endeavors.

All of the enforcement measures described above could be instituted only if none of the five permanent members used their VETO power, as all decisions under Chapter VII are substantive (Article 27). Although the United States sought a Chapter VII approval for its war against Iraq initiated in 2003, all permanent members of the Security Council—with the exception of the UNITED KINGDOM—and non-permanent members resisted Washington's urgings; thus the U.S. invasion was conducted without UN authorization. In 2006 when the U.S. government sought sanctions against IRAN for its continuing nuclear enrichment program, the RUSSIAN FEDERATION and CHINA would only agree to measures under Article 41 of the Charter, thus eliminating the possible use of military force.

See also APPEALS TO THE SECURITY COUNCIL, COLLEC-
TIVE SELF-DEFENSE, EMERGENCY SPECIAL SESSIONS OF THE
GENERAL ASSEMBLY, KOREAN WAR, SUSPENSION AND EXPUL-
SION OF MEMBERS, TIMOR-LESTE.

Further Reading: Conlon, Paul. *United Nations Sanction
Management: A Case Study of the Iraq Sanctions Committee,
1990–1994.* Ardsley, N.Y.: Transnational Publishers, 2000.
Freudenschuss, Helmut. "Between Unilateralism and Col-
lective Security: Authorizations of the Use of Force by the
UN Security Council." *European Journal of International Law*
5, no. 4 (1994): 492–531. Maley, William. "The UN and
Afghanistan: 'Doing Its Best' or Failure of a Mission?" *Fun-
damentalism Reborn: Afghanistan and the Taliban.* Edited by
William Maley. New York: New York University Press, 1998.
Roberts, Adam, and Benedict Kingsbury, eds. *United Nations,
Divided World: The UN's Roles in International Relations.* 2nd
ed. New York: Oxford University Press, 2000.

environment

Nothing in the United Nations CHARTER specifically authorizes the organization to deal with global environmental issues.
In 1945 the founders of the United Nations were primarily
concerned with creating an institution that could maintain
international peace and security. While the Charter's Preamble
committed UN members "to promote social progress, and better standards of life in larger freedom," and "to employ international machinery for the promotion of the economic and
social advancement of all peoples," environmental issues were
perceived to be matters for national governments and organizations outside the UN STRUCTURE. Yet, beginning in the 1970s
the United Nations became the initiator and primary sponsor
of global efforts to protect the environment from detrimental
human activities, and to assure that its protection was compatible with social and economic DEVELOPMENT. Pressured by
NON-GOVERNMENTAL ORGANIZATIONS (NGOs), SPECIALIZED
AGENCIES, developed states, and growing scientific evidence of
environmental damage, the United Nations sponsored WORLD
CONFERENCES, panels of experts, the initiation of environmental CONVENTIONS, and the creation of new environmental
law and concepts that came to define the international regime
of environmental politics by the end of the century.

Interest by the United Nations in environmental affairs
was part of the emerging "Other UN," as contrasted with the
primary institutional focus on questions of war and peace. In
the context of a COLD WAR that limited UN success in political and military areas, environmental policy became part of
the United Nations's growing "THEMATIC DIPLOMACY," which
emphasized areas of functional human activity and included,
in addition to the environment, HUMAN RIGHTS, economic
development, health, humanitarian assistance, the transfer
of technology, and issues involving WOMEN and dependent
populations.

The United Nations's active and direct participation in
environmental politics began with the 1972 UNITED NATIONS
CONFERENCE ON THE HUMAN ENVIRONMENT (UNCHE),
held in Stockholm. Earlier meetings, sponsored by private
groups and by some of the UN's specialized agencies—particularly the 1968 Biosphere Conference convened by the
UNITED NATIONS EDUCATIONAL SCIENTIFIC AND CULTURAL
ORGANIZATION (UNESCO)—had put pressure on the GEN-
ERAL ASSEMBLY to convene a world conference focused on
natural resource conservation. Also, at the 1968 U.S.–Soviet
Summit meeting in Glassboro, New Jersey, the two superpowers called for international cooperation on environmental matters as a way to promote cooperation in East-West
diplomacy. Finally, growing European concerns that unrestricted development in the Third World would damage the
global commons and, consequently, the quality of life in the
developed world led the United Nations to accept a Swedish
invitation to host the Stockholm Conference.

UNCHE focused on conservation and pollution issues,
viewing the natural environment as fundamentally under
threat from economic development. The conference issued
the "Stockholm Declaration," outlining the environmental
obligations and duties of states, and a Plan of Action with
109 recommendations. The conference documents suggested that development and environmental protection were
laudable movements that unfortunately required trade-offs
between the two. Furthermore, because economic development was essentially within the domestic JURISDICTION of
states, protecting the environment on a global scale constituted an assault on the principle of state SOVEREIGNTY.
The Stockholm meeting attempted to balance the conflicting interests in the final DECLARATION. Principle 21 asserted
that "States have . . . a sovereign right to exploit their own
resources pursuant to their own environmental policies
. . . [States have] the responsibility to ensure that activities
within their jurisdiction or control do not cause damage to
the environment of other States, or of areas beyond the limits
of national jurisdiction."

The most important institutional outcome of the meeting was the establishment of a new environmental agency. In
December 1972 the General Assembly created the UNITED
NATIONS ENVIRONMENT PROGRAMME (UNEP). Its expenses
were to be paid through a voluntary FUND, and its HEAD-
QUARTERS was located in Nairobi, Kenya, to ease concerns
in the developing world that the UN body might represent
developed states' desires to limit development policies. During its first decade of activity UNEP became an effective and
visible actor in promoting environmental awareness and in
attracting major contributions from the industrialized states
to international environmental projects. It formed partnerships with the WORLD BANK and the UNITED NATIONS
DEVELOPMENT PROGRAMME (UNDP).

On the 10th anniversary of the Stockholm Conference,
70 government representatives met in Nairobi to assess the

amount of progress that had been made on environmental matters. They concluded that a reinvigorated international effort was needed, and they called on the General Assembly to initiate a new study of the relationship between the environment and development. In 1983 the Assembly established the WORLD COMMISSION ON ENVIRONMENT AND DEVELOPMENT (WCED). SECRETARY-GENERAL JAVIER PÉREZ DE CUÉLLAR appointed Norwegian prime minister GRO HARLEM BRUNDTLAND as the commission's chairperson. The Secretary-General charged the commission with establishing "a global agenda for change."

The 21-member commission, and its panel of experts, held open hearings and interviewed thousands of individuals and groups over a two-year period. The commission's final report (1987), entitled OUR COMMON FUTURE, proved to be one of the most widely read and influential UN publications. The report recognized the direct links between development and the environment. It called for SUSTAINABLE DEVELOPMENT, defined as "development that meets the needs of the present without compromising the ability of future generations to meet their own needs." Sustainable development became the bedrock objective for all future UN efforts to address global environmental challenges. While imprecisely defined, "sustainable development" appealed to political leaders in states with environmental concerns because it seemed to put a natural limit on economic development strategies. For DEVELOPING COUNTRIES it officially recognized for the first time the legitimate competing claims of environmental preservation and development.

Dr. Brundtland's commission called upon the United Nations to convene another world conference, this one with the expressed purpose of drafting an international convention on the rights and duties of states in terms of sustainable development. The General Assembly, in its 44th session (1989), authorized the calling of the UNITED NATIONS CONFERENCE ON ENVIRONMENT AND DEVELOPMENT (UNCED), later known as the Earth Summit. When it convened in Rio de Janeiro in 1992, it proved to be the largest, most expensive, and most widely covered UN meeting in history. National delegations from 178 countries and two-thirds of the world's heads of state attended. More than 1,400 NON-GOVERNMENTAL ORGANIZATIONS (NGOs) were accredited to UNCED. The NGOs, with UN blessing, also staged a Global Forum in tandem with the conference that attracted 30,000 participants.

The field of environmental politics has provided an expanding opportunity for non-governmental organizations to be involved in UN affairs. At the Stockholm Conference more than 400 NGOs participated. Stockholm's secretary-general, Maurice Strong, also appointed to chair the subsequent Earth Summit in Rio, made sure that NGOs would have an even greater presence at the 1992 meeting. Strong believed that NGOs were critical to the formation of international public opinion and to effective implementation on the subnational level of international environmental programs.

UNCED produced three important international agreements—the RIO DECLARATION, AGENDA 21, and the STATEMENT OF FOREST PRINCIPLES—and served as the venue for the signing of the FRAMEWORK CONVENTION ON CLIMATE CHANGE (UNFCCC) and the CONVENTION ON BIOLOGICAL DIVERSITY (CBD). It also called upon the United Nations to create a new institutional body to oversee the successful implementation of sustainable development in all of its dimensions. This led to the General Assembly's establishment of the COMMISSION ON SUSTAINABLE DEVELOPMENT (CSD) in 1993. UNCED directed key UN bodies to make sustainable development a central part of their responsibilities (Chapter 38). In particular, it identified the United Nations Environment Programme, the United Nations Development Programme, the World Bank, the UNITED NATIONS CONFERENCE ON TRADE AND DEVELOPMENT (UNCTAD), the GLOBAL ENVIRONMENT FACILITY (GEF), the INTERNATIONAL DEVELOPMENT ASSOCIATION (IDA), and the REGIONAL DEVELOPMENT BANKS as the central agencies for future UN activity.

The primary documents produced by the Earth Summit attempted to balance the concerns of developed states for greater environmental protection—and their desire to avoid huge new financial responsibilities associated with the global effort—with the LESS DEVELOPED COUNTRIES' (LDCs) efforts to protect their sovereignty and pursue unrestrained national economic policies. LDCs also demanded increased international aid to cover additional costs imposed by sustainable development requirements. However, led by the UNITED STATES, which remained largely hostile to the UNCED negotiations, major powers refused to include increased environmental aid in the final conference report.

The Rio Declaration proclaimed that "human beings are at the centre of concerns for sustainable development." It recognized the right to development. The declaration gave support to the creation of international environmental law and standards. It recognized the "Polluter Pays Principle" (PPP), which required states to pay not only for pollution prevention on their territory but also for damage costs from pollution. It reaffirmed the idea, first asserted in principle 21 of the 1972 Stockholm Declaration, that states were accountable for practices that injured the environment beyond their borders. Agenda 21, an 800-page document filled with more than 1,000 specific recommendations to achieve a "comprehensive plan for global action in all areas of sustainable development," set international and national objectives, and provided programmatic suggestions on how to fulfill the objectives. The areas for action included world trade, poverty eradication, population, cities, atmospheric pollution, deforestation, drought, DESERTIFICATION, marine resource management, waste management, agriculture, biodiversity, and the transfer of technology. UNCED also issued the "Non-legally binding authoritative statement of principles for a global consensus on the management, conservation and sustainable development of all types of forests." The document fell far short of the World Convention on Forests that developed states and NGOs sought. Developing states resisted international restrictions on the use of forests. With no possibility of an agreement between developing and developed states, the Statement of Forest Principles simply called for the protection of forests, but recognized the right of states to use their forests as they wished.

The signing by 153 nations and the European Union (EU) of the United Nations Framework Convention on Climate Change, and by the EU and 155 countries of the Convention on Biological Diversity provided much of the perceived "success" of the Rio conference. Global media coverage, particularly of the CLIMATE CHANGE agreement, provided impetus for many national governments to establish domestic environmental programs and agencies. It also encouraged the General Assembly to endorse the negotiation of additional environmental conventions. The United Nations Conference on Environment and Development laid the foundation for UN activity in many fields of environmental policy. Over the succeeding decade the United Nations and its affiliated bodies sponsored environmental meetings, conventions, and implementation programs in each of the following areas:

SUSTAINABLE DEVELOPMENT

Between 1994 and 1996 the Commission on Sustainable Development reviewed each area identified by Agenda 21, including desertification, health, toxic chemicals and hazardous waste, biodiversity, human settlements, the atmosphere, and oceans and seas. It also held sessions on the overlapping issues of trade and the environment, poverty, demographic pressures on the environment, financial resources and mechanisms, and the transfer of environmentally sound technology to the underdeveloped world. In 1997 the Earth+5 SPECIAL SESSION OF THE GENERAL ASSEMBLY directed CSD to monitor carefully a few major identified provisions of Agenda 21. Earth+5 also directed the commission to begin work on the identification of "Indicators of Sustainable Development" that could be used to measure progress toward the goals of the Rio Declaration.

While the UN created the commission specifically to oversee sustainable development goals laid out at the Earth Summit, CSD deliberations were plagued by two perennial dilemmas: first, the recurring conflict between environmental protection and economic development strategies, and second, the intrusive character of international environmental efforts and the inviolability of national sovereignty. Faced with these countervailing pressures, the commission had limited success, and it was soon eclipsed by other UN agencies.

UNEP took the lead in promoting sustainable development projects. In 1997 UNEP approved the Nairobi Declaration, which declared it the "principal United Nations body in the field of environment." In the 1990s UNEP was assigned responsibility for providing SECRETARIAT, scientific, and technical assistance for several environmental agreements

and MECHANISMS. The success of UNEP could be credited in significant part to its development of scientific and technical expertise, which it employed in a number of successful monitoring and information-sharing programs. For example, through its *Infoterra* network it provided a national environmental information service to more than 170 states.

In January 1999 SECRETARY-GENERAL KOFI ANNAN proposed a GLOBAL COMPACT between the United Nations and multinational corporations to fulfill the environmental principles established in the Rio Declaration. In particular, he called upon those companies joining the compact to support sustainable development's precautionary approach to environmental challenges, and to undertake greater diffusion of environmentally friendly technologies to the developing world. Within a year more than 50 transnational corporations had signed the compact. Secretary-General Annan wrote in 1998 that the United Nations was "focusing on the importance of sustainability—on sustainable development—in all aspects of [its] work, [even] including peace and security."

The MILLENNIUM SUMMIT in September 2000 marked a watershed in the promotion of sustainable development. The participating nations agreed to eight MILLENNIUM DEVELOPMENT GOALS (MDGs); Goal Seven was to "Ensure Environmental Sustainability." MDG #7 set three targets to be achieved no later than 2020, including the reversal of policies that were leading to the loss of environmental resources, the halving of the proportion of people without sustainable access to drinking water, and the achievement of a significant improvement in living environment of at least 100 million slum dwellers. Given the broad commitment of the UN System to the MDGs, nearly all agencies involved with the developing world made a commitment to environmentally friendly policies.

Secretary-General Annan's March 2005 report, *IN LARGER FREEDOM*, urged nations to meet the Millennium targets and to make investments in resource management. A month after his report, Annan released a Millennium Ecosystem Assessment, a document produced by more than 1,400 experts from 95 countries. The panelists warned that human activity had so stressed the global ecosystem that achieving the MDGs would be very difficult. They called on governments to include the costs to the environment in all estimates of planned development projects, to include local communities in development planning, and to give central focus to the protection of natural assets in national decision-making.

ATMOSPHERE AND CLIMATE CHANGE

The WORLD METEOROLOGICAL ORGANIZATION (WMO) and the United Nations Environment Programme played the central roles in the 1980s and 1990s in the world's efforts to halt the interrelated problems of ozone layer depletion and global warming. Under their sponsorship the VIENNA CONVENTION FOR THE PROTECTION OF THE OZONE LAYER was adopted in

1985. The convention, ratified by 190 states as of October 2006, made a general commitment to protect the ozone layer by reducing ozone-depleting chemical compounds from the atmosphere. It was amended several times at subsequent Meetings of the Parties (MOPs). The most important was the MONTREAL PROTOCOL in 1987, which set specific production and consumption limits on refrigerant and industrial substances known as CFCs.

Ozone depletion and its recovery are closely associated with climate change. In the late 1980s UNEP and WMO launched two important initiatives to deal with the deleterious aspects of the latter. The first was the creation of the INTERGOVERNMENTAL PANEL ON CLIMATE CHANGE (IPCC) in 1988, made up of more than 1,000 scientists, policy makers, legal experts, and climate specialists from more than 60 nations. The two organizations hoped the IPCC would bring new attention to the growing phenomenon and would produce momentum toward a new international convention. The work of the panel led to the United Nations Framework Convention on Climate Change. The second was the promotion of a World Climate Conference that convened in November 1990, setting the stage for several climate agreements during the decade. The most important was the KYOTO PROTOCOL to the UNFCCC. Adopted in 1997 the PROTOCOL set specific greenhouse gas (GHG) emission targets for industrialized states to be achieved by 2012. The goal was to lower overall emissions of carbon dioxide, nitrous oxide, methane, hydrofluorocarbons, perfluorocarbons, and sulphur hexafluoride to at least 5 percent below 1990 levels. Kyoto's provisions were specifically directed at the industrialized states, which produced the overwhelming bulk of effluents responsible both for global warming and ozone depletion.

Post-Kyoto meetings were aimed at developing operational plans for implementing the Protocol, but the unwillingness of the United States and several other major states to ratify the agreement delayed the Protocol from entering into force. For the protocol to go into effect, it had to be ratified by 55 states that were party to the UNFCCC and it had to be ratified by sufficient "Annex I" countries (major developed states) to account for 55 percent of carbon dioxide (CO_2) emissions in 1990. The United States produces more than one-third of all CO_2, and, thus, without U.S. ratification it would take nearly all other developed states' assent to achieve the agreement. After much vacillation, the RUSSIAN FEDERATION accepted the protocol in November 2004, and Kyoto entered into force the following February. Participants at subsequent meetings of the parties in Canada and GERMANY recognized, however, that the protocol was insufficient to reverse global warming, and they encouraged a follow-on process with the goal of achieving larger cuts in greenhouse gases.

MARINE RESOURCES AND WATER POLLUTION

The Stockholm Declaration gave special emphasis to protecting the marine environment. Consequently, its successor organization, the United Nations Environment Programme, developed a number of programs to improve marine fish stocks, ocean and freshwater bodies, and transboundary waterways. Under UNEP auspices, efforts to protect the world's oceans resulted in a number of regional seas agreements. Nine were signed in the 1970s, beginning with an agreement among countries bordering the Mediterranean. Six more agreements were signed in the 1980s covering many of the regional seas of the world. In addition to UNEP, the ECONOMIC COMMISSION FOR EUROPE (ECE) played a critical role in developing the 1992 Convention on the Protection and Use of Transboundary Watercourses and International Lakes.

Central to the UN's activity to protect the ocean environment was the LAW OF THE SEA Convention, adopted in 1982. By the mid-20th century, various pressures on the oceans brought about several challenges to the long-standing custom of "freedom of the seas." Specifically, concerns over exploitation of global fish stocks by expanded distant fishing fleets, the realization that offshore areas contained significant supplies of natural resources (especially oil and natural gas), and increased potential for damage to the marine environment from various sources (especially increased oil tanker traffic) contributed to the realization that there was a need for modification of the existing law of the sea. Part XII of the convention dealt specifically with the protection of the marine environment. It was augmented in 1995 with an Agreement for the Implementation of the Provisions of the UNCLOS (UNITED NATIONS CONFERENCE ON THE LAW OF THE SEA) of December 10, 1982, Relating to the Conservation and Management of Straddling Fish Stocks and Highly Migratory Fish Stocks.

The effort to build on the Law of the Sea Convention in order to enhance marine protection included litigation. Among other provisions, the convention created an international tribunal to adjudicate cases among the parties. In 2001 Ireland sued the United Kingdom in hopes of halting the operation of a British nuclear reprocessing facility on the west coast of the Irish Sea. Dublin feared the dumping of waste material in the ocean or a terrorist attack that could pollute key fishing grounds for the Irish economy. The tribunal found that the convention requires cooperation among governments in such matters, and ordered the two states to exchange information, monitor any continuing risks, and devise collective measures to prevent pollution.

Of equal importance with a healthy oceanic biosphere is the preservation of freshwater sources. The Millennium Development Goals highlighted the desperate circumstances of nearly two billion people who were without access to potable water. The United Nations declared 2003 the International Year of Freshwater, and the UN Environment Programme convened in August the latest International Fresh Water Forum. The first of these had been held in 1977. Further meetings in 1990 and 1992 established international principles to govern the protection of fresh water and to provide sanitation. In 1997 a World Water Council was established with its headquarters in Marseilles, FRANCE. The Council included representation not only from UN agencies such as UNDP, the World Bank, and UNESCO, but also private firms, foundations, national government agencies, academic and research institutes, and banks.

BIODIVERSITY AND NATURAL RESOURCES

Pressed to do so by many environmental NGOs, UNEP sponsored negotiations beginning in 1987 on a convention to protect biological diversity. Those negotiations resulted in the Convention on Biological Diversity being opened for signature at the 1992 Earth Summit. The convention, while couched in general terms, sought to conserve biodiversity and to provide for the fair and equitable sharing of genetic resources and technology. Under the terms of the convention nations were required to make national inventories of biodiversity, develop national plans for the sustainable use of biodiversity, restore degraded ecosystems, and regulate the release of genetically modified organisms. The convention established a Conference of the Parties (COP) to implement and enhance the PACT through subsequent negotiations. By 2006, 188 nations had ratified the agreement and joined the COP.

The most significant accomplishment of the COP was the passage of the Cartagena protocol in January 2000. The protocol created a regulatory system for the transfer and use of genetically modified organisms. By fall 2006, 135 parties had accepted the protocol. Under the Cartagena agreement standards were established primarily on altered farm products meant for human consumption and animal feed.

In addition to UNEP, the United Nations Conference on Trade and Development (UNCTAD) played an important role in promoting the CBD. At the 1996 conference of the CBD signatories, UNCTAD launched its "Biotrade Initiative," meant to stimulate trade and investment in biological resources in the developing world. UNCTAD established Biotrade country programs to help governments identify opportunities for sustainable resource development. Based on a 1997 Memorandum of Understanding between the Convention on Biological Diversity Secretariat and UNCTAD, the two organs identified partnerships that could be developed among governments, NGOs, and international agencies that had the potential to turn the protection of biodiversity into a development asset for LDCs.

DEFORESTATION AND DESERTIFICATION

While there often has been a conflict between economic development and environmental protection, one area where the two reenforced each other was the slowing of land degradation. In Africa the steady growth of the Sahara Desert has diminished arable land and, thus, undercut agricultural production and lowered the standard of living. According to a 2000 FOOD AND AGRICULTURE ORGANIZATION (FAO) report,

44 percent of sub-Saharan Africa was at high risk of devastating drought. Led by states in the Sahel region during the 1980s, African nations pressed for international action. The 1992 Earth Summit recommended that the United Nations create a negotiating committee to draft a convention on the problem of desertification. The product of the committee's work was the CONVENTION TO COMBAT DESERTIFICATION (CCD), which was opened for signature in Paris in October 1994. The TREATY entered into force in December 1996 following ratification by 50 states.

The CCD established its secretariat headquarters in Bonn, Germany, in 1999. Activities recommended by the convention required extensive new funding, which proved difficult to raise. The Conference of Parties, which directed the work of the convention, set up a "Global Mechanism" in conjunction with the INTERNATIONAL FUND FOR AGRICULTURAL DEVELOPMENT (IFAD) in Rome to seek funds and channel them into desertification projects. Major goals of these projects included efforts to reduce poverty in arid and semi-arid areas in the belief that poverty led to agricultural practices that exacerbated desertification. The COP also encouraged non-governmental organizations to participate in its work. By 2003 more than 650 NGOs had achieved observer status with the organization and were pressuring their national governments to aid CCD programs. The funding crisis, however, led the CCD to seek financial support from the Global Environment Facility of the World Bank. GEF, in turn, established desertification and deforestation as central thematic areas of its work.

At the time of the Rio meeting, the positive connections between environmentally sound policies concerning forests and economic development in the underdeveloped world were not as clear. Industrialized states had become concerned by reports of significant damage to the rain forests and to tropical stands of timber as the result of land clearing, the sale of mahogany and other precious lumber, and development practices that threatened this part of the global commons. While deforestation produced land degradation, often in the form of erosion, LDCs argued that this was a necessary practice if, first, land were going to be made available for agricultural and industrial development, and, second, if forest products were going to comprise a part of the nation's export production. Led by Brazil and INDONESIA, developing states not only blocked a convention on forests in 1992 but subsequently kept any consensus from emerging on how to meet Agenda 21's call for the protection of forested terrain. In May 1999 the UN Forum on Forests (UNFF) met in Geneva and discussed the incentives created by the Kyoto Protocol's "sinks" provisions, which would reward states for planting and restoring forests. The forum hoped to establish a funding mechanism to emulate Kyoto's incentives, but no agreement was reached. While the UNFF put forward nearly 300 proposals to attain "sustainable forest management," little progress could be made as long as lumber-producing nations such as the United States, Brazil, JAPAN, Mexico, and INDIA opposed the recommendations.

FINANCING

At the conclusion of UNCED the conference secretariat estimated that $125 billion in foreign assistance to developing countries would be needed to implement all of the recommendations in Agenda 21. This was nearly 10 times the 1992 level of global aid. Yet no large contributions to a "Green Fund" were made at the conference by the major industrialized states. One of the reasons that LDCs urged the creation of the Commission on Sustainable Development was their hope that the new UN body could be used to encourage greater financial aid from the donor states. When it became clear that the rich nations were not going to give any significant new funds to implement Agenda 21, and that the CSD could not raise the sums needed, the world community fell back on using the World Bank's Global Environment Facility as an interim mechanism.

In 1990 the World Bank set up the Global Environment Facility to meet the Brundtland Commission's concerns about insufficient international financing of environmentally friendly development projects. The bank provided $1.4 billion in initial funding for projects focused on biodiversity, global warming, ocean pollution, and ozone depletion. Following the Earth Summit the agency was designated as the financial mechanism for the implementation of both the Convention on Biological Diversity and the United Nations Framework Convention on Climate Change.

As of December 2005, the facility included 175 member states and was based in Washington, D.C. In developing funding projects, GEF worked closely with the United Nations Environment Programme, the United Nations Development Programme, the WORLD TRADE ORGANIZATION, and UNCTAD. The primary work of GEF is to provide grants to developing countries for environment-related projects, and to encourage cooperation among donor nations. The facility also leverages several billion dollars in cofinancing. The World Bank serves as the trustee of the GEF Fund, and along with UNDP and UNEP is one of the implementing agencies. The four REGIONAL DEVELOPMENT BANKS and several UN specialized agencies serve as the "executing" bodies for funded projects. GEF is directed by an Assembly of its member governments, which meets every three years, and a council of directors. By 2006, GEF had provided $6.2 billion in grants and generated over $20 billion in cofinancing. These resources had funded more than 1,800 projects in 140 countries.

See also COMMITTEE OF INTERNATIONAL DEVELOPMENT INSTITUTIONS ON THE ENVIRONMENT.

Further Reading: Chasek, Pamela S. *The Global Environment in the Twenty-first Century: Prospects for International Cooperation.* New York: United Nations University Press, 2000. Elliott, Lorraine. *The Global Politics of the Environment.* New York: New York University Press, 1998. Moore, John Allphin, Jr., and Jerry Pubantz. *The New United Nations: International Organization in the Twenty-first Century.* Upper Saddle River, N.J.: Prentice Hall, 2006. Victor, David G., Kal Raustiala, and Eugene B. Skolnikoff. *The Implementation and Effectiveness of International Environmental Commitments: Theory and Practice.* Cambridge, Mass.: MIT Press, 1998. Werksman, Jacob. *Greening International Institutions.* London: Earthscan Publications, 1996. World Commission on Environment and Development. *Our Common Future.* New York: Oxford University Press, 1987. United Nations Environment Programme web site: <www.unep.org>. UNFCCC and Kyoto Protocol Web site: <www.unfccc.de/>. Commission on Sustainable Development Web site: <www.un.org/esa/sustdev/index.html>. Global Environment Facility Web site: <www.gefweb.org>.

Executive Committee on Economic and Social Affairs *See* DEPARTMENT OF ECONOMIC AND SOCIAL AFFAIRS.

Expanded Program of Technical Assistance (EPTA)

U.S. president Harry S. Truman proposed in his 1949 inaugural address a new American program of economic assistance under the aegis of Article 56 of the UN CHARTER. Responding to this initiative, the GENERAL ASSEMBLY created the Expanded Program of Technical Assistance in November of that year. Based on a U.S. proposal, EPTA was placed under the JURISDICTION of the UN's ECONOMIC AND SOCIAL COUNCIL (ECOSOC). It commenced operations in 1950 as the UN's single largest program, with $20 million contributed by 54 nations. The UNITED STATES initially provided 60 percent of the agency's BUDGET. By 1964, the last year of EPTA's existence, pledges from 108 NATION-STATES brought its budget to $50 million.

EPTA was made up of "participating organizations," which included the United Nations itself, the FOOD AND AGRICULTURE ORGANIZATION (FAO), the INTERNATIONAL LABOUR ORGANIZATION (ILO), the WORLD HEALTH ORGANIZATION (WHO), the INTERNATIONAL CIVIL AVIATION ORGANIZATION (ICAO), the UNIVERSAL POSTAL UNION (UPU), the INTERNATIONAL ATOMIC ENERGY AGENCY (IAEA), the UNITED NATIONS EDUCATIONAL, SCIENTIFIC AND CULTURAL ORGANIZATION (UNESCO), the WORLD METEOROLOGICAL ORGANIZATION (WMO), the INTERNATIONAL TELECOMMUNICATION UNION (ITU), and the INTERNATIONAL MARITIME ORGANIZATION (IMO). These SPECIALIZED AGENCIES were represented on EPTA's Technical Assistance Board. In an effort to limit ideological controversy over its work, the board met in private, debated possible funding projects, and then submitted the list as a package for an up or down vote. The Expanded Program provided technical training for people in the Third World. It also sponsored experts who could contribute development advice in LESS DEVELOPED COUNTRIES. Since it did not make capital grants or loans, developing countries often criticized EPTA for constituting a limited effort by the developed world. It was merged with the SPECIAL UNITED NATIONS FUND FOR ECONOMIC DEVELOPMENT (SUNFED) in 1965 to form the UNITED NATIONS DEVELOPMENT PROGRAMME (UNDP).

See also POINT FOUR PROGRAM.

Further Reading: Riggs, Robert E., and Jack C. Plano. *The United Nations. International Organization and World Politics.* Pacific Grove, Calif.: Brooks/Cole Publishing Company, 1988. Stoessinger, John G. *The United Nations and the Superpowers: China, Russia, and America.* 4th ed. New York: Random House, 1977.

expulsion from the United Nations *See* SUSPENSION AND EXPULSION OF MEMBERS.

F

Fifth Committee of the General Assembly

The Fifth Committee of the GENERAL ASSEMBLY, one of its six main committees, considers an agenda relating to the budgetary and administrative matters of the United Nations. Like all General Assembly main committees, it consists of representatives of every member state, each with an equal vote. Its function is to consider and negotiate draft RESOLUTIONS before they are placed before the full General Assembly.

Budgetary matters are highly specialized and detailed, requiring expert representatives. The Fifth Committee functions by consensus, adopting all measures in this manner. It addresses the financing of the various UN bodies, and each year spends extensive time dealing with lengthy reports on the Regular, PEACEKEEPING, and PROGRAMME BUDGETS of the United Nations. It examines and approves the institution's financial audits, prepared by the UN Board of Auditors, and its procurement procedures. It also considers resolutions concerning the financing of all peacekeeping missions, programme planning, and international WAR CRIMES TRIBUNALS. In its deliberations, the committee depends heavily on the oral and written reports of the ADVISORY COMMITTEE ON ADMINISTRATIVE AND BUDGETARY QUESTIONS (ACABQ), which is one of the two standing committees of the General Assembly.

Since the United Nations and its bodies are dependent on contributions from member states, the Fifth Committee has the responsibility of recommending to the General Assembly the SCALE OF ASSESSMENTS every three years, which establishes how much each state must pay to the organization. Many states have failed to pay their assessed contributions, or have been slow in doing so. Thus the committee has focused on methods to cover the continuing expenses of the United Nations, while reforming the assessment procedure. The committee also makes recommendations to the General Assembly on the appointment of individuals to fill vacancies on the COMMITTEE ON CONTRIBUTIONS, the ACABQ, the Board of Auditors, the United Nations ADMINISTRATIVE TRIBUNAL, the International Civil Service Commission, and the Staff Pension Committee.

See also COMMITTEE SYSTEM OF THE GENERAL ASSEMBLY, STRUCTURE OF THE UNITED NATIONS.

Further Reading: Fifth Committee Web site: <www.un.org/ga/fifth/>.

— *K. J. Grieb*

financing the United Nations   *See* BUDGET, SCALE OF ASSESSMENTS.

First Committee of the General Assembly

The First Committee is one of the six main committees that present RESOLUTIONS to the GENERAL ASSEMBLY (GA) for final approval or rejection. Each of these committees consists of equal representation from all member states of the United Nations. The First Committee was known originally as the Political and Security Committee. However, the committee, quickly overwhelmed by the range of issues assigned to it, came to focus its work on the field of DISARMAMENT. Given the importance of disarmament and, in particular, issues of nuclear arms reduction, the General Assembly decided in the wake of the 1978 SPECIAL SESSION on Disarmament that the First Committee should concentrate on this topic. Political issues were shunted to the SPECIAL POLITICAL COMMITTEE, and subsequently the title of the First Committee was changed to "Disarmament and International Security."

Debates about disarmament were highly contentious during the COLD WAR and particularly in the early years of nuclear weapons development, when international diplomats were trying to work out a set of rules and agreements to deal with a new and frightening topic that threatened global survival. Key negotiations occurred among the two superpowers and the five nuclear powers (UNITED STATES, UNITED KINGDOM, Union of Soviet Socialist Republics, FRANCE, and the People's Republic of CHINA). The First Committee and the CONFERENCE OF THE COMMITTEE ON DISARMAMENT offered the only forums where the non-nuclear states could express their views and be heard by the larger world community.

The First Committee considers all disarmament related topics on the agenda of the General Assembly's regular session. Annually it adopts more than 40 resolutions dealing with the NUCLEAR NON-PROLIFERATION regime, the various proposals for regional NUCLEAR-WEAPONS-FREE ZONES, nuclear test bans, all aspects of the arms trade, chemical and BIOLOGICAL WEAPONS, and all types of WEAPONS OF MASS DESTRUCTION and conventional arms. It also considers the implementation of existing disarmament agreements and General and Complete Disarmament. At the turn of the century the committee emphasized the need for full ratification of the COMPREHENSIVE TEST BAN TREATY. Beyond disarmament, the General Assembly often asks the First Committee to consider other security agenda items: such as the violent disintegration of NATION-STATES, developments in telecommunications in the context of international security, and confidence-building measures in central Africa.

See also COMMITTEE SYSTEM OF THE GENERAL ASSEMBLY, STRUCTURE OF THE UNITED NATIONS.

Further Reading: First Committee Web site: <www.un.org/ga/55/first/>. For preceding and succeeding years, substitute the GA session number in the Web site URL.

— *K. J. Grieb*

First Development Decade *See* DEVELOPMENT DECADES.

First and Third Worlds

In 1952 the French demographer Alfred Sauvy coined the expression "Third World" (*tiers monde*) to distinguish the world's poorer countries from its richer and more dominant ones. Sauvy saw the term as analogous to the "third estate," or the class of commoners in FRANCE before and during the French Revolution. In that historical case, the First Estate and the Second Estate (equivalent to the First World and SECOND WORLD of the late 20th century) consisted of the most dominant classes, such as priests and nobles.

While Third World came to refer to the economically underdeveloped countries of Asia, Africa, Oceania, and LATIN AMERICA, the "First World" signified the richer developed capitalist world, including countries such as the UNITED STATES, Canada, Western European nations, JAPAN, Australia, and New Zealand. Unlike the last two, most First World nations reside in the northern hemisphere, while the bulk of Third World countries are in the south. The "Second World" comprised the communist bloc, led by the Soviet Union; with the collapse of the USSR in the early 1990s, the Second World ceased to exist.

The First World typically refers to those NATION-STATES that historically were in the forefront of economic and political modernization, that is, those who benefited most from the industrial revolution. Several First World nations were also colonial powers. And, many Third World nations were those that had been colonized. While some observers prefer the terms "developed" and "developing" to denote differences, the terms First and Third World were widely used as the 20th century ended.

Within the United Nations, particularly in the GENERAL ASSEMBLY and the ECONOMIC AND SOCIAL COUNCIL, these classifications have had some procedural meaning. For example, the GROUP OF 77 was originally organized by Third World nations as a CAUCUS GROUP to promote common interests and highlight common concerns. During the COLD WAR, these nations tended to be non-aligned, refusing to join either Western alliances of the First World, such as NATO, or Soviet-inspired alliances, such as the Warsaw PACT. Within the UNITED NATIONS SYSTEM, these Third World countries often acted together as the largest bloc, frequently frustrating more powerful First World nations, who, interestingly, had been most active in initiating the United Nations in the mid-1940s. To promote their interests within UN bodies, most of the First World states joined the West European and Other States caucus group.

See also LEAST DEVELOPED COUNTRIES, LESS DEVELOPED COUNTRIES, NEW INTERNATIONAL ECONOMIC ORDER, NORTH-SOUTH RELATIONS.

Five Power Disarmament Committee *See* DISARMAMENT.

Food and Agriculture Organization (FAO)

One of the largest SPECIALIZED AGENCIES in the UNITED NATIONS SYSTEM, the Food and Agriculture Organization is an intergovernmental organization that, as of 2006, comprised 189 member countries plus one member organization, the European Union. The FAO is located in Rome and carries a mandate to raise levels of nutrition and standards of living, aid productivity in agriculture, and enhance living conditions in rural areas of the world.

In 1943, 44 governments met in Hot Springs, Virginia, and committed themselves to setting up a permanent organization for the support of food and agricultural improvements worldwide. The first session of the FAO Conference, attended by the original 44 nations, convened in Quebec City, Canada, in 1945 to create the Food and Agriculture Organization as a UN Specialized Agency. The founding date of October 16, 1945, was observed after 1981 as WORLD FOOD DAY. In 1951, FAO headquarters moved from Washington, D.C., to Rome.

A conference of member nations governs the Food and Agriculture Organization and meets every two years to review the organization's work, approve a program of work, and determine a BUDGET for the next two years. The conference elects a DIRECTOR-GENERAL for a six-year term, and a council, made up of 49 member nations, that acts as an interim body to direct the FAO's operations between conference meetings. Elected members of the council serve three-year terms. In 2006 Dr. Jacques Diouf of Senegal was reelected director-general for a third six-year term.

More than 3,700 staff personnel worked for the FAO by the turn of the century. The organization had five regional offices, five subregional ones, five liaison offices, and almost 80 country offices in addition to its Rome headquarters. At any given time it had about 1,800 field operations in place. Its budget was $765 million in 2006–2007.

The FAO is active in promoting SUSTAINABLE DEVELOPMENT. It provides help to developing nations by way of a range of assistance programs; it collects, analyzes, and disseminates information about nutrition, food production, agricultural issues, and forestry and fisheries matters; and it acts as a clearinghouse for farmers, scientists, and governments in food and agriculture developments. It encourages nations to seek its advice on strategies for rural development, food security, and reducing poverty, particularly in rural areas. In 1996 the FAO hosted the WORLD FOOD SUMMIT in Rome, where 186 nations approved a DECLARATION and Plan of Action on World Food Security, outlining a set of commitments intended to achieve universal food security and halve hunger by 2015. However, in June 2002 the FAO announced that without the commitment of an additional $24 billion annually by the world community, this goal could not be met. Nearly 600 million hungry people would remain without additional contributions.

In 1962 the organization joined with the WORLD HEALTH ORGANIZATION (WHO) to establish the FAO/WHO Codex Alimentarius (Food Code) Commission, to set international food standards. The commission seeks to protect the health of consumers and promote fair practices in the food trade by way of a set of international standards of behavior and by coordinating world food standards.

See also ADMINISTRATIVE TRIBUNALS; CHIEF EXECUTIVES BOARD; CONSULTATIVE STATUS; DESERTIFICATION; EISENHOWER, DWIGHT D.; EXPANDED PROGRAM OF TECHNICAL ASSISTANCE; INTER-AGENCY COMMITTEE ON SUSTAINABLE DEVELOPMENT; INTERNATIONAL TRADE CENTRE; PEARSON, LESTER; SOMALIA; STATEMENT OF FOREST PRINCIPLES; UNITED NATIONS ASSOCIATION; UNITED NATIONS ENVIRONMENT PROGRAMME; UNITED NATIONS OFFICE FOR PROJECT SERVICES; WORLD FOOD PROGRAMME.

Further Reading: New Zealand Ministry of Foreign Affairs United Nations Handbook. Wellington, N.Z.: Ministry of Foreign Affairs and Trade, published annually. FAO web site: <www.fao.org>.

former Yugoslavia

Yugoslavia emerged as a nation by way of the Paris Peace Conference ending World War I, realizing a long dream of Serbs to create a country for South Slav peoples. It united a mix of ethnic groups in the Balkan regions under a Serb monarch, and the country remained a monarchy until World War II. The ultimate breakup of Yugoslavia may well have been destined in 1919, and clearly the balancing act required to hold the nation together was at best difficult, at worst, monumental. During World War II, the Axis powers conquered Yugoslavia and pitted nationality against nationality. Italy occupied KOSOVO and Macedonia and gave the areas to Albania, and encouraged the Albanians to display their national icons. Croat Ustache collaborated with the Nazis and waged a bitter war against both Serbs and Muslims. The largely Serb, pro-royalist Chetnik resistance waged war with both the Nazis and communist partisans, led by Marshal Josip Tito and drawing from all nationalities as a class-based movement.

The success of the communists by the end of the war, and the subsequent trial and execution of Chetnik militia leader Dragoljub (Draza) Mihailovic, signaled the end of nationalist politics. Mihailovic had promised a Yugoslav kingdom led by the Serb royal family. Tito countered with the need for a federalist state under communist rule. Tito won the day politically, but the contradictions of his politics could not outlast his rule. On one hand, he called for a strong central state, consistent with the communist program. Also consistent with communism was his call for a new Yugoslav identity, and his assertion that nationalism was an ideology of capitalism. The six republics—BOSNIA and Herzegovina, Croatia, Macedonia, Montenegro, Serbia, and Slovenia—each contained different ethnic and different religious populations, including Roman Catholics in Slovenia and Croatia, Orthodox Christians in Serbia, a plurality of Muslims in Bosnia (and a large majority of Muslim Albanians in Kosovo province). Tito insisted that workers of all nations shared a common bond, and therefore brotherhood and unity were the keys to the state. But he also provided for governments at the republic level, and he rotated key positions within the state to placate the different nationalities. The Tito-led Yugoslav postwar government entered the United Nations as an original member on October 24, 1945. Tito's personality was strong enough to hold this contradiction together for many years, but upon his death, the foundation was shaken considerably. After his death in 1980, the call was "After Tito, Tito," but the stage was set for the breakup of the country.

The course of the breakup was set as the COLD WAR was ending, at the height of MIKHAIL GORBACHEV's perestroika and glasnost in 1987. The rise of SLOBODAN MILOŠEVIĆ within the Serb Republic in Yugoslavia signaled an end of Tito's dream of a multiethnic socialist state. Milošević's speech to a group of Serbs in Kosovo on April 24, 1987, in which he declared to the Serbian minority of the province that "no one should dare beat you," vaulted the nationalist to the forefront of Yugoslav politics, marshaled the ouster of then-president Ivan Stambolic, and sparked the violence that finally tore the country apart.

By the time that Milošević made his famous speech in Kosovo, tensions in every republic had risen. The federal government seized on Milošević's stirring of Serb emotions to end Kosovo's autonomy. Kosovo occupied a unique place in Yugoslavia because historically it was a part of Serbia. The battle of Kosovo in 1389 marked the foremost political date on the Serb calendar. But Kosovo was predominantly Albanian. The abolition of Kosovar autonomy signaled the other republics that Serbia intended to use the federal government as a means to dominate Yugoslavia.

Following Tito's death in 1980 the Yugoslav federal presidency became a collective of the heads of the different republics, each taking a turn in the presidential chair. In spring 1991 the Serb president, Borisav Jovic, refused to step down in order to allow the Croat Stipe Mesić to hold the presidency as scheduled. Because Serbia controlled four of the eight votes in the collective presidency (Kosovo, Montenegro, and Vojvodina were controlled by Milošević allies), the

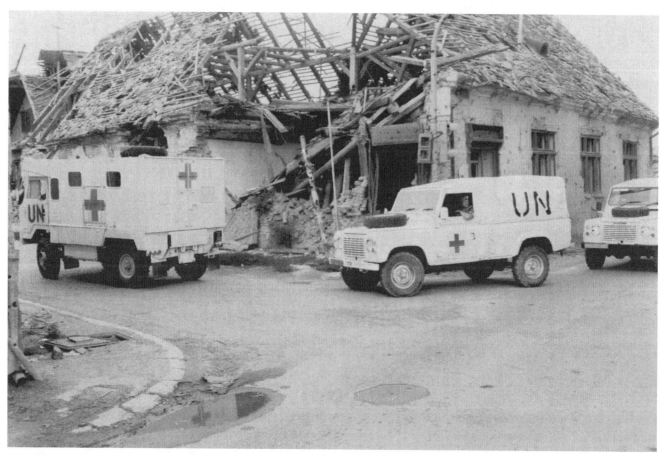

UNPROFOR ambulances in Croatia, 1992 (UN PHOTO 159206/S. WHITEHOUSE)

vote to seat Mesić was deadlocked and Jovic was granted an additional term. This was, in essence, a Serb coup d'état, and on May 19, 1991, Croatia first voted for independence from Yugoslavia. Despite intense lobbying from both the European Union and the UNITED STATES, Croatia and Slovenia carried through with their DECLARATIONS of independence. Milošević responded with force and "ethnic cleansing" in Serb-dominated parts of Croatia.

The first fighting took place in Slovenia, which had a very small percentage of Serbs. To placate Yugoslavia's largest ethnic group, Tito had allowed Serbs to dominate the officer corps of the Yugoslav National Army (JNA), and by 1991 Serbs represented the dominant group in the army. As the country verged on collapse, the strongest pro-unity sentiment was in the army. Milošević used this to his advantage as he shifted from a policy of Serb-dominated unity of Yugoslavia to one of disintegration but with the largest "rump" state remaining. At first, the JNA attacked Slovenia to maintain the state's unity, but as the war progressed badly for the JNA, Milošević quickly withdrew the army and prepared to unite all Serbs in the rump state. Slovenia gained its independence by the time the JNA withdrew on July 18, 1991.

Croats and Serbs had been bitter enemies in World War II. Croat Ustache militia had, with the help of the German army, rounded up Serbs and placed them in the Jasenovac concentration camp. This history served as the backdrop for the violence of the war, in which the JNA forcibly resettled (ethnically cleansed) Croats out of the Krajina region of Croatia and united that area with the rump state. Croatian militia responded by driving Serb farmers off their land. By December 1991, Croatia gained international recognition but lost about one-third of its prewar territory. On May 22, 1992, both Slovenia and Croatia became members of the United Nations. The low-level guerrilla war that ensued claimed countless lives, and, by May 1995, most of the Krajina territory was under Croatian control.

The hope for Western unity on policy toward Yugoslavia disintegrated in 1991. The United States and most of its European allies worked to hold Yugoslavia together as a loosely bound democracy. Involved in war with IRAQ, the United States left the matter to European resolution, and the European Union sought United Nations action, largely of a humanitarian character. It was GERMANY, however, that first broke ranks with the Western effort to maintain the federal Yugoslav state. Faced with massive Serbian HUMAN RIGHTS violations in Slovenia and Croatia, and little evidence that international efforts were succeeding, the government of Chancellor Helmut Kohl announced that it would support independence for the two republics. That Germany was leading the recognition charge only further fueled Serb suspicions about the European Union's intentions. In December, German foreign minister Hans Dietrich Genscher announced to the European Union that, if there was no unified policy about how and when to recognize

the new states, Germany would act unilaterally. On December 17, the European Union rushed into place a policy of recognition, and the key component was that any republic wishing independence had to state that intention by December 24, 1991. With a timetable set by the European Union, Croatia and Slovenia immediately confirmed their intention to become independent, and Bosnia, under the leadership of Alija Izetbegovic, made clear its intention to hold a referendum on independence in the spring. The European Union recognized Slovenia and Croatia, while the United States withheld recognition.

The UN's initial involvement came in September 1991, as the SECURITY COUNCIL imposed an arms embargo on Yugoslavia. The SECRETARY-GENERAL then appointed a personal envoy, former U.S. secretary of state Cyrus Vance (replaced later by Thorvald Stoltenberg) to coordinate UN cooperation with European Union peace efforts, led by veteran British diplomat and politician Lord Owen. The Vance-Owen Plan concentrated on finding a solution to the brewing Bosnian crisis. In the end they recommended the cantonization of Bosnia, dividing the republic among Bosnian Muslim, Bosnian Serb, and Bosnian Croatian communities. None of the parties was willing to accept the proposed subdivisions, and the mission failed. In 1993 the Security Council created the INTERNATIONAL CRIMINAL TRIBUNAL FOR THE FORMER YUGOSLAVIA (ICTY) as the first institution of international criminal prosecution since the end of World War II. The ICTY issued its first indictment on November 11, 1994. It cited Dragan Nikolic, a Bosnian Serb who was alleged to have been the commander of a small prison camp in eastern Bosnia.

Bosnia proved to be the battleground for the most brutal fighting and the most violent war crimes. Bosnia and Herzegovina declared independence in March 1992 and also became a member of the United Nations on May 22, 1992. Because Bosnia was an ethnically mixed republic, the principle that all Serbs should live in a rump Yugoslavia was considerably more difficult to achieve than in Krajina. Muslim populations were removed and driven to the smaller center of the Republic as the Serb militias moved to ethnically cleanse areas and make them majority Serb. The Serb militias, led by General Ratko Mladić, killed Muslim men, WOMEN, and children, carried out a systematic campaign of rape and terror, and created death and detention centers at Omarska, Trnopolje, and Manjaca. When images of these camps were displayed in Western media centers, it reminded the international community of Nazi concentration camps. Western governments were aware of the camps in April 1992, and the press publicized them in July, raising the demand for justice to a fever pitch.

UN efforts proved unsuccessful in attempting to end the violence. The North Atlantic Treaty Organization (NATO) also proved incapable of a consensus on military measures that would halt the Serbian attacks. Throughout 1992 and 1993, Bosnian calls for stronger action were met with international indifference, and the Serb violence continued. Bosnian Croats joined their Pale counterparts in declaring an independent state in southwestern Bosnia, and the nation threatened to break up along ethnic and religious lines. A PEACEKEEPING force, the United Nations Protection Force (UNPROFOR), established by the Security Council in early 1992, was sent to Yugoslavia, but proved ineffective. The Muslim populations moved from the countryside to UNPROFOR "protected areas" or safe havens in Mostar, Gorazde, Srebrenica, and elsewhere, believing in the UN promise of protection, only to find the peacekeepers unable to fight off the Serb militias. At Srebrenica, Mladić's forces rounded up men and boys, marched them out of the town as UN peacekeepers were held hostage, and summarily executed the civilians in the surrounding fields.

After a brutal mortar attack on the marketplace in Sarajevo, NATO bombed Serb positions around the capital in August 1995. Coupled with a successful Croatian offensive that reclaimed large territories held by the Serbs, the NATO action forced Milošević to the bargaining table. Invited by U.S. president BILL CLINTON to Dayton, Ohio, the leaders of Serbia, Croatia, and Bosnia hammered out an agreement. The Bosnian war ended with negotiation of the DAYTON PEACE ACCORDS, which provided that the United Nations monitor the agreement through the Implementation Force (IFOR) made up of NATO troops, to be replaced by the Stabilization Force (SFOR). In October 2001 the parliament of the Bosnian Serb enclave approved the arrest of individuals under indictment by the international tribunal in The Hague.

Milošević, constitutionally banned from an additional term as president of Serbia, manipulated an election in July 1997 to have himself elected president of Yugoslavia, by then made up only of the former republics of Serbia and Montenegro, as well as, presumably, Kosovo. He then moved to crush the ethnic Albanian drive for independence in Kosovo. Fighting between Serbia's JNA and the Kosovo Liberation Army (KLA) reached fever pitch in 1999 with thousands of Kosovar refugees forced to flee to the Albanian mountains and to Macedonia. When a peace proposal (arranged by Richard Holbrooke, U.S. PERMANENT REPRESENTATIVE to the United Nations) could not be negotiated between the two sides, NATO, citing UN RESOLUTIONS empowering it to promote peace in the region and protect civilian victims from ethnic cleansing, bombed Yugoslav targets in both Kosovo and Serbia, beginning on March 25, 1999. Milošević accepted a UN-approved peace agreement on June 3. By then, according to the UN HIGH COMMISSIONER FOR REFUGEES, at least 850,000 people had been displaced from their homes in Kosovo. The final settlement called for a UN force—called the Kosovo Force (KFOR)—to monitor that peace.

Tensions ran high in Macedonia as well, a former Yugoslav republic that had declared its independence and become a UN member in 1992. By summer 2001, Macedonia faced a potential civil war between its majority of Macedonians and minority Muslim Albanians. A NATO/European Union negotiated settlement concluded in the late summer called for an end to conflict and internal reforms to allow more equitable representation in government for Albanian Macedonians. By the agreement, the United Nations joined with troops from NATO, largely veterans of KFOR, to monitor the DISARMAMENT of all sides.

Earlier, in September 2000, Vojislav Koštunica, a Serb reformer, was elected president of Yugoslavia, finally ending the reign of Milošević, who in 2001 was arrested and handed over to the UN's International Criminal Tribunal for the Former Yugoslavia, in The Hague, to be tried for war crimes. Kostunica committed his government to internal democracy and to resolving tensions in Kosovo peacefully. Yet, in February 2008, Kosovo, against the opposition of Serbia, declared its independence. Yugoslavia, which had not been allowed automatically to accede to the UN MEMBERSHIP of the defunct Yugoslav Socialist Republic, was admitted to membership on November 1, 2000. The arms embargo imposed in March 1998 was lifted by the Security Council on September 10, 2001, ending all international SANCTIONS on the regime. In March 2002, leaders from the two remaining republics of the former Yugoslavia signed a PACT creating a weak confederation to be called Serbia and Montenegro. By thus abandoning the name Yugoslavia, the rump confederation officially ended the eight decade long attempt to create a unification of south Slavs.

At The Hague, Milošević's trial was long and complex. As it proceeded, his popularity rose in Serbia. On March 11, 2006, he was found dead in his cell at the detention center in The Hague. An autopsy established that he had died of a heart attack. As of May of that year, the court had indicted 161 people and completed 95 trials, with 37 convictions. At the time of Milošević's death, only six indicted suspects remained at large, and it appeared the work of the tribunal would soon be concluded. Among the six, however, were General Mladić and Radovan Karadžić, the former leader of the Bosnian Serbs.

See also ANNAN, KOFI; CONVENTION ON THE PREVENTION AND PUNISHMENT OF THE CRIME OF GENOCIDE; INTERNATIONAL COURT OF JUSTICE; INTERNATIONAL RESEARCH AND TRAINING INSTITUTE FOR THE ADVANCEMENT OF WOMEN; SUSPENSION AND EXPULSION OF MEMBERS; UNITED NATIONS INTERIM ADMINISTRATION MISSION TO KOSOVO; UNITED NATIONS MISSION IN BOSNIA AND HERZEGOVINA; UNITED NATIONS PREVENTIVE DEPLOYMENT FORCE IN THE FORMER YUGOSLAVIA REPUBLIC OF MACEDONIA; UNITED NATIONS SPECIAL COMMITTEE ON THE BALKANS; UNITED NATIONS VOLUNTEERS; WAR CRIMES TRIBUNALS.

Further Reading: Holbrooke, Richard. *To End a War.* New York: Random House, 1998. Meier, Viktor. *Yugoslavia: A History of Its Demise.* London: Routledge Books, 1999. Rogel, Carole. *The Breakup of Yugoslavia and the War in Bosnia.* Westport, Conn.: Greenwood Press, 1998. Silber, Laura, and Allan Little. *Yugoslavia: Death of a Nation.* New York: Penguin Books, 1995. Udovicki, Jasminka, and James Ridgeway, eds. *Burn This House: The Making and Unmaking of Yugoslavia.* Revised and expanded. Durham, N.C.: Duke University Press, 2000.

— *D. J. Becker*

"Four Policemen" proposal

U.S. president FRANKLIN ROOSEVELT first used this term in reference to the four major powers that initially had signed the DECLARATION BY UNITED NATIONS on January 1, 1942. Following the UNITED STATES, the UNITED KINGDOM, CHINA, and the Soviet Union, representatives of 22 other nations at war with the Axis powers signed the document the next day in Washington, D.C. This distinction between great and small nations soon became a fundamental axiom in Roosevelt's thinking about postwar planning for peace.

Determined to avoid the excessive idealism of Woodrow Wilson's plan for a universal family of nations, the president emphasized the need for the use of military power by the Big Four of the wartime Grand Alliance in order to insure postwar peace. With a growing indication of public approval for some sort of organization of nations after the war, Roosevelt, in November 1942, revealed his plan for the Four Policemen to disarm and patrol the postwar world to Clark Eichelberger, one of the leading internationalist leaders in the nation.

During the course of 1943, Roosevelt shared his views of a great power–dominated association of nations with WINSTON CHURCHILL (a supporter of regional security arrangements), JOSEPH STALIN (soon a convert) at the TEHERAN CONFERENCE, and, in veiled terms, with the American people in a series of public speeches from January to December 1943. That year marked the turning point of the world conflict and, thus, 1944 and 1945 were the critical years of postwar planning for peace. At the State Department a planning group proposed a "United Nations Authority" with a security commission consisting of the four great powers, thus incorporating Roosevelt's idea into a more general universal organization.

During 1944, policy makers in Washington carefully monitored American public opinion regarding international organization. The Hollywood feature film *Wilson* sparked a popular internationalist revival, while best-selling books and articles by Wendell Willkie, Sumner Welles, Walter Lippmann, and Nicholas Spykman prompted a lively debate about the nature and goals of U.S. foreign policy. By mid-1944 American public opinion had moved quite far from the idealism of Wendell Willkie's *One World* and other internationalists' proposals. Although accepting the need for a universal world organization, Americans seemed to reject the ideal of the full equality of all nations and embraced instead Roosevelt's realpolitik of Big Four hegemony. The president finally revealed publicly his concept of the "Four Policemen" in a two-part interview in *The Saturday Evening Post* in May

1944. The author, Forrest Davis, concluded that the new United Nations "presupposes that the powers able to make war are convinced their self-interest demands peace."

Roosevelt thus enjoyed overwhelming public support in his struggles against both liberal internationalists and conservative opponents of postwar cooperation with the Soviet Union. As the century turned, the STRUCTURE of the UN SECURITY COUNCIL remained a testament to the durability of the concept of the "Four Policemen."

See also CAIRO DECLARATION.

Further Reading: Divine, Robert A. *Second Chance: The Triumph of Internationalism in America during World War II.* New York: Atheneum, 1967. Hoopes, Townsend, and Douglas Brinkley. *FDR and the Creation of the U.N.* New Haven, Conn.: Yale University Press, 1997. Kimball, Warren F. *Forged in War: Roosevelt, Churchill, and the Second World War.* New York: William Morrow, 1997. Ostrower, Gary. *The United Nations and the United States.* New York: Twayne, 1998.

— *E. M. Clauss*

Four Power Declaration   *See* RUSSIAN FEDERATION.

Fourteen Points

In a speech to both houses of the U.S. Congress on January 8, 1918, President Woodrow Wilson introduced the Fourteen Points by which he sought to build a peace at the conclusion of the "war to end all war." His statement of "what we demand in this war" declared that the Allies sought to make the world safe for democracy, one that was "safe for every peace-loving nation." Wilson's Fourteen Points unveiled the idea of an international organization through which the nations of the world would preserve peace, thereby leading directly to the LEAGUE OF NATIONS, the predecessor of the United Nations.

Wilson was president of the UNITED STATES from 1913 to 1921. In the early 20th century, Americans viewed Europe with suspicion and initially sought to stay out of World War I, but the effort proved hopeless. In early 1917, while the United States was still officially neutral, Wilson called for a "peace without victory" and enunciated what he considered the kind of peace the American people would support.

Once the United States was in the war, the Fourteen Points appeared to express distinctive American views about war and international relations and changed public opinion about the nature of diplomacy. Wilson listed objectives that became the basis of U.S. foreign policy in the American public mind and influenced the role of the United States in the world well beyond World War I. Although the president presented the Fourteen Points as Allied objectives, he did not consult any of the Allied governments prior to his speech to Congress.

The first five points reflected Wilson's desire for the rule of law in international politics. He called for (1) open COVENANTS of peace, openly arrived at, and an end to all secret diplomacy and secret treaties, (2) freedom of the seas, meaning the right of the ships of all nations to sail on any international waters, (3) removal of economic barriers and the establishment of equal trading rights for all nations, constituting one of the initial statements of the most-favored-nation trading principle that became the basis of international trade rules after World War II, (4) reduction of armaments "to the lowest point consistent with domestic safety," thus stating the American objective of DISARMAMENT, and (5) adjustment of all colonial claims based on the interests of the colonial peoples, which were to be considered equally with the claims of the colonial powers.

Points 6 through 13 dealt with European territorial settlements among the combatants, based on the principles of nationality and self-determination. Boundaries should now be established in order to unite peoples of a given nationality (or ethnicity) within a single state where they would constitute the majority of the population and hence be guaranteed the right to govern themselves. Such "self-determined" nations would replace political entities based on natural features, conquest, and dynasties, and be an important step toward worldwide decolonization. Achieving this would entail the breakup of GERMANY, Austria-Hungary, and the Ottoman Empire. The latter two multinational states would be carved up into several new states whose frontiers would be based on nationality. When implemented after the conclusion of the war, this restructuring required the forced relocation of large populations. Nations based on ethnically kindred populations would replace the empires of central Europe that had ignored nationalities in order to unite within a single state all the resources needed to achieve economic security and power.

Most significant, the 14th point called for the establishment of "A general association of nations . . . for the purpose of affording guarantees of political independence and territorial integrity" to all countries. This point became the basis of the League of Nations, embodying the principle of COLLECTIVE SECURITY through universal action against AGGRESSION, whereby all members would agree to protect the boundaries of all other members.

The League of Nations, established by the Allies at the 1919 Versailles Peace Conference, launched a new era in international organization. Ironically, after President Wilson forced inclusion of the League in the peace settlement over the objections of the reluctant Europeans, the U.S. Senate rejected the TREATY. Thus the United States did not join the entity it had helped create. World War II exposed the weaknesses of the League, but, for many Americans, the collapse of international order leading to the war likewise revealed the need for their country to enter forcefully into international affairs in a leadership role as anticipated by Wilson in his Fourteen Points. A major result was the establishment of the United Nations.

See also ATLANTIC CHARTER, NATION-STATE.

Further Reading: Bailey, Thomas A. *Wilson and the Peacemakers.* New York: Macmillan, 1947. Cooper, John Milton, Jr. *Breaking the Heart of the World: Woodrow Wilson and the Fight for the League of Nations.* New York: Cambridge University Press, 2001. Hoover, Herbert. *The Ordeal of Woodrow Wilson.* New York: McGraw Hill, 1958. Knock, Thomas J. *To End All War: Woodrow Wilson and the Quest for a New World Order.* Princeton, N.J.: Princeton University Press, 1995. Link, Arthur S. *Wilson the Diplomatist.* Baltimore: Johns Hopkins University Press, 1957.

— *K. J. Grieb*

Fourth Committee of the General Assembly

The Fourth Committee of the GENERAL ASSEMBLY (GA) is one of the GA's six main committees, and is also known as the Special Political and Decolonization Committee. Like all General Assembly main committees, it has representatives from every member state, each with an equal vote. Its function is to consider and negotiate draft RESOLUTIONS before they are placed before the full General Assembly. By GA Resolution 233 in 1993 the General Assembly merged the Special Political Committee (formerly the Seventh Committee) with that of the Fourth Committee, adding the work of the former to the latter's existing agenda on trusteeship issues. This was done because, with the independence of most colonial, and all trust territories, there was little business left for the Fourth Committee. The Special Committee itself had been created in the early years of the United Nations, when the FIRST COMMITTEE found that it needed to devote its attention to DISARMAMENT.

Since the end of the COLD WAR, despite the existence of an expanding number of ethnic conflicts and the increasing involvement of the United Nations in internal civil wars, the newly merged Fourth Committee has developed a high level of cooperation and consensus on its agenda topics. The committee addresses all conflict situations appearing before the General Assembly, invariably passing resolutions on each one. It also deals with all aspects of PEACEKEEPING, and the issues of NON-SELF-GOVERNING TERRITORIES. Each year it invariably passes several resolutions relating to various aspects of the situation in the Middle East. It also considers matters relating to the Geneva CONVENTIONS regarding the laws of war, and issues concerning cooperation in outer space.

See also COMMITTEE SYSTEM OF THE GENERAL ASSEMBLY, STRUCTURE OF THE UNITED NATIONS, TRUSTEESHIP COUNCIL.

Further Reading: Fourth Committee Web site: <www.un.org/ga/54/fourth/fourth.htm>. (Substitute annual session number for details of specific sessions.)

— *K. J. Grieb*

Fourth Development Decade *See* DEVELOPMENT DECADES.

Fourth World Conference on Women *See* WORLD CONFERENCES ON WOMEN.

Framework Convention on Climate Change (UNFCCC) *See* UNITED NATIONS FRAMEWORK CONVENTION ON CLIMATE CHANGE.

France

The French Republic has been a PERMANENT MEMBER OF THE SECURITY COUNCIL from the commencement of the United Nations. Thus, France has, since 1945, consistently been a major player in UN-associated international relations. Moreover, French is one of the official LANGUAGES of the organization, the UNITED NATIONS EDUCATIONAL, SCIENTIFIC, AND CULTURAL ORGANIZATION (UNESCO) resides in Paris, and, as of 2006, France was the fourth largest contributor to the UN BUDGET.

That France, occupied by GERMANY for almost the entirety of World War II, would become one of the five VETO-wielding great powers of the UN was due to the geopolitical decisions made by U.S. president FRANKLIN ROOSEVELT and British leader WINSTON CHURCHILL at war-end conferences where, with a skeptical JOSEPH STALIN, the major victors planned the postwar world. Roosevelt and Churchill saw a stalwart, resuscitated, and capitalist France as crucial to rebuilding a war-ravished Europe. However, eventually France evinced a disposition to conduct its own, independent foreign policy, at the UN and elsewhere, sometimes to the displeasure of the Americans and British. Nonetheless, by the middle of the 21st century's first decade, American, British, and French positions at the UN (with the clear exception of the IRAQ war begun in 2003) were not all that far apart. In addition, in the last half of the 20th century France joined willingly, indeed had become a leader in, two ground-breaking developments in Europe: the German-French harmony that effectively signaled the end of a centuries-long European civil war and the crafting of a comprehensive European unity in the European Union.

Known in ancient times as Gaul and peopled by Celtic tribes, France was conquered by the Roman leader Julius Caesar in the first century B.C.E. During the fifth century barbarian incursions resulted in the formation of a modest unified polity in 486 under Clovis, the leader of the Franks. Clovis founded the Merovingian dynasty and acknowledged Christianity as the country's religion. In 732, at a historic battle near Poitiers, Charles Martel defeated the Muslim Saracens, paving the way for the reign of Charlemagne, who, in 800, became emperor of a large area in Western Europe.

After his death, Charlemagne's dynasty—the Carolingians—fractured into various independent and aristocratically ruled estates, some of which would eventually combine to become the area we now see as modern France. In the 10th century, the Capetians replaced the Carolingian dynasty, after which Paris became a major university, trade, and religious center. In the 14th century, France was weakened by the Black Death plague and the Hundred Years' War with England (1337–1453), when the two countries fought over rival claims on the Continent. Full consolidation and centralization of political power came with the Bourbon dynasty, culminating in the reign of Louis XIV in the 17th century. In the 18th century, France became the center of the Enlightenment, but by the end of the century the French Revolution (beginning in 1789) had overthrown the monarchy, established France's first republic, executed King Louis XVI, and devolved into a Reign of Terror.

As the 19th century dawned, Napoléon Bonaparte contained the revolution, declared himself emperor, transformed civil and legal practices with the Code Napoléon, and set out to expand French influence throughout Europe. Major war with several countries was the consequence. By 1815 Napoléon had been defeated by a large coalition of forces, led by the English. At the Conference of Vienna, the victors sought to establish a stable peace on the Continent, in the event restoring the monarchy to France. The peace launched at Vienna prevented a Europe-wide war until 1914 through a device known as the Concert of Europe. The major powers (GREAT BRITAIN, Prussia, Austria, and Russia) committed their governments to regular consultation—signaling the so-called "congress" system of European affairs. From the beginning the restored French government was included in the Concert of Europe's deliberations. France and its partners agreed on a new and transformed balance of power, complemented by territorial compromise among all the former belligerents.

In 1848, France established the brief Second Republic, soon replaced by Napoleon III's Second Empire. Also, during the 19th century, the country became a colonial empire, gaining overseas possessions in north and west AFRICA and in Indochina. Another grievous defeat occurred in 1870 in the Franco-Prussian War, this time at the hands of a German army. The Second Empire disappeared and the Third Republic replaced it, lasting until World War II.

In the Great War of 1914–18, France joined with Great Britain and Russia to fight the Germans (and their allies) again. Although surfacing from the war on the winning side, France had suffered immensely, since the fiercest fighting had taken place on French soil. The peace conference ending the war took place at Louis XIV's grandiose palace at Versailles, confirming France's symbolic leadership role of the war's winners. Here, in 1919, conference participants, including French premier Georges Clemenceau, signed a complex peace agreement that included provisions for the LEAGUE OF

NATIONS, U.S. president Woodrow Wilson's plan for a world organization to end war. The UNITED STATES never joined the League because the U.S. Senate never ratified the Versailles Treaty. France, however, became a permanent member of the League Council (forerunner to the UN's SECURITY COUNCIL) and was a member for the duration of the organization, until Vichy France, a puppet regime under German domination following the Nazi conquest of France in 1940, withdrew. During the interwar period France administered a League mandate over the former Ottoman Empire's region of Lebanon, establishing a special relationship with that multireligious MIDDLE EAST country (granted independence from League mandate in 1943).

During World War II, the Vichy government ruled in the south, while Germany occupied northern France, including Paris. In London, General Charles de Gaulle led the anti-Fascist exiled Free French movement. After the liberation of Paris a provisional government that included de Gaulle's followers established the Fourth Republic. Aided by Marshall Plan funds from the United States, the new government presided over postwar recovery and joined in organizing the European Economic Community (EEC), precursor to the European Union.

The SUEZ CRISIS of 1956 proved something of a defining moment for French diplomacy and, indeed, the future configuration of international affairs. France allied with the United Kingdom and Israel in an attack on Egypt in late October to recover control of the Suez Canal, which had been nationalized by Egyptian president GAMAL ABDUL NASSER. The three allies achieved considerable early success, occupying the Gaza Strip and the Sinai Peninsula. French and British paratroopers landed in the canal zone at Port Said on November 5. However, to the chagrin of Paris and London, their NATO ally in Washington joined with the Soviet Union to insist that the incursion end. The EISENHOWER administration even threatened UN SANCTIONS on Israel if she did not withdraw from conquered territory. The consequent pull-out of the aggressors marked a clear shift in the global balance of power from European locales such as France and Britain to the United States and the USSR. Moreover, in France, de Gaulle became convinced that his country could not depend on supposed allies like the United States.

The Suez debacle took place in the midst of the breakup of France's overseas colonial empire in northern Africa and Southeast Asia during the postwar period of NATIONAL LIBERATION MOVEMENTS. This dissolution confronted the Fourth Republic with disruptive domestic strains. France lost a colonial war in Vietnam in 1954; Morocco and Tunisia became independent in 1956; and the Front de Libération Nationale in Algeria (FLN) fought effectively to end French control there. The Algerian War was particularly polarizing in France and led to the threat of a military coup by a pro-colonial military group. In 1958 the National Assembly granted Charles de Gaulle emergency powers to deal with

the situation. De Gaulle negotiated a withdrawal from Algeria, leaving the FLN in control (full transfer was completed by 1962). He then guided the country to a new constitution that resulted in the establishment of the Fifth Republic, with a strong presidency, a post assumed by de Gaulle. The newly empowered president pursued an independent foreign policy, seeking closer ties with the Soviet bloc and DEVELOPING COUNTRIES. He also opposed British entry into the Common Market (EEC), developed an autonomous nuclear force, advanced momentous rapprochement with Germany, recognized the People's Republic of CHINA, and withdrew French forces from the North Atlantic Treaty Organization (NATO). In the wake of student riots in 1968 de Gaulle called for new elections, which he won. Nonetheless, in 1969 he resigned the presidency. Former premier Georges Pompidou won election to the presidency that same year and retained the position until his death in 1974. In the late years of his service, France reversed policy and endorsed British MEMBERSHIP in the EEC. From 1974 to 1981 Valéry Giscard d'Estaing served as president. During these years, France joined in the steady progress of European integration and the development of the European Parliament. Socialist François Mitterrand defeated Giscard d'Estaing in the 1981 election, ending the long Gaullist era. The new president restored French military collaboration with NATO and vigorously supported UN intervention in the Balkans (FORMER YUGOSLAVIA). In 1995, Mitterrand's 14-year Socialist rule in the presidency came to an end with the electoral victory of Jacques Chirac, leader of the Gaullists, the majority party in the legislature during the later stages of Mitterrand's presidency. Chirac remained president until the elections of 2007. Chirac suffered a serious political embarrassment when French voters rejected a proposed EU constitution in a referendum in 2005. Former president Giscard d'Estaing had been one of the main authors of the constitution and Chirac's government a robust proponent.

At the United Nations, while it served as one of the five permanent powers on the Security Council, France often was overshadowed by U.S., Russian, Chinese, and British diplomacy. The stinging defeat in the Suez crisis and France's limited military capability reinforced this circumstance. UN DISARMAMENT negotiations were monopolized by the United States and the Soviet Union. In the ARAB-ISRAELI DISPUTE France supported general efforts to achieve a negotiated settlement, but played no direct role other than in Lebanon. In the post–COLD WAR era it tended to support the Palestinian cause against what it perceived to be Israeli heavy-handedness. However, when it supported resolutions to this end, the French government often found its position rejected by a U.S. veto. Its most important contribution to UN activities proved to be in support of UN DEVELOPMENT programs and PEACEKEEPING missions.

In early 2003, France joined with Germany and others on the Security Council to oppose American and British efforts to gain UN approval for their invasion of IRAQ. When GEORGE W. BUSH's administration proceeded with military action despite the rebuff, trans-Atlantic, as well as UN-U.S., tensions reached a high pitch. In Washington, an anti-French mood escalated as conservative members of Congress supported legislative resolutions to rename French fries "freedom fries." However, what may have been obscured by the clamor was that Chirac's government (and much of the world) had supported American action in AFGHANISTAN following the terrorist attacks in New York and Washington, D.C., on September 11, 2001. France had also joined with NATO in the 1995 attacks that ultimately led to the DAYTON ACCORDS ending the civil war in the FORMER YUGOSLAVIA and then again supported NATO air strikes that in 1999 finally ended Serb occupation of KOSOVO. Recently France has also been a committed participant in meetings of the GROUP OF EIGHT and has joined with other Security Council members (including the United States and the United Kingdom) in (1) crafting with the United States SC Resolution 1701, passed on August 11, 2006, calling for an end to hostilities in France's former mandate Lebanon and the insertion of an expanded peacekeeping force there (UN INTERIM FORCE IN LEBANON—UNIFIL), (2) passing SC Resolution 1718 (October 14, 2006) condemning nuclear tests conducted by North Korea (Democratic Republic of Korea), and (3) leading efforts to direct the international community's attention to the conflict in DARFUR and to press Sudan to accept UN peacekeepers there.

The election of President Nicolas Sarkozy in 2007 brought a shift in French foreign policy. Sarkozy endorsed U.S. efforts at the United Nations to pressure IRAN to forego the development of nuclear weapons. He supported harsh sanctions on Iran for refusing to suspend uranium enrichment and urged that country to return to negotiations on its nuclear program.

See also ANNAN, KOFI; ANTARCTICA TREATY; APARTHEID; APPENDIX A; CAMBODIA; CHIEF EXECUTIVES BOARD FOR COORDINATION; CONFERENCE ON DISARMAMENT; DAYTON PEACE ACCORDS; EIGHTEEN NATION DISARMAMENT COMMITTEE; EMERGENCY SPECIAL SESSIONS OF THE GENERAL ASSEMBLY; GUATEMALA; GULF WAR; INTERNATIONAL LABOUR ORGANIZATION; INTERNATIONAL MONETARY FUND; JURISDICTION OF THE UNITED NATIONS; NAMIBIA; NUCLEAR NONPROLIFERATION TREATY; NUCLEAR-WEAPONS-FREE ZONES; OIL-FOR-FOOD SCANDAL; QUANTICO MEETING, RWANDA CRISIS; SCALE OF ASSESSMENTS; SOUTHEAST ASIA TREATY ORGANIZATION; SUSPENSION AND EXPULSION OF MEMBERS; THANT, U; TREATY OF RAROTONGA; TREATY OF TLATLELOCO; TRUSTEESHIP COUNCIL; TRUSTEESHIP SYSTEM; UNITED NATIONS CONFERENCE ON INTERNATIONAL ORGANIZATION; UNITED NATIONS EMERGENCY FORCE; UNITED NATIONS RELIEF AND WORKS AGENCY FOR PALESTINE REFUGEES IN THE NEAR EAST; WORLD HEALTH ORGANIZATION; YALTA CONFERENCE.

Further Reading: Ardagh, John. *France in the New Century.* New York: Penguin, 2000. Gildea, Robert. *France since 1945.* New York: Oxford University Press, 2002. Gildea, Robert. *The Past in French History.* New Haven, Conn.: Yale University Press, 1994. Judt, Tony. *Burden of Responsibility: Blum, Camus, Aron, and the French 20th Century.* Chicago: University of Chicago Press, 2006. French Mission to the UN Web site: <www.franceonu.org/sommaire.php3?id_rubrique=2>.

Fréchette, Louise (1946–)

On March 2, 1998, Louise Fréchette became the first DEPUTY SECRETARY-GENERAL of the United Nations. The post had been created in December 1997 by the GENERAL ASSEMBLY as part of the REFORM package put forward by SECRETARY-GENERAL KOFI ANNAN. According to the plan set forth in *RENEWING THE UNITED NATIONS,* the Deputy Secretary-General would serve as the Secretary-General's primary adviser, have assigned responsibilities for daily administration of the SECRETARIAT—particularly of the reform process—coordinate coherence and cooperation among UN bodies, represent the Secretary-General at conferences and official functions, and take on special assignments. With her appointment, Fréchette became the highest-ranking woman within the institution in UN history.

Louise Fréchette was born in Montreal, Canada, on July 16, 1946. She earned a bachelor of arts degree from College Basile Moreau and a history degree from the University of Montreal (1970). She also earned a diploma in economic studies from the College of Europe in Bruges, Belgium. Following her graduation from the University of Montreal, Fréchette commenced a long career in the Canadian government, rising to the position of deputy minister of national defense immediately prior to her appointment as Deputy Secretary-General. As a member of Canada's Department of External Affairs in 1972 she served on the delegation to the UN General Assembly. She then served as second secretary in the Canadian embassy in Athens. Following a tour of service in the External Affairs Department's European Division (1975–77), Fréchette became Canadian first secretary at its UN mission in Geneva until 1982. In 1985 she was appointed ambassador simultaneously to Argentina, Uruguay, and Paraguay. Her work in South America led to an appointment as assistant deputy minister for Latin American and Caribbean affairs. From 1992 to 1995 Fréchette served as Canada's PERMANENT REPRESENTATIVE to the United Nations in New York.

In addition to overseeing the UN reform process, Fréchette served on Annan's SENIOR MANAGEMENT GROUP and other secretariat leadership committees. Her primary responsibilities centered on social, economic, and development activities. She supervised the Office for Development Financing in the effort to find additional financial support for UN projects. She was also given a major role in Annan's

Deputy Secretary-General Louise Fréchette (UN/DPI PHOTO BY ESKINDER DEBEBE)

these liaison relationships for which Fréchette had special responsibility was with American broadcast entrepreneur Ted Turner's United Nations Foundation, which bestowed a gift of $1 billion to the UN in 1999. In the area of peace and security, the Secretary-General put his deputy in charge of implementing the recommendations of the BRAHIMI REPORT, a sweeping set of reforms in the area of UN PEACEKEEPING.

Fréchette became an ardent spokesperson for what she called the emerging "New" United Nations, an institution increasingly focused on "human beings, respect for their rights, and the satisfaction of their basic needs," and for gender equality in all societies. Speaking in April 2001, she argued for the THEMATIC DIPLOMACY of the UN that went "beyond the CHARTER," and was enshrined in the DECLARATION of the MILLENNIUM SUMMIT, convened in September 2000. Beyond the traditional concerns of NATION-STATE diplomacy the United Nations in her view was now rightly focused on human problems associated with peace missions, globalization, poverty, DEMOCRATIZATION, environmental activities, human settlements, population growth, drug trafficking, disease, migration, CLIMATE CHANGE, and the information revolution. Noting the critical importance of the United Nations to a topic "that is dear to me," namely, women's rights, Fréchette suggested that the UN's engagement with INTERNATIONAL CIVIL SOCIETY had "created for the WOMEN of world a set of standards against which to measure performance in their own countries."

During the IRAQ OIL-FOR-FOOD SCANDAL, Fréchette found herself facing criticism, from among others, former U.S. Federal Reserve chairman PAUL VOLCKER, who cited mismanagement of the program. In the event, Fréchette in 2005 announced her resignation from the post of deputy secretary-general. On March 3, 2006, Secretary Annan appointed Mark Malloch Brown to succeed her.

Further Reading: Hampson, Fen Osler, and Maureen Appel Molot, eds. *Big Enough to Be Heard: Canada among Nations.* Ottawa: Carleton University Press, 1996. UN Biography Web site: <www.un.org/events/women/iwd/2003/frechette.html>.

funds   *See* PROGRAMMES AND FUNDS.

efforts to develop cooperation between the United Nations and "civil society," including partnerships with NONGOVERNMENTAL ORGANIZATIONS and private businesses. She was a major advocate of the UN's GLOBAL COMPACT, an initiative by Annan to obtain the formal commitment by world business leaders to respect UN-established HUMAN RIGHTS, labor, and environmental norms. The most important of

G

General Agreement on Tariffs and Trade (GATT)

The General Agreement on Tariffs and Trade was a PACT originally adopted at Geneva on October 30, 1947. It governed tariff concessions on industrial products as agreed to among its 23 original signatories. These initial GATT partners included the most important countries allied in World War II against the Axis powers. The negotiations were driven by the postwar agenda of the main Allied powers, the UNITED STATES, the United Kingdom, and Canada, to create postwar institutions to prevent a reemergence of war and depression. This aim could be accomplished, in their view, only by ending economic nationalism and the extensive protectionist policies that had characterized the interwar period.

The GATT was supposed to be an "interim" agreement until an International Trade Organization (ITO), which would provide a more ambitious regulatory framework for world trade, was established to join the INTERNATIONAL MONETARY FUND (IMF) and the INTERNATIONAL BANK FOR RECONSTRUCTION AND DEVELOPMENT (IBRD), also known as the WORLD BANK, in overseeing the international economy. While the Final Act of the United Nations Conference on Trade and Employment at Havana, CUBA, establishing an ITO, was signed on March 24, 1948, this so-called Havana Charter was withdrawn from consideration by the Truman administration in 1950 because of the almost certain defeat it faced in the U.S. Senate. This left the GATT by default as the mainstay of the international trading system. It, along with the IMF and the World Bank, was intended to promote a global free trade system.

To underline its "interim" status, secretarial support for the GATT was provided by the UN's Interim Committee for International Trade Organization. Over its almost 50-year lifetime, the GATT SECRETARIAT, which remained very small by UN standards, had four executive secretaries (subsequently upgraded to the more prestigious title of DIRECTOR-GENERAL): Eric Wyndham White, Olivier Long, Arthur Dunkel, and Peter Sutherland. Another sign of the provisional nature of GATT was that its secretariat did not actually have a permanent home until 1977 when it moved into the Centre William Rappard on the shores of Lake Geneva in Switzerland.

There were several key principles embodied in the various articles of GATT. It established the principle of nondiscrimination in international trade as expressed in most-favored-nation (MFN) treatment (Article I) and national treatment (Article III). Under "MFN treatment," signatories to GATT agreed to extend the lowest tariff rate that was generally applicable to the imports from all other GATT countries. Under "national treatment," member countries agreed that tax and regulatory policies should not be applied to imported or domestic products so as to afford protection to domestic production. Additionally, the agreement required the publication and transparency of trade regulations (Article X); the use of tariffs—not nontariff barriers—to regulate trade (Articles III through XXIII); the objective of a progressive reduction of tariffs (Article XXVIII); the private, and not governmental, nature of trade; the acceptance of barriers against dumped or subsidized imports (Article VI); the settlement of disputes through consultation and negotiation (Articles XXII and XXIII); and the avoidance of retaliation.

Over eight rounds of negotiations, culminating in the 1986–94 Uruguay Round, progress was made in lowering average tariff rates on manufactured goods levied by industrialized countries from 40 percent before GATT to around 4 percent. Progress was also made in eliminating barriers to trade such as exchange controls, import licensing, quotas, and other quantitative restrictions that were even more damaging than tariffs. But it was not until the Uruguay Round that significant separate agreements were reached covering the two key excluded areas of agriculture and services.

In its negotiations, the GATT employed an easy three-step recipe to reduce the overall level of protectionism in the world economy. First, less visible nontariff trade barriers were, wherever possible, replaced with tariffs or, better still, eliminated. Second, maximum (or "bound") tariff rates were negotiated. The "binding of tariffs" results in countries agreeing not to increase a tariff after it has been lowered. Third, the bound rates continued to be lowered over time in subsequent rounds of negotiations.

For most industrialized countries, under GATT rules bound tariff rates were the same as MFN tariff rates. But for DEVELOPING COUNTRIES, bound tariff rates were often much higher than the actual "applied" rates, that is, the existing rates then in place, and consequently the bound rates served as a ceiling. This gave these poorer countries the flexibility to raise tariffs arbitrarily and unexpectedly if they so chose. In contrast, countries that bound their tariffs at applied levels were required to compensate their trading partners if for any reason they raised their tariffs. During the Uruguay Round, there were detailed schedules of bound tariffs by Harmonized System classification for each individual country participating in the negotiations.

The Uruguay Round tariff cuts, which were fully phased in by the year 2000, averaged almost 40 percent and lowered the average tariff on industrial products levied by developed countries from 6.3 percent to 3.8 percent. The proportion of the value of these products that were duty free rose from 20 percent to 44 percent. The proportion facing high tariffs—above 15 percent—fell from 7 percent to 5 percent. The proportion of these tariff lines that were bound increased from 78 percent to 99 percent.

According to a 1997 Organization for Economic Cooperation and Development (OECD) study, average tariffs would be reduced substantially when the Uruguay Round cuts were fully in place. For the four largest economies (the United States, the European Union, JAPAN, and Canada), tariffs would average in the 4 to 7 percent range and be higher in the European Union and Canada than in Japan and the United States. Excepting Switzerland and Sweden, bound tariff rates would be significantly higher in other advanced OECD countries, averaging from 9 to 25 percent. And bound tariffs would be even higher in the developing countries of Mexico and Turkey, averaging 35 to 45 percent, which would be representative of bound tariff rates in the developing world. Applied tariff rates only averaged 14 percent in Mexico and 10 percent in Turkey.

While much progress had been made in eliminating or lowering nontariff barriers (NTBs), at the turn of the century they still existed and were important. The OECD examined the prevalence of NTBs among OECD countries. The NTBs considered fell under two rubrics: price controls and quantitative restrictions (QRs). Price controls covered Voluntary Export Restrictions (VERs) like those used for automobiles and textiles, variable charges, and antidumping and countervailing duties. QRs included nonautomatic licensing, export restraints, and other quotas and import prohibitions. The OECD study showed that QRs were still very prevalent.

The GATT and its secretariat were subsumed into the WORLD TRADE ORGANIZATION (WTO) on January 1, 1995. The GATT and its related understandings and agreements became parts of Annex 1A to the "Marrakesh Agreement Establishing the World Trade Organization." Consequently, future GATT negotiations will take place under the auspices of the WTO, the GATT will be administered by the WTO, and disputes will be resolved under the new rules of the WTO's dispute settlement understanding.

See also ANNAN, KOFI; BRETTON WOODS.

Further Reading: Hart, Michael. *Fifty Years of Canadian Statecraft: Canada at the GATT 1947–1997.* Ottawa: Centre for Trade Policy and Law, 1998. Organization for Economic Cooperation and Development. *Indicators of Tariff and Nontariff Trade Barriers: Update 1997.* Paris: Organization for Economic Cooperation and Development, 1997.

— *P. M. Grady*

General and Complete Disarmament (GCD)
See DISARMAMENT.

General Assembly (GA)
CHAPTER IV, Articles 9 through 22 of the UN CHARTER, provides for the composition, functions, powers, and procedures of the General Assembly. The GA, meeting in formal session every fall at UN HEADQUARTERS in New York, is the single most important of the six PRINCIPAL ORGANS OF THE UNITED NATIONS. It is the sole forum in which all member states are represented and in which each member state, regardless of its physical size or population, has an equal vote. For this reason most nations consider the Assembly the focal point of the United Nations. Its importance has grown with the expansion of United Nations MEMBERSHIP, which has ensued following

the end of Western colonialism, particularly during the 1960s. The consequence has been a dramatic increase in the number of independent nations in the world, and hence in the UN membership, which reached 192 in the year 2006. The General Assembly prepared to act in 2002 on yet two more membership applications—from Switzerland and TIMOR-LESTE.

The General Assembly is often referred to as the "Town Meeting of the World," where all residents of the planet theoretically are represented by their governments. Small and middle-sized nations place a great value on the equality of VOTING, reflecting the principle of the sovereign equality of states, which constitutes the basis of INTERNATIONAL LAW and, hence, of the UNITED NATIONS SYSTEM. Each member state is allowed five representatives and five alternate representatives to the General Assembly, with these individuals serving on the various committees as well as meeting in the full Assembly.

Since four of the remaining principal organs report to the General Assembly, it plays a role in all the main functions of the United Nations. Only the SECURITY COUNCIL (SC) and the INTERNATIONAL COURT OF JUSTICE (ICJ) do not submit their decisions for review. The General Assembly deals with a wide range of topics spanning all fields of international affairs. It employs a system of plenary committees, with all topics originally debated, reviewed, and voted upon by these committees. Committee RESOLUTIONS are then presented to the Assembly for plenary consideration.

There are six main committees. The FIRST COMMITTEE, designated the Political and Security Committee under its original mandate, in fact deals almost exclusively with DISARMAMENT affairs. The member states found that this topic was so central to the international system that it required its own committee. The First Committee is now charged with addressing "disarmament and international security." A sepa-

General Assembly Hall, New York City (UN/DPI PHOTO BY ESKINDER DEBEBE)

rate Special Political Committee was established early in the history of the United Nations to consider all other political questions. The other main committees are the SECOND COMMITTEE: Economic and Financial (ECOFIN); THIRD COMMITTEE: Social, Humanitarian, and Cultural (SOCHUM); FOURTH COMMITTEE: Trusteeship, which in the late 1990s was merged with the Special Political Committee to become the Special Political and Decolonization Committee; FIFTH COMMITTEE: Administrative and Budgetary; and SIXTH COMMITTEE: Legal. The General Assembly also has established special committees and working groups to deal with specific issues, or to carry out procedural and administrative duties. The most important are the GENERAL COMMITTEE, the CREDENTIALS COMMITTEE, the ADVISORY COMMITTEE ON ADMINISTRATIVE AND BUDGETARY QUESTIONS (ACABQ), and the COMMITTEE ON CONTRIBUTIONS. The General Assembly may also call SPECIAL SESSIONS to deal with specific issues.

The annual meeting usually convenes on the first or second Tuesday after the first Monday of September each year, and usually concludes in mid-December. This three and a half month period includes the most intense portion of the session when the majority of the agenda items are considered. It is not unusual for less frequent meetings to resume in January and continue through April to deal with additional items. The September session begins with each nation making an opening statement in what is called a period of GENERAL DEBATE. These statements constitute formal policy DECLARATIONS regarding the items that nations consider the most important issues before the United Nations and in the international arena. Opening statements are of such importance that most nations send their president, prime minister, or minister of foreign affairs to deliver the address.

The agenda of the General Assembly consists of matters proposed by any member state, as well as continuing items resulting from previously adopted General Assembly resolutions. Hence, the member states determine the agenda, although the SECRETARY-GENERAL can also suggest additional items for consideration. Some continuing items are brought directly to the General Assembly without reference to a committee. The overwhelming majority of the resolutions considered by the full Assembly have been previously discussed in detail and passed by the various committees. The Assembly elects its own president annually, along with 17 vice presidents. The latter are chosen on a proportional basis according to geographical regions, to assure representation of all areas of the world. Collectively they, along with the president and the elected chairmen of each of the six main committees, constitute the General Committee, which functions as a steering committee of the session and sets the agenda order.

The General Assembly functions by consensus rather than by majority vote. While a majority vote can assure passage, the United Nations is not a sovereign body, meaning that General Assembly resolutions are not binding but are dependent on the will of the participating governments to carry them out. Whereas in a government of a sovereign state the majority may have the right to impose its will on the minority through binding laws, in the greater global community, as represented in the United Nations, only those nations agreeing to be bound by a resolution are committed to carrying out its provisions. A majority vote can therefore be meaningless unless all member states are willing to abide by the terms of the approved resolution. As a result, the General Assembly functions as a negotiating body rather than a parliamentary body; the objective is to seek the agreement of all participating nations to the resolution, which is the only way to ensure that all sovereign nations agree to carry it out. This necessity often requires lengthy negotiations among representatives of all member states in order to establish language that is acceptable—or at least tolerable—to all, and to reach agreement on declarations that all member states are willing and likely to fulfill. Usually, the General Assembly negotiations continue until the initial proposals by the various nations are combined to reach agreed compromise on a single resolution on each agenda topic. As a result, negotiations regarding the wording continue until unanimous agreement is achieved, or until it is evident that unanimous consent is impossible and that the number of nations dissenting is reduced to a handful. Only after negotiations reach these stages is an item brought to a vote. Generally, a resolution that lacks the support of an overwhelming majority of the body will be withdrawn rather than being brought to a vote, and votes take place only when there are only a small number of holdouts that cannot accept the language of the resolution.

Consensus agreement is frequently reached on global issues, and since the end of the COLD WAR more than 70 percent of the resolutions adopted by the General Assembly each year have been adopted by unanimous consent, without a formal recorded vote. In about half the cases where votes are necessary, only a handful of negative votes (fewer than 10) are recorded, along with a larger group of abstentions, as nations vote negatively only in cases where their national interests or perceived national security is endangered. Abstentions are far more common than are negative votes. Thus, while the Charter provides that the Assembly make decisions by majority rule, it in fact functions by unanimous consent, and therefore does indeed serve as a town meeting of the world. The Charter further stipulates that "IMPORTANT QUESTIONS" must pass in the GA by a two-thirds majority. Yet, this requirement has little impact, since resolutions are rarely adopted with less than a two-thirds majority, especially in the years since the end of the cold war. Important questions are those involving international peace and security, trusteeship questions, questions involving membership and the SUSPENSION of the rights and privileges of membership, budgetary questions, and various electoral functions for the other principal organs of the United Nations.

The General Assembly elects the NON-PERMANENT MEMBERS OF THE SECURITY COUNCIL, the members of the ECONOMIC AND SOCIAL COUNCIL, and the TRUSTEESHIP COUNCIL, and, acting upon the recommendation of the SECURITY COUNCIL, elects the Secretary-General, as well as the judges of the International Court of Justice in concurrence with the Council. A two-thirds vote of the General Assembly is also required to propose AMENDMENTS TO THE CHARTER, which then must be ratified by the governments of the member states, or to set the place and time of a General Conference to be held for the purpose of proposing Charter amendments. While the Security Council normally deals with questions affecting international peace and security, the General Assembly may consider such questions and make recommendations to the Security Council, and under the 1950 UNITING FOR PEACE RESOLUTION may make recommendations in cases when a VETO prevents the Security Council from taking action, although this latter measure is rarely invoked.

In addition to its official functions, the General Assembly offers a meeting place for the governments of the world to share ideas on global concerns. It also can be the vital setting for informal, behind-the-scenes diplomacy, even between nations that have technically broken relations or may be at war. The resulting opportunities for confidential exchanges can play, and have played, a central role in enabling nations to cooperate in addressing a wide range of global, multilateral, and bilateral issues.

See also PROCEDURAL COMMITTEES, REFORM OF THE UNITED NATIONS.

Further Reading: Bailey, Sydney D. *The United Nations: A Concise Political Guide.* 3d ed. Lanham, Md.: Barnes and Noble, 1995. Mingst, Karen A., and Margaret P. Karns. *The United Nations in the Twenty-first Century.* 3d ed. Boulder, Colo.: Westview, 2006. Muldoon, James P. Jr., et al., eds. *Multilateral Diplomacy and the United Nations Today.* 2d ed. Boulder, Colo.: Westview, 2005. Peterson, M. J. *The UN General Assembly.* New York: Routledge, 2006.

— *K. J. Grieb*

General Committee

The General Committee is one of the PROCEDURAL COMMITTEES of the GENERAL ASSEMBLY (GA), and consists of the Assembly's president, 21 vice presidents, and the elected chairmen of the six main committees of the General Assembly. Members are elected at the beginning of the GA session in September. The president serves for one annual session, and is usually a leading statesman from a middle power or small state, with the position rotating by region. No representative of the PERMANENT MEMBERS OF THE SECURITY COUNCIL has ever been elected to the presidency.

Following selection of the president, the General Assembly elects 17 vice presidents for one-year terms. They are

allocated by geographical region, according to a formula that assures equitable representation reflecting the VOTING strength of each region in the MEMBERSHIP of the United Nations. Specifically, there are seven vice presidents from AFRICA and Asia, three from LATIN AMERICA, two from the Western Europe and Other States CAUCUS GROUP, and one from Eastern Europe (reflecting the fact that the distribution was agreed upon during the COLD WAR). Since the Middle East is not considered a "geographical area" in UN parlance, one of the seven seats assigned to Asia and Africa is by agreement held by a Middle Eastern country, thereby allowing accommodation to a significant political bloc within a formula based exclusively on geographical representation. Thus, the seat allocated to the Middle East rotates between Africa and Asia. The "Other" category is used to add the Western democracies located outside Western Europe and includes Canada, Australia, and New Zealand. In 2000 Israel was added to the Other group, becoming eligible for election as a vice president for the first time since the United Nations was formed. The region from which the president of the General Assembly is drawn receives one less vice president. The five remaining vice presidencies are allotted to the permanent members of the SECURITY COUNCIL.

The General Committee functions as the steering committee for the annual session of the General Assembly, making decisions regarding the agenda and the order in which items will be considered. Items are placed on the agenda at the request of member states, or by previous decisions and continuing actions of the General Assembly.

Further Reading: United Nations Department of Public Information. *Basic Facts about the United Nations.* New York: United Nations Department of Public Information, periodically.

— *K. J. Grieb*

General Debate

Each session of the GENERAL ASSEMBLY (GA) opens in September with what is called General Debate. During this two- or three-week period, each member state makes an opening address before the full General Assembly in the GA Hall at UN HEADQUARTERS. These statements are formal policy DECLARATIONS regarding the items that each government considers the most important issues before the United Nations and in the international arena. The speeches are not confined to items on the agenda, nor do they attempt to address all agenda topics. Rather each nation has the option to focus on a single item, or on several issues that it regards as of particular consequence.

Opening statements are of such importance that most nations send their president, prime minister, or minister of foreign affairs to deliver the address. The length of general debate speeches has varied over the years. While diplomatic courtesy requires limiting the length of statements, it is difficult to silence a head of state once at the podium. However, as the number of member states has expanded over the years, limits have been agreed upon and are generally respected.

— K. J. Grieb

Geneva Headquarters of the United Nations

Considered the second UN center in the world after the UN HEADQUARTERS in New York, the Palais des Nations in Geneva, Switzerland, became the headquarters of the LEAGUE OF NATIONS in 1936. At its initiation in 1919 the League chose Geneva as its central location. Designed by a team of architects from four European countries, the Palais was built between 1929 and 1936. When, after World War II the United Nations assumed the place of the League as the universal COLLECTIVE SECURITY organization of the world's nations, it took possession of the Palais des Nations as its European seat. Officially called the UN Office at Geneva (UNOG), the Palais is situated in Ariana Park overlooking Lake Geneva. Since 1936 it has remained a major center of international activity, and surrounding it in the city of

Geneva are several international organizations, almost all of which are affiliated with the United Nations. More than 300 conferences convene annually at the Palais, and, as of 2007, national representatives from more than 160 nations were accredited to the Geneva Office. Here as well are found several OBSERVER missions, intergovernmental organizations such as the European Union, the AFRICAN UNION, and the Arab League. A DIRECTOR-GENERAL appointed by the SECRETARY-GENERAL administers the Geneva Office. There is a library at the headquarters, established by a donation from American entrepreneur John D. Rockefeller Jr., containing more than one million volumes and, since 1997, state-of-the-art connections with the World Wide Web. The Palais also serves as Geneva's international press center and contains a post office, bank, restaurants, media services, and a UN philatelic museum.

In the Palais's most spacious room—the Assembly Hall, accommodating more than 2,000 delegates—SPECIAL SESSIONS of the United Nations, such as the WORLD SUMMIT FOR SOCIAL DEVELOPMENT of 2000, as well as annual plenary gatherings of several UN SPECIALIZED AGENCIES have been held over the years. The CONFERENCE ON DISARMA-

Palais des Nations (UN/DPI PHOTO BY P. KLEE)

MENT usually holds its annual sessions in the smaller Council Chamber, where other historic conferences have occurred, including the conference on Indochina in 1954, the conference on Korea in 1954, and the AFGHANISTAN peace conference of 1988.

Like the New York Headquarters the Palais is open to the public and provides guided tours and information programs. Secretary-General Kofi Annan appointed Sergei Ordzhonikidze as the new UNOG DIRECTOR-GENERAL beginning March 1, 2002, succeeding Vladimir Petrovsky, who had held the post for the previous nine years.

See also INTERNATIONAL LAW COMMISSION, INTERNATIONAL TRADE CENTRE UNCTAD/WTO, UNITED NATIONS ASSOCIATION, UNITED NATIONS RESEARCH INSTITUTE FOR SOCIAL DEVELOPMENT.

Further Reading: Eco'Diagnostic, Geneva. *International Geneva Yearbook*. Geneva: United Nations, published annually. UNOG Web site: <www.unog.ch>. Geneva Headquarters Guide Web site: <www.genevabriefingbook.com/chapters/palais.html>

genocide   *See* CONVENTION ON THE PREVENTION AND PUNISHMENT OF THE CRIME OF GENOCIDE.

Germany

The Federal Republic of Germany (then called "West Germany") entered the United Nations on September 18, 1973, at the precise time that the German Democratic Republic (referred to at the time as "East Germany") also assumed MEMBERSHIP. These unusual, arranged ADMISSIONS were the consequence of a compromise between the opposing antagonists in the COLD WAR. Divided Germany, resulting from the settlement engineered by the victors in World War II, was the epicenter of the long cold war. In November 1989 perhaps the most stunning event that marked the unraveling of that bipolar competition occurred: the dismantling of the Soviet-built wall that since 1961 had separated East and West Berlin. Within less than a year, the two formerly divided rivals had merged into a single nation, now a powerful and influential member of the United Nations. When the former East Germans combined with their western compatriots they also instantly entered the European Union and the North Atlantic Treaty Organization. United Germany, populated by 80 million citizens, was now unquestionably a major player in international affairs. These striking developments took place within only half a century of the cataclysmic end of World War II, which had been accompanied by the utter devastation of Germany, military occupation by her powerful wartime enemies, and the ensuing division of the erstwhile proud people into two confrontational minions at the very heart of the global cold war.

Ancient and dispersed German tribes first appeared in history on the fringes of the Roman empire, occasionally resisting incursions by Roman armed forces, infiltrating the empire, and, by some accounts, causing the collapse of the empire in 476 C.E., when the German chieftain Odoacer deposed the last western Roman emperor. Whether the empire actually "fell" is a point of scholarly contention, since the Eastern Empire continued until 1453 and the Roman Catholic Church maintained a kind of unity of Christians in the West. Within this switching historical milieu "Germany" emerged. Charlemagne brought most of the area containing ethnic Germans into his large empire, which, at his death in 843, broke into three parts to his three sons. The eastern portion of that division contained mostly Germans. By the end of the 10th century, most Germans found themselves in scattered political entities within the feudal domain of the Holy Roman Empire. Fragmentation of the German people would continue to be a feature of central Europe until the late 19th century.

The Reformation of the 16th century, highlighted by Martin Luther's break with the Roman Catholic Church, exacerbated divisions. The Thirty Years' War (1618–48) was in large part a religious struggle between Protestant and Catholic leaders that took place chiefly in and around German lands. The war concluded with the Treaty of Westphalia and the European-wide concession of state SOVEREIGNTY as the underlying principle of international relations. At the same time it left Germany prostrate and shattered. During the Napoleonic wars of the early 19th century, FRANCE conquered much of Germany. The Vienna Congress of 1814–15, attempting to restore European order after Napoléon, created a German League with 39 distinct states. Of these, the most prominent was the Kingdom of Prussia, which, by war and diplomacy, finally, during the last third of the century, brought unity to the bewildering assortment of German political entities. Led by its shrewd chancellor, Otto von Bismarck, Germany achieved industrial prowess and military might, and even began to accumulate a few overseas colonies, thus ascending to great power status.

Under Kaiser Wilhelm II, Germany entered World War I, which it lost, in the event losing its colonial empire and some of its border lands. The Treaty of Versailles, which included a proposal for the LEAGUE OF NATIONS, contained, as well, provisions asserting German blame for the war (Article 231) and calling for the vanquished nation to pay reparations to the victors, irritants that provided a grievance for exploitation by extremist political movements, such as Adolf Hitler's National Socialists. Hitler's movement gained power into the early 1930s, and he was able to manipulate his appointment as chancellor in January 1933, leading to the effective dismantling of the Weimar Republic that had been established in 1919.

Hitler called his polity the "Third Reich." ("Reich" is German for empire; the Holy Roman Empire is considered the

First Reich, unified Germany from 1871 to 1918 was called the Second Reich.) The new chancellor (1) pressed through a compliant Reichstag an "Enabling Law" giving him the power to rule by decree, (2) withdrew from the League of Nations in October 1933 (Germany had been a member since 1926), (3) began to rearm, contrary to the Treaty of Versailles (which he denounced in 1936), (4) contrived *Anschluss* (merger) with Austria in 1938, (5) annexed Czechoslovakia in March 1939, (6) invaded Poland in September 1939, launching World War II, and (7) led his country during the years of war and the mass slaughter called the Holocaust.

Despite early successes, Hitler and his partners—chiefly JAPAN and Italy—found themselves eventually overwhelmed by the Allies, led by GREAT BRITAIN, the Soviet Union, and the UNITED STATES. The war concluded disastrously for Germany. Her cities lay in ruins and famine and energy shortages plagued the country; the Third Reich was over. At the YALTA CONFERENCE in February 1945 the three major powers—the United States, United Kingdom, and USSR—dealt with postwar Germany while at the same time refining plans for the new United Nations. That is, the history of Germany and the history of the United Nations were conjoined, as the birth of a new Germany and the birth of the new international organization occurred simultaneously. Moreover, the key motive for the new organization was to avoid in the future any cataclysmic world conflict such as the one the Third Reich was charged with having brought on.

Yalta divided Germany into four occupation zones, managed by France, Britain, the United States, and the Soviet Union. By 1949 the occupation zones had morphed into two separate nations—East (the Soviet sphere) and West Germany. Berlin, the capital of prewar Germany, was likewise occupied and then divided into East and West Berlin. Because Berlin was inside the Soviet sphere, Moscow persistently sought to unify the city under its puppet regime. When the USSR imposed a blockade on West Berlin in 1948 the Western powers, for several months, supplied the beleaguered city by way of a dramatic airlift. West Berlin survived to remain a major irritant in the Soviets' eastern bloc empire.

Konrad Adenauer became the dominant political figure in the postwar Federal Republic, serving as chancellor for 14 years, long enough to witness his country's obtaining full sovereignty in 1954. In 1951 the country evinced its commitment to European integration by joining the Council of Europe and the European Coal and Steel Community. In 1955 West Germany was admitted into NATO and in 1957 she became one of the six founding members of the European Economic Community, the forerunner of the European Union. The consequent German-French rapprochement at the heart of Western Europe underscored the momentous, certain end of the centuries-long European civil war that had culminated in the 1945 *Götterdämmerung*. Meantime, with aid from the Marshall Plan as an initial stimulus, West Germany realized a remarkable economic revival, sometimes called the

"German Miracle." In less than two decades following the war the country's industrial production rose by 60 percent, gross national product (GNP) tripled, and unemployment dropped to a negligible 1 percent. Next door, East Germany became the second-largest industrial economy in Eastern Europe, and in 1968 its GNP outpaced Czechoslovakia's.

Despite the apparent economic successes in the East, migration to the West, especially through Berlin, continued. To stem the flow, East Germany's Communist Party leader Walter Ulbricht, with the approval of Soviet leader NIKITA KHRUSHCHEV, began construction of a wall on August 13, 1961. The completed wall separated the two halves of Berlin for the next 28 years. It became a widely recognized, notorious symbol of the cold war as well as the most popular tourist attraction in West Berlin. Nonetheless, from 1969 to 1982, the Social Democrats, led for most of those years by Willy Brandt and Helmut Schmidt, governed the country and pursued policies to ease tensions between East and West. From 1982 to 1998 West Germany's politics was dominated for the most part by Chancellor Helmut Kohl of the conservative Christian Democratic Party, who presided over the years that witnessed the end of the cold war, the dismantling of the Berlin Wall, and the reunification of Germany on October 3, 1990. Then, conforming to a cyclical pattern in German politics, the Social Democrats returned to power in 1998, electing Gerhard Schröder chancellor for two election cycles.

Schröder's government joined with close ally France in 2002 and 2003 to oppose the U.S. policy in IRAQ, denying Washington the UN SECURITY COUNCIL support for invasion of SADDAM HUSSEIN's country. Thus Germany became a key player in the standoff that caused transcontinental bitterness and serious angst within the United Nations, as the administration of GEORGE W. BUSH, bypassing support from key traditional allies in the Security Council, engaged in unilateral military and diplomatic actions. The diplomatic twitter surrounding the fray obscured Germany's support of the United States in AFGHANISTAN (in early 2007 almost 3,000 German forces were serving with NATO in Afghanistan), support in the earlier GULF WAR of 1991, and her accommodating actions within the UN and with the United States in a number of challenging international matters. Indeed, Germany, a NON-PERMANENT MEMBER OF THE SECURITY COUNCIL in the middle of the first decade of the 21st century, proved to be a major leader in crafting RESOLUTIONS in a number of cases, including, crucially, resolutions seeking to restrain and abort IRAN's nuclear WEAPONS program (Berlin was particularly active in fashioning SC Resolution 1686 of July 31, 2006 and SC Resolution 1737 of December 23, 2006). Also, Germany was the largest donor ($600 million) to the UN-initiated global fund-raising effort to finance relief projects for victims of the December 2004 tsunami, which ravaged INDONESIA and surrounding areas.

Because of its extensive activity on the international stage and its contribution to UN programs, Germany sought to upgrade its position within UN bodies in the new millennium. The German government campaigned for permanent membership on the Security Council in conjunction with UN SECRETARY-GENERAL Kofi ANNAN'S REFORM proposals in 2005. While the United States had endorsed this revision of the UN CHARTER in earlier times, the Bush administration now opposed it. Other states worried about the addition of yet another European state to the Council and about Germany's ability and willingness to use force at the behest of the United Nations. German representatives joined ambassadors from INDIA, Brazil, and Japan in making the case for all four gaining permanent membership, but the initiative died for lack of international support.

Under the Chancellorship of Christian Democrat Angela Merkel, whose party won the September 2005 elections, Germany's ascension into world politics seemed to continue. Moreover, the country's economy began to accelerate in 2006 after several years of apparent stagnation. Long the economic powerhouse in the EU, with the largest population of all the members, Germany was, in early 2007, the third leading economy in the world, with a per capita GNP of 26,856 euros (over $35,000) as well as the world's leading exporter. She ranked number one in Europe in patent registrations and, together with Japan and the United States, was among the world's three most innovative countries in the first decade of the 21st century.

By early 2007 Chancellor Merkel had launched diplomatic initiatives addressing a wide range of issues, from dealing with conflict in the Middle East to resolving the EU's budget problems. Berlin assumed the presidency of the EU at the close of 2006 as well as the chairmanship of the GROUP OF EIGHT industrial powers. In September 2006 the German cabinet agreed to send 2,400 air and naval troops to join the projected 15,000-strong UN PEACEKEEPING mission in Lebanon (augmenting, by way of SC Resolution 1697, the UN INTERIM FORCE IN LEBANON—UNIFIL). Merkel called this a "historic decision." The nation seemed more eager than ever to be involved in world affairs.

See also ANTARCTIC TREATY; BIOLOGICAL WEAPONS; DAYTON PEACE ACCORDS; DESERTIFICATION; ENVIRONMENT; FORMER YUGOSLAVIA; INTERNATIONAL ATOMIC ENERGY AGENCY; INTERNATIONAL COURT OF JUSTICE; INTERNATIONAL LABOUR ORGANIZATION; INTERNATIONAL MONETARY FUND; KYOTO PROTOCOL; NAMIBIA; ROOSEVELT, FRANKLIN D.; RWANDA; STALIN, JOSEPH; TEHERAN CONFERENCE; UN SECURITY COUNCIL RESOLUTION 1441; UNIFIED TASK FORCE; UNITED NATIONS CONFERENCE ON THE LAW OF THE SEA; UNITED NATIONS ENVIRONMENT PROGRAMME; UNITED NATIONS FRAMEWORK CONVENTION ON CLIMATE CHANGE; UNITED NATIONS VOLUNTEERS; WEAPONS OF MASS DESTRUCTION; WORLD BANK.

Further Reading: Fuibrook, Mary. *The Divided Nation: A History of Germany 1918–1990.* New York: Oxford University Press, 1991. Irving, Ronald. *Adenauer.* New York: Pearson Education, 2002. Kettenacker, Lothar. *Germany since 1945.* New York: Oxford University Press, 1997. "Newly Confident Germany Takes Over EU Presidency, G-8 Chair." *International Herald Tribune,* December 27, 2006. Found at: <www.iht.com/articles/ap/2006/12/28/europe/EU_GEN_Germany_Great_Expectations.php>. Pulzer, Peter. *Germany 1870–1945: Politics, State Formation, and War.* New York: Oxford University Press, 1997. Schissler, Hanna, ed. *The Miracle Years: A Cultural History of West Germany, 1949–1968.* Princeton, N.J.: Princeton University Press, 2001. Permanent Mission of Germany to the UN Web site: <www.new-york-un.diplo.de/Vertretung/newyorkvn/en/Startseite.html>.

Global Compact

The United Nations is an international organization of sovereign NATION-STATES that serves as a forum for interstate diplomacy and collective action. However, in the new millennium the organization expanded its involvement with the private sector and NON-GOVERNMENTAL ORGANIZATIONS (NGOs). Particularly in the area of development, there was a new UN effort to engage private corporations and NGOs in the work of the United Nations. Decreases in donor state funding made this a necessity. The focus on private actors in the international arena was also recognition by the UN leadership that an emerging INTERNATIONAL CIVIL SOCIETY would have a significant impact on the success or failure of UN initiatives. It was within this context that SECRETARY-GENERAL KOFI ANNAN proposed a Global Compact between the United Nations and multinational corporations to protect HUMAN RIGHTS, international labor standards, and the global ENVIRONMENT. Speaking on January 31, 1999, to the World Economic Forum in Davos, Switzerland, Annan urged corporations to work directly with the world body, bypassing national governments, to fulfill nine principles established in the RIO DECLARATION of the Earth Summit, the INTERNATIONAL LABOUR ORGANIZATION'S Fundamental Principles on Rights of Work, and the UNIVERSAL DECLARATION OF HUMAN RIGHTS.

The Compact is a purely voluntary initiative. Corporations joining the Global Compact commit themselves to: (1) support and respect the protection of international human rights within their sphere of influence, (2) make sure their own corporations are not complicit in human rights abuses, (3) uphold freedom of association and the right to collective bargaining, (4) promote the elimination of all forms of forced and compulsory labor, (5) work for the effective abolition of child labor, (6) support the elimination of discrimination in respect to employment and occupation, (7) support a precautionary approach to environmental challenges, (8) undertake initiatives to promote greater environmental responsibility, and (9) encourage the development and diffusion of environmentally friendly technologies. In

2004, the Secretary-General added a 10th principle: to fight corruption. The program requires the chief executive officer to submit a letter to the executive office of the Secretary-General committing the corporation to these 10 principles and agreeing to post them on the premises of the enterprise. Other private organizations, ranging from chambers of commerce and labor organizations to activist environmental and human rights NGOs are allowed to join as well.

Within a year of Annan's speech more than 50 transnational corporations had signed onto the program, and by early 2007 there were 3,800 participants in the Global Compact, including 2,900 businesses in 100 countries. Annan established a Global Compact office within his executive office, which began operations on July 26, 2000 and was at the time responsible for overall management of the Global Compact.

After a review during 2004–05 of the Global Compact's governance procedures, a new framework was established. The so-called Global Compact Governance Framework was designed to be more efficient and less bureaucratic, and to encourage greater involvement by participants. Six entities share in governance, each with distinct tasks to perform. The six are (1) Global Compact Leaders Summit, (2) Local Networks, (3) Annual Local Networks Forum, (4) Global Compact Board, (5) Global Compact Office, and (6) Inter-Agency Team. Also responding to recommendations that were generated by the mid decade review, the Secretary-General, on April 20, 2006, appointed a new Global Compact Board (number 4 above) made up of 20 members, which was given a mandate to encourage synergetic cooperation among the six entities and to improve management of the enterprise. Six UN Agencies continued to support the Global Compact Office: the UN HIGH COMMISSIONER FOR HUMAN RIGHTS, the UN ENVIRONMENT PROGRAMME, the International Labour Organization, the UN DEVELOPMENT PROGRAMME, the UN INDUSTRIAL DEVELOPMENT ORGANIZATION, and the UN OFFICE ON DRUGS AND CRIME.

The Global Compact set as its overall goals the promotion of international corporate citizenship and social responsibility, the establishment of corporate "good practices," and the development of the United Nations, the "world's only truly global political forum, as authoritative convener and facilitator" of international civil societal organizations.

See also CARDOSO REPORT; FRÉCHETTE, LOUISE; SUBSIDIARITY SUSTAINABLE DEVELOPMENT; THEMATIC DIPLOMACY.

Further Reading: Tessitore, John, and Susan Woolfson, eds. *A Global Agenda. Issues before the 55th General Assembly of the United Nations.* New York: Rowman and Littlefield, 2000. Global Compact Web site: <www.unglobalcompact.org>.

Global Environment Facility (GEF)

The GEF is one of the leading international agencies for the global ENVIRONMENT. It was established in November 1990 by the WORLD BANK, with participation by the UNITED NATIONS DEVELOPMENT PROGRAMME (UNDP) and the UNITED NATIONS ENVIRONMENT PROGRAMME (UNEP). The Global Environment Facility's primary purpose is to provide grants to DEVELOPING COUNTRIES for environment-related projects and to facilitate networking and cooperation among donors. Also, the agency serves as the financial MECHANISM for the implementation of two international CONVENTIONS adopted at the 1992 UNITED NATIONS CONFERENCE ON ENVIRONMENT AND DEVELOPMENT (UNCED) in Rio: the Convention on Biological Diversity and the UNITED NATIONS FRAMEWORK CONVENTION ON CLIMATE CHANGE.

As of early 2007, the facility had 177 member states. GEF's operations are directed by an assembly, composed of all member states, which meets every four years, and a council, functioning as a board of directors and representing 32 constituencies (16 from developing countries, 14 from developed countries, and two from transitional economies), that meets twice a year and also conducts business by mail. Daily activities are managed by a permanent SECRETARIAT consisting of a staff of 40, headed by a chief executive officer, and based in Washington, D.C. The World Bank is the trustee of the GEF trust FUND. It acts as one of the facility's three implementing agencies, and it provides administrative support for the secretariat. The other two GEF implementing agencies are UNDP and UNEP.

Restructured in 1994, GEF implements 12 operational programs (OPs) through which it provides grants. Eleven of these reflect the facility's primary focal areas: four on biodiversity, four on CLIMATE CHANGE, and three on international waters. OP 12—integrated ecosystem management—encompasses cross-sectoral projects. In addition, GEF funds projects to combat ozone depletion that are not grouped among the OPs. Biodiversity OPs include: arid and semi-arid zone ecosystems; coastal, marine, and freshwater ecosystems; forest ecosystems; and mountain ecosystems. Climate change OPs include: removal of barriers to energy efficiency and energy conservation; promoting the adoption of renewable energy by removing barriers and reducing implementation costs; reducing the long-term costs of low greenhouse gas emitting energy technologies; and promoting environmentally sustainable transport. International waters OPs include: waterbody-based, integrated land and water multiple focal area and contaminant-based operational programs. Between 1991 and 1999 GEF provided $991 million in grants for biological diversity projects, and $884 million for climate change projects, as well as $1.5 billion and $4.7 billion in co-financing in these same areas, respectively. It also allocated $360 million to international water initiatives. In addition, it provided $155 million to projects to phase out ozone depleting substances.

From 1991 to 2004, GEF provided almost $1.75 billion to various climate change projects. Matching funds in excess of $9 billion helped co-finance these activities. Since the report of the INTERGOVERNMENTAL PANEL ON CLIMATE CHANGE was issued in early 2007, GEF has moved to expand its activities in the area of combating global warming. Based on a recommendation from the WORLD SUMMIT ON SOCIAL DEVELOPMENT in 2002, it also took over the funding mechanism for DESERTIFICATION as a central area of its work and invested $63 million by 2004 to reverse the phenomenon.

In accordance with the Global Environment Facility's policy, any individual or group may propose a project, which must meet two key criteria: it must improve the global environment or advance the prospect of reducing risks to it and it must reflect national or regional priorities and have support of the country or countries involved. GEF project ideas may be proposed directly to any of its implementing agencies. Country eligibility to receive funding is determined in two ways. Developing countries that have ratified the relevant convention are eligible to propose biodiversity and climate change projects. Other countries, primarily those with economies in transition, are eligible if the country is a party to the appropriate TREATY and is eligible to borrow from the World Bank or receives technical assistance grants from UNDP.

See also AGENDA 21, SUSTAINABLE DEVELOPMENT, WORLD COMMISSION ON ENVIRONMENT AND DEVELOPMENT, WORLD SUMMIT ON SUSTAINABLE DEVELOPMENT.

Further Reading: Aggarwal-Khan, Sheila. *Promoting Coherence: Towards an Effective Global Environment Facility.* Amsterdam: Netherlands Committee for IUCN, 1997. Chasek, Pamela S. *The Global Environment in the Twenty-first Century: Prospects for International Cooperation.* New York: United Nations University Press, 2000. *Introduction to the GEF.* Washington, D.C.: The Global Environment Facility, 2000. Sjeoberg, Helen. *From Idea to Reality: The Creation of the Global Environment Facility.* Washington, D.C.: The Global Environment Facility, 1994. GEF Web site: <www.gefweb.org>

— A. I. Maximenko

Global Fund to Fight AIDS, Tuberculosis and Malaria

Established in January 2002, the Global Fund to Fight AIDS, Tuberculosis and Malaria seeks to increase funding worldwide to combat these three pandemics. By 2007 the Global Fund was providing two-thirds of all funding for programs contending with malaria and tuberculosis, and 20 percent of funding to battle HIV/AIDS. As of April 2007 the fund had been instrumental in saving up to 1.6 million lives in 136 countries where it had provided about $7 billion to over 540 grants.

Acting on a recommendation by UN SECRETARY-GENERAL KOFI ANNAN, the conferring heads of state at the 2001 summit of the GROUP OF EIGHT in Genoa established the new funding arrangement. The first executive director of the fund was Sir Richard Feachem, a professor of international

health from the United Kingdom. In 2007 the successor executive director was Dr. Michel Kazatchkine of FRANCE, who oversaw a SECRETARIAT of 238 employees from more than 68 nations, administering day-to-day operations in the Secretariat HEADQUARTERS in GENEVA, Switzerland. Less that 3 percent of annual commitments to the fund were, in 2007, earmarked for administration and management. There is also an international Board which meets at least twice annually and is responsible for the overall governance of the program. The Board is composed of representatives from both donor and recipient nations, as well as from NON-GOVERNMENTAL ORGANIZATIONS (NGOs), the private sector, and specifically affected communities. In addition, the fund has participating international partners, including the WORLD HEALTH ORGANIZATION, the JOINT UN PROGRAMME ON HIV/AIDS, and the WORLD BANK, which serves as the Global Fund's trustee. Unlike the World Bank, however, the Global Fund provides grants rather than loans to suffering poor countries.

The fund provides financing, not specific implementation of programs. Implementation is done by Country Coordinating MECHANISMS, meaning committees made up of local stakeholder groups within countries, and may include government representatives, relevant NGOs and UN organizations, as well as faith-based and private sector actors. The Global Fund makes an initial grant on the basis of the quality of applications received. An independent Technical Review Panel evaluates applications. Grants are provided for a period of two years, but disbursements are made only on the basis of proven performance, and follow-up funding is normally approved only after careful review of achieved results. The Global Fund, a novel example of the principle of INTERNATIONAL CIVIL SOCIETY, is a public-private partnership incorporated as a foundation under Swiss law.

See also GLOBAL COMPACT.

Further Reading: Attaram, Amir, and Jeffrey Sachs. "Defining and Refining International Donor Support for Combating the AIDS Pandemic." *The Lancet,* January 6, 2001. Found at: <www.earth.columbia.edu/about/director/pubs/lancet010601.pdf>. Global Fund Web site: <www.theglobalfund.org/en/>.

Global Warming   *See* CLIMATE CHANGE.

globalization   *See* BRETTON WOODS, GLOBAL COMPACT, INTERNATIONAL MONETARY FUND, MILLENNIUM SUMMIT, WORLD TRADE ORGANIZATION.

Goldberg Reservation

In 1960 the United Nations intervened with PEACEKEEPING forces in the Congolese civil war. Meant to restore order, the

UN operation was seen by the Soviet Union as an effort on the part of UN SECRETARY-GENERAL DAG HAMMARSKJÖLD to support Western forces in the CONGO. In protest, and despite a ruling by the INTERNATIONAL COURT OF JUSTICE that peacekeeping expenses could be drawn from the regular BUDGET OF THE UNITED NATIONS, the USSR refused to pay its associated UN assessment. According to Article 19 of the UN CHARTER, "A Member of the United Nations which is in arrears to the payment of its financial contributions to the Organization shall have no vote in the GENERAL ASSEMBLY if the amount of its arrears equals or exceeds the amount of the contributions due from it for the preceding two full years." Once the Soviet Union fell far enough behind in payments to trigger the implementation of Article 19 the UNITED STATES pressed for the denial of Soviet VOTING privileges.

Led first by Adlai Stevenson, and then by Arthur J. Goldberg, U.S. PERMANENT REPRESENTATIVES to the United Nations during the LYNDON JOHNSON administration, the American effort made little progress since the growing pro-Soviet majority in the United Nations, largely from the developing world, saw no value in excluding the Soviet Union from the General Assembly. The United States gave up its effort in 1965, but Ambassador Goldberg took the occasion to assert a new American policy toward the world body. He told the SECURITY COUNCIL, "If any member can insist on making an exception to the principle of collective financial responsibility with respect to certain activities of the United Nations, . . . the United States reserves the same option to make exceptions if, in our view, strong and compelling reasons exist to do so."

This threat, known as the Goldberg Reservation, simply appeared to be an expression of disgust and an admission of defeat. By the end of Lyndon Johnson's term as president of the United States, the U.S. government was paying nearly one-third of all UN bills. However, following the 1980 election of President RONALD REAGAN, the Goldberg Reservation was exercised. Disillusionment with the United Nations led the administration to withdraw U.S. MEMBERSHIP from some UN agencies, charging that they had been "politicized," and to limit payment of its assessment, particularly for peacekeeping, until institutional REFORMS were made. The Goldberg Reservation was reenforced with the Kassebaum Amendment, which cut U.S. payments to UN organs until their staffs were reduced significantly, and until they made revisions to their charters in order to allow weighted representation based on the size of the financial contributions of the members. In 1985, 20 years after Goldberg enunciated U.S. policy, President Reagan signed congressional legislation unilaterally reducing the U.S. contribution to the UN budget from 25 percent to 20 percent. This action led to a growing U.S. debt owed to the United Nations that by 2000 left the United States on the verge of losing its vote in the General Assembly. Only a final compromise between

Washington and the United Nations led to a payment of U.S. arrearages in 2001.

See also SCALE OF ASSESSMENTS.

good offices

In international affairs when a party independent of a disagreement intervenes to help bring about negotiation and eventual resolution of the disagreement, the third party is expected to act with "good offices." That is, the outsider's "good offices" suggest impartiality, a desire to avoid conflict and initiate discussions, and a genuine commitment to an eventual resolution of the dispute. Good offices should be distinguished from MEDIATION and ARBITRATION, both of which imply active participation by the third party in reaching settlement. Good offices is less participatory and is usually limited to offering channels of communication between those in disagreement. Thus it seeks to create diplomatic conversation preliminary to any possible settlement.

While the "good offices" function of the SECRETARY-GENERAL is not mentioned in the UN CHARTER, each Secretary-General has exercised this function, authorized to do so by the SECURITY COUNCIL or the GENERAL ASSEMBLY, by agreement of the parties to a dispute, or on his own initiative. Secretaries-General have exercised "good offices" in disputes involving Cyprus, Libya, CAMBODIA, TIMOR-LESTE, NAMIBIA, the FORMER YUGOSLAVIA, the Falkland Islands, SOMALIA, IRAN, LEBANON, and IRAQ. The first-ever summit meeting of the Security Council in 1992 recommended that the Secretary-General "make greater use . . . of his good offices in settling post–COLD WAR disputes."

See also AFGHANISTAN; APPENDIX F (UN Security Council Resolution 1325); APPENDIX G (Convention against Torture and Other Cruel, Inhuman or Degrading Treatment or Punishment); AFRICAN UNION; ARAB-ISRAELI DISPUTE; CONCILIATION; CONFLICT RESOLUTION; DEPARTMENT OF PEACEKEEPING OPERATIONS; EL SALVADOR; INDIA; INDONESIA; INTERNATIONAL COVENANT ON CIVIL AND POLITICAL RIGHTS (Articles 41 and 42); IRAN HOSTAGE CRISIS; IRAN-IRAQ WAR; KASHMIR; PERMANENT COURT OF ARBITRATION; SPECIAL REPRESENTATIVE OF THE SECRETARY-GENERAL; UNITED NATIONS COMMISSION FOR INDONESIA; UNITED NATIONS MISSION IN THE SUDAN; UNITED NATIONS SUPPORT OFFICE IN GUINEA-BISSAU; WALDHEIM, KURT.

Gorbachev, Mikhail (1931–   )

Mikhail Sergeyevich Gorbachev was the last leader of the Soviet Union, serving as the general secretary of the Communist Party of the country from 1985 to 1991 and as president from 1990 to 1991, the year the Soviet Union collapsed into 15 independent nations. Gorbachev, a Russian reformer unlike any other (with the possible exceptions of Peter the Great and Catherine the Great), sought to reform his country both economically and politically, liberalized Russian relations with Eastern Bloc countries, pursued a foreign policy of accommodation and cooperation with the West that ended the COLD WAR, and emphasized the importance of the United Nations in world affairs. For his efforts he was rewarded with the Nobel Prize for Peace in 1990. Two years earlier, *Time* magazine had named him "Man of the Year." As of 2008 he still headed the Gorbachev Foundation, a respected think-tank that deals with issues of international affairs.

The future world leader was born to a peasant family on March 2, 1931, in Privolye, Stavropol territory, Russia. Russia was then the largest state in the USSR. In his twenties he joined Komsomol, the Young Communist League. In 1955 he graduated from the law program at Moscow State University, where he had become a member of the Communist Party. By 1970 he had risen to the post of first secretary of the Stavropol regional party committee. He continued a rapid rise within party circles, being named a member of the party's Central Committee in 1971, secretary of agriculture by 1978, and, in 1980, when he was 49, a member of the Politburo (that is, the "political bureau" that was the executive organization of the Communist Party). Two years later brought the death of long-time Soviet boss Leonid Brezhnev (who served as party general secretary from 1964 to 1982) and a quick progression of followers—Yuri Andropov died after only 15 months as general secretary, and his successor, Konstantin Chernenko barely survived for one more year, dying on March 10, 1985. The very next day, the Politburo elected Gorbachev the party's general secretary. After years of what the world had viewed as sclerotic leadership from Moscow, the 54-year-old Gorbachev seemed a breath of fresh air. Accompanied by an urbane wife—Raisa Maksimovna Titarenko, a professor of philosophy at Moscow State University—Gorbachev set out to charm not only his nation but also the world. He was always more successful in the latter endeavor than in the former.

Within a few months of his ascension to ultimate power in the USSR, the new leader submitted to a lengthy interview with *Time* magazine, revealing a surprisingly accommodating demeanor. He insisted that he wished to "bring the process of arms limitation out of the dead end" and announced a unilateral moratorium on nuclear explosions, asking the UNITED STATES to join him and then proceed to "a complete ban on nuclear tests, as well as . . . peaceful cooperation and the prevention of an arms race in space." When asked if he might be making such proposals because of the economic strain the arms race caused to his country, he responded: "As I understand, you in the U.S. could also make better use of the money consumed nowadays by arms productions."

Gorbachev's fresh ideas were to lead to dramatic changes in international relations. In the interim, he set in motion equally unexpected domestic policies designed to bring deep reform to Soviet politics and economics. *Glasnost* (translated as "openness") led to expanded freedom of expression in the

Soviet Union, which eventually resulted in open repudiation of Stalinist totalitarian policies, as well as secret ballots and open elections. *Perestroika* ("restructuring") attempted to reform both politics and, especially, the economic situation in the USSR. Moving with caution away from command economics, perestroika encouraged a modest introduction of market principles. However, resistance to these reforms began to surface within entrenched government and bureaucratic circles.

Meantime, Gorbachev was charming the world. British prime minister Margaret Thatcher found him a "man we can work with." President RONALD REAGAN's hard-line ambassador to the United Nations, Jeane Kirkpatrick, was also won over, seeing Gorbachev as a "man of history." Gorbachev and Reagan met officially five times, exceeding by far the encounters by their predecessors. And they continued to meet after Reagan left office. In late 1988, as the U.S. president's term was drawing to a close, Gorbachev came to the United Nations to deliver one of his most important speeches. On December 7 the Soviet leader spoke to an overflow audience in the Great Hall of the GENERAL ASSEMBLY. He insisted that it was "high time to make use of the opportunities provided by this universal organization," calling the UN "a unique international centre serving the cause of peace and security." The UN, he asserted, was crucial for 21st-century advances in PEACEKEEPING, DEVELOPMENT, environmental reform, DISARMAMENT, and moving from an "armaments economy" to a "disarmament economy." He then emphasized HUMAN RIGHTS, democracy, and ending the arms race, and asserted that no country in the modern age could be "closed," that the world economy was becoming "a single entity." Then, in an unforgettable signal, he said that no nation should be denied "the freedom of choice, regardless of the pretext or the verbal guise in which it is cloaked. . . . Freedom of choice is a universal principle. It knows no exceptions." Gorbachev's biographer Archie Brown has maintained that this last statement at the United Nations "paved the way for the independence of the countries of Eastern Europe."

What followed astonished the world. The Soviet Union (1) cooperated with Western nations in the SECURITY COUNCIL to end the brutal IRAN-IRAQ WAR (SC RESOLUTION 598), (2) signed on to the breakthrough Intermediate Nuclear Forces agreement, dismantling tactical nuclear weapons on both sides of the now concluding cold war, (3) left AFGHANISTAN, which had been invaded nine years earlier during the rule of Leonid Brezhnev, and, most unexpectedly, (4) allowed the overthrow of communist regimes throughout Eastern Europe to proceed peacefully, never hinting at military intervention, as had been done repeatedly during the post–World War II Soviet dominance of the region. By the end of the 1980s there was no more Soviet Empire in Eastern Europe. By the early 21st century, most countries that had been part of the Russian-led Warsaw Pact were NATO members and participants in the European Union. An unprecedented international revolution had taken place in the center of Europe with virtually no violence. All of this was accomplished on Gorbachev's watch.

Within the USSR a new Congress of People's Deputies was created, with some members directly elected in contested elections. In 1989, this newly elected Congress chose a new Supreme Soviet that elected Gorbachev its chair, making him effectively president of a much democratized country. In early 1990 an official post of president was established, and Gorbachev assumed the position.

Then, from August 19 to 21, 1991, a conspiratorial group of hard-liners attempted to engineer a coup, dismiss Gorbachev, and, particularly, negate what they believed was an accelerating move toward autonomy for many of the constituent republics that made up the Soviet Union. The coup failed because of overwhelming resistance led by the Russian president Boris Yeltsin (Gorbachev at the time was president of the whole Soviet Union, Yeltsin of the Russian republic, the largest entity in the USSR). Although the coup collapsed, Gorbachev now was bereft of substantive authority. Effectually, his reforms had stimulated movements that had gone well beyond his control. Yeltsin became the popular leader within Russia. Gorbachev found himself with no choice but to enter an uncomfortable alliance with the Russian president. He resigned from the Communist Party, disbanded it, and eventually agreed to the break-up of the 75-year-old Soviet Empire. On December 25, 1991, this "man of history" resigned the presidency of the Soviet Union, which that same day ceased to exist.

See also BRUNDTLAND, GRO HARLEM; ARAB-ISRAELI DISPUTE; PÉREZ DE CUÉLLAR, JAVIER.

Further Reading: Brown, Archie. *The Gorbachev Factor.* New York: Oxford University Press, 1996. Gorbachev official Web site: <www.mikhailgorbachev.org/>. English, Robert D. *Russia and the Idea of the West: Gorbachev, Intellectuals, and the End of the Cold War.* New York: Columbia University Press, 2000. Gorbachev Foundation Web site: <www.gorby.ru/en/default.asp>. Gorbachev, Mikhail. *Memoirs.* New York: Doubleday, 1995. Matlock, Jack F. *Reagan and Gorbachev: How the Cold War Ended.* New York: Random House, 2004. Moore, John Allphin, Jr., and Jerry Pubantz. *To Create a New World?: American Presidents and the United Nations.* New York: Peter Lang, 1999. "Special Report: An Exclusive Interview." *Time.* September 9, 1985, 16–33.

Great Britain

The United Kingdom of Great Britain and Northern Ireland (U.K.), sometimes called Great Britain, was one of the three great powers leading the Allies during World War II. The nation—a constitutional monarchy—worked with the UNITED STATES and the Soviet Union to guide a cooperative prosecution of the war against the Axis powers. The prime minister of wartime Great Britain, WINSTON CHURCHILL, joined with American president FRANKLIN D. ROOSEVELT and Soviet leader JOSEPH STALIN at several wartime conferences to plan the conduct of the war, the postwar settlement, and the initiation of the United Nations. Most significantly, in February 1945 the three leaders met at the Crimean city of YALTA in southern Ukraine where they settled the remaining differences on the basic STRUCTURE and functions of the new organization. The previous year the three powers had fleshed out the basic elements of the United Nations at the DUMBARTON OAKS CONFERENCE in Washington, D.C., but remained divided on the future use of the VETO and on Stalin's demand that all of the USSR's Union Republics be admitted to the organization as independent member states. Dumbarton Oaks and Yalta made the core decisions about the proposed United Nations in anticipation of its creation at the SAN FRANCISCO CONFERENCE in the spring and summer of 1945. Thus, the United Kingdom was from the first a key player in the UN's history.

Although no longer the leading great power (as many had considered her in the 19th century), Britain was, in the early 21st-century, still a major force in world affairs and at the United Nations. In 2007 the appointed diplomatic personnel of the U.K. Mission to the UN numbered 36, making it one of the largest contingents at the organization's central HEADQUARTERS. The United Kingdom, with a population of over 60 million, was one of the five PERMANENT MEMBERS OF THE SECURITY COUNCIL, was a member of the GROUP OF EIGHT richest nations in the world, had the world's fifth largest economy (with a per capita income of over $30,000), was the second highest military defense-spending country (after the United States), was an active member of the European Union, and continued to be the central country in the voluntary Commonwealth of Nations—inclusive of Great Britain and over 50 sovereign states that formerly had made up the vast British Empire.

In 43 C.E., Roman invaders conquered and then ruled tribal groups in what is now the United Kingdom. Roman legions withdrew from the area in the fifth century, leaving ethnic groups such as Jutes, Angles, and Saxons to compete for political control of England, while Celtic peoples lived in Wales, Scotland, and Ireland. William the Conqueror crossed from Normandy in 1066 to defeat a Saxon kingdom. In 1215, King John agreed to the legendary Magna Carta (Great Charter), announcing legal rights and initiating the embryonic features of parliamentary government. The War of the Roses (1455–85) brought to the throne the Tudor dynasty, whose second king, Henry VIII, broke with the church of Rome (Catholic Church) in 1534, bringing the kingdom into the Protestant zone during the Reformation. His daughter, Elizabeth I, by defeating the Spanish Armada (1588), laid the foundation for England's rising sea power. Elizabeth's long rule (1558–1603) was followed by the Stuart dynasty, a civil war, a brief experiment with republican government (under

Oliver Cromwell during the 1650s), and the Glorious Revolution of 1688–89, which brought the reign of William and Mary, the English Bill of Rights, and parliamentary supremacy to English governance. In 1707, by the Act of Union, the United Kingdom was officially created when Scotland joined a common parliament (with England and Wales). By definition deriving from that act, the "United" Kingdom was, as of 2007, made up of England, Wales, Scotland, and Northern Ireland.

In the 18th century Great Britain became the greatest sea power in the world and, despite the loss of its 13 colonies in North America, the grandest imperial nation. By the end of the century, she became the first nation to experience the stirrings of the industrial revolution. In the 19th century industrialization accelerated and the empire grew until it included the Indian subcontinent, Canada, Australia, New Zealand, Malaya, Hong Kong, and several areas in sub-Saharan Africa, all displaying allegiance to Queen Victoria (the British monarch from 1837 to 1901). The United Kingdom was on the winning side in World War I, but suffered an unbearable death toll. The country emerged from the war an important member of the LEAGUE OF NATIONS, and preserved and even expanded its empire, adding—from former possessions of the defeated Ottoman and German Empires—the League mandates of Tanganyika, Jordan, Palestine, and IRAQ. In the interwar period Britain continued to fund the largest navy in the world. In 1939 she went to war against GERMANY again and the Axis powers, and by 1942 was partnered with several allies according to the announced DECLARATION BY UNITED NATIONS. Although once more a winner in world war, the United Kingdom found itself of second rank internationally as the COLD WAR elevated the governments in Moscow and Washington to the position of dominant great powers. Still, London retained considerable stature as a cofounder of the United Nations, an original member of NATO, and as one of the few nations in the postwar world to develop its own nuclear weapons arsenal. At the same time, the British Empire experienced a quick demise at the end of the war. INDIA obtained independence in 1947; shortly thereafter Burma, Ceylon, and Palestine (where the ARAB-ISRAEI DISPUTE began) left British control; and the African colonies realized independence in the 1960s.

The failed Anglo-French invasion of EGYPT in 1956 sparked the SUEZ CRISIS and strained relations with the United States; Britain was further humbled in 1963 when her application for MEMBERSHIP in the European Economic Community (EEC—the forerunner of the European Union) received a highly public veto by French president Charles de Gaulle. The UK finally entered the EEC in 1973, three years after de Gaulle's retirement from office. In 1982 Great Britain scored a military and diplomatic victory when it launched a successful counteroffensive against Argentina's military leaders who had ordered the occupation of the British Falkland Islands (called the Malvinas by Argentina). The Falklands

triumph had been achieved during the tenure of Conservative Party leader Margaret Thatcher, the first (and so far only) female prime minister in British history. She led her party to three consecutive electoral victories, served as prime minister from 1979 until 1990, energized the British economy, and was an instrumental world leader in bringing an end to the cold war. Thatcher's successor, John Major, joined willingly with other allies, including the United States, in the GULF WAR of 1991 and, again with NATO allies, in BOSNIA, to bring the warring parties to the DAYTON PEACE ACCORDS.

In 1997 the Labour Party returned to power with Tony Blair as prime minister. Blair, abiding by a decision of 1985, presided over the return of Hong Kong—a British possession for a full century—to Chinese SOVEREIGNTY. In April 1998 Blair, assisted by the American administration of President BILL CLINTON, negotiated the Good Friday Accord, establishing the outlines for a final settlement to the Northern Ireland Catholic-Protestant violence that had so long troubled that British enclave. By the time of the prime minister's retirement in 2007, Northern Ireland had implemented the accord fully and peace genuinely seemed at hand. In May 1999 the first election of a Scottish parliament and a Welsh assembly took place, complying with a decision of the Blair government to institute what was called "devolution," meaning the initiation of a system similar to America's "federalism," whereby regional areas had their own governmental responsibilities. Until this reform, the United Kingdom (like FRANCE) was a unitary government, meaning that full political sovereignty rested with the central government. London also participated in the spring of 1999 in the NATO bombardments of Serb positions during the KOSOVO conflict, eventually forcing Serb president SLOBODAN MILOŠEVIĆ to cease his efforts to subdue the province. In 2001, the United Kingdom joined with others in the international community in occupying AFGHANISTAN in the aftermath of the terrorist attacks of September 11, 2001. Then, in March 2003, Prime Minister Blair made the fateful decision to join the United States and its president, GEORGE W. BUSH, in the invasion of Iraq, even without UN Security Council approval. British forces were still in the country in mid-2007 when Blair resigned in the face of the growing unpopularity in Britain over the United Kingdom's involvement in the war.

Within the UN SYSTEM, the United Kingdom has been a supporter of PEACEKEEPING and PEACEBUILDING and has urged the development of the UN's capabilities in conflict prevention. In this regard, Britain was the first permanent member of the Security Council to declare the availability of its police and armed forces for use in UN Rapid Reaction Units. As of 2006, the United Kingdom had 430 troops, police officers, and military observers involved in UN peacekeeping missions in Cyprus, Democratic Republic of CONGO, Liberia, Kosovo, SUDAN, Georgia and SIERRA LEONE, plus 800 additional personnel serving in Bosnia, 190 in Kosovo, and 600 in Afghanistan, all working with UN-authorized operations. During the first years of the 21st century, the United Kingdom was the fourth largest contributor to the UN's peacekeeping operations, accounting for approximately a 7.4 percent share of the assessed BUDGET.

Within the British government, the Department of International Development (DFID), established in 1997, has concentrated on helping to achieve the UN's MILLENNIUM DEVELOPMENT GOALS (MDGs). The DFID is headed by a secretary of state with cabinet rank, manages Britain's aid to poor countries, and seeks to help in eliminating extreme poverty. Under the Blair government, the United Kingdom was one of the most enthusiastic promoters of the MDGs.

Although by the middle of the first decade of the 21st century the United Kingdom was seen as a close ally of the United States, there were differences between the two governments over certain issues of importance to the UN community. For example, while the Bush administration refused to ratify the INTERNATIONAL CRIMINAL COURT (ICC), the United Kingdom was one of its strongest supporters. In 2004, Britain provided 11 percent of the ICC's budget. Moreover, while the United States disapproved of, and refused to run for an elected position on, the new HUMAN RIGHTS COUNCIL, Great Britain embraced the new organ and became one of 47 governments to be elected to the Council in May 2006. London was an active participant in the work of the new Council, both as a sovereign nation and through its affiliation with the European Union. Finally, with reference to the issue of CLIMATE CHANGE, Washington, as of 2008, refused to ratify the KYOTO PROTOCOL. Prime Minister Blair, on the other hand, convinced of the seriousness of global warming, invited CHINA, Brazil, India, Mexico, and South Africa to join G8 nations in a G8+5 Climate Change Dialogue. The group reached agreement on February 16, 2007, on the "Washington DECLARATION," a nonbinding outline of a successor to the Kyoto Protocol. Admitting that man-made climate change existed "beyond doubt," the signatories proposed a global system of emission caps and carbon emissions trading that would apply to both industrialized and DEVELOPING COUNTRIES.

See also ARBITRATION, ATLANTIC CHARTER, CYPRUS DISPUTE, DISARMAMENT, DOUBLE VETO, EIGHTEEN NATION DISARMAMENT COMMITTEE, "FOUR POLICEMEN" PROPOSAL, INTERNATIONAL COURT OF JUSTICE, INTERNATIONAL MONETARY FUND, IRAN, MIDDLE EAST WAR OF 1967, MOSCOW CONFERENCE OF FOREIGN MINISTERS, MOSCOW DECLARATION, NAMIBIA, QUADRANT CONFERENCE, UN SECURITY COUNCIL RESOLUTION 242, TEHERAN CONFERENCE.

Further Reading: Ferguson, Niall. *Empire: The Rise and Demise of the British World Order and the Lessons for Global Power.* New York: Basic Books, 2003. Green, E. H. H. *Thatcher.* New York: Oxford University Press, 2006. "How Will History Judge Him?" *The Economist,* May 12, 2007, 11, 57–62. Murphy, Kim. "To the Last, Blair Defends Iraq War." *Los Angeles Times,* May 11, 2007, A1, 8, 9. Robbins, Keith. *The Eclipse of a Great Power: Modern Britain, 1870–1992.* 2nd ed. London: Longman, 1994. U.K. Foreign and Commonwealth Office Web site: <www.fco.gov.uk>. U.K. Mission to the UN Web site: <//www.ukun.org/>. Wilson, A. N. *After the Victorians: The Decline of Britain in the World.* New York: Farrar, Straus, and Giroux, 2005.

Group of 77

The Group of 77 is a CAUCUS of the nations of the Third World or the global south within the United Nations that came into being in 1964 during the first meeting of the UNITED NATIONS CONFERENCE ON TRADE AND DEVELOPMENT (UNCTAD). The group, which originally consisted of 75 Third World nations, became officially the Group of 77 at its first ministerial meeting in 1977 that issued the Charter of Algiers. Although the MEMBERSHIP grew to 133 by the end of the century, the name was retained for its historic significance. The organizational STRUCTURE of the Group has gradually expanded and chapters have been established in several locations in association with United Nations agencies most significant to the concerns of developing nations, including New York (at UN HEADQUARTERS), Rome (at the FOOD AND AGRICULTURAL ORGANIZATION [FAO]), Vienna (at the UN INDUSTRIAL DEVELOPMENT ORGANIZATION [UNIDO]), and Paris (at the UN EDUCATIONAL, SCIENTIFIC AND CULTURAL ORGANIZATION [UNESCO]). There is also a Committee of 24 located in Washington, D.C., to represent the group's interests at the INTERNATIONAL MONETARY FUND and WORLD BANK. Its objectives are to articulate and promote the collective interests of the nations of the Third World and to enhance their joint negotiating capacity on economic issues in the UNITED NATIONS SYSTEM. This committee, however, should not be confused with the Special Committee on the Implementation of the Declaration on Decolonization, also known as the COMMITTEE OF 24. The latter is also made up of many members from the Group of 77, but it is an official committee of the GENERAL ASSEMBLY, with responsibilities for implementing the 1960 DECLARATION on decolonization. In addition to their presence in these UN bodies, Group of 77 nations seek to expand economic and technical cooperation among themselves.

Important to the effectiveness of the ministerial meetings of the Group of 77 have been preliminary meetings on a regional basis in LATIN AMERICA, AFRICA, and Asia. At first the activities of the group related primarily to negotiations with industrialized nations; the importance of South to South cooperation was recognized in 1976 when a Conference on Economic Co-operation among DEVELOPING COUNTRIES was held in Mexico City. Despite the many forces that have existed to undermine the group's cohesiveness—regional differences, differences in size and wealth that confer advantages on larger nations, privileged economic relationships of former colonies with their one-time colonizers, and ideological disagreements—the value of the group to its members has been demonstrated by its continued existence.

In April 2000 the first meeting of the heads of state of the Group of 77 was held in Havana. The issues highlighted at this South Summit were the need for renewed North-South dialogue, the North's domination of the BRETTON WOODS organizations (the IMF and the World Bank), the nontransparency of the WORLD TRADE ORGANIZATION (WTO), the need for food security and rural employment, and the problem of AIDS. A Second South Summit was held in Doha, Qatar, in June 2005. It attracted the largest gathering of heads of state from the membership of the Group of 77.

See also NON-ALIGNED MOVEMENT, NORTH-SOUTH RELATIONS.

Further Reading: Sauvant, Karl P. *The Group of 77: Evolution, Structure, Organization*. New York: Oceana, 1981. ———. *Chronology, Bibliography and Index for the Group of 77 and the Non-Aligned Movement*. New York: Oceana, 1993. Sauvant, Karl P., and Joachim Miller, eds. *The Third World without Superpowers: The Collected Documents of the Group of 77, 2nd Series*. New York: Oceana, 1891–1995. Williams, Marc. *Third World Cooperation: The Group of 77 in UNCTAD*. New York: St. Martin's, 1991. Group of 77 Web site: <www.g77.org>.

— M. W. Bray

Group of Eight (G8)

The Group of Eight is a CAUCUS GROUP of those nations with the world's largest economies, plus the RUSSIAN FEDERATION. In addition to Russia, the MEMBERSHIP includes the UNITED STATES, Canada, GREAT BRITAIN, FRANCE, GERMANY, JAPAN, and Italy. G8 is an informal economic and financial decision-making group of the nations most involved in and most affected by the global economy. The eight member countries account for more than half the world's economic production and trade, and half the assets of the INTERNATIONAL MONETARY FUND. The "Group of 6" was formed initially in 1975 to coordinate economic policies in response to the oil crisis following the MIDDLE EAST WAR OF 1973, the recent collapse of the original BRETTON WOODS system, and concomitant economic decline in the industrialized world. It sought to separate economic and financial decision-making from political factors, and to coordinate informally the activities of global economic organizations, including the WORLD BANK, the International Monetary Fund, and the GENERAL AGREEMENT ON TARIFFS AND TRADE, now the WORLD TRADE ORGANIZATION. Canada was added to the group in 1976. In 1997, after the COLD WAR had ended, Russia was admitted, chiefly for geopolitical purposes, since Russia is not one of the eight or even ten largest economies in the world.

The most visible activity of the G8 is an annual summit meeting of the heads of state or government. At the summit the leaders talk directly to each other, accompanied by their finance ministers. Ministers such as the secretary of the Treasury in the United States and the chancellor of the Exchequer in the United Kingdom are responsible for carrying out the decisions of the summit, and are in contact with each other on a continuing basis. The ministers meet at least four times during the succeeding year to coordinate monetary and economic policy. They often set up working groups and task forces—consisting of economic experts—to focus on particular problems and issues. Often at the annual summit national leaders are joined by the central bank governors of their nations for at least one of their meetings, and bank governors frequently meet separately during the summit sessions. The president of the European Commission is also often present or represented at the summit, though he meets with officials outside the central sessions. The G8 frequently invites representatives of international organizations or other heads of state to attend a portion of their meeting to discuss specific actions or initiatives.

During the 1970s and 1980s, the summit agendas included economic and financial matters exclusively. By the 1990s discussions were broadened to include political affairs. The leaders issued a closely watched statement at the end of each meeting, which addressed a broad range of current problems, both political and economic. In particular crises, the G8 also created "Contact Groups" consisting of several caucus members. The Contact Group then would conduct negotiations and organize G8 peacemaking efforts. The G8 was most successful with its Contact Groups for BOSNIA and KOSOVO.

The Group of Eight is not a formal international organization or SPECIALIZED AGENCY. Unlike an international organization, it is not based on a TREATY, and has no formal MEMBERSHIP criteria and no staff. The host of the annual summit serves as the informal chair of the group for the following year, in addition to preparing the agenda for the summit. While the G8 is not a part of the UNITED NATIONS SYSTEM, it is clearly involved in making international policy, and cooperates closely with several UN bodies and supports several key UN initiatives. The summit established the G8 Africa Action Plan after meeting with the four African heads of state who were instrumental in drawing up the NEW PARTNERSHIP FOR AFRICA'S DEVELOPMENT (NEPAD), specifically to support NEPAD and provide some of the resources needed to carry it out. The G8 established the Global Partnership against the Spread of WEAPONS OF MASS DESTRUCTION, which provided funds for the destruction of NUCLEAR WEAPONS in Russia and from those newly independent states of the former Soviet Union. The G8 also set up the GLOBAL FUND TO FIGHT AIDS, TUBERCULOSIS AND MALARIA, in close cooperation with the United Nations. In addition, the G8 played a central role in launching the Heavily Indebted Poor Countries Initiative (HIPC), which established an agreed upon process for canceling the external debt of the world's poorest countries. This was an essential element in promoting SUSTAINABLE DEVELOPMENT. The G8 provides strong support for the United Nations Terrorism CONVENTIONS, and works closely with the SECURITY COUNCIL Counter-Terrorism Committee. The G8 has been particularly active in preventing the transfer of funds by terrorist organizations and in cutting off the sources of financing for TERRORISM.

See also CAUCUS GROUPS, WORLD SUMMIT ON THE INFORMATION SOCIETY.

Further Reading: Baker, Andrew. *The Group of Seven: Finance Ministries, Central Banks and Global Financial Governance.* New York: Routledge, 2006. Penttilä, Risto E. J. *The Role of the G8 in International Peace and Security.* New York: Oxford University Press, 2003.

— *K. J. Grieb*

Guatemala

Guatemala joined the United Nations as one of the body's original members on October 24, 1945. It became a concern of the SECURITY COUNCIL in 1954 as a result of a military coup mounted against the democratically elected president, Jacobo Arbenz Guzman. The UNITED STATES provided military, financial, and diplomatic support for the coup. Protest over U.S. involvement and support led Guatemala to request the intervention of the Security Council. Honduras, Nicaragua, Colombia, and Brazil challenged the request. Citing Article 33 of CHAPTER VI and Article 52 (2) of Chapter VIII of the UN CHARTER, Guatemala's opponents argued that as a regional dispute the matter fell under the JURISDICTION of the ORGANIZATION OF AMERICAN STATES (OAS). A VETO by the USSR blocked a RESOLUTION offered by Brazil and Colombia that would have officially called on the OAS to open discussion concerning the situation in Guatemala. In its place, FRANCE authored a resolution that called for an end to military action and a commitment from all parties to block any and all assistance to the disputing parties. This resolution passed unanimously.

The Soviet Union and Guatemala continued to call for UN action, but a U.S. veto stalled Security Council deliberations. The fall of the Arbenz government led to an end of UN discussion of the crisis.

Conflict between the Guatemalan government and indigenous communities residing in the country generated extended concern within the United Nations after 1980. Systematic HUMAN RIGHTS violations and political corruption led first to GENERAL ASSEMBLY Resolution 184 on December 17, 1982, that expressed the body's concern over the human rights situation in the country. With the formation of the Rio Group in 1986, which involved representatives from the Contadora Group, the Contadora Support Group, the secretary-general of the OAS, and the SECRETARY-GENERAL of the United Nations, the latter organization became directly involved in the push to bring peace to Guatemala. In 1994 the General Assembly established the United Nations Verification Mission in Guatemala (MINUGUA) to monitor the human rights treatment of INDIGENOUS PEOPLES.

Both the Guatemalan government and its civilian opposition preferred UN involvement in the peace process over that of the OAS. Following the successfully negotiated settlements in Nicaragua and EL SALVADOR, the United Nations Observer Group in Central America helped coordinate talks involving the Guatemalan government and the guerrilla movement. These efforts culminated with the signing of a peace accord in 1996. MINUGUA then took responsibility for verifying that the agreement was being fulfilled.

The Guatemalan Republican Front won the elections of 1999, but in 2003 VOTING, the more conservative Great National Alliance proved victorious, winning control of both the presidency and the parliament. Such peaceful political transition suggested relative stability. The growth of tourism in the country (1.4 million visitors in 2006) further underscored that, as of 2007, the country had benefited by, among other factors, UN involvement.

Further Reading: McCoubrey, Hilaire, and Justin Morris. *Regional Peacekeeping in the Post–Cold War Era.* Boston: Kluwer Law International, 2000. Permanent Mission of Guatemala to the United Nations Web site: <www.un.int/guatemala>.

— *D. K. Lewis*

Gulf War

On August 2, 1990, 150,000 Iraqi armed forces invaded the neighboring country of Kuwait, claiming its territory as an integral part of IRAQ, driving the ruling al-Sabah family into exile, occupying all of Kuwait within less than two days, and marshaling a huge military force on the Kuwait–Saudi Arabia border. The invasion culminated several months of growing tension between the Iraqi government, headed by SADDAM HUSSEIN, and the Kuwaiti regime. The invasion was met with an unprecedented coalition of Western and Arab nations, led by the UNITED STATES, that first defended Saudi Arabia and then liberated Kuwait in the spring of 1991. Iraq was branded the "aggressor" in the war by the UN SECURITY COUNCIL and subjected to a series of Council RESOLUTIONS mandating CHAPTER VII ENFORCEMENT MEASURES—the most dramatic exercise of UN authority and power since the KOREAN WAR.

Despite an historical objection by Iraq to the legitimacy of Kuwait's independence and SOVEREIGNTY, the two countries had maintained good relations during the IRAN-IRAQ WAR (1980–87). Kuwait lent several billion dollars to Iraq in an effort to keep Iranian Shi'ite influence in the Gulf region confined. When the war was over, however, old tensions reemerged. War-torn Iraq balked at requested repayment of

Burning oil well and destroyed Iraqi tank (UN/DPI PHOTO 158181/J. ISAAC)

Kuwaiti loans. Instead, it accused Kuwait of keeping international oil prices low (to the detriment of Iraqi postwar reconstruction) by selling oil in excess of Kuwait's OPEC–approved quotas, by opposing higher cartel prices on the world market, and by using slant drilling techniques to "steal" Iraqi oil from the transboundary Rumeilah fields. Arguing that it had defended the Gulf Arab states from Iranian domination, Baghdad sought concessions from Kuwait, including control of two strategic Kuwaiti islands at the northern end of the Persian Gulf. The al-Sabah rulers declined to lease the islands or to make any concessions on oil policy. As the confrontation escalated in the summer of 1990, Hussein held a fateful meeting with the U.S. ambassador to Iraq, April Glaspie. Based on that discussion, including her reference to the nonexistence of a mutual defense PACT between the United States and Kuwait, Hussein and his advisers miscalculated that the international reaction to an Iraqi invasion would be muted.

On August 2 U.S. president GEORGE H. W. BUSH directed the U.S. PERMANENT REPRESENTATIVE to the United Nations, Thomas Pickering, to request an emergency meeting of the Security Council. The occupation of Kuwait directly threatened American interests, it endangered a significant proportion of the world's oil supply, and it jeopardized the security of several American allies in the region. The American initia-tive found near unanimity of support among UN members and a consensus for action among the Council's five PERMANENT MEMBERS. Over the next three months the Security Council passed 10 RESOLUTIONS meant to isolate Iraq, and to prepare the legal groundwork for collective military action. Among the most important were Resolutions 660 (a condemnation of the invasion), 661 (the imposition of mandatory economic SANCTIONS), 662 (a DECLARATION that the annexation of Kuwait was null and void), 665 (the establishment of a naval blockade and the invitation to member states to make use of the UN MILITARY STAFF COMMITTEE for military preparations), and 678. This last resolution was passed on November 29 and gave Iraq 48 days to withdraw from Kuwait or face military retaliation. For only the second time in its history the United Nations authorized member states to use "all necessary means . . . to restore peace and security in the area." RESOLUTION 678 legitimized the American sponsored military coalition then massing in the Saudi desert. The UN action was reinforced by equivalent condemnations from other international organizations: the ORGANIZATION OF AFRICAN UNITY (August 3), the Gulf Cooperation Council (August 3), the Organization of the Islamic Conference (August 5), and the League of Arab States (August 10).

By August 9 the U.S. military had accepted an invitation from the Saudi government and took up defensive positions along the Saudi-Kuwaiti border. Dubbed "Desert Shield," the first phase of preparations included the dispatch of more than 200,000 U.S. troops to Saudi Arabia. President Bush adroitly worked to put together a coalition of states, unusual in its combination. By January 1991 troop levels had grown to 715,000, with personnel from the United States, the United Kingdom, FRANCE, EGYPT, Syria, Italy, Morocco, Bangladesh, Bahrain, Qatar, Algeria, Kuwait, Turkey, Senegal, the United Arab Emirates, Saudi Arabia, Oman, Niger, and Pakistan. During the buildup U.S. secretary of state James Baker secured the nonmilitary support of the Soviet Union and Israel. At Bush's direction, he also met with Iraq's foreign minister Tariq Aziz to warn of the consequences of noncompliance with UN resolutions. UN SECRETARY-GENERAL JAVIER PÉREZ DE CUÉLLAR also traveled to Baghdad to urge compliance. Iraq could count on support only from Libya and the Palestine Liberation Organization, with neutral positions taken by Jordan and Yemen.

The deadline established in Resolution 678 having passed, the coalition commenced Desert Storm on January 16, 1991, a military effort that drove Iraq from Kuwait, beginning with a powerful five and a half week air campaign. Using the most technologically advanced WEAPONS, the UN coalition carried out more than 10,000 sorties in the first week, dropping more than 800,000 tons of munitions. Targets in all parts of Iraq were hit, including civilian sites in Baghdad. Two days into the fighting Iraq launched SCUD missiles against sites in Israel, hoping to draw the Israelis into the war, and to transform the conflict into an Arab struggle against Israel and the United States. Promising to address the ARAB-ISRAELI DISPUTE when the war was over, and dissuading the Israelis from retaliation, President Bush maintained the coalition's resolve to liberate Kuwait. On February 24 the land phase of military operations began. With unexpected ease the coalition forces liberated Kuwait in four days and moved into the southern quarter of Iraq.

Offensive operations ended on February 28 following Iraq's announcement that it would accept all UN resolutions passed since August 2. There was some criticism, especially in the United States, that the allied forces had not marched all the way to Baghdad to force the removal of Saddam Hussein. However, nothing in the UN resolutions that held the multilateral coalition together authorized such action. Arab states in particular would not support efforts beyond the liberation of Kuwait and the implementation of penalties contained in the relevant Security Council resolutions.

In the spring of 1991 the Security Council adopted Resolution 687 establishing the conditions and modalities of a cease-fire. It affirmed Iraq's liability under INTERNATIONAL LAW "for any direct loss, damage, . . . or injury to foreign governments, nationals and corporations, as a result of Iraq's unlawful invasion and occupation of Kuwait." The resolution created a number of bodies to implement its directives. Pursuant to Resolution 687, the Security Council created a Compensation fund to pay claims, its assets coming from 30 percent of Iraqi oil export revenues. As of 2001 the fund had paid more than $300 billion to satisfy 2.6 million claims. The resolution also authorized the Council's Sanctions Committee, created in August 1990 to enforce the mandated embargo, to supply humanitarian materials for civilian use. Also created was the UN Iraq-Kuwait Observation Mission (UNIKOM) to monitor the demilitarized border between the two countries. In addition the Council created the UN SPECIAL COMMISSION ON IRAQ (UNSCOM) to verify Iraqi compliance with all UN resolutions and to carry out no-notice inspections inside of Iraq for the purpose of finding and destroying all WEAPONS OF MASS DESTRUCTION. Finally, UNSCOM was charged with establishing a permanent system of monitoring and verification to assure that Iraq could not rebuild nuclear, biological, or CHEMICAL WEAPON capabilities. UNSCOM conducted its work under continuing challenge and obstruction from the Baghdad government until Iraq ended all cooperation with the UN agency in 1998. During its seven years of operation UNSCOM's demands on the regime often were buttressed with air reprisals, largely carried out by U.S. and British warplanes, before Hussein would allow the commission's inspections.

The collapse of Iraqi resistance to the coalition assault sparked secessionist efforts in both southern and northern Iraq. The Shia community in the Basra area seized the oppor-

tunity to break with Baghdad. In the north Kurds sought to fulfill their long sought goal of an independent Kurdish state. Hussein responded with air attacks against both groups. At the end of March 1991 the Iraqi army launched a massive attack against rebels in the northern part of the country. The attack produced more than 200,000 Kurdish REFUGEES fleeing to the region along Iraq's border with Turkey and 500,000 crossing into IRAN. On April 5 the Security Council condemned the attacks and called upon "the Secretary-General to use all the resources at his disposal . . . to address urgently the critical needs of the refugees." The United States, with the assistance of Turkey, Great Britain, and France, established "no-fly" zones in both the north and the south. The four powers launched Operation Provide Comfort, creating a massive humanitarian air-drop operation and protective "enclaves" for Kurds inside Iraq. Almost immediately thereafter the allies urged the United Nations to take over administration of the enclaves. Pérez de Cuéllar was hesitant to do so without the consent of the Iraqi government. To this end he negotiated an agreement with Baghdad on April 18, 1991. With the agreement in place the allied states ceded control of the camps. Unwilling to allow the destabilization of the region that a breakup of Iraq would produce, the United Nations imposed a near protectorate over large parts of the country. Iraq remained a serious international problem with which the UN dealt for the remainder of the 1990s and into the next century, when yet another war—this one more controversial—would take place on the country's soil.

See also ANNAN, KOFI; ARAFAT, YASSER; BLIX, HANS; BOUTROS-GHALI, BOUTROS; COLD WAR; COLLECTIVE SELF-DEFENSE; GERMANY; INTERNATIONAL ATOMIC ENERGY AGENCY; JAPAN; PERMANENT MEMBERS OF THE SECURITY COUNCIL; SANCTIONS; UN SECURITY COUNCIL RESOLUTION 1441; UNITED NATIONS RELIEF AND WORKS AGENCY FOR PALESTINE REFUGEES IN THE NEAR EAST; ZIONISM IS RACISM RESOLUTION.

Further Reading: Blix, Hans. *Disarming Iraq.* New York: Pantheon, 2004. Hiro, Dilip. *Desert Shield to Desert Storm: The Second Gulf War.* London: Paladin, 1992. Sifry, Micah L., and Christopher Cerf. *The Gulf War Reader: History, Documents, Opinions.* New York: Times Books, 1991. Malone, David M. *The International Struggle over Iraq: Politics in the UN Security Council, 1980–2005.* New York: Oxford University Press, 2006. Moore, John Allphin, Jr., and Jerry Pubantz. *To Create a New World?: American Presidents and the United Nations.* New York: Peter Lang Publishing, 1999. Andersen, Roy R., Robert F. Seibert, and Jon G. Wagner. *Politics and Change in the Middle East: Sources of Conflict and Accommodation.* 6th ed. Upper Saddle River, N.J.: Prentice Hall, 2001.

habitat See UNITED NATIONS CENTRE FOR HUMAN SETTLEMENTS.

Hague Academy of International Law

Housed in the Peace Palace at The Hague, Netherlands, with its neighbors the INTERNATIONAL COURT OF JUSTICE (ICJ) and the PERMANENT COURT OF ARBITRATION (PCA), the Hague Academy of International Law provides training for advanced students of INTERNATIONAL LAW. It was established in 1923 with funds provided by the Carnegie Foundation in Washington, D.C. Admission to the academy's programs is granted only to those who have studied law for at least four years or have an equivalent qualification acceptable to the curatorium of the academy, and who are fluent in one of the two working LANGUAGES of the academy—English or French, the same languages used by the ICJ. After his service as UN SECRETARY-GENERAL, BOUTROS BOUTROS-GHALI was appointed president of the Curatorium's Administrative Council, which hires the professors for the academy and sets its scientific research program.

The academy's highly regarded summer course program in public international law is open to a selective number of scholars, who are usually supported in their applications by references made to the academy's SECRETARIAT. Participants in the summer program, numbering about 300, come from a wide range of countries and backgrounds, and include law professors, diplomats, judges, and practicing lawyers. Lectur-

ers in the program are among the best known and eminent of international lawyers, including judges from the International Court of Justice. Additionally, the academy has established a respected diploma for those candidates who possess advanced knowledge of international law and pass a rigorous qualifying examination. Since 1950 the academy has awarded the diploma to a limited number of applicants from 57 countries.

Responding in part to the needs of decolonized and DEVELOPING COUNTRIES, and to contribute to efforts to promote "life-long learning" in international law, the academy, in 2004, inaugurated a new program entitled "Seminar for Advanced Studies in Public and Private International Law for Professionals." The seminar was designed for those who wished to update their understanding of international law's steady evolution.

Further Reading: The Hague Academy of International Law Web site: <www.hagueacademy.nl/>.

Haiti

Haiti joined the United Nations as an original member on October 24, 1945. Regarded as the LEAST DEVELOPED COUNTRY in the Western Hemisphere, its government first requested assistance from the UN ECONOMIC AND SOCIAL COUNCIL (ECOSOC) in 1948 in an effort to identify and recommend solutions that would assist in the improvement of Haitian economic conditions.

In the 1990s, a political and military crisis in Haiti led to the intervention of UN PEACEKEEPING forces. In the wake of a military coup against the democratically elected government of Father Jean-Bertrand Aristide in September 1991, the United Nations acted in concert with the ORGANIZATION OF AMERICAN STATES (OAS) to defend the right of self-determination and preserve democracy. The GENERAL ASSEMBLY approved economic and trade SANCTIONS and established an embargo against oil and fuel shipments in June 1993. The sanctions led to the Governors Island Accord in July that committed the Haitian military to a gradual relinquishing of power and to Aristide's eventual return to office. As part of the agreement the United Nations established the UN Mission in Haiti (UNMIH) for the purpose of assisting the returned democratic government. However, the continued resistance of the Haitian military and police forces to any return to civilian rule led first to an extension of economic and military sanctions and then to a postponement of UNMIH's deployment. In July 1994, the SECURITY COUNCIL approved the use of military force against the Haitian dictatorship. Before an invasion of U.S. armed forces took place, Haitian officers agreed to a peace settlement on September 17, 1995.

The UN peacekeeping force, comprised of troops from the UNITED STATES, Bangladesh, and INDIA, supervised the transition to civilian rule, which resulted in the election of René Préval as the new president on December 17, 1995. UNMIH was replaced in July 1996 by the United Nations Support Mission in Haiti (UNSMIH) with the mandate of assisting in the professionalization of the Haitian National Police. Under UNSMIH's command, foreign soldiers remained on duty in Haiti until July 1997, and police from Canada and other nations recruited and trained police and security forces within Haiti that would reinforce the authority of the new government. UNSMIH was succeeded by yet four more UN peacekeeping operations to assure Haitian domestic stability to the end of the century: United Nations Transition Mission in Haiti—UNTMIH (August to November, 1997), UNITED NATIONS CIVILIAN POLICE MISSION IN HAITI—MIPONUH (December 1997 to March 2000), International Civilian Support Mission in Haiti—MICAH (succeeded MIPONUH in March 2000), and INTERNATIONAL CIVILIAN MISSION IN HAITI—MICIVIH (a joint UN/OAS operation).

Aristide returned to the presidency in the irregular election of November 2000. However, he was deposed by an armed coup in February 2004 and was taken to AFRICA in U.S. custody. The Security Council then unanimously resolved to deploy a Multinational Interim Force (MIF) to the island following an urgent appeal by acting president Boniface Alexandre. In April 2004 the Security Council, acting under CHAPTER VII of the UN CHARTER, passed RESOLUTION 1542 creating the United Nations Stabilization Mission in Haiti (MINUSTAH) to replace the MIF. Delayed elections took place in early 2006 as MINUSTAH patrolled the country. René Préval narrowly won the presidency.

See also CARTER, JIMMY; CLINTON, WILLIAM JEFFERSON; DEPARTMENT OF PEACEKEEPING OPERATIONS; ENFORCEMENT MEASURES; LATIN AMERICA.

Further Reading: Perusse, Roland I. *Haitian Democracy Restored, 1991–1995.* Lanham, Md.: University Press of America, 1995. *Mission to Haiti: Report of the United Nations Mission of Technical Assistance to the Republic of Haiti.* United Nations Publication 1949, IIB, 2. Lake Success, N.Y.: United Nations Publications, 1949. MICIVIH Web site: <www.un.org/rights/micivih/first.htm>. MIPONUH Web site: <www.un.org/Depts/dpko/dpko/co-mission/miponuh.htm>. MINUSTAH Web site: www.un.org/Depts/dpko/missions-minustah/>.

— D. K. Lewis

Hammarskjöld, Dag Hjalmar Agne Carl (1905–1961)

The second SECRETARY-GENERAL of the United Nations served from April 10, 1953, until his untimely death on September 18, 1961, while on a peace mission to the recently independent CONGO. Hammarskjöld was born in 1905 in Jönköping, Sweden. The son of the Swedish prime minister during World War I—Hjalmar Hammarskjöld—he was brought up in the university town of Uppsala, near Stockholm. At the university in Uppsala he studied French literature, political economy, and law, and in 1934 he completed a doctor's degree in economics at the university in Stockholm. He then joined the Swedish civil service, served in the Ministry of Finance, and eventually became chairman of the board of the bank of Sweden. As World War II ended, he was appointed adviser to the cabinet on financial and economic matters. In 1947 he entered the Foreign Office with the rank of under-secretary, that year participating as a delegate to the Paris Conference that organized the Marshall Plan program for Europe. The following year he was Sweden's head delegate to the Paris Conference that initiated the Organization for European Economic Cooperation. By 1951 he had ascended to the post of deputy foreign minister, and from 1951 to 1953 he represented Sweden at the Sixth and Seventh GENERAL ASSEMBLY sessions held, consecutively, in Paris and New York. In early April 1953, five months after the resignation of TRYGVE LIE of Norway as Secretary-General, the General Assembly, on the recommendation of the SECURITY COUNCIL, unanimously appointed Hammarskjöld to the post Lie had vacated. In September 1957, the General Assembly, again unanimously, reelected him to a five-year term.

Hammarskjöld's term as Secretary-General was marked by considerable activity, and he approached the job with vigor and dedication. Although tactful and quiet, Hammarskjöld demonstrated an energetic commitment to international diplomacy, and, in the event, extended the influence of the United Nations and enhanced the reputation and visibility of the institution's Secretary-General. On several occasions he criticized the superpowers for ignoring the UN's role in the maintenance of COLLECTIVE SECURITY. In 1954, for example, he urged the UNITED STATES, to no avail, to bring its dispute with the Arbenz government in GUATEMALA to the Security Council. The DWIGHT EISENHOWER administration, however, kept the matter out of the Council, preferring the friendlier setting of the ORGANIZATION OF AMERICAN STATES (OAS). Hammarskjöld also complained on several occasions that the UN's responsibility for DISARMAMENT and arms control was being undermined by the American and Soviet monopolization of negotiations.

The Secretary-General traveled extensively in his efforts to lessen tensions in the world. In 1955 he visited Beijing, after which CHINA released 15 detained U.S. flyers who had served with the United Nations forces in Korea. Twice he visited the Middle East in ongoing efforts to stabilize armistice agreements between Israel and the Arab states and to promote peace in the region. Following his efforts (with cooperation from Canadian prime minister LESTER PEARSON) to resolve the SUEZ CRISIS of 1956, he guided the launching of the UNITED NATIONS EMERGENCY FORCE (UNEF), sent to the Middle East to help maintain peace and order after the crisis; he led in the creation of the UNITED NATIONS OBSERVATION GROUP IN LEBANON (UNOGIL), dispatched to Lebanon in 1957, and he appointed a SPECIAL REPRESENTATIVE to Jordan in 1958.

His continuing travels took him to numerous countries throughout the world. On one trip, from mid-December 1959 to the end of January 1960, he visited 21 countries and territories in Africa, a "study" trip, he called it, to obtain a "cross-section of every sort of politically responsible opinion in the Africa of today." In fact, Hammarskjöld was committed to making the United Nations a truly universal organization. When, in April 1955, 25 African and Asian countries initiated the "NON-ALIGNED MOVEMENT," pressure for expanding UN MEMBERSHIP grew. In December 1955 Hammarskjöld presided over an agreement between the opposing sides in the COLD WAR—each fearing that the other would profit by membership growth—and realized a dramatic increase in membership, as 16 new nations were admitted, four from the Soviet bloc and the rest from Africa, Asia, and the Arab world. But the biggest challenge confronting the Secretary-General, the one that would result in his death, emerged from the center of Africa.

The Belgian Congo became the independent country of the Congo on June 30, 1960, and almost immediately civil strife broke out between various factions, some eventually associated with the major cold war competitors. Hopes for stability were particularly endangered when soldiers in the national army revolted against remaining Belgian soldiers, and the southern province of Katanga, led by Moise Tshombe, seceded. The Secretary-General, fearful that Wash-

ington and Moscow might once again circumvent the UN, quickly assumed an active role in the crisis. The Congo's new president, Joseph Kasavubu, and his prime minister, Patrice Lumumba, both issued a cable to New York on July 12 urging immediate UN military assistance. In a novel but dramatic moment, Hammarskjöld, exercising Article 99 of the UN CHARTER, convened a night meeting of the Security Council on July 13, urging "utmost speed" in meeting the request. The Security Council called on Belgian forces to withdraw and opposed the secession of Katanga province. Hammarskjöld then helped craft the UN force in the Congo, and personally made four trips to the area in connection with UN operations there. In the meantime, the Secretary-General obtained authority to replace Belgian troops and, going beyond a neutral PEACEKEEPING role, moved to support the central government. But Belgian forces delayed leaving, and Prime Minister Lumumba sent an appeal to Soviet leader NIKITA KHRUSHCHEV for help. Khrushchev began airlifting WEAPONS and technical advisers to the Congo and called for the United Nations to leave the country. The United States saw Lumumba as a tool of the Soviet Union and persuaded President Kasavubu to dismiss him. Lumumba refused to go and, in the midst of the chaos, Congolese general Joseph Mobutu seized power. The United States now gave its full support to Hammarskjöld's efforts to shore up the central government. At one point, UN forces arrested Lumumba and turned him over to the Kasavubu government, now backed by Mobutu. Kasavubu then callously turned the former prime minister over to Katangan rebels, who promptly executed him. By September 1960, the Soviet Union had determined that the Secretary-General was a tool of U.S. foreign policy, pursuing policies in the Congo that were unneutral and antithetical to its interests. Moscow denounced Hammarskjöld and demanded that he be replaced by a three-person board (the TROIKA PROPOSAL), equally representing the West, Soviet bloc nations, and neutral countries. But

Secretary-General Dag Hammarskjöld in the Congo (UNITED NATIONS)

Hammarskjöld, with Western support, persisted in his efforts to bring peace and stability to central Africa.

On September 12, 1961, he began what would be the last trip of his unusually vigorous diplomatic career. He was on his way to urge Moise Tshombe, leader of the breakaway province of Katanga, to pursue peace and to drop his plans to secede. He died on September 18, when his plane crashed in a remote area of Northern Rhodesia (now Zambia). Almost immediately, Hammarskjöld became a martyred symbol of the noblest, yet most frustrating, possibilities of international cooperation. His writings, including his popular *Markings,* published in English in 1964, enhanced his fame and further elevated his reputation. Initially, some Third World countries, aggravated by the murder of Patrice Lumumba, and angry Soviet leaders, would not join in the praise. Meantime, a widely performed play by the Irish writer Conor Cruise O'Brien (who had been the Secretary-General's representative in Katanga in 1961) entitled *Murderous Angles; A Political Tragedy and Comedy in Black and White* (1968) raised doubts about the late Secretary-General's character and his Congo policy. Nonetheless, Hammarskjöld's reputation survived. Posthumously he was awarded the 1961 Nobel Peace Prize, and today the DAG HAMMARSKJÖLD MEMORIAL LIBRARY at UN HEADQUARTERS in New York and the nearby Dag Hammarskjöld Plaza reflect the legacy of the second Secretary-General.

See also ARAB-ISRAELI DISPUTE, SECRETARIAT, UNITING FOR PEACE RESOLUTION.

Further Reading: Cordier, Andrew W., and Wilder Foote. *Public Papers of the Secretaries-General of the United Nations.* New York: Columbia University Press, 1969–1977. Foote, Wilder, ed. *Servant of Peace; A Selection of the Speeches and Statements of Dag Hammarskjöld, Secretary-General of the United Nations, 1953–1961.* New York: Harper and Row, 1962. Hammarskjöld, Dag. *Markings.* New York: Knopf, 1964. Urquhart, Brian. *Hammarskjöld.* New York: Knopf, 1972. Zacher, Mark W. *Dag Hammarskjöld's United Nations.* New York: Columbia University Press, 1970.

Hammarskjöld Library *See* DAG HAMMARSKJÖLD LIBRARY.

Headquarters of the United Nations

Although the United Nations maintains operations in various parts of the world and several of its PROGRAMMES, SPECIALIZED AGENCIES, and other organizations have headquarters in major international cities—for example, in Paris, The Hague, Rome, Vienna, Nairobi, Washington, D.C. and, most significantly, in GENEVA—the official headquarters is in New York City, on First Avenue, between 42nd and 48th Streets. This scenic location adjacent to the East River is the permanent

nerve center of the organization, and includes the GENERAL ASSEMBLY building—featuring the GA's magnificent Assembly Hall—the Conference Building, with the SECURITY COUNCIL, TRUSTEESHIP COUNCIL, and ECONOMIC AND SOCIAL COUNCIL chambers; the DAG HAMMARSKJÖLD LIBRARY; and the 39-story SECRETARIAT building.

The inaugural UN General Assembly met in Central Hall, Westminster, London, on January 10, 1946; the Security Council met for the first time in London exactly one week later. There was at that time no permanent location for the new organization. In December 1946, John D. Rockefeller, Jr., offered a gift of $8.5 million to the United Nations to purchase the present site, an 18-acre area known as Turtle Bay. Construction costs, provided in most part by an interest-free loan from the UNITED STATES, came close to $70 million. The complex was designed by a group of international architects led by Wallace K. Harrison of New York, and included Charles Edouard Jeanneret (known as Le Corbusier) of FRANCE, Oscar Niemeyer of Brazil, and Sven Markelius of Sweden. Under the direction of city planner Robert Moses, New York made way for the buildings by diverting First Avenue's through traffic into a tunnel under United Nations Plaza on the west side of the avenue. SECRETARY-GENERAL TRYGVE LIE and chief architect Harrison laid the cornerstone on October 24, 1949 (the second anniversary of official UNITED NATIONS DAY). The Secretariat building opened in 1950 and the General Assembly and Security Council were able to begin meeting there two years later. By 1953 the headquarters was declared finished and ready for full occupancy, but the Library was not completed until 1962.

The final product became a major feature of the New York skyline, and an early example of the so-called international style of architecture, represented by tall, unadorned rectangular structures typically sheathed in glass. The Secretariat building gave evidence of the new style. A 544-foot-high slab only 72 feet thick, it dominates the group of buildings, with the Library to the south and the General Assembly building to the north. Constructed of white Vermont marble and glass and aluminum panels, the Secretariat building, by the turn of the 21st century, accommodated an extensive operation, including the office of the Secretary-General and over 3,600 international civil servants from many countries, counting among its employees interpreters and translators, experts in INTERNATIONAL LAW and economics, press officers, security officers, tour guides, and more.

Visitors enter the headquarters via one of seven doors at the northern side of the low-lying General Assembly building. Here one finds the great Assembly Hall, the setting for annual fall meetings of the largest organ of the United Nations. From its speaker's podium, the world has heard from the most powerful, most famous, and most infamous of national and international leaders, watched over by representatives from nearly 200 countries, observer groups, and NON-GOVERNMENTAL ORGANIZATIONS (NGOs) who fill the

UN Headquarters, New York City (UN Photo/Y. Nagata/ARA)

hall, as well as by the PRESIDENT OF THE GENERAL ASSEMBLY, an UNDER SECRETARY-GENERAL for political affairs, and the Secretary-General, who are perched above the speakers on a high dais surmounting the rostrum. Behind them is a large emblem of the United Nations, placed between two illuminated boards that indicate the electronic VOTING of members. To either side, in an upper floor behind glassed panels, reside simultaneous translators and representatives of the media. At the back of the hall, on either side, are giant murals in abstract style of alternating orange, black, and white color on one flank, with beige, blue, and white on the other, done by the French cubist painter Fernand Léger and donated anonymously to the headquarters. No matter where one is in the great hall, one has a panoramic view of the 75-foot high, 165 feet by 115 feet oval interior.

Entering the United Nations complex is to enter international territory. The land belongs not to just one country, but to all member countries. It has its own security and fire forces, issues its own postage stamps, and conducts business in the six official LANGUAGES of the United Nations. The site is one of the most visited tourist destinations in the world. By 2006, almost 40 million people had taken the tour of the headquarters. Tour guides from some 30 countries conduct tours in more than 20 different languages. Visitors see the Assembly Hall, conference rooms, including the Secu-

rity Council meeting chamber, and the many exhibits of art, sculpture, and photographs bequeathed to the United Nations by several countries.

In 2006 the United Nations developed tentative plans to have the headquarters undergo a major renovation at a cost of about $1.6 billion; however, as of early 2007 the General Assembly had not yet agreed on a comprehensive and detailed plan. The original building had been constructed under 1938 building codes and it was in need of major overhaul to remove asbestos, to install a fire sprinkler system, to improve plumbing and electric systems, and to repair leaking roofs. During the proposed restoration most of the UN staff planned to move to nearby buildings. The cost would be met by added dues assessments for all member states over a five-year period.

Further Reading: Churchill, Henry Stern. "United Nations Headquarters." *Architectural Record* 112 (July 1952). Dudley, George A. *A Workshop for Peace: Designing the United Nations Headquarters.* Cambridge, Mass.: MIT Press, 1994. United Nations Headquarters Web site: <www.greatbuildings.com/buildings/United_Nations_Headquarter.html>.

health *See* WORLD HEALTH ORGANIZATION.

High-Level Panel on Threats, Challenges and Change

In November 2003 SECRETARY-GENERAL KOFI ANNAN appointed a High-level Panel on Threats, Challenges and Change. Chaired by Anand Panyarachun, former prime minister of Thailand, the panel included 15 other prominent national leaders, such as Brent Scowcroft, National Security Advisor to president GEORGE H. W. BUSH; Yevgeny Primakov, former Russian prime minister; GRO HARLEM BRUNDTLAND, former prime minister of Norway; and Amre Moussa, secretary-general of the League of Arab States.

In his charge to the committee, Annan indicated that the past year—marked by, among other challenges, the U.S. invasion of IRAQ without SECURITY COUNCIL approval—had "shaken the foundations of COLLECTIVE SECURITY, and undermined confidence in the possibility of collective responses to our common problems." He gave the panel 10 months to recommend "clear and practical measures" that would REFORM the UN's PRINCIPAL ORGANS in such a way that the organization could respond to new threats effectively and collectively. He asked the panel to assess future threats to peace and security and to appraise current approaches and MECHANISMS, particularly those used by UN organs. Specifically, the panel was to study current global threats, anticipate future challenges to international peace and security, suggest what changes were necessary to make the United Nations more effective in anticipation of future difficulties, and propose contributions collective action could make in meeting these challenges. Implicit in the charge to the panel was a stern review of the effectiveness of the UN's principal organs. Thus, the entire exercise fit well into Annan's desire to bring reform to the United Nations.

The High-Level Panel issued its final report in December 2004. Entitled *A More Secure World: Our Shared Responsibility,* the report forwarded a number of recommendations within six areas of concern: (1) war between states, (2) violence within states (including violations of HUMAN RIGHTS), (3) poverty, infectious diseases, and environmental degradation, (4) nuclear, radiological, chemical, and BIOLOGICAL WEAPONS, (5) TERRORISM, and (6) transnational organized crime. Perhaps the panel's most striking recommendation was with reference to the second area of concern listed above: the establishment of a PEACEBUILDING COMMISSION as a subsidiary body of the Security Council, which would "identify countries which are under stress and risk sliding toward state collapse," and assist in planning and implementing transition to post-conflict peacebuilding in such countries.

The panel also called for "a new security consensus" that would allow for a broader definition of collective security than currently understood in the UN CHARTER. To this end, the group urged an enlargement of the Security Council, but could not come to universal agreement about the formula for increasing its size. Secretary-General Annan later incorporated the panel's proposal to increase the Council's size to 24 members in his own reform recommendations to the 2005 WORLD SUMMIT and put forward two possible models first suggested by the panel for changing the body's composition. The group additionally recommended that the Security Council make more use of ENFORCEMENT MEASURES under the Charter's CHAPTER VII to address the full range of security threats. It endorsed the emerging principle of the RESPONSIBILITY TO PROTECT those threatened with GENOCIDE or serious violations of international humanitarian law. In response to the growing controversy surrounding U.S. president GEORGE W. BUSH's doctrine of preemption, the panel acknowledged that Article 51 of the Charter gave every state the right to self-defense, but resolutely noted that it did not authorize any state to use preventive force in the international system. Faced with an American unilateral war in Iraq that shook the 60-year-old principle of collective security, the panel—in a restatement of Just War Theory— argued that the decision to use force should turn on the seriousness of the threat, the belief that the proposed war addressed the threat, that any use of force be proportional to that threat, that the calculated benefits of war far outweigh the costs of inaction, and finally that any use of force be a last resort.

See also HUMAN RIGHTS COUNCIL, *IN LARGER FREEDOM.*

Further Reading: *A More Secure World: Our Shared Responsibility. Report of the Secretary-General's High Level Panel on*

Threats, Challenges and Change Web site: <//www.un.org/secureworld/>.

Hiss, Alger (1904–1996)

Alger Hiss was an active participant in the U.S. State Department's efforts to create the United Nations, and the central figure in one of the most celebrated espionage cases in early COLD WAR America. A Harvard Law School graduate and protégé of Felix Frankfurter, Oliver Wendell Holmes, and DEAN ACHESON, he rose rapidly through the ranks of FRANKLIN ROOSEVELT's New Deal agencies, entering the State Department in 1936.

With the outbreak of World War II in 1939, the State Department began an effort at postwar planning, which intensified when CORDELL HULL appointed LEO PASVOLSKY, a special assistant to the secretary, to head a new Division of Special Research. Assisted by Sumner Welles, Pasvolsky became the major architect of what came to be the UN CHARTER. Alger Hiss served as the deputy director of the division and in that role was one of Roosevelt's advisers at the YALTA CONFERENCE. In 1945 he was appointed the secretary-general of the UN's founding San Francisco Conference. Indeed, the Soviet Union proposed that he be elected the first SECRETARY-GENERAL of the United Nations. Leaving the State Department, he went on to serve as president of the Carnegie Endowment of International Peace until 1949.

In 1948 the liberal establishment in America was stunned when Hiss was accused of being a Communist Party member as well as a Soviet spy by *Time* magazine editor Whittaker Chambers, a former party member. Although denying the charge until his death, Hiss was convicted of perjury and jailed for several years. The case became an important icon in the rise of McCarthyism in postwar America, pitting liberals against conservatives for decades to come.

Evidence gleaned from Soviet archives after the end of the cold war convinced most historians that Hiss, indeed, had been an agent of Soviet military intelligence (GRU) since the mid-1930s. With access to the records of the State, War, and Navy Departments, he was a major source for Soviet intelligence operations in the UNITED STATES. During the course of 1945 and 1946 Hiss made extraordinary efforts to acquire top secret reports on atomic energy that were clearly outside of his duties as a specialist on United Nations diplomacy. Occasional suspicions of Alger Hiss were always allayed by his impeccable credentials and ties to the New Deal–Fair Deal elite.

Further Reading: Haynes, John, and Harvey Klehr. *Venona: Decoding Soviet Espionage in America.* New Haven, Conn.: Yale University Press, 1999. Weinstein, Allen, and Alexander Vassiliev. *The Haunted Wood: Soviet Espionage in America— The Stalin Years.* New York: Random House, 1999.

— *E. M. Clauss*

HIV/AIDS (Human Immunodeficiency Virus/ Acquired Immune Deficiency Syndrome)

AIDS was first identified in 1981 among homosexual men in the UNITED STATES. After 20 years, AIDS had become a pandemic disease with cases diagnosed in most regions of the world and primarily among heterosexuals through either sexual intercourse or intravenous drug use. By the year 2007 the disease would infect over 65 million people, killing 25 million of them. By 2002, the disease had become the primary cause of mortality in Africa from an infectious agent.

There have been distinctive phases in the spread of HIV/AIDS and the subsequent global response. In the first phase, from the mid-1970s until 1981, the epidemic spread silently since its presence was unknown. When AIDS was authoritatively defined in 1981, cases began appearing in various parts of the world—Africa, the Caribbean, Europe, LATIN AMERICA, and the United States. The scientific community embarked upon a sustained effort to identify the cause of this mysterious illness. The period of discovery of HIV lasted from 1981 to 1984 during which time the medical community was able to identify modes of transmission and those behaviors associated with increased risk of HIV infection. The next phase of global mobilization started in 1985 when the WORLD HEALTH ORGANIZATION (WHO) drafted the global strategy for the prevention and control of HIV/AIDS. Many countries also created national AIDS programs. On a local level, community-based organizations sprang up with programs to deal with HIV prevention and to administer to the needs of those suffering and dying from AIDS.

A gradual realization that HIV/AIDS was rapidly affecting every corner of the world provoked calls for a more concerted international response. The UNITED NATIONS SYSTEM, with its experience in health as well as social and economic DEVELOPMENT issues, was soon compelled to mount an international plan of action. Many believed that the United Nations was best equipped to help mobilize national governments and international organizations, including NON-GOVERNMENTAL ORGANIZATIONS (NGOs), to develop policies both for prevention of HIV transmission and for the mitigation of social and economic consequences of the growing pandemic. The UN response to HIV/AIDS began in the mid-1980s with a coordinated effort between the UNITED NATIONS DEVELOPMENT PROGRAMME (UNDP) and WHO. In February 1987, WHO set up its Special Programme on AIDS, which later received the more permanent title of the Global Programme on AIDS (GPA). In October 1987, the UN GENERAL ASSEMBLY held an extraordinary session on AIDS calling for all parts of the UN system to become engaged in a coordinated effort to address global HIV/AIDS problems.

Despite inter-agency agreements under the leadership of the World Health Organization, coordinating policies, strategies, and support activities became increasingly difficult. In response to these difficulties and to the growing awareness that HIV/AIDS was not only a medical problem but also an epidemic with social, economic, and political complexities, a new UN program, the JOINT UNITED NATIONS PROGRAMME ON HIV/AIDS (UNAIDS), was created in 1996. With seven originating agencies that grew to 10 organizations by 2007 operating under the leadership of a program SECRETARIAT, UNAIDS recognized the need for greater program coordination to combat the increasingly complex nature of this global pandemic. Important features of the UNAIDS program design included cooperation with the numerous NGOs active in HIV prevention worldwide as well as the active participation of national HIV/AIDS programs.

The UN SECURITY COUNCIL also recognized the potentially destabilizing force of HIV/AIDS, particularly among those communities ravaged by conflicts and warfare. Through a number of RESOLUTIONS, AIDS was identified by the Security Council as the first health and development issue to be considered a threat to global peace and security. Particular attention was focused on the links between regional conflicts in sub-Saharan Africa and the incidence of HIV/AIDS.

The United Nations continued to evolve in its response to the HIV/AIDS pandemic. A "Country Response Monitoring Project" launched in 2000 was just one of the UN's efforts, in collaboration with national governments and NGOs, to provide the latest information on the epidemic in specific countries. In June 2001, the United Nations General Assembly held its first SPECIAL SESSION on HIV/AIDS. The Final Document, known as the Declaration of Commitment, recognized the HIV/AIDS pandemic as much more than a medical problem. With references to political challenges, HUMAN RIGHTS, and economic threats posed by the pandemic, the DECLARATION called for an increased emphasis on prevention efforts bearing in mind the particular vulnerability of WOMEN to HIV disease. In addition, the Special Session called for the immediate implementation of the Heavily Indebted Poor Country Initiative (HIPC) and cancellation of all bilateral debts of HIPC countries, especially those heavily impacted by HIV/AIDS.

Despite these efforts, as of 2007 the AIDS pandemic continued unabated in regions hardest hit. The developing world bore the brunt of this pandemic with about 95 percent of those living with HIV/AIDS residing in the Third World. Africa alone accounted for over 60 percent of the almost 50 million people living with HIV/AIDS. South, Southeast, and East Asia were also hard hit; by 2005 infections had increased ominously in INDIA and CHINA. DEVELOPING COUNTRIES lacked the resources to overcome the HIV/AIDS challenges and, less able to take advantage of medical and scientific developments, experienced reverses in many of the economic and social gains achieved through decades of efforts. According to the WORLD BANK, widespread international support was required to help these countries establish viable national HIV/AIDS programs that included basic prevention, treatment, and care. And while promising antiviral drugs had extended the lives of some infected with the HIV virus, the overwhelming majority in the developing world were too poor ever to expect this type of treatment. Most government health programs were incapable of providing the necessary drugs and infrastructure to deal with AIDS in the developing world. Recognizing the urgency of the poorer countries facing the devastation of AIDS, the United Nations called for a Global AIDS and Health Fund to generate between $8 billion and $10 billion annually to respond to the AIDS pandemic. At the 2000 MILLENNIUM SUMMIT participants agreed to halt the spread of AIDS by 2015, making the target a MILLENNIUM DEVELOPMENT GOAL.

In addition, AIDS activists put political pressure on international pharmaceutical companies to lower the price on HIV/AIDS drug therapies for the developing world, making some progress in the new millenium when former U.S. president BILL CLINTON negotiated a new price arrangement between the United Nations and the companies. Still, prevention efforts constituted the mainstay in the fight against AIDS. Yet these too were hampered, primarily by poverty but also by cultural norms in some instances and by political considerations in others. The UN General Assembly's Declaration of Commitment in 2001 reflected the controversies surrounding prevention efforts with its notable omission of language on certain "high risk" groups such as homosexuals and sex workers. UNAIDS/WHO reported that at the new millennium 16,000 people—almost half of whom were between the ages of 15 and 24 years old—became newly infected everyday with HIV.

See also APPENDIX G (MILLENNIUM DECLARATION).

Further Reading: Bastos, Cristiana. *Global Responses to AIDS: Science in Emergency.* Bloomington: Indiana University Press, 1999. Feldman, Douglas, and Julia Wang Miller. *The AIDS Crisis: A Documentary History.* Westport, Conn.: Greenwood Press, 1998. Joint United Nations Programme on HIV/AIDS. *From Advocacy to Action: A Progress Report on UNAIDS at Country Level.* Geneva: Joint United Nations Programme on HIV/AIDS, 2005. Mann, Jonathan, and Daniel Tarantola, eds. *AIDS in the World II.* New York: Oxford University Press, 1996. Smith, Raymond. *Encyclopedia of AIDS: A Social, Political, Cultural, and Scientific Record of the HIV Epidemic.* Chicago: Fitzroy Dearborn Publishers, 2000. UNAIDS *Report on the Global AIDS Epidemic 2006* Web site: <www.unaids.org/en/HIV_data/2006GlobalReport/default.asp>.

— R. E. McNamara

Hull, Cordell (1871–1955)

In 1945 Cordell Hull was awarded the Nobel Peace Prize for his role in establishing the United Nations. Appointed secretary of state by President FRANKLIN ROOSEVELT in 1933, Hull served until 1944, longer than any other secretary in U.S. history. Roosevelt, joining in wide recognition, called him the "Father of the United Nations."

Hull was born in a log cabin in Pickett County, Tennessee. He was educated at the Montvale Academy at Celina, Tennessee, the Normal School at Bowling Green, Kentucky, and the National Normal University at Lebanon, Ohio. He obtained a law degree in 1891 upon completing a one-year course at Cumberland University at Lebanon, Tennessee. Elected to the Tennessee House of Representatives in 1893, he later fought in the Spanish-American War, served in the U.S. Congress from 1907 to 1931, and was elected to the U.S. Senate in 1930, but he resigned upon his appointment as secretary of state in 1933. He actively pursued the Roosevelt administration's "Good Neighbor" policy with LATIN AMERICA, attending several hemispheric meetings during the 1930s. A proponent of liberalized international trade, Hull urged the Reciprocal Trade Agreements Act of 1934, which reversed the high tariff policies of the 1920s. He negotiated numerous treaties under authority of the act that lowered tariff barriers and stimulated international commerce.

Shortly after the outbreak of World War II, Hull proposed that a new international organization be created to replace the failed LEAGUE OF NATIONS. A supporter and admirer of President Woodrow Wilson's moralistic and legalistic visions of world affairs, Hull was also keenly mindful of that president's failure with the League. Determined to have the UNITED STATES participate in the new postwar organization, Hull in 1941 formed a bipartisan Advisory Committee on Postwar Foreign Policy to assure that a wide spectrum of the country's political views were represented in discussions. The committee included members of Congress, senators, experts from the private sphere, and State Department officials. Hull, chairman of the group, pressed for public discussions of the plans being considered, and oversaw the formulation of detailed proposals.

Hull's efforts within the State Department began as early as 1939. He was approached by the Council on Foreign Relations (CFR) with a proposal that the CFR form a group of experts to research postwar issues under the "general guidance" of the department. Hull accepted the idea, and the Council established the War and Peace Studies Project. Hull set up a department committee for postwar planning in December 1939, and he appointed Under Secretary of State Sumner Welles to chair it. In early 1943 he appointed a close confidant—LEO PASVOLSKY—as his "special adviser" in charge of preparatory work for the proposed international organization. His efforts resulted in composition of a State Department draft document in August 1943, entitled "CHARTER of the United Nations." This document became the basis for discussions at the DUMBARTON OAKS CONFERENCE in 1944.

At the MOSCOW CONFERENCE OF FOREIGN MINISTERS in October 1943, Hull successfully brought the issue forward, and for the remainder of his service in the department he was chiefly occupied with forwarding plans for a United Nations. Following the conference, the Secretary of State established an "Informal Political Agenda Group," which crafted the outlines of the world body. President Roosevelt approved the group's recommendations early in 1944.

Although President Roosevelt and Prime Minister WIN-STON CHURCHILL early indicated a penchant for a postwar world of more or less independent regional councils and SPE-CIALIZED AGENCIES, with all but four nations—the United States, the United Kingdom, the Soviet Union, and CHINA—disarmed, Hull insisted that the new peace organization be universal in character, and that no parts be greater than the whole. With the Four-Power Declaration of the Dumbarton Oaks Conference, Hull's views triumphed in language that called for "a general international organization, based on the . . . sovereign equality of all peace-loving states, and open to MEMBERSHIP by all such states, large and small."

On November 27, 1944, Hull, citing ill health, resigned, and he was replaced by EDWARD STETTINIUS, who faithfully carried on his predecessor's work. Hull, who had seemed to lose influence with the president as the war proceeded, nonetheless received from Roosevelt praise as "the one person in all the world who has done the most to make this great plan for peace an effective fact."

See also DECLARATION BY UNITED NATIONS, INTERNATIONAL COURT OF JUSTICE, MOSCOW DECLARATION, TRUST-EESHIP SYSTEM.

Further Reading: Drummond, Donald F. "Cordell Hull." In *An Uncertain Tradition: American Secretaries of State in the Twentieth Century.* Edited by Norman A. Graebner. New York: McGraw Hill, 1961. Gellman, Irwin F. *Secret Affairs: Franklin Roosevelt, Cordell Hull, and Sumner Welles.* Baltimore: Johns Hopkins University Press, 1995. Hull, Cordell. *The Memoirs of Cordell Hull.* Two vols. New York: Macmillan, 1948. Pratt, Julius W. *Cordell Hull, 1933–1944.* New York: Cooper Square Publishers, 1964. Schlesinger, Stephen C. *Act of Creation: The Founding of the United Nations; A Story of Superpowers, Secret Agents, Wartime Allies and Enemies and Their Quest for a Peaceful World.* Boulder, Colo.: Westview Press, 2003.

human rights

The United Nations was the first international organization to address the issue of human rights, and it has remained a central concern of the institution since its founding. Before World War II, human rights were rarely addressed in international relations. For example, the COVENANT of the LEAGUE OF NATIONS did not use the term "human rights." International diplomats previously had addressed only narrow questions of what might be called "worst practices," such as when banning the slave trade in 1815, which led much later to the Slavery Convention of 1926. The Hague Convention of 1907 dealt with a government's treatment of foreign nationals, but the document said nothing about treatment of its own citizens. Under the principle of SOVEREIGNTY, the relations between a government and its people were considered an internal matter, and, even in the view of a number of nations at the turn of the 21st century, outside intrusion on that relationship continued to be regarded as a violation of INTERNATIONAL LAW.

Addressing human rights on an international level involved two problematic challenges. The first was that NATION-STATES held different views regarding the role of the international community in the area of rights. Second, while many people agreed that there was a set of basic human rights, not all agreed on what was included under the term "rights." Dissimilar cultures placed different definitions and different priorities on the claim of rights, and indeed even on the basis from which such rights derived. Initially, the impetus for the idea of human rights was Western-based, and since the CHARTER was drawn up by a small group of wartime allies, it reflected Western views of this concept.

Although the UN Charter did not contain specific definitions and procedures regarding this issue, it was the first international agreement in which the signatory nations made a commitment to promote human rights at the international level. The fundamental nature of this issue was indicated in the Preamble. It declared that one of the UN's purposes was "to reaffirm faith in the fundamental human rights, in the dignity and worth of the human person, in equal rights of men and WOMEN and of nations large and small."

The Charter contains several references to human rights. The term is used in Articles 13, 55, 56, 62, 68, and 76. The Charter authorizes the United Nations to make recommendations to member states regarding human rights policies, and it declares that the states have an obligation to consider its proposals carefully. The Charter limits the organization to making recommendations, since only treaties can create legally binding obligations. Under the Charter all the PRINCIPAL ORGANS of the United Nations can deal with human rights, and each of them has addressed this topic at one time or another.

Yet while Article 68 of the Charter empowers the ECONOMIC AND SOCIAL COUNCIL (ECOSOC) to set up commissions to promote human rights it made no effort to define the term "Human Rights," and reaching agreement on what constituted such rights required a prolonged effort that gradually expanded the meaning of the term. The deliberations reflected the sensitivity of the issue and the new departure represented by the Charter. The founding San Francisco Conference shunned proposals to define the term, reflecting the challenge posed by the concept of national sovereignty. At its initial session in 1946, the COMMISSION ON HUMAN RIGHTS, created that year by ECOSOC, established a small drafting group to prepare the UNIVERSAL DECLARATION OF HUMAN RIGHTS (UDHR). ELEANOR ROOSEVELT, widow of former U.S. president FRANKLIN D. ROOSEVELT, chaired the drafting committee. Mrs. Roosevelt played a central role in the evolution of the document, along with John Humphrey of Canada, the first director of the SECRETARIAT's Division of Human Rights, Charles Malik, rapporteur of the commission, Dr. Peng-chun Chang, who represented an Asian perspective on rights, and Frenchman René Cassin, who in 1968 won the Nobel Peace Prize for his involvement in the drafting of the DECLARATION. Throughout the drafting, the Soviet Union and its Eastern European allies resisted the idea of defining human rights.

Western nations and their citizens, drawing on a tradition of democratic politics that accentuates the primacy of the individual, place strong emphasis on civil and political rights. That is, they stress the rights of the person, and tend to view human rights as protecting the individual from actions by the state. They emphasize protection of minority groups against overweening majority power. This viewpoint advocates that human rights be articulated and proclaimed in print, and, furthermore, ascertained and protected by judicial process. Such an outlook emphasizes rights such as free speech, freedom of religion, freedom of assembly, specific rights of the accused, and the right to organize.

Developing nations, on the other hand, emphasize economic, social, and cultural rights. In part, this viewpoint is based on their living conditions. Theirs is a collective outlook that holds that societies, as groups, have rights, and that the rights of the group as a whole supersede the rights of the individual. In this view, the good of the majority transcends the protection of the minority. Developing nations and their citizens also believe that the state offers the only prospect for DEVELOPMENT of the society, and hence view human rights as the basis for state action, rather than as designed to protect the individual from the state. This approach to human rights speaks to the goals and responsibilities of the state, requiring government action to provide citizens with the conditions and facilities essential for the full realization of rights. Developing nations view economic rights, particularly the right to development, as the most basic rights, and therefore essential to the exercise of all other rights. Developing nations also view these rights as creating obligations for the international system as a whole, including the provision of needed resources for development. Developing nations have emphasized the primacy of rights such as adequate food, tolerable living standards, and requisite shelter, which they regard as essential to human dignity. Western nations tend to reject development as a right equivalent to individual freedoms. The Western nations have resisted elevating economic rights to a position of primacy, since they view this as an effort to redistribute wealth to their disadvantage.

On December 10, 1948, the GENERAL ASSEMBLY adopted the Universal Declaration of Human Rights as "a common standard of achievement for all peoples and all nations, to the end that every individual and every organ of society, keeping this Declaration constantly in mind, shall strive by teaching and education to promote respect for these rights and freedoms and by progressive measures, national and international, to secure their universal and effective recognition and observance, both among the peoples of Member States themselves and among the peoples of territories under their JURISDICTION." Reflecting the predominantly Western MEMBERSHIP of the United Nations in 1948, prior to decolonization, 22 of the Declaration's 30 articles deal with individual, civil, and political rights, and only six articles deal with economic, social, and cultural rights. The declaration stresses the "inherent dignity" of the individual, the principle of equality, and the three interrelated fundamental rights of life, liberty, and the security of the person. It also recognizes the need for social order, and therefore that individuals also have duties, which impose certain limitations on the exercise of their rights. Since those limitations are determined by national law, the declaration accepts the principle that states can limit human rights, providing that such laws are "solely for the purpose of securing due recognition and respect for the rights" of others, and establishing "the just requirements of morality, public order and the general welfare in a democratic society." The Universal Declaration set the direction for all subsequent agreements in the field of human rights.

It required elaborate negotiations spanning another 18 years to produce the other documents that comprise the composite "International Bill of Human Rights." In 1948, the CONVENTION ON THE PREVENTION AND PUNISHMENT OF THE CRIME OF GENOCIDE was opened for signature. The much more specific INTERNATIONAL COVENANT ON CIVIL AND POLITICAL RIGHTS (ICCPR) and the INTERNATIONAL COVENANT ON ECONOMIC, SOCIAL, AND CULTURAL RIGHTS (ICESCR), which, with the Universal Declaration, collectively comprise the International Bill of Human Rights, were only adopted by the General Assembly in 1966. Another 10 years elapsed Ibefore the covenants were ratified by the requisite 35 nations to come into force, and then they were binding only on those nations that had ratified them. The International Covenants were adopted as two separate documents rather than as a single CONVENTION because Western nations objected to the inclusion of economic, social, and cultural rights, which they contended were goals that were not enforceable. Developing nations insisted on including economic and social rights, since they considered these to be the most fundamental. As a compromise, two separate documents were composed and introduced simultaneously. Reflecting the NORTH-SOUTH controversy, there were a few "no" votes to each.

The two covenants spelled out in more detail the rights involved in each category. Unlike the Universal Declaration, they were written in the form of treaties, requiring ratification by the member states, and consequently creating legally binding obligations. The ICCPR detailed the freedoms of speech, press, worship, assembly, security of person and property, political participation, and procedural due process, protecting the individual against arbitrary and unreasonable government action. Each state assumed the obligation to submit regular reports to the HUMAN RIGHTS COMMITTEE, which reviewed them in detail and made recommendations to governments for improvement and additional legislation. The ICESCR provided guarantees of "the right of everyone to the enjoyment of an adequate standard of living for himself and his family, including adequate food, clothing, and housing, and to the continuous improvement of living conditions." It also guaranteed access by all to adequate education, social security, medical care, employment, shelter, mental health, and leisure, requiring an expansion of governmental functions. At the insistence of the developing nations, which by 1966 made up a majority of UN membership, both documents recognized the right of self-determination. By December 31, 1995, ratifications of the two covenants had reached 132, or about two-thirds of the member states of the United Nations.

Regional efforts revealed the differing viewpoints regarding human rights. The Western Hemisphere acted first, when the ORGANIZATION OF AMERICAN STATES unanimously approved the American Declaration on the Rights and Duties of Man on May 2, 1948. It was the first international human rights document to include a detailed enumeration of those rights. The document reflected the region's Western heritage, and consequently emphasized civil and political rights. But it insisted on an individual's duties as well. Reflecting Western traditions, it included the right to life and to asylum. However, it also stressed the protection of the family, its mothers and children, and the inviolability of the home. In 1948 the Western Hemisphere nations also adopted the Inter-American Charter of Social Guarantees, protecting workers' rights and stressing the goal of raising the standard of living. The American Convention on Human Rights of 1969, also known as the PACT of San José, entered into force in 1976. It established the Inter-American Court of Human Rights and the Inter-American Commission of Human Rights. The commission investigates complaints and makes recommendations to signatory governments. The court can adjudicate complaints brought by other states. Individual complaints can be made to the commission, which has the power to place cases before the Inter-American Court.

The European Convention for the Protection of Human Rights and Fundamental Freedoms was drafted by the Council of Europe and entered into force in 1953. At the time, its application was confined to Western Europe, since it was written when the COLD WAR divided the continent. It established the European Commission of Human Rights, which reviewed complaints by individuals as well as NON-GOVERNMENTAL ORGANIZATIONS (NGOs), and the European Court of Human Rights, whose decisions were binding among signatories. Individuals could bring complaints before the court.

In many respects the most significant regional agreement was the African Charter of Human and Peoples' Rights, also known as the Banjul Charter, signed in 1981, which came into force in 1986. The African Charter was a major document reflecting the views of the developing nations and former colonies. It was notable for its statement of the collective rights of peoples, as revealed in its title, pointing out that the rights of the nation as a collective take primacy over the rights of individuals. It stressed that individuals have duties to their families and the society as a whole, and consequently that the "rights and freedoms of each individual, shall be exercised with due regard to the rights of others, COLLECTIVE SECURITY, morality, and common interest." The charter placed considerable emphasis on economic, social, and cultural rights. The African Charter was the first international agreement to include both classes of rights, civil and political, as well as economic, social, and cultural, within a single document. It was also the first international document to identify the right to development as the most fundamental right of all. It included the right of peoples to peace and security, and the right to an ENVIRONMENT supportive of the health of its citizens. In 1988 the ORGANIZATION OF AFRICAN UNITY established the African Commission on Human and Peoples' Rights, which was primarily a body to study and collect information on "African problems in human and peoples' rights."

Other regions acted in a more limited manner. In the Middle East, the issue of human rights has been more contentious than in other regions, echoing the conflict that has polarized the region since the end of World War II. Middle Eastern countries were divided in their attitudes toward the adoption of the Universal Declaration. Initial resistance came from fundamentalist Islamic states that objected to the right of religious conversion. However, the League of Arab States established the Arab Commission on Human Rights in 1968 that was empowered to draft regional agreements in this field. The Islamic Conference adopted the broader Cairo Declaration on Human Rights in Islam in 1990.

Countries in Asia have shown the strongest inclination to abstain from Western notions of the universality of human rights. Asian states' firmness on asserting the inviolability of national sovereignty has meant that no agreement on an Asian human rights instrument has ever been reached. At the turn of the century Asia remained the only continent without such a document.

The UN's role has been to formulate standard and voluntary norms through conferences and declarations, and then to encourage conformity, while having little enforcement power. It carries out its mission by promoting international agreements that set standards, and then urges member states to report on their progress. The United Nations supplies information and assists nations in meeting human rights standards through technical missions and by developing model codes and programs. These procedures depend on monitoring to encourage states to develop legislation to implement the rights involved. Until 2006 the Commission on Human Rights served as the main monitoring body. Compliance with universal standards was voluntary, and implementation was up to individual governments. In March 2006 a new HUMAN RIGHTS COUNCIL replaced the Human Rights Commission as part of an attempt to REFORM the UN's handling of human rights issues.

In 1967, the Economic and Social Council authorized the Commission on Human Rights to move beyond general discussion, and to consider human rights violations in individual countries. While no enforcement was possible, both the commission and the General Assembly passed RESOLUTIONS condemning the worst abuses on a country-specific basis each year. In 1979–80 the commission expanded its efforts by establishing special procedures to enable investigations, which led to the appointment of SPECIAL RAPPORTEURS to investigate and compile reports for the commission. Rapporteurs were employed both to investigate thematic issues such as torture, summary executions, violence against women, racial discrimination, and religious discrimination, and to investigate the situation in particular countries. This procedure ensured discussion of the topic, and often led to resolutions on the subject. In 2007 there were 23 special rapporteurs (plus several independent experts and special representatives) covering a range of topical and country situations and reporting to the new Human Rights Council. A number of non-governmental organizations, which served as advocates for human rights, also monitored situations throughout the world and submitted their own reports to the various UN bodies.

Throughout its existence the United Nations has negotiated and adopted a long list of conventions and declarations regarding specific rights that have sought to extend and clarify the meaning of "human rights." Some were drafted by the commission, some by other bodies, and several resulted from UN conferences or came from SPECIALIZED AGENCIES. Among the principal documents on the long list are the conventions on the Elimination of All Forms of Racial Discrimination (1966), the Suppression and Punishment of the Crime of APARTHEID (1973), the Political Rights of Women (1953), the Elimination of All Forms of Discrimination Against Women (1979), the Suppression of the Traffic in Persons (1950), the Status of Refugees (1951), the Status of Stateless Persons (1954), against Torture and other Cruel and Inhuman or Degrading Treatment or Punishment (1984), the Rights of the Child (1989), and the Protection of the Rights of All Migrant Workers (1990). Declarations were issued dealing with the Eradication of Hunger and Malnutrition (1974), the Protection of Women and Children in Emergency and Armed Conflict (1974), the Rights of Disabled Persons (1975), the Right to Development (1986), and the Rights of Persons Belonging to National, Ethnic, Religious, and Linguistic Minorities (1992). These joined the initial Convention on Genocide to constitute a body of humanitarian law. Additional PROTOCOLS were added to several of the existing covenants. All set standards and required reporting by governments, although all nations had not ratified all agreements.

Other agencies and organizations within the UNITED NATIONS SYSTEM also have negotiated agreements relating to human rights. For example, several treaties regarding the rights of labor, including the right to organize, were formulated through the INTERNATIONAL LABOUR ORGANIZATION (ILO). Other agencies include the UNITED NATIONS CHILDREN'S FUND (UNICEF), the United Nations COMMISSION ON THE STATUS OF WOMEN, and the UNITED NATIONS HIGH COMMISSIONER FOR REFUGEES (UNHCR). In 1993 the WORLD CONFERENCE ON HUMAN RIGHTS, known as the Vienna Conference, conducted a global review of human rights and the UN work in this area. The Vienna Declaration and Program of Action, adopted by participants representing 171 nations, highlighted the links among development, democracy, and the promotion of human rights, bridging the differing interpretations of the West and the developing nations. It emphasized the universality, indivisibility, and interdependence of civil, cultural, economic, political, and social rights, declaring all to be the responsibility of governments and requiring governments to promote all human rights and fundamental freedoms. The declaration reaffirmed the right to development as a universal, inalienable, integral, and fundamental part of human rights. The signatories of the Vienna Declaration agreed that the development of the poorest nations was the collective responsibility of the international community. The Final Document asserted that extreme poverty and social exclusion constituted a "violation of human dignity." The declaration emphasized the rights of all vulnerable groups, especially women, and extended this protection to INDIGENOUS PEOPLES.

In one of its most controversial decisions, the Vienna Declaration recommended the creation of the position of UN HIGH COMMISSIONER FOR HUMAN RIGHTS, a new office to advocate human rights and to coordinate UN programs, agencies, and offices involved in this field. Established in 1993, the High Commissioner serves as the focal point for all United Nations human rights activities, and acts as the SECRETARIAT for all treaty bodies monitoring compliance with human rights covenants and agreements. The CENTRE FOR HUMAN RIGHTS became part of the Office of the High Commissioner. Located in Geneva, the centre conducts studies and provides recommendations, information, and analysis to all UN organs dealing with human rights issues.

Seven years after the world's governments gathered in Vienna, they convened in New York City for the MILLENNIUM SUMMIT. Reasserting the Vienna declaration's commitment to human rights, the attending delegates established MILLENNIUM DEVELOPMENT GOALS (MDGs) that were postulated on the assumption that human rights and development were inextricably linked. Among the MDGs were commitments to achieve gender equality, education for all, and the eradication of poverty. SECRETARY-GENERAL KOFI ANNAN later in his 2005 UN reform report, *IN LARGER FREEDOM*, argued that only in a world where all states sought human rights and development simultaneously could the maintenance of peace and security be achieved.

The various UN and regional human rights bodies are assisted by a large number of non-governmental organizations that serve as advocates of human rights and work to protect them. At times the NGOs intervene to protect individuals who are denied their rights. These NGOs constantly monitor the situation in each of the world's nations, and they submit informative reports to the various monitoring bodies. While functioning separately, they therefore are indirectly a part of the global monitoring system for human rights. Human rights is an area of concern for one of the largest number of non-governmental organizations.

In the course of developing human rights treaties, the United Nations adopted the Nuremberg Tribunal Charter, under which World War II war criminals were tried for "crimes against humanity." These were defined as crimes of "murder, extermination, enslavement, deportation, and other inhumane acts committed against any civilian population, before or during a war . . . whether or not in violation of the domestic law of the country where perpetrated." Both the Convention on Genocide and the Convention on the Suppression and Punishment of the Crime of Apartheid (1973) defined these as crimes against humanity.

Following the conclusion of the cold war, the United Nations established judicial bodies to deal with this type of crime. The SECURITY COUNCIL established the INTERNATIONAL CRIMINAL TRIBUNAL FOR THE FORMER YUGOSLAVIA in 1993, with headquarters in The Hague. The INTERNATIONAL CRIMINAL TRIBUNAL FOR RWANDA, with headquarters in Arusha, Tanzania, was established in 1994. Each had JURISDICTION involving only the specified countries, and in the Rwandan case for Rwandan citizens who may have committed war crimes in neighboring states. The creation of these tribunals embodies an expression of the worldwide horror at the GENOCIDE practiced in both crises, which differentiated them from other conflicts. The tribunals became the precedents for the establishment of extraordinary mixed— national and international—courts in CAMBODIA and SIERRA LEONE to address human rights abuses by the Khmer Rouge and the Revolutionary United Front, respectively, in their particular countries. In 1998, a conference of 100 countries approved the Rome Statute of the INTERNATIONAL CRIMINAL COURT (ICC) establishing a permanent court, independent of the United Nations, to investigate and decide cases involving individuals responsible for the most serious crimes of concern to the international community. Its statute extended the court's jurisdiction to genocide, war crimes, and crimes against humanity, and provided definitions for these crimes. On April 11, 2002, 10 nations deposited their ratifications of the statute, bringing the ICC into existence as of July 1. While there was considerable controversy about the jurisdiction and powers of the court, its creation constituted a significant new departure in the enforcement and definition of human rights. These developments occurred as the General Assembly declared 1995–2004 the UN Decade for Human Rights Education. The decade sought to encourage the establishment of national committees composed of representatives from both public and private sectors in each country to promote education about and awareness of human rights.

See also AFGHANISTAN, AGENDA FOR DEVELOPMENT, BEIJING +5, BRICKER AMENDMENT, CHAPTER VI ½, COMMITTEE OF 24, CONGO, CONVENTION AGAINST TORTURE AND OTHER CRUEL, INHUMAN OR DEGRADING TREATMENT OR PUNISHMENT, CONVENTION ON THE ELIMINATION OF ALL FORMS OF DISCRIMINATION AGAINST WOMEN, CONVENTION ON THE ELIMINATION OF ALL FORMS OF RACIAL DISCRIMINATION, CONVENTION ON THE POLITICAL RIGHTS OF WOMEN, DECLARATION BY UNITED NATIONS, GLOBAL COMPACT, *JUS COGENS*, OFFICE FOR THE COORDINATION OF HUMANITARIAN AFFAIRS, PEACEKEEPING, RWANDA CRISIS, UNITED NATIONS DEVELOPMENT FUND FOR WOMEN, UNITED NATIONS MISSION IN BOSNIA AND HERZEGOVINA, UNITED NATIONS TRANSITIONAL ADMINISTRATION IN EAST TIMOR.

Further Reading: Alston, Philip, ed. *The United Nations and Human Rights: A Critical Appraisal.* Oxford: Oxford University Press, 1992. Alston, Philip, and James Crawford, eds. *The Future of UN Human Rights Treaty Monitoring.* Cambridge: Cambridge University Press, 2000. Donnelly, Jack. *International Human Rights.* Boulder, Colo.: Westview Press, 1998. Langley, Winston E. *Encyclopedia of Human Rights Issues since 1945.* Westport, Conn.: Greenwood Press, 1999. Lauren, Paul Gordon. *The Evolution of International Human Rights: Visions Seen.* 2nd ed. Philadelphia: University of Pennsylvania Press, 2004. Mertus, Julie A. *The United Nations and Human Rights: A Guide for a New Era.* New York: Routledge, 2005. United Nations. *The United Nations and Human Rights: 1945–1995.* New York: United Nations, 1995.

— *K. J. Grieb*

Human Rights Commission *See* COMMISSION ON HUMAN RIGHTS.

Human Rights Committee (HRC)

Article 28 of the INTERNATIONAL COVENANT ON CIVIL AND POLITICAL RIGHTS established the Human Rights Committee to monitor the progress made by signatory states in ensuring "the equal rights of men and WOMEN to the enjoyment of all civil and political rights." The 18 committee members are elected by the states party to the COVENANT, but they do not represent their states. They serve in their personal capacity as individuals of high moral character and with expertise in the field of HUMAN RIGHTS. Sometimes confused with the UN COMMISSION ON HUMAN RIGHTS, which was created in 1946 and drafted the UNIVERSAL DECLARATION OF HUMAN

RIGHTS, the Human Rights Committee was established in 1976, meets three times yearly in New York or Geneva, and considers reports on human rights conditions in the specific nations that have signed the covenant.

The International Covenant detailed the freedoms of speech, press, worship, assembly, security of person and property, political participation, procedural due process, and individual protection against arbitrary and unreasonable government action. Each state assumed the obligation to submit regular reports to the Human Rights Committee, which reviews them in detail and makes recommendations to governments for improvement and additional legislation. In addition, as of 2007, 143 states had accepted the covenant's First Optional PROTOCOL that gave the committee the COMPETENCE to receive petitions from individuals alleging human rights abuses by their own governments. The committee also has oversight of the Second Optional Protocol, which entered into force in 1991, seeking to eliminate the use of the death penalty. Ninety-five states had approved that protocol by 2007.

Under the committee's rules of procedure, the HRC provides guidelines to signatory states for the preparation of national reports. Those reports are then discussed by the committee with the state's representatives present. The committee publishes a summary of its findings in what are called "general comments." These commentaries are written in broad, vague terms. Specific criticisms and recommendations are conveyed under terms of confidentiality to the government concerned.

Further Reading: Langley, Winston E. *Encyclopedia of Human Rights Issues since 1945.* Westport, Conn.: Greenwood Press, 1999. United Nations Centre for Human Rights, and United Nations Institute for Training and Research. *Manual on Human Rights Reporting under Six Major International Human Rights Instruments.* New York: United Nations, 1991. UN Human Rights Committee Web site: <www.ohchr.org/english/bodies/hrc/index.htm>.

Human Rights Conventions   *See* HUMAN RIGHTS.

Human Rights Council

The UN GENERAL ASSEMBLY inaugurated the Human Rights Council on March 15, 2006, in Resolution 251, as part of an effort to REFORM the United Nations. The specific recommendation for the new body originated in the 2004 report of the HIGH-LEVEL PANEL ON THREATS, CHALLENGES AND CHANGE, and was endorsed by SECRETARY-GENERAL KOFI ANNAN in March 2005 and by the WORLD SUMMIT in September of that year. The Human Rights Council replaced the COMMISSION ON HUMAN RIGHTS (CHR), and its mandate differs considerably from that of the CHR. Western nations and Western-oriented advocacy NON-GOVERNMENTAL ORGA-

NIZATIONS (NGOs) viewed the establishment of the Human Rights Council as a way to give new prominence to HUMAN RIGHTS throughout the UN system, and as a progressive alternative to the much maligned CHR. In doing so, this coalition emphasized the value of the new body in promoting civil and political rights. The effort to create the new council brought into high relief the differing views of human rights in different parts of the world. Developing nations, which consider economic, social, and cultural rights as important as civil and political rights, questioned the need for a new body.

Lengthy negotiations and a number of compromises proved necessary before agreement was reached between Western and developing nations. Among the issues debated were the size of the body, its purpose, the method of selecting its members, and its place within the United Nations. Secretary-General Annan proposed a small working body, modeled on the SECURITY COUNCIL, which would become one of the PRINCIPAL ORGANS OF THE UNITED NATIONS. The NON-ALIGNED MOVEMENT (NAM) and the GROUP OF 77 (G77), insisting on the prerogatives of the General Assembly as the hub of the UN, successfully pressed to make the new council a subsidiary body of the Assembly. The NAM/G77 coalition also insisted on broader, regionally balanced, MEMBERSHIP for the new council than that proposed by the developed states. During the course of the negotiations, proposed membership schemes ranged from a small working body with 15 members to a plenary body with universal membership. The agreement eventually reached established a council with 47 members—not much smaller than the 53 member Commission on Human Rights that it replaced.

Western states contended that election of members to the CHR by group VOTING on candidates as put forward by regional CAUCUS GROUPS had resulted in a commission whose members included several states that were well known to be human rights violators and who sought membership to prevent a review of their countries' records. They proposed a secret ballot on each candidate state, with a two-thirds vote of the General Assembly required for election to the new council. The NAM/G77 group insisted on regionally balanced membership and rejected the at-large two-thirds vote proposal. The resulting prolonged deadlock was broken only when the PRESIDENT OF THE GENERAL ASSEMBLY proposed a compromise formula. As thus established, while membership is regionally balanced, each candidate is voted on separately in a secret ballot and must receive the affirmative votes of an absolute majority of the General Assembly. In 2006, that meant that countries were elected only if they received 96 affirmative votes. This also meant that abstentions hurt a nation's chances of election to the council. Each country serving on the Human Rights Council will be required to undergo a review of its human rights record by the council during its term of membership. Member states are limited to two consecutive terms on the new council. In addition, the General Assembly can suspend the council membership of any state that "commits gross and systematic violations of human rights," though this requires a two-thirds vote.

Election of the initial 47 member states, which required three ballots, was conducted on March 9, 2006, with the initial session of the Human Rights Council conducted June 19, 2006. Lots were drawn after the election to determine the terms of those elected, with some serving for three years, others for two or for one, so as to stagger the expiration of the terms. Ensuing elections will be for three-year terms, with one-third of the Council elected each year, as is the case of other UN bodies, such as the ECONOMIC AND SOCIAL COUNCIL and the Security Council.

Annan's original proposal to give the new council the status of a main organ of the UN would have required a CHARTER amendment, which would have taken a protracted time to accomplish due to the requirement that sufficient member states ratify the AMENDMENT. The UNITED STATES, which had forcefully backed the original proposal, rejected the compromises and voted against forming the new council, because it felt the agreements had weakened the power of the new body. The U.S. government was particularly disappointed by the rejection of the at-large election process it had put forward, concluding that the finally accepted method would still allow states with weak human rights records to serve on the council. The United States, in protest, declined to be a candidate for membership on the original Human Rights Council.

The council is based in Geneva, where it meets more frequently that its predecessor, with no fewer than three annual sessions for a total of at least 10 weeks. It carries a broader mandate than its predecessor. It has the power (if one-third of the council agrees) to call additional SPECIAL SESSIONS at the request of any of its members. It is supposed to promote "effective coordination and the mainstreaming of human rights within the UNITED NATIONS SYSTEM," and it works closely with the OFFICE OF THE HIGH COMMISSIONER FOR HUMAN RIGHTS. The Human Rights Council is "responsible for promoting universal respect for the protection of all human rights and fundamental freedoms for all, without distinction of any kind," and is "guided by the principles of universality, impartiality, objectivity . . . with a view to enhancing the promotion and protection of all human rights, civil, political, economic, social and cultural rights, including the RIGHT TO DEVELOPMENT." The new council assumed the mandate of the Commission on Human Rights and continued its special procedures. Moreover, the new council serves as a forum for dialogue on all human rights, and seeks to advance international cooperation to enhance the abilities of states to implement human rights commitments, including promoting educational programs and providing advisory and technical assistance to states. It also "address[es] situations of violations of human rights," and conducts "universal periodic review" of all UN member states. At its second meeting in September 2006 the council

took up the task of framing a uniform procedure to be used in these reviews. The HRC submits an annual report to the General Assembly.

See also APPENDIX F (General Assembly Resolution 251); BUSH, GEORGE W.; CHINA; *IN LARGER FREEDOM*.

Further Reading: Annan, Kofi. Report of the Secretary-General: *In Larger Freedom: Towards Development, Security and Human Rights for All.* March 21, 2005, A/59/2005. *2005 World Summit Outcome.* A/RES/60/1. 24 October 20: <www.ohchr.org/english/bodies/hrcouncil1>.

— *K. J. Grieb*

Human Rights Day
Celebrated on December 10 annually, Human Rights Day marks the anniversary of the GENERAL ASSEMBLY's adoption of the UNIVERSAL DECLARATION OF HUMAN RIGHTS in 1948. It has been celebrated since 1950.

human trafficking
Human trafficking refers to the recruiting, transporting, enslaving, or receiving of people in order to exploit and abuse them. Such trafficking often uses threats, force, abduction, deception, and fraud to compel vulnerable people into situations clearly violating their fundamental HUMAN RIGHTS. Persons so exploited find themselves in abhorrent conditions of forced labor, prostitution, slavery, servitude, illegal international adoption, child soldiering, begging, and even coerced removal of organs. WOMEN and children are particularly affected by this vile practice. The U.S. State Department has estimated that between approximately 600,000 and 800,000 humans are trafficked over international boundaries every year; 80 percent are women and girls and 50 percent are minors. Victims usually are from poor areas of the world, often being displaced during internal civil wars (as in BOSNIA, CONGO, DARFUR, and KOSOVO). Refugees are also targets. Poorer women may be enticed into trafficking by fraudulent promises of marriage or legitimate work. Children may be sold by poor parents, or find themselves trafficked after being abandoned (as in AFRICA, should both parents die from AIDS). The collapse of the SOVIET UNION and the civil wars in the FORMER YUGOSLAVIA, creating porous borders among unstable new countries, exacerbated transnational trafficking, which became a profitable international criminal enterprise. Human rights critics point out that there are too few national or international penalties against the practice. As for sexual trafficking, the UN OFFICE ON DRUGS AND CRIME (UNODC, formerly called UN OFFICE FOR DRUG CONTROL AND CRIME PREVENTION) has found that too many governments, and some human rights organizations, simply judge women as guilty of prostitution and thus minimize the illicit role of traffickers.

In November 2000, the UN GENERAL ASSEMBLY adopted the CONVENTION against Transnational Organized Crime (the so-called Palermo Convention) and two Palermo PROTOCOLS: the Protocol to Prevent, Suppress and Punish Trafficking in Persons, Especially Women and Children, and the Protocol against the Smuggling of Migrants by Land, Sea and Air. The protocol dealing with trafficking falls under the JURISDICTION of the UN Office on Drugs and Crime (UNODC). It entered into force in December 2003 and by 2006 it had 117 signatories and 110 ratifications. The protocol requires participating states to prevent and combat human trafficking, protect and assist victims, and cooperate with the international community and other states to meet all the obligations of the protocol.

See also DECLARATION ON THE ELIMINATION OF VIOLENCE AGAINST WOMEN, INTERNATIONAL CONVENTION ON THE PROTECTION OF THE RIGHTS OF ALL MIGRANT WORKERS AND MEMBERS OF THEIR FAMILIES, INTERNATIONAL ORGANIZATION ON MIGRATION, UNITED NATIONS INTERREGIONAL CRIME AND JUSTICE RESEARCH INSTITUTE.

Further Reading: Protocol to Prevent, Suppress and Punish Trafficking in Persons Especially Women and Children, Web site: <www.ohchr.org/english/law/protocoltraffic.htm>. UN Office on Drugs and Crime Report on Trafficking in Human Beings, Web site: <www.unodc.org/unodc/en/trafficking/human_beings.html>. U.S. Department of State. *Trafficking in Persons Report,* Web site: <www.state.gov/g/tip/rls/tiprpt/2005/46606.htm>.

Hussein, Saddam (1937–2006)

Saddam Hussein was born in 1937 in Tikrit, IRAQ. He was educated at the Universities of Cairo and Baghdad and became a member of Iraq's Ba'ath Socialist Party in 1957. Following imprisonment in 1964, Hussein participated in General Bakr's 1968 revolution. Hussein succeeded Bakr to become chairman of Iraq's Revolution Command Council and, in 1979, president of Iraq. He proceeded to establish a harsh system of one-man rule, making use of an extended family from Tikrit and favored military personnel to maintain tight control on the country.

In 1980 Hussein initiated the IRAN-IRAQ WAR (1980–88) by ordering Iraqi forces into IRAN. It was during this conflict that Hussein used poison gas against Iranian troops as well as Kurds in northern Iraq. The muted UN response to this conflict stands in stark contrast to the international outcry that accompanied Hussein's 1990 invasion of Kuwait.

During the Iran-Iraq War, Saudi Arabia, Kuwait, and several Western states, desiring to preserve a balance of power in the Gulf region between Iraq and the larger Islamic revolutionary government of Iran, provided financial and military assistance to Hussein's regime. One factor that prompted Hussein to invade Kuwait in August 1990 was a Kuwaiti refusal to forgive $14 billion in loans extended to Iraq to help fight Iran. Hussein's invasion of Kuwait was met with an avalanche of UN SECURITY COUNCIL resolutions. In accordance with these resolutions, a U.S.-led coalition forcibly removed Iraqi forces from Kuwait.

Following a March 1991 cease-fire, the United Nations imposed crippling SANCTIONS on Iraq. American administrations, and their allies in the Security Council, maintained that these sanctions were necessary to prevent Hussein from replenishing his arsenal of WEAPONS OF MASS DESTRUCTION. As such, the UNITED STATES refused to allow the Security Council to revisit the RESOLUTION that imposed the sanctions, despite the hardship they caused to ordinary Iraqi citizens. Hussein used the unpopularity of the sanctions to maintain his grip on power in Iraq. Repeatedly he challenged the inspections regime imposed by the United Nations, and the no-fly zones maintained by the coalition partners both in the northern and southern areas of Iraq.

Hussein continued to repress Shi'a and Kurdish POPULATIONs, which he feared were planning to overthrow his government or gain full independence from Iraq. The president was then deposed by the United States during the invasion starting in March 2003. He immediately went into hiding, but on December 13, 2003, U.S. forces captured him. He was incarcerated, eventually turned over to the interim Iraqi government that had been established by the United States, and faced trial on a variety of charges of "crimes against humanity" and other offenses. On November 5, 2006, a court in Baghdad convicted him of charges related to the 1982 execution of 148 Shi'ites, whom he had suspected of trying to assassinate him. The former president was sentenced to death by hanging and was executed December 30, 2006.

See also ANNAN, KOFI; BUSH, GEORGE W.; GULF WAR; UNITED NATIONS IRAQ-KUWAIT OBSERVER COMMISSION; UNITED NATIONS MONITORING, VERIFICATION, AND INSPECTION COMMISSION; UNITED NATIONS SPECIAL COMMISSION ON IRAQ; UN SECURITY COUNCIL RESOLUTION 598; UN SECURITY COUNCIL RESOLUTION 678; UN SECURITY COUNCIL RESOLUTION 1441.

Further Reading: Makiya, Kanan. *Republic of Fear: The Politics of Modern Iraq.* Berkeley: University of California Press, 1998. Moore, John Allphin Jr., and Jerry Pubantz. *To Create a New World?: American Presidents and the United Nations.* New York: Peter Lang Publishers, 1999. ———. *The New United Nations: International Organization in the Twenty-first Century.* Upper Saddle River, N.J.: Prince Hall, 2006. Pérez de Cuéllar, Javier. *Pilgrimage for Peace: A Secretary General's Memoir.* New York: St. Martin's, 1997.

— *S. F. McMahon*

I

IAEA Safeguards *See* INTERNATIONAL ATOMIC ENERGY AGENCY.

Implementation Force (IFOR) *See* BOSNIA.

important question

Article 18 of the UN CHARTER has three paragraphs. The second of these refers to "important questions" which require a two-thirds vote of those "present and VOTING" in any session of the GENERAL ASSEMBLY (GA). The GA's Rules of Procedure define the words "members present and voting" as "members casting an affirmative or negative vote. Members which abstain from voting are considered as not voting." Thus, the two-thirds vote mandated for Important Questions could actually be less than a majority of all the members of the General Assembly.

The distinction in Article 18 between "important" and "other" questions is detailed in the second paragraph, where Important Questions are specified, and in the third paragraph, which allows the General Assembly, by majority vote, to determine what "other" questions must be decided by a two-thirds vote of those present and voting. According to the second paragraph, a two-thirds vote must be obtained on the following Important Questions: matters relating to international peace and security, electing NON-PERMANENT MEMBERS to the SECURITY COUNCIL (SC) and all members of the ECONOMIC AND SOCIAL COUNCIL (ECOSOC) and the TRUSTEESHIP COUNCIL, the ADMISSION OF MEMBERS to the United Nations, the SUSPENSION AND EXPULSION OF MEMBERS, issues regarding the operation of the TRUSTEESHIP SYSTEM, and budgetary questions. Also, the General Assembly Rules of Procedure require a two-thirds vote in order to reconsider proposals that have been adopted or rejected, and in order to add items to the supplementary list or the agenda of an EMERGENCY SPECIAL SESSION. By Rule 84 of the Rules of Procedure, amendments to proposals relating to Important Questions must obtain a two-thirds vote of those present and voting.

Over the years the General Assembly, using the provisions of the third paragraph of Article 18, has, by a simple majority vote, determined that "other" questions are, in fact, "important" and require a two-thirds vote of those present and voting. (This is a practice only recognized in the General Assembly; none of the GA main committees has such a rule; their decisions are made by a simple majority.) Numerous examples include: consideration of new trusteeship agreements, questions relating to racial conflict in South Africa, questions relating to South-West Africa, and issues of decolonization. Perhaps the most legendary use of this procedure dealt with the representation of CHINA in the United Nations. From 1961 on the UNITED STATES used the third paragraph of Article 18 to make any consideration of changing Chinese representation an Important Question, requiring a two-thirds vote. By assuring a simple majority vote to resolve that the issue of representation was an "important question," Washington was able to insist on an insurmountable two-thirds vote to seat the People's Republic of China and to remove the government of the Chinese Republic on Taiwan from the United Nations (and the Security Council). The procedure worked until 1971. On October 25 of that year the vote on the Important Question RESOLUTION regarding Chinese representation narrowly lost for the first time, 59 to 55, with 15 abstentions, and on the next vote, the General Assembly seated Beijing as the official Chinese representative and removed Taiwan.

Further Reading: Simma, Bruno, ed. *The Charter of the United Nations: A Commentary.* 2nd ed. New York: Oxford University Press, 2002.

In Larger Freedom

In Larger Freedom is the title of a pivotal report published by SECRETARY-GENERAL KOFI ANNAN in March 2005 that offered a blueprint for UN REFORM. This particular reform effort stemmed from the Secretary-General's *Renewing the United Nations* program of 1997, the 2004 HIGH-LEVEL PANEL ON THREATS, CHALLENGES AND CHANGE—originally charged with making proposals to strengthen the COLLECTIVE SECURITY system—and the expert group that produced a plan of action to achieve the MILLENNIUM DEVELOPMENT GOALS, which were adopted by the MILLENNIUM SUMMIT in 2000. The Secretary-General selected from the accumulated list of proposals those that he considered most important and most likely to be implemented. Annan acknowledged that he had included only those items that were "both vital and achievable in the coming months."

Annan had to walk a fine line between competing reform agendas. Western nations spearheaded by the UNITED STATES, who contribute the largest financial support to the UN BUDGET, demanded reforms to make the organization more efficient, in accord with a Western business model rather than with diplomatic practices. The developing nations, constituting a majority of UN MEMBERSHIP, were far more concerned with equal representation assuring all nations the opportunity to state their views and have an equal influence on decisions. They also wanted to guarantee equitable geographical representation in all bodies and in the UN staff. Consequently, they often advocated practices to achieve these ends which the United States and Western nations regarded as time consuming and inefficient. As a result, the topic of UN reform, although frequently on the agenda and regularly negotiated, meant different things at different times. Each side emphasized different priorities, saw the alternative proposals as either ineffective or discriminatory, and resisted consensus.

Annan couched his proposals in the context of updating the United Nations for facing the realities of the new century by way of a systematic review of the institutions created at the founding of the organization at the end of World War II. He accentuated implementing the already agreed upon Millennium Development Goals, which the Secretary-General described as "a shared vision of DEVELOPMENT." Achieving these goals required actions at both the international and the national levels and attention to the special needs of AFRICA. His report also suggested new means of increasing collective action to meet contemporary and novel security threats, such as TERRORISM, and to improve collective security actions to reduce conflict and organized crime. He recommended the creation of a PEACEBUILDING COMMISSION that would address problems in post-conflict regions, the establishment of a HUMAN RIGHTS COUNCIL to replace the COMMISSION ON HUMAN RIGHTS, and the strengthening of the OFFICE OF THE HIGH COMMISSIONER FOR HUMAN RIGHTS and the recently created INTERNATIONAL CRIMINAL COURT. His recommendations also included strengthening the ECONOMIC AND SOCIAL COUNCIL (ECOSOC) through annual high-level ministerial meetings to assure that ECOSOC remained the central organ focused on development cooperation. The recommendations encompassed streamlining GENERAL ASSEMBLY procedures and its committee STRUCTURE, and increasing the Assembly's interaction with INTERNATIONAL CIVIL SOCIETY. The plan included steps for a comprehensive review of budget and human resources rules, strengthening the resident coordinator system in countries receiving UN assistance, and new arrangements to enable faster and more effective response to humanitarian crises. Recommended CHARTER amendments included deleting the "enemy states" clauses, and abolishing the MILITARY STAFF COMMITTEE, though the precise wording of the AMENDMENTS was to be worked out later. The report also called for enlarging the SECURITY COUNCIL (SC) to 24 members according to one of two plans earlier put forward.

Even after his narrowing down to the principal options for SC reform, Annan's propositions faced further, likely debilitating, deliberation. The Security Council expansion proposals became bogged down in a debate regarding establishing new PERMANENT MEMBERS, and whether they would have the VETO. JAPAN, GERMANY, INDIA, and Brazil made early bids for membership, but other states not only opposed their inclusion but also recommended an alternative regional approach to adding new members. There were also broader questions about the wisdom of enlarging the Council altogether.

Finally, Annan proposed strengthening his office. Disagreement on this idea surfaced between Western states and DEVELOPING COUNTRIES. The latter group was reluctant to give the Secretary-General greater administrative and budgetary powers, fearing a concomitant weakening of the General Assembly's authority, where they had a working majority.

These deliberations ultimately led to the adoption of a series of specific measures in 2006—following the WORLD SUMMIT—as well as the abandonment of some of the recommendations. After extensive negotiations and modification of the proposals, the United Nations created both the Peacebuilding Commission and the Human Rights Council, although it proved impossible to reach agreement on Security Council reform.

Further Reading: Annan, Kofi. Report of the Secretary-General: *In Larger Freedom: Towards Development, Security and Human Rights for All.* March 21, 2005, A/59/2005. Moore, John Allphin, Jr., and Jerry Pubantz. *The New United Nations: International Organization in the Twenty-first Century.* Upper Saddle River, N.J.: Prentice Hall, 2006.

— *K. J. Grieb*

India

While still part of the British Empire, the Indian government—then known as the Raj—was a founding member of the United Nations in 1945. India's participation in the world body was notable from the beginning for its steady commitment to DISARMAMENT, economic DEVELOPMENT in the post-colonial regions of the world, the enhanced participation of small powers, and the resolution of COLD WAR disputes between Western and communist nations. To these ends, India was one of the founders of the NON-ALIGNED MOVEMENT (NAM). Under Jawaharlal Nehru, its first prime minister, India regularly criticized great power domination of UN deliberations, and was a strong advocate for enhancing the role of the majority in the GENERAL ASSEMBLY. To this end, Prime Minister Nehru conducted the critical negotiations with Soviet representatives in 1955 that broke the logjam that had blocked increased UN representation from the developing world.

In 1945 India was the world's second most populous state and fourth largest industrial power. Yet it was not considered one of the major powers that should have a permanent seat on the UN SECURITY COUNCIL. Indian leaders themselves were focused on the attainment of independence. Also under discussion was partition of the subcontinent into Hindu and Muslim states. When the British parliament passed the Indian Independence Act of July 18, 1947, the Republic of India assumed the seat of the Raj, and under the British partition plan the new state of PAKISTAN was established in the western Punjab region of the subcontinent and also in East Bengal. Pakistan was then admitted as a member of the United Nations as well. The partition led to one of the largest human migrations in history, with more than 14.5 million people crossing the borders between Muslim Pakistan and Hindu India in search of safety among their co-religionists. As many as a half a million people lost their lives and more than 12 million found themselves homeless as a result of the dislocations.

Each of the 565 princely states of the subcontinent was allowed to choose affiliation with either Pakistan or India. The most contentious of these province distributions occurred in the territories of KASHMIR and Jammu. In a heavily Muslim region, the local leader opted for inclusion in India. This decision was challenged by Pakistan. Local Muslim fighters and Pakistani troops invaded the territory, producing the first of four wars over Kashmir. The UN SECURITY COUNCIL established the United Nations Commission for India and Pakistan (UNCIP), which proposed a cease-fire, troop withdrawals, and a plebiscite to decide the controversy, and deployed the UNITED NATIONS MILITARY OBSERVER GROUP IN INDIA AND PAKISTAN (UNMOGIP), which in 2007 was still monitoring the original cease-fire.

During the summer of 1965 hostilities between India and Pakistan occurred again over the issue of Kashmir. The skirmish led to Security Council Resolution 211 calling for a cease-fire and a withdrawal of military forces to pre-conflict lines. Secretary-General U THANT established the UNITED NATIONS INDIA-PAKISTAN OBSERVATION MISSION (UNIPOM), which provided GOOD OFFICES for the arranged withdrawal. In 1972, the two countries signed an agreement defining a Line of Control in Kashmir. India then took the position that the mandate of UNMOGIP had lapsed; Pakistan insisted that it had not. The SECRETARY-GENERAL decided that only the Security Council could terminate the mandate, leaving the UN force in place.

Again in 1999, Pakistani forces invaded unoccupied mountain areas of Kashmir only to be pushed back by the Indian military. Perhaps a dozen Islamic militant groups were fighting Indian security forces in Kashmir by the turn of the century. India continued to charge that Pakistan was providing funding and training to the guerrilla groups, while Pakistan insisted that it only provided diplomatic and moral support to "freedom fighters."

Beyond Kashmir, India and Pakistan confronted each other during the latter's 1971 civil war that resulted in the loss of East Pakistan to an independence movement that created the state of Bangladesh. India sided with the revolutionaries and blocked any effort by Pakistani forces to reimpose control. Because of a Soviet VETO in the Security Council, a proposal for a cease-fire had to be carried to the General Assembly, where, under the UNITING FOR PEACE RESOLUTION, it passed overwhelmingly. India also appealed to UN SECRETARY-GENERAL U Thant to deal with the refugee crisis occasioned by the hostilities. U Thant was conflicted. His authority was limited to what member states on the Security Council would give consent. Yet, the Council did not act and the humanitarian crisis grew worse. The Secretary-General, once he had Pakistani agreement, acted on his own to create two relief operations: the UN Relief Operation in East Pakistan (UNEPRO) and the UN Relief Operation in Dacca (UNROD). He raised more than $1 billion for these efforts. Pakistan permanently lost its eastern provinces on December 16, 1971, when it surrendered to Bangladeshi and Indian forces, and a UN-decreed cease-fire went into effect.

The successive wars between Pakistan and India grew more ominous for international peace and security as each developed a nuclear weapons capability. In paradoxical fashion, India advocated global DISARMAMENT plans from the earliest days of the United Nations, but joined the club of nuclear nations in 1974, conducting underground tests that year and again in 1998. Despite its active participation in UN disarmament, such as in the CONFERENCE ON DISARMAMENT and the EIGHTEEN NATION DISARMAMENT COMMITTEE, it had not signed by 2007 either the NUCLEAR NON-PROLIFERATION TREATY or the COMPREHENSIVE TEST BAN TREATY. Indian governments rejected overtures for India's compliance with these agreements until Pakistan, which also became a nuclear power, agreed to be a signatory. Also, India has argued that these TREATIES are unequal agreements, imposing conditions on non-nuclear states that limit their sovereign right to develop nuclear WEAPONS while placing no requirements on the most powerful nuclear states to diminish their military stockpiles and to end the arms race.

India's military might, coupled with the country's impact on the world economy, and its prominence in UN-sponsored programs and missions led government leaders to seek in the 21st century a more significant role in UN decision-making bodies. Beginning with its participation in the PEACEKEEPING force stationed in Egypt following the 1956 SUEZ CRISIS, India contributed more than 55,000 troops to 35 UN operations over the next 50 years. In the new millennium India sought a permanent seat on the Security Council. Using the initiative of Secretary-General KOFI ANNAN to REFORM UN STRUCTURES in 2005, India joined with JAPAN, GERMANY, and Brazil in bids for MEMBERSHIP on the Council. The opposition of other states with claims to membership, the lack of support from the existing PERMANENT MEMBERS, and the desire of many countries to see the expansion of the Security Council by way of new regional representation, thwarted India's campaign of inclusion.

See also ANTARCTIC TREATY; APARTHEID; APPENDIX F (Uniting for Peace Resolution); ATOMS FOR PEACE PROPOSAL; BASEL CONVENTION ON THE CONTROL OF TRANSBOUNDARY MOVEMENTS OF HAZARDOUS WASTES AND THEIR DISPOSAL; CHINA; CONVENTION ON THE PROHIBITION OF THE USE, STOCKPILING, PRODUCTION AND TRANSFER OF ANTI-PERSONNEL MINES AND THEIR DESTRUCTION; DEPARTMENT OF DISARMAMENT AFFAIRS; DEPARTMENT OF PEACEKEEPING OPERATIONS; DESERTIFICATION; ENVIRONMENT; HAITI; *IN LARGER FREEDOM;* INQUIRY; INTERNATIONAL LABOUR ORGANIZATION; NUCLEAR-WEAPONS-FREE-ZONES; THANT, U; TREATY OF BANGKOK, UNIFIED TASK FORCE; UNITED NATIONS CHILDREN'S FUND; UNITED NATIONS CIVILIAN POLICE MISSION IN HAITI; UNITED NATIONS COMMISSION FOR INDONESIA; UNITED NATIONS CONFERENCE ON INTERNATIONAL ORGANIZATION; UNITED NATIONS MISSION IN ETHIOPIA AND ERITREA; WAR CRIMES TRIBUNALS; WEAPONS OF MASS DESTRUCTION; WORLD SUMMIT 2005.

Further Reading: Cohen, Stephen Philip. *India: Emerging Power.* Washington, D.C.: Brookings Institution Press, 2001. Ghose, Arundhati. "Negotiating the CTBT: India's Security Concerns and Nuclear Disarmament." *Journal of International Affairs* (Summer 1997). Singh, Lalita Prasad. *India and Afro-Asian Independence: Liberation Diplomacy in the United Nations.* New Delhi: National Book Organization, 1993.

indigenous peoples

The United Nations defines indigenous peoples as "those people having a historical continuity with pre-invasion and pre-colonial societies, [who] consider themselves distinct from other sectors of the societies now prevailing in those territories or parts of them." Indigenous peoples consider themselves "non-dominant sectors of society" and are usually determined "to preserve, develop and transmit to future generations, their ancestral territories, and their ethnic identity."

Indigenous peoples can be found in many areas of the world. As of 2001 they numbered about 300 million and lived in about 70 countries on five continents. Indigenous, or "aboriginal" peoples are considered descendants of those who lived in a region before new and different peoples arrived. The new arrivals typically became dominant by way of conquest or settlement. Indigenous peoples include the Indians of the Americas, the Inuit and Aleutians of the polar regions, the Saami in Scandinavia, the Aborigines and Torres Strait Islanders of Australia, and the Maori of New Zealand.

Between March 1997 and August 2001, 15 organizations of indigenous peoples gained CONSULTATIVE STATUS with the ECONOMIC AND SOCIAL COUNCIL (ECOSOC). Representatives of other indigenous peoples have come to participate in UN meetings, particularly in the UN Working Group on Indigenous populations, established in 1982, following the first international conferences of NON-GOVERNMENTAL ORGANIZATIONS on indigenous issues held in Geneva in 1977 and again in 1981. The Working Group meets for one week each year before the annual session in Geneva of the UN Sub-commission on Prevention of Discrimination and Protection of Minorities. The Working Group has two formal tasks: first, to review national developments regarding protection of HUMAN RIGHTS for indigenous peoples, and second, to develop international standards concerning the rights of indigenous peoples.

In 1990 the GENERAL ASSEMBLY (GA) proclaimed 1993 to be the International Year of the World's Indigenous People. And in 1993 the GA proclaimed the International Decade of the World's Indigenous People to be 1995–2004. The goal of the decade was to strengthen international cooperation in seeking solutions to the problems confronting indigenous populations. The Assembly declared a second international decade to begin on January 1, 2005, to be coordinated by the UNDER SECRETARY-GENERAL for Economic and Social Affairs.

In 1995, the COMMISSION ON HUMAN RIGHTS and the Economic and Social Council established an open-ended inter-sessional Working Group to develop a draft DECLARA-TION on the rights of indigenous peoples. The group was composed of representatives of member states, and NGOs and indigenous organizations that had gained consultative status. On July 29, 2006, the new UN HUMAN RIGHTS COUN-CIL, convening for the first time, recommended the working group's draft to the General Assembly for adoption. Also in 1995 the General Assembly established the UN Voluntary fund for the International Decade of the World's Indigenous People, and directed it to administer voluntary contributions during the decade and to assist indigenous communities and organizations to participate in the activities of the Working Group on the draft declaration. A successor fund was established to support the activities of the second international decade. Also, the General Assembly designated August 9 of each year as International Day of the World's Indigenous People for the duration of the first International Decade.

In 2001, the Commission on Human Rights appointed Rodolfo Stavenhagen (Mexico) as the SPECIAL RAPPORTEUR on the situation of the human rights and fundamental freedoms of indigenous people. Mr. Stavenhagen concentrated on three main areas of work: thematic research on issues that have an impact on the human rights situation and the fundamental freedoms of indigenous peoples, country visits, and communications with governments concerning allegations of violations of human rights. By 2007, the special rapporteur had submitted two reports to the General Assembly and had made specific recommendations to UN agencies and programs on steps that they could take to improve the lot of indigenous peoples.

Growing out of recommendations adopted at the 1993 WORLD CONFERENCE ON HUMAN RIGHTS in Vienna, the General Assembly urged the creation of a Permanent Forum on Indigenous Issues (UNPFII). The Permanent Forum convened its first meeting in May 2002. Holding annual 10-day sessions, the forum serves as an advisory body to the UN ECONOMIC AND SOCIAL COUNCIL. It is comprised of 16 independent experts, eight of whom are nominated by national governments and eight by regional indigenous organizations. The forum has its own SECRETARIAT housed in the UN DEPARTMENT OF ECONOMIC AND SOCIAL AFFAIRS.

See also AGENDA FOR DEVELOPMENT, AGENDA 21, APPENDIX G (CONVENTION ON THE RIGHTS OF THE CHILD), COMMISSION ON SOCIAL DEVELOPMENT, COMMITTEE OF 24, COMMITTEE SYSTEM OF THE GENERAL ASSEMBLY, GUATE-MALA, INTERNATIONAL CIVIL SOCIETY, LATIN AMERICA, RIO DECLARATION, THIRD COMMITTEE OF THE GENERAL ASSEM-BLY, WORLD SUMMIT ON SUSTAINABLE DEVELOPMENT.

Further Reading: Anaya, S. James. *Indigenous Peoples in International Law.* New York: Oxford University Press, 2000. New Zealand Ministry of Foreign Affairs. *United Nations* *Handbook.* Wellington, N.Z.: Ministry of Foreign Affairs and Trade, published annually. UNHCR Indigenous Peoples Web site: <www.ohchr.org/english/issues/indigenous/index.htm>. Permanent Forum on Indigenous Issues Web site: <www. un.org/esa/socdev/unpfii/index.html>.

Indonesia

The struggle between the Netherlands, which sought to reassert its control over the East Indies after JAPAN'S defeat in World War II, and Indonesian nationalists, who had declared a republic in 1945, was one of the first colonial disputes to elicit extensive United Nations involvement. Security Council Resolution 27 of August 1, 1947, called for a cease-fire in the armed conflict and urged the parties "to settle their disputes by ARBITRATION or other peaceful means." By Resolution 31 (August 21, 1947), the SECURITY COUNCIL created the Committee of GOOD OFFICES (the Committee of Three, composed of the UNITED STATES, Belgium, and Australia) to facilitate an agreement. The continued use of force by the Dutch, however, negated the Renville Agreement of January 1948 and signified that the Security Council could no longer persevere with its good offices approach. Instead, through Resolution 67 (January 28, 1949), the Security Council outlined a detailed recommendation for a settlement of the dispute and established the UNITED NATIONS COMMISSION FOR INDONESIA (UNCI). The Netherlands, under pressure from the United States, ultimately accepted the RESOLUTION and, on December 27, 1949, transferred SOVEREIGNTY to the Republic of Indonesia. Indonesia was admitted to the United Nations on September 29, 1950.

The subsequent conflict between the Netherlands and Indonesia over the status of West New Guinea (West Irian) was also resolved with UN assistance. Indonesia brought the issue to the United Nations in 1954, claiming that West New Guinea should have come under its JURISDICTION in 1950 as stipulated by the 1949 agreement that recognized Indonesian independence. The Netherlands contended that the Papuans of West New Guinea were not Indonesians and that they should be permitted to decide their own fate at some future date. After years of resistance to Indonesian claims that the territory should be freed from Dutch colonial rule, the Netherlands, under pressure from the United States, finally agreed to give up West New Guinea and to use the United Nations as a MECHANISM for the transfer. The August 1962 agreement—reached through the good offices of UN SECRETARY-GENERAL U THANT and the MEDIATION of Ellsworth Bunker—committed the Netherlands to transfer the administration of West New Guinea to a UNITED NATIONS TEMPORARY EXECUTIVE AUTHORITY (UNTEA) on October 1. In May of the following year, New Guinea was placed under Indonesian jurisdiction, subject to the right of the native Papuans to determine their own political fate by a plebiscite before the end of 1969. At the initiative of U Thant, but ultimately with the approval of the UN GENERAL ASSEMBLY, a UNITED NATIONS SECURITY FORCE (UNSF) was assembled to effect a cease-fire and to serve as the "police arm" of UNTEA in maintaining order during the transfer of authority. Comprised largely of 1,500 Pakistani troops, UNSF was a supplement to the Papuan police force in preserving law and order. UNTEA transferred full administrative control over West New Guinea (Irian Jaya) to Indonesia on May 1, 1963. In 1969, the government of Indonesia reported to the UN Secretary-General that consultative councils representative of the Papuan population had "expressed their wish to remain with Indonesia."

In January 1965, President Sukarno ordered Indonesia to leave the United Nations in protest against the election of Malaysia to a seat on the Security Council. Sukarno viewed Malaysia as a neocolonial creation of what he termed the "old established forces" of the West and, in 1963, he declared a policy of "confrontation" toward its Southeast Asian neighbor. While Indonesia is the only state to have announced its withdrawal from the United Nations, the Jakarta government reversed its position on September 19, 1966, and resumed full participation in UN activities.

In the 1990s, Indonesia served a term on the UN Security Council and joined the UN COMMISSION ON HUMAN RIGHTS. Indonesia was elected, as well, to chair the NON-ALIGNED MOVEMENT for a three-year term and, in September 1992, President Suharto addressed the UN General Assembly as a representative of the DEVELOPING COUNTRIES. Indonesia played a key role in getting the warring factions in CAMBODIA to agree to UN-sponsored elections in 1993 and contributed troops to UN PEACEKEEPING efforts in BOSNIA and Cambodia. Indonesia also was engaged in regional affairs, playing an active role in the Association of South East Asian Nations (ASEAN). President Suharto hosted the 1994 heads-of-state meeting of the Asia Pacific Economic Cooperation (APEC) forum and was instrumental in securing the agreement of APEC states (the Bogor DECLARATION) to create a tariff-free trading regime in the region by 2020 for developing countries and 2010 for developed countries. In UN-sponsored WORLD CONFERENCES Indonesia was a central participant defending the position of developing countries on economic and environmental issues. At the EARTH SUMMIT in 1992 Indonesia led the opposition to a CONVENTION on forests that would have limited these states' use of critical lumber resources.

Yet Indonesia's international reputation in the 1990s was marred by its continued and brutal occupation of East Timor, known as TIMOR-LESTE following its independence from Indonesia. The United Nations repeatedly denounced Indonesia's 1975 invasion of East Timor and demanded that Indonesia withdraw its forces from the eastern portion of the island. In March 1993, a UN Human Rights Commission resolution censured Indonesia for its poor HUMAN RIGHTS record in the territory. With the fall of the Suharto govern-

ment in 1998 and the new government's openness to possible independence for East Timor, the UN Security Council established the UNITED NATIONS MISSION IN EAST TIMOR (UNAMET) to oversee a popular consultation on the question of autonomy for the Timorese. The UNITED NATIONS TRANSITIONAL ADMINISTRATION IN EAST TIMOR (UNTAET) was formed to administer the territory during the transition to independence after the majority of East Timorese voters rejected autonomy within Indonesia. East Timor proclaimed its independence on May 31, 2002.

On December 26, 2004, Indonesia and surrounding countries were hit by a devastating tsunami. More than 125,000 people were killed in the Indonesian province of Aceh, and at least 650,000 were displaced. The country suffered massive agricultural destruction and environmental degradation. A "flash appeal" for funds was issued by the United Nations so that the UN HIGH COMMISSIONER FOR REFUGEES (UNHCR) could help more than 5 million affected people, sheltering more than 100,000 individuals within a month of the disaster. Other SPECIALIZED AGENCIES, departments, and UN programs intervened with aid under the general supervision of Jan Egeland, head of the OFFICE FOR THE COORDINATION OF HUMANITARIAN AFFAIRS. Among the UN bodies providing assistance were UN-HABITAT, UN CHILDREN'S FUND, UN OFFICE FOR PROJECT SERVICES, WORLD FOOD PROGRAMME, FOOD AND AGRICULTURE ORGANIZATION, and UN EDUCATIONAL, SCIENTIFIC AND CULTURAL ORGANIZATION. The last of these undertook the initial steps to build a tsunami early warning system in the Indian Ocean. Former U.S. president BILL CLINTON was appointed by the UN to lead a global fundraising effort to finance these projects. In excess of $6 billion was contributed by governments and private sources. GERMANY was the largest donor ($600 million), followed by the ASIAN DEVELOPMENT BANK and Japan.

The 2004 tsunami hastened the peace process between the Indonesian government and separatist movement in Aceh province, resulting in a 2005 cease-fire agreement. In the effort to attract foreign aid, the government also continued its national DEMOCRATIZATION program. It was rewarded for its efforts with election to the Security Council for 2007–08.

See also ANNAN, KOFI; MILLENNIUM SUMMIT; QAEDA, AL-; STATEMENT OF FOREST PRINCIPLES; UNITED NATIONS CONFERENCE ON ENVIRONMENT AND DEVELOPMENT; UNITED NATIONS OPERATION IN SOMALIA.

Further Reading: Hainsworth, Paul, and Stephen McCloske. *The East Timor Question: The Struggle for Independence from Indonesia.* London and New York: I.B. Tauris, 2000. Järvinen, Taina. *Human Rights and Post-Conflict Transitional Justice in East Timor: UPI Working Papers 47 (2004).* Helsinki: Finnish Institute of International Affairs, 2004. McMullen, Christopher J. *Mediation of the West New Guinea Dispute, 1962: A Case Study.* Washington, D.C.: Institute for the Study of Diplomacy, Edmund A. Walsh School of Foreign Service,

Georgetown University, 1981. Romano, Cesare P. R., André Nollkaemper, and Jann K. Kleffner, eds. *Internationalized Criminal Courts: Sierra Leone, East Timor, Kosovo, and Cambodia.* New York: Oxford University Press, 2004. Schwarz, Adam. *A Nation in Waiting: Indonesia's Search for Security.* 2d ed. Boulder, Colo.: Westview Press, 2000.

— *G. S. Silliman*

inquiry

One of the methods for the pacific settlement of disputes available to states under Article 33 of the UN CHARTER, inquiry is a fact-finding process conducted by reputable neutral observers meant to provide the basis for the resolution of a contentious issue between parties to a dispute. The Charter's reference to inquiry, along with negotiation, MEDIATION, and other traditional diplomatic means to resolve conflicts between states, was a continuation of 20th-century international practice beginning with the Hague CONVENTIONS of 1899 and 1907, and maintained by the LEAGUE OF NATIONS. The parties to a dispute might appoint or agree to a third-party appointment of a "commission of inquiry," which would investigate the factual matters underlying the beginnings of a conflict and then prepare a report for the disputants. The hope is that the elucidation of the objective circumstances will provide the basis for a negotiated settlement. In addition to the UN's authorization of this peaceful resolution method, the 1949 Geneva Conventions for the Protection of Victims of War, and their 1977 PROTOCOL endorsed the method, going further than the Charter by laying out specific procedures for its use.

While a century of diplomatic practice made inquiry an accepted principle of INTERNATIONAL LAW, the frequency of its use has been limited. By its nature it allows third-party involvement in a dispute with the likelihood that the neutral party will produce a report injurious to the interests of one of the disputants. It is also the case that most disputes arise not from a misunderstanding between states over factual matters but rather from a conflict of perceived national interests that inquiry cannot resolve. Most successfully used in 1904 to resolve a dispute between Russia and GREAT BRITAIN over a mistaken Russian attack on British fishing ships, inquiry was used on several occasions between 1945 and 2007. The first time was in January 1948, when the UN SECURITY COUNCIL appointed the United Nations Commission for INDIA and PAKISTAN (UNCIP) to conduct an inquiry and to provide mediation between the parties over their recent fighting in the disputed region of KASHMIR. The second time was in 1962 in the "*Red Crusader* Incident," when a panel of legal experts investigated an incident between British and Danish military ships. In 1973, the GENERAL ASSEMBLY established a Commission of Inquiry on the Reported Massacres in MOZAMBIQUE, consisting of five member states, to carry out an investigation of the reported atrocities by rebel groups

and to report its findings to the Assembly as soon as possible. In connection with a complaint by Seychelles, the SECURITY COUNCIL adopted, on December 15, 1981, Resolution 496 by which it decided to send a commission of inquiry composed of three members of the Council to investigate the origin, background, and financing of mercenary AGGRESSION against the Republic of Seychelles, as well as to assess and evaluate economic damages, and to report to the Council with recommendations. The method of inquiry was also part of the resolution of the IRAN-IRAQ WAR (1980–87). The two sides accepted a cease-fire demanded by the Security Council in part on the condition that the United Nations establish a fact-finding commission to determine who started the hostilities. The commission reported in 1993 that IRAQ was responsible for the commencement of the war.

Separate from its pacific settlement context, inquiry as a non-judicial process has found increased use in UN bodies as a means of bringing world public attention to HUMAN RIGHTS abuses, or to circumstances that could produce ethnic or religious conflict. Reversing a 1947 decision by the UN COMMISSION ON HUMAN RIGHTS (CHR) that "it had no power to take any action in regard to any complaints concerning human rights" by individuals against their own governments (Doctrine of Impotency), the ECONOMIC AND SOCIAL COUNCIL (ECOSOC) in 1967 directed the commission, as a matter of importance and urgency, to take up these allegations. After that both ECOSOC and CHR asserted the authority of UN bodies to protect individual rights.

In its 1979–80 session, the commission established special procedures, known as "MECHANISMS," to facilitate such investigations. These procedures led to the appointment of SPECIAL RAPPORTEURS to investigate and prepare reports for the commission. Through the appointment of special rapporteurs, an organ of the United Nations or a SPECIALIZED AGENCY seeks an inquiry into a specific global problem or area of concern. The rapporteur's report is normally extensive and consists of an explanation of the historical background, economic, social, political, and demographic information, assessment of the current situation, information received from relevant countries, reports of field or site visits, and, frequently, recommendations for UN action. The commission has appointed special rapporteurs to investigate thematic issues, such as torture, summary executions, violence against WOMEN, racial discrimination, and religious discrimination. In 2000 there were 15 special rapporteurs conducting inquiries into a broad range of topics and inspecting specific countries.

See also APPEAL TO THE SECURITY COUNCIL, CHAPTER VI, CONCILIATION, CONVENTION ON THE ELIMINATION OF ALL FORMS OF DISCRIMINATION AGAINST WOMEN, IRAN HOSTAGE CRISIS, RWANDA CRISIS, SECRETARY-GENERAL.

Further Reading: Shaw, Malcolm N. *International Law.* 3d ed. Cambridge: Cambridge University Press, 1994. Simma,

Bruno, ed. *The Charter of the United Nations. A Commentary.* 2nd ed. New York: Oxford University Press, 2002. United Nations. *Report of the Independent Inquiry into the Actions of the United Nations during the 1994 Genocide in Rwanda.* New York: United Nations, 1999.

Inter-Agency Committee on Sustainable Development (IACSD)

From 1993 to 2001 inter-agency coordination in the area of SUSTAINABLE DEVELOPMENT was undertaken through the Inter-Agency Committee on Sustainable Development (IACSD). The United Nations ADMINISTRATIVE COMMITTEE ON COORDINATION (ACC), renamed the UN System CHIEF EXECUTIVES BOARD FOR COORDINATION (CEB) in 2002, created the IACSD in October 1993 to advise it on ways that the UNITED NATIONS SYSTEM might coordinate efforts to carry out the decisions of the UNITED NATIONS CONFERENCE ON ENVIRONMENT AND DEVELOPMENT (UNCED), including AGENDA 21 and the Plan of Action for the sustainable development of small island developing states (SIDS). The Inter-Agency Committee met semi-annually and included among its members most of the important UN funds, PROGRAMMES, and SPECIALIZED AGENCIES working in the fields of ENVIRONMENT and DEVELOPMENT. Sessions of the IACD were also open to all CEB members at the level of senior officials, and, as observers, to related organizations such as the GLOBAL ENVIRONMENT FACILITY (GEF). The CEB Subcommittees on Water Resources and on Oceans and Coastal Areas report to the IACSD.

The SECRETARIAT was located at UN HEADQUARTERS in New York. It prepared analytical studies and reports for the COMMISSION ON SUSTAINABLE DEVELOPMENT (CSD), promoted joint programming among UN agencies, and fulfilled assessment and reporting functions for the Inter-Agency Committee. The IACSD monitored financing requirements associated with Agenda 21. It also issued directives to "task managers" from each of the represented organizations who then were expected to take responsibility for implementing specific aspects of the UNCED and CSD agendas. For example, the UNITED NATIONS EDUCATIONAL, SCIENTIFIC, AND CULTURAL ORGANIZATION (UNESCO) was responsible for trade and environment, the UNITED NATIONS DEVELOPMENT PROGRAMME (UNDP) for capacity building, and the FOOD AND AGRICULTURE ORGANIZATION (FAO) for land management, forestry, sustainable mountain development, and agriculture. The Inter-Agency Committee was chaired by an UNDER SECRETARY-GENERAL; in 2001 the chair was Nitin Desai from the UN Secretariat DEPARTMENT OF ECONOMIC AND SOCIAL AFFAIRS (DESA).

When the ACC was renamed the United Nations System Chief Executives Board for Coordination (CEB) in 2001 in order to better reflect the scope of its functions and composition, the newly reformed body decided that coordina-tion should be pursued through more informal and flexible MECHANISMS rather than formal subsidiary bodies. It abolished the IACSD. In its place the CEB took steps to establish or strengthen inter-agency collaborative arrangements in the key areas of freshwater, water and sanitation, energy, oceans and coastal areas, and consumption and production patterns. These initiatives included a mandate for "UN-Water" to serve as the inter-agency group to implement the MILLENNIUM DEVELOPMENT GOALS concerning freshwater and sanitation issues. CEB established "UN-Oceans" to coordinate UN efforts on ocean and coastal issues, in accordance with the WORLD SUMMIT FOR SOCIAL DEVELOPMENT's (WSSD) call for such a mechanism within the UN System. The board also set up "UN-Energy" to address the energy-related issues found in WSSD's Johannesburg Plan of Implementation.

Inter-Agency Network on Women and Gender Equality (IANWGE)

Although WOMEN have found a voice and recognition in the work of the United Nations, most female UN employees have served in gender-traditional and junior level positions. Studies of the bureaucracy, professional ranks, and SPECIALIZED AGENCY staffs demonstrated at the beginning of the 21st century that women were significantly underrepresented. In pursuit of gender parity, which the GENERAL ASSEMBLY set as a goal to be achieved by 2000, the SECRETARY-GENERAL reported that year the disappointing fact that women accounted for only 33.5 percent of the professional and higher-level staff of the UNITED NATIONS SYSTEM as a whole. The percentages were slightly better in the SECRETARIAT (40.2 percent as of July 2001). By the end of 2001, only one UN agency—the UN POPULATION FUND—had a majority of women (50.4 percent) on its staff. At the slow rate of growth in female employment, it was likely that parity would not be reached until 2012.

To address the imbalance and to improve working conditions for women in the United Nations, and to coordinate all UN activities on behalf of women around the world, an Inter-Agency Committee on Women and Gender Equality was established in 1996. Following administrative REFORMS of the CHIEF EXECUTIVES BOARD, formerly known as the Administrative Committee on Coordination, the Inter-Agency Committee became the Inter-Agency Network with a SECRETARIAT in the DEPARTMENT OF ECONOMIC AND SOCIAL AFFAIRS's Division for the Advancement of Women. The IANWGE convened its first annual session in February 2002. The network is chaired by the special adviser to the Secretary-General on gender issues. On August 12, 2004, Secretary-General KOFI ANNAN appointed Rachel N. Mayanja (Uganda) to the post. IANWGE consists of approximately 25 entities in the UN System, including the OFFICE OF INTERNAL OVERSIGHT SERVICES, the OFFICE OF LEGAL AFFAIRS, the

WORLD HEALTH ORGANIZATION, the WORLD INTELLECTUAL PROPERTY ORGANIZATION, the INTERNATIONAL ATOMIC ENERGY AGENCY, the JOINT UNITED NATIONS PROGRAMME ON HIV/AIDS, the INTERNATIONAL LABOUR ORGANIZATION, and the UNITED NATIONS CHILDREN'S FUND.

The network monitors and oversees the mainstreaming of a gender perspective in all agencies and bodies of the United Nations. In terms of UN policies and programs, IANWGE takes as its mandate the implementation of the Beijing Plan of Action approved by the FOURTH WORLD CONFERENCE ON WOMEN in 1995. The network was charged in 2002 with implementing a system-wide medium-term plan for the advancement of women for the period 2002–05 under the rubric of the Plan of Action. The plan identified twelve areas of critical concern: women and poverty, education, women and decision-making, women and armed conflict, health, violence against women, women and the economy, the girl-child, ENVIRONMENT, media, HUMAN RIGHTS, and institutional MECHANISMS for the advancement of women.

Further Reading: Web site of the Inter-Agency Network on Women and Gender Equality: <www.un.org/womenwatch/ianwge>.

Inter-American Development Bank (IDB) *See* REGIONAL DEVELOPMENT BANKS.

Intergovernmental Maritime Consultative Organization (IMCO) *See* INTERNATIONAL MARITIME ORGANIZATION.

Intergovernmental Panel on Climate Change (IPCC)

In November 1988 the UNITED NATIONS ENVIRONMENT PROGRAMME (UNEP) and the WORLD METEOROLOGICAL ORGANIZATION (WMO) jointly sponsored the creation of the Intergovernmental Panel on Climate Change, that by 2004 interconnected more than 2,500 scientists, policy makers, legal experts, and climate specialists in more than 60 nations. The two organizations hoped the IPCC would bring new attention to the growing phenomenon of CLIMATE CHANGE, and would produce momentum toward a new international CONVENTION in response to the problem. UNEP and WMO charged IPCC with assessing the scientific, technical, and socioeconomic information relevant to understanding the risks of human-induced climate change, its potential impact, and the options for adaptation and mitigation. Its reports were to be neutral with respect to policy, although objective in their analysis of the effects of policies currently employed.

The IPCC published its *First Assessment Report* in August 1990, noting the dangers implicit in climate change due to global warming. Its report provided the basis of discussion for the World Climate Conference convened by the WMO the following November. It also created the impetus for the establishment of the Intergovernmental Negotiating Committee (INC) that, in turn, made the commitment to the negotiation of a climate change TREATY by the time of the contemplated 1992 Earth Summit. Officially known as the UNITED NATIONS CONFERENCE ON ENVIRONMENT AND DEVELOPMENT (UNCED), the meeting in Rio provided the venue for signing the UNITED NATIONS FRAMEWORK CONVENTION ON CLIMATE CHANGE (UNFCCC).

Since 1992, the Intergovernmental Panel on Climate Change has continued its preparation of Assessment Reports—the second and third reports were released in 1995 and 2001. On April 6, 2007, IPCC issued its fourth report, which predicted widening droughts in the Middle East, Africa, the American Southwest, and Mexico. The report's authors estimated a rise of three to five degrees Fahrenheit over the next century if remedial steps were not taken immediately. Blaming a significant proportion of the rise in temperatures on human activity, the group suggested there would be other deleterious effects on the Earth's climate: instability in permafrost areas, rock avalanches in mountain regions, changes in ecosystems worldwide, enlargement of glacial lakes, poleward and upward shifts in the ranges of plant and animal life, earlier migration of fish in rivers, the earlier advent of spring in moderate climes, and the reduced lengths of growing seasons in hot climates. In recognition of its fourth report, the IPCC received the 2007 Nobel Peace Prize. The agency also issues special studies on aspects of climate change. In 2005 IPCC issued reports on safeguarding the ozone layer and the global climate system and on carbon dioxide capture and storage.

Of special importance, the IPCC develops methods for calculating greenhouse gas emissions through its National Greenhouse Gas Inventories Programme, and its Task Force on Scenarios for Climate Impact Assessment (TGCIA) facilitates cooperation among experts on modeling future climate change. The panel meets yearly in plenary session to approve work done by the organization's working groups, of which there are three. Special attention is given to geographical representation on all of the units of the IPCC. The three working groups conduct no independent research or data collection. They review public scientific data and research results. Working Group I assesses the scientific aspects of climate change. Working Group II focuses on the impact of climate change on socioeconomic and natural systems, and the possibilities for adaptation to the changed conditions. Working Group III analyzes options for mitigating climate change and limiting greenhouse gases. The IPCC SECRETARIAT is hosted at WMO headquarters in Geneva, and the organization's work is directed by the IPCC secretary and bureau. The WMO and UNEP provide much of the funding for the IPCC, although member states of both organizations also make contributions to the IPCC Trust Fund based on their SCALE OF ASSESSMENT set by the UN GENERAL ASSEMBLY.

IPCC reports have had a significant impact on international policy-making concerning climate change. Its *Second Assessment Report* in 1995 led to the 1997 KYOTO PROTOCOL of the UNFCCC that set specific greenhouse gas emission limits on individual countries, which they agreed to meet by 2002. Its third report in 2001 found "there [was] stronger evidence [that greenhouse gases produced by human activity] have contributed substantially to the observed warming over the last 50 years." Preliminary word of the IPCC's warning in the report that if emissions were not lowered significantly temperatures could climb 50 percent higher than predicted in its 1995 report put intense pressure on the representatives of 180 countries meeting at the UN Climate Change Summit in The Hague during November 2000. The IPCC has also worked with specific sectors of the world economy to find mitigation strategies. Its 1999 report on the effects of aviation on climate change was the first to be undertaken in partnership with airlines, air industries, and air transportation engineers, with the consequence that its recommendations reflected an implicit commitment by those groups to implement the mitigation proposals. Furthermore, the report was forwarded to the parties of the UNFCCC and the INTERNATIONAL CIVIL AVIATION ORGANIZATION (ICAO) for additional action by those bodies.

See also ENVIRONMENT.

Further Reading: Elliott, Lorraine. *The Global Politics of the Environment.* New York: New York University Press, 1998. Grubbs, Michael, Matthias Koch, Koy Thomson, Abby Manson, and Francis Sullivan. *The 'Earth Summit' Agreements: A Guide and Assessment.* London: Earthscan Publications Ltd., 1993. Imber, Mark F. *Environment, Security and UN Reform.* New York: St. Martin's, 1994. Young, Oran B. *International Governance. Protecting the Environment in a Stateless Society.* Ithaca, N.Y.: Cornell University Press, 1994. IPCC Web site: <www.ipcc.ch/>.

International Atomic Energy Agency (IAEA)

U.S. president DWIGHT EISENHOWER delivered his "ATOMS FOR PEACE" speech to the UN GENERAL ASSEMBLY in December 1953 and proposed that the nuclear powers gradually transfer a percentage of their fissionable materials to a new INTERNATIONAL ATOMIC ENERGY AGENCY, which would be under the authority of the United Nations. After nearly four years of diplomatic efforts, the required 18 nations had ratified the Statute of the IAEA, and it went into force on July 29, 1957. Because of the arms race at the time between the UNITED STATES and the Soviet Union, there was never a serious possibility that the superpowers would turn over part of their nuclear arsenals to the proposed agency. Instead, the only common ground that could be found was for a

body committed to cooperation in the use of nuclear science and technology for peaceful DEVELOPMENT purposes. It was also not to be a subsidiary organ of the United Nations, but rather an independent inter-governmental organization under UN aegis. By 2007, 143 states had joined the International Atomic Energy Agency. Best known for its "Safeguards" system, the IAEA was increasingly used as a monitor in international agreements to guarantee that states were not diverting nuclear materials from peaceful purposes to military WEAPONS.

The IAEA's Statute commits the agency "to accelerate and enlarge the contribution of atomic energy to peace, health and prosperity throughout the world." To that end the agency maintains programs on verification, nuclear safety, the uses of nuclear energy, and technological exchange. Its Safeguards system was developed to implement the verification provisions of the 1968 NON-PROLIFERATION TREATY (NPT). Since then NATION-STATES have employed the system to enforce the compliance terms of international TREATIES, including NUCLEAR-WEAPONS-FREE ZONE agreements in Africa, LATIN AMERICA, and the South Pacific. Following the 1991 GULF WAR, IAEA safeguard inspectors enforced nuclear provisions of the armistice agreement imposed on IRAQ. By 2007, more than 1,000 nuclear facilities were under IAEA Safeguards.

IAEA headquarters is in Vienna, Austria. It has additional offices in Toronto, New York, Trieste, Monaco, and Tokyo. The agency employs more than 2,300 people. Its General Conference and Board of Governors are the policy-making bodies of the IAEA. They approve the programs and budget, and appoint the DIRECTOR-GENERAL. The General Conference is the agency's plenary organ, consisting of all member states. It meets annually to debate the report of the Board of Governors and other agenda items presented by individual states. The board meets five times yearly, and its 35 members have reflected due regard for geographical representation. In 1999 the General Conference approved an expansion of the board to 43 members, which will occur when the approval process is completed. Among other duties, the board considers applications for MEMBERSHIP and nominates the director-general to the General Conference. The IAEA's regular budget reached $283.6 million in 2007, and it sought an additional $80 million in voluntary contributions during that same year.

The increasing budget for the organization in the first decade of the 21st century reflected the world community's heightened concern about WEAPONS OF MASS DESTRUCTION (WMD), and its particular interest in using IAEA structures to address potential WMD development in Iraq, IRAN, and North Korea. Ousted from Iraq in 1998, IAEA inspectors returned in 2002 at the behest of the UN SECURITY COUNCIL to verify whether SADDAM HUSSEIN's regime still had a nuclear program. In 2002, the Security Council passed RESOLUTION 1441, replacing the IAEA monitoring group with inspectors headed by HANS BLIX. His monitoring commission found no WMD.

By 2004, Iran and North Korea seemed poised to join the nuclear club. Two years earlier North Korean officials had admitted that the country was developing these weapon systems in secret. The government also barred IAEA inspectors in violation of its commitments under the agency's safeguards program. The IAEA referred the North Korean case to the Security Council in February 2003. As the product of six-party talks in Beijing, CHINA, North Korea agreed in February 2007 to halt its nuclear enrichment program in return for economic assistance and the normalization of relations with the United States. A high-level IAEA delegation visited North Korea in March to begin negotiations on returning the Korean facilities to the organization's inspection regime. While Iran signed the additional PROTOCOL to the NPT on November 26, 2003, giving the IAEA the right to make unannounced inspections and to access sensitive Iranian information concerning the country's nuclear program, the Iranian government claimed sovereign authority to continue its nuclear research program. It asserted that the enrichment of uranium then underway was purely for peaceful purposes. However, the United States and several European nations claimed Tehran was seeking a NUCLEAR WEAPONS capability. Negotiations between Iran and three European governments—GREAT BRITAIN, FRANCE, and GERMANY—were unable to persuade Tehran to halt uranium enrichment. As it had earlier with North Korea, the IAEA referred the Iranian case to the Security Council at the end of March 2006.

As a result of reviewing Iranian documentation, the IAEA discovered a Pakistani nuclear ring consisting of individuals, companies and at least seven governments that had exported Pakistani nuclear components and expertise to Iran and other countries. At the center of the clandestine export of nuclear know-how was Dr. A. Q. Khan, the "father" of PAKISTAN's nuclear bomb. The IAEA had been unaware of the nuclear network when the evidence was discovered. IAEA Director-General Mohamed ElBaradei acknowledged the failings of the organization in not knowing about the export network, nor about a secret Libyan nuclear program and the breadth of the Iranian effort. Despite these shortcomings, Mr. ElBaradei and the IAEA were awarded the Nobel Peace Prize in 2005 for their willingness to press for the end of nuclear enrichment by dangerous states in the world.

See also ACHESON-LILIENTHAL REPORT, ADMINISTRATIVE TRIBUNALS; APARTHEID; APPENDIX F (SECURITY COUNCIL RESOLUTIONS 1441, 1540, and 1718); BUSH, GEORGE W.; CHIEF EXECUTIVES BOARD FOR COORDINATION; COMPREHENSIVE NUCLEAR TEST BAN TREATY; DEPARTMENT FOR DISARMAMENT AFFAIRS; DISARMAMENT; EXPANDED PROGRAM OF TECHNICAL ASSISTANCE; INTER-AGENCY NETWORK ON WOMEN AND GENDER EQUALITY; TREATY OF BANGKOK; TREATY OF PELINDABA; TREATY OF TLATLELOCO; UNITED NATIONS INDUSTRIAL DEVELOPMENT ORGANIZATION.

Further Reading: Imber, Mark. *The USA, ILO, UNESCO, and IAEA: Politicization and Withdrawal in the Specialized Agencies.* London: Macmillan, 1989. Pruden, Caroline. *Conditional Partners: Eisenhower, the United Nations, and the Search for a Permanent Peace.* Baton Rouge: Louisiana State University Press, 1998. *United Nations Handbook 2000.* Wellington, N.Z.: New Zealand Ministry of External Affairs and Trade, 2000. IAEA Web site: <www.iaea.org/>.

International Bank of Reconstruction and Development (IBRD)   *See* WORLD BANK.

International Centre for Settlement of Investment Disputes   *See* WORLD BANK.

International Civil Aviation Day

In 1996, the GENERAL ASSEMBLY proclaimed December 7 as International Civil Aviation Day. It marks the anniversary of the adoption of the Chicago CONVENTION in 1944, which brought into being the INTERNATIONAL CIVIL AVIATION ORGANIZATION (ICAO).

International Civil Aviation Organization (ICAO)

The International Civil Aviation Organization became a SPECIALIZED AGENCY of the United Nations in October 1947. It originated three years earlier at the International Civil Aviation Conference hosted by the UNITED STATES in Chicago. Fifty-two nations signed the Chicago Convention on December 7, 1944, which served as the constitution of the new organization. With the receipt of the required 26th ratification the ICAO came into being on April 4, 1947. The CONVENTION dedicated the organization to providing safety in civilian air travel and cooperation among NATION-STATES to assure standard air transport principles and regulations. The ICAO headquarters was established in Montreal, Canada. As of September 2006, 189 nations belonged to the ICAO.

The organization is made up of an assembly, a council, and a SECRETARIAT. The assembly is the plenary body, made up of all members, which sets ICAO policies and approves the budget. It meets every three years, with its 36th session set for the fall of 2007. The council is the agency's executive body, has 33 members elected for three-year terms, and meets three times a year. Members are elected from three categories: states of chief importance in air transport, states that make the largest contribution to facilities for air travel, and states whose election will assure that all regions of the globe are represented. This last category is a reflection of an early decision to provide a universal organization dealing with air travel while also grouping states in regions where common air travel networks exist. The council has a number of committees that assist with policy making in areas of the organization's responsibilities. They are the Air Navigation Commission, the Air Transport Committee, the Legal Committee, the Committee on Unlawful Interference, and the Technical Cooperation Committee. The ICAO secretariat is headed by a SECRETARY-GENERAL. Dr. Taïeb Chérif served in this position in 2007. Senior secretariat personnel are selected based on technical expertise and regard for geographical representation. The secretariat in Montreal works closely with regional offices around the world. It also works with specialized agencies and NON-GOVERNMENTAL ORGANIZATIONS that can contribute to air safety such as the WORLD METEOROLOGICAL ORGANIZATION, the INTERNATIONAL TELECOMMUNICATION UNION, the INTERNATIONAL MARITIME ORGANIZATION, the International Air Transport Association, and the International Federation of Air Line Pilots' Associations.

The primary work of the International Civil Aviation Organization is standardization of air rules and practices. Once the organization adopts a standard, it is then put into practice by all member states. Areas of standardization include operation of aircraft, personnel licensing, air traffic services, navigation rules, aeronautical communications, search and rescue, accident investigation, airworthiness, and regulating transport of dangerous goods. ICAO is also involved in the development of satellite-based navigation systems, regional planning, the facilitation of passenger movement through national terminals of entry and egress, and the development of international air law. Additionally, ICAO convenes diplomatic conferences for the purpose of developing consensus on important areas of civil aviation. The organization held a conference in 2001 to adopt a Mobile Equipment Convention, in 2003 to consider ways to liberalize air transport as part of the development of globalization, and in 2007 on ways to use aviation to enhance economic DEVELOPMENT in Africa. Since the terrorist attacks on September 11, 2001, the ICAO has also emphasized security measures in air traffic management systems that would assure they could not be compromised. It maintains 10 aviation security training centers to promote regional cooperation in this area.

The ICAO works with individual countries to resolve aviation issues and to develop air transport capabilities. In 2003 it brought about an agreement between Greece and Turkey that would facilitate air traffic services in the previously contested route network over the Aegean Sea. This was an important settlement in preparation for the 2004 Olympic Games in Greece. Each year the ICAO dispatches more than 100 experts to oversee nearly 120 projects totaling approximately $54 million in expenditures.

The ICAO convened its first security conference in February 2002 with delegates from 144 countries and 22 international organizations attending the meeting in Montreal. Chaired by ICAO president Assad Kotaite, the conference urged a security audit for all member states in the wake of the September 11, 2001, terrorist attacks on New York City and Washington, D.C. The conference marked a shift in the organization's focus from safety issues to security both for airline passengers and people on the ground. ICAO estimated that the proposed audits would cost $17 million over three years. Initially the organization planned to seek voluntary donations to cover these costs but would include continuing audit expenses in its regular budget after the first three-year period.

See also EXPANDED PROGRAM OF TECHNICAL ASSISTANCE, INTERGOVERNMENTAL PANEL ON CLIMATE CHANGE, INTERNATIONAL CIVIL AVIATION DAY, IRAN-IRAQ WAR, JOINT INSPECTION UNIT.

Further Reading: *Yearbook of the United Nations. Special Edition, UN Fiftieth Anniversary, 1945–1995.* The Hague: Martinus Nijhoff Publishers, 1995. ICAO Web site: <www.icao.int>.

international civil society

In 1997 SECRETARY-GENERAL KOFI ANNAN defined international civil society as the "sphere in which social movements organize themselves around objectives, constituencies and thematic interests. These movements include specific groups such as WOMEN, youth and INDIGENOUS PEOPLE. Other actors . . . include local authorities, mass media, business and industry, professional associations, religious and cultural organizations and the intellectual research communities." During his tenure, Annan encouraged greater participation of these groups in UN activities, believing the UN's achievement of thematic goals such as DEMOCRATIZATION, HUMAN RIGHTS protection, and SUSTAINABLE DEVELOPMENT depended on non-state actors playing an escalating role in UN decision-making processes.

In 1999 Secretary-General Annan launched an initiative to bring private enterprises into a special relationship with the United Nations through the GLOBAL COMPACT. Corporations could commit to 10 principles established in important UN CONVENTIONS, and in so doing be given recognition and involvement in the work of the world body. He established a special bureau in his office for this liaison relationship, and a 17-member advisory board. Six sponsoring organizations supported the work of the new office: the UNITED NATIONS ENVIRONMENT PROGRAMME, the UNITED NATIONS DEVELOPMENT PROGRAMME, the INTERNATIONAL LABOUR ORGANIZATION, the UN OFFICE ON DRUGS AND CRIME, the UNITED NATIONS INDUSTRIAL DEVELOPMENT ORGANIZATION, and the UNITED NATIONS HIGH COMMISSIONER FOR HUMAN RIGHTS. The Global Compact set as its overall goals the promotion of international corporate citizenship and social responsibility, the establishment of corporate "good practices," and the development of the United Nations, the "world's only truly global political forum, as authoritative convener and facilitator" of international civil societal organizations.

Secretary-General Annan's "stakeholder" strategy engaged three broad categories of non-state participants: NON-GOVERNMENTAL ORGANIZATIONS (NGOs), civil society members (including private individuals and sub-national organizations), and the international business community. Together these three components of international civil society grew dramatically in number and influence in the post–COLD WAR era, largely as a product of GLOBALIZATION and new communications technologies like the Internet. Also a new sense of world citizenship and transnational globalism contributed to the growth of strong advocacy networks for addressing thematic issues. Annan hoped to harness these networks in support of UN initiatives.

Article 71 of the UN CHARTER urges the ECONOMIC AND SOCIAL COUNCIL (ECOSOC) to grant "CONSULTATIVE STATUS" to non-governmental organizations that are involved with issues addressed by the United Nations. In the late 1980s and 1990s NGO participation in the United Nations grew quickly. The number of non-governmental organizations granted consultative status by ECOSOC was 41 in 1948. This number only rose to 377 by 1968. However, NGO association with ECOSOC reached 1,200 in 1997, and 2,700 in mid 2006. In 1996 ECOSOC passed RESOLUTION 31, giving NGOs expanded access to the Council. Those organizations granted "General" consultative status were allowed observers at ECOSOC meetings and permitted to submit written statements to both the Council and subsidiary bodies. They could also address the Council on subjects of interest. As a result, these organizations regularly circulated materials to member-state missions, providing an opportunity for enhanced interest group advocacy.

The ECOSOC process was replicated in other bodies of the UN SYSTEM. Annan's REFORM proposals encouraged NGO participation in the work of the GENERAL ASSEMBLY. Civil society organizations were also included in UN WORLD CONFERENCES, on agencies such as the JOINT UNITED NATIONS PROGRAMME ON HIV/AIDS (UNAIDS), and in SPECIAL SESSIONS OF THE GENERAL ASSEMBLY. A total of 47,000 people attended the EARTH SUMMIT in Rio de Janeiro; 50,000 attended the FOURTH WORLD CONFERENCE ON WOMEN in Beijing; 30,000 were accredited to the 1996 Istanbul Second World Conference on Human Settlements (HABITAT II), and 3,744 NGOs, along with 17,000 individuals, were accredited to the 2001 WORLD CONFERENCE TO COMBAT RACISM in Durban, South Africa.

Expanding international civil society's role in UN bodies and deliberative processes is not universally lauded, nor is it seen in some quarters as particularly democratic. Critics, including member-state delegations at the United Nations, have pointed out that NGO representatives are unelected and often do not reflect majority opinion either internationally or in the countries of their origin. They argue that only representatives of sovereign states may make that claim. They also contend that civil society organizations often do not use the accepted channels for influencing global policy and are therefore disruptive in the effort to address important international issues. Particular criticism was directed by many governments at civil society's involvement in the 1999 street protests directed at the WORLD TRADE ORGANIZATION (WTO) ministerial meeting in Seattle, Washington, and subsequent WTO conferences that led to many arrests and several deaths.

In February 2003, the Secretary-General appointed a panel of eminent persons, headed by Fernando Henrique Cardoso, the former president of Brazil, to look at UN-international civil society relations and to make recommendations on how they might be improved. The panel issued the CARDOSO REPORT in June 2004. The report encouraged the involvement of a wide range of civil society actors in UN affairs. Panel members called for a "paradigm shift" in the work of the UN. They urged the United Nations to become an "outward-looking organization," serving as the "convener" of multiple constituencies. The panel asserted that the UN needed to go beyond its intergovernmental nature and become an actor itself in international civil society.

See also APPENDIX F; COMMITTEE ON NON-GOVERNMENTAL ORGANIZATIONS; DEPARTMENT OF ECONOMIC AND SOCIAL AFFAIRS; FRÉCHETTE, LOUISE; *IN LARGER FREEDOM*; THEMATIC DIPLOMACY.

Further Reading: Alger, Chadwick. "The Emerging Roles of NGOs in the UN System: From Article 71 to a People's Millennium Assembly." *Global Governance* 8, no. 1 (January–March 2002): 93–117. Anheier, Helmut K., Mary H. Kaldor, and Marlies Glasius, eds. *Global Civil Society: 2005/6*. Oxford: Oxford University Press, 2005. Edwards, Michael. *Civil Society*. Cambridge: Polity Press, 2004. Kaldor, Mary. *Global Civil Society: An Answer to War*. Cambridge: Polity Press, 2003. Malena, Carmen. *Strategic Partnership: Challenges and Best Practices in the Management and Governance of Multi-Stakeholder Partnerships Involving UN and Civil Society Actors*. Background Paper for the Multi-Stakeholder Workshop on Partnerships and UN–Civil Society Relations, February 2004. Panel of Eminent Persons on United Nations–Civil Society Relations. Report: *We the Peoples: Civil Society, the United Nations and Global Governance*. June 21, 2004, A/58/817. "Partners with the United Nations" Web site: http://www.un.org/partners/.

International Civilian Mission in Haiti (MICIVIH)

Initiated February 1993, the International Civilian Mission in Haiti was the first joint mission between the United Nations and a REGIONAL ORGANIZATION, the ORGANIZATION OF AMERICAN STATES (OAS). MICIVIH's director, an OAS representative, and its deputy director from the UN were jointly appointed by the two organizations, and an equal number of staff from each organization was assigned to its work. In the wake of the military seizure of power in September 1991, MICIVIH's mandate was to verify Haitian compliance with the human rights CONVENTIONS to which the country was a party. At its peak in 1995 the operation had more than 193 HUMAN RIGHTS monitors (89 OAS, 104 UN) in HAITI, including 26 UNITED NATIONS VOLUNTEERS, posted in 13 offices throughout the country.

The 1991 overthrow of Haiti's president, Jean-Bertrand Aristide, challenged the OAS commitment to the maintenance of democracy in the Western Hemisphere asserted just three months earlier in the Santiago Commitment to Democracy and the Renewal of the Inter-American System. The Santiago Commitment required the OAS Permanent Council to respond to "sudden or irregular interruptions of the democratic process." The organization already had been involved in assuring the fair election process that had brought Aristide to power in 1990. Following the coup, the Organization of American States sent several high-level delegations to Port-au-Prince to pressure the de facto leader of Haiti, Lieutenant-General Raoul Cédras, to accept an OAS presence on the island. In July 1992 OAS secretary-general Joán Baena Soares extended an invitation to UN SECRETARY-GENERAL BOUTROS BOUTROS-GHALI to send a representative as part of a joint delegation, an invitation Boutros-Ghali accepted. In January 1993 ousted president Aristide asked first the OAS and then the United Nations to expand the international presence in Haiti. The GENERAL ASSEMBLY responded with a RESOLUTION directing the UN Secretary-General to work out the modalities of a joint UN/OAS Mission.

MICIVIH's assignment was to verify that the regime was honoring Haiti's commitments under the INTERNATIONAL COVENANT ON CIVIL AND POLITICAL RIGHTS and the American Convention on Human Rights. It worked in tandem with the separately deployed UNITED NATIONS CIVILIAN POLICE MISSION IN HAITI (MIPONUH), which sought to professionalize the Haitian National Police as a neutral security force in the country, and provided security for MICIVIH's personnel. MICIVIH's duties included assisting the judicial system in its administration of justice, receiving complaints from Haitian citizens and groups about violations of human rights, conducting unannounced inspections of any site in Haiti (mission observers regularly used this power to inspect Haitian prisons), and making recommendations to the Haitian government concerning ways to ameliorate human rights abuses.

Following the restoration of the Aristide government in October 1994, MICIVIH added to its responsibilities democratic institution-building and civic education. It held workshops and seminars for local residents in preparation for parliamentary and local elections. At the time of elections OAS representatives served as election monitors and UN personnel provided technical assistance in staging the elections. With the restoration of civilian domestic government MICIVIH

presence was reduced and finally withdrawn in early 2000, when it and MIPONUH were both replaced with the International Civilian Support Mission in Haiti (MICAH). The latter was not a usual SECURITY COUNCIL mandated PEACEKEEPING operation, but a special mission, without any military or police component, created by consensus vote of the GENERAL ASSEMBLY to oversee upcoming parliamentary elections.

Further Reading: MICIVIH Web site: <www.un.org/rights/micivih/first.htm>.

International Commission of Inquiry *See* RWANDA CRISIS.

International Conference on Population and Development (ICPD)

The International Conference on Population and Development convened in Cairo, September 5–13, 1994. Chaired by Dr. Safis Nadik, executive director of the UNITED NATIONS POPULATION FUND (UNFPA), the conference attracted 179 government participants, and 4,200 representatives of 1,500 NON-GOVERNMENTAL ORGANIZATIONS (NGOs). The WORLD CONFERENCE was the fifth global meeting on population, with the previous conferences having been held in Rome (1954), Belgrade (1965), Bucharest (1974), and Mexico City (1984). The conference sought to demonstrate the reenforcing links between population policies and DEVELOPMENT. It endorsed the rights of all people to reproductive freedom, and it encouraged policies that would slow population growth, including the empowerment of WOMEN, expanded educational opportunities, gender equality, and the reduction of poverty.

The conference adopted a program of action to guide international population efforts for the next 20 years. It called for universal availability of family planning by 2015—calling it a basic HUMAN RIGHT—and encouraged adolescent access to reproductive and family planning information. ICPD called upon individual countries and the international community to commit up to $21 billion by 2015 to population projects and services. UNFPA was decreed the lead agency for the implementation of the ICPD recommendations and an Inter-Agency Task Force was established to coordinate efforts throughout the UNITED NATIONS SYSTEM. The agency became part of the UN's ADMINISTRATIVE COMMITTEE ON COORDINATION in 1996.

The Cairo meeting, while reasserting many of the consensus recommendations of previous conferences, found itself embroiled in controversy over the issues of abortion and reproductive rights. Nations with sizable Roman Catholic populations, Right to Life NGOs, and the Vatican opposed any LANGUAGE in the final conference statement that might imply endorsement of abortion. Compromise language was achieved that urged governments "to deal with the health impact of unsafe abortion as a major public health concern and to reduce the recourse to abortion through expanded and improved family planning services." It also declared that "in no case should abortion be promoted as a method of family planning." Islamic nations sought to limit conference recommendations that might interfere with gender relationships and laws distinctive to certain cultures and nations. The Programme of Action sought a middle ground by affirming "the right of men and women to be informed and to have access to safe, effective, affordable and acceptable methods of family planning of their choice, as well as other methods of their choice for the regulation of fertility *which are not against the law.*" [Italics added.]

As follow-up to the Cairo Conference, the Intergovernmental Commission on Population was renamed in 1995 the UN Commission on Population and Development, and given responsibility for monitoring progress on different aspects of the Programme of Action. It approached its work in much the same way that its parallel body, the ECONOMIC AND SOCIAL COUNCIL's COMMISSION FOR SOCIAL DEVELOPMENT (CSocD) approached review of the outcomes from the WORLD SUMMIT FOR SOCIAL DEVELOPMENT (WSSD). That is, it established a topical yearly agenda and focused its assessment on one set of recommendations at a time. In 1999 a full review of progress was released as a report (ICPD+5). An international forum organized by UNFPA was held in The Hague the same year, leading to a SPECIAL SESSION OF THE UN GENERAL ASSEMBLY, June 30 to July 2, 1999, that considered ICPD+5 and made some specific recommendations for future action. The Assembly set benchmarks for measuring progress through 2015. The session adopted recommendations that the 1990 illiteracy rate for women and girls should be halved by 2005, the primary school enrollment ratio for all children should be 90 percent by 2010, 60 percent of all family planning facilities should offer comprehensive services by 2005 (80 percent by 2010, and 100 percent by 2015), and the gap between the proportion of individuals using contraceptives and the proportion expressing a desire to space or limit their families should be reduced gradually to zero percent by 2015. On the matter of HIV/AIDS the Special Session called for 90 percent of men and women between the ages of 15 and 24 to have access to preventive methods by 2005. Many of these recommendations became part of the MILLENNIUM DEVELOPMENT GOALS established by the United Nations in 2000.

See also DEPARTMENT OF ECONOMIC AND SOCIAL AFFAIRS.

ICPD meets in Cairo, 1994 (UN/DPI PHOTO)

Further Reading: Johnson, Stanley. *The Politics of Population: The International Conference on Population and Development, Cairo 1994.* London: Earthscan Publications, 1995. Schechter, Michael G. *United Nations-Sponsored World Conferences. Focus on Impact and Follow-up.* Tokyo: United Nations University Press, 2001. Taub, Nadine. *International Conference on Population and Development.* Washington, D.C.: American Society of International Law, 1994. United Nations Department of Public Information. *UN Briefing Papers: The World Conferences, Developing Priorities for the 21st Century.* New York: United Nations Department of Public Information, 1997. United Nations Population Fund. *Investing in People: National Progress in Implementing the ICPD Programme of Action, 1994–2004.* New York: UNFPA, 2004. ICPD Web site: <www.unfpa.org/icpd/index.htm>.

International Convention on the Protection of the Rights of All Migrant Workers and Members of Their Families

The UN GENERAL ASSEMBLY adopted the International Convention on the Protection of the Rights of All Migrant Workers and Members of Their Families on December 18, 1990. The CONVENTION entered into force on July 1, 2003, when sufficient states (20) had acceded to or signed the agreement. By March 1, 2007, 35 nations were parties to the TREATY. Meant to protect the HUMAN RIGHTS, working and living conditions, and access to social services that are often denied to migrant workers, the international convention was the first major extension of international human rights law in the new millennium.

Annually there are 175 million international migrant workers—approximately 2 percent of the world's POPULATION. The convention defines a migrant worker as "a person who is to be engaged, is engaged or has been engaged in a remunerative activity in a State of which he or she is not a national." Asserting the fundamental principle of non-discrimination, the convention protects migrants' right to life, liberty, free expression, urgent medical care, trade unions, and other associations. It also requires parties to the agreement to give the children of migrant workers the right to their name, nationality, and education. It also prohibits slavery, torture, or mistreatment. Article 31 requires states to ensure respect for the cultural identity of migrant workers and to allow them to maintain their cultural links to their state of origin. Article 32 gives migrant workers the right to transfer their earnings, savings, and personal property to their home country or elsewhere. The convention covers migrant workers' rights before departure from their home countries, in transit, and in the country of employment, and it establishes obligations for countries of origin, transit, and final working place.

One of the innovative aspects of the convention is that it not only covers the rights of individual migrant workers, but also establishes a framework for the orderly and safe transit of these workers and their families. Article 66 restricts the recruitment of workers for employment in another state to public services, state bodies, and authorized private agencies. Article 67 calls upon states to cooperate in the orderly return of migrants to their home countries. Article 68 invites states to collaborate in the prevention of illegal or secret trafficking and employment of migrants.

The United Nations first expressed concern about the lives of migrant workers in 1972 when the ECONOMIC AND SOCIAL COUNCIL and the General Assembly condemned conditions akin to slavery and forced labor in the misuse of African laborers in some European countries. In 1976, the Sub-Commission on Prevention of Discrimination and Protection of Minorities adopted a report by a SPECIAL RAPPORTEUR on clandestine trafficking in migrant workers that recommended the drafting of a convention. This proposal was endorsed by the WORLD CONFERENCE TO COMBAT RACISM AND RACIAL DISCRIMINATION in Geneva in 1978. The working group to draft an international agreement was established in 1980. Following UN adoption of the draft convention in 1990, a steering committee was established to encourage governments to sign the accord.

The terms and conditions of the convention are implemented by a Committee on the Protection of All Migrant Workers and the Members of Their Families (CMW), which consists of 10 experts elected by the parties to the convention. This number will rise to 14 when state ratifications of the convention reach 41. States must submit regular reports every five years to the committee on the nation's fulfillment of the provisions of the convention. Individuals may also submit complaints that their rights under the convention have been violated by one of the parties. The committee held its first session in March 2004. It meets annually in Geneva.

See also APPENDIX F, APPENDIX G, INTERNATIONAL MIGRANTS DAY.

Further Reading: Web site for the Convention: <www.ohchr.org/english/law/cmw.htm>.

International Court of Justice (ICJ)

Established in 1945 in the CHARTER OF THE UNITED NATIONS (Chapter XIV) as the successor to the PERMANENT COURT OF INTERNATIONAL JUSTICE (PCIJ), the ICJ is the UN's principal judicial organ. While the Court functions as the UN's legal arm, it is an independent institution. Its governing document—the STATUTE OF THE INTERNATIONAL COURT OF JUSTICE—accentuates that independence. The Statute is an integral part of, and usually appended to, any published copy of the UN Charter and itself is based on the 1922 Statute of the Permanent Court of International Justice. The Statute details the organization, procedures, and JURISDICTION of the Court. The ICJ, like the PCIJ, is often called the "World Court," which draws attention to its ancestral connection to the earlier institution.

The outbreak of general European war in 1939 damaged the reputation not only of the LEAGUE OF NATIONS but also the Permanent Court of International Justice, which met for the last time on December 4, 1939. In 1942 U.S. secretary of state CORDELL HULL and the foreign minister of the United Kingdom, ANTHONY EDEN, declared their support for a postwar reestablishment of an international court. In early 1943 the United Kingdom invited a number of experts to London to discuss the subject. Forming the so-called Inter-Allied Committee, under the chairmanship of Sir William Malkin, the group held 19 meetings and published a report on February 10, 1944. Among other recommendations, the committee suggested that the statute of any new court be based on that of the PCIJ. Later that year, at the DUMBARTON OAKS CONFERENCE in the U.S. capital, the four attending powers agreed on including an international court of justice into the emerging STRUCTURE OF THE UNITED NATIONS. In April 1945, a meeting of jurists from 44 nations convened in Washington, D.C. Chaired by G. H. Hackworth of the UNITED STATES, the committee composed a draft statute for the new court, which was then submitted to the UN's organizing conference in San Francisco in the spring of 1945. At this meeting the delegates determined on creating a new court, with its own statute, to become the principal judicial organ of the United Nations. In order to retain a sensible continuity with evolving INTERNATIONAL LAW, the authors of the UN Charter made clear in Article 92 that the ICJ Statute was based on that of the PCIJ. The old Court convened in October 1945 in order to dissolve itself and transfer its archives to the new Court. The sixth and last president of the Permanent Court of International Justice, Judge J. Gustavo Guerrero, presided over this closing session and then became the first elected president of the new International Court of Justice.

The ICJ is the only PRINCIPAL ORGAN OF THE UNITED NATIONS not based in New York. The seat of the Court, like that of the PCIJ, is at the Peace Palace (a gift of American entrepreneur Andrew Carnegie) in The Hague, the Netherlands. It may hold sessions elsewhere if it so determines, but as of 2008 it had not. Its first session took place on April 18, 1946. Since then the ICJ has been considered in continuous session. As an autonomous body it determines its own rules of procedure, elects its own president and vice president, and appoints a registrar (with the equivalent rank of an assistant secretary-general of the United Nations) and other registry staff and officers. The registry maintains all records of the Court, makes available its publications, communicates with outside organizations, acts as a press office, and keeps a Web site. Appointees to the registry must be proficient in both French and English, the official LANGUAGES of the Court.

All UN members are parties to the ICJ's Statute. Additionally, a non-member may become a party to the Statute on conditions recommended by the SECURITY COUNCIL (SC) and approved by the GENERAL ASSEMBLY (GA). There are 15 judges on the Court, elected by the General Assembly and the Security Council for nine-year terms. The procedure of nominating and electing candidates for judgeships on the court is complex and is detailed in Article 4 of the Statute. All NATION-STATES party to the ICJ Statute are allowed to put forward candidates, although the nominations are made not by a government but by a group of four members from the PERMANENT COURT OF ARBITRATION who are from the nominating state. If a country is not represented on the Permanent Court of Arbitration it may still make a nomination through a similar national group of legal experts that would clearly qualify to serve on the ARBITRATION tribunal. Each group can propose up to four candidates, not more than two of its own nationality. The names are then forwarded to the UN SECRETARY-GENERAL who submits the names to the General Assembly and the Security Council for vote. For this election the PERMANENT MEMBERS OF THE SECURITY COUNCIL retain no right of VETO; the required majority vote for a judge in that body is eight. Both the General Assembly and the Security Council vote simultaneously but separately. To be elected, a candidate must obtain an absolute majority in both chambers (in 2008 that amounted to 97 votes in the GA, eight in the SC). As a consequence, there often must be several votes before an election is decided. The elections are almost always held—in three-year cycles—at the HEADQUARTERS in New York during the annual fall session of the General Assembly. The term of office begins on February 6 of the next year. Judges may be reelected, but no two from the same country may serve simultaneously. (Should two candidates of the same nationality be elected at the same time, the elder of the two receives the appointment.) In accord with Article 13 of the Statute, elections for the first Court, meeting in 1946, resulted in three groups of five judges each being selected for first a three-year, then a six-year, and finally the normal nine-year term, initiating staggered terms to be filled every three years hence. Judges of the Court may not, according to Article 16 of the Statute, engage in any other administrative or political position nor in any other occupation of a professional nature. Members of the Court do not represent their governments; they are independent. Still, they should have qualifications for appointment to the highest judicial offices in their respective countries or be recognized as experts in international law. No judge may be dismissed except by the unanimous decision of the other judges. The United Nations has persistently tried to apportion the judgeships on an equitable geographical basis. In 2007 the allocation of seats on the Court was three Africans, two Latin Americans, three Asians, one east European, and six from Western Europe and Other States. There is no entitlement to MEMBERSHIP, but normally, with the exception of CHINA, the Court has always had judges from the permanent members of the Security Council.

International Court of Justice (UNITED NATIONS PHOTO/170055)

The Court considers itself an organ of and contributor to international law. It decides disputes consistent with international law, the sources of which, according to Article 38 of the Statute, are international CONVENTIONS, international custom, general principles of law recognized by civilized nations, and judicial decisions and teachings of the most qualified publicists on the topic. All judgments of the Court are published in French and English. The Court's rules of procedure were updated on December 5, 2000.

The Court deals only with disputes between sovereign states; no private party may present a case. Moreover, the Court is not expected to resolve all international conflicts, but only specific legal disputes brought before it. It has COMPULSORY JURISDICTION in cases involving countries that have signed OPTIONAL CLAUSE 36 (paragraphs 2 and 3) of the ICJ's Statute, allowing the Court to adjudicate legal disputes concerning (1) the interpretation of a TREATY, (2) any question of international law, (3) the existence of any fact which may constitute a breach of an international obligation, or (4) the nature and extent of a reparation for such a breach. This is the so-called optional clause, allowing "DECLARATIONS of acceptance of the compulsory jurisdiction of the Court." More than 300 treaties and conventions require parties aris-

ing under the agreements to settle legal disputes by recourse to the ICJ. But the two affected states usually must agree to bring the case, and no state may be sued before the Court unless it consents to such an action. In fact, the jurisdiction of an international tribunal depends on the consent of the states concerned. The Court's effectiveness also is affected by states' consent; however, since 1984 there has not been a single instance of open defiance to ICJ final judgments. In the new millennium there was a marked increase in the number of cases brought before the Court. The ICJ established new regulations in hope of cutting the backlog, but by May 2004, 21 cases were pending.

Most often cases are initiated either by the disputants, who notify the Court of a special agreement reached by each to seek Court action, or by the unilateral initiation of one party, acknowledging that the opposing party has not recognized the Court's jurisdiction, but asking it to do so. In the latter case, the lone litigant writes to the Court's registrar. Nation-states have no permanent official representatives at the ICJ. As a rule, a state's foreign minister, or ambassador to the Netherlands, communicates with the Court's registrar. Parties before the Court are not required to pay fees or administrative expenses; these costs fall to the United Nations.

In proceedings before the Court, there is both a written phase, when the parties file and exchange pleadings, and an oral stage, when there are public hearings and when counsel address the Court. The Court may hear witnesses and authorize investigations by commissions of experts. The Court deliberates in private, but all judgments—arrived at by majority vote—are made public in the Court's chambers. A judge in the minority may file a dissenting opinion, although majority judgments are final; there is no appeal. Yet the Court has no power of enforcement. Article 94 of the UN Charter provides recourse to the Security Council for a successful disputant unhappy at non-compliance with a decision. The Council then may forward recommendations or take measures to effect the judgment. But, in fact, given the reality of a world of sovereign nations, the Court's verdicts depend wholly on compliance by the litigants. Nonetheless, as of 2000 there had been only two recorded instances in which a disappointed party to a decision had failed to comply with the Court. The very first decision, in the *Corfu Channel* case of 1946, was rebuffed by Albania when it failed to pay the United Kingdom the £843,947 mandated by the Court as compensation for damages suffered. And the United States, reacting to the 1984 case of *Nicaragua v. U.S.A.,* refused for two years to accept prior compulsory jurisdiction of the Court in matters relating to Central America and, following the Court's insistence (by a 12–3 majority) that the United States had violated international law in its dealings with Nicaragua and should pay reparations to that country, blocked any APPEAL TO THE SECURITY COUNCIL. Yet one must bear in mind that on several occasions, by request of one of the litigants, cases have been removed from the Court's list before a judgment has been rendered.

Under provisions of Article 26 of the Statute, the Court may establish a special chamber composed of three or more judges. This might be done either at the request of the parties in an individual case, or in order to deal with particular categories of cases. Such a procedure was used for the first time in 1982 and has been used infrequently since. However, in July 1993 the Court set up a special seven-member chamber to deal with environmental cases falling within its jurisdiction.

Article 65 of the Statute also authorizes the Court to deliver "advisory opinions" if so requested by one of the five principal organs of the United Nations, or by a SPECIAL-IZED AGENCY. After receiving such a request, the Court seeks useful information from various organizations and requests written and oral statements on the issue. Otherwise, the procedures for dealing with advisory opinions and the legal sources employed are the same as for adversarial cases. Nonetheless, advisory opinions are consultative in nature and thus not binding. A nation may simply disregard an advisory opinion, as happened, for example, when in 1948 the Court advised the General Assembly that the Soviet Union could not use its veto to deny membership in the United Nations to the qualified states of Italy and Finland. Moscow ignored the decision and ultimately struck a compromise with Western nations that resulted in the two countries being admitted along with several other nations.

By the first decade of the 21st century the Court had rendered 24 advisory opinions concerning a variety of topics, including issues of UN membership, reparation for injuries in the service of the United Nations, the territorial status of NAMIBIA and Western Sahara, expenses of various UN operations, the status of human rights SPECIAL RAP-PORTEURS, and the legality of the threat or use of nuclear weapons. In 2003 an EMERGENCY SPECIAL SESSION OF THE GENERAL ASSEMBLY referred to the ICJ the matter of a security wall being built by Israel to separate Palestinian and Israeli communities in the West Bank occupied territories. In July 2004, the Court voted 14 to 1 to declare the wall illegal under international law. It ordered Israel to remove the barrier—a mandate that Tel Aviv rejected. The Court called on the General Assembly and Security Council to take additional actions to insure the enforcement of the ICJ's ruling. Subsequently, the General Assembly voted 150 to 6 to urge all members to acknowledge the illegality of the barrier and to render no aid to Israel in its construction. The Security Council took no action.

From 1946 to 2001, more than 95 contentious cases were referred to the Court, although several were subsequently removed from the Court's list or were still pending. Of the 75 countries that had been litigants in these cases, the United States was involved most often (about 20), with the United Kingdom and the FORMER YUGOSLAVIA ranking second and third.

Three specific cases give example to the Court's workings. In its first case, *Corfu Channel (United Kingdom v. Albania),* the Court proffered three judgments. First, on March 25, 1948, it asserted its jurisdiction over the case—involving a British grievance against Albania for explosions in the Corfu Channel in 1946 that had damaged a British warship and killed members of the crew. Second, on April 9, 1949, it found Albania responsible under international law for the explosions. And third, on December 15, 1949, the Court assessed Albania a reparation payment to be paid to the United Kingdom. However, as noted above, Albania refused to observe the judgment.

In 1979 the United States requested that the Court take the case *U.S. Diplomatic and Consular Staff in Tehran (U.S.A. v. Iran).* Washington brought the case following the occupation of its embassy by Iranian militants on November 4, 1979, and the capture and holding of hostages of its diplomatic and consular staff. The Court immediately held that there was no more fundamental requirement for international relations than the inviolability of diplomatic envoys and embassies. In a judgment of May 24, 1980, the Court found that IRAN had violated obligations to the United

States according to international law and under existing conventions. However, the Court was not called upon to deliver any further judgment on reparation, and, on May 12, 1981, the case was removed from the Court's list. Ultimately negotiations between Iran and the United States took place to resolve outstanding grievances on both sides. The result was the establishment of the Iran–U.S. Claims Tribunal to handle claims by nationals of either country. By the end of the century the tribunal had dealt with more than 3,900 cases.

A final example is the *LaGrand Case (GERMANY v. United States of America)*, decided on June 27, 2001. Citing Article 36 of the Statute (explained above) the Court determined that the United States had violated international law when it failed to grant consular services to two German brothers executed in Arizona in 1999. Also, the Court found that the United States had ignored an ICJ order to stay one of the executions. The two brothers were charged with murder in a 1982 holdup. Washington conceded during the proceedings that it had neglected the 1963 Vienna Convention on Consular Relations in prosecuting the LaGrand brothers without informing diplomats from their homeland, but insisted that the brothers had received a fair trial and that the verdicts would have been unaffected by consular intervention. But ICJ president Gilbert Guillaume, speaking for the Court's overwhelming majority, reprimanded the United States for denying defendants their international rights regardless of the likely outcome of a trial. The ruling was also noteworthy because it pronounced, for the first time in the Court's history, that provisional orders of the ICJ, such as the ignored injunction against Walter LaGrand's execution, were legally binding.

The LaGrand case provided precedent for a Mexican claim against the United States in January 2003. In *Mexico v. United States,* the Mexican government claimed the United States had violated the rights of 52 nationals in connection with their arrests, trials, and convictions, which included in several cases a sentence of death. Mexico charged that the defendants were never informed of their right to consult with Mexican consular officials. The Court ruled that the United States had violated its treaty obligations, and determined that U.S. courts should reconsider all of the cases. In one case—that of Osvaldo Torres Aguilera—the governor of Oklahoma pardoned the accused five days before his scheduled execution, after a court granted a hearing on the state's failure to notify him of his consular rights.

See also ADMINISTRATIVE TRIBUNALS, ADMISSION OF MEMBERS, ANTARCTIC TREATY, APARTHEID, APPEAL TO THE SECURITY COUNCIL, APPENDIX A, APPENDIX E, APPENDIX G (Convention on the Prevention and Punishment of the Crime of Genocide, Convention against Torture), CHAPTER VI, CHINA, COMPETENCE OF UNITED NATIONS ORGANS, GOLDBERG RESERVATION, IRAN HOSTAGE CRISIS, *JUS COGENS,* SCALE OF ASSESSMENTS, TREATY OF BANGKOK, TREATY OF PELINDABA, UNITED NATIONS CONFERENCE ON THE LAW OF THE SEA, VOTING, WOMEN, YALTA CONFERENCE.

Further Reading: Bowett, D. W., et al. *The International Court of Justice: Process, Practice and Procedure.* London: British Institute of International and Comparative Law, 1997. International Court of Justice. *Yearbook.* The Hague, published annually. Llamzin, Aloysius P. "Jurisdiction and Compliance in Recent Decisions of the International Court of Justice (March 12, 2007). *Yale Law School. Yale Law School Student Scholarship Series.* Paper 3. Rosenne, Shabtai. *The Law and Practice of the International Court, 1920–1996.* Boston: Martinus Nijhoff Publishers, 1997. ICJ Web site: <www.icj-cij.org/icjwww/icjhome.htm>.

International Covenant on Civil and Political Rights (ICCPR)

The International Covenant on Civil and Political Rights codified and expanded on rights listed in the UNIVERSAL DECLARATION OF HUMAN RIGHTS. As a formal TREATY, the COVENANT carried the force of INTERNATIONAL LAW, requiring signatories to live up to its terms. It was adopted by the GENERAL ASSEMBLY on December 16, 1966, and went into force in 1976. At the time of its adoption, the Assembly also opened for signature the INTERNATIONAL COVENANT ON ECONOMIC, SOCIAL AND CULTURAL RIGHTS (ICESCR), which together with the Universal Declaration and the ICCPR form what is often called the "International Bill of Human Rights." Excerpts from the covenant follow.

> PREAMBLE
> *The States Parties to the present Covenant,*
> *Considering* that, in accordance with the principles proclaimed in the CHARTER OF THE UNITED NATIONS, recognition of the inherent dignity and of the equal and inalienable rights of all members of the human family is the foundation of freedom, justice and peace in the world,
> *Recognizing* that these rights derive from the inherent dignity of the human person,
> *Recognizing* that, in accordance with the Universal Declaration of Human Rights, the ideal of free human beings enjoying civil and political freedom and freedom from fear and want can only be achieved if conditions are created whereby everyone may enjoy his civil and political rights, as well as his economic, social and cultural rights,
> *Considering* the obligation of States under the Charter of the United Nations to promote universal respect for, and observance of, HUMAN RIGHTS and freedoms,
> *Realizing* that the individual, having duties to other individuals and to the community to which he belongs, is under a responsibility to strive for the promotion and observance of the rights recognized in the present Covenant,

Agree upon the following articles:

PART I

Article 1

1. All peoples have the right of self-determination. By virtue of that right they freely determine their political status and freely pursue their economic, social and cultural DEVELOPMENT.

2. All peoples may, for their own ends, freely dispose of their natural wealth and resources without prejudice to any obligations arising out of international economic cooperation, based upon the principle of mutual benefit, and international law. In no case may a people be deprived of its own means of subsistence.

3. The States Parties to the present Covenant, including those having responsibility for the administration of NON-SELF-GOVERNING and Trust Territories, shall promote the realization of the right of self-determination, and shall respect that right, in conformity with the provisions of the Charter of the United Nations.

PART II

Article 2

1. Each State Party to the present COVENANT undertakes to respect and to ensure to all individuals within its territory and subject to its JURISDICTION the rights recognized in the present Covenant, without distinction of any kind, such as race, colour, sex, LANGUAGE, religion, political or other opinion, national or social origin, property, birth or other status.

2. Where not already provided for by existing legislative or other measures, each State Party to the present Covenant undertakes to take the necessary steps, in accordance with its constitutional processes and with the provisions of the present Covenant, to adopt such legislative or other measures as may be necessary to give effect to the rights recognized in the present Covenant.

3. Each State Party to the present Covenant undertakes:

(a) To ensure that any person whose rights or freedoms as herein recognized are violated shall have an effective remedy, notwithstanding that the violation has been committed by persons acting in an official capacity;

(b) To ensure that any person claiming such a remedy shall have his right thereto determined by competent judicial, administrative or legislative authorities, or by any other competent authority provided for by the legal system of the State, and to develop the possibilities of judicial remedy;

(c) To ensure that the competent authorities shall enforce such remedies when granted.

Article 3

The States Parties to the present Covenant undertake to ensure the equal right of men and WOMEN to the enjoyment of all civil and political rights set forth in the present Covenant.

Article 4

1. In time of public emergency which threatens the life of the nation and the existence of which is officially proclaimed, the States Parties to the present Covenant may take measures derogating from their obligations under the present Covenant to the extent strictly required by the exigencies of the situation, provided that such measures are not inconsistent with their other obligations under international law and do not involve discrimination solely on the ground of race, colour, sex, language, religion or social origin.

2. No derogation from articles 6, 7, 8 (paragraphs 1 and 2), 11, 15, 16 and 18 may be made under this provision.

3. Any State Party to the present Covenant availing itself of the right of derogation shall immediately inform the other States Parties to the present Covenant, through the intermediary of the SECRETARY-GENERAL of the United Nations, of the provisions from which it has derogated and of the reasons by which it was actuated. A further communication shall be made, through the same intermediary, on the date on which it terminates such derogation.

Article 5

1. Nothing in the present Covenant may be interpreted as implying for any State, group or person any right to engage in any activity or perform any act aimed at the destruction of any of the rights and freedoms recognized herein or at their limitation to a greater extent than is provided for in the present Covenant.

2. There shall be no restriction upon or derogation from any of the fundamental human rights recognized or existing in any State Party to the present Covenant pursuant to law, CONVENTIONS, regulations or custom on the pretext that the present Covenant does not recognize such rights or that it recognizes them to a lesser extent.

PART III

Article 6

1. Every human being has the inherent right to life. This right shall be protected by law. No one shall be arbitrarily deprived of his life.

2. In countries which have not abolished the death penalty, sentence of death may be imposed only for the most serious crimes in accordance with the law in force at time of the commission of the crime and not contrary to the provisions of the present Covenant and to the CONVENTION ON THE PREVENTION AND PUNISHMENT OF THE CRIME OF GENOCIDE. This penalty can only be carried out pursuant to a final judgement rendered by a competent court.

3. When deprivation of life constitutes the crime of genocide, it is understood that nothing in this article shall authorize any State Party to the present Covenant

to derogate in any way from any obligation assumed under the provisions of the Convention on the Prevention and Punishment of the Crime of Genocide.

4. Anyone sentenced to death shall have the right to seek pardon or commutation of the sentence. Amnesty, pardon or commutation of the sentence of death may be granted in all cases.

5. Sentence of death shall not be imposed for crimes committed by persons below eighteen years of age and shall not be carried out on pregnant women.

6. Nothing in this article shall be invoked to delay or to prevent the abolition of capital punishment by any State Party to the present Covenant.

Article 7

No one shall be subjected to torture or to cruel, inhuman or degrading treatment or punishment. In particular, no one shall be subjected without his free consent to medical or scientific experimentation.

Article 8

1. No one shall be held in slavery; slavery and the slave-trade in all their forms shall be prohibited.

2. No one shall be held in servitude.

3. (a) No one shall be required to perform forced or compulsory labour;

(b) Paragraph 3 (a) shall not be held to preclude, in countries where imprisonment with hard labour may be imposed as a punishment for a crime, the performance of hard labour in pursuance of a sentence to such punishment by a competent court;

(c) For the purpose of this paragraph the term "forced or compulsory labour" shall not include:

(i) Any work or service, not referred to in subparagraph (b), normally required of a person who is under detention in consequence of a lawful order of a court, or of a person during conditional release from such detention;

(ii) Any service of a military character and, in countries where conscientious objection is recognized, any national service required by law of conscientious objectors;

(iii) Any service exacted in cases of emergency or calamity threatening the life or well-being of the community;

(iv) Any work or service which forms part of normal civil obligations.

Article 9

1. Everyone has the right to liberty and security of person. No one shall be subjected to arbitrary arrest or detention. No one shall be deprived of his liberty except on such grounds and in accordance with such procedure as are established by law.

2. Anyone who is arrested shall be informed, at the time of arrest, of the reasons for his arrest and shall be promptly informed of any charges against him.

3. Anyone arrested or detained on a criminal charge shall be brought promptly before a judge or other officer authorized by law to exercise judicial power and shall be entitled to trial within a reasonable time or to release. It shall not be the general rule that persons awaiting trial shall be detained in custody, but release may be subject to guarantees to appear for trial, at any other stage of the judicial proceedings, and, should occasion arise, for execution of the judgement.

4. Anyone who is deprived of his liberty by arrest or detention shall be entitled to take proceedings before a court, in order that that court may decide without delay on the lawfulness of his detention and order his release if the detention is not lawful.

5. Anyone who has been the victim of unlawful arrest or detention shall have an enforceable right to compensation.

Article 10

1. All persons deprived of their liberty shall be treated with humanity and with respect for the inherent dignity of the human person.

2. (a) Accused persons shall, save in exceptional circumstances, be segregated from convicted persons and shall be subject to separate treatment appropriate to their status as unconvicted persons;

(b) Accused juvenile persons shall be separated from adults and brought as speedily as possible for adjudication.

3. The penitentiary system shall comprise treatment of prisoners the essential aim of which shall be their reformation and social rehabilitation. Juvenile offenders shall be segregated from adults and be accorded treatment appropriate to their age and legal status.

Article 11

No one shall be imprisoned merely on the ground of inability to fulfill a contractual obligation.

Article 12

1. Everyone lawfully within the territory of a State shall, within that territory, have the right to liberty of movement and freedom to choose his residence.

2. Everyone shall be free to leave any country, including his own.

3. The above-mentioned rights shall not be subject to any restrictions except those which are provided by law, are necessary to protect national security, public order (*ordre public,*) public HEALTH or morals or the rights and freedoms of others, and are consistent with the other rights recognized in the present Covenant.

4. No one shall be arbitrarily deprived of the right to enter his own country.

Article 13

An alien lawfully in the territory of a State Party to the present Covenant may be expelled therefrom only in pursuance of a decision reached in accordance with law and shall, except where compelling reasons of national security otherwise require, be allowed to submit the reasons against his expulsion and to have his case reviewed by, and be represented for the purpose before, the competent authority or a person or persons especially designated by the competent authority.

Article 14

1. All persons shall be equal before the courts and tribunals. In the determination of any criminal charge against him, or of his rights and obligations in a suit at law, everyone shall be entitled to a fair and public hearing by a competent, independent and impartial tribunal established by law. The press and the public may be excluded from all or part of a trial for reasons of morals, public order (*ordre public*) or national security in a democratic society, or when the interest of the private lives of the parties so requires, or to the extent strictly necessary in the opinion of the court in special circumstances where publicity would prejudice the interests of justice; but any judgement rendered in a criminal case or in a suit at law shall be made public except where the interest of juvenile persons otherwise requires or the proceedings concern matrimonial disputes or the guardianship of children.

2. Everyone charged with a criminal offence shall have the right to be presumed innocent until proved guilty according to law.

3. In the determination of any criminal charge against him, everyone shall be entitled to the following minimum guarantees, in full equality:

(a) To be informed promptly and in detail in a language which he understands of the nature and cause of the charge against him;

(b) To have adequate time and facilities for the preparation of his defence and to communicate with counsel of his own choosing;

(c) To be tried without undue delay;

(d) To be tried in his presence, and to defend himself in person or through legal assistance of his own choosing; to be informed, if he does not have legal assistance, of this right; and to have legal assistance assigned to him, in any case where the interests of justice so require, and without payment by him in any such case if he does not have sufficient means to pay for it;

(e) To examine, or have examined, the witnesses against him and to obtain the attendance and examination of witnesses on his behalf under the same conditions as witnesses against him;

(f) To have the free assistance of an interpreter if he cannot understand or speak the language used in court;

(g) Not to be compelled to testify against himself or to confess guilt.

4. In the case of juvenile persons, the procedure shall be such as will take account of their age and the desirability of promoting their rehabilitation.

5. Everyone convicted of a crime shall have the right to his conviction and sentence being reviewed by a higher tribunal according to law.

6. When a person has by a final decision been convicted of a criminal offence and when subsequently his conviction has been reversed or he has been pardoned on the ground that a new or newly discovered fact shows conclusively that there has been a miscarriage of justice, the person who has suffered punishment as a result of such conviction shall be compensated according to law, unless it is proved that the non-disclosure of the unknown fact in time is wholly or partly attributable to him.

7. No one shall be liable to be tried or punished again for an offence for which he has already been finally convicted or acquitted in accordance with the law and penal procedure of each country.

Article 15

1. No one shall be held guilty of any criminal offence on account of any act or omission which did not constitute a criminal offence, under national or international law, at the time when it was committed. Nor shall a heavier penalty be imposed than the one that was applicable at the time when the criminal offence was committed. If, subsequent to the commission of the offence, provision is made by law for the imposition of the lighter penalty, the offender shall benefit thereby.

2. Nothing in this article shall prejudice the trial and punishment of any person for any act or omission which, at the time when it was committed, was criminal according to the general principles of law recognized by the community of nations.

Article 16

Everyone shall have the right to recognition everywhere as a person before the law.

Article 17

1. No one shall be subjected to arbitrary or unlawful interference with his privacy, family, home or correspondence, nor to unlawful attacks on his honour and reputation.

2. Everyone has the right to the protection of the law against such interference or attacks.

Article 18

1. Everyone shall have the right to freedom of thought, conscience and religion. This right shall include freedom to have or to adopt a religion or belief of his choice, and freedom, either individually or in community with others and in public or private, to manifest his religion or belief in worship, observance, practice and teaching.

2. No one shall be subject to coercion which would impair his freedom to have or to adopt a religion or belief of his choice.

3. Freedom to manifest one's religion or beliefs may be subject only to such limitations as are prescribed by law

and are necessary to protect public safety, order, health, or morals or the fundamental rights and freedoms of others.

4. The States Parties to the present Covenant undertake to have respect for the liberty of parents and, when applicable, legal guardians to ensure the religious and moral education of their children in conformity with their own convictions.

Article 19

1. Everyone shall have the right to hold opinions without interference.

2. Everyone shall have the right to freedom of expression; this right shall include freedom to seek, receive and impart information and ideas of all kinds, regardless of frontiers, either orally, in writing or in print, in the form of art, or through any other media of his choice.

3. The exercise of the rights provided for in paragraph 2 of this article carries with it special duties and responsibilities. It may therefore be subject to certain restrictions, but these shall only be such as are provided by law and are necessary:

(a) For respect of the rights or reputations of others;

(b) For the protection of national security or of public order (*ordre public*), or of public health or morals.

Article 20

1. Any propaganda for war shall be prohibited by law.

2. Any advocacy of national, racial or religious hatred that constitutes incitement to discrimination, hostility or violence shall be prohibited by law.

Article 21

The right of peaceful assembly shall be recognized. No restrictions may be placed on the exercise of this right other than those imposed in conformity with the law and which are necessary in a democratic society in the interests of national security or public safety, public order (*ordre public*), the protection of public health or morals or the protection of the rights and freedoms of others.

Article 22

1. Everyone shall have the right to freedom of association with others, including the right to form and join trade unions for the protection of his interests.

2. No restrictions may be placed on the exercise of this right other than those which are prescribed by law and which are necessary in a democratic society in the interests of national security or public safety, public order (*ordre public*), the protection of public health or morals or the protection of the rights and freedoms of others. This article shall not prevent the imposition of lawful restrictions on members of the armed forces and of the police in their exercise of this right.

3. Nothing in this article shall authorize States Parties to the INTERNATIONAL LABOUR ORGANIZATION Convention of 1948 concerning Freedom of Association and

Protection of the Right to Organize to take legislative measures which would prejudice, or to apply the law in such a manner as to prejudice, the guarantees provided for in that Convention.

Article 23

1. The family is the natural and fundamental group unit of society and is entitled to protection by society and the State.

2. The right of men and women of marriageable age to marry and to found a family shall be recognized.

3. No marriage shall be entered into without the free and full consent of the intending spouses.

4. States Parties to the present Covenant shall take appropriate steps to ensure equality of rights and responsibilities of spouses as to marriage, during marriage and at its dissolution. In the case of dissolution, provision shall be made for the necessary protection of any children.

Article 24

1. Every child shall have, without any discrimination as to race, colour, sex, language, religion, national or social origin, property or birth, the right to such measures of protection as are required by his status as a minor, on the part of his family, society and the State.

2. Every child shall be registered immediately after birth and shall have a name.

3. Every child has the right to acquire a nationality.

Article 25

Every citizen shall have the right and the opportunity, without any of the distinctions mentioned in article 2 and without unreasonable restrictions:

(a) To take part in the conduct of public affairs, directly or through freely chosen representatives;

(b) To vote and to be elected at genuine periodic elections which shall be by universal and equal suffrage and shall be held by secret ballot, guaranteeing the free expression of the will of the electors;

(c) To have access, on general terms of equality, to public service in his country.

Article 26

All persons are equal before the law and are entitled without any discrimination to the equal protection of the law. In this respect, the law shall prohibit any discrimination and guarantee to all persons equal and effective protection against discrimination on any ground such as race, colour, sex, language, religion, political or other opinion, national or social origin, property, birth or other status.

Article 27

In those States in which ethnic, religious or linguistic minorities exist, persons belonging to such minorities shall not be denied the right, in community with the other members of their group, to enjoy their own culture, to profess and practice their own religion, or to use their own language.

PART IV

Article 28

1. There shall be established a HUMAN RIGHTS COM-MITTEE (hereafter referred to in the present Covenant as the Committee). It shall consist of eighteen members and shall carry out the functions hereinafter provided.

2. The Committee shall be composed of nationals of the States Parties to the present Covenant who shall be persons of high moral character and recognized COMPE-TENCE in the field of human rights, consideration being given to the usefulness of the participation of some persons having legal experience.

3. The members of the Committee shall be elected and shall serve in their personal capacity . . .

Article 40

1. The States Parties to the present Covenant undertake to submit reports of the measures they have adopted which give effect to the rights recognized herein and on the progress made in the enjoyment of those rights:

(a) Within one year of the entry into force of the present Covenant for the States Parties concerned;

(b) Thereafter whenever the Committee so requests.

2. All reports shall be submitted to the Secretary-General of the United Nations, who shall transmit them to the Committee for consideration. Reports shall indicate the factors and difficulties, if any, affecting the implementation of the present Covenant.

3. The Secretary-General of the United Nations may, after consultation with the Committee, transmit to the SPECIALIZED AGENCIES concerned copies of such parts of the reports as may fall within their field of competence.

4. The Committee shall study the reports submitted by the States Parties to the present Covenant. It shall transmit its reports, and such general comments as it may consider appropriate, to the States Parties. The Committee may also transmit to the ECONOMIC AND SOCIAL COUN-CIL these comments along with the copies of the reports it has received from States Parties to the present Covenant.

5. The States Parties to the present Covenant may submit to the Committee observations on any comments that may be made in accordance with paragraph 4 of this article.

Article 41

1. A State Party to the present Covenant may at any time declare under this article that it recognizes the competence of the Committee to receive and consider communications to the effect that a State Party claims that another State Party is not fulfilling its obligations under the present Covenant. Communications under this article may be received and considered only if submitted by a State Party which has made a declaration recognizing in regard to itself the COMPETENCE of the Committee.

No communication shall be received by the Committee if it concerns a State Party which has not made such a DECLARATION. Communications received under this article shall be dealt with in accordance with the following procedure:

(a) If a State Party to the present Covenant considers that another State Party is not giving effect to the provisions of the present Covenant, it may, by written communication, bring the matter to the attention of that State Party. Within three months after the receipt of the communication the receiving State shall afford the State which sent the communication an explanation, or any other statement in writing clarifying the matter, which should include, to the extent possible and pertinent, reference to domestic procedures and remedies taken, pending, or available in the matter;

(b) If the matter is not adjusted to the satisfaction of both States Parties concerned within six months after the receipt by the receiving State of the initial communication, either State shall have the right to refer the matter to the Committee, by notice given to the Committee and to the other State;

(c) The Committee shall deal with a matter referred to it only after it has ascertained that all available domestic remedies have been invoked and exhausted in the matter, in conformity with the generally recognized principles of international law. This shall not be the rule where the application of the remedies is unreasonably prolonged;

(d) The Committee shall hold closed meetings when examining communications under this article;

(e) Subject to the provisions of subparagraph (c), the Committee shall make available its GOOD OFFICES to the States Parties concerned with a view to a friendly solution of the matter on the basis of respect for human rights and fundamental freedoms as recognized in the present Covenant . . .

Article 42

1. (a) If a matter referred to the Committee in accordance with article 41 is not resolved to the satisfaction of the States Parties concerned, the Committee may, with the prior consent of the States Parties concerned, appoint an *ad hoc* CONCILIATION Commission (hereinafter referred to as the Commission). The good offices of the Commission shall be made available to the States Parties concerned with a view to an amicable solution of the matter on the basis of respect for the present Covenant . . .

7. When the Commission has fully considered the matter, but in any event not later than twelve months after having been seized of the matter, it shall submit to the Chairman of the Committee a report for communication to the States Parties concerned . . .

Article 44

The provisions for the implementation of the present Covenant shall apply without prejudice to the procedures prescribed in the field of human rights by or under the constituent instruments and the conventions of the United Nations and of the specialized agencies and shall not prevent the States Parties to the present Covenant from having recourse to other procedures for settling a dispute in accordance with general or special international agreements in force between them.

Article 45

The Committee shall submit to the General Assembly of the United Nations, through the Economic and Social Council, an annual report on its activities.

PART V

Article 46

Nothing in the present Covenant shall be interpreted as impairing the provisions of the Charter of the United Nations and of the constitutions of the specialized agencies which define the respective responsibilities of the various organs of the United Nations and of the specialized agencies in regard to the matters dealt with in the present Covenant.

Article 47

Nothing in the present Covenant shall be interpreted as impairing the inherent right of all peoples to enjoy and utilize fully and freely their natural wealth and resources. . .

International Covenant on Economic, Social and Cultural Rights (ICESCR)

The International Covenant on Economic, Social and Cultural Rights codified and expanded on rights listed in the UNIVERSAL DECLARATION OF HUMAN RIGHTS. As a formal TREATY, the COVENANT carried the force of INTERNATIONAL LAW, requiring signatories to live up to its terms. It was adopted by the GENERAL ASSEMBLY on December 16, 1966, and went into force in 1976. At the time of its adoption, the Assembly also opened for signature the INTERNATIONAL COVENANT ON CIVIL AND POLITICAL RIGHTS (ICCPR), which together with the Universal Declaration and the ICESCR form what is often called the "International Bill of Human Rights." The text of the covenant follows.

PREAMBLE

The States Parties to the present Covenant,

Considering that, in accordance with the principles proclaimed in the CHARTER OF THE UNITED NATIONS, recognition of the inherent dignity and of the equal and inalienable rights of all members of the human family is the foundation of freedom, justice and peace in the world,

Recognizing that these rights derive from the inherent dignity of the human person,

Recognizing that, in accordance with the Universal Declaration of Human Rights, the ideal of free human beings enjoying freedom from fear and want can only be

achieved if conditions are created whereby everyone may enjoy his economic, social and cultural rights, as well as his civil and political rights,

Considering the obligation of States under the Charter of the United Nations to promote universal respect for, and observance of, HUMAN RIGHTS and freedoms,

Realizing that the individual, having duties to other individuals and to the community to which he belongs, is under a responsibility to strive for the promotion and observance of the rights recognized in the present Covenant,

Agree upon the following articles:

PART I

Article 1

1. All peoples have the right of self-determination. By virtue of that right they freely determine their political status and freely pursue their economic, social and cultural DEVELOPMENT.

2. All peoples may, for their own ends, freely dispose of their natural wealth and resources without prejudice to any obligations arising out of international economic cooperation, based upon the principle of mutual benefit, and international law. In no case may a people be deprived of its own means of subsistence.

3. The States Parties to the present Covenant, including those having responsibility for the administration of NON-SELF-GOVERNING and Trust Territories, shall promote the realization of the right of self-determination, and shall respect that right, in conformity with the provisions of the Charter of the United Nations.

PART II

Article 2

1. Each State Party to the present Covenant undertakes to take steps, individually and through international assistance and cooperation, especially economic and technical, to the maximum of its available resources, with a view to achieving progressively the full realization of the rights recognized in the present Covenant by all appropriate means, including particularly the adoption of legislative measures.

2. The States Parties to the present Covenant undertake to guarantee that the rights enunciated in the present Covenant will be exercised without discrimination of any kind as to race, colour, sex, LANGUAGE, religion, political or other opinion, national or social origin, property, birth or other status.

3. DEVELOPING COUNTRIES, with due regard to human rights and their national economy, may determine to what extent they would guarantee the economic rights recognized in the present Covenant to non-nationals.

Article 3

The States Parties to the present Covenant undertake to ensure the equal right of men and WOMEN to the enjoyment of all economic, social and cultural rights set forth in the present Covenant.

Article 4

The States Parties to the present Covenant recognize that, in the enjoyment of those rights provided by the State in conformity with the present Covenant, the State may subject such rights only to such limitations as are determined by law only in so far as this may be compatible with the nature of these rights and solely for the purpose of promoting the general welfare in a democratic society.

Article 5

1. Nothing in the present Covenant may be interpreted as implying for any State, group or person any right to engage in any activity or to perform any act aimed at the destruction of any of the rights or freedoms recognized herein, or at their limitation to a greater extent than is provided for in the present Covenant.

2. No restriction upon or derogation from any of the fundamental human rights recognized or existing in any country in virtue of law, CONVENTIONS, regulations or custom shalt be admitted on the pretext that the present Covenant does not recognize such rights or that it recognizes them to a lesser extent.

PART III

Article 6

1. The States Parties to the present Covenant recognize the right to work, which includes the right of everyone to the opportunity to gain his living by work which he freely chooses or accepts, and will take appropriate steps to safeguard this right.

2. The steps to be taken by a State Party to the present Covenant to achieve the full realization of this right shall include technical and vocational guidance and training programmes, policies and techniques to achieve steady economic, social and cultural development and full and productive employment under conditions safeguarding fundamental political and economic freedoms to the individual.

Article 7

The States Parties to the present Covenant recognize the right of everyone to the enjoyment of just and favourable conditions of work which ensure, in particular:

(a) Remuneration which provides all workers, as a minimum, with:

(i) Fair wages and equal remuneration for work of equal value without distinction of any kind, in particular women being guaranteed conditions of work not inferior to those enjoyed by men, with equal pay for equal work;

(ii) A decent living for themselves and their families in accordance with the provisions of the present Covenant;

(b) Safe and healthy working conditions;

(c) Equal opportunity for everyone to be promoted in his employment to an appropriate higher level, subject to no considerations other than those of seniority and competence;

(d) Rest, leisure and reasonable limitation of working hours and periodic holidays with pay, as well as remuneration for public holidays.

Article 8

1. The States Parties to the present Covenant undertake to ensure:

(a) The right of everyone to form trade unions and join the trade union of his choice, subject only to the rules of the organization concerned, for the promotion and protection of his economic and social interests. No restrictions may be placed on the exercise of this right other than those prescribed by law and which are necessary in a democratic society in the interests of national security or public order or for the protection of the rights and freedoms of others;

(b) The right of trade unions to establish national federations or confederations and the right of the latter to form or join international trade-union organizations;

(c) The right of trade unions to function freely subject to no limitations other than those prescribed by law and which are necessary in a democratic society in the interests of national security or public order or for the protection of the rights and freedoms of others;

(d) The right to strike, provided that it is exercised in conformity with the laws of the particular country.

2. This article shall not prevent the imposition of lawful restrictions on the exercise of these rights by members of the armed forces or of the police or of the administration of the State.

3. Nothing in this article shall authorize States Parties to the INTERNATIONAL LABOUR ORGANIZATION Convention of 1948 concerning Freedom of Association and Protection of the Right to Organize to take legislative measures which would prejudice, or apply the law in such a manner as would prejudice, the guarantees provided for in that Convention.

Article 9

The States Parties to the present Covenant recognize the right of everyone to social security, including social insurance.

Article 10

The States Parties to the present Covenant recognize that:

1. The widest possible protection and assistance should be accorded to the family, which is the natural and fundamental group unit of society, particularly for its establishment and while it is responsible for the care and education of dependent children. Marriage must be entered into with the free consent of the intending spouses.

2. Special protection should be accorded to mothers during a reasonable period before and after childbirth. During such period working mothers should be

accorded paid leave or leave with adequate social security benefits.

3. Special measures of protection and assistance should be taken on behalf of all children and young persons without any discrimination for reasons of parentage or other conditions. Children and young persons should be protected from economic and social exploitation. Their employment in work harmful to their morals or health or dangerous to life or likely to hamper their normal development should be punishable by law. States should also set age limits below which the paid employment of child labour should be prohibited and punishable by law.

Article 11

1. The States Parties to the present Covenant recognize the right of everyone to an adequate standard of living for himself and his family, including adequate food, clothing and housing, and to the continuous improvement of living conditions. The States Parties will take appropriate steps to ensure the realization of this right, recognizing to this effect the essential importance of international cooperation based on free consent.

2. The States Parties to the present Covenant, recognizing the fundamental right of everyone to be free from hunger, shall take, individually and through international cooperation, the measures, including specific programmes, which are needed:

(a) To improve methods of production, conservation and distribution of food by making full use of technical and scientific knowledge, by disseminating knowledge of the principles of nutrition and by developing or reforming agrarian systems in such a way as to achieve the most efficient development and utilization of natural resources;

(b) Taking into account the problems of both food-importing and food-exporting countries, to ensure an equitable distribution of world food supplies in relation to need.

Article 12

1. The States Parties to the present Covenant recognize the right of everyone to the enjoyment of the highest attainable standard of physical and mental health.

2. The steps to be taken by the States Parties to the present Covenant to achieve the full realization of this right shall include those necessary for:

(a) The provision for the reduction of the stillbirthrate and of infant mortality and for the healthy development of the child;

(b) The improvement of all aspects of environmental and industrial hygiene;

(c) The prevention, treatment and control of epidemic, endemic, occupational and other diseases;

(d) The creation of conditions which would assure to all medical service and medical attention in the event of sickness.

Article 13

1. The States Parties to the present Covenant recognize the right of everyone to education. They agree that education shall be directed to the full development of the human personality and the sense of its dignity, and shall strengthen the respect for human rights and fundamental freedoms. They further agree that education shall enable all persons to participate effectively in a free society, promote understanding, tolerance and friendship among all nations and all racial, ethnic or religious groups, and further the activities of the United Nations for the maintenance of peace.

2. The States Parties to the present Covenant recognize that, with a view to achieving the full realization of this right:

(a) Primary education shall be compulsory and available free to all;

(b) Secondary education in its different forms, including technical and vocational secondary education, shall be made generally available and accessible to all by every appropriate means, and in particular by the progressive introduction of free education;

(c) Higher education shall be made equally accessible to all, on the basis of capacity, by every appropriate means, and in particular by the progressive introduction of free education;

(d) Fundamental education shall be encouraged or intensified as far as possible for those persons who have not received or completed the whole period of their primary education;

(e) The development of a system of schools at all levels shall be actively pursued, an adequate fellowship system shall be established, and the material conditions of teaching staff shall be continuously improved.

3. The States Parties to the present Covenant undertake to have respect for the liberty of parents and, when applicable, legal guardians to choose for their children schools, other than those established by the public authorities, which conform to such minimum educational standards as may be laid down or approved by the State and to ensure the religious and moral education of their children in conformity with their own convictions.

4. No part of this article shall be construed so as to interfere with the liberty of individuals and bodies to establish and direct educational institutions, subject always to the observance of the principles set forth in paragraph 1 of this article and to the requirement that the education given in such institutions shall conform to such minimum standards as may be laid down by the State.

Article 14

Each State Party to the present Covenant which, at the time of becoming a Party, has not been able to secure in its metropolitan territory or other territories under its JURISDICTION compulsory primary education, free of charge, undertakes, within two years, to work out and adopt a detailed plan of action for the progressive implementation, within a reasonable number of years, to be fixed in the plan, of the principle of compulsory education free of charge for all.

Article 15

1. The States Parties to the present Covenant recognize the right of everyone:

(a) To take part in cultural life;

(b) To enjoy the benefits of scientific progress and its applications;

(c) To benefit from the protection of the moral and material interests resulting from any scientific, literary or artistic production of which he is the author.

2. The steps to be taken by the States Parties to the present Covenant to achieve the full realization of this right shall include those necessary for the conservation, the development and the diffusion of science and culture.

3. The States Parties to the present Covenant undertake to respect the freedom indispensable for scientific research and creative activity.

4. The States Parties to the present Covenant recognize the benefits to be derived from the encouragement and development of international contacts and cooperation in the scientific and cultural fields.

PART IV

Article 16

1. The States Parties to the present Covenant undertake to submit in conformity with this part of the Covenant reports on the measures which they have adopted and the progress made in achieving the observance of the rights recognized herein.

2. (a) All reports shall be submitted to the SECRETARY-GENERAL of the United Nations, who shall transmit copies to the ECONOMIC AND SOCIAL COUNCIL for consideration in accordance with the provisions of the present Covenant;

(b) The Secretary-General of the United Nations shall also transmit to the SPECIALIZED AGENCIES copies of the reports, or any relevant parts therefrom, from States Parties to the present Covenant which are also members of these specialized agencies in so far as these reports, or parts therefrom, relate to any matters which fall within the responsibilities of the said agencies in accordance with their constitutional instruments.

Article 17

1. The States Parties to the present Covenant shall furnish their reports in stages, in accordance with a programme to be established by the Economic and Social Council within one year of the entry into force of the present Covenant after consultation with the States Parties and the specialized agencies concerned.

2. Reports may indicate factors and difficulties affecting the degree of fulfillment of obligations under the present Covenant.

3. Where relevant information has previously been furnished to the United Nations or to any specialized agency by any State Party to the present Covenant, it will not be necessary to reproduce that information, but a precise reference to the information so furnished will suffice.

Article 18

Pursuant to its responsibilities under the Charter of the United Nations in the field of human rights and fundamental freedoms, the Economic and Social Council may make arrangements with the specialized agencies in respect of their reporting to it on the progress made in achieving the observance of the provisions of the present Covenant falling within the scope of their activities. These reports may include particulars of decisions and recommendations on such implementation adopted by their competent organs.

Article 19

The Economic and Social Council may transmit to the COMMISSION ON HUMAN RIGHTS for study and general recommendation or, as appropriate, for information the reports concerning human rights submitted by States in accordance with articles 16 and 17, and those concerning human rights submitted by the specialized agencies in accordance with article 18.

Article 20

The States Parties to the present Covenant and the specialized agencies concerned may submit comments to the Economic and Social Council on any general recommendation under article 19 or reference to such general recommendation in any report of the Commission on Human Rights or any documentation referred to therein.

Article 21

The Economic and Social Council may submit from time to time to the General Assembly reports with recommendations of a general nature and a summary of the information received from the States Parties to the present Covenant and the specialized agencies on the measures taken and the progress made in achieving general observance of the rights recognized in the present Covenant.

Article 22

The Economic and Social Council may bring to the attention of other organs of the United Nations, their subsidiary organs and specialized agencies concerned with furnishing technical assistance any matters arising out of the reports referred to in this part of the present Covenant which may assist such bodies in deciding, each within its field of COMPETENCE, on the advisability of international measures likely to contribute to the effective progressive implementation of the present Covenant.

Article 23

The States Parties to the present Covenant agree that international action for the achievement of the rights recognized in the present Covenant includes such methods as the conclusion of conventions, the adoption of recommendations, the furnishing of technical assistance and the holding of regional meetings and technical meetings for the purpose of consultation and study organized in conjunction with the Governments concerned.

Article 24

Nothing in the present Covenant shall be interpreted as impairing the provisions of the Charter of the United Nations and of the constitutions of the specialized agencies which define the respective responsibilities of the various organs of the United Nations and of the specialized agencies in regard to the matters dealt with in the present Covenant.

Article 25

Nothing in the present Covenant shall be interpreted as impairing the inherent right of all peoples to enjoy and utilize fully and freely their natural wealth and resources.

PART V

Article 26

1. The present Covenant is open for signature by any State Member of the United Nations or member of any of its specialized agencies, by any State Party to the STATUTE OF THE INTERNATIONAL COURT OF JUSTICE, and by any other State which has been invited by the General Assembly of the United Nations to become a party to the present Covenant.

2. The present Covenant is subject to ratification. Instruments of ratification shall be deposited with the Secretary-General of the United Nations.

3. The present Covenant shall be open to ACCESSION by any State referred to in paragraph 1 of this article.

4. Accession shall be effected by the deposit of an instrument of accession with the Secretary-General of the United Nations.

5. The Secretary-General of the United Nations shall inform all States which have signed the present Covenant or acceded to it of the deposit of each instrument of ratification or accession.

Article 27

1. The present Covenant shall enter into force three months after the date of the deposit with the Secretary-General of the United Nations of the thirty-fifth instrument of ratification or instrument of accession.

2. For each State ratifying the present Covenant or acceding to it after the deposit of the thirty-fifth instrument of ratification or instrument of accession, the present Covenant shall enter into force three months after the date of the deposit of its own instrument of ratification or instrument of accession.

Article 28

The provisions of the present Covenant shall extend to all parts of federal States without any limitations or exceptions.

Article 29

1. Any State Party to the present Covenant may propose an amendment and file it with the Secretary-General of the United Nations. The Secretary-General shall thereupon communicate any proposed amendments to the States Parties to the present Covenant with a request that they notify him whether they favour a conference of States Parties for the purpose of considering and VOTING upon the proposals. In the event that at least one third of the States Parties favours such a conference, the Secretary-General shall convene the conference under the auspices of the United Nations. Any amendment adopted by a majority of the States Parties present and voting at the conference shall be submitted to the General Assembly of the United Nations for approval.

2. AMENDMENTS shall come into force when they have been approved by the General Assembly of the United Nations and accepted by a two-thirds majority of the States Parties to the present Covenant in accordance with their respective constitutional processes.

3. When amendments come into force they shall be binding on those States Parties which have accepted them, other States Parties still being bound by the provisions of the present Covenant and any earlier amendment which they have accepted.

Article 30

Irrespective of the notifications made under article 26, paragraph 5, the Secretary-General of the United Nations shall inform all States referred to in paragraph 1 of the same article of the following particulars:

(a) Signatures, ratifications and accessions under article 26;

(b) The date of the entry into force of the present Covenant under article 27 and the date of the entry into force of any amendments under article 29.

Article 31

1. The present Covenant, of which the Chinese, English, French, Russian and Spanish texts are equally authentic, shall be deposited in the archives of the United Nations.

2. The Secretary-General of the United Nations shall transmit certified copies of the present Covenant to all States referred to in article 26.

International Criminal Court (ICC)

The International Criminal Court is a permanent court that investigates and brings to justice individuals, not countries, who commit the most serious crimes of concern to the international community, such as GENOCIDE, war crimes, and crimes against humanity—including widespread murder of civilians, TORTURE, and mass rape. The Rome Statute, negotiated by the world community over a two-year period and adopted on July 17, 1998, created the ICC as a global judicial institution with an international JURISDICTION complementing national legal systems. The key elements of the ICC are that it is designed to be permanent, rather than an ad hoc body, and that it tries individuals, not states as in other more traditional international courts. The current tribunals for the FORMER YUGOSLAVIA and for Rwanda are ad hoc, created by the United Nations SECURITY COUNCIL, with defined historical periods and geographical areas as jurisdiction. The ICC has no restrictions on time or geography.

The precedents for the International Criminal Court were the International Military Tribunal at Nuremberg and the Tokyo War Crimes Trial that concluded World War II. As early as October 1946, international legal meetings discussed the possibility of a permanent WAR CRIMES TRIBUNAL to sustain the momentum created at Nuremberg and Tokyo. By 1948, the INTERNATIONAL LAW COMMISSION (ILC) of the United Nations began discussions for the creation of a criminal court, and this sentiment was given greater momentum with the signing of the Geneva CONVENTIONs on December 9, 1948. The issue remained on the ILC agenda throughout the COLD WAR. In 1993, the ILC submitted a draft statute RESOLUTION to the GENERAL ASSEMBLY to create an international criminal court.

The General Assembly passed several resolutions that led to the Rome Conference. These included Resolution 73 on December 9, 1994, creating the initial ad hoc committee for the conference; Resolution 46 on December 11, 1995, making this committee permanent; and Resolution 160 on December 15, 1997, establishing the dates of the conference and selecting Rome as the host city. Between June 15 and July 17, 1998, 160 countries participated in the UN Diplomatic Conference of Plenipotentiaries on the Establishment of an International Criminal Court. On February 2, 1999, Senegal became the first country to ratify the Rome Statute. By April 2007, 145 nations had signed the statute, and 104 had ratified it. It required 60 ratifications to take effect. The Court commenced operations on July 1, 2002.

The most serious controversy to arise over the negotiation of the Rome Statute centered on U.S. objections to the jurisdiction of the court. The UNITED STATES declared that it would ratify the statute only if its jurisdiction were limited to cases referred to it by the UN Security Council. The statute, as opened for signature in 1998, had no such provisions and claimed universal jurisdiction on the basis of INTERNATIONAL LAW. In December 2000, President BILL CLINTON signed the Rome Statute, but noted the need for amendments to it. Clinton's successor, President GEORGE W. BUSH, refused to submit the Statute to the U.S. Congress for ratification until U.S. concerns were met. The United States pressured governments that were parties to the statute to sign separate bilateral agreements with Washington promising to bring no cases in the Court against U.S. citizens. It also sought to limit any diplomatic actions that would legitimize the ICC. In Africa, the United States delayed UN proposals for intervention in the DARFUR region of Sudan because the UN plan called for prosecuting suspected war criminals in the Court. The American government preferred to establish a separate ad hoc tribunal in Africa, possibly under the authority of the AFRICAN UNION.

While the United Nations sponsored the negotiations that led to the creation of the International Criminal Court and plays a role in administratively supporting the operation, and in bringing cases to its attention, the ICC is not a subordinate UN agency. It is an independent international organization that has a diplomatic agreement with the United Nations on the modalities of their relationship. Cases may be referred by the Security Council under CHAPTER VII of the UN CHARTER, by one of the parties to the Rome Statute, or by the chief prosecutor with the approval of three judges. Its jurisdiction extends to cases that national governments refuse or are unable to prosecute. The Court has 18 judges elected to nine-year terms by the Assembly of the statute's state parties. No two judges may come from the same country. The Assembly also elects the chief prosecutor. The judges elect the president of the Court. The ICC has pretrial, trial, and appeals divisions. It may impose fines, forced compensation to victims, or imprisonment, but not the death penalty. The provision of compensation to victims broke new ground in INTERNATIONAL LAW. This compensation is paid through a Victim's Trust Fund established by the Rome Statute. In addition to forced contributions by convicted perpetrators, nations, individuals, and other international organizations may contribute to the FUND.

Immediately following its organization, the Court received several hundred referrals for the prosecutor to investigate. Some of the more high-profile allegations came from the Democratic Republic of the CONGO and from the Sudan. In June 2004 the chief prosecutor announced formal investigations into the atrocities associated with the Congolese civil war, and on March 15, 2005, the ICC's Pre-Trial Chamber held its first-ever session to assess the investigation's progress. The first person charged and brought before the Court was Thomas Lubanga Dyilo, leader of the Union of Congolese Patriots. He was arrested on March 17, 2006, and transferred to The Hague. He was charged with conscripting children under the age of 15 and using them as child soldiers. The prosecutor also launched an investigation into alleged HUMAN RIGHTS abuses in Uganda. After meetings with government officials and representatives of the Ugandan rebel Lord's Resistance Army, he announced that he might suspend the investigation if it served "the interests of justice" by reconciling the parties to the growing conflict in the country.

The UN Security Council made its first referral to the Court in the case of Darfur, Sudan. The mounting evidence of genocide and other war crimes by the janjaweed militia, with the complicity of the Sudanese government, and the intransigence of Khartoum on accepting a UN PEACEKEEPING force in the area, led Council members to seek ICC investigations of human rights violations. The prosecutor received a sealed list of suspects from the UN Commission of INQUIRY on Darfur. On February 27, 2007, Court Prosecutor Luis Moreno-Ocampo lodged 51 counts of war crimes and crimes against humanity against the former Sudanese state interior minister Ahmed Muhammad Harun and janjaweed leader Ali Muhammed Ali Abd-al-Rahman. The Sudanese government immediately rejected the ICC's indictments and jurisdiction, and refused to turn over the suspects.

See also INTERNATIONAL CRIMINAL TRIBUNAL FOR RWANDA, INTERNATIONAL CRIMINAL TRIBUNAL FOR THE FORMER YUGOSLAVIA.

Further Reading: Beigbeder, Yves, and Theo Von Boven. *Judging War Criminals: The Politics of International Justice.* New York: St. Martin's, 1999. Drakulich, Angela, ed. *A Global Agenda: Issues Before the 60th General Assembly of the United Nations.* New York: United Nations Association of the United States of America, 2005. Frye, Alton. *Toward an International Criminal Court?: A Council Policy Initiative.* New York: Council on Foreign Relations, 2000. Lee, Roy S., ed. *The International Criminal Court: The Making of the Rome Statute Issues, Negotiations, Results.* The Hague: Kluwer Law International, 1999. Romano, Cesare P. R., André Nollkaemper, and Jann K. Kleffner, eds. *Internationalized Criminal Courts: Sierra Leone, East Timor, Kosovo, and Cambodia.* New York: Oxford University Press, 2004. Sewall, Sarah B., and Carl Kaysen, eds. *The United States and the International Criminal Court: National Security and International Law.* Lanham, Md.: Rowman and Littlefield Publishers, 2000. Thakur, Ramesh Chandra, and Peter Malcontent. *From Sovereign Impunity to International Accountability: The Search for Justice in a World of States.* New York: United Nations University Press, 2004. International Criminal Court Web site: <www.un.org/law/icc/>.

— *D. J. Becker*

International Criminal Tribunal for Rwanda (ICTR)

The UN SECURITY COUNCIL created the International Criminal Tribunal for Rwanda on November 8, 1994 (Res. 955), as the second institution of international criminal prosecution since the Nuremberg Tribunal at the end of World War II. It followed the establishment of the INTERNATIONAL CRIMINAL TRIBUNAL FOR THE FORMER YUGOSLAVIA (ICTY) and closely resembled it in STRUCTURE and procedures. Article 1 of its statute states that "The International Tribunal for Rwanda shall have the power to prosecute persons responsible for serious violations of international humanitarian law committed in the territory of Rwanda and Rwandan citizens responsible for such violations committed in the territory of neighbouring states between 1 January 1994 and 31 December 1994." As such, it had a limited time JURISDICTION, but its mandates extend beyond the borders of Rwanda to incor-

porate crimes against Rwandans in refugee camps in the Republic of CONGO and in Burundi. The crimes it specifically was empowered to prosecute included grave breaches of the 1949 Geneva Convention, war crimes, GENOCIDE, and crimes against humanity.

The ICTR operated with primary jurisdiction over national courts under the principle of *non-bis-in-idem*, which holds that one may not be tried twice for the same crime, and prohibits national courts from hearing the cases of those standing trial in the WAR CRIMES TRIBUNAL. At any time the ICTR formally could request that national courts surrender their jurisdiction over an individual to be tried at the tribunal. The ICTR was organized like the ICTY, with three offices: the chambers of judges (with both a trial chamber and an appeals chamber), the office of the prosecutor, and the registry. The two tribunals shared the judges of the appeals chamber as well as the lead prosecutor—in 2001, the Swiss jurist Carla del Ponte. In September 2003, however, the UN Security Council removed del Ponte, and replaced her with Hassan Bubacar Jallow of Gambia.

The ICTR issued its first indictments, charging eight persons, on November 28, 1995. The tribunal also charged Jean-Paul Akayesu, a high government official, with inciting others to commit rape, recognizing the offense as a "war crime" for the first time in history. Former Rwandan prime minister Jean Kambanda was tried and convicted by the tribunal on September 4, 1998. The first head of government to be convicted for such crimes, Kambanda was sentenced to life imprisonment. The convictions of Akayesu and Kambanda were the first ever rendered by an international court for genocide. By 2007, the tribunal had secured the arrest of more than 60 individuals accused of involvement in the 1994 Rwandan massacre.

Mali was the first country to provide prison facilities for the enforcement of the tribunal's sentences. Benin, Swaziland, Belgium, Denmark, Norway, and some other African countries subsequently indicated their willingness to incarcerate persons convicted by the tribunal, under certain conditions. The ICTR was authorized to give a maximum punishment of life in prison, but no death penalty.

The budget for the ICTR in 2006–07 was $260 million for operations. The International Criminal Tribunal for Rwanda was housed at Arusha, Tanzania, and the Office of the Prosecutor was in Kigali, Rwanda. According to the ICTR's Completion Strategy, all first-instance cases were to have completed trial by the end of 2008 and the Tribunal was to end operations by 2010.

See also HUMAN RIGHTS, INTERNATIONAL CRIMINAL COURT, RWANDA CRISIS.

Further Reading: Gourevitch, Philip. *We Wish to Inform You That Tomorrow We Will Be Killed with Our Families: Stories from Rwanda.* New York: St. Martin's, 1999. Morris, Virginia, and Michael P. Scharf. *International Criminal Tribunal* *for Rwanda.* Vols. 1 and 2. Irvington, N.Y.: Transnational Publishers, 1998. Jones, John R. W. D. *The Practice of the International Criminal Tribunals for the Former Yugoslavia and Rwanda.* Irvington, N.Y.: Transnational Publishers, 1999. Romano, Cesare P. R., André Nollkaemper, and Jann K. Kleffner, eds. *Internationalized Criminal Courts: Sierra Leone, East Timor, Kosovo, and Cambodia.* New York: Oxford University Press, 2004. ICTR Web site: <www.ictr.org>.

— *D. J. Becker*

International Criminal Tribunal for the Former Yugoslavia (ICTY)

The United Nations SECURITY COUNCIL created the International Criminal Tribunal for the Former Yugoslavia in 1993 (Res. 827) as the first institution of international criminal prosecution since the Nuremberg Tribunal at the end of World War II. An earlier decision by the Council (Res. 780) had created the Kalshoven Commission of Experts to study and document crimes committed in the FORMER YUGOSLAVIA. The commission, headed by Mr. Cherif Bassiouni from Egypt, recommended that the Security Council establish an international tribunal to try those responsible for war crimes in the conflict. Both RESOLUTIONS passed unanimously. The tribunal was located in The Hague. The tribunals at Nuremberg and Tokyo were the precedents for this court. Article 1 of its statute stated that "The International Tribunal shall have the power to prosecute persons responsible for serious violations of international humanitarian law committed in the territory of the former Yugoslavia since 1991" until the UN Security Council decided to withdraw its mandate. The crimes it specifically was empowered to prosecute included grave breaches of the 1949 Geneva Convention, violations of the laws and customs of war, GENOCIDE, and crimes against humanity.

The ICTY, operating under the principle of *non-bis-in-idem*, which holds that one may not be tried twice for the same crime, prohibits national courts from hearing the cases of those standing trial in the WAR CRIMES TRIBUNAL. The ICTY could also prosecute persons already under accusation in a national court if the accused was charged only with an "ordinary" offense (that is, not a war crime), or if the national trial had not been impartial.

The ICTY had three organs: the chambers of judges (with both a trial chamber and an appeals chamber), the office of the prosecutor, and the registry. Each of these bodies was established under the terms of the international agreement that created the tribunal. The trial chamber had five judges, and the appeals chamber had three judges. The Security Council, upon recommendation of the SECRETARY-GENERAL, selected the judges and the lead prosecutor. The prosecutor in 2007 was the Swiss jurist Carla del Ponte, who followed South African Richard Goldstone and Canadian Louise Arbour in this role. The president of the tribunal, elected in November 2005, was Judge Fausto Pocar of Italy, and the vice-president was Judge Kevin Parker of Australia. The registry was the bookkeeping office of the tribunal, and served as the repository of all motions, arguments, judgments, and organizational records of the ICTY.

The International Criminal Tribunal for the Former Yugoslavia could not try defendants in absentia, but a Rule 61 proceeding allowed the prosecutor to present evidence publicly and to call witnesses. The stated purpose was to reconfirm the indictment against the defendant and to permit the judges to issue an international arrest warrant. Rule 61 served two functions. First, it provided a documentary account of alleged acts. Second, it increased pressure on alleged war criminals who would not be able to travel out of the country without fear of detention by a UN member.

The ICTY issued its first indictment on November 11, 1994. It was for Dragan Nikolić, a Bosnian Serb who was alleged to have been the commander of a small prison camp in eastern BOSNIA. The first conviction was Duško Tadić, who was convicted of every count established by the statute except genocide. Other notable indictments included former Yugoslav president SLOBODAN MILOŠEVIĆ, and Bosnian Serb leaders Radovan Karadžić and General Ratko Mladić, the latter two of whom remained at large by early 2007. The ICTY relied on other institutions, most notably the North Atlantic Treaty Organization (NATO), to apprehend and extradite indicted individuals. As of August 2006, the tribunal had publicly indicted 161 individuals and completed proceedings in 94 cases with 34 convictions. Of those found guilty, Radislav Krstić (chief of staff of the Bosnian Serb forces that attacked the UN peacekeepers and local POPULATION in the safe haven of Srebrenica) received the most severe sentence. The ICTY sentenced him to 46 years' imprisonment for crimes against humanity, violations of the laws of war, and genocide. The most important trial, however—that of Slobodan Milošević—ended abruptly with his death in his holding cell in the spring of 2006. His case was made even murkier in February, 2007, when the INTERNATIONAL COURT OF JUSTICE ruled that Serbia could not be held guilty of genocide in Bosnia for the actions of Bosnian Serbs.

The ICTY could pronounce a maximum punishment of life in prison. Once sentenced, defendants served their terms in nations that volunteered prison space and were approved by the tribunal. Once a criminal passed into the prison system of one of these countries, the ICTY relinquished JURISDICTION.

In 2003 the Security Council approved a Completion Strategy for the ICTY and the INTERNATIONAL CRIMINAL TRIBUNAL FOR RWANDA. Under the plan, all initial trials would be completed by the end of 2008, and the tribunal would finish all of its work by December 2010. Faced with these deadlines, the tribunal president sought, and obtained consent to add several new judges in order to hear cases more quickly. The ICTY also started returning cases to national jurisdiction in order to clear its docket. The first referral to a national court came in May 2005, when the tribunal referred the case of Radovan Stankković, a Bosnian Serb, to the State Court of Bosnia and Herzegovina on charges of crimes against humanity.

See also INTERNATIONAL CRIMINAL COURT, UNITED NATIONS MISSION IN BOSNIA AND HERZEGOVINA, UNITED NATIONS PROTECTION FORCE.

Further Reading: Ackerman, John E., and Eugene O'Sullivan. *Practice and Procedure of the International Criminal Tribunal for the Former Yugoslavia.* Boston: Kluwer Law International, 2000. Ball, Howard. *Prosecuting War Crimes and Genocide: The Twentieth Century Experience.* Lawrence: University of Kansas Press, 1999. Boas, Gideon, and William A. Schabas, eds. *International Criminal Law Developments in the Case Law of the ICTY.* Leiden, Netherlands: Brill Academic Publishers, 2003. Minow, Martha. *Between Vengeance and Forgiveness: Facing History after Genocide and Mass Violence.* Boston: Beacon Press, 1998. Neier, Aryeh. *War Crimes: Brutality, Genocide, Terror, and the Struggle for Justice.* New York: Times Books, 1998. Osiel, Mark. *Mass Atrocity, Collective Memory, and the Law.* New Brunswick, N.J.: Transaction Publishers, 1997. Paust, Jordan J., et al., eds. *International Criminal Law: Cases and Materials.* Durham, N.C.: Carolina Academic Press, 1996. Romano, Cesare P. R., André Nollkaemper, and Jann K. Kleffner, eds. *Internationalized Criminal Courts: Sierra Leone, East Timor, Kosovo, and Cambodia.* New York: Oxford University Press, 2004. ICTY Web site: <www.un.org/icty/>.

— D. J. Becker

International Day against Drug Abuse

First observed in 1988, the International Day against Drug Abuse is held annually on June 26.

International Day for Biological Diversity

The GENERAL ASSEMBLY has proclaimed May 22 of each year as the International Day for Biological Diversity. The date marks the anniversary of the adoption of the Convention on Biological Diversity in 1992.

International Day for Preventing the Exploitation of the Environment in War and Armed Conflict

The GENERAL ASSEMBLY declared this day of recognition initially for November 6, 2001, and for each following year on that date. By doing so, the General Assembly hoped to raise awareness of the long-term consequences that armed conflict has on the world's ecosystem. The damage affects territories far from the battleground and lasts long after the conflict ends.

International Day for the Elimination of Racial Discrimination

Observed annually on March 21, this International Day was proclaimed in 1966 in remembrance of the 69 people killed by police gunfire on March 21, 1960, in Sharpeville, South Africa. They were part of a peaceful demonstration against APARTHEID.

International Day for the Elimination of Violence against Women

The GENERAL ASSEMBLY designated November 25 as International Day for the Elimination of Violence against WOMEN. That date was chosen to remember the 1961 assassination of three Mirabal sisters, political activists in the Dominican Republic, on orders of Dominican ruler Rafael Trujillo.

International Day for the Eradication of Poverty

Observed on October 17 annually, the day replaced the World Day for Overcoming Extreme Poverty, observed in many countries. The GENERAL ASSEMBLY created the day to promote awareness of the need to eradicate poverty and destitution in all nations, particularly in DEVELOPING COUNTRIES.

International Day for the Preservation of the Ozone Layer

Observed on September 16 annually, the day marks the anniversary of the signing of the MONTREAL PROTOCOL ON SUBSTANCES THAT DEPLETE THE OZONE LAYER in 1987.

International Day in Support of Victims of Torture

Observed on June 26, the date in 1987 when the CONVENTION AGAINST TORTURE AND OTHER CRUEL, INHUMAN OR DEGRADING TREATMENT OR PUNISHMENT entered into force, the day raises world public attention to the continuing problem of torture.

International Day of Commemoration in Memory of the Victims of the Holocaust

Observed on January 27 annually, the day marks the date on which the Soviet army liberated the Nazi death camp in Auschwitz-Birkenau (Poland). The day was established by the UN GENERAL ASSEMBLY, and first observed in 2006.

International Day of Cooperatives

In 1994, recognizing that cooperatives were becoming an indispensable factor in the economic and social development of the Third World, the GENERAL ASSEMBLY declared the first Saturday of July every year as the International Day of Cooperatives. The date marks the anniversary of the founding of the International Cooperative Alliance, an umbrella group of organizations comprising 760 million members of cooperatives in 100 countries in 1892.

International Day of Disabled Persons

The International Day of Disabled Persons is observed annually on December 3. Beginning in 2005, the day took on new importance as the world community entered final negotiations on an international CONVENTION to protect the rights of the disabled.

International Day of Older Persons

First celebrated in 1991, the International Day of Older Persons is held annually on October 4.

International Day of Peace

In 1981, the UN GENERAL ASSEMBLY declared that the opening day of its regular session in September each year "shall be officially dedicated and observed as the International Day of Peace and shall be devoted to commemorating and strengthening the ideals of peace both within and among all nations and peoples." The General Assembly convenes each year, usually on the first Tuesday after September 1.

International Day of Solidarity with the Palestinian People

Celebrated annually on November 29, the day marks the anniversary of RESOLUTION 181, passed by the GENERAL ASSEMBLY in 1947 calling for the partition of Palestine.

International Day of the World's Indigenous People

In 1994 the GENERAL ASSEMBLY proclaimed August 9 for the duration of the International Decade of the World's Indigenous People (1995–2004) as the day in the UN calendar to recognize INDIGENOUS PEOPLES. On that day in 1982 the UN Working Group on Indigenous Populations of the SUB-COMMISSION ON THE PROMOTION AND PROTECTION OF HUMAN RIGHTS convened for the first time.

International Day of United Nations Peacekeepers

The UN GENERAL ASSEMBLY established May 29 as the day to be observed annually as the International Day of UN Peacekeepers. The day marks the anniversary of SECURITY COUNCIL Resolution 50 of May 29, 1948, that authorized the creation of the first United Nations PEACEKEEPING operation.

International Development Association (IDA)

See WORLD BANK.

International Finance Corporation (IFC) *See* WORLD BANK.

International Fund for Agricultural Development (IFAD)

The 1974 World Food Conference initiated the International Fund for Agricultural Development as a UN SPECIALIZED AGENCY. The conference sought to respond to the food crises of the early 1970s that especially affected the Sahelian area of Africa. Believing that economic structural problems and the concentration of poor POPULATIONS in remote rural areas accounted for much food deficiency, insecurity, and famine, the conference advanced a RESOLUTION stating that "an International Fund for Agricultural Development should be established immediately to finance agricultural DEVELOPMENT projects primarily for food production in the DEVELOPING COUNTRIES." Thus, to ease scarcity in rural settings, improve nutrition, and deal with poverty and hunger, IFAD was to target the poorest people in the world. The FUND began operation as an international financial institution in 1977.

IFAD works with other institutions, including the WORLD BANK, REGIONAL DEVELOPMENT BANKS, and regional and UN agencies. Many of these bodies co-finance projects initiated by IFAD. Low-income countries obtain loans and grants from the fund on concessional terms, repaid usually over 40 years, with an initial grace period of 10 years and a very low annual service charge. From the time it began work in 1977 through February 2007, IFAD financed more than 732 projects in more than 115 countries and territories. The cost of these projects was $9.5 billion in grants and loans. IFAD played a central role in the fight against DESERTIFICATION. The agency contributed more than $750 million in grants and loans to assist governments fighting the environmental phenomenon. It also financed specific programs in 25 African nations. The fund's resources come, in roughly equal share, from three major sources: member contributions, loan repayments, and investment income.

MEMBERSHIP in IFAD is open to any member of the United Nations or one of its specialized agencies. A Governing Council—made up of all 165 members (as of 2007)—is the fund's highest authority. The council holds sessions annually and may call SPECIAL SESSIONS. A governor and alternate governor represent the council when it is not in session. An executive board of 18 members and 18 alternates oversees daily operations and approves loans and grants. The Governing Council elects a president for a four-year term, renewable for one further term. In 2007, the council elected Mr. Lennart Båge its president. Its HEADQUARTERS is in Rome.

See also CHIEF EXECUTIVES BOARD, ENVIRONMENT, FOOD AND AGRICULTURE ORGANIZATION, UNITED NATIONS RESEARCH INSTITUTE FOR SOCIAL DEVELOPMENT, WORLD FOOD PROGRAMME.

Further Reading: McGovern, George. *The Third Freedom, Ending Hunger in Our Time.* New York: Simon and Schuster, 2001. Talbot, Ross B. *The Four World Food Agencies in Rome.* Ames: Iowa State University Press, 1990. IFAD Web site: <www.ifad.org>.

International Labour Organization (ILO)

The constitution of the International Labour Organization was incorporated in Part XIII of the 1919 Versailles Peace Treaty ending World War I. International commitment to such an organization grew out of the strong labor and social movements of the late 19th century. The first meeting of the ILO was in Washington, D.C., on October 29, 1919. It subsequently opened its permanent headquarters—operated by its SECRETARIAT, the International Labour Office—in Geneva. On December 14, 1946, the International Labour Organization became the first SPECIALIZED AGENCY of the newly created United Nations. With an original MEMBERSHIP of 45 countries, the ILO grew to near universal NATION-STATE participation by 2007, with 180 members. In 1969, during its 50th anniversary year, the agency was awarded the Nobel Peace Prize.

Not only governments are represented in the organization but also employer and worker delegates participate with equal VOTING rights. Each member state has four representatives to the ILO: two government delegates, one employer and one worker delegate. Members of the delegation are not required to speak or vote with one national voice, but may and do cast differing votes on issues brought before the organization. This arrangement is unique among UN specialized agencies. Delegates meet annually in the International Labour Conference, held each June in Geneva. Approximately 3,000 people participate. The conference is the chief legislative body. Each year the conference adopts several CONVENTIONS and RESOLUTIONS focused on international labor standards and working conditions.

Between sessions of the conference, the work of the ILO is directed by the Governing Body, a committee that meets three times a year (March, June, and November) and has 56 members (28 government, 14 employer, and 14 worker representatives). Ten of the government seats are held by "members of chief industrial importance": the UNITED STATES, the United Kingdom, FRANCE, CHINA, RUSSIAN FEDERATION, Brazil, Italy, JAPAN, INDIA, and GERMANY. The remaining 18 seats are allocated on the basis of equitable geographical distribution: Africa (6), Americas (5), Asia (4), and Europe (3). Member countries are elected for three-year terms. The Governing Body prepares the agenda for the annual conference, drafts the budget, and undertakes ILO initiatives. It also elects the DIRECTOR-GENERAL.

The third important body in the ILO is the International Labour Office. As of 2007, it had been headed by nine directors-general since 1919: Albert Thomas (France, 1919–32), Harold Butler (GREAT BRITAIN, 1932–38), John G. Winant (United States, 1939–41), Edward Phelan (Ireland, 1941–48), David Morse (United States, 1948–70), C. Wilfred Jenks (Great Britain, 1970–73), Francis Blanchard (France, 1974–89), Michel Hansenne (Belgium, 1989–99), and Juan Somavia (Chile, 1999–   ). The director-general oversees a staff of approximately 2,000, working both in Geneva and in 40 field offices around the world, and administers the organization's budget, which was $594 million in 2008–09. The office directs research and training programs, prepares reports, and provides secretariat services to the many committees of the organization. Among the most important of these subordinate bodies is the Committee on Freedom of Association (CFA). Created in 1951, the nine-member CFA meets three times a year to hear complaints (more than 2,000 since its founding) about violations of freedom of association. The secretariat carries out investigations and writes reports on these complaints, as well as preparing reports on individual countries' compliance with ILO standards and conventions.

The work of the ILO is guided by three of its most important documents: the constitution found in the Versailles Treaty, its 1944 "Philadelphia DECLARATION," and the 1998 "Declaration on Fundamental Principles and Rights at Work and its Follow-up." These statements of purpose give the organization three broad duties. First, throughout its history the ILO has drafted and promoted conventions and treaties that establish international labor standards. By 2001 it had promulgated 183 conventions, and made 191 official "recommendations" to the international community. Once a member state ratified an ILO convention, it was obligated to implement its recommendations in domestic law. These conventions covered such topics as occupational safety and health, working conditions, industrial relations, minimum wage, social security, HUMAN RIGHTS, the employment of WOMEN, children, and the disabled, and collective bargaining. Second, the ILO provides technical assistance to national governments and the private sector, particularly in the developing world. To this end it works closely with the UNITED NATIONS DEVELOPMENT PROGRAMME. It also became one of the sponsoring organizations for UN SECRETARY-GENERAL

KOFI ANNAN'S "GLOBAL COMPACT" program, launched in 1999 and meant to bring private companies into a working relationship with the United Nations. Under the program, participating enterprises commit themselves to uphold nine principles, four of them (freedom of association and the right to collective bargaining, promotion of the elimination of all forms of forced and compulsory labor, effective abolition of child labor, and the elimination of discrimination in respect to employment and occupation) coming directly from the ILO's 1998 Declaration. Third, the ILO sponsors research, training, education, and publication of labor related materials. In 1960, the organization created the International Institute for Labour Studies in Geneva to conduct much of the research function. In 1965 it set up the International Training Centre in Turin, Italy, in order to train senior and mid-level managers in both private and public enterprises. During its first 35 years of operation, the Centre trained more than 70,000 individuals.

The work of the ILO has not been without controversy. Given the differences in labor laws and ideologies among nations, ILO standards have often offended particular member states. During the COLD WAR, when the world community had both capitalist and socialist systems vying for international dominance, the International Labour Organization was often accused of being "politicized." From 1977 to 1980 the United States refused to participate in the ILO for this reason and withdrew its funding, accounting for nearly one-fourth of the organization's BUDGET. Successive American governments insisted on major reforms in the ILO, along with several other specialized agencies, before it would pay past and continuing assessments. Most of these had been met by the end of the century under Secretary-General Annan's REFORM program, and U.S. arrearages were paid in 2001.

See also ADMINISTRATIVE TRIBUNALS, APARTHEID, CHIEF EXECUTIVES BOARD, EXPANDED PROGRAM OF TECHNICAL ASSISTANCE, INTERNATIONAL COVENANT ON CIVIL AND POLITICAL RIGHTS.

Further Reading: Imber, Mark. *The USA, ILO, UNESCO, and IAEA: Politicization and Withdrawal in the Specialized Agencies.* London: Macmillan, 1989. Lubin, Carol Riegelman, and Anne Winslow. *Social Justice for Women: The International Labor Organization and Women.* Durham, N.C.: Duke University Press, 1990. ILO Web site: <www.ilo.org>.

international law

The body of rules and norms regulating activities between and among NATION-STATES—often called "the law of nations"—was entitled "International Law" by the English philosopher Jeremy Bentham (1748–1832). Bentham's became the preferred term by the middle of the 20th century, although it was often expanded to "public international law" to contrast it with "private international law,"

or the "conflict of laws," regulating private matters affected by more than one legal JURISDICTION. By the beginning of the 21st century, due in part to quickening developments in the international community, and particularly due to activities within the UNITED NATIONS SYSTEM, international law's province experienced an expansion, in some instances including areas of jurisdiction once thought to be outside its realm. For example, recent years have witnessed a development in the field of international economic law that constitutes a mix of public and private international law. The expansion can be seen also in the establishment of WAR CRIMES TRIBUNALS to take to court individuals accused of violating HUMAN RIGHTS, even within their own country. Nonetheless, the apparent applicability of international law has not resulted in any comparable super-national means of enforcement. Whereas law within nations is enforced via the police function of the state, there is no such MECHANISM in an international community that continues to be composed of sovereign nations.

According to Article 38 of the STATUTE OF THE INTERNATIONAL COURT OF JUSTICE, the sources of international law are international CONVENTIONS, international custom, general principles of law recognized by civilized nations, judicial decisions, and teachings of the most qualified publicists on the topic. Of these, ratified international conventions and treaties tend to carry the most weight. Some legal experts also consider ARBITRATION awards and decisions by the ICJ as precedents for developing law in the international arena. International law is usually considered part of national or municipal law. (For example, Article 6, paragraph two of the U.S. Constitution declares "all treaties made, or which shall be made, under the authority of the UNITED STATES, shall be the supreme law of the land; and the Judges in every State shall be bound thereby, anything in the Constitution or laws of any State to the contrary notwithstanding.")

The development of formal relations between and among nations, empires, and peoples has characterized human activity since the millennia before the common era. The diffusion and ultimate availability of texts and TREATIES dealing with such relations suggests a pattern in world history of cross-cultural intercourse among political elites the world over that led to what might be called international affairs or even "international law." Basic principles and precedents emerged as different communities sought to impose order on their mutual relations, and to resolve disagreements without the resort to force, except as those principles might allow or require it.

Although law-like relations existed among political units in antiquity and throughout the world, the modern concept of international law emerged at the end of the Middle Ages in European history. It referred to a body of rules considered binding in relations among princely states. Typically, international law regulated diplomatic practices (that is, protection of diplomatic personnel, rules of seniority among ambassadors to a specific country, and related diplomatic matters), maritime intercourse, restrictions on WEAPONS, and the commencement and conduct of war. In 1625, the Dutch jurist Hugo Grotius (1583–1645) published his *De jure belli ac pacis* (Concerning the law of war and peace), the first comprehensive text of international rules. His views were frequently studied and on occasion applied in subsequent international interactions.

It is of note that Grotius, and many early publicists on international law who followed him—including Dutchman Cornelius van Bynkershoek (1673–1743), German philosopher Christian von Wolff (1679–1754), Swiss jurist Emerich de Vattel (1714–67), and German Georg Friedrich von Martens (1756–1821)—highlighted the SOVEREIGNTY and legal equality of states, principles later ensconced in the UN CHARTER (Article 2, paragraph 1). The concept of the sovereign state was enshrined in the 1648 Treaty of Westphalia, which prohibited interference by outside powers in a state's internal affairs. In the Westphalian system states took on obligations in the international community only by their voluntary commitments made largely through treaties. By the late 18th century, the mounting use of treaty agreements had furthered the course of international law considerably. Even the newly independent United States, emphasizing the value of treaty arrangements, contributed to its elaboration in the areas of international trade, freedom of the seas, and the meaning of neutrality.

Grotius developed many of his concepts of modern international law from an empirical study of what nations actually did in his time. For example, his rules on the Law of the Sea were drawn from contemporaneous Dutch practice that emphasized oceanic free trade. But the Dutch scholar also premised his work on the assertion that international law was a reflection of the natural law, divorced from earlier theological conceptions of higher law, but nonetheless a reflection of the law of nature based on reason. Accordingly, Grotius's 1625 work invigorated an already existing "naturalist" school of international law. Found in the works of Francisco Vitoria (1480–1546), Father Suarez (1548–1617), and Samuel Pufendorf (1632–94), naturalists argued that international law should codify not simply what states do, but rather what states *should* do to conform to the principles of justice. Pufendorf in particular denied the value of treaties and urged a conception of international law that recognized absolute values. The natural law tradition espoused by these scholars remained a secondary thread of Grotius's teachings until the 1940s, when the horror of the Nazi era produced a new interest in using international law to defend HUMAN RIGHTS, protect values even if states had not officially agreed to them in treaties, and punish states for "crimes against humanity." In this spirit, the Preamble of the UN Charter "reaffirm(ed) faith in fundamental human rights, in the dignity and worth of the human person, [and] in the equal rights of men and WOMEN."

The period of the Napoleonic Wars in the early 19th century witnessed a disregard for the law of nations, until the Congress of Vienna (1814–15), which concluded those wars, attempted a reassertion of European order through the restoration of older rules of diplomacy, and introduced newer and more standardized legal principles, such as respect for the freedom of navigation on international waterways and the more precise classification for and protection of diplomatic personnel. What had been "customary" international law—accepted practice—was clarified in legally binding international agreements. This marked the beginning of the long era of "legal positivism." The DECLARATION of Paris (1856) following the Crimean War represented the first major attempt to codify the rules of maritime warfare. It made privateering illegal, determined that a neutral flag protected all goods on board a ship—except contraband of a belligerent during times of war—and made neutral goods free from capture even when under an enemy's flag. A blockade was considered binding only if it was functional; that is, a belligerent could no longer APPEAL to a "paper" blockade. The Declaration of Paris was the accepted rule of law on the high seas until it became unfeasible with the introduction of submarines in World War I. As the century proceeded, multilateral agreements were negotiated establishing international rules for weights and measures, trademarks, copyrights, patents, and other matters for which legal uniformity was desirable. New technologies resulted in international conferences that established the International Telegraph Union (at Paris in 1865) and the UNIVERSAL POSTAL UNION (at Berne, Switzerland, in 1874). In the post–World War II period these became the UN SPECIALIZED AGENCIES of the INTERNATIONAL TELE-COMMUNICATIONS UNION and the Universal Postal Union, respectively.

Meantime, arbitration as a means of settling disputes became fashionable. With the Jay Treaty of 1794, the United States and GREAT BRITAIN initiated the practice of setting up mixed commissions to settle disagreements unyielding to normal diplomacy. The post–American Civil War *Alabama Claims* arbitration in 1872 between the United Kingdom and the United States marked a decisive phase in the arbitration movement that culminated with the establishment of the PERMANENT COURT OF ARBITRATION at the Hague Conference of 1899. A second Hague Conference in 1907 expanded rules governing arbitral procedures. The two Hague Conferences also issued a number of declarations and conventions dealing with the laws of war, including banning aerial bombardment, submarine mines, and poison gas. Meantime, Pan American Congresses in the Western Hemisphere established several continent-wide diplomatic practices.

But the onset of World War I brought this progress to a halt. Many provisions of international law were violated and new problems arose—for example, submarine warfare and the use of CHEMICAL WEAPONS—for which existing standards of international behavior were inadequate. The creation of the LEAGUE OF NATIONS and the PERMANENT COURT OF INTERNATIONAL JUSTICE following the war were attempts to create multinational institutions to deal with the extraordinary problems that had arisen during the conflict. The League represented the first attempt in history to maintain a permanent organization committed to a sustained effort to develop and codify international law. That is, unlike functional organizations of the 19th century dealing with a single purpose, and unlike time-bound congresses or conferences, the League was a multipurpose, permanent organization, with a SECRETARIAT, and a mandate to deal with all international law matters. League conferences brought forth more than 120 international understandings covering a range of subjects. Although many failed of full ratification, they became a model for the future United Nations, and some—such as those dealing with control of narcotics, traffic in persons, economic statistics, and slavery—remained in force with UN AMENDMENTS or further treaty action. Moreover, the UN SECRETARY-GENERAL's office became responsible for the depository of extant League documents.

Also in the interwar period other multilateral activities extended the reach of international law. The Washington Naval Conference of 1921–22 disarmed the world's most powerful navies (the last actual "DISARMAMENT" agreement until the 1987 Intermediate Nuclear Forces Agreement signed by the Soviet Union and the United States, although in the interim there were "arms limitations" and "arms control" initiatives), abolished the Anglo-Japanese alliance, provided for mutual respect for Pacific territories, and endorsed the Open Door Policy in CHINA to preserve China's territorial integrity and assure equal trade in the country. The Kellogg-Briand PACT (Paris Pact) of 1928, ultimately signed by 62 nations, outlawed war as national policy. These multilateral agreements had no enforcement mechanisms. They depended on compliance or moral suasion. The rise of fascism and nazism in Europe and of militarism in JAPAN and then the collapse of international order in the 1930s wrought discredit to the agreements of the 1920s and damaged the reputation of the League of Nations. The advent of World War II tainted international law with the darkest of hues.

Yet, phoenix-like, out of the war came the United Nations, the new INTERNATIONAL COURT OF JUSTICE (ICJ), a congeries of international economic institutions, and a renewed dedication to reclaim and build upon the efforts of former years. Indeed, during the post–World War II period, the concepts and procedures constituting international law were to undergo considerable maturation and affect the entire globe. From those early concerns with state practices during wartime through the development of a balance of power conception of international relations, international law was, by the 21st century, a remarkably transformed system, featuring a permanent multilateral framework for the resolution of disputes; preservation of the peace; the rules of war; the establishment of WAR CRIMES TRIBUNALS; financial, economic,

environmental, and technological cooperation; and even the promulgation of individual and human rights. While this momentum clearly did not and could not promise a world utopia, the long-term crafting of such an international framework represented one of the extraordinary achievements of human endeavor. And, from 1945, the United Nations stood at the heart of these developments.

Since the end of World War II there have been differing opinions about exactly what international law is and how it is to be executed. One straightforward view is that all nations should obey international law, just as individuals should obey domestic (or "municipal") law. Yet some lofty thinkers—Samuel Pufendorf and Thomas Hobbes in the 17th century, John Austin in the 19th, and Henry Kissinger in the 20th—have challenged the very notion of an international "law," because there is no legitimate enforcer. Sociological responses have emphasized the behavior of states rather than overarching principle. Thus, since states seek first their own preservation, then their increased power, and only afterward world order, international law, according to some sociologists, cannot shape international politics but merely adjust to it. Marxists have regarded international law as but an instrument of class oppression; Chinese scholars, whether or not followers of MAO ZEDONG, have described international law as a set of platitudes that historically have been ruinous to non-Western cultures such as China's; many citizens of Third World nations have felt themselves victimized by Eurocentered notions of international law (as SADDAM HUSSEIN said he was in 1990 while trying to correct a British-dictated boundary line between IRAQ and Kuwait); feminists have argued that "the rules of international law privilege men," that women are "marginalized," and that international law is "a thoroughly gendered system"; and "post modernism," emphasizing relativism, difference, and the problematic nature of LANGUAGE itself, has questioned any "universalist" assumption of a fundamental international law deriving from a narrow, elitist political tradition in the Western First World. And, of course, a common commitment to a single conception of legal principles is less likely when one nation's core interests diverge from the interests of other nations.

Yet in practice international law is widely recognized and most nations have participated in its evolution. The penalties for failing to comply, although less severe than in national cases, and often unenforceable, are economic SANCTIONS, the constraint of public opinion, intervention by third states, international condemnation—as by way of UN RESOLUTIONS—and, as a last resort, war.

The wider reach of international law by the late 20th century was due in no small part to the activities of UN-related organizations. The International Court of Justice, which replaced the Permanent Court of International Justice after World War II and is popularly known as the World Court, has made modest but significant contributions to the development of international law, through countless judgments and advisory opinions that, although usually narrow, have affected maritime law, questions of diplomatic immunity, the legitimacy of mandates under the League of Nations, the COMPETENCE of the United Nations, the jurisdiction of its PRINCIPAL ORGANS, and other matters. Article 102 of the UN Charter requires member states to register all treaties with the Secretariat, which must then publish them. This represents a continuation of the practice of the League of Nations. It means that there is a central depository for all international agreements and that there should be no "secret" arrangements unobserved by the international community. By Article 13, paragraph 1 of the Charter, the GENERAL ASSEMBLY (GA) acquired the obligation to initiate studies and make recommendations for "encouraging the progressive development of international law and its codification." In 1947 the Assembly entrusted this Charter function to the INTERNATIONAL LAW COMMISSION, an auxiliary but autonomous organ of the Assembly, which began the slow but steady process of codification. The General Assembly SIXTH COMMITTEE works closely with the International Law Commission; it reviews the work of the UN COMMISSION ON INTERNATIONAL TRADE LAW (UNCITRAL), negotiates relevant treaties and agreements to submit to the General Assembly Plenary (the Sixth Committee spent 30 years in intricate negotiations to determine an internationally acceptable definition of AGGRESSION), and deals with reports from all UN bodies regarding legal matters. UNCITRAL, created by the General Assembly in 1966, develops conventions, rules, and legal guides to harmonize international trade law. The UN OFFICE OF LEGAL AFFAIRS (OLA), initiated in 1946, serves the Secretariat and provides legal advice to the Secretary-General. The WORLD INTELLECTUAL PROPERTY ORGANIZATION (WIPO), established in 1970, promotes the protection of intellectual property worldwide, and the INTERNATIONAL MARITIME ORGANIZATION (IMO), begun in 1959, is the only UN agency solely involved with issues of shipping safety and securing environmentally sound oceans.

The UN's efforts to internationalize outer space and bring it into the realm of recognized international law resulted in the 1966 Treaty on Principles Governing the Activities of States in the Exploration and Use of Outer Space, including the Moon and Other Celestial Bodies (Outer Space Treaty) and the 1979 Agreement Governing Activities of States on the Moon and Other Celestial Bodies (the MOON AGREEMENT). The COMMITTEE ON THE PEACEFUL USES OF OUTER SPACE, set up by the General Assembly in 1959 to review and encourage international cooperation, has adopted several additional treaties and conventions to regulate outer space, and in 1974 the committee set up the Office for Outer Space Affairs, which maintains a registry of space objects.

Other important areas of developing international law less directly connected with the United Nations derived from various arms agreements (beginning with the Limited Test Ban Treaty of 1963), from the internationalization of Ant-

arctica (1959), and from a number of agreements regarding international economic and financial relations. The GENERAL AGREEMENT ON TARIFFS AND TRADE (GATT), a negotiating regime initiated in 1948 to encourage lowering trade barriers around the world, became the WORLD TRADE ORGANIZATION (WTO) in 1995. GATT/WTO, along with related organizations (the INTERNATIONAL MONETARY FUND and the WORLD BANK) founded at the BRETTON WOODS Conference (the UN Monetary and Financial Conference) in 1944, sought to bring harmonization and common rules to world trade and finance. The Bretton Woods institutions and the WTO became controversial in the late 1990s as some environmentalists, labor activists, and socialists came to view these institutions as promoting only the interests of wealthy capitalist nations to the disadvantage of DEVELOPING COUNTRIES, laboring people, and the ecosystem. Defenders insisted that these institutions, by bringing the rule of law to the world economy, providing banking resources for troubled economies, establishing transparent rules of trade among ever more nations, and lowering barriers to trade, travel, and investment, offered the best antidote to persistent poverty and the most sensible stimulus to economic growth worldwide.

One of the most comprehensive agreements affecting the development of international law was the UN CONVENTION ON THE LAW OF THE SEA. The convention, affording a uniform rule in the uses of the sea, established a framework to deal with questions of sovereignty, jurisdiction, use, and national rights and obligations in ocean areas. The convention was opened for signature in 1982 and entered into force in 1994. In like manner, the United Nations has been involved in the growth of international environmental law. Usually the UNITED NATIONS ENVIRONMENT PROGRAMME administers the many treaties brokered by the United Nations, including agreements on DESERTIFICATION, biological diversity, movement of hazardous wastes, protection of the ozone layer, and controlling acid rain. The KYOTO PROTOCOL, negotiated at a UN conference in 1997, set standards for states to curtail greenhouse emissions in order to combat global warming.

Undoubtedly, the most celebrated contribution by the United Nations to the creation of new international law is in the broad area of human rights. The contemporary effort to develop international law as an expression of a higher law that governs all human activity found its first modern expression in the international war crimes trials at Nuremberg and for Japanese enemies in Tokyo. Whereas a precedent of sorts had been established in the Versailles Treaty after World War I (providing for international tribunals for offending Germans, but left to German courts, where prosecution dissipated), nothing like them had happened before and nothing like them took place again until the late 20th century. Captured German and Japanese leaders were not charged with violating any particular treaty commitment, or even with violating their own domestic laws. They were tried, convicted, and punished for crimes against humanity. Following the trials, there developed over time an abundance of international agreements and rules that seemed to proscribe those atrocities classified as human rights violations.

In 1946 the General Assembly affirmed "the principles of international law recognized by the Charter of the Nuremberg Tribunal and the judgment of the Tribunal." At the same time the Assembly declared that "GENOCIDE is a crime under international law," and in 1948 the GA approved the Genocide Convention (CONVENTION ON THE PREVENTION AND PUNISHMENT OF THE CRIME OF GENOCIDE). In 1946 the ECONOMIC AND SOCIAL COUNCIL (ECOSOC) established the UN COMMISSION ON HUMAN RIGHTS, which was chaired by ELEANOR ROOSEVELT and given a mandate to compose a UNIVERSAL DECLARATION OF HUMAN RIGHTS. Working with a group of celebrated international legal minds from a variety of cultures, Mrs. Roosevelt discovered that conceptualizing rights and fleshing out international law were multicultural, even multicivilizational endeavors. Peng-chung Chang, a Chinese philosopher, brought an Asian and Confucianist perspective to discussions; Charles Malik a view from the Arab Middle East; Hernan Santa Cruz was from Chile and from the Latin American political left; and Hansa Mehta brought an Indian outlook and an insistence that women's equality be clearly articulated. René Cassin, a French Jew, possessed a unique outlook, colored by the most recent, and appalling, example of human rights violations, When, in late 1948, the General Assembly passed the Universal Declaration without a dissenting vote, no longer could it be asserted without challenge that the notion of rights and the practice of international law were strictly Western conceits. René Cassin noted the most significant, if subtle, breakthrough in his 1968 acceptance speech upon receiving the Nobel Peace Prize: After the Universal Declaration, nations still retained jurisdiction over their citizens, he said, but it would "no longer be exclusive." From the 17th century to 1948, absolute state sovereignty had been the underpinning of international law. With the ascension of the primacy of rights, international law had entered a new, uncertain, phase. Combined with the declaration, the INTERNATIONAL COVENANT ON ECONOMIC, SOCIAL AND CULTURAL RIGHTS, and the INTERNATIONAL COVENANT ON CIVIL AND POLITICAL RIGHTS, both opened for signature in 1966 and both brought into force in 1976, made up the "International Bill of Human Rights." Other conventions and declarations announcing an assortment of human rights continued to pass in UN organs. By the summer of 1993, more than 170 nations, meeting in Vienna, adopted a sweeping declaration affirming the principle that "all human rights are universal," and that "it is the duty of states, regardless of their political, economic and cultural systems, to promote and protect all human rights and fundamental freedoms." Add to this the establishment of war crimes tribunals (the INTERNATIONAL TRIBUNAL FOR RWANDA, the SPECIAL COURT FOR SIERRA LEONE, the international human rights courts in CAMBODIA, and the INTERNATIONAL CRIMINAL TRIBUNAL FOR THE FORMER YUGOSLAVIA) that in the early 21st century were prosecuting individuals for crimes against humanity perpetrated *in their own countries,* and the adoption in Rome in 1998 of a statute calling for an INTERNATIONAL CRIMINAL COURT to try individuals for genocide, crimes against humanity, war crimes, and aggression, and the implication Cassin discerned comes into fuller relief.

The use of the International Criminal Court (ICC) and the companion tribunals to punish government officials for crimes against their own people tested the existing three-century paradigm for international order by challenging the sovereignty of the state. It also introduced morality into the considerations of international relations. Particularly in the area of human rights enforcement, state sovereignty progressively gave way to what UN Secretary-General KOFI ANNAN called "personal sovereignty," the international legal defense of people's rights against their own governments. By the early 21st century, the United Nations asserted a "RESPONSIBILITY TO PROTECT" these populations under international law.

Not only in the human rights area, but in economic and environmental policy arenas international law is taking on new enforceability. Rulings by the World Trade Organization that limit or reject a government's trade policies cannot be ignored without the offending nation paying very high domestic economic costs in the form of trade retaliation, sanctions, and denial of access to capital in the world market. In the DEVELOPMENT of their own societies, states must also consider the environmental consequences of their policies on other countries. Even without formal signature on existing environmental treaties states find it counterproductive to violate new consensual environmental rules. International law today is increasingly reflective of a global community and its standards rather than solely the product of sovereign states' decisions.

See also ACCESSION, APPENDIX A, APPENDIX E, CHAPTER VI, CHAPTER VII, COMPULSORY JURISDICTION, CONVENTION RELATING TO THE STATUS OF REFUGEES, DIRECTOR-GENERAL, GULF WAR, HAGUE ACADEMY OF INTERNATIONAL LAW, INQUIRY, IRAN HOSTAGE CRISIS, *JUS COGENS,* MILLENNIUM SUMMIT, NATION-STATE, PEACEKEEPING, SECURITY COUNCIL, STIMSON DOCTRINE, STRUCTURE OF THE UNITED NATIONS, TERRORISM TREATIES, UNITED NATIONS CONFERENCE ON THE HUMAN ENVIRONMENT, WORLD SUMMIT (2005).

Further Reading: Anaya, S. James. *Indigenous Peoples in International Law.* New York: Oxford University Press, 2000. Beck, Robert J., et al., eds. *International Rules: Approaches from International Law and International Relations.* New York: Oxford University Press, 1996. Bentham, Jeremy, "Principles of International Law" (original, 1786–1789). In Bowring, John, ed. *The Works of Jeremy Bentham.* Vol. 2. New York:

Russell and Russell, 1962. Elagab, Omer Y. *International Law Documents Relating to Terrorism.* London: Cavendish Publishers, 1995. Glendon, Mary Ann. *A World Made New: Eleanor Roosevelt and the Universal Declaration of Human Rights.* New York: Random House, 2001. Gross, Leo. "The Development of International Law through the United Nations." In *The United Nations; Past, Present, and Future.* Ed. by John Barros. New York: Free Press, 1972. Hannikainen, Lauri. *Peremptory Norms (Jus Cogens) in International Law: Historical Development, Criteria, Present Status.* Helsinki: Finnish Lawyers' Publishing Company, 1988. Oxman, Bernard H. "Complementary Agreements and Compulsory Jurisdiction," *American Journal of International Law* 95, no. 2 (April 2001): 277–312. Romano, Cesare P. R., André Nollkaemper, and Jann K. Kleffner, eds. *Internationalized Criminal Courts: Sierra Leone, East Timor, Kosovo, and Cambodia.* New York: Oxford University Press, 2004. Singh, Nagendra. "The UN and the Development of International Law." In Roberts, Adam, and Benedict Kingsbury, eds. *United Nations, Divided World.* New York: Oxford University Press, 1993. Research on international law Web site: <www.lib.uchicago.edu/~llou/forintlaw>. UN International Law Web site: <www.un.org/law>.

International Law Commission (ILC)

Article 13, paragraph 1 of the UN CHARTER directs the GENERAL ASSEMBLY (GA) to "initiate studies and make recommendations" to promote "the progressive development of INTERNATIONAL LAW and its codification." In response, GA RESOLUTION 174, in 1947, created an International Law Commission. The new permanent commission, charged with fulfilling the mandate of Article 13, began meeting on June 17, 1948. Since then, it has sought to make international law clear and acknowledged and to encourage its evolution. The commission's task is to forward the principles of the UN Charter. It engages chiefly in drafting articles on aspects of international law that may at some future point be acceptable in international CONVENTIONS or treaties.

The commission's MEMBERSHIP, initially 15, was increased three times and as of 2007 consisted of 34 individuals of "recognized COMPETENCE" in international law, elected by the General Assembly to reflect "the principal forms of civilization and the principal legal systems of the world." Members serve for five-year terms, no two of which may be nationals of the same NATION-STATE, and they may be reelected. The General Assembly receives nominees in the same manner as it does nominees to the INTERNATIONAL COURT OF JUSTICE, that is, from lists provided by UN member states. And as in the case of the ICJ, members of the commission serve as individuals, not as representatives of a specific government. Notwithstanding the requirement of impartiality, in 1981 the GA mandated the following geographical pattern of representation: nine members from African states, eight from Asia, three from Eastern

Europe, six from LATIN AMERICA and the Caribbean, and eight from Western Europe and Other States. The commission is instructed by a statute that was drafted by the GA SIXTH COMMITTEE and adopted by the General Assembly on November 21, 1947. It usually meets in UN HEADQUARTERS in Geneva (Palais des Nations). The topics handled by the commission are often forwarded to it by the General Assembly or the Sixth Committee, or, on occasion, by other UN bodies. Since its founding, the commission has been one of the UN bodies to make use of SPECIAL RAPPORTEURS in aiding its research. When the commission completes draft articles on a particular topic, the General Assembly may convene an international conference of plenipotentiaries to consider incorporating the articles into a convention, and then open the convention to signature.

The idea of codifying and developing international law derives from long historic desires. For example, the British 18th-century philosopher Jeremy Bentham, who is credited with having coined the phrase "international law," proposed a full codification of all international laws. In 1924, the assembly of the LEAGUE OF NATIONS, with a view to fostering codification, created a committee of experts to compile a list of laws and obtain comments by various world governments on its work. In the spring of 1930, at The Hague, 47 governments participated in a "Codification Conference," which, however, ended with little in the way of accomplishment. Within a decade world war had broken out, and the labors of law codifiers seemed gravely weakened. But the UN's founders, with Article 13 of the Charter, determined to undertake another effort. The International Law Commission became a permanent manifestation of that endeavor.

By October 2006, the commission had completed drafts on 33 topics and was considering six more. Its work was reflected in a number of agreements. For example, a UN conference in 1958 adopted the four conventions on the Law of the Sea. In New York, the General Assembly adopted the Convention on the Prevention and Punishment of Crimes against Internationally Protected Persons, including Diplomatic Agents (1973) and the Convention on the Non-navigational Uses of International Watercourses (1997). Vienna has been the site of numerous meetings to consider and consolidate the commission's labors, including the Conventions on Diplomatic Relations (1961), on Consular Relations (1963), on the Law of Treaties (1969), on the Succession of States in Respect of State Property, Archives and Debts (1983), and on the Law of Treaties between States and International Organizations or between International Organizations (1986). In 1992 the General Assembly instructed the commission to provide a draft statute for an INTERNATIONAL CRIMINAL COURT (ICC), which led to the 1998 Rome conference that adopted the statute for the new court.

See also ARBITRATION, *JUS COGENS,* SIXTH COMMITTEE, UNITED NATIONS CONFERENCE ON THE LAW OF THE SEA.

Further Reading: *Analytical Guide to the Work of the International Law Commission, 1949–1997.* New York: United Nations, 1998. Morton, Jeffrey S. *The International Law Commission of the United Nations.* Columbia: University of South Carolina Press, 2000. *United Nations Handbook.* Wellington, N.Z.: Ministry of External Affairs, published annually. International Law Commission Web site: <www.un.org/law/ilc>.

International Maritime Organization (IMO)

The increase in international trade coupled with the growing number and size of the world's merchant fleets after World War II significantly heightened concerns about maritime safety. To address these concerns, a UN conference meeting in Geneva in 1948 established the Convention on the Inter-Governmental Maritime Consultative Organization (the name changed to International Maritime Organization in 1982). The CONVENTION entered into force in 1958 and the first meetings were held in 1959. Originally charged with updating existing maritime TREATIES and creating new ones to improve maritime safety and the efficiency of navigation, the IMO has since dealt with the prevention and control of marine pollution at sea, maritime traffic control, maritime education, technical issues, liability and compensation issues relating to marine pollution and accidents, and the prevention of crime on the high seas. The IMO is a SPECIALIZED AGENCY of the United Nations, and, as such, reports on its activities to the ECONOMIC AND SOCIAL COUNCIL.

The 167 member states, as of February 2007, constitute the Assembly, which meets every two years. The 40-member Council is the IMO's governing body and oversees the operations of the organization. There are five main committees (Maritime Safety, Environmental Protection, Legal, Technical Co-operation, and Facilitation) which deal with the organization's major areas of responsibility. Headquartered in London, the IMO has a permanent staff of 300. Since its inception, the IMO has produced 10 major conventions dealing with maritime safety, four with marine pollution, six with liability and compensation, two with maritime crime prevention, and three that address technical maritime issues. For example, in February 2004, after more than 10 years of negotiations, the IMO adopted a convention on the management of ships' ballast water in order to prevent effluents from damaging fragile marine organisms. Many of these conventions have been ratified by more than 95 percent of the member states. Today most of the world's merchant vessels involved in international trade adhere to IMO building, maintenance, and operating regulations. As a result, the number and frequency of maritime accidents have been reduced considerably.

The IMO was the first UN agency to implement a Technical Co-operation Committee to assist member states in implementing the organization's conventions. This committee also has aided LESS DEVELOPED COUNTRIES with the development of their merchant fleets in accordance with IMO conventions.

To facilitate further the implementation and maintenance of its regulatory and legislative work, the IMO has established the world's premier network of maritime educational institutions, including the International Maritime University in Malmö, Sweden, the International Maritime Academy in Trieste, Italy, and the International Maritime Law Institute in Valletta, Malta.

See also ADMINISTRATIVE TRIBUNALS, CONSULTATIVE STATUS, EXPANDED PROGRAM FOR TECHNICAL ASSISTANCE, INTERNATIONAL CIVIL AVIATION ORGANIZATION.

Further Reading: Degenhardt, Henry W. *Maritime Affairs—A World Handbook: A Reference Guide to Maritime Organizations, Conventions, and Disputes and to the International Politics of the Sea.* Harlow, U.K.: Longman, 1985. International Maritime Organization. *IMO: The First 50 Years.* London: International Maritime Organization, 1999. ———. *Convention on the IMO,* IMO 013E, London: International Maritime Organization Publishing Service, 1984. Simmonds, K. R. *The International Maritime Organization.* London: Simmonds and Hill Publishers, 1994. IMO Web site: <www.imo.org/home.asp>.

— M. S. Lindberg

International Migrants Day

Observed annually on December 18, the day commemorates the GENERAL ASSEMBLY's adoption on December 18, 1990, of the INTERNATIONAL CONVENTION ON THE PROTECTION OF THE RIGHTS OF ALL MIGRANT WORKERS AND MEMBERS OF THEIR FAMILIES. In 2006 the General Assembly highlighted the problems facing migrants by holding a High-Level Dialogue on International Migration and DEVELOPMENT.

International Monetary Fund (IMF)

Created at the BRETTON WOODS Conference in New Hampshire in 1944, the International Monetary Fund is a UN SPECIALIZED AGENCY designed to promote international monetary cooperation; facilitate economic expansion, world trade, high employment, and income growth; promote stability and eliminate restrictions in international money exchange; and assist its members with temporary financial resources to solve balance of payments problems and other financial difficulties. It came into existence on December 27, 1945, when 29 nations signed the Articles of Agreement that had been proposed at Bretton Woods. The IMF often finds itself in close collaboration with the WORLD BANK, a group of four institutions made up of the International Bank for Reconstruction and Development (IBRD, initiated as well at the Bretton Woods Conference), the International Finance Corporation (IFC, founded in 1956), the International Development Association (IDA, founded in 1960), and the Multilateral Investment Guarantee Agency (MIGA, founded in 1988). These entities, all headquartered in Washington,

D.C., along with the GENERAL AGREEMENT ON TARIFFS AND TRADE, which became the WORLD TRADE ORGANIZATION in 1995, serve as the primary international monetary and financial institutions in the global financial framework initiated after World War II.

At the conclusion of that war, economists, financiers, diplomats, and political leaders were determined to avoid the economic and financial pitfalls they believed had helped cause the collapse of international order leading to global conflict. They agreed to establish institutions to encourage freer trade in goods, money, and people, international rules to effect such liberalization, transparency in economic and financial arrangements, and the ability to locate and rectify sudden economic troubles in discrete areas of the world, so as to avoid their spreading infection. For the most part, these aims were astonishingly successful as the world economy grew substantially through the end of the 20th century. However, during the 1990s the work of the IMF, the World Bank, and the WTO became increasingly controversial because they were seen as promoters of a process called "GLOBALIZATION" that, critics believed, only benefited corporations in the wealthiest capitalist nations at the expense of Third World countries, laboring people, distinctive native cultures, and the ENVIRONMENT. Moreover, critics contended that IMF, World Bank, and WTO decisions were not those of democratically chosen governments, but rather of high-powered bankers and financiers, removed from the concerns and wishes of most people. The IMF was a particularly clear target because of its mode of operation and because of its role in setting financial terms for debt-ridden nations and imposing on them stringent conditions in order to receive help. Deep crises in Mexico (1995), throughout Asia (1997–98), and in Argentina (2001) led to IMF involvement, and to strong disagreement with its policies by national governments, NON-GOVERNMENTAL ORGANIZATIONS, other international institutions, and citizens' groups.

The IMF has tried to combine several roles that in their complexity, and possible incompatibility, make the institution controversial. It has taken on the role of an international bank, an insurance company, a regulator, and a charity. To begin, one may think of the IMF exactly as it is entitled: that is, it is a FUND. The member countries of the IMF (184 as of February 2007) grant an assessed quota to the IMF much as individuals deposit money into a bank or a credit union. The amount of the quota is based on each member's relative size in the world economy. The quotas so subscribed determine VOTING power in the IMF. So, richer nations wield more voting power when the IMF makes decisions. Based on its proportion of the total assets, the UNITED STATES held slightly over 16 percent of the voting power in the IMF in 2007. This was the largest vote bloc in the fund and a sufficient amount to block most proposals with which the U.S. government disagreed. Members pay 25 percent of their quota subscription in acceptable international reserve assets (U.S. dollars,

euros, Japanese yen, British pound sterling, or so-called Special Drawing Rights; see below for a definition). The remaining 75 percent is in the country's own currency. As with a bank or credit union, members may draw from the general resources of the fund derived from these quota subscriptions. Members with "structural maladjustments" (an inability to meet payments, an accelerating public debt, a dangerously fluctuating currency, a balance of trade problem, and so on) may enter into extended arrangements with the IMF for longer periods. The IMF can supplement its resources by borrowing from member countries that have strong economies. This may happen when the fund is in need of added capital to deal with an immediate and costly problem that endangers international financial stability. Finally, there is the "Structural Adjustment Facility" of the "Special Disbursement Account," under which funds may be made available on "concessional" terms to low-income, DEVELOPING COUNTRIES, at lower interest rates. Usually, these developing countries are engaged in fundamental structural REFORM of their economies. During the late 20th century, such structural readjustment normally meant moving from a more or less command style, socialist economy in which the government played the major role and outside trade was restricted by protectionist policies to a free market economy emphasizing private enterprise, freer trade, and an internationally convertible currency. Such "structural readjustments" typically were the conditions the IMF imposed on the borrowing countries, whose citizens, accustomed to government sustenance, sometimes suffered transitory discomfort or even prolonged hardship.

The IMF is governed by its member states. At the top is the Board of Governors, composed of one representative from each member, and an equal number of alternate governors. Governors are almost always the minister of finance or the head of the central bank of their country. Thus they represent their government. They gather only at annual meetings. Otherwise the governors stay in touch with the IMF executive board stationed at the headquarters in Washington. Twenty-four executive directors meet at least three times a week in formal session and carry out the policies of the Board of Governors. In 2007, eight executive directors represented individual countries: CHINA, FRANCE, GERMANY, JAPAN, the RUSSIAN FEDERATION, Saudi Arabia, the United Kingdom, and the United States. The 16 remaining directors represented groupings of the other member states. The executive board often makes decisions on the basis of consensus rather than majority vote. There is a staff of about 2,700 and a managing director (Rodrigo de Rato y Figaredo of Spain in 2007), who is also chair of the executive board.

So-called Special Drawing Rights (SDR) are a novel creation of the IMF. The term implies that they can be "drawn" by a member state, much as one would "draw" a loan from a bank in which one had deposits. SDRs are a form of reserve asset invented by the IMF's Board of Directors in 1967. By

1969 enough members had ratified the new system to bring it into practice. SDRs are now the principal unit of account of the IMF. In the practice of international finance, SDRs have replaced more traditional reserves such as gold. The value of the IMF's SDRs is measured against a "basket" of a few strong currencies (the dollar, yen, pound sterling, and euro), and it is based on current market exchange rates. Countries are accorded SDR allotments in the IMF, and consider them as assets within the fund. Although technically a paper reserve, SDRs have many of the characteristics of money. For example, SDRs are interest-bearing assets, and interest can be charged on IMF loans made in SDRs. In effect, SDRs represent a movement away from using the dollar as the world's reserve currency, implicit in the Bretton Woods system.

The IMF engages in several activities. It conducts "surveillance," which means that it constantly monitors, appraises, and reports its members' exchange rates to assure that they remain stable. It offers financial assistance, including credits and loans to members with financial needs. As of August 31, 2006, the fund had credit and loans outstanding to 74 countries for about $28 billion. And it provides technical assistance to its members to help with fiscal and monetary policy and structural reforms.

The IMF does not lend for specific purposes or projects as do REGIONAL DEVELOPMENT BANKS. Reserve assets that a member may borrow are normally deposited in the borrowing country's central bank and are available to the country as would be any other international reserves. When lending, the IMF provides reserve assets (in accepted foreign currencies and Special Drawing Rights) taken from other members of the fund. A borrower uses its own currency to "purchase" these assets from the fund that are obtained from quota subscriptions. To repay, the borrower "repurchases" its own currency with international reserve assets. So, from an accounting perspective, there is no variation in the fund's total resources. But financial aid is usually linked to specific, and sometimes onerous, conditions that the borrowing country must meet. This was the case with Mexico and afflicted Asian countries in the mid-1990s, and with Argentina in 2001. In each of these instances, because the richer nations of the world—most importantly the United States—held the controlling voting power in the IMF, and feared instability in world financial markets, the fund voted to provide "bailout" loans, determined to avert a serious world financial crisis.

As a specialized agency of the United Nations, the IMF often coordinates its activities with other UN agencies and on behalf of UN programs. In March 2002 the IMF was one of the major participants in the UN-sponsored International Conference on Financing for DEVELOPMENT, also known as the Monterrey Conference. IMF officials cochaired economic issue roundtable discussions among heads of government; ministers of finance, trade, and foreign affairs; and business representatives. Conference participants decided to continue the discussions on an annual basis in the effort to develop common strategies toward achieving SUSTAINABLE DEVELOPMENT. The IMF also participates in the Heavily Indebted Poor Country Initiative through which, in cooperation with the World Bank, it provides debt relief to exceptionally poor nations. Additionally, it has provided financial assistance to countries in which UN PEACEKEEPING operations have been inserted, working closely with the UN PEACEBUILDING COMMISSION.

See also ADMINISTRATIVE TRIBUNALS; BOSNIA; CLINTON, WILLIAM JEFFERSON; DEVELOPMENT DECADES; GROUP OF EIGHT; MULTILATERALISM; NEW PARTNERSHIP FOR AFRICA'S DEVELOPMENT; SIERRA LEONE; UNITED NATIONS COMMISSION ON INTERNATIONAL TRADE LAW; UNITED NATIONS CONFERENCE ON TRADE AND DEVELOPMENT; UNITED NATIONS DEVELOPMENT PROGRAMME.

Further Reading: Matejka, Harriet, and Mihály Sima. *Aspects of Transition.* Helsinki: United Nations University, 1999. Micklethwait, John, and Adrian Wooldridge. *Future Perfect: The Challenge and Hidden Promise of Globalization.* New York: Crown Publishers, 2000. New Zealand Ministry of Foreign Affairs. *United Nations Handbook.* Wellington, N.Z.: Ministry of Foreign Affairs and Trade, published annually. O'Brien, Robert, et al. *Contesting Global Governance: Multilateral Institutions and Global Movements.* New York: Cambridge University Press, 2000. "Winners and Losers." *The Economist.* April 26, 2001. IMF Web site: <www.imf.org>.

International Mother Language Day

Observed on February 21 annually to promote linguistic and cultural diversity and multilingualism, the day was proclaimed by the UNITED NATIONS EDUCATIONAL, SOCIAL AND CULTURAL ORGANIZATION's General Conference in November 1999, and was first observed in 2000.

International Organization on Migration (IOM)

The International Organization on Migration (IOM) was created in 1951 to promote orderly migration, to find solutions to serious migrant problems, and to provide advice to both migrants and governments. In 2007, 120 governments belonged to the organization. While not one of the UN's SPECIALIZED AGENCIES, IOM achieved OBSERVER STATUS in the GENERAL ASSEMBLY and became a "standing invitee" in the Inter-Agency Standing Committee in 1992. In 1996 IOM and the United Nations signed a Cooperation Agreement to enhance collaboration between the SECRETARIATs of the two organizations.

IOM was first created to deal with European migration problems following World War II. However, as new crises arose, it expanded its mission and services. By the turn of the millennium, the agency had more than 100 offices worldwide,

5,400 personnel, and an annual BUDGET of approximately $1 billion. The end of the COLD WAR and the pervasiveness of GLOBALIZATION meant new waves of economic migrants, largely moving from the developing world of the SOUTH to the industrialized north or from former communist societies to the market economies of Europe and North America. Estimates put the total number of migrants at more than 191 million. To respond to migration challenges, IOM instituted several new programs, including the "1035 Facility," which allocated FUNDs for the voluntary return and integration of migrants, labor migration, health issues of migrants, and training programs.

The organization is headed by a DIRECTOR-GENERAL who is elected to a five-year term by the IOM Council. The director-general presides over a highly decentralized organizational STRUCTURE, with most of the staff in field offices and operations. In addition to the plenary Council, IOM has an Executive Committee, and a Sub-committee on Budget and Finance.

The UN General Assembly convened a High-Level Dialogue on International Migration and Development on September 14, 2006. In its RESOLUTION calling the session, it specifically encouraged a central role for the International Organization on Migration. The High-Level Dialogue recommended the creation of a global, informal, and voluntary forum to explore ways to tie migration to DEVELOPMENT. Belgium offered to convene the first forum in the summer of 2007. The Belgian government specifically called on IOM to provide information for the forum to consider.

Further Reading: IOM Web site: <www.iom.int/jahia/jsp/index.jsp>.

International Research and Training Institute for the Advancement of Women (INSTRAW)

The UN ECONOMIC AND SOCIAL COUNCIL (ECOSOC) created the International Research and Training Institute for the Advancement of Women in 1976, fulfilling a recommendation made the previous year by the WORLD CONFERENCE of the International Women's Year, held in Mexico City. ECOSOC established INSTRAW as an autonomous institute within the framework of the UNITED NATIONS SYSTEM, joining by the end of the century the Division for the Advancement of Women (DAW), and the UNITED NATIONS DEVELOPMENT FUND FOR WOMEN (UNIFEM) as the three UN entities committed solely to promoting the advancement of WOMEN. In 1983 INSTRAW accepted the offer of facilities from the Dominican Republic for its permanent HEADQUARTERS, situating it within the developing world, the focus of most of its efforts.

A board of 11 directors selected on the basis of equitable geographical distribution governs the Institute. Nominated by ECOSOC member states and appointed by the Council

to three-year terms, they are individuals with international reputations and expertise in gender equity issues. The board meets annually to review the work of the staff, headed by a director appointed by the UN SECRETARY-GENERAL. It also approves the program, activities, and BUDGET (approximately $4 million in 1999) of the Institute. The new millennium brought serious funding difficulties for INSTRAW. In late 2003, it had income of little more than $1 million, including a grant of $250,000 by the UN GENERAL ASSEMBLY, and a year later the Assembly had to provide an additional $500,000. To address its financial difficulties, INSTRAW undertook a revitalization process that included a new strategic plan for 2004–07. Central to the plan was a concerted effort to raise additional outside FUNDs. The Institute's training, research, and information dissemination programs were to be financed completely by voluntary contributions from governments, NON-GOVERNMENTAL ORGANIZATIONS, and private contributors.

In 1999 the GENERAL ASSEMBLY approved a new working method for INSTRAW that allowed it to make maximum use of information technology systems. Its Gender Awareness Information and Networking System (GAINS) served as a "virtual workshop," producing and distributing information about women. GAINS also provided a MECHANISM for interactive research and training projects. With the new system INSTRAW set as one of its strategic work programs for 2001–02 "Closing the Digital Divide between Women and Men." Close to its headquarters in the Dominican Republic, for example, it undertook in the Caribbean region two demonstration projects on developing women's skills in information and communications technologies. Other strategic topics established for the period were "Building Partnerships for Gender Equity," and "The Impact of Globalization." The latter of these was directed not only at the opportunities that GLOBALIZATION raises for women but also at the threats it can pose. Among other research agenda, INSTRAW undertook a study of the increasing role the Internet played in the migration of women as "e-mail order brides" worldwide, as well as research on the role of gender in the cycle of conflict in the FORMER YUGOSLAVIA.

INSTRAW also sponsors conferences on critical issues involving women and gender equity. In October 2001, it worked with the UNITED NATIONS CHILDREN'S FUND (UNICEF) and the UNITED NATIONS DEVELOPMENT PROGRAMME (UNDP) to organize a four-day conference on "Working with Men to End Gender-Based Violence." The meeting was held in Bellagio, Italy. In February 2007 INSTRAW hosted 10 national conferences in LATIN AMERICA on women's political participation at the local level.

See also DEPARTMENT OF ECONOMIC AND SOCIAL AFFAIRS, WORLD CONFERENCES ON WOMEN.

Further Reading: Anand, Anita, with Gouri Salvi. *Beijing! UN Fourth World Conference on Women.* New Delhi: Women's

Feature Service, 1998. United Nations Department of Public Information. *The United Nations and the Advancement of Women, 1945–1996.* New York: United Nations Department of Public Information, 1996. ———. *Basic Facts about the United Nations.* New York: United Nations Department of Public Information, published periodically. INSTRAW Web site: <www.un-instraw.org>.

International Seabed Authority

On November 16, 1994, the United Nations CONVENTION on the Law of the Sea entered into force, some 12 years after it had been adopted following three rounds of meetings of the UN CONFERENCE ON THE LAW OF THE SEA. There were 153 states that were parties to the convention by February 2007. An Implementing Agreement of July 28, 1994, on the application of provisions on seabed mining, supplemented the full convention. This latter agreement was meant to address requests for a more market-oriented approach to seabed issues, and refine decision-making procedures connected with the convention. The convention had established the International Seabed Authority, which, by virtue of the provisions of the convention, and the complementary Implementing Agreement, became responsible for organizing and controlling exploration for and exploitation of the mineral resources of the deep seabed.

Members of the International Seabed Authority are the parties to the convention on the Law of the Sea. They elect a Seabed Authority Council with representatives coming from geographical groupings identified in the UN Convention on the Law of the Sea. Council members serve for a term of four years. In 2007 the authority's SECRETARIAT had an authorized strength of 37 people. Its managing SECRETARY-GENERAL was Mr. Satya N. Nandan from Fiji, and its headquarters was in Kingston, Jamaica.

See also OBSERVER STATUS.

Further Reading: International Seabed Authority Web site: <www.isa.org.jm>.

International Telecommunication Union (ITU)

Founded in 1865 in Paris by 20 European nations as the International Telegraph Union, the ITU received its present name in 1934 and in 1947 became a SPECIALIZED AGENCY of the United Nations. It is the oldest intergovernmental organization in the world, with HEADQUARTERS in Geneva. It encourages the development and efficient use of telecommunications and the seamless exchange of information around the world, promotes technical assistance in the field of telecommunications to DEVELOPING COUNTRIES, and endorses a broad approach to issues of telecommunications in the changing environment of the global information society. The ITU is particularly interested in assuring that progress

in telecommunications advances the global movement and coordination of services, banking, tourism, transportation, and information.

As of 2007, in addition to its 191 member NATION-STATES, the ITU was also composed of more than 600 non-governmental members (called "sector members") that included scientific and business groups, public and private operators, broadcasters, and regional and international organizations. It is governed by a plenipotentiary conference that convenes every four years, often amends its constitution, its CONVENTION, and its rules of procedure, establishes a budget, and elects a 46-member council that meets annually. The ITU is administered by a SECRETARY-GENERAL who in 2007 was Hamadoun Touré.

The ITU seeks public-private cooperation in the development and use of telecommunications worldwide. The ITU has been involved in helping to develop a new system called "international freephone numbers" to help lower costs and make international communication more efficient. It has participated in the introduction of the third-generation mobile phone system (called MT-2000), developed global standards for connecting different telecommunications systems, and been active in the effort to restructure the domain-of-names system of the worldwide Internet.

In 1998, the International Telecommunications Union, meeting in its plenipotentiary conference in Minneapolis, Minnesota, called for the convocation of a WORLD CONFERENCE on the global information society. The ITU was concerned primarily about the limited access to information and communication technologies (ICTs) by peoples in poor countries. The G-8 (GROUP OF EIGHT Developed Economic Powers) endorsed the ITU proposal at its July 2000 meeting in Okinawa, JAPAN. The UN GENERAL ASSEMBLY, in December 2001, formally authorized the gathering. The WORLD SUMMIT ON THE INFORMATION SOCIETY met in two phases: the first phase in Geneva, Switzerland, from December 10 through 12, 2003, and in Tunis, Tunisia, November 16–18, 2005.

See also ADMINISTRATIVE TRIBUNALS, CHIEF EXECUTIVES BOARD, EXPANDED PROGRAM OF TECHNICAL ASSISTANCE.

Further Reading: United Nations Department of Public Information. *Basic Facts about the United Nations.* New York: United Nations Department of Public Information, 1998. ITU Web site: <www.itu.int>.

International Trade Centre UNCTAD/WTO (ITC)

The International Trade Centre is a "joint subsidiary organ" of the WORLD TRADE ORGANIZATION (WTO) and the United Nations, the latter acting through the UNITED NATIONS CONFERENCE ON TRADE AND DEVELOPMENT (UNCTAD). Created in 1964, the ITC provides technical assistance to enterprises in the field of trade promotion, being designated in 1973 by the UN GENERAL ASSEMBLY as the focal point in the UNITED NATIONS SYSTEM for this purpose. In particular, it implements trade promotion projects financed by the UNITED NATIONS DEVELOPMENT PROGRAMME (UNDP) in LEAST DEVELOPED COUNTRIES (LDC) and economies in transition (EITs). It also works closely with SPECIALIZED AGENCIES in the UN system, including the FOOD AND AGRICULTURE ORGANIZATION (FAO) and the UNITED NATIONS INDUSTRIAL DEVELOPMENT ORGANIZATION (UNIDO), and with REGIONAL DEVELOPMENT BANKS.

Among its other tasks, the International Trade Centre, headquartered at the Palais des Nations in Geneva, attempts to expand exports from DEVELOPING COUNTRIES. It also advises them on how to improve import operations. It provides trade information, needs assessment, and human resource development expertise. ITC specialists work with national and regional groups at the request of individual governments; projects last from several weeks to years. The International Trade Centre also sponsors World Trade Promotion Conferences, holding its sixth such meeting in March 2007 in Buenos Aires, Argentina.

ITC's executive director—in April 2007, Patricia Francis of the UNITED STATES—oversees a staff of more than 200, and several hundred consultants. The SECRETARIAT receives its funds in equal parts from the WTO and the United Nations. Project allocation of the funds is made on the recommendation of ITC's Joint Advisory Group (JAG), an intergovernmental board that meets annually. JAG also reviews the International Trade Centre's medium-term plan, which covers consecutive six-year periods. ITC's annual BUDGET is approximately $33 million.

See also PROGRAMMES AND FUNDS.

Further Reading: New Zealand Ministry of Foreign Affairs. *United Nations Handbook.* Wellington, N.Z.: Ministry of Foreign Affairs and Trade, published annually. ITC Web site: <www.intracen.org/>.

International Tribunal for the Law of the Sea
See UNITED NATIONS CONFERENCE ON THE LAW OF THE SEA.

Iran
Iran, about the size of the state of Alaska, with a POPULATION of almost 70 million people, derives from a large Persian Empire dating from antiquity. In the seventh century of the common era Arabs conquered the country and introduced Islam, which replaced indigenous Zoroastrianism. Persians eventually reclaimed control over their country and adopted the Shi'ite form of Islam, not the Sunni faith of much of the surrounding Arab world. During the 19th century Persia came under the influence of GREAT BRITAIN and

Russia. In the 1920s the Pahlavi family leaders declared a hereditary monarchy and changed the name of the country to Iran. During World War II Britain occupied Iran, and for a brief time after the war a National Front government ran the country, which was populated by a majority of Persians, but with a sizable minority of Azerbaijanis and other ethnic groups.

Two days after the UN SECURITY COUNCIL convened for the first time (January 17, 1946) the Iranian government brought to the Council the UN body's first complaint. Iran called on the Council to force Soviet troops out of northern Iran, where they had been stationed as World War II partners in the 1942 Tripartite Treaty of Alliance. Under that agreement, the Soviet Union was authorized to establish a northern security zone in Iran, while the British maintained one in the south. With the end of World War II, the TREATY's terms required that all Soviet troops be out of the country by March 2. While British forces were withdrawing from Iran, there was no evidence of a Soviet pullout in the spring of 1946.

Soviet representatives responded to the Iranian charges by submitting their own complaints about British forces in Greece and INDONESIA. The Council met 11 times between March 2 and May 22 on the issue. In early May, the UNITED STATES increased diplomatic and military pressure on the Kremlin, notifying JOSEPH STALIN's government that Washington could not "remain indifferent to the USSR's refusal to withdraw," and sending an American warship to the eastern Mediterranean to signal U.S. concern. By May 21, the Iranian government informed the Security Council that all Soviet personnel had left the country.

Most COLD WAR era Iranian interactions with the UN Security Council were over Iran's claims to territory either along or outside its traditional borders. Iran had long disputes with IRAQ over their common border, particularly over the Shatt al-Arab (Arab Canal), a narrow waterway that empties into the Gulf. In 1969 Iran asserted a right to half of the Shatt al-Arab, a claim Iraq disputed. Both sides appealed to the Security Council. Largely under American aegis, the dispute was settled by treaty in 1975 in favor of the Iranian position. In the Gulf itself, in 1970, Iran claimed SOVEREIGNTY over the sheikdom of Bahrain, as the British withdrew their protection of the emirate. Bahrain made an APPEAL TO THE SECURITY COUNCIL. RALPH BUNCHE was asked to mediate the controversy. In the last major international assignment of his storied career before his imminent death from a terminal illness, Bunche managed to obtain the withdrawal of the Iranian claim and, in 1971, UN MEMBERSHIP for Bahrain. By the fall of 1971, however, Iran made further claims to territory in the Gulf. It asserted its right to three small islands in the Straits of Hormuz: Abu Musa, Greater Tunb, and Lesser Tunb. Each of these ostensibly belonged to one of the Trucial States that subsequently became the United Arab Emirates (UAE). In late November Iran invaded and occupied the islands. The Security Council took up the Iranian action on December 9, one day after endorsing the UN membership application of the UAE. While there was significant criticism of the Iranian occupation by many Council members, the United Nations took no action as the United Kingdom tacitly supported the invasion.

The Islamic Revolution of 1979 in Iran set in train events that brought Iran under UN scrutiny and even condemnation. The deleterious domestic consequences of the revolution led Iran's neighboring Iraqi government of SADDAM HUSSEIN to believe that the balance of power between the two countries had shifted in favor of Iraq. Hussein attacked Iran in September 1980 in order to reclaim territory earlier lost to the Iranians. The IRAN-IRAQ WAR lasted eight years and cost hundreds of thousands of lives. While the apparent victim of AGGRESSION, the Iranian government found little sympathy at the United Nations during much of the conflict. First, the revolutionary regime of Ayatollah Khomeini regularly condemned the policies of the major powers on the Security Council and encouraged Islamic revolutionary movements throughout the Middle East. Also, when the war began, Iran was already in the midst of a serious diplomatic confrontation with the world community. The previous November Iranian students had overrun the U.S. embassy in Tehran, taking captive more than 50 American personnel. The student action was soon endorsed by the regime, leading to what became known as the IRAN HOSTAGE CRISIS. The standoff between the United States and Iran would last 444 days. It badly damaged Iranian standing in the United Nations because the protection and inviolability of a country's diplomats is one of the most sacrosanct principles in INTERNATIONAL LAW. Consequently, when Iranian officials appealed to the United Nations for support in the war with Iraq, they found preliminary demands that Iran release the American diplomats.

In the summer of 1987 the United States and the Soviet Union jointly sponsored Security Council Resolution 598 demanding an immediate cease-fire between Iran and Iraq. The RESOLUTION threatened unspecified consequences against either party should it not accept its terms. Iraq accepted immediately. Iran condemned the resolution as one-sided since it did not identify Iraq as the aggressor. However, after several days the Khomeini government accepted Resolution 598 "in principle." It would take another year before fighting ended. The war came to a close in August 1988 as a consequence of an Iranian collapse at the front and a dire assessment by the Iranian government of possible American military action following what Washington claimed was an accidental downing of an Iranian civilian airplane over the Gulf with a large loss of life. As part of the final cease-fire negotiations, however, Iran did extract the establishment of a UN INQUIRY into which side had started the war. Several years later the UN commission would uphold Iran's position that Iraq had begun the war.

Mahmoud Ahmadinejad, President of the Islamic Republic of Iran, addresses the general debate of the sixtieth session of the General Assembly at UN Headquarters. (UN PHOTO 92922/PAULO FILGUEIRAS)

Twenty-four months after hostilities ended in the Iran-Iraq War Iraqi forces invaded Kuwait. Iran played no role in the conflict, but sought to break out of its diplomatic isolation once the war ended. Moderate Iranian governments in the 1990s tried to ease relations with the United States and European states. Domestic opposition to this opening and outside suspicions that Iran continued to finance anti-Israeli and terrorist organizations tempered the possibilities for a normalization of Iran's relations with former enemies. Five months after the September 2001 terrorist attacks in the United States, U.S. president GEORGE W. BUSH named Iran one of three states in what he termed "the Axis of Evil," because of its apparent support for TERRORISM and reported development of nuclear weapons.

In 2005 Iranian voters elected Mahmoud Ahmadinejad as president of the Islamic Republic. Ahmadinejad represented nationalist and revolutionary forces in the country. On foreign policy matters, he took a confrontational approach that caused fresh tensions with outside powers, including the United States. Of particular concern was the president's decision to accelerate Iran's nuclear enrichment program.

Iran had first begun nuclear research in the 1950s. A signatory of the NUCLEAR NON-PROLIFERATION TREATY, Iran informed the INTERNATIONAL ATOMIC ENERGY AGENCY (IAEA) in the early 1980s that it intended to develop indigenously made nuclear fuel for its civilian energy program. Russia and CHINA provided technical and material assistance in the 1990s.

Following the revelation in 2002 of secret nuclear enrichment facilities at Natanz and Arak, FRANCE, GERMANY, and

Great Britain undertook a diplomatic initiative to obtain Iranian commitments to suspend its nuclear enrichment program. In October 2003 Iran reached agreement with the European negotiators. The country promised to suspend its enrichment efforts, sign the IAEA's stringent Additional PRO-TOCOL, and cooperate with agency inspectors in return for modern energy technology and assistance. Nonetheless, an IAEA report in November 2004 found a "pattern of conceal-ment" in Iran's nuclear program. In 2006 the IAEA Board of Directors referred the matter to the UN Security Council, which imposed SANCTIONS banning the supply of nuclear materials and freezing the assets of individuals and compa-nies associated with the Iranian program. Insisting that Iran had a sovereign right to develop peaceful nuclear energy, President Ahmadinejad announced in April 2006 that his country's scientists had successfully enriched uranium. Later he declared that Iran would accelerate its production of the nuclear fuel. Addressing the UN GENERAL ASSEMBLY in Sep-tember 2007, Ahmadinejad declared his country's nuclear program no longer a matter for international discussion.

See also AFGHANISTAN; APPENDIX F (Security Coun-cil Resolution 598); ARBITRATION; CARTER, JIMMY; CHAP-TER VII; CLINTON, WILLIAM JEFFERSON; COMPREHENSIVE NUCLEAR TEST BAN TREATY; DEPARTMENT OF PEACEKEEP-ING OPERATIONS; DISARMAMENT; ENFORCEMENT MEASURES; GOOD OFFICES; INTERNATIONAL COURT OF JUSTICE; MIL-LENNIUM SUMMIT; PÉREZ DE CUÉLLAR, JAVIER; WALDHEIM, KURT; WEAPONS; WEAPONS OF MASS DESTRUCTION; WORLD SUMMIT ON THE INFORMATION SOCIETY.

Further Reading: Christopher, Warren, et al. *American Hos-tages in Iran: The Conduct of a Crisis.* New Haven, Conn.: Yale University Press, 1985. Hume, Cameron R. *The United Nations, Iran and Iraq: How Peacemaking Changed.* Blooming-ton: Indiana University Press, 1994. Pérez de Cuéllar, Javier. *Pilgrimage for Peace: A Secretary-General's Memoirs.* New York: St. Martin's, 1997.

Iran hostage crisis

The Iran hostage crisis began on November 4, 1979, with the seizure of the American embassy in Tehran by followers of Ayatollah Khomeini. Students seized the embassy in response to an American decision to allow the deposed shah of Iran, Mohammad Reza Pahlavi, to receive medical treatment in the UNITED STATES. The embassy grounds were occupied and 66 American citizens taken hostage; 13 hostages were released shortly after the embassy was occupied while the remaining hostages were detained for a total of 444 days.

In 1979 there existed in the Iranian polity residual anger with U.S. involvement in the 1953 coup that reinstituted the shah, and as the crisis continued this discontent was exacerbated by Iranian fears that the United States would again intervene to reinstall the deposed shah. This anger

was also compounded by American moves to freeze Iranian assets controlled by U.S. banks, the imposition of economic SANCTIONS on IRAN, and an unwillingness on the part of the United States to return the shah to Iran to face prosecution.

On November 9, 1979, U.S. permanent representative Donald McHenry asked the UN SECURITY COUNCIL to take up the matter. The Council was gravely concerned with the hostage crisis, seeing it as a serious threat to international peace. This sentiment is evident in Security Council Resolu-tions 457 and 461. Urgent calls for the release of the hos-tages appeared in both RESOLUTIONS as did demands that issues outstanding between the two states be resolved in accordance with the principles of the UN CHARTER. Resolu-tion 457 in particular mentioned the Vienna CONVENTIONS of 1961 and 1963 on Diplomatic and Consular Relations as they pertain to the inviolability of diplomatic personnel. Council members asked SECRETARY-GENERAL KURT WALD-HEIM to use his GOOD OFFICES. Waldheim traveled to Iran in January 1980, but he achieved little progress in gaining the diplomats' freedom.

Waldheim kept open channels of communication, met privately with U.S. secretary of state Cyrus Vance and with Iran's Revolutionary Council. He appointed a Commission of INQUIRY that visited Iran in early 1980 with no more success than he had achieved in his personal efforts. The INTERNA-TIONAL COURT OF JUSTICE (ICJ) was also involved in the crisis. On December 15, 1979, the Court ordered that the government of Iran should immediately release all American nationals held in Iran and that neither government should undertake any action that would aggravate extant tensions.

Following a failed rescue mission by the American gov-ernment in April 1980, little progress toward a resolution occurred until Iran's prime minister, Muhammed Ali-Rajai, visited UN HEADQUARTERS in New York. He came seeking support for Iran in the war that had just broken out with IRAQ. Secretary-General Waldheim explained to him that as long as Tehran held the American hostages in violation of INTERNATIONAL LAW and UN resolutions, he could expect little support from member states. While in New York, Ali-Rajai addressed the Security Council, seeking help against Iraq. Unanimously all Council members condemned Iran's seizure of the U.S. diplomats and largely ignored Iran's com-plaints about Iraq. Within days of his return to Iran, Ali-Rajai designated Algeria as its official intermediary to negotiate a settlement with the United States. Waldheim wrote later that the prime minister's visit to the UN had been the turning point in the crisis. The highly negative attitude toward Iran presented by Third World countries in particular convinced Ali-Rajai of the need to settle the matter. After lengthy nego-tiations the hostages were released on January 20, 1981.

See also IRAN-IRAQ WAR.

Further Reading: Puchala, Donald, ed. *Issues Before the 35th General Assembly of the United Nations: 1980–1981.* New

York: United Nations Association of the USA, 1980. Waldheim, Kurt. *In the Eye of the Storm: A Memoir.* Bethesda, Md.: Adler and Adler, 1986.

Iran-Iraq War

The Iran-Iraq war started in 1980 and raged until a UN-mediated cease-fire was agreed to by the combatants in July 1988. In accordance with UN SECURITY COUNCIL RESOLUTION 598, passed unanimously during that month, a peace settlement between IRAN and IRAQ, which tried to address issues such as an exchange of prisoners and the settlement of their shared international border, was agreed to in August 1990. The RESOLUTION also marked a high-water mark in American-Soviet cooperation on Middle East issues. The resolution imposed a threat of retaliation against either combatant who refused to comply.

Iraq initiated the Iran-Iraq war at the height of the IRAN HOSTAGE CRISIS but the conflict had its genesis in the imperial division of the Middle East earlier in the century. The border separating Iraq and Iran was a hotly contested issue in the region's immediate postcolonial period. Again in 1969, both sides disputed each other's claims to the waterway. In 1975 the boundary was fixed down the middle of the Shatt al Arab estuary. The repudiation of this agreement—on September 17, 1980, SADDAM HUSSEIN declared the Shatt al-Arab "totally Iraqi and totally Arab"—coupled with Iraq's invasion of Iran sparked the 1980 Iran-Iraq war.

Considering that the Iran-Iraq war was one of the longest and most costly conflicts of the 20th century, both in financial and human terms (estimates place total number of casualties as high as two million), the international community remained surprisingly silent on the conflagration. The UN SECURITY COUNCIL passed Resolution 479 a few weeks after hostilities were initiated and passed Resolutions 514, 522, 540, 582, 588, 598, 612, 616, 619, 620, 631, 642, 651, 671, 676, and 685 over the subsequent eight years; but while doing so (and calling on all states not to undertake actions that would contribute to the continuation and/or widening of the conflict) members of the Security Council were perpetuating, and profiting from, the conflict by rearming the combatants. American involvement in this enterprise was exposed as the Iran-contra affair.

UN silence and inaction resulted not because of apathy on the part of the SECRETARY-GENERAL but rather because of political calculations on the part of the permanent five (P5) in the Security Council. The Security Council did meet several days after the initial invasion but this was after Secretary-General KURT WALDHEIM, under article 99 of the UN CHARTER, called the Security Council's attention to the conflict. Waldheim also immediately appealed to both sides to cease hostilities and offered the services of his GOOD OFFICES. As the conflict bogged down into a protracted stalemate the Secretary-General appointed as his SPECIAL REPRESENTA-

TIVE—and sent to negotiate with both Iran and Iraq—the Swedish politician Olof Palme. Some of the political machinations that precluded Security Council action were American preoccupation with the hostages held in Iran; Soviet insistence that the Iraqi AGGRESSION had been launched at the behest of the West; and Chinese, Japanese, and West German concerns for their economic relations with the combatants.

Several of the Security Council's resolutions explicitly invoked the Geneva CONVENTIONS of 1949 as well as the 1925 Geneva PROTOCOL. The 1949 Geneva Convention prohibited attacks on civilian centers as well as the targeting of neutral shipping, both of which were occurring in the region. The council reaffirmed the Geneva Protocol of 1925 and its Protocol for the Prohibition of the Use in War of Asphyxiating, Poisonous or Other Gases, and of Bacteriological Methods of Warfare because of Iraq's repeated use of poison gas on Iranian troops, probably as early as 1983 and most certainly by 1986. It is in the context of this deployment of CHEMICAL WEAPONS that the UN CONFERENCE ON DISARMAMENT (CD) was cited in Resolution 620.

Also found in these documents—several of which merely extend the mandate of the UN Iran-Iraq Military Observer Group—is UN Security Council Resolution 616. This resolution, passed in July of 1988, expressed deep distress at the downing of Iran Air flight 655 over the Straits of Hormuz by a missile fired from the UNITED STATES warship USS *Vincennes* and welcomed an investigation by the INTERNATIONAL CIVIL AVIATION ORGANIZATION (ICAO) into the events that led to the destruction of the aircraft.

On July 20, 1987, U.S. secretary of state George Shultz traveled to New York for informal discussions with Secretary-General JAVIER PÉREZ DE CUÉLLAR and the PERMANENT MEMBERS OF THE SECURITY COUNCIL. At the end of the day the Council unanimously passed Resolution 598, calling for a cease-fire and the withdrawal of belligerents to internationally recognized borders, and deploring the bombing of civilian POPULATIONs. It also threatened unspecified retaliation against the combatants if they did not agree to a cease-fire. The resolution was adopted under Articles 39 and 40 of CHAPTER VII of the UN CHARTER, which give the Council authority to use force to implement its decisions. Iran, angry that the international community had not found Iraq to be the aggressor in the war, criticized the RESOLUTION, calling it a "vicious American diplomatic maneuver." Tehran, nonetheless, invited Pérez de Cuéllar to visit in mid-September and explain Resolution 598. Within days, Iran informed the secretary-general that it would act within the "framework" of 598. Yet the war dragged on for almost a year. Finally, both sides acceded to a UN settlement, and on August 9, 1988, again by unanimous vote, the Security Council approved Resolution 619, setting up a UN Iran-Iraq Military Observer Group to implement the cease-fire and withdrawal. By August 20, UN observers were in place to monitor the now effected cease-fire.

Further Reading: Hume, Cameron R. *The United Nations, Iran and Iraq: How Peacemaking Changed.* Bloomington: Indiana University Press, 1994. Malone, David M. *The International Struggle over Iraq: Politics in the UN Security Council, 1980–2005.* New York: Oxford University Press, 2006. Pérez de Cuéllar, Javier. *Pilgrimage for Peace: A Secretary-General's Memoirs.* New York: St. Martin's, 1997. Simons, Geoff. *The United Nations: A Chronology of Conflict.* New York: St. Martin's, 1994. Urquhart, Brian. *Decolonization and World Peace.* Austin: University of Texas Press, 1989. *Yearbook of the United Nations.* New York: United Nations Office of Public Information, 1987 and 1988.

— S. F. McMahon

Iraq

Iraq is situated in Mesopotamia, the site of one of the oldest civilizations in history. Converted to Islam in the seventh century, the area was, in the 16th century, absorbed into the Islamic Ottoman Empire, which was destined to be on the losing side in World War I. GREAT BRITAIN occupied Iraq during that war and obtained a LEAGUE OF NATIONS Mandate there. The country, which was cobbled together by Britain in the aftermath of the collapse of the Ottoman Empire, was made up of a large Arab majority of Islamic worshipers, split however between a preponderance of Shi'ite practitioners and a substantial minority of rival Sunni Muslims. In addition, ethnic Kurds represented a minority of about 15 percent of the POPULATION. British influence continued until after World War II. In 1948, Iraq joined the Arab League in the first Arab-Israeli War. In 1958 a pan-Arab revolutionary coup overthrew the monarchy. The resultant republic was replaced by the Ba'ath Socialist Party in 1968.

Iraq's first encounter with the UN SECURITY COUNCIL occurred in 1961 when Iraq's premier Abd al Karim Qasim laid claim to the southern border state of Kuwait. The British government had recently cancelled the TREATY of 1899, which made Kuwait a British protectorate, and began removing its troops from the country. Qasim argued that Kuwait was an integral part of the Iraqi state and he unilaterally announced that Iraq's southern border now extended through the "province of Kuwait," with the ruler of Kuwait now the new province governor. Even though not a UN member, Kuwait asked for a Security Council session. Iraq countered with a complaint against Great Britain, accusing it of threatening Iraqi independence and security. Both the Kuwaiti and Iraqi items were put on the agenda.

In the meantime, Britain moved more than 4,000 troops back into Kuwait. In the fall these forces were replaced by League of Arab States personnel. Qasim's inability to deliver on the conquest of Kuwait led to his overthrow in February 1963 by the Baathist Party. The new regime moved toward a diplomatic resolution of the crisis. In May, the Security Council voted for Kuwaiti MEMBERSHIP in the United Nations, and

in October, Iraq "recognized the independence and complete SOVEREIGNTY of the State of Kuwait."

It was as a member of the Baathist Party that SADDAM HUSSEIN came to power in a 1968 coup and then succeeded to the Iraqi presidency in 1979. Within a year of his ascendancy Saddam took Iraq into war with IRAN's Islamic government, although the Iraqi ambassador at the United Nations described the war as purely an act of self-defense. The IRAN-IRAQ WAR lasted eight years and claimed more than a half million lives. During the conflict the Iraqi regime took the occasion to use poison gas against its own Kurdish population and to launch missiles against civilian targets in and around Tehran, Iran. While the Iranian government regularly sought UN condemnation of the Iraqi war of AGGRESSION, the SECURITY COUNCIL proved largely uninterested in taking the Iranian side. During the early months of the war the Iranian government continued to hold 52 American diplomats as a result of the seizure of the U.S. embassy in Tehran in November 1979. Most nations were outraged by this action since it violated one of the most important and protected principles of INTERNATIONAL LAW, namely, diplomatic immunity. Most Arab and Western nations generally "tilted" toward Iraq in the war, fearful that an Iraqi loss would lead to the spread of "Khomeinism," a reference to the radical ideas of Iran's revolutionary leader Ayatollah Khomeini.

Reduced to calls for cease-fires and admonitions to both parties to honor CONVENTIONS relevant to the rules of war, the Security Council took no serious action until summer 1987. This lackluster performance probably encouraged President Hussein in his belief that the UNITED STATES and other major powers on the Council were not to be feared as he pursued an expansionist foreign policy. Only with the prodding of UN SECRETARY-GENERAL JAVIER PÉREZ DE CUÉLLAR did the United States, the Soviet Union, and the other PERMANENT MEMBERS OF THE SECURITY COUNCIL reach a consensus embodied in Resolution 598. The RESOLUTION called for a cease-fire and an end to the war. It threatened unspecified actions against either party if it did not agree to the resolution's terms. Iraq accepted immediately, and Iran grudgingly followed suit. Saddam Hussein did have to agree to the formation of a UN Commission of INQUIRY to determine which country had started the war, but little else in the conclusion of hostilities penalized Iraq.

During the war, many states provided financial and military assistance to Hussein's regime. One factor that prompted Iraq to invade Kuwait in August 1990 was a Kuwaiti refusal to forgive $14 billion in loans extended to Iraq to help fight Iran. Saddam also criticized Kuwait for stealing Iraqi oil by its drilling techniques and selling oil on the world market in greater amounts than it had agreed to do, thus, driving down the world price on oil and severely affecting Iraq's ability to earn enough foreign exchange to prop up the Iraqi economy. This time Hussein's invasion of another country was met with an avalanche of UN Security Council resolutions declaring Iraq the aggressor and calling upon member states to take all necessary means to liberate Kuwait. In accordance with these resolutions, a U.S.-led coalition forcibly drove Iraqi forces from Kuwait in the spring of 1991.

Following a March 1991 cease-fire—in return for which Saddam was forced to recognize the independence of Kuwait, allow coalition forces on Iraqi territory, and agree to verifiable DISARMAMENT, particularly of his supposed nuclear and CHEMICAL WEAPONS—the United Nations imposed economic SANCTIONS and WEAPONS inspections on Iraq. There was some hope, particularly in the American government, that the imposition of sanctions coupled with the shame of the war's loss would lead to the overthrow of the Hussein regime. However, when Shi'ite and Kurdish rebellions broke out in the southern and northern parts of the country respectively, Hussein used his remaining military capabilities to crush the revolts. The United Nations, led by the U.S. government, imposed "no-fly" zones in

these regions and launched a humanitarian effort to assist the affected populations.

The imposed sanctions did not undermine the regime. Instead, Hussein used the unpopularity of the sanctions to maintain his grip on power in Iraq. Repeatedly he challenged the inspections regime imposed by the United Nations and the no-fly zones maintained by the coalition partners, and he pointed to these foreign impositions as the reasons so many common Iraqi citizens were suffering. The sanctions severely impinged on the supply of food, medicines, and everyday necessities. Iraqi popular opinion tended to agree with Hussein on the foreign causes for their condition.

In response, the Security Council established the "Oil-for-Food" program that allowed Iraq to sell a quota of its oil and to use the proceeds for the purchase of humanitarian supplies. The Council authorized the sale of $1.6 billion worth of oil in six-month increments, even though the humanitarian need was placed by most estimates at more than $2 billion. In addition to the shortfall, the Hussein

Workers and soldiers search through the rubble of United Nations headquarters, Baghdad, after an explosion. (UN PHOTO 26788)

regime took kick-backs on the oil sales and diverted earnings to its own purposes. The program was also plagued with poor bookkeeping and corruption, leading to little relief for the population. In 2000, the Council retooled its restrictions on Iraq by the imposition of "SMART SANCTIONS," restructured economic limitations on the country in a fashion meant to affect the well-being of the leadership rather than the general citizenry.

From 1991 to 2001, the United States and the United Kingdom blocked any effort in the UN Security Council to ease restrictions on the Iraqi government. They pursued a policy of "containment" in hopes of bringing about a domestic undermining of the Hussein regime. Shortly after the war ended the Council created the UN SPECIAL COMMISSION ON IRAQ (UNSCOM) to verify Iraqi compliance with all UN resolutions and to carry out no-notice inspections inside of Iraq for the purpose of finding and destroying all WEAPONS OF MASS DESTRUCTION (WMD). UNSCOM also was charged with establishing a permanent system of monitoring and verification to assure that Iraq could not rebuild nuclear, biological, or chemical weapon capabilities. UNSCOM conducted its work under continuing challenge and obstruction from the Baghdad government. During its seven years of operation, UNSCOM's demands on the regime often were buttressed with air reprisals, largely carried out by U.S. and British warplanes.

A critical moment came in 1998 when U.S. president BILL CLINTON ordered four days of bombing in retaliation for Iraqi unwillingness to allow inspectors into requested sites. The UN withdrew the inspectors for the duration, citing safety considerations. Baghdad then announced that it would not allow the return of UNSCOM. The United Nations did not try to reinsert the inspection teams, but rather replaced UNSCOM with a new agency, the United Nations Monitoring, Verification, and Inspection Commission (UNMOVIC), which UN authorities hoped would be more acceptable in its personnel and leadership to Baghdad. The Swedish diplomat, Dr. HANS BLIX, was appointed executive secretary, and only one of UNMOVIC's 16 commissioners was an American. Hussein still refused to allow the reentry of the inspectors.

The policy of containment, despite Hussein's unwillingness to cooperate with UN agencies and past resolutions, remained the consensus strategy of the world community until the terrorist attacks on the World Trade Center in New York City and the Pentagon outside Washington, D.C., on September 11, 2001. After those events, the American administration of GEORGE W. BUSH, supported by the British government of Prime Minister Tony Blair, increasingly made Iraq a target of their anti-TERRORISM policies. The remaining permanent members on the Security Council, however, saw little connection between the attacks launched by AL-QAEDA and Hussein's regime.

In January 2002, the Bush administration announced that there were some unwelcome nations who made up an "axis of evil," and later that year the president argued that one of them—Iraq—needed to be struck immediately, preemptively, even unilaterally if the other members of the Security Council refused to accede to U.S. demands for military action. During much of 2002 and into early 2003, disagreements within the Security Council on the reasonableness of war with Iraq became public. Washington began warning of the certain "irrelevancy" of the UN should the Security Council fail to accede to war. Led by FRANCE, most of the members of the Security Council urged that UN arms inspectors be allowed to complete their work in Iraq. In November 2002, the United States acceded to a new resolution that would give the Iraqi regime one more chance to account for suspected weapons of mass destruction. UN SECURITY COUNCIL RESOLUTION 1441 found the Baghdad government in "material breach" of past UN resolutions, but provided for another arms inspection team under Dr. Blix. Until that team reported on compliance or non-compliance by Iraq with UN resolutions there could be no invasion of the country. France and the RUSSIAN FEDERATION argued that regardless of whether Blix found weapons or not, another Council resolution would be needed to authorize an attack. When Blix gave his report in the spring, he noted that the Iraqi regime had not been fully forthcoming, but that there was no conclusive evidence that Saddam Hussein had such weapons. When the United States sought an authorizing resolution in the wake of the Blix report, France indicated that it would VETO the proposal. After making its case for military action in a globally televised presentation by Secretary of State Colin Powell before the Security Council, the United States went to war in March 2003. Secretary-General KOFI ANNAN would later call the invasion illegal under the UN CHARTER.

While the U.S.-led coalition seemed to win the 2003 war in Iraq, postwar challenges proved more intractable than originally thought. Saddam was toppled and went into hiding, but no weapons of mass destruction were found. David Kay, who resigned in late January 2004 as head of the U.S. Iraq Survey Group trying to find weapons, declared before the U.S. Senate Armed Services Committee that there were no chemical, biological, or nuclear weapons in Iraq and no evidence that Baghdad had transferred any such weapons to al-Qaeda or any other terrorist group. Additionally, the American military and civilian administration of Iraq did not go as hoped. By spring 2007, more than 3,000 Americans had been killed in the country since the U.S. invasion and over 90 percent of those deaths had occurred after President Bush announced the end of combat on May 1, 2003. For the United Nations, the postwar reconstruction proved equally painful. On August 19, 2003, the UN suffered one of its most mortifying and heartbreaking moments when a bomb exploded at the UN compound in Baghdad, killing 22 personnel, including SERGIO VIEIRA DE MELLO, the UN HIGH COMMISSIONER FOR HUMAN RIGHTS and the Secretary-General's SPECIAL REPRESENTATIVE to Iraq. The UN Mission had been authorized by a unanimous Security Council resolution (1483) passed on May 22 of that year. In Resolution 1483 the Council empowered a UN presence to provide much needed humanitarian relief and help in NATION-BUILDING after the war. The bomb attack undercut the UN effort in Iraq, and by the end of September nearly all UN personnel were withdrawn from the country.

By early 2004, American Iraqi policy shifted, as officials announced the U.S. intention to transfer SOVEREIGNTY to an interim Iraqi government by June 30—a government selected by secretary-general Annan's Special Representative Lahkdar Brahimi. To contain the certain confusion and possible instability that might result, Washington made urgent appeals to the UN to take an active role in restoring order. On June 1, 2004, Brahimi and President Bush acceded to decisions by Iraqi Governing Council members to appoint immediately their own selections for a new government, with authority to manage Iraqi affairs until scheduled elections in January 2005. The United Nations then assisted in staging and monitoring those elections.

Despite new cooperation between Washington and the United Nations, the UN presence in Iraq remained meager. Amidst a growing insurgency against the American-backed government, occupying forces, and foreign agencies, Saddam Hussein was captured in December 2003. There were calls for the former leader to be tried for crimes against humanity in the UN-sponsored INTERNATIONAL CRIMINAL COURT, but instead he was tried and convicted in an Iraqi special court. Hussein was hanged on December 30, 2006.

Through the UNITED NATIONS ASSISTANCE MISSION IN IRAQ (UNAMI), first created in the summer of 2003, the UN attempted to maintain a presence in Iraq under the leadership of Annan's special representative, Ashraf Jehangir Qazi of PAKISTAN. Security Council Resolution 1546 established the UNAMI's mandate, which included assisting in the convocation of a conference to select an Iraqi Governing Council once sovereignty was transferred from the occupying forces on June 30, 2004, advising and supporting the Iraqi electoral commission that would administer VOTING for a national assembly, and contributing "to the coordination and delivery of reconstruction, DEVELOPMENT, and humanitarian assistance." UNAMI was also asked to promote HUMAN RIGHTS, judicial and legal REFORM, and national reconciliation. To carry out its wide-ranging responsibilities UNAMI coordinated the work of 16 UN agencies, most important among them the WORLD BANK, the WORLD FOOD PROGRAMME, the UN HIGH COMMISSIONER FOR REFUGEES, the UN CHILDREN'S FUND, the UN ENVIRONMENT PROGRAMME, the FOOD AND AGRICULTURE ORGANIZATION, and the UN DEVELOPMENT PROGRAMME. Critical to its work was raising sufficient funds from donor states and organizations. In partnership with the World Bank, UNAMI created the UN-WB International Reconstruction Trust Fund Facility for Iraq. The facility funneled donor resources to critical reconstruc-

tion projects, investment efforts, and technical assistance. Donor states began depositing resources in the FUND in 2004 and by 2007 more than $410 million had been expended. But the continuing security crisis in the country made it extremely difficult for the UN and other international actors to achieve their goals. By mid 2007 there seemed little hope at anytime in the near future of a peaceful, democratic, and economically successful Iraq emerging from the devastating events of the previous four years.

See also APPENDIX F (Uniting for Peace Resolution, Security Council Resolution 242, Security Council Resolution 678); ARAB-ISRAELI DISPUTE; BIOLOGICAL WEAPONS; BUSH, GEORGE H. W.; CHAPTER VII; COLD WAR; DEPARTMENT OF PEACEKEEPING OPERATIONS; GULF WAR; INTERNATIONAL ATOMIC ENERGY AGENCY; MIDDLE EAST WAR OF 1967; OIL-FOR-FOOD SCANDAL; ORGANISATION FOR THE PROHIBITION OF CHEMICAL WEAPONS; SANCTIONS COMMITTEES OF THE SECURITY COUNCIL; SPECIAL RAPPORTEUR; TRUSTEESHIP SYSTEM; UN SECURITY COUNCIL RESOLUTION 678; UNITED NATIONS OFFICE FOR PROJECT SERVICES; ZIONISM IS RACISM RESOLUTION.

Further Reading: Blix, Hans. *Disarming Iraq.* New York: Pantheon, 2004. Butler, Richard. *Iraq. Weapons of Mass Destruction, and the Growing Crisis of Global Security.* New York: Public Affairs, 2000. Conlon, Paul. *United Nations Sanctions Management: A Case Study of the Iraq Sanctions Committee 1990–1994.* Ardsley, N.Y.: Transnational Publishers, 2000. Dobbins, James, Seth G. Jones, Keith Crane, Andrew Rathmell, Brett Steele, and Richard Teltschik. *The UN's Role in Nation-Building: From the Congo to Iraq.* Santa Monica, Calif.: RAND Corporation, 2004. Hume, Cameron R. *The United Nations, Iran and Iraq: How Peacemaking Changed.* Bloomington: Indiana University Press, 1994. Malone, David M. *The International Struggle over Iraq: Politics in the UN Security Council, 1980–2005.* New York: Oxford University Press, 2006. Moore, John Allphin, Jr., and Jerry Pubantz. *The New United Nations: International Organization in the Twenty-first Century.* Upper Saddle River, N.J.: Prentice Hall, 2006. Pubantz, Jerry, and John Allphin Moore, Jr. "Best of Times, Worst of Times: The Fortunes of the United Nations in the Middle East." In *War in the Gardens of Babylon,* edited by Bülent Aras, 89–106. New York: Tasam Publications, 2004. Ritter, Scott. *Endgame: Solving the Iraq Problem—Once and For All.* New York: Simon & Schuster, 1999.

Islamic Development Bank (IDB)

On March 28, 2007, the UN GENERAL ASSEMBLY granted OBSERVER STATUS to the Islamic Development Bank (IDB). The financial institution is a MULTILATERAL DEVELOPMENT BANK located in Jeddah, Saudi Arabia, and committed to economic DEVELOPMENT in Islamic member states and in Muslim communities in non-member countries. The IDB operates according to the principles of shari'a (Islamic law). During its first three decades the IDB added specialized entities to create an Islamic Bank Group. These included the International Islamic Trade Finance Corporation (ITFC), the Islamic Corporation for the Development of the Private Sector (ICD), the Islamic Corporation for the Insurance of Investment and Export Credit (ICIEC), the World WAQF Foundation (WWF), and the Islamic Research and Training Institute (IRTI).

The bank was the brainchild of Saudi king Faisal and was created by the Organization of the Islamic Conference (OIC) in December 1973. It began operations on October 20, 1975. Beginning with 22 members, at the end of 2006 the bank had 56 member countries. Each member state must be a member of the OIC. Members place assets in the bank that are then used for development projects. VOTING in the bank is weighted to reflect the percentage of bank assets held by each member. As of April 2007, among the MEMBERSHIP the most significant contributors were EGYPT, IRAN, Kuwait, Libya, Saudi Arabia, Turkey, and the United Arab Emirates. In September 2006 the IDB's capital fund stood at $4.1 billion.

The bank is governed by its 10 member Board of Governors, Board of Executive Directors, and president. Each of the seven largest shareholders in the bank appoints one of the executive directors. An additional seven directors are elected to three-year renewable terms by the remaining member states. In 2007 the bank president was Ahmad Mohamed Ali Al-Madani (Saudi Arabia) who had held the post since the IDB's founding.

In his letter of acceptance of UN observer status, IDB Bank president Ali noted the bank's commitment to the MILLENNIUM DEVELOPMENT GOALS. In particular, the IDB sought to alleviate poverty in Islamic states by emphasizing human, agricultural, and infrastructure development. It also sought to expand trade among member countries. To achieve these ends, the bank launched in 2006 its "1440 Hijira Vision" Initiative, and it explored the possibility of creating a "Poverty Reduction Fund." A serious challenge, however, that the bank faced in achieving its goals was the existing tension between typical banking practices and Shari'a proscriptions against the charging of interest. Islamic religious principles barred interest payments and earnings as akin to gambling. Islamic jurisprudence, however, does not prohibit profit and loss on goods, property, and services. Consequently, the IDB uses a multiple-contract and strict collateral system to make possible the issuance of what in practical terms would be loans and a normal return on those loans.

See also ECONOMIC COMMUNITY OF WEST AFRICAN STATES, REGIONAL DEVELOPMENT BANKS.

Further Reading: IDB Web site: <www.isdb.org/irj/portal/anonymous>.

J

Japan

Japan is composed of a chain of numerous islands at the edge of East Asia. Approximately the size of California, the country in 2005 had a POPULATION of about 130 million people and a gross national product of over $4 trillion, making it one of the wealthiest of the world's nations. Following the accession of the Meiji emperor in 1868, the island nation rejected its traditional policy of isolationism from the rest of the world, underwent a rapid modernization, and became a military rival of, and diplomatic participant with, the imperial Western powers. Japan defeated RUSSIA in the Russo-Japanese War of 1904–05, becoming the dominant power in East Asia. Japan was one of the great powers that founded the LEAGUE OF NATIONS following World War I. The country served on the League's Council, and its government regularly participated in cooperative relations with Council members. It signed the Kellogg-Briand PACT in 1928 that outlawed the use of force in international politics. But the shift toward militarism, Japan's invasion of Manchuria in 1931, and her withdrawal from the League in 1933 led to her isolation from the multilateral diplomacy of the period. As one of the "enemy states" of World War II, identified as such in Articles 53 and 107 of the UN CHARTER, Japan was not allowed to join the new organization in 1945. In the early 1950s the country sought MEMBERSHIP on several occasions, but was regularly blocked by the Soviet Union, which feared that Japan would constitute another vote in favor of U.S. positions.

Despite not being admitted to the United Nations until 1956, Japan quickly joined other international organizations and UN SPECIALIZED AGENCIES in the immediate postwar era. These included the WORLD HEALTH ORGANIZATION in 1951, UNIVERSAL POSTAL UNION (1948), INTERNATIONAL COURT OF JUSTICE (1954), and UN EDUCATIONAL, SCIENTIFIC AND CULTURAL ORGANIZATION (1951). These memberships in prelude to joining the United Nations reflected a broad commitment by the Japanese elite, reflected in public opinion, to rebuild the country's international reputation and influence through a "UN-centered diplomacy." In 1951 Japanese foreign minister Kishi Nobusuhe identified support for the United Nations as a central "pillar" of his country's foreign policy. It would remain so beyond the next half century.

Once admitted, Japan voted with the UNITED STATES and other Western industrialized nations on nearly all critical issues until the early 1970s. However, as the VOTING majority in the GENERAL ASSEMBLY steadily shifted to anti-American positions, Japan, in an effort to remain effective within the world body, slowly diverged from its Western partners. The evolution was clear on MIDDLE EAST issues. While Japan abstained on the "ZIONISM IS RACISM" resolution in deference to U.S. and Western opposition, it supported granting the Palestine Liberation Organization OBSERVER STATUS at the UN. Japan, however, did support the American-led GULF WAR to liberate Kuwait from Iraqi control in 1990–91, but only provided humanitarian assistance to the UN-authorized military action.

Its enthusiasm for UN diplomacy as a method of reintegrating the Pacific nation into the world community led Japan to steadily increase its funding of the world body through both direct financial contributions and the underwriting of UN initiatives. In 1975 the government offered a home in Tokyo for the new UNITED NATIONS UNIVERSITY and provided continuing funding for the research institution. It also was a strong supporter of the UN ENVIRONMENT PROGRAMME, UN DEVELOPMENT PROGRAMME (UNDP), and UN HIGH COMMISSIONER FOR REFUGEES. In October 1993 it convened the first Tokyo International Conference on African Development (TICAD-I) in association with UNDP, the Global Coalition for AFRICA, and the WORLD BANK. TICAD provided a framework for Asian-African DEVELOPMENT cooperation. Subsequent meetings in 1998 and 2003 emphasized foreign investment in Africa, particularly by the private sector in agriculture. Japan also worked closely with the UN Economic Commission for Asia and the Pacific to alleviate poverty in the region. Tokyo contributed ¥120 million to the effort.

By the turn of the century Japan was the second largest financial contributor to UN PEACEKEEPING. But given the deep sense of antimilitarism in Japanese political culture, it was reluctant to send personnel as members of an operation. It first provided funds in 1974 for the UNITED NATIONS FORCE IN CYPRUS. It also supported operations in IRAQ, CAMBODIA, SOMALIA, BOSNIA, and KOSOVO. The first Japanese civilian participants in UN peacekeeping took part in NAMIBIA in the late 1980s. Subsequently, Japan participated in missions to MOZAMBIQUE (1993), the Golan Heights (1996), and TIMOR-LESTE (1999). Japanese personnel observed elections, undertook humanitarian work, provided medical care, and organized communications in these settings.

Japan has been a strong supporter of DISARMAMENT and arms control agreements. It signed and ratified both the ANTARCTIC TREATY, which prohibited the militarization of the continent, and the NUCLEAR NON-PROLIFERATION TREATY shortly after its promulgation. As a member of the CONFERENCE ON DISARMAMENT, Japan regularly proposed new WEAPONS reduction plans. In 1998, Japan submitted to the UN General Assembly a RESOLUTION seeking the complete phase-out of nuclear weapons tests with the goal of ultimately eliminating this category of weapons. In the 1990s it helped fund the dismantling of nuclear arsenals possessed by the former Soviet Union and denounced the nuclear tests conducted by INDIA and PAKISTAN. Japan encouraged all powers to become parties to the COMPREHENSIVE NUCLEAR TEST BAN TREATY. Finally, in the first decade of the 21st century the Japanese government actively participated in the "six party" talks meant to dissuade North Korea from developing a nuclear bomb.

A regular NON-PERMANENT MEMBER OF THE SECURITY COUNCIL Japan, having held that position more than any other country, has sought permanent membership on the Council as its financial contributions to the United Nations have risen. It has also threatened to pull its considerable financial support from UN agencies that do not have sufficient Japanese representation on their staffs and in senior positions. Its most bruising fight came in 1993 when Tokyo threatened to withhold its contribution to the World Health Organization if the members did not reelect Nakajima Hiroshi as the organization's DIRECTOR-GENERAL. Outside of WHO Japan pressured major trading partners to support Hiroshi.

Japan's encouragement of UN REFORM programs has been driven in part by its desire to enlarge its role in UN affairs. When SECRETARY-GENERAL KOFI ANNAN proposed in 2005 the enlargement of the Security Council, Japan joined GERMANY, Brazil, and India in campaigning for the group's inclusion as permanent members, first with the VETO, then, as opposition grew to their candidacies, without it. While the United States supported Japan's application for a seat, most Asian states, particularly CHINA, opposed adding it to the PERMANENT MEMBERS OF THE SECURITY COUNCIL. On substantive grounds several nations questioned whether Japan could fulfill the responsibilities of permanent membership, given its constitutional prohibitions against maintaining military forces and its regular opposition to the use of force. Other nations demurred on adding yet another representative of the developed world to the Council. Japan failed in its bid, raising calls in Japanese politics for a diminution of the country's financial support of the world body.

See also ADVISORY COMMITTEE ON ADMINISTRATIVE AND BUDGETARY QUESTIONS; AGENDA 21; APPENDIX F (Security Council Resolution 1718); BUDGET OF THE UNITED NATIONS; CHINA; DESERTIFICATION; ENVIRONMENT; FIRST AND THIRD WORLDS; GENERAL AGREEMENT ON TARIFFS AND TRADE; G-8; INTERNATIONAL LABOUR ORGANIZATION; INTERNATIONAL LAW; INTERNATIONAL MONETARY FUND; KYOTO PROTOCOL; STIMSON DOCTRINE; STALIN, JOSEPH; TRUSTEESHIP SYSTEM; UNITED NATIONS RELIEF AND WORKS AGENCY FOR PALESTINE REFUGEES IN THE NEAR EAST; WAR CRIMES TRIBUNALS; WEAPONS OF MASS DESTRUCTION; WORLD FOOD PROGRAMME; WORLD SUMMIT (2005), WORLD TRADE ORGANIZATION; YALTA CONFERENCE.

Further Reading: Clark, William, Jr., and Ryukichi Imai, eds. *Next Steps in Arms Control and Non-Proliferation: Report of the U.S.-Japan Study Group on Arms Control and Non-Proliferation after the Cold War.* Washington, D.C.: Carnegie Endowment for International Peace, 1997. Drifte, Reinhard. *Japan's Quest for a Permanent Security Council Seat: A Matter of Pride or Justice?* New York: St. Martin's, 2000. Hook, Glenn D., Julie Gilson, Christopher W. Hughes, and Hugo Dobson. *Japan's International Relations: Politics, Economics, and Security.* New York: Routledge, 2001. Kawashima,

Yutaka. *Japanese Foreign Policy at the Crossroads: Challenges and Options for the Twenty-first Century.* Washington, D.C.: Brookings Institution, 2003. Permanent Mission of Japan to the UN Web site: <www.un.int/japan/>. Takashi, Inoguchi, and Purnendra Jain, eds. *Japanese Foreign Policy Today: A Reader.* New York: Palgrave, 2000.

Jarring, Gunnar (1907–2002)

Gunnar Jarring was born in Sweden in 1907. Trained at Lund University, he earned the Doctor of Philosophy degree in 1933 and went on to a distinguished career as a linguist who specialized in Turkic languages, and as a world renowned diplomat. As a member of the Swedish foreign service, he served in IRAN, IRAQ, INDIA, the UNITED STATES, the Soviet Union, and Ethiopia. He was Sweden's UN ambassador from 1956 to 1958, sitting as his country's representative on the SECURITY COUNCIL.

Following the MIDDLE EAST WAR OF 1967, UN SECRETARY-GENERAL U THANT appointed Jarring his SPECIAL REPRESENTATIVE for Middle East peace. At the time, he was posted as his country's ambassador in Moscow, but he was recommended to U Thant by a long-time friend, U.S. secretary of state Dean Rusk. By late 1970 Jarring's mission had reached an impasse because of differing interpretations in Israeli and Arab capitals of UN SECURITY COUNCIL RESOLUTION 242, which had been approved in 1967 as the basis for a settlement of the ARAB-ISRAELI DISPUTE. Israel refused to make any territorial concessions until peace agreements were struck with the Arab states that recognized Israel's right to exist. On the other hand, Arab governments insisted that Israel return to its pre-1967 borders before they would enter any negotiations with Tel Aviv.

Jarring's mission would continue until hostilities once again broke out in 1973. On February 8, 1971, the ambassador issued an aide-memoire to both sides proposing that each give its preliminary and simultaneous commitment to him that it would meet the demands of the other side, and, thus, break the impasse. The proposal was unacceptable to both Israelis and Arabs. After the 1973 war, while Jarring continued as the Secretary-General's special representative (which he did until March 1991), his role was largely marginalized by the direct diplomatic intervention of the United States. For the most part, Jarring returned to his academic studies of Turkic languages. In 1982 he donated his personal collection of manuscripts from eastern Turkestan—at the time the third largest collection in the world—to his alma mater. Among his more important writings was *Return to Kashgar: Central Asian Memoirs in the Present*, published in 1986. Jarring also served as the chairman of the Swedish Research Institute in Istanbul (SRII). He died at his home in Helsingborg, Sweden, on May 29, 2002. SRII subsequently established the Gunnar Jarring Lectures to be given annually on eastern Turkic languages and cultures.

Further Reading: Korn, David A., *Stalemate: The War of Attrition and Great Power Diplomacy in the Middle East, 1967–1970.* Boulder, Colo.: Westview Press, 1992.

Johnson, Lyndon B. (1908–1973)

Lyndon Baines Johnson, often referred to as "LBJ," served as the 36th president of the UNITED STATES from November 22, 1963, to January 20, 1969. Rising from humble beginnings in the Hill Country of Texas, Johnson ascended to the powerful position of Majority Leader of the U.S. Senate and contested for the presidential nomination in 1960. Serving as vice president under President JOHN F. KENNEDY, LBJ succeeded to the presidency following Kennedy's assassination.

A protégé of FRANKLIN D. ROOSEVELT, Johnson entered politics in the 1930s. He was a strong advocate of Roosevelt's New Deal liberalism. Throughout his career Johnson promoted national social welfare programs to assist the poor and disadvantaged. As president he launched a "War on Poverty," proposed strong civil rights laws, and pushed through Congress national health care programs for the elderly and poor.

It is understandable that Johnson's first inclinations as president were to apply his social and political philosophy to both domestic and foreign policy. For Johnson, who was attuned to the social and economic problems of disadvantaged people, the expansion of DEVELOPMENT aid was naturally appealing, either directly from Washington or multilaterally through the United Nations. Twenty-five days after becoming president, Johnson addressed the UN GENERAL ASSEMBLY. He emphasized the importance of the UN's fight against hunger, poverty, and disease, and applauded the UN for its "Decade of Development" and its maintenance of agencies and programs that alleviated the suffering of people. During his five years in office, Johnson expanded American aid programs out of a personal conviction that such actions were important on their own merits, not primarily as tactics in the COLD WAR. He sought additional congressional funding for the FOOD AND AGRICULTURE ORGANIZATION and for food contributions to Asian and African food programs, and to specific LEAST DEVELOPED COUNTRIES facing shortages. To make the United Nations more effective in promoting prosperity, the administration urged it to merge its assistance programs. Accordingly, in 1965 the United Nations combined the SPECIAL UNITED NATIONS FUND FOR ECONOMIC DEVELOPMENT (created in 1958) and the EXPANDED PROGRAM FOR TECHNICAL ASSISTANCE (established during Truman's presidency) into the UNITED NATIONS DEVELOPMENT PROGRAMME (UNDP). The president in turn asked Congress to augment the U.S. contribution to UNDP in proportion to other nations' allocations.

Johnson's focus on the development process and support of a UN role in it was an increasingly unpopular position in American politics. Faced with a backlash among voters,

LBJ found ways to enlarge U.S. assistance to the underdeveloped states without endangering his base of support in Congress or in the nation at large. His strategy was to emphasize the efficiency and effectiveness of UN programs, to promote regional economic development outside the UN machinery, and to expand American unilateral projects where it could be demonstrated that U.S. help would make the recipient nation quickly independent of outside support.

At the United Nations he endorsed the Third World's demand for greater inclusion in the decision-making organs. Four days before his first address to the General Assembly, that body voted overwhelmingly to enlarge the SECURITY COUNCIL's membership from 10 delegates to 15. The new NON-PERMANENT MEMBERS were meant to give the Council a broader geographical and political representation, diluting the dominance of the PERMANENT MEMBERS and representing the interests of the many new states admitted since 1945. Although the United States abstained from VOTING, Johnson lobbied Congress to approve the AMENDMENT TO THE CHARTER, as well as to ratify an enlargement of the ECONOMIC AND SOCIAL COUNCIL from 18 to 27 nations.

The REFORM of UN STRUCTURES eased the political problems Johnson faced with the public and with DEVELOPING COUNTRIES, but it did not convince him that the United Nations should be the sole channel for delivering U.S. aid to recipient states. For that, he concluded, REGIONAL ORGANIZATIONS and agreements provided the longest-lasting benefit. LBJ supported expanding the regional principle that President Kennedy had initiated in LATIN AMERICA with the "Alliance for Progress" program. In Africa the president was impressed with the work of the ORGANIZATION OF AFRICAN UNITY (OAU). Johnson pressed the WORLD BANK to organize a donors' committee of developed states that would work closely with the OAU. The committee met for the first time in 1967; its membership consisted of the United States, the United Kingdom, Italy, Belgium, and Canada. In Asia Johnson's most important economic assistance goal was the completion of plans for the ASIAN DEVELOPMENT BANK, which began operation in late 1967. The original capitalization for the bank was $1 billion, with the United States subscribed for 20 percent of the total. In East Asia the United States joined with South Korea, Nationalist CHINA, Malaysia, and several other nations to form the Asian and Pacific Council (ASPAC), which committed itself to promoting regional prosperity through freer trade and assistance programs.

Beyond development issues, Johnson believed that the UN provided a useful venue for the pursuit of DISARMAMENT and arms control agreements. The most important success achieved by the United Nations during his tenure in this regard was the NUCLEAR NON-PROLIFERATION TREATY (NPT) of 1968. Applauded by Johnson as the most important international disarmament agreement since the dawn of nuclear weapons, the TREATY was largely the product of secret earlier negotiations between the United States and the Soviet Union. The parties submitted a joint draft agreement to the EIGHTEEN NATION DISARMAMENT COMMITTEE (ENDC) in 1967. Under the terms of the joint proposal states who possessed nuclear weapons promised not to give those WEAPONS to states that did not already have them, and non-nuclear states gave up their right to obtain nuclear armaments.

Weaker states on the ENDC understood that any agreement that limited the spread of nuclear technology was an inherently "unequal" treaty. It would freeze the gulf between those nations that already possessed these weapons and states that would be permanently barred from obtaining them. The United Nations's imprimatur was being used to solidify the dominance of nuclear states in world affairs. Consequently, nonaligned states insisted on a balance of mutual responsibilities for nuclear and non-nuclear powers. The group was especially concerned about the "vertical proliferation" represented in the huge arsenals of the superpowers. Any ban on "horizontal proliferation" to non-nuclear states that allowed the United States and the USSR to continue stockpiling nuclear weapons would only exacerbate the gulf between the "haves" and "have-nots." A coalition of these states, led by Nigeria and Brazil, insisted on language in the treaty that required the United States and the USSR to begin negotiations on diminishing the size of their nuclear arsenals. Without the agreement of the many threshold states, a nonproliferation agreement would be worthless. Articles Six and Seven were added to the NPT, which called upon the parties to "pursue negotiations in good faith on effective measures relating to the cessation of the nuclear arms race at an early date and to nuclear disarmament."

Even prior to this demand, Lyndon Johnson had attempted to engage the Soviets in talks on strategic arms limitations (SALT), and, as early as January 1964, he proposed to the ENDC a "verified freeze" on arms stockpiling. In January 1967, the president wrote directly to Soviet premier Kosygin proposing secret negotiations. Those discussions led to agreement on the provisions of a SALT treaty. However, the Soviet invasion of Czechoslovakia in August 1968 cut short movement toward a signing ceremony.

One glaring omission from the draft Nuclear Non-Proliferation Treaty was any system of international control or verification. The Soviets had urged the use of the INTERNATIONAL ATOMIC ENERGY AGENCY (IAEA) for this purpose. Initially, the United States welcomed the IAEA's authority, except in Western Europe—where, it argued, Euratom should provide verification. However, Washington found itself in the minority on the inspection issue and had to retreat before strong Third World complaints. The final compromise included provision that in exchange for giving up the pursuit of nuclear weapons, non-nuclear countries would receive international assistance in the development of nuclear technology for peaceful purposes and would be subject to the IAEA Safeguard inspection system.

While development and disarmament seemed appropriate issues areas for the United States to address through UN auspices, most of the serious cold war disputes between the superpowers, in President Johnson's view, made the United Nations more a battleground than an instrument for easing tensions and required direct bilateral negotiations with Moscow rather than multilateral discussion. As an example of the former phenomenon, when Johnson succeeded to the Oval Office, the United Nations was deeply involved in the civil war then underway in the CONGO. The United States had supported the UN operation over Soviet objections. Fighting the war was made more difficult by the withholding of UN contributions by several nations, including the USSR. Johnson tried to force the Soviet government to pay its required dues by attempting to take away the USSR's vote in the General Assembly as allowed by the UN CHARTER if a nation falls more than two years behind in its assessed contributions. Finding insufficient support in the Assembly, the United States finally dropped the matter in 1964.

Vietnam was the most serious item on the president's foreign policy agenda in the weeks and years following the assassination. Like his predecessors, LBJ perceived this second Indochinese war as a struggle with international communism on the periphery of the traditional cold war terrain. As early as February 1954, Johnson assured President DWIGHT D. EISENHOWER of his support for the administration's decision to take over the French commitment as long as Vietnam was granted its independence and there were allies in the region to join the United States in the effort. Kennedy had expanded the American policy to hold the line against falling dominoes in Southeast Asia, and Johnson saw no reason to disrupt the continuity. As vice president, he told reporters that deserting Vietnam would mean "the United States, inevitably, must surrender the Pacific and take up our defenses on our own shores."

Johnson was not in a frame of mind to find a diplomatic solution in the first months of his presidency. UN SECRETARY-GENERAL U THANT, nonetheless, pressed for a negotiated settlement. Thant, meeting with Johnson in August 1964, proposed that he quietly organize talks among the principal parties. When U Thant's efforts seemed to bear fruit in October—with a tentative commitment from the North Vietnamese to participate in talks—U.S. secretary of state Dean Rusk dismissed the initiative because it would mean rewarding AGGRESSION.

Only in support of the U.S. war effort did Johnson consider UN involvement helpful. In May 1964, the administration suggested that the UN put a PEACEKEEPING or observer group along the Vietnamese-Cambodian border to stabilize conditions upset by Viet Cong operations. In August it also agreed to a Security Council invitation to North Vietnam to participate in the Council's sessions called to hear the American complaint about the Tonkin Gulf incidents. Beyond these small nods to the United Nations, Johnson was unwilling to

go. Even when good friends and advisers suggested that he look to the United Nations for a possible diplomatic avenue, he rejected it. U.S. ambassador to the UN Adlai Stevenson urged an APPEAL TO THE SECURITY COUNCIL before the decision to bomb targets in North Vietnam, but Johnson rejected the idea.

It was only in the later stages of Johnson's presidency that the United States sought a route out of Vietnam by way of the United Nations. By then, the United States was dealing from a position of weakness. Neither the Soviet Union nor North Vietnam saw any merit in employing the United Nations to diminish the likelihood of an American defeat. When the president asked members of the United Nations at the 20th anniversary of the signing of the UN Charter "to individually and collectively bring to the table those who seem determined to make war," there was no meaningful response. At the end of January 1966 the United States asked the Security Council to call for immediate unconditional talks, but that was vetoed by the USSR. In September 1967 U.S. ambassador Arthur Goldberg circulated a draft Security Council RESOLUTION calling for a cease-fire and the withdrawal of foreign troops from South Vietnam. The Soviets and their allies kept it off the agenda.

It was the perceived centrality to American national interests of this particular fight on the periphery of the Soviet-American confrontation that made the use of the United Nations so unappealing to Johnson, as it had to Kennedy and Eisenhower. The president took the same stance on other critical U.S.-Soviet matters. In Europe, disputes over divided GERMANY and its former capital, Berlin, were left to bilateral negotiations. In surrogate confrontations in Latin America and Africa, Johnson preferred to act with allies or unilaterally. Only when disputes seemed not to involve the cold war dynamic was Johnson predisposed to turn to the UN. For example, he sought UN assistance when fighting broke out on the island of CYPRUS, exacerbating tensions between two NATO allies, Greece and Turkey. In March 1964 the administration supported the creation of a UN peacekeeping force to separate the Turkish and Greek Cypriots on the island. And in the MIDDLE EAST WAR OF 1967 President Johnson initially left the crisis to UN resolution until it appeared there might be Soviet intervention in the conflict. Then Johnson's government moved quickly to find at least a temporary formula for settlement.

See also ARAB-ISRAELI DISPUTE, GOLDBERG RESERVATION, UNITED NATIONS CONFERENCE ON THE HUMAN ENVIRONMENT.

Further Reading: Bloomfield, Lincoln P. *The UN and Vietnam.* New York: Carnegie Endowment for International Peace, 1968. Dallek, Robert. *Flawed Giant: Lyndon B. Johnson and His Times, 1961–1973.* Oxford: Oxford University Press, 1998. Johnson, Lyndon B. *The Vantage Point: Perspectives of the Presidency, 1963–1969.* New York: Holt, Rinehart and

Winston, 1971. Kearns, Doris. *Lyndon Johnson and the American* Dream. New York: Signet, 1976. Moore, John Allphin, Jr., and Jerry Pubantz. *To Create a New World?: American Presidents and the United Nations.* New York: Peter Lang, 1999. Packenham, Robert A. *Liberal America and the Third World.* Princeton, N.J.: Princeton University Press, 1973.

Joint Inspection Unit (JIU)

Located at the GENEVA HEADQUARTERS OF THE UNITED NATIONS, the Joint Inspection Unit is an external oversight body and subsidiary organ of the UN GENERAL ASSEMBLY (GA) that makes recommendations on improving management and coordination within the UNITED NATIONS SYSTEM. The General Assembly established JIU in 1968, giving it broad authority to investigate all SPECIALIZED AGENCIES and other bodies of the UN system, and to draft independent reports for consideration by the GA FIFTH COMMITTEE. By the turn of the century, the Joint Inspection Unit had produced more than 300 reports on management issues, including personnel policy, planning, career development, budgeting, development cooperation, and performance assessment. Over four decades, JIU's guidelines and procedures became the standards used throughout the UN system.

The Joint Inspection Unit has 11 inspectors elected by the General Assembly to once-renewable five-year terms. In addition to assuring equitable geographical representation, the Assembly elects individuals with strong experience in administrative and financial matters. The inspectors have broad powers of investigation, using on-the-spot reviews of specialized agencies to assure that these organs are working efficiently and providing effective service. Among the bodies reviewed were the WORLD INTELLECTUAL PROPERTY ORGANIZATION (WIPO), INTERNATIONAL LABOUR ORGANIZATION (ILO), NEW PARTNERSHIP FOR AFRICA'S DEVELOPMENT (NEPAD), and PAN-AMERICAN HEALTH ORGANIZATION (PAHO). Its projected investigations for 2006 and beyond included the WORLD METEOROLOGICAL ORGANIZATION (WMO) and INTERNATIONAL CIVIL AVIATION ORGANIZATION (ICAO). Since 2004, each of the organizations reviewed by JIU has been expected to report to the General Assembly on the steps taken to implement any recommendations the unit made in its report. The change in procedure in 2004 reflected a REFORM program put in place that year by JIU that included a new strategic framework for its operations and the development of a series of common questions to be answered by all agencies reviewed. JIU also prepares reports on system-wide administrative and financial issues. It produced 27 such reports between 1994 and 1999. Its provisional work program at the beginning of the new century included studies on the administration of the UN OFFICE AT GENEVA (UNOG), the handling of oversight reports by legislative bodies in the UN system, the management of buildings,

planning and budgeting in the UN system, a comparative analysis of the management of junior professionals in the system, and the administration of justice in UN ADMINISTRATIVE TRIBUNALS. The specialized agencies and the UN BUDGET cover the expenses of JIU, which generally range from $3 million to $9 million annually.

Further Reading: Eco'Diagnostic, Geneva. *International Geneva Yearbook, 2005–2006.* Geneva: United Nations, 2005. United Nations. *Reports of the Joint Inspection Unit: General Assembly Official Records,* Supplement No. 34 (each session). JIU Web site: <www.jiu.org>.

Joint United Nations Programme on HIV/AIDS (UNAIDS)

The Joint United Nations Programme on HIV/AIDS (UNAIDS) acts as the leading coordinating body for the United Nations's response to the worldwide AIDS epidemic. Prior to its creation in 1996, the WORLD HEALTH ORGANIZATION (WHO) was the primary agency responsible for addressing the epidemic. In 1987, the United Nations established a Special Programme on AIDS within WHO, later to be called the Global Programme on AIDS (GPA). Despite the leadership role of WHO and its coordinating efforts with the UNITED NATIONS DEVELOPMENT PROGRAMME (UNDP) and the WORLD BANK, it was decided within the United Nations that an expanded coordinating program was warranted to address the multifaceted nature of the AIDS epidemic. The consensus among the various UN organizations addressing the AIDS epidemic was that there needed to be one source of policy and technical guidance within the UN system that recognized the underlying causes and impact of AIDS, which go far beyond the health sector. The result was the creation of UNAIDS, which initially brought together six agencies belonging to or affiliated with the UN system—WHO, UNDP, UNICEF (UNITED NATIONS CHILDREN'S FUND), UNFPA (UNITED NATIONS POPULATION FUND), UNESCO (UNITED NATIONS EDUCATIONAL, SCIENTIFIC AND CULTURAL ORGANIZATION), and the World Bank—to coordinate their individual efforts in addressing the AIDS epidemic. In April 1999, recognizing the increasing impact of HIV transmission through needles shared by injecting drug users, the UN INTERNATIONAL DRUG CONTROL PROGRAMME (UNDCP), later known as the OFFICE ON DRUGS AND CRIME, joined the Joint United Nations Programme on AIDS. In October 2001 the INTERNATIONAL LABOUR ORGANIZATION (ILO) became the eighth co-sponsor on UNAIDS, joined soon thereafter by the WORLD FOOD PROGRAMME (WFP) and the UN HIGH COMMISSIONER FOR REFUGEES (UNHCR).

The goal of UNAIDS is to strengthen and orchestrate the expertise, resources, and influence that each of its constituent organizations offers. As the main advocate for global action on HIV/AIDS, the UNAIDS mission is to support a coordinated effort aimed at HIV prevention, provide care and support for people living with HIV/AIDS, and help alleviate the socioeconomic and human impact of AIDS. With this mission in mind, UNAIDS has identified four objectives: (1) To foster expanded national responses to HIV/AIDS, particularly in developing countries; (2) To promote strong commitment by governments to an expanded response to HIV/AIDS; (3) To strengthen and coordinate UN action on HIV/AIDS at the global and national levels; and (4) To identify, develop, and advocate international best practices for HIV prevention.

UNAIDS is governed by a Programme Coordinating Board (PCB) with representatives of 22 governments from all regions of the world. In addition, the board includes representatives from the 10 participating agencies and five representatives from NON-GOVERNMENTAL ORGANIZATIONS (NGOs), which include associations of people living with AIDS. As such, UNAIDS is the first United Nations program to include NGOs in its governing body. At its 19th meeting in December 2006 the PCB agreed to undertake a REFORM review of its operations in order to determine how it could restructure in order to be more effective in its leadership role in the fight against the disease.

With a relatively modest BUDGET in 2000 of $60 million, funding to UNAIDS rose dramatically to $320.5 million in 2006. These resources were put to the task of carrying out UNAIDS 2004 "Three Ones" principles. These included one international framework to coordinate all HIV/AIDS partner organizations, endorsement of each country having one national authority to coordinate domestic programs, and the creation of one global country-level monitoring and evaluation system. Remaining resources went to support the UNAIDS SECRETARIAT, based in Geneva. The Secretariat operates on behalf of the participating agencies to provide the following services: (1) policy development and research; (2) technical support; (3) advocacy; and (4) coordination. Priority areas identified by the UNAIDS secretariat include: young people, high-risk POPULATIONS, prevention of mother-to-child HIV transmission, development and implementation of community standards of AIDS care, vaccine development, and the creation of special initiatives for heavily impacted regions in the developing world where approximately 95 percent of HIV cases are found. In March 2005, the Secretariat was charged with facilitating two new working groups: the Global Task Team charged with improving ties among multinational organizations and international donors, and a working group to review the operating assumptions underlying estimates for future financial needs in the fight against HIV/AIDS.

In the developing nations, UNAIDS operates through a United Nations Theme Group on AIDS, consisting of representatives of the participating UN agencies. The representatives work with national government agencies as well as NGOs to support the host governments' efforts to develop a comprehensive response to HIV/AIDS.

Further Reading: Bastos, Cristiana. *Global Responses to AIDS: Science in Emergency*. Bloomington: Indiana University Press, 1999. Feldman, Douglas, and Julia Wang Miller. *The AIDS Crisis: A Documentary History*. Westport, Conn.: Greenwood Press, 1998. Joint United Nations Programme on HIV/AIDS. *From Advocacy to Action: A Progress Report on UNAIDS at Country Level*. Geneva: Joint United Nations Programme on HIV/AIDS, 2005. Stine, Gerald. *AIDS Update 2000*. Upper Saddle River, N.J.: Prentice Hall, 1999. UNAIDS Web site: <www.unaids.org.>

— R. E. McNamara

judicial settlement *See* CHAPTER VI OF THE UN CHARTER, INTERNATIONAL COURT OF JUSTICE.

jurisdiction of the United Nations

Jurisdiction is the exercise of legitimate "authority"—rather than "force" or "power"—over people, territory, or a particular human activity. In international affairs, jurisdiction is associated with the legal principle of state SOVEREIGNTY, which gives NATION-STATES unfettered control over domestic affairs, and requires of them non-interference in the affairs of other states. Within a political system itself, jurisdiction over aspects of political, social, and economic life may be assigned by constitutional arrangement to different government agencies, bodies, or individuals.

The jurisdiction of the United Nations arises from an agreement among independent states, enshrined in the UN CHARTER and approved at the 1945 San Francisco Conference. According to the Preamble of the Charter, the world's "people," represented by their governments, established the United Nations to maintain international peace and security, granting it broad jurisdiction in world affairs. Historically, the domestic jurisdiction of the nation-state shielded it from regulation by international organizations and INTERNATIONAL LAW. The Charter recognized this reality in Article 2, Section 7, stating "nothing contained in the present Charter shall authorize the United Nations to intervene in matters which are essentially within the domestic jurisdiction of any state." The article made only one exception to this proviso, allowing for Security Council ENFORCEMENT MEASURES under CHAPTER VII. Nonetheless, from its founding to the turn of the millennium the United Nations promoted policies and took decisions that increasingly brought into question the dividing line between its jurisdiction and that of its member states.

In the 1903 *Nationality Decrees in Tunis and Morocco* case, the PERMANENT COURT OF INTERNATIONAL JUSTICE (PCIJ) ruled that "the question of whether a certain matter is or is not solely within the jurisdiction of a state is an essentially relative question, it depends on the development of international relations." This position was reenforced by the authors of the UN Charter who substituted in Article 2, Section 7 the word "essentially" for the LEAGUE OF NATIONS Covenant's formulation "solely." Thus, domestic jurisdiction could be decided according to political considerations. Secondly, since the Charter did not state who should determine the question, the principal organs of the United Nations were competent to decide the meaning of the DOMESTIC JURISDICTION CLAUSE or even to ignore it in appropriate cases.

State sovereignty became increasingly constrained in the latter half of the 20th century by many factors, not the least of which was the assertion by the United Nations of its authority in certain areas. The United Nations passed RESOLUTIONS condemning states' internal policies such as APARTHEID, colonial rule, HUMAN RIGHTS violations, environmental degradation, and the treatment of dependent POPULATIONS. In the case of war crimes, crimes against humanity, and crimes against peace, the United Nations asserted the same "universal jurisdiction" that every state had under international law to bring perpetrators to account. Having officially accepted in 1946 the legal principles established in the Nuremberg Trials, the United Nations created its own tribunals in the 1990s (INTERNATIONAL CRIMINAL TRIBUNAL FOR THE FORMER YUGOSLAVIA, INTERNATIONAL CRIMINAL TRIBUNAL FOR RWANDA, INTERNATIONAL CRIMINAL COURT) to try suspected violators. It also sponsored the negotiating process that brought about the creation of the International Criminal Court, which began operations on July 1, 2002.

From the beginning, UN efforts to assert its jurisdiction engendered disputes. They took three forms: disputes about which organs of the United Nations were competent to exercise jurisdiction in a particular case, disagreements between the United Nations and other international organizations over which group's jurisdiction applied in a given area, and disputes between the United Nations and specific states concerning, from the state's point of view, an illegal intervention by the world body in the nation's domestic affairs.

An organization may have an overarching jurisdiction, but this quality is usually exercised in its parts by different organs within the larger entity. The Charter assigned jurisdiction for different activities to its six principal organs: the GENERAL ASSEMBLY, the SECURITY COUNCIL, the SECRETARIAT, the TRUSTEESHIP COUNCIL, the INTERNATIONAL COURT OF JUSTICE, and the ECONOMIC AND SOCIAL COUNCIL. The Security Council was the only body given COMPULSORY JURISDICTION over threats to the peace, with the power to use force to restore peaceful conditions. In 1950, however, faced with a deadlock among the PERMANENT MEMBERS of the council, the General Assembly passed the UNITING FOR PEACE RESOLUTION, giving the Assembly authority to recommend measures when the VETO blocked council action. The Resolution was rejected by the SOVIET UNION as a violation of the Charter. FRANCE later also rejected any responsibility for the costs of UN operations that came from an invocation of the resolution, causing a serious financial crisis for the organization.

The UN's most serious jurisdictional disputes with other international organizations have been with REGIONAL ORGANIZATIONS and alliances. Under the Rio PACT of 1947 and the Pact of Bogotá (1948), the ORGANIZATION OF AMERICAN STATES (OAS) claimed jurisdiction when disputes arose among its members. The OAS also pointed to Article 52 of the UN Charter, which approved the existence of regional organizations and encouraged "pacific settlement of local disputes through such regional arrangements." However, during crises in GUATEMALA (1954), CUBA (1960), and the Dominican Republic (1965), various UN members invoked Articles 34, 35, and 39, which appeared to give the Security Council immediate jurisdiction whenever it determined there was a threat to international peace and security. Jurisdictional disputes in these cases arose out of the COLD WAR politics of the time, and made UN action nearly impossible. Following the close of the cold war, however, jurisdictional questions arose over the role of the North Atlantic Treaty Organization (NATO) in KOSOVO, as opposed to UN undertakings there. When NATO forces attacked Yugoslavian installations and occupied Kosovo, Russia and other states opposed to the operation asserted that NATO actions usurped UN jurisdiction and were, therefore, illegal.

The final form of jurisdictional dispute has been between individual states, or their leaders, and the United Nations as a whole. The UN's condemnation of apartheid and its call for SANCTIONS against South Africa in the 1960s and 1970s were labeled illegitimate by the South African government. Pretoria also rejected the jurisdiction of the United Nations, and particularly of the International Court of Justice, in the matter of South Africa's control of NAMIBIA. UN efforts to encourage decolonization led Portugal and other colonial powers to question UN jurisdiction under the Charter. More recently, the UN's pursuit of war criminals, and their forcible detention and trial before international tribunals, brought the defense by those charged that the United Nations had no jurisdiction in their cases. In July 2001, the former president of Yugoslavia, SLOBODAN MILOŠEVIĆ, made that argument after his transfer to The Hague for trial, claiming his actions were solely a matter of domestic jurisdiction, protected by the principle of state sovereignty.

Further Reading: *Repertory of Practice of United Nations Organs: Articles 1–8 of the Charter.* New York: United Nations, 2002. Repertory Web site: <www.un.org/law/repertory>.

jus cogens

Article 53 of the 1969 Vienna Convention on Treaties recognized the existence of *jus cogens*, defined as a "peremptory norm of INTERNATIONAL LAW." The CONVENTION voided all TREATY provisions in violation of these universal principles "accepted and recognized by the international community of states as a whole as [norms] from which no derogation is permitted." Based on this principle, the INTERNATIONAL LAW COMMISSION had earlier held that any treaty provision in violation of the UN CHARTER was null and void, relying on Article 103's admonition that "In the event of a conflict between the obligations of the Members of the United Nations under the present Charter and their obligations under any other international agreement, their obligations under the present Charter shall prevail."

The Vienna convention's Article 64 allowed the INTERNATIONAL COURT OF JUSTICE (ICJ) to accept any dispute brought to it by a party to a treaty in which an issue of *jus cogens* arose, and for which the parties were unable to agree to ARBITRATION. The ICJ's JURISDICTION arose from the STATUTE OF THE INTERNATIONAL COURT OF JUSTICE's Article 38, which required it to apply "the general principles of law recognized by civilized nations" as a source of international law.

First suggested by Hugo Grotius in the 16th century, the revival of *jus cogens* by UN bodies and conferences represented a renewed interest in the natural law theory of international law. Instead of law solely arising from the consent of states, *jus cogens* asserted a set of fundamental principles that reflected higher law and were binding on all governments. The principle became closely associated with the efforts to develop HUMAN RIGHTS law that could limit state discretion against its own citizens or other peoples.

The development of *jus cogens* proved to be controversial as to both content and the method of creation. Since "universal acceptance" was the bedrock for the assertion of these peremptory norms, the list of accepted general principles remained short. The INTERNATIONAL LAW COMMISSION (ILC) served as the forum of *jus cogens* debate within the UNITED NATIONS SYSTEM after 1969. Many examples of universal norms were cited and discussed, including prohibitions against GENOCIDE, AGGRESSION, slave-trading, piracy, and APARTHEID, as well as positive norms such as the sovereign equality of states, and self-determination. The Soviet Union often proposed DISARMAMENT and peaceful coexistence as *jus cogens,* but they never achieved the broad acceptance across ideological and regional blocs necessary to be so designated. By the time of the UN MILLENNIUM SUMMIT in 2000, the right of development was being promoted within the ILC, among developing states, and in many reports of UN bodies, including the SECRETARIAT, as an emerging general norm of international law, and therefore as part of *jus cogens.*

See also CHINA.

Further Reading: Hannikainen, Lauri. *Peremptory Norms (Jus Cogens) in International Law: Historical Development, Criteria, Present Status.* Helsinki: Finnish Lawyers' Publishing Company, 1988. *Repertory of Practice of United Nations Organs: Articles 1–8 of the Charter.* New York: Office of Legal Affairs, 2002. Shaw, Malcolm N. *International Law.* 3d ed. Cambridge: Cambridge University Press, 1994.

K

Kampuchea *See* CAMBODIA.

Kashmir

Controversy between PAKISTAN and INDIA over the territory of Kashmir and Jammu has been a concern of the United Nations since the dispute surfaced in the 1940s. When the British *raj*—that is, colonial control over the subcontinent exercised from London—ended in 1947 with the grant of independence to the two separate nations of India and Pakistan, the partition resulted in the largest migration in human history. As many as 17 million people fled across the borders in both directions, Muslims to Pakistan, Hindus to India, all in a desperate effort to escape bloody riots among sectarian groups. Simultaneously, conflict broke out over competing claims to the princely states of Jammu and Kashmir, initiating the longest running dispute between the two nations. India gained sovereign control over most of the area, which had a majority Islamic POPULATION. For the United Nations this quarrel would become one of the oldest, comparable to the ARAB-ISRAELI DISPUTE. Both began in 1947 and both continued to plague the world in the new century.

The SECURITY COUNCIL first addressed the Kashmir issue in 1948, responding to an Indian complaint that forces had invaded the province. Pakistan denied the allegation and further declared the ACCESSION of Kashmir to India to be unlawful. The Security Council forwarded recommendations for ending the fighting. It established the United Nations Commission for India and Pakistan (UNCIP), which proposed a cease-fire, troop withdrawals, and a plebiscite to decide the controversy. Although both sides appeared to accept the proposal generally, they could not agree on details and modalities. However, the disputants did accept the deployment of the UNITED NATIONS MILITARY OBSERVER GROUP IN INDIA AND PAKISTAN (UNMOGIP), which remained in place for the next half century and as of 2007 was still monitoring the original cease-fire. Thus UNMOGIP was one of the longest peace operations in UN history.

In 1962 India found itself at war with CHINA over a border dispute along the Kashmir and Assam frontiers. During the summer of 1965 hostilities between India and Pakistan occurred again over the issue of Kashmir. The skirmish led to Security Council Resolution 211 calling for a cease-fire and a withdrawal of military forces to pre-conflict lines. Secretary-General U THANT then established an adjunct mission to UNMOGIP, the UNITED NATIONS INDIA-PAKISTAN OBSERVATION MISSION (UNIPOM). With the Tashkent Agreement of January 10, 1966, the parties agreed to withdraw their forces to lines recommended by the Security Council. UNIPOM provided GOOD OFFICES for the arranged withdrawal, and then the mission was terminated in March of that same year.

By 1971 Indian-Pakistani relations had degenerated further. A civil war that year in Pakistan, aggravated by Indian interference, resulted in the loss of East Pakistan, which became Bangladesh. When the war began, Pakistani president Yahya Khan requested that the United Nations send observers to the Pakistani side of the line and take over refugee facilities in East Pakistan. But the great powers resisted making use of the organization at the initiation of fighting. By December 4, 1971, when it was clear that India was on the march and that Pakistan was to be truncated, a Security Council resolution called for an immediate cease-fire. Because of a Soviet Union VETO, the proposal had to be carried to the GENERAL ASSEMBLY, where, under the UNITING FOR PEACE formula, it passed overwhelmingly. Pakistan would lose its eastern province once the UN-decreed cease-fire went into effect.

In 1972, following the war of the previous year, the two countries signed an agreement defining a line of control in Kashmir. India then took the position that the mandate of UNMOGIP had lapsed; Pakistan insisted that it had not. The SECRETARY-GENERAL insisted that only the Security Council could terminate the mandate, and consistently recommended that both sides seek UN MEDIATION to resolve the conflict.

In 1989, Muslim separatists in Kashmir called for an end to Indian rule and either independence or merger with Pakistan. India accused Islamabad of supporting the rebels and called their guerrilla activities "TERRORISM"; tension accelerated. A Hindu nationalist party in India, the Bharatiya Janata Party (BJP), became more potent during the 1990s by proposing a stronger assertion of Indian claims over Kashmir and it advocated a more hardened policy toward separatists there. In 1999 Muslim insurgents mounted attacks on Indian forces in Kashmir that were met with strong retaliation. That summer in Indian elections the BJP won control of the parliament and Atal Behari Vajpayee became prime minister. Meantime in Pakistan, the military took an equally inflexible position on Kashmir and, in October 1999, General Pervez Musharraf executed a coup, overthrowing the civilian government. Still more ominous, in the previous year both India and Pakistan, to the distaste of other major nations and the United Nations, each conducted successful nuclear WEAPONs tests, clearly raising the stakes in the ongoing battle over Kashmir. With both rivals now governed by hard-liners, the situation seemed more unpromising than ever. In July 2001, Prime Minister Vajpayee and General Musharraf met for the first time, in Agra in Uttar Pradesh, India. For a moment there was some optimism, but the talks collapsed. Pakistan had always sought the independence of the province from India and from the beginning supported the notion of a plebiscite to determine Kashmir's future, but India considered the issue of Kashmir to be an internal issue and rejected a plebiscite, such as that recommended as early as 1948 by the United Nations.

The issue was complicated by the crisis brought on with the terrorist attacks on the UNITED STATES on September 11, 2001. Washington brought intense pressure on AFGHANISTAN to extradite alleged terrorist Osama bin Laden, and then, on October 7, the United States commenced an air attack on the

ruling Taliban in the country. Even though Pakistan had been one of the few nations to recognize the Taliban, President Musharraf made the crucial decision to support the United States. On October 1, less than a week before the U.S. offensive, a Pakistan-based group was implicated in a terrorist attack on the state legislature in the Indian part of Kashmir. Harsh comments flowed from both New Delhi and Islamabad and violence mounted in Kashmir at the very time that U.S. strikes against the Taliban accelerated. U.S. secretary of state Colin Powell made a hurried visit to the area in mid October, hoping to defuse the tension so as to solidify support from both Pakistan and India for America's antiterrorist campaign. His efforts, however, were eclipsed by a dramatic escalation of the violence on December 13. Five gunmen entered the parliament building in New Delhi and killed seven people, injuring 18 others. Indian officials blamed Lashkar-e-Taiba, a radical Islamic group with headquarters in Pakistan, for the attack. New Delhi demanded that Pakistan close down the operation of the group and arrest militant terrorists in the Pakistani parts of Kashmir. President Musharraf was also under pressure from the United States to disband separatist and militant groups operating out of the country. By December 24, Pakistan and India had moved troops to the border and sporadic exchanges of gunfire were reported. Secretary-General KOFI ANNAN made a hurried trip to both capitals and achieved limited commitments from both governments not to resort to war. Nonetheless, tensions remained high well into spring 2002, exacerbated by the continuing military activity in bordering Afghan territories. Despite determined diplomatic efforts by Secretary of State Powell in May and June to defuse the situation, both sides redeployed military forces in large numbers along the Kashmir border.

Perhaps a dozen Islamic militant groups were fighting Indian security forces in Kashmir by 2002. India continued to charge that Pakistan was providing funding and training to the guerrilla groups, while Pakistan insisted that it provided only diplomatic and moral support to "freedom fighters." Official tallies estimate that 30,000 lives had been lost since the latest insurgency began in 1989. Some HUMAN RIGHTS groups insisted that the toll was double those numbers.

In a hopeful turn, Pakistan and India commenced negotiations over Kashmir in mid-2004. As a product of those talks, several confidence-building measures were contemplated. The first tangible result was the reopening, in April 2005—after 60 years—of bus service across the cease-fire line. The underlying tensions, however, were evident even in that small step. The first bus trip had to be delayed a day because of a separatist bomb attack on the terminal on the planned inaugural day of service. The easing of Indian-Pakistani relations, however, made way for limited Indian assistance to Pakistan when the latter suffered a massive earthquake that left 3.3 million people homeless in its northwest provinces and Kashmir on October 8, 2005. Additionally, both countries allowed UN teams from the UN Disaster

Assessment and Coordination agency (UNDAC), UN OFFICE FOR COORDINATION OF HUMANITARIAN AFFAIRS (OCHA), UN CHILDREN'S FUND (UNICEF), and UN POPULATION FUND (UNFPA) to expand their operations in the region.

See also DEPARTMENT OF PEACEKEEPING OPERATIONS, NUCLEAR-WEAPONS-FREE ZONES, PEACEKEEPING.

Further Reading: United Nations. *The Blue Helmets: A Review of United Nations Peace-Keeping.* 3d ed. New York: United Nations Department of Public Information, 1996. UNMOGIP Web site: <www.un.org/Depts/DPKO/Missions/unmogip/index.html>.

Kassebaum Amendment *See* REFORM OF THE UNITED NATIONS.

Kennedy, John F. (1917–1963)

John Fitzgerald Kennedy, elected in 1960 as the 35th president of the UNITED STATES, was the youngest person in American history elected to the presidency, the first president born in the 20th century, and the first Roman Catholic to hold the office. "JFK," as he was often called in public life, was the second son of a wealthy and politically connected family in Massachusetts. His father had served as President FRANKLIN ROOSEVELT's ambassador to the United Kingdom. Kennedy graduated from Harvard University in June 1940 with a degree in international relations. He joined the U.S. Navy in September 1941 on the eve of America's entrance into World War II. Kennedy commanded a patrol torpedo (PT) boat in the Pacific, and earned medals for heroism after saving the life of one of his crewmen when the boat was sunk by an enemy ship.

After the war, Kennedy considered a career in journalism, attending as a reporter for the *Chicago Herald-American* the SAN FRANCISCO CONFERENCE that founded the United Nations. But in 1946 he entered politics, winning a seat in the U.S. House of Representatives. In 1952 Massachusetts elected him to the U.S. Senate. His rising political prominence and ambition led to a second place finish for the vice presidential nomination in the balloting at the 1956 Democratic National Convention. In 1960 he defeated well-known democratic contenders Hubert Humphrey and LYNDON B. JOHNSON for the presidential nomination. Choosing Johnson as his running mate, JFK went on to a narrow victory in the general election, defeating sitting vice president Richard M. Nixon.

The COLD WAR struggle with the Soviet Union was at the center of U.S. foreign policy as Kennedy took the oath of office on January 20, 1961. At the United Nations the United States was in a deadlock with the Soviet government over the ongoing PEACEKEEPING operation in the CONGO, and was fending off a proposal by Soviet leader NIKITA KHRUSH-

CHEV to amend the UN CHARTER by replacing the position of SECRETARY-GENERAL with a three-person executive called the TROIKA. Beyond UN HEADQUARTERS, the U.S.-Soviet confrontation was focused on the divided city of Berlin, GERMANY, and on problems in Asia and LATIN AMERICA. In the Western Hemisphere, the new Cuban government under Fidel Castro had declared its allegiance to communism, leading to a break in relations with the United States. The United States also faced an apparently unified Sino-Soviet bloc that sought to reunite the Chinese Nationalist stronghold on Taiwan and the outlying islands of Formosa and Quemoy with the mainland communist government. In Indochina, President DWIGHT D. EISENHOWER bequeathed to his successor a growing U.S. involvement in Vietnam. President Kennedy took notice of these dangers in a stirring inaugural address, which called the nation to "defend any friend, [and] oppose any foe to assure the survival . . . of liberty." He reminded the world that the "torch has been passed" to a new generation of Americans "tempered by war, [and] disciplined by a hard and bitter peace." To the United Nations he gave a new vote of confidence, "to prevent it from becoming merely a forum for invective—to strengthen its shield of the new and the weak—and to enlarge the area in which its writ may run."

Early in his term Kennedy laid down a litmus test for Soviet responsibility in the cold war, calling for a cease-fire and settlement of the growing conflict near the border of Vietnam in Laos, cooperation with the United Nations in the Congo, and the "speedy conclusion" of a nuclear test-ban TREATY. The last item was of particular interest to the president, because he believed that some easing of the Soviet-American confrontation might make progress possible on the most disconcerting aspect of the post-1945 era, the arms race between the superpowers. In this regard, he saw little substitute for direct American engagement of the adversary. Kennedy opted for bilateral discussions rather than working through intermediaries such as the United Nations. During his first year in office the president held a summit with Nikita Khrushchev in Vienna, Austria. The two leaders reviewed all of the important issues between the two countries but made little progress on Kennedy's priorities.

The president first addressed the UN GENERAL ASSEMBLY on September 25, 1961. He made clear his commitment to maintain the organization and to VETO the Soviet troika plan. The president emphasized the practical merits of diplomacy that the UN provided. He pointed out that the United Nations was at its best in the defense of the weak, of those states powerless to defend their own interests. The new nations of Africa and Asia needed the United Nations as a platform for their views and as an institution capable of tempering the unilateral actions of powerful states. He went on to talk about the role the United Nations could play in DISARMAMENT negotiations, peacekeeping, and DEVELOPMENT.

Under the articles of the UN Charter, members are obligated to bring to the attention of the SECURITY COUNCIL "threats to the peace," so that the UN COLLECTIVE SECURITY system might respond effectively. Kennedy had no intention, however, of putting either Berlin or Vietnam before the United Nations. The matter of Berlin and divided GERMANY was to be kept solely within the purview of the occupying powers. Khrushchev's recurring threats to sign a peace treaty with the German Democratic Republic, presumably to cut off Western access to West Berlin, were seen as direct challenges to Western interests in divided Europe. Kennedy responded to Khrushchev's initiatives by indicating that the United States and its allies would remain in Berlin no matter what arrangement the USSR imposed on East Germany. Even when the East German government abruptly erected the Berlin Wall on August 13, 1961—to keep its citizens from fleeing to the West—Kennedy's recourse was not to the United Nations. At best he used the UN for back-channel negotiations with the Soviets and with European allies. Far more important, he sent 1,500 American military personnel to Berlin via the Autobahn, past East German checkpoints, to test Soviet intentions. In June 1963 the president traveled to Berlin to demonstrate American resolve to defend the western parts of the city.

The American role in Vietnam and Southeast Asia was another matter President Kennedy did not feel comfortable leaving to multilateral diplomacy at the United Nations. After several months in office the president was able to negotiate with the Soviet Union and parties in the region a settlement on Laos that established that country's neutrality in the East-West confrontation. For Vietnam—unlike Laos—the president disregarded advice to find a neutrality arrangement. The defense of Vietnam was an "alliance commitment" growing out of the Eisenhower administration's promises in 1954. The administration was interested in victory, not a UN-brokered compromise. The consequence was that the U.S. government never seriously brought its most tragic cold war initiative to the councils of the world organization, which it had created for exactly such conflicts. Denying the Soviet Union a public relations victory, and possibly a strategic victory, was too important to consider such an option.

Probably no single event better illustrated Kennedy's unwillingness to trust strategic interests to UN deliberations than the CUBAN MISSILE CRISIS of 1962. Coming at the end of the tensest four years of the cold war, and a period marked by increasing hostility between Washington and Havana, the Cuban crisis seemed to threaten the most important purpose of the UN. The United Nations had been created to ensure that the world would never again experience a global holocaust like World War II. Yet almost no use was made of the UN during a crisis that Kennedy later estimated had put the possibility of a nuclear exchange at one out of four.

In the last months of the Eisenhower administration, the CIA had developed contingency plans for the invasion of CUBA by Cuban exiles financed and encouraged by the U.S. government. President Kennedy did little to review the

components of the plan critically, and, shortly after entering office, he gave the go-ahead, reserving the right to terminate the invasion at any point and making clear that he did not intend to allow direct military action by U.S. forces. The operation was a failure. On April 17, 1961, Cuban nationals went ashore at the Bay of Pigs; by April 19 the invasion had been defeated by Castro's forces. The president was forced to admit American complicity and his responsibility for the debacle.

Castro appealed his case to the United Nations. World public opinion condemned the invasion, and several RESOLUTIONS to that effect were circulated. In the end, no resolutions passed and discussion of the incident at the United Nations devolved into lengthy cold war recriminations. The following July Nikita Khrushchev forged an alliance with Cuba, and Castro shortly thereafter declared himself a communist.

Kremlin leaders and Castro, fearing another U.S. mission to topple the Cuban government, decided to place Soviet offensive missiles on the island. By the fall of 1962 several missiles and their launchpad facilities had been secretly moved to Cuba, and they were about to become operational when U.S. overflights discovered them in October. The president believed that the placement of missiles in Cuba altered the strategic balance. He convened a secret group of advisers to assess the threat and the options available to remove the missiles.

U.S. secretary of state Dean Rusk, who had been assistant secretary for UN Affairs in the Truman administration, expressed no interest in taking the matter to the United Nations, and only slightly more in taking it to the ORGANIZATION OF AMERICAN STATES. At best, he proposed communicating with Castro through his representative at the UN. Only U.S. ambassador to the UN Adlai Stevenson among those in the inner circle made the case for UN diplomacy. Briefed by Kennedy personally, Stevenson counseled negotiations before any military action. The president rejected Stevenson's approach. In Kennedy's view, it was, in fact, important to act in secret so that the Soviets did not bring the matter to the United Nations before the United States acted. At one point the president even indicated that he wanted to "frighten" UN delegations through ambiguity about possible U.S. retaliation, thus making more likely the future achievement of an Assembly resolution favorable to American interests.

Kennedy's advisers eventually developed six policy options. Of those, three—doing nothing, negotiating secretly with Fidel Castro, and appealing to the Security Council—were rejected as ineffective. The remaining options involved the use of force. The president decided on a naval blockade of the island and a demand that the missiles be removed.

Once having quarantined Cuba, only then did President Kennedy look for ways to incorporate the United Nations into his efforts to avoid war with the Soviet Union while achieving the removal of the missiles. In the Security

Council Stevenson presented photographic evidence of the missile sites and demanded an explanation from the Soviet representative. Working privately with Acting Secretary-General U THANT, the American ambassador explored ways in which U Thant might serve as an intermediary. The United States proposed that the United Nations provide observation teams to oversee any missile withdrawal. Kennedy also let Stevenson suggest to the Secretary-General that if it became necessary to trade U.S. installations in Turkey for those in Cuba, it should be U Thant who "spontaneously" proposed it. Thus, the trade would not appear to be an American concession to the Russians. Khrushchev also suggested using the Secretary-General as the principal "intermediary" to resolve the dispute.

Despite overtures to U Thant, the substantive negotiation of the crisis was conducted through correspondence between the two leaders and secret back-channel contacts. The confrontation concluded on November 26, when the Kremlin ordered its ships carrying missiles to Cuba to reverse course and Khrushchev agreed to withdraw the ones already in place. In return, Kennedy indicated that the United States would not invade Cuba and would remove its missiles from Turkey. The crisis had been concluded with little UN involvement. Even in the aftermath of the confrontation the administration demonstrated caution in employing the United Nations, reneging on its earlier suggestion to use UN observation teams to monitor the removal of the missiles. Kennedy decided to depend on surveillance flights for this purpose.

The Cuban crisis marked the nadir of U.S.-Soviet relations in the cold war. The ultimate confrontation that both sides thought they could avoid while pursuing brinkmanship around the world had nearly happened. The events in the Caribbean had a cathartic effect on Moscow and Washington. Afterward, both sides looked for ways to lessen the tension between them. A telephone "hot line" that allowed direct communication between the Kremlin and the White House was established. As 1963 began, both Khrushchev and Kennedy spoke about the necessity of what the former called "peaceful coexistence." A step-by-step retreat from the precipice seemed to be under way. Most important, both sides quietly moved toward some accommodation on the arms race by intensifying the effort to get a nuclear test ban in place, culminating in the Partial Test Ban Treaty of August 1963.

There was a reasonable prospect, as Kennedy looked forward to his reelection campaign (set to begin in the fall), that the two superpowers might move forward on disarmament. If that could happen, then the saved resources of the diminished arms race could be turned to development in the Third World, areas of the globe Kennedy worried would be a breeding ground for war if the overwhelming human problems were not addressed. In the arena of development the United Nations could play a broader role than it had played in the contest with Moscow. One might have expected that within a year Khrushchev and Kennedy could be employing the United Nations in effective ways. Tragically, John F. Kennedy was assassinated on November 22, 1963, as he rode in a motorcade through the streets of Dallas, Texas. It was left to his successor, President Johnson, to forge if possible a Kennedy legacy in foreign policy.

See also ACHESON, DEAN; ROOSEVELT, ELEANOR; UNITED NATIONS CONFERENCE ON TRADE AND DEVELOPMENT.

Further Reading: Dallek, Robert. *An Unfinished Life: John F. Kennedy, 1917–1963.* Boston: Little, Brown, 2003. Kennedy, John. *Why England Slept.* Westport, Conn.: Greenwood Press, 1981. May, Ernest R., and Philip D. Zelikow. *The Kennedy Tapes: Inside the White House during the Cuban Missile Crisis.* Cambridge, Mass.: Belknap, 1998. Schlesinger, Arthur, Jr. *A Thousand Days: John F. Kennedy in the White House.* Boston: Houghton Mifflin, 2002.

Khmer Rouge Trials

Nearly 3 million people died at the hands of the Khmer Rouge regime in CAMBODIA between April 1975 and January 1979. The magnitude of executions and deaths due to maltreatment shocked world opinion, which in turn brought pressure on the international community and succeeding Cambodian governments to punish those responsible for the killings. After lengthy negotiations between the United Nations and a hesitant Cambodia, the two parties reached an agreement in March 2003 "concerning the prosecution under Cambodian law of crimes committed during the period of Democratic Kampuchea." Among the likely defendants were Ke Pauk, Khieu Samphan, and Nuon Chea. The leader of the Kampuchean government, Pol Pot, died in April 1998. The agreement established a mixed national-international court known as the Extraordinary Chambers in the Courts of Cambodia (ECCC).

Signing of the "UN-Cambodia Agreement" did not lead to immediate prosecution of suspected war criminals. Since the Cambodian government insisted that the tribunal operate inside Cambodia with Cambodian personnel, working out the modalities for international participation in the trials and approving a JURISDICTION for the Court that would meet international standards proved to be protracted. Under the agreement, the Court would have both Cambodian and international judges, the latter nominated by the UN SECRETARY-GENERAL. Co-investigating judges and co-prosecutors—one Cambodian and the other non-Cambodian in both cases—were to be appointed.

The jurisdiction of the Court extended to the crime of GENOCIDE as defined in the 1948 CONVENTION on Genocide, crimes against humanity, war crimes, TORTURE, religious persecution, and violations of the Cambodian penal code. The use of the Genocide Convention raised a difficult issue for the Court, since the convention defines genocide as an act against a group to which the perpetrator does not belong. At best, the slaughter in Cambodia amounted to auto-genocide, Cambodian on Cambodian. Nonetheless, the sheer dimension of mass killing led the negotiators to include the charge. With a majority of Cambodian nationals serving as the judges on the Court, all decisions of guilt or innocence required a super majority that included at least one international judge's vote.

To support the operation of the Court the United Nations created UNAKRT (United Nations Assistance to the Khmer Rouge Trials) Mission. It also encouraged voluntary contributions from member states. A pledging conference held in New York City produced offers of assistance of more than $38 million, with the largest contributions coming from FRANCE, GERMANY, JAPAN, Canada, and the Netherlands. The first trials were expected to take place in 2007. The first charges were brought against Nuon Chea, the second-ranking leader of the Khmer Rouge after Pol Pot, and Kaing Guek Eav, commandant of Tuel Sleng prison where 14,000 people suffered torture and execution.

Further Reading: Etcheson, Craig. *After the Killing Fields: Lessons from the Cambodian Genocide.* Westport, Conn.: Greenwood Publishing Group, 2005. Romano, Cesare P. R., André Nollkaemper, and Jann K. Kleffner, eds. *Internationalized Criminal Courts: Sierra Leone, East Timor, Kosovo, and Cambodia.* New York: Oxford University Press, 2004. UNAKRT Web site: <www.unakrt-online.org>. EEEC Web site: <www.eccc.gov.kh/>.

Khrushchev, Nikita S. (1894–1971)

Nikita Sergeyevich Khrushchev succeeded JOSEPH STALIN as General Secretary of the Communist Party of the Soviet Union in 1953, and in that role was the effective leader of the USSR until his ouster in 1964. For the last six years of his rule he also served as chairman of the Council of Ministers, the equivalent of national prime minister. Born into a peasant family, Khrushchev joined the Communist Party in 1918. By 1931 the rising leader was directing the Moscow City Committee where he made his mark in leading the construction of the Moscow subway system. In 1938 he became the First Secretary of the Central Committee of the Ukrainian Central Committee. From Kiev he guided the Ukrainian war effort against the Nazi invaders.

Nikita Khrushchev first joined the party's most senior leadership body—the Politburo—in 1939. A beneficiary of Stalin's purges of the party's "Old Bolsheviks," Khrushchev faithfully carried out Stalin's orders and participated in the "Cult of Personality" that surrounded the aging dictator. When Stalin died in March 1953, Khrushchev was one of several potential successors. Initially he participated in a collective leadership of the state and party with himself in the party secretary's position, Georgy Malenkov as head of state, and Nikolai Bulganin as premier. In traditional Communist Party fashion, he spent the next several years outmaneuvering his colleagues, emerging as the country's leader at the 20th Party Congress in 1956.

The Khrushchev regime faced the challenge of adapting the Leninist-Stalinist model of government and politics to contemporary COLD WAR conditions. The command economy system coupled with totalitarian terror in the 1930s and 1940s had gotten the country through the horrors of World War II and had built—albeit highly inefficiently—an industrialized Russia. But they had also overburdened the Soviet economy with military expenditures and excessive administrative control from the central ministries. Postwar circumstances forced the Soviet Union to compete with the UNITED STATES on a global stage and to confront a superpower far better suited to that competition in nearly all arenas of policy-making. Stalin had also saddled the USSR with the maintenance of an untenable empire in Eastern Europe. Under the conditions of global competition, Khrushchev sought ways to undo the terror at home, decentralize the economy, and expand Soviet influence abroad. These tasks aggravated the already difficult but permanent need in the Marxist-Leninist Soviet Union to balance ideology against national interest.

In a secret speech to the 20th Party Congress in 1956, Khrushchev criticized Stalin. He accused the former ruler of crimes against the party, state, and POPULATION. He rejected the use of terror and Stalin's cult of personality. He argued that Stalin had eclipsed the Communist Party with a police state. The government eased censorship, and new efforts were made to revitalize the Soviet economy. He launched a program of "de-stalinization" that, in foreign affairs, jettisoned Stalin's theory of inevitable war with the capitalist world. Khrushchev contended that the birth of the nuclear age made inevitable war unthinkable. In place of inevitable war, Khrushchev proposed "peaceful coexistence," a form of permanent but peaceful struggle between the two world systems, in which cooperation and conflict would be viewed as interpenetrating, dialectically compatible phenomena.

Khrushchev also sought a new relationship with NON-ALIGNED states of the Third World. At the United Nations the USSR became a strong advocate for DECOLONIZATION and causes supported by developing states. Following 1955, as increasing numbers of DEVELOPING COUNTRIES joined the UN, the Soviet Union moved from a position in the VOTING minority to being able to pass RESOLUTIONS in the GENERAL ASSEMBLY supportive of its foreign policy goals. Khrushchev became the first Soviet leader to visit states in the developing South, a region he described as an emerging "peace zone," with many nations following the "non-capitalist path of DEVELOPMENT." Early in his term he traveled to INDIA in order to signal the decision to compete with the United States in the newly liberated parts of the globe. The Soviet government also provided significant military and economic assistance to potential allies in the developing world. In the Middle East, Khrushchev provided military aid to EGYPT and funds to build the High Dam at Aswan.

Toward the United States, Khrushchev followed a peripatetic course, sometimes seeking better relations—he visited the United States in 1959, establishing with President DWIGHT D. EISENHOWER the "spirit of Camp David"—and other times confronting Washington in terms that suggested likely war. He and Eisenhower agreed to pursue DISARMAMENT discussions in the UN's EIGHTEEN NATION DISARMAMENT COMMITTEE (ENDC). Within this setting, however, the Soviet government rejected the American proposal for international verification of disarmament commitments. When President Eisenhower proposed in 1955 that the two superpowers provide "OPEN SKIES" to the surveillance planes of the other nation, Khrushchev rejected it as "spying." Crises arose over Berlin, the CONGO, the Suez Canal, and U.S. spy flights over the USSR, but Russia also purchased Western agricultural goods, and sought better relations with Western European states.

In 1960 a U.S. spy plane commanded by Francis Gary Powers was shot down over Soviet territory. In addition to bringing a quick end to a planned summit with Eisenhower and the leaders of FRANCE and GREAT BRITAIN, Khrushchev mounted a show trial of the pilot and attended the fall session of the UN General Assembly in order to excoriate the United States. On September 29, Khrushchev interrupted a speech by British prime minister Harold Macmillan by taking off one of his shoes and banging it on his desk in the Assembly Hall. In his own address, Khrushchev protested American spying and accused UN SECRETARY-GENERAL DAG HAMMARSKJÖLD of serving only Western interests.

Khrushchev's ire toward Hammarskjöld was occasioned in large part by the UN's involvement at the time in the Congolese civil war. When the Congo became independent from Belgium in 1960, internecine conflict broke out. With the support of the General Assembly, the Secretary-General organized a PEACEKEEPING operation to support the central government of President Kasavubu, an American ally. The USSR refused to pay its ASSESSMENT, arguing the mission had not been authorized by the SECURITY COUNCIL. Khrushchev's anger at the apparent tilt by Hammarskjöld in favor of the American-supported faction in the Congo reached a breaking point when the Soviet-sponsored Congolese prime minister, Patrice Lumumba, was assassinated after being released from UN protective custody. The Soviet delegation refused to have any further working relationship with the Secretary-General. In his 1960 speech to the United Nations Khrushchev charged Hammarskjöld with being in the service of the United States and its cold war partners. He demanded Hammarskjöld's resignation and a reorganization of the office of Secretary-General, replacing the single secretary with a TROIKA, whereby there would be

a three-person executive with equal representation from the Western bloc, the Eastern bloc, and the neutral countries in the United Nations. Only some months after Hammarskjöld died in a plane crash in Africa did Khrushchev relent and allow the election of a new Secretary-General—U THANT of Burma.

Khrushchev believed that peaceful confrontation with the West, liberalization at home, and defense of socialism within the Soviet bloc would ultimately produce the global victory of socialism over the capitalist system without the resort to nuclear war. Instead his policies seemed to undermine party control at home and within the Soviet bloc. In Eastern Europe Khrushchev's de-stalinization campaign undermined hard-line communist leaders. In October 1956, the Soviet Union had to install a more moderate government in Poland to quell disturbances, and to use force to crush the demands for freedom in Hungary. President Eisenhower took the Hungarian incident to the UN Security Council, seeking condemnation of Soviet intervention. But given the possession of the VETO by the USSR, little cost adhered to Khrushchev's decision to invade and occupy Budapest. Beyond Eastern Europe, the criticisms of Stalin and the pursuit of peaceful coexistence also made an enemy of Mao Zedong, the leader of Communist CHINA, arguably the most Stalinist of rulers in the communist camp.

During Khrushchev's years in office the most dangerous encounter between the superpowers occurred in October 1962. The CUBAN MISSILE CRISIS proved a humiliating defeat for Soviet foreign policy. Khrushchev had decided to place nuclear missiles in Cuba for strategic reasons. Given the encirclement of the Soviet Union with U.S. allies, military bases, and U.S. WEAPONS systems, the Soviet leader reportedly considered deployment of Soviet missiles in CUBA to be, for Americans, a "taste of their own medicine." The Cuban government, led by Fidel Castro, sought to use the missiles as a way to defend against another American invasion similar to the abortive U.S.-backed effort to overthrow the regime in 1961.

Following the discovery of the missiles, American president JOHN F. KENNEDY, imposed a naval blockade of the island and demanded the removal of the missiles. Khrushchev floated the idea of using UN Secretary-General U Thant as an intermediary, but the Kennedy administration demurred. The most important diplomatic exchanges were kept directly between Moscow and Washington. At UN HEADQUARTERS the United States requested a session of the Security Council. During that televised meeting, U.S. PERMANENT REPRESENTATIVE Adlai Stevenson presented surveillance photographs of the missiles. Beyond the drama, however, negotiations in New York were limited to out-of-view discussions.

Khrushchev demanded a "no-invasion" pledge regarding Cuba and the removal of American missiles in Turkey as the quid pro quo for Soviet withdrawal of the missiles. Kennedy met on October 27 with Soviet ambassador to the United States Anatoly Dobrynin and agreed to both conditions, but insisted that the Soviets keep the second condition confidential. The next day both sides announced that the crisis had been defused; the missiles would be withdrawn and the United States would make clear it had no intention of invading Cuba in the future. As a result of the crisis, the two countries agreed to the installation of a "hot line" telephone connection so that in the future negotiations could be initiated instantly, before an awkward situation became a crisis. Shortly thereafter Khrushchev's government entered into negotiations with the United States on a limited nuclear test ban TREATY that was signed in August 1963. Recognizing the precipice the two sides had come to in the Cuban missile crisis, Kennedy and Khrushchev took the first steps toward a "détente"—relaxation—in their countries' relations.

In the Soviet Union Khrushchev found his foreign and domestic policies under rising challenge. The confrontation in the Caribbean had ended in an embarrassing diplomatic and strategic failure. Faced with a simmering revolt by party bureaucrats, old Stalinists, and conservatives worried about unrestrained liberalization, Khrushchev moved to reorganize the party and to stack it with his supporters. The reorganization only alerted his opponents. They successfully removed him from all of his government and party posts in October 1964. While he had defeated an "anti-party" group opposed to his policies in 1957, it would be Khrushchev's closest colleagues in the Politburo who would oust him in 1964, charging him with "hare-brained schemes." Restoring stability at home and Soviet prestige abroad fell to the new leaders increasingly under the direction of Leonid Brezhnev, Khrushchev's successor as general secretary of the party.

Party leaders declared Khrushchev a "special pensioner" of the state and he was allowed to retire to his country home, albeit with secret police surveillance for the rest of his life. Prior to his death he wrote and recorded his memoirs, which were smuggled out of the USSR and published in the West. When he died in 1971, Khrushchev was not buried in the Kremlin Wall like other esteemed party leaders of the past, but in a Moscow cemetery. Nonetheless, large crowds and a stream of admirers gathered at the cemetery over many months following his interment.

See also GERMANY.

Further Reading: Gaddis, John Lewis. *We Now Know, Rethinking Cold War History.* Oxford: Clarendon Press, 1998. Garthoff, Raymond L. *Reflections on the Cuban Missile Crisis.* Washington: Brookings Institution, 1990. Kennedy, Robert F. *Thirteen Days: A Memoir of the Cuban Missile Crisis.* New York: W.W. Norton, 1999. Khrushchev, Nikita S. *Khrushchev Remembers.* Boston: Little, Brown, 1974. Zubok, Vladislav, and Constantine Pleshakov. *Inside the Kremlin's Cold War: From Stalin to Khrushchev.* Cambridge, Mass.: Harvard University Press, 1997.

Kim Il-Sung (1912–1994)

Known as the "Great Leader" and, since his death, "Eternal Leader" of the Democratic People's Republic of Korea (North Korea), Kim Il-Sung provoked the only military conflict that directly involved the United Nations by his attack on the Republic of Korea (South Korea) on June 25, 1950. The KOREAN WAR or "police action" lasted from 1950 to 1953 with 17 UN members contributing troops and supplies, while the People's Republic of CHINA (PRC) intervened on behalf of Kim and the Soviet Union provided surreptitious military assistance.

With the sudden collapse of JAPAN in mid-August 1945 in the wake of two nuclear attacks by the UNITED STATES and the long-promised Soviet DECLARATION of war, Washington proposed that Japanese-dominated Korea be assigned a northern Soviet occupation zone and an American southern zone, divided at the 38th parallel. In the postwar climate of the COLD WAR, the Soviets supported a leftist North Korean regime headed by former anti-Japanese partisan Kim Il-sung, while the United States supported the rightist elder nationalist Syngman Rhee in the south. As the two superpowers prepared to leave the peninsula in 1948–49, the United States turned to the United Nations as an avenue of multilateral withdrawal, in hopes of avoiding chaos and civil war.

Despite Soviet opposition, the UN GENERAL ASSEMBLY approved a RESOLUTION calling for elections in the spring of 1948 throughout Korea to establish a national assembly. A UN Temporary Commission on Korea (UNTCOK) was created to oversee the process. When the Soviets carried out their threat to deny UNTCOK entry into the north, Washington secured UN sanction, through the Interim Committee of the General Assembly, for elections in the south alone to create a "National Government." Consequently, the Syngman Rhee regime in the south was confirmed as the legitimate government of all Korea while the Kim Il-Sung regime remained isolated and drew close to both the PRC and the USSR. It sought military assistance in order to carry out a forceful unification of the two Koreas.

After repeated political efforts to gain support for unification among southerners as well as efforts to foment rebellion, Kim Il-Sung, with the permission of Moscow and Beijing, launched a massive military assault on the Republic of Korea. Under U.S. pressure the United Nations quickly branded North Korea the aggressor and called upon all member states to render assistance to South Korea to repel armed attack and "to restore international peace and security in the area."

The Korean War soon stalemated and finally ended in an armistice in July 1953 between the Kim regime (and China) and the United Nations forces (most notably U.S. forces, who made up the preponderance of military personnel and who were led by U.S. commanders). A major international conference at Geneva in 1954 failed to bring a final resolution to the Korean imbroglio. For the next 20 years Kim

Il-Sung routinely denounced the United Nations as a tool of American imperialism.

In 1972 Kim initiated a North-South Coordinating Committee to discuss the issue of reunification but it was soon apparent that he sought northern control of the south. Given this impasse, President Chung Hee Park, in June 1973, announced his willingness to have both Koreas admitted to the United Nations as separate entities. Kim condemned Park's proposal as a formula for permanent national division and urged a union of the two regimes under a Confederal Republic of Koryo that could join the United Nations as a single state. Seoul's rejection of the proposal led to an assassination attempt on President Park by Kim's government and to a relentless North Korean tunneling program under the demilitarized zone between north and south.

During the 1970s Kim Il-Sung sought to distance himself from his wartime allies (and superiors) by reaching out to the non-aligned nations for recognition and support in the United Nations. Slowly he gained acceptance as the legitimate ruler of an independent nation in the eyes of the world, especially following South Korea's proposed simultaneous and separate UN MEMBERSHIP. With the support of Algeria and other non-aligned nations and the replacement at the United Nations of the Republic of China (Taiwan) by PRC representatives in 1971, Kim Il-Sung managed to gain a foothold for North Korea to secure status as an official UN observer, and he succeeded in having his government admitted as a full member in a number of SPECIALIZED AGENCIES, beginning with membership in the WORLD HEALTH ORGANIZATION. In 1991 both Koreas became full members of the United Nations.

Kim Il-Sung's policy of rapprochement with South Korea and the world community did not extend to North Korea's nuclear ambitions. On March 12, 1993, Kim's government announced that it would exercise its right to withdraw from the NUCLEAR NON-PROLIFERATION TREATY. The United States responded with diplomatic pressure, including a trip to Pyongyang by former president JIMMY CARTER, and back channel threats from the administration of President WILLIAM JEFFERSON CLINTON that Washington would use military force if necessary to keep North Korea from obtaining nuclear weapons. Kim agreed to negotiations with the United States that concluded, following Kim's sudden and unexpected death on July 8, 1994, with both sides signing an "Agreed Framework" under which North Korea promised to end its nuclear enrichment program in return for light-water reactors from the United States. Succeeding his father, as Kim Il-Sung had planned since the early 1970s, his son, Kim Jong-Il, became the new leader of the North Korean regime.

Further Reading: Cumings, Bruce. *Korea's Place in the Sun: A Modern History.* New York: Norton, 1997. Stueck, William. *The Korean War: An International History.* Princeton, N.J.: Princeton University Press, 1995. Suh, Dae-Sook. *Kim Il-Sung: The North Korean Leader.* New York: Columbia University Press, 1988.

— *E. M. Clauss*

Korean War

The United Nations initially became involved in Korea in the autumn of 1947 when the American government presented a RESOLUTION to the GENERAL ASSEMBLY calling for the Soviet Union and the UNITED STATES to hold elections in their respective post–World War II occupation zones in order to select members of a national assembly and a Korean national government. In November the General Assembly approved the proposal and established a United Nations Temporary Commission on Korea (UNTCOK) to supervise the elections and report to the Assembly. As the COLD WAR surfaced, the United States and its allies became convinced that the Soviet Union would never cooperate with an American-sponsored plan under the auspices of the United Nations. Thus Washington's policy was aimed at creating a separate South Korean government under conservative Syngman Rhee and shielded by United Nations legitimacy.

Other members of UNTCOK, including U.S. allies Australia and Canada, opposed the decision for elections until they could be administered throughout the peninsula. Under pressure from the American military government, the General Assembly in February 1948 approved an American-sponsored resolution giving UNTCOK authority to supervise elections "in such parts of Korea as might be accessible to the Commission."

Elections were held in May 1948 and Rhee won a significant victory despite mixed assessments of its fairness by the members of UNTCOK. In July, the newly created legislative assembly promptly elected Syngman Rhee as the first president of the Republic of Korea (ROK). Although a separate regime, the Democratic People's Republic (DPR), headed by KIM IL-SUNG, was established in North Korea, the General Assembly declared the South Korean government to be the only lawful government in that part of Korea where UNTCOK had observed elections and thus the only legitimate government in Korea. As both regimes claimed JURISDICTION over the entire peninsula, violence loomed as the only available path to national unification. International politics mirrored the stalemate in Korea as Soviet-U.S. relations deteriorated into a cold war characterized by an American foreign policy of containment. The fate of the troubled peninsula was to be left in the hands of the United Nations.

When North Korea, with the foreknowledge and approval of the Soviet Union and the People's Republic of CHINA, invaded South Korea on June 25, 1950, the United States responded immediately, sending combat troops to defend Seoul and calling for an emergency meeting of the UN SECURITY COUNCIL. A UN resolution of June 27 provided for military SANCTIONS against North Korea and

U.S. Marines in Korea, 1951 (UNITED NATIONS)

called for member states to assist the Republic of Korea. The Security Council was able to act decisively because the Soviet ambassador was boycotting council meetings at the time. Protesting the seating of the Nationalist Government as the representative of China, his absence meant the Soviet VETO was not an obstacle to action. Once the Soviets returned to the table, the American delegation had to appeal to the General Assembly to legitimize military actions in Korea. The Truman administration pushed through the Assembly the UNITING FOR PEACE RESOLUTION, which allowed the members to "discuss" threats to the peace and "recommend" UN action or a response from individual states when the Security Council was deadlocked over an issue. Eventually 16 nations, including the United States, provided armed forces. Another Security Council resolution of July 7 established a unified command under the UN FLAG and delegated the authority for the command

to the United States. President Harry S. Truman appointed General Douglas MacArthur as the Supreme United Nations Commander, and the UNITED NATIONS COMMAND (UNC) became the official title of the force.

After enduring initial defeats that drove UN forces to the southern tip of Korea in the Pusan perimeter, MacArthur's forces mounted spectacular counterattacks at Inchon and Pusan, resulting in the recapture of Seoul on September 28 and the pursuit by UN armies of North Korean forces fleeing across the 38th parallel. The Truman administration decided that, absent evidence of a major Soviet or Chinese intervention in the war, UN forces would pursue the North Koreans beyond the 38th parallel and unite the peninsula by force. Thus began the period of the UN offensive, approved by the Security Council on October 7, 1950.

Despite repeated Chinese warnings that it would not tolerate an advance toward its borders, MacArthur's forces moved deeper into North Korea and made preparations to establish a government of national unification.

In early November, the Chinese acted, hurling hundreds of thousands of veteran troops across the Yalu River to confront U.S. and ROK forces approaching the border. As UN forces reeled in retreat, President Truman shocked the world by raising the possibility of using nuclear weapons to stem the tide. Britain's prime minister Clement Attlee flew to Washington to secure assurances from Truman that nuclear decisions would not be made unilaterally.

At the United Nations in New York, efforts were underway to seek a negotiated settlement of the conflict, including, for the first time, representatives of the People's Republic of China. The United States was adamant, however, that a cease-fire must not include discussions of such outstanding issues as diplomatic recognition, Formosa, or a seat at the United Nations. Consequently, the Chinese departed the talks and declared on December 21, 1950, that all actions taken by the United Nations without Chinese participation were illegal.

As UN forces retreated south toward the 38th parallel in the freezing winter of 1950–51, a major foreign policy debate erupted in the United States that made Europeans apprehensive that Washington would retreat from its postwar role of world leadership. While encouraging a dialogue between Washington and Moscow, Western European governments were appalled over an American resolution at the United Nations to brand China as an "aggressor nation" and to impose sanctions on Beijing. On February 1, 1951, the General Assembly approved the American resolution. It was seen as a call to Beijing to desist from offensive action, yet it was also perceived as an indication of a potential peaceful settlement of the issue. An early end to the conflict, however, was precluded by Washington's insistence that outstanding East Asian issues be deferred until after a cease-fire.

During the late winter and early spring of 1951, the pressing military crisis facing the UN Command (UNC) was contained when the Chinese offensive was halted south of Seoul and UN forces were able to launch a counteroffensive, led by General Matthew Ridgeway, which regained territory above the 38th parallel once more. Officially, UN forces still operated on the basis of the October 7, 1950, directive to establish "a unified, independent, and democratic Korea." In reality, however, the Chinese intervention caused both the U.S. State Department and Defense Department to reevaluate their objectives in Korea. The State Department made it clear that it now sought to use military pressure to achieve a cease-fire agreement followed by UN negotiations leading to reimposition of the status quo before June 25, 1950. Offensive operations north of the 38th parallel would only be initiated with the approval of coalition partners, an unlikely prospect.

As the tide of battle appeared to be turning, a mood of optimism pervaded American public opinion. In March 1951, the Western allies, SECRETARY-GENERAL TRYGVE LIE,

and the State Department and Defense Department convinced Truman to undertake a major peace initiative toward North Korea and China through the United Nations Command. When informed of the initiative, the commander of UN forces, General Douglas MacArthur, was irate. He directly challenged U.S. policy and urged an expansion of the war to force a Chinese surrender, thus precipitating the Truman-MacArthur crisis, which ended with President Truman's dismissal of the celebrated general.

Hopes for a negotiated settlement were further delayed by the renewal of fierce Chinese offensives in April and May 1951. After UN forces repelled this drive and once again reentered North Korea, the Truman administration decided to halt the UN advance in order to probe the possibilities for a cease-fire.

Responding to the growing pressure of world opinion and confident that it could negotiate from a position of military strength, the Truman administration resumed the search for a diplomatic settlement. In May the State Department instructed diplomat George Kennan to meet with Jacob Malik, Soviet ambassador to the UN, and indicate that Washington was interested in seeking an armistice or cease-fire along the 38th parallel. On June 22, Moscow responded with a statement of interest. Despite determined resistance by South Korean president Syngman Rhee, negotiations between the United Nations and communist forces began on July 10, 1951, at Kaesong, the ancient capital of Korea.

A cease-fire, much less an armistice, was not close at hand. The military stalemate that had developed between the summer of 1951 and the winter of 1952 was reflected in the diplomatic impasse at the negotiation site in Panmunjom. In November, the U.S. National Security Council drafted a new policy statement on Korea (NSC-118/2), which concluded that the United States should continue its limited war in Korea while seeking an armistice. Flexibility in negotiations with the Chinese would be made possible by a "greater sanction" statement which threatened China with prompt retaliation in case of renewed AGGRESSION. The military stalemate was further complicated by heated controversies over the status of prisoners-of-war as well as charges of germ warfare lodged against the United States.

In November 1952, Republican DWIGHT EISENHOWER won the U.S. presidential election in part because of a widespread belief that a new administration was necessary to bring a conclusion to the unpopular war in Korea. Keeping his campaign pledge, the president-elect flew to Korea in early December where he visited the troops and met with President Syngman Rhee and U.S. commander Mark Clark, making it clear that any escalation of the conflict would risk global war. Confident that the pivot of the cold war was Europe and not Asia, he was determined to take new initiatives to end the conflict in Korea.

Syngman Rhee's refusal to accept an armistice agreement and his threats to pursue a unilateral course forced the UN

Command—and U.S. administration officials—to prepare plans for the possible withdrawal of ROK forces from the coalition. The U.S. 8th Army prepared plan EVERREADY that envisioned a military takeover if Rhee became openly hostile to UN forces. At the same time, the United States offered a mutual security PACT with South Korea if it would accept a UN proposed armistice and leave Korean forces under the control of the UN Command. In addition, Eisenhower subtly, but never directly, warned China of the possibility of nuclear retaliation.

The communists and the UN Command, but not Syngman Rhee, agreed to armistice terms in June 1953. Both President Eisenhower and his secretary of state, John Foster Dulles, sent notes to the South Korean leader indicating that the United States and the United Nations were prepared to conclude peace with or without the Seoul government. When armistice talks resumed on July 10, 1953, a leading issue involved the United States's ability to guarantee South Korea's conduct in the post-armistice period. The UN Command negotiators assured the Chinese and North Koreans that the UN Command would withdraw all military aid and support if ROK forces violated the armistice agreement. To insure good conduct, the Chinese launched a massive final assault against the ROK positions. Finally, the United States renewed its promise of a defense pact, a commitment from Eisenhower to South Korea to respond immediately to an unprovoked attack with a UN force and a pledge of major economic assistance.

The armistice ending the Korean War was signed in silence at Panmunjom on July 27, 1953. The next day, the 16 nations with armed forces in Korea signed the "greater sanction" statement reaffirming their intent to resist any attacks on South Korea from the north. In a report to the Security Council on August 7, 1953, General Mark Clark revealed that the allied nations had warned that a breach of the armistice would have consequences "so grave that in all probability, it would not be possible to confine hostilities within the frontiers of Korea."

A United Nations resolution of August 28, 1953, approving the armistice agreement, limited attendance to a postwar political conference to the former belligerents only, and the Soviet Union, which could participate "provided the other side desires it." Immediate postwar acrimony among China, North Korea, and South Korea prevented the realization of a postwar conference. Eventually, in 1954, agreement was reached to hold a conference of the Korean belligerents in Geneva in April of that year in order to discuss the final resolution of both the Korean and Indochina wars. The lack of a successful peace accord between the belligerent parties in Korea left the future unification of the nation in the hands of the United Nations, where it remains today.

See also CHAPTER VII OF THE UN CHARTER.

Further Reading: Foot, Rosemary. *The Wrong War: American Policy and the Dimensions of the Korean Conflict, 1950–1953.*

Ithaca, N.Y.: Cornell University Press, 1985. Kaufman, Burton. *The Korean War: Challenges in Crisis, Credibility and Command.* New York: McGraw-Hill, 1997. Mazuzan, George. *Warren R. Austin at the UN, 1946–1953.* Kent, Ohio: Kent State University Press, 1977. Stueck, William. *Rethinking the Korean War: A New Diplomatic and Strategic History.* Princeton, N.J.: Princeton University Press, 2002. Stueck, William, ed. *The Korean War in World History.* Lexington: University Press of Kentucky, 2004.

— E. M. Clauss

Kosovo *See* FORMER YUGOSLAVIA, UNITED NATIONS INTERIM ADMINISTRATION MISSION FOR KOSOVO, WAR CRIMES TRIBUNALS.

Kyoto Protocol

Adopted on December 11, 1997, by the Third Conference of the Parties (COP-3), the directing body of the UNITED NATIONS FRAMEWORK CONVENTION ON CLIMATE CHANGE (UNFCCC), the Kyoto Protocol set specific greenhouse gas (GHG) emission targets for industrialized states to achieve by 2012. Known as "Annex 1 Parties" to the UNFCCC, the developed states and states with economies in transition from socialist to capitalist systems agreed to lower overall emissions of six GHGs (carbon dioxide, nitrous oxide, methane, hydrofluorocarbons, perfluorocarbons, and sulphur hexafluoride) to at least 5 percent below 1990 levels between 2008 and 2012. Within this group individual states committed to realize differentiated emission reductions below the 1990 ceiling. Among them the UNITED STATES accepted a target of 7 percent reduction, Italy 6.5 percent, GERMANY 21 percent, JAPAN and Canada 6 percent each, and the United Kingdom 12.5 percent, Non-Annex 1 states were not required by the PROTOCOL to meet any specific targets.

Because of objections by industrialized states to the lack of mandated emission reductions by the LESS DEVELOPED COUNTRIES (LDCs), the PROTOCOL also established a number of innovative, flexible techniques for developed states to reach their targets. For example, it provided for "emissions trading," by which a country might transfer to another state emission reduction credits resulting from its own projects. Also, it had a "sinks" provision that provided credits to countries that planted forests or undertook other carbon dioxide absorbing activities. In addition, Kyoto allowed for "joint implementation" credits whereby an industrialized state could count emission reduction units achieved in another developed state if it helped finance the GHG-reducing project. Finally, at the urging of the United States and Brazil, negotiators created a "Clean Development MECHANISM" that enabled a country to receive credit for emissions-avoiding projects that it undertook or that its private corporations undertook in other countries, presumably in the developing world.

In February 2005, the Kyoto Protocol entered into force after being ratified by a minimum of 55 states, among which were to be sufficient developed countries to account for at least 55 percent of global carbon dioxide (CO_2) emissions in 1990. The ratification of the agreement by the Russian Duma provided the needed participation to initiate the protocol's provisions. The long delay in implementing the protocol was due in large part to the strong opposition of the United States. Since the United States produced nearly 40 percent of the world's CO_2 emissions at the time of the Kyoto Protocol's signing, the requirement that 55 percent of 1990 CO_2 emissions be represented in the states that ratified the accord gave Washington a near VETO over the measure. In July 1997 the U.S. Senate voted 95 to 0 to oppose ratification of any climate TREATY that did not include limitations on LDC emissions, effectively postponing early implementation of the agreement. While President BILL CLINTON later signed the protocol, chances for American ratification became nil with the election of President GEORGE W. BUSH, who announced, in early 2001, that he would not submit it to the Senate without significant changes.

Post-Kyoto annual meetings of the UNFCCC Conference of the Parties were aimed at developing operational plans for implementing the protocol and at generating public pressure on the United States and other developed countries to meet their Kyoto commitments. At COP-4 (1998) in Argentina, negotiators drew up the Buenos Aires Plan of Action, which established a calendar of negotiations on all outstanding issues. In November 2000, more than 7,000 participants gathered for the sixth COP meeting in The Hague, Netherlands. Despite two weeks of intense negotiations, however, the conference broke up without an agreement that would meet the needed requirements for the protocol to go into force. Delegates agreed to suspend the meeting until later in 2001, giving time for UN SECRETARY-GENERAL KOFI ANNAN and others to bring public pressure to bear on the United States and other states that had not ratified the Kyoto Protocol.

Once the protocol entered into force without U.S. participation so much time had passed that the likelihood of the parties reaching their targets by the agreed dates seemed unlikely. In an effort to reinvigorate emissions-cutting as a method of slowing global warming and to entice American participation, GREAT BRITAIN's prime minister Tony Blair invited CHINA, Brazil, INDIA, Mexico, and South Africa to join G8 (GROUP OF EIGHT) nations in a G8+5 Climate Change Dialogue. The group reached agreement on February 16, 2007, on the "Washington DECLARATION," a non-binding outline of a successor to the Kyoto Protocol. Admitting that man-made CLIMATE CHANGE existed "beyond doubt," the signatories proposed a global system of emission caps and carbon emissions trading that would apply to both industrialized and DEVELOPING COUNTRIES. The group hoped to put the new arrangement in place by 2009. American willingness to support the new agreement was due in part to the decline in U.S. emissions relative to the rest of the world. Kyoto Protocol signatories accounted for 61.6 percent of total emissions by the end of 2006, meaning that U.S. emissions had fallen well below their earlier high of 40 percent.

See also ENVIRONMENT, INTERGOVERNMENTAL PANEL ON CLIMATE CHANGE, MONTREAL PROTOCOL ON SUBSTANCES THAT DEPLETE THE OZONE LAYER.

Further Reading: Fletcher, Susan R. *Congressional Research Service Report for Congress. 98-2: Global Climate Change Treaty: The Kyoto Protocol.* Washington, D.C.: National Council for Science and the Environment, 2000. Victor, David G. *The Collapse of the Kyoto Protocol and the Struggle to Slow Global Warming.* Princeton, N.J.: Princeton University Press, 2001. Kyoto Protocol Web site: <www.unfccc.int/essential_background/kyoto_protocol/items/2830.php>.

L

land mines

As of 2001, there were between 60 million and 110 million land mines deployed in more than 60 countries around the world. Some of the most heavily mine-affected states included AFGHANISTAN, BOSNIA, and CAMBODIA. By 2001, according to international experts, including those from the United Nations, land mines had caused 10,000 deaths and 15,000 injuries in those 60 states annually.

Land mines as a class of WEAPONS do not distinguish between combat forces and civilians. In fact, 80 to 90 percent of land mine victims have been civilians. Furthermore, land mines continue to kill and maim long after emplacement, well after hostilities have ended. In addition to their savage civilian toll, land mines hinder economic DEVELOPMENT and the repatriation of refugees and displaced persons. These devastating effects have prompted the United Nations to support numerous mine clearing projects. The UN Mine Action Service is a cooperative effort between the UN and NON-GOVERNMENTAL ORGANIZATIONS such as Handicap International and the Vietnam Veterans of America Foundation. The UN Mine Action Service has been involved in de-mining activities in states such as Azerbaijan, Cambodia, and LEBANON. The UNITED NATIONS OFFICE OF PROJECT SERVICES also provides extensive de-mining services in states where UN PEACEKEEPING operations are underway.

The SECRETARY-GENERAL and GENERAL ASSEMBLY have addressed the issue of land mines in reports and RESOLU-TIONS. In 1995, the Secretary-General issued a report entitled "Assistance in Mine Clearance." During the 1990s the General Assembly adopted resolutions 48/75K, 49/75D, 50/70O, 51/45S, 52/38A, 53/77N and 54/54B. Resolutions 49/75D and 50/70O made the elimination of anti-personnel land mines a goal of the international community. Together with resolution 48/75K, these resolutions urged a moratorium on a export of anti-personnel land mines. Resolution 51/45S urged states to pursue vigorously an effective, legally binding international agreement to ban the use, stockpiling, production, and transfer of anti-personnel land mines. This international agreement was realized in 1997 with the signing of the CONVENTION ON THE PROHIBITION OF THE USE, STOCKPILING, PRODUCTION AND TRANSFER OF ANTI-PERSONNEL MINES AND THEIR DESTRUCTION in Ottawa, Canada. Resolutions 52/38A, 53/77N, and 54/54B invited all states to sign the Ottawa Convention and urged signatories to ratify the CONVENTION without delay.

As required by the convention, the first review conference, known as the Nairobi Summit for a Mine Free-World, convened on November 29, 2004. The Geneva International Centre for Humanitarian Demining (GICHD) provided the SECRETARIAT for the meeting. The largest number of NON-GOVERNMENTAL ORGANIZATIONS (NGOs)—350—to ever participate in a de-mining conference attended the Nairobi Summit. The plan of action emanating from the gathering listed 70 specific recommendations to rid the world more quickly of land mines.

By summer 2007, 153 states had become parties to the CONVENTION. Of the three dozen or so governments that remained outside the land mines agreement, the UNITED STATES and the RUSSIAN FEDERATION were the most important. They were also two of 13 countries that continued to produce the weapon. The others were IRAN, CUBA, Burma, CHINA, INDIA, Nepal, North and South Korea, PAKISTAN, Singapore, and Vietnam. Additionally, several non-state groups were producing home-made versions, such as the improvised explosive device used regularly in IRAQ by insurgents resisting the occupying forces following the invasion of 2003. For its part, Russia continued to lay land mines in the separatist province of Chechnya. When the convention was signed in 1997, the U.S. administration of President BILL CLINTON expressed support for the accord, but indicated it could not sign until a workable substitute was found for the many land mines it maintained along the demilitarized zone between the two Koreas. President Clinton's successor, GEORGE W. BUSH, also disapproved of American participation, but in February 2004 his administration indicated that the United States would eliminate from its arsenal all land mines that were not capable of automatically turning off after a limited period in the ground.

Despite nonparticipation and continued production by several states, the Landmine Convention could claim some success after 10 years in force. The international trade in land mines had nearly dried up. Of those states reporting stockpiles, the total number of land mines had fallen to below a quarter million. Each month new states reported destruction of significant percentages of their munitions.

See also APPENDIX F (Security Council Resolution 1701), DEPARTMENT FOR DISARMAMENT AFFAIRS, DISARMAMENT.

Further Reading: Cameron, M., R. Lawson, and B. Tomlin. *To Walk without Fear: The Global Movement to Ban Landmines.* Toronto: Oxford University Press, 1998. *Landmine Monitor Report, 2006 and annually: Toward A Mine-Free World. Portfolio of Mine Action Projects, 2006.* 9th ed. New York: United Nations Mine Action Service, 2006. Short, N. "The Role of NGOs in the Ottawa Process to Ban Landmines." *International Negotiation* 4, no. 3 (1999): 481–500. Sundararaman, S. "The Landmines Question: An Overview of the Ottawa Process." *Strategic Analysis* 22, no. 1 (April 1998): 17–33. Thakur, Ramesh, and W. Maley. "The Ottawa Convention on Landmines: A Landmark Humanitarian Treaty in Arms Control?" *Global Governance: A Review of Multilateralism and International Organizations* 5, no. 3 (July–September 1999): 273–302. Vines, A., and H. Thompson. "Beyond the Landmine Ban: Eradicating a Lethal Legacy." *Conflict Studies,* 316 (March 1999): 1–37. International Campaign to Ban Landmines Web site: <www.icbl.org>.

— *S. F. McMahon*

languages, United Nations official and working

The official languages of the United Nations are Arabic, Chinese, English, French, Russian, and Spanish. Simultaneous translation into the official languages is provided in official meetings of UN organs and conferences. The UN Web site also is accessible in these languages. The working languages of the United Nations, however, are French and English. All UN documents are translated into these two languages. They, therefore, have more prominence in UN meetings, publications, and activities than the other four. There is even an intermixing of French and English in official titles and documents. For example, British English terms such as *centre* and *programme* are used universally in UN documents and publications.

See also APPENDIX F (Economic and Social Council Resolution 31), DEPARTMENT OF PUBLIC INFORMATION, HAGUE ACADEMY OF INTERNATIONAL LAW, INTERNATIONAL COURT OF JUSTICE, SECRETARIAT.

Deactivating mines in Cambodia (UN PHOTO 159491/ J. BLEIBTREU)

Latin America

As a result of the region's participation in World War II as part of the Grand Alliance, 20 countries within the Western Hemisphere entered the United Nations as charter members on October 24, 1945: Argentina, Bolivia, Brazil, Chile, Colombia, Costa Rica, CUBA, the Dominican Republic, Ecuador, EL SALVADOR, GUATEMALA, HAITI, Honduras, Mexico, Nicaragua, Panama, Paraguay, Peru, Uruguay, and Venezuela.

Latin American leaders have been active in the leadership of the United Nations since its inception. Most notably, JAVIER PÉREZ DE CUÉLLAR served as SECRETARY-GENERAL between 1982 and 1992.

The region and its problems have been important concerns for a number of UN organizations. The Economic Commission for Latin America (ECLA), founded in 1948, helped promote policy shifts that aimed at the creation of sustained economic expansion and modernization within the region. In 1985, the body evolved into the ECONOMIC COMMISSION FOR LATIN AMERICA AND THE CARIBBEAN (ECLAC). Other UN bodies that have become involved in Latin American economic, social, and cultural issues include: UNESCO (UNITED NATIONS EDUCATIONAL AND CULTURAL ORGANIZATION, established in 1945), UNICEF (UNITED NATIONS CHILDREN'S FUND, 1946), UNIDO (UNITED NATIONS INDUSTRIAL DEVELOPMENT ORGANIZATION, 1966), and WHO (WORLD HEALTH ORGANIZATION, 1948).

Three controversies affecting the region marked the early history of the United Nations. The strained diplomatic relations between the UNITED STATES and Argentina as a result of the latter's neutrality in World War II led to a push to block Argentina from UN MEMBERSHIP. The Argentine government's decision on March 27, 1945, to declare war against the remaining Axis powers, and its subsequent ratification of the RESOLUTIONS issued at the Inter-American Conference on War and Peace Problems at Chapultepec Palace in Mexico City (February 11, 1945) settled existing differences and cleared the way for Argentina's membership.

The push for hemispheric solidarity involving the American states during the years preceding the UN's formation created a second and more serious problem. Latin American leaders sought special recognition from the body for their region's status, as well as guarantees that UN obstruction, resulting from the use of a VETO by a permanent member of the SECURITY COUNCIL or other means, would not interfere with inter-American issues and concerns. Facing an impasse, the United States orchestrated a compromise that recognized the authority of "regional arrangements" to manage local or regional affairs, provided that their activities were "consistent with the Purposes and Principles of the United Nations" (Chapter VIII, Article 52). Additionally, under Article 51 states were permitted to undertake "COLLECTIVE SELF-DEFENSE" until the Security Council had taken sufficient steps to restore peace. The new wording in the CHARTER, however, limited this grant of autonomy by asserting the right of the council to investigate and take action on any threat to the peace. It also allowed any state to bring any dispute directly to the council. Following its establishment in 1948, the ORGANIZATION OF AMERICAN STATES (OAS) took on primary responsibility for ensuring peace and security within Latin America in accordance with the Charter provisions.

Regional interests and concerns over the power of the PERMANENT MEMBERS OF THE SECURITY COUNCIL led to a third impasse. Latin American representatives sought a greater role within the Security Council from the outset. This push generated an effort, led by El Salvador and Brazil, to have Latin America guaranteed representation within the Security Council. El Salvador recommended the addition of more members to the council, which would have raised its original membership from 11 to 15. While the proposal gained support from small states in other regions, Brazil determined instead to seek a permanent seat on the Security Council for one Latin American country. The United States effectively blocked this proposed REFORM. Fearing that expansion would create concerns over a Western bloc within the council, Washington successfully argued that any attempt to alter the council's composition would upset existing settlements and delay the establishment of the United Nations. An informal compromise occurred. Latin American countries were in practice reserved two seats on the Security Council that the regional members shared through a regular rotation. Later, in 1965, the UN GENERAL ASSEMBLY adopted a resolution that increased the size of the Security Council to 15 and formally reserved two of the non-permanent seats for Latin American representatives.

While regional conflicts occasionally gained the attention of the United Nations, Latin America fell into a close partnership with the United States in almost all UN affairs. Rising COLD WAR tensions and the efforts of U.S. policy makers to orchestrate Latin American support, produced a significant American VOTING bloc within the General Assembly that effectively countered challenges through the 1950s. In the first years of the body's operations, the Latin American bloc demonstrated its loyalty to Western interests through its votes on the ADMISSION of new members. Solidly supporting the candidates backed by the United States and its European allies, and voting with near unanimity against those put forward by the Soviet Union, the Latin American countries consistently demonstrated their allegiance to the anticommunist position. Latin American support for the series of resolutions that led to UN intervention in the KOREAN WAR in 1950 demonstrated the success of American efforts to cultivate regional support.

The Guatemala crisis of 1954 strained the ties between the American members of the United Nations. Claiming that the Arbenz administration then ruling Guatemala was communist in its actions and character, the U.S. government helped foment a military coup. Guatemala sought the intervention of the United Nations. It claimed that the invasion of U.S.-backed mercenary groups from Nicaragua and Honduras was an act of AGGRESSION and it requested UN assistance. Honduras, Nicaragua, Colombia, and Brazil challenged the request. Citing Article 33 of CHAPTER VI and 52 (2) of Chapter VIII of the UN Charter, Guatemala's opponents argued that as a regional dispute the matter fell under the JURISDICTION of the Organization of American States. A veto by the USSR blocked a resolution offered by Brazil and Colombia that would have officially called on the OAS to open discussion concerning the situation in Guatemala. In its place, FRANCE authored a resolution that called for an end to military action and a commitment from all parties to block any and all assistance to the disputing parties. This resolution passed unanimously. The Soviet Union and Guatemala continued to call for UN action, but a U.S. veto stalled Security Council deliberations. The collapse of the Arbenz government led to an end of UN discussion of the crisis.

The fall of Fulgencio Batista in 1959 transformed Cuba into a catalyst of dramatic shifts in Latin America's role in the United Nations. The CUBAN MISSILE CRISIS of October 1962 brought about an emergency session of the UN Security Council. The United States used the session to justify its actions and establish a UN commission that was to supervise the removal of missiles and missile facilities from Cuba. The representatives of the Latin American delegations, with the exception of Cuba, supported the U.S. position. While a settlement negotiated by the United States and the USSR ended the crisis, the status of Cuba within Latin America and the United Nations generated challenges to the authority of the United States.

Rafael Trujillo's dictatorship in the Dominican Republic also created a crisis that altered inter-American relations. Declaring that civil war in the Dominican Republic threatened regional peace and its own national interests, the United States invaded the island in April 1965. In the wake of such a military intervention, the United Nations authorized its first observer mission. In May 1965 a resolution of the Security Council called for a cease-fire and for the UN Secretary-General to send a representative who would report on the situation. The Mission of the SPECIAL REPRESENTATIVE OF THE SECRETARY-GENERAL to the Dominican Republic remained in place until October 1966, after elections and the withdrawal of an inter-American PEACEKEEPING force had taken place.

Rising nationalist sentiment created a new source of tensions in Panama. Resentment over the continued control of the Canal Zone by the United States led to civil disturbances in the 1950s. Escalating riots in 1964 and the forceful response by U.S. military forces moved the Panamanian government to sever relations with the United States and appeal to the United Nations for redress. Stalled negotiations and intermittent violence led the UN Security Council to meet in Panama City in March 1973. The council aired a proposal to

support Panamanian claims of SOVEREIGNTY over all its territories, but a threatened U.S. veto stalled any action. Bilateral negotiations eventually produced a TREATY that accelerated the transfer of authority over the Canal Zone in 1977.

Popular revolutions and fear of U.S. military interventions led Latin America to use the United Nations as a venue for negotiated settlements of recent and long-standing disagreements. The Nicaraguan revolution of 1979 toppled a regime closely allied with the United States. The U.S. government's concerns over the ideological orientation of the revolutionary government and its potential influence over politics in neighboring states led it to sponsor the Contra War. To bring peace and head off greater U.S. involvement in the military and political affairs of Central America, Latin American leaders launched the Contadora Peace Project. The UN issued resolutions first in 1983 supporting this effort. When the Contadora process stalled, Latin American leaders enlisted the involvement of the Secretary-General's office in an attempt to develop a regional settlement. The result was christened in 1986 the Rio Group, which launched negotiations and brokered settlements in Nicaragua, El Salvador, and Guatemala. The United Nations Observer Group in Central America, operating between 1989 and 1992, also established a system to demobilize and resettle combatants, verify elections, and reintegrate rebel groups into the political systems of the countries involved.

U.S. diplomatic and military actions weakened the allegiance of Latin America to the American position within the United Nations. The 1982 U.S. decision to aid GREAT BRITAIN and to defend the British position in the United Nations in relation to the Malvinas (Falklands) Islands War angered many Latin American nations. The U.S. invasion of Grenada in 1983 led to a General Assembly resolution, supported by most Latin American nations, that condemned the intervention. A U.S. veto killed a similar proposal in the Security Council. The December 1989 invasion of Panama by the United States also generated broad criticism within Latin America. A Security Council resolution calling for the immediate withdrawal of U.S. forces failed to gain approval only as a result of vetoes from the United States, Great Britain, and France.

Latin American issues remained of primary importance within the United Nations as the new century began. The mounting debt of Latin American and other developing nations, which the interventions of the WORLD BANK and the INTERNATIONAL MONETARY FUND had not solved, became a growing concern of the United Nations beginning in the 1970s. In 1993, the General Assembly declared the "International Year of the World's INDIGENOUS PEOPLE," and in 1994 it inaugurated the "International Decade of the World's Indigenous People." Focusing UN attention on the rights and contributions of indigenous communities to world affairs, the General Assembly became increasingly active in Latin American conflicts. This attention was most pronounced concerning the central Andes, southern Mexico, and Central America, as a result of discussions concerning government repression, the drug trade, and SUSTAINABLE DEVELOPMENT.

Within the United Nations, Latin America remained an important part of two recognized blocs. First, regional issues molded a Latin American and Caribbean group that often used the General Assembly as a venue for challenging the authority of the United States. Second, from the 1960s, Latin America increasingly joined in the NON-ALIGNED MOVEMENT when issues concerning economic development and the disparity between the Northern and Southern Hemispheres arose. These blocs were useful in the General Assembly for challenging U.S. policies. However, they have proven to be not particularly cohesive. During the first decade of the new millennium, Latin American cohesiveness disintegrated further as several states in the region elected governments ideologically to the left of their predecessors. Led by the Hugo Chávez government in Venezuela, these states criticized the impact of GLOBALIZATION on the region, and opposed U.S. efforts to expand free trade policies through BRETTON WOODS institutions and new free trade zones. In the latter case, Brazil took the lead. The divisions in the region came to a head in the UN General Assembly in 2006 when Venezuela sought election to the Security Council. Fully anticipating victory, Venezuela lost the seat after an intemperate speech to the Assembly by President Chávez and after the longest voting process in the history of the chamber.

See also APARTHEID; CAUCUS GROUPS; COMMISSION ON SUSTAINABLE DEVELOPMENT; DEMOCRATIZATION; DESERTIFICATION; DISARMAMENT; FIRST AND THIRD WORLDS; GENERAL COMMITTEE; GROUP OF 77; INTER-AMERICAN DEVELOPMENT BANK; INTERNATIONAL COURT OF JUSTICE; INTERNATIONAL LAW COMMISSION; NON-PERMANENT MEMBERS OF THE SECURITY COUNCIL; NUCLEAR-WEAPONS-FREE ZONES; ORGANISATION FOR THE PROHIBITION OF CHEMICAL WEAPONS; PREBISCH, RAÚL; REGIONAL ORGANIZATIONS; TREATY OF TLATLELOCO; UNITED NATIONS CONFERENCE ON THE LAW OF THE SEA; UNITED NATIONS CONFERENCE ON TRADE AND DEVELOPMENT; UNITED NATIONS ENVIRONMENT PROGRAMME; YALTA CONFERENCE.

Further Reading: Cayuela, Jose. *ECLAC 40 Years (1948–1988)*. Santiago, Chile: Economic Commission for Latin American and the Caribbean, 1988. Houston, John A. *Latin America in the United Nations*. New York: Carnegie Endowment for International Peace, 1956. Mingst, Karen A., and Margaret P. Karns. *The United Nations in the Post–Cold War Era*. 2d ed. Boulder, Colo.: Westview Press, 2000. Roberts, Adam, and Benedict Kingsbury, eds. *United Nations, Divided World: The UN's Roles in International Relations*. 2d ed. Oxford: Clarendon Press, 1993. Rosenthal, Gert. "The United Nations and ECLAC at the Half-Century Mark." *CEPAL Review*, no. 57 (December 1995): 7–15.

— *D. K. Lewis*

Law of the Sea   *See* UNITED NATIONS CONFERENCE ON THE LAW OF THE SEA (UNCLOS).

League of Nations

Precursor to the United Nations, the League was founded at the end of World War I on the initiative of U.S. president Woodrow Wilson, who included in his FOURTEEN POINTS of 1918 (at number 14) a proposed league that would be the first world organization for maintaining peace and security, international cooperation, and the development of INTERNATIONAL LAW. The League virtually ceased to function with the outbreak of World War II and in 1946 it officially dissolved itself.

The unrivaled bloodshed and carnage of World War I convinced many leaders of the necessity of a world organization to avert another such conflict, but the intellectual and practical origins of the League preceded the eruption of war in 1914. Eighteenth-century German philosopher Immanuel Kant had envisioned a global organization, and the 19th century had witnessed the growth of numerous international cooperative ventures, including the International Telegraph Union, initiated in 1865, the UNIVERSAL POSTAL UNION, established in 1874, and the International Red Cross, urged by Swiss doctor Jean-Henri Dunant after he witnessed the suffering of the wounded in the battle of Solferino in 1859. The Hague Peace Conferences at the beginning of the 20th century and the establishment of the PERMANENT COURT OF ARBITRATION gave further impetus to international cooperation. The war solidified opinion among an active group of diplomats, including South African Jan Smuts, Britain's Lord Robert Cecil, and Frenchman Léon Bourgeois, all advocating a society of nations. As early as 1914 Wilson had spoken with his closest adviser, Colonel Edward House, about the merits of a world association to avoid the kind of war just underway. The president may also have been influenced by the British writer Norman Angell with whom he spoke before publicly articulating his ideas on a league. In 1917, the American Institute of International Law issued a recommendation in Havana, CUBA, calling for a world organization that dovetailed agreeably with Wilson's proposal.

At the Paris Peace Conference in 1919, Wilson insisted on including the COVENANT of the new League in the text of the TREATY of Versailles, designed to end the war. The U.S. president headed a special committee at the conference that crafted the Covenant of the League and made it an "integral part of the General Peace Treaty." The Covenant, coming into force on January 10, 1920, included 26 articles, provided for an Assembly composed of all members, a Council to include permanent members from the great powers (at first the United Kingdom, FRANCE, Italy, and JAPAN, later joined by GERMANY and the Soviet Union), and a SECRETARIAT. Both the Assembly and the Council required unanimity on any decision. The Covenant called for DISARMAMENT, territorial integrity and political independence of NATION-STATES, the establishment of a PERMANENT COURT OF INTERNATIONAL JUSTICE, the end of colonialism by means of a mandate system (whereby existing colonial administrators would prepare colonial areas for independence), international cooperation in humanitarian affairs, and provisions for amending the Covenant. The most controversial provision of the Covenant, highlighted in Article 10, called for COLLECTIVE SECURITY to assure nations League protection against AGGRESSION.

The inaugural session of the League Council was held in Paris in January 1920, but Geneva became the permanent home of the new League, which met at first in the Hôtel National (before construction of the Palais des Nations, which opened in 1936). MEMBERSHIP could be extended to any state, dominion, or even self-governing colony by a two-thirds vote of the Assembly. The original members were the victorious nations from the war. There were 32 such countries, and 29 came into the League initially. The largest victor not to join was the UNITED STATES, which refused to ratify the Treaty of Versailles. In 1920 membership stood at 42 states. Several neutral nations, and the Soviet Union—isolated from world affairs following the Bolshevik Revolution—did not become members in 1920. Germany, unhappy with the peace treaty, did not enter the League until 1926. The Soviet Union joined in 1934, at the very time the strains on the organization were becoming unbearable. The greatest number of members, achieved in 1937, was 58; by 1943 there were only 10. The League's secretaries-general were Sir James Eric Drummond of GREAT BRITAIN (1920–33), Joseph Avenol of France (1933–40), and Sean Lester of Ireland (1940–46).

The offices of the League Secretariat were in a building along Lake Geneva that in 1924 was renamed the Palais Wilson, following the death of the former president. Sir Eric Drummond, the first, and longest serving, SECRETARY-GENERAL, assembled a genuinely international secretariat, and early on the League realized some successes. It settled a Finnish-Swedish dispute over the Aland Islands in the Gulf of Bothnia (1920–21), guaranteed the security of Albania (1921), aided Austria's economic reconstruction after the war, guided the peaceful division of Upper Silesia between Germany and Poland (1922), and helped prevent hostilities between Greece and Bulgaria in the Balkans (1925). It also extended help to refugees, worked to suppress the white slave trade and to restrain the traffic in opium, and published surveys and data on a number of pressing international issues such as world health, labor conditions, and economics. But intractable problems confronted the League. For one, without the United States as a member, the League lacked an influential player in world affairs. The problem of including the Soviet Union in international diplomacy was not resolved until quite late in the League's history. Moreover, the worldwide depression that engulfed most countries by the 1930s made it even more difficult to deal with nations

seeking to look out for their own interests. Then, as the dismantling of world order ensued, the League seemed destined to sit aside as aggressions proceeded. The League could do nothing as the French and Belgians occupied the Ruhr in 1923, the Japanese invaded Manchuria in 1931 (when the League accepted the U.S. policy—called the STIMSON DOCTRINE—of simply not recognizing the occupation), the Japanese withdrew from League membership (1933), and Bolivia and Paraguay fought the Chaco War (1932–35). In 1935 the League completed a 15-year administration of the Saar territory with a plebiscite, but Germany had already left the League (1933), and in 1935 Italy invaded Ethiopia in defiance of League SANCTIONS. Adolf Hitler's remilitarization of the Rhineland and censure of the Treaty of Versailles foreshadowed an ominous future for the organization. The Spanish Civil War (1936–39), the Japanese invasion of mainland CHINA (1937), appeasement of Hitler at Munich concerning the dismemberment of Czechoslovakia (1938), and German demands on Danzig, Poland, which a League commissioner in the city could not resist, culminated in the outbreak of World War II and the end of the League experiment. The impotence of the League became obvious when in 1939 the Council—for the only time in the League's history—expelled a nation, the Soviet Union, for its attack on Finland, following the German-Soviet PACT of August 23, 1939, by which the two totalitarian regimes agreed to divide Eastern Europe. At the moment of the agreement, war became inevitable, as did the end of the League. Several affiliated organizations and powerful ideas of international cooperation did survive the crisis of World War II, and they merged with the new United Nations after that conflict.

Although the League served as a model for the later United Nations, in important respects the two organizations were different. The League had been ensconced in the full Treaty of Versailles; thus to reject the League the U.S. Senate of necessity had to reject the entire peace agreement. The United Nations, conversely, was purposely separated from the peace treaties that ended World War II; U.S. president FRANKLIN ROOSEVELT, informed by Wilson's lack of success, determined on a separate process of ratification in the United States. The League Covenant had been a traditional agreement among governments, called in the Covenant "The High Contracting Parties." The Preamble of the UN CHARTER began, "We the *peoples* of the United Nations." The League required unanimous votes in both the League Assembly and the League Council, but decision making in the United Nations was deliberately made more flexible. Parties to a dispute before the League were prohibited from VOTING because of the obvious conflict of interest. In the United Nations, in a concession to the realities of power politics, member states have no such limitations. When coupled with the VETO, this means that a PERMANENT MEMBER OF THE SECURITY COUNCIL can block UN action. Finally, it is significant to note that in 1945 the United States, never a member of the League or the Permanent Court of International Justice, eagerly entered the United Nations and determined to play a major role in all the post–World War II international organizations.

See also ADMINISTRATIVE TRIBUNALS; CHAPTER VII; DAG HAMMARSKJÖLD LIBRARY; DOMESTIC JURISDICTION CLAUSE; ELECTION ASSISTANCE DIVISION; HUMAN RIGHTS; INQUIRY; INTERNATIONAL LAW COMMISSION; JURISDICTION OF THE UNITED NATIONS; MULTILATERALISM; NAMIBIA; PASVOLSKY, LEO; STATUTE OF THE INTERNATIONAL COURT OF JUSTICE; TERRORISM; TRUSTEESHIP SYSTEM; UNITED NATIONS INTERIM FORCE IN LEBANON; WORLD HEALTH ORGANIZATION.

Further Reading: Carr, E. H. *International Relations between the Two World Wars (1919–1939)*. London: Macmillan, 1963. Moore, John Allphin, Jr., and Jerry Pubantz. *To Create a New World?: American Presidents and the United Nations*. New York: Peter Lang, 1999. Northedge, F. S. *The League of Nations; Its Life and Times, 1920–1946*. New York: Holmes and Meier, 1986. Ostrower, Gary B. *Collective Insecurity: The United States and the League of Nations during the Early Thirties*. Lewisburg, Pa.: Bucknell University Press, 1979. Rovine, Arthur W. *The First Fifty Years: The Secretary-General in World Politics, 1920–1970*. Leiden, Netherlands: A. W. Sijthoff, 1970.

least developed countries (LDC)

The term "Least Developed Country" is an official UN designation identifying the "poorest of the poor" countries with the greatest need of development assistance. The expression emerged in recognition of the inadequacy of the terms "THIRD WORLD" and "developing nations," which served only to distinguish these nations from developed states, more correctly called industrialized countries. In recognition of the reality that the general category of "DEVELOPING COUNTRIES" included large numbers of nations with great differences among them, specialists regularly separated them into several subcategories. The United Nations Committee for Development Policy (CDP), a group of experts established by the ECONOMIC AND SOCIAL COUNCIL (ECOSOC), decided in 1971 that those nations ranking at the bottom of global living standards should be called "Least Developed." The governments of these countries are impoverished by a limited national economy and consequently have the fewest resources to assist their citizens. The committee reviews the list every three years to determine which nations should be added to or removed from it.

The United Nations has developed a set of specific criteria for listing least developed countries. The first is a state's level of DEVELOPMENT as demonstrated by a GDP (gross domestic product) per capita of $750 (U.S.) or less. Despite the official $750 ceiling, the vast majority of least developed countries had incomes under $400 in 2002. Indeed, the average per capita GDP of least developed countries is one-quarter of that of all developing countries, with 75 percent of the POPULATION in LDCs having an income of less than $2 per day. The second criterion is weak human resources and infrastructure, as measured by a Human Assets Index (HAI) that combines life expectancy at birth, per capita calorie intake, combined primary and secondary school enrollment, and adult literacy. This category underscores the fact that such countries cannot afford to spend adequately on education or HEALTH care and usually are unable to produce enough food to feed their people. For example, primary school enrollment rates in least developed countries average 30 percentage points below the overall rate for all developing countries. Secondary school enrollments average 50 percentage points below, and adult literacy rates are less than two-thirds that of all developed countries. Least developed countries average four telephone lines per thousand people, which is one-fiftieth the average in all developing countries. The third criterion is a nation's economic vulnerability to internal and external pressures, measured by the Economic Vulnerability Index (EVI), which combines the share of manufacturing in GDP, the share of the labor force employed in industry, annual per capita commercial energy consumption, and the UNCTAD (UNITED NATIONS CONFERENCE ON TRADE AND DEVELOPMENT) Merchandise Export Concentration Index, measuring the degree of dependence on the export of single commodities and raw materials. Low performance relative to this standard indicates that such nations have very little industrialization and are dependent on the agricultural sector and the export of unprocessed or semi-processed primary commodities. Reflecting this single commodity dependence, the export instability price index of least developed countries is over 50 percent higher than that for all developing countries. LDCs derive the bulk of their energy from fuel-wood. Moreover, the per capita consumption of combined coal, natural gas, oil, and electricity in least developed countries averages one-tenth of the levels of developing countries as a whole.

To be classified as "Least Developed," a nation must meet the inclusion thresholds for all three criteria. Countries qualify for "graduation" from the category when they surpass the thresholds for two of the three criteria. The number of least developed countries has remained surprisingly constant, with 50 countries so designated as of 2006. The majority of least developed countries are located in Africa, where more than 30 nations have been so classified, constituting more than half the nations on the continent.

At the 2006 review, the committee noted several changes and recommended that the Republic of the CONGO, Papua New Guinea, and Zimbabwe be added to the list of least developed countries at the 2007 session, having met the criteria. The government of each country must accept this designation, however, and Zimbabwe immediately notified the committee that it "does not give its consent to be downgraded to LDC status," halting the process. During the 2006 review, the committee identified Samoa as eligible for graduation, pending approval by ECOSOC and the General Assembly in 2007. The committee also found that four countries, Equatorial Guinea, Kiribati, Tuvalu, and Vanuatu had met the necessary criteria for graduation for the first time, and hence were embarking on the second phase of the six-year graduation process They were to be considered for graduation during the 2009 review. The fact that countries were graduating from Least Developed status indicated that a few countries were making significant progress in development.

In 2007 the 50 countries officially classified as least developed include: AFGHANISTAN, ANGOLA, Bangladesh, Benin, Bhutan, Burkina Faso, Burundi, CAMBODIA, Cape Verde, Central African Republic, Chad, Comoros, Democratic Republic of the CONGO, Djibouti, Equatorial Guinea, Eritrea, Ethiopia, The Gambia, Guinea, Guinea-Bissau, HAITI, Kiribati, Lao People's Democratic Republic, Lesotho, Liberia, Madagascar, Malawi, Maldives, Mali, Mauritania, Mozambique, Myanmar, Nepal, Niger, Rwanda, Samoa, São Tomé and Príncipe, Senegal, SIERRA LEONE, Solomon Islands, SOMALIA, Sudan, TIMOR-LESTE, Togo, Tuvalu, Uganda, United Republic of Tanzania, Vanuatu, Yemen, and Zambia. Nigeria meets all the criteria for inclusion, but is disqualified by its large population, which exceeds the allowable limits for the list.

Only Botswana has ever been declared to have "graduated" from the "Least Developed" to the "Middle Income" Category, although in 2003 Maldives and Cape Verde were under consideration for the same change in designation. The destruction wrought by the Asian tsunami of December 2004 caused the GENERAL ASSEMBLY to postpone consideration of Maldives until 2008, leaving only Cape Verde eligible for "graduation" consideration in 2007. The Economic and Social Council upon recommendation by the CDP assigns countries to the LDC category, reviewing the list every three years. Eritrea was added to the list when it separated from Ethiopia in 1993. Timor-Leste was added in 2003.

Aid donors are expected to grant special consideration to least developed countries, providing them with more development assistance, and granting duty-free trade access to the home markets of industrialized donor states. LDCs also qualify for preferential debt relief terms. UN poverty eradication programs are especially targeted at least developed countries.

In order to bring world attention and assistance to LDCs, the United Nations has sponsored three WORLD CONFERENCES on least developed countries—in Paris (1981 and 1990) and in Brussels (2001). These conferences have evaluated progress and developed programs and plans of action to address LDCs' problems. Least developed countries are considered so significant that the United Nations established a special office to assist these countries in addressing their development problems, and to represent them in UN bodies to assure that their concerns were addressed. Originally titled the Office of the Coordinator for Africa and Least Developed Countries, the office was modified by UN reorganization. African concerns were separated into the Office of the Special

Adviser on Africa and new categories of developing countries with special problems were added to produce the present lead agency for LDCs, the Office of the High Representative for Least Developed, Landlocked Developing Countries, and Small Island Developing States. The least developed countries themselves have established their own CAUCUS GROUP at the UN. The chair of the LDC caucus speaks for the entire group in the General Assembly and all UN bodies.

See also SCALE OF ASSESSMENTS, SUSTAINABLE DEVELOPMENT, UNITED NATIONS DEVELOPMENT PROGRAMME.

Further Reading: United Nations Conference on Trade and Development. *The Least Developed Countries Report.* New York and Geneva: United Nations, issued annually. UN Office of the High Representative for the Least Developed Countries, Landlocked Developing Countries and Small Island Developing States Web site: <www.un.org/ohrlls/>. LDC Web site: <www.unctad.org/Templates/StartPage.asp?intItemID=3 617&lang=1>.

— *K. J. Grieb*

Lebanon   *See* APPENDIX F (Security Council Resolution 1701), ARAB-ISRAELI DISPUTE, UNITED NATIONS INTERIM FORCE IN LEBANON.

Legal Committee   *See* SIXTH COMMITTEE OF THE GENERAL ASSEMBLY.

less developed countries (LDC)

"Less Developed Country" is a designation that applies to the middle segment of DEVELOPING COUNTRIES. The inclusive category of "developing countries" describes all states that are not classified as "industrialized countries," or "EITs" (Economies in Transition in the former socialist states of Eastern Europe). Developing countries, often referred to as the Third World, are in UN parlance divided into subcategories.

Congregated within the GROUP OF 77 (G 77) and the NON-ALIGNED MOVEMENT (NAM), developing countries nonetheless differ significantly in their economies and social infrastructure. The United Nations acknowledges these differences by enumerating several categories within the developing group. The official UN terms designate those with the most DEVELOPMENT as "Middle Income Countries," and the poorest as "LEAST DEVELOPED COUNTRIES." Nations that do not fall under either of these categories, but rather in between them, are the less developed countries. The WORLD BANK refers to them as "Lower-Middle Income Countries," defined as nations with a per capita annual gross domestic product (GDP) of between $750 and $2,995. The World Bank distinguishes this group from what it calls "Upper-

Middle Income Countries." Less developed countries comprise about half of all developing countries.

Less developed countries are characterized by a lack of significant industrialization, the export of unprocessed or minimally processed primary commodities, single commodity dependence, a young POPULATION, widespread poverty, low government income, low spending in the education and health sectors, a lack of social services, a high degree of illiteracy, the absence of a social safety net for the populace, high debts, and a chronic negative balance of payments.

Less developed countries are not eligible for special aid programs targeted at least developed countries, but they are the recipients of extensive UN programmatic assistance. They are often exempt from international obligations, such as environmental rules, that are imposed on developed states.

See also ADMISSION OF MEMBERS, AGENDA FOR PEACE, AGENDA 21, ENVIRONMENT, EXPANDED PROGRAM OF TECHNICAL ASSISTANCE, FIRST AND THIRD WORLDS, KYOTO PROTOCOL, NEW INTERNATIONAL ECONOMIC ORDER, RIO DECLARATION, SPECIAL UNITED NATIONS FUND FOR ECONOMIC DEVELOPMENT, UNITED NATIONS CONFERENCE ON THE ENVIRONMENT AND DEVELOPMENT, UNITED NATIONS CONFERENCE ON THE HUMAN ENVIRONMENT, UNITED NATIONS DEVELOPMENT PROGRAMME, UNITED NATIONS FRAMEWORK CONVENTION ON CLIMATE CHANGE, UNITED NATIONS OFFICE FOR PROJECT SERVICES.

— *K. J. Grieb*

Lessons Learned Unit   *See* DEPARTMENT OF PEACEKEEPING OPERATIONS.

Lie, Trygve Halvadan (1896–1968)

The first SECRETARY-GENERAL of the United Nations was born in Oslo, Norway, in 1896. He studied at Oslo University where he received a law degree in 1919. He became active in the Norwegian Labor Party as a youth, subsequently serving the party as legal adviser to the Norwegian Trade Union Federation and then as national executive secretary. During the 1930s, Lie won a seat in the Norwegian parliament and served as minister of justice in a labor government. When World War II broke out he became minister of supply and shipping, performing a crucial role in saving the Norwegian fleet for the Allies after the Germans had commenced their invasion in 1940. He then fled Norway and, during the war, acted as foreign minister for his homeland's exiled government in London. Lie was head of the Norwegian delegation to the San Francisco UN organizing conference in April 1945, where he played a prominent role in drafting the SECURITY COUNCIL provisions in the new CHARTER. Shortly after the San Francisco meeting, he was reelected to parliament and then chosen foreign minister in a new postwar Labor government, in which capacity he headed the Norwegian

Trygve Lie (UNITED NATIONS)

delegation to the UN GENERAL ASSEMBLY meeting in London in early 1946. Lie was elected the UN's first Secretary-General on February 1, 1946, being formally installed the next day by the General Assembly.

Lie considered the job of Secretary-General to be one of energetic leadership. During the crisis of the KOREAN WAR his active efforts in negotiations and his support of UN prosecution of the war annoyed the Soviet Union, which perceived him as a tool of American foreign policy. During the McCarthy era of the early 1950s Secretary-General Lie's willingness to fire American employees of the SECRETARIAT who came under suspicion as communist infiltrators reenforced the Soviet view. When 18 American employees asserted their fifth amendment rights against self-incrimination and refused to testify before the Senate Subcommittee on Internal Security in October 1952, Lie fired them on the grounds that they had violated Article 1.4 of the staff regulations, which required that they act in a manner befitting their status as international civil servants. Lie even allowed the U.S. Federal Bureau of Investigation to fingerprint and question all American UN officials at the UN HEADQUARTERS building in New York City.

At the close of his term in 1951 the USSR indicated it would VETO the reelection of Lie. The U.S. government responded that it would support no other candidate. The impasse was finessed by the General Assembly deciding by a vote of 46 in favor, 5 opposed, and 8 abstentions to "continue in office" the Secretary-General for another three years. The Soviet delegation considered the vote illegitimate and subsequently refused to work with Lie, hastening his early retirement. In 1953 he returned to Norway where, before his death in 1968, he continued an active political and diplomatic life, serving as governor of Oslo, minister of industries, and minister of commerce. In 1959 Norwegian king Olav V, asked by the General Assembly to expedite a settlement of a dispute between Italy and Ethiopia over the borders of SOMALIA, appointed Lie as mediator.

See also ADMINISTRATIVE TRIBUNALS; BUNCHE, RALPH; STALIN, JOSEPH; UN FLAG; URQUHART, BRIAN.

Further Reading: Barnes, James. *Trygve Lie and the Cold War: The UN Secretary-General Pursues Peace.* DeKalb: Northern Illinois University Press, 1989. Chesterman, Simon, ed. *Secretary or General? The UN Secretary-General in World Affairs.* Cambridge: Cambridge University Press, 2007. Cordier, Andrew W., and Wilder Foote. *Public Papers of the Secretaries-General of the United Nations.* New York: Columbia University Press, 1969–1977. Kille, Kent J. *From Manager to Visionary: The Secretary-General of the United Nations.* New York: Palgrave Macmillan, 2006. Lie, Trygve. *In the Cause of Peace.* New York: Macmillan, 1954.

MacArthur, Douglas *See* KOREAN WAR.

Main Committees *See* COMMITTEE SYSTEM OF THE GENERAL ASSEMBLY.

Mao Zedong *See* CHINA, KOREAN WAR.

Marrakesh Protocol

On April 15, 1994, finance ministers from 123 participating governments at a meeting in Marrakesh, Morocco, signed the Marrakesh PROTOCOL that established the WORLD TRADE ORGANIZATION (WTO). The WTO entered into force on January 1, 1995, effectively replacing the GENERAL AGREEMENT ON TARIFFS AND TRADE (GATT) that had been the world's chief trade regime since the end of World War II.

GATT's members had concluded that the postwar system was under strain to adapt to forces of accelerating GLOBALIZATION. The eighth GATT round—called the Uruguay Round—initiated in 1986 in Punta del Este, Uruguay, represented the most ambitious effort to that time to liberalize international trade. Talks during the Uruguay Round were intended to amplify the international trading system's province in order to deal with new areas of economic and financial activity, including trade in services and intellectual property, and to effect extensive reform in agriculture and textiles trade policy. Also, all of the GATT's articles were scheduled for review. Disagreements, principally over agricultural trade, resulted in the talks being extended beyond the proposed conclusion in December 1990. In November 1992 the UNITED STATES and the European Union came to agreement on most outstanding issues at the so-called Blair House Accord, which was seen as preliminary to wholesale reform of the international trading system. The main features of the Blair House Accord then became the basis for the Marrakesh Protocol. Annexed to the "Final Act" of the protocol was the "Understanding on Rules and Procedures Governing the Settlement of Disputes" (DSU). The WTO's Dispute Resolution MECHANISM is the vital feature of the new multilateral trade system initiated at Marrakesh. That is, WTO members are committed to using the multilateral means of the DSU—instead of unilateral actions—to settle disputes should they believe other members are violating agreed-upon trade rules. The WTO calls the DSU a "unique contribution to the stability of the global economy" since it assures enforcement of international rules.

Further Reading: Marrakesh Protocol Web site: <www.wto.org/english/docs_e/legal_e/13-mprot_e.htm>. The WTO's DSU Web site: <www.wto.org/english/thewto_e/whatis_e/tif_e/disp1_e.htm>.

mechanism

A mechanism, according to the Oxford English Dictionary, is a "structure or way of working of the parts of a system," or "the mode of operation of a process." In the United Nations, mechanisms are formalized procedures to make possible the desired functioning of a UN organ. For example, in its 1979–80 session, the COMMISSION ON HUMAN RIGHTS established special procedures, or *mechanisms,* to facilitate its HUMAN RIGHTS investigations. The mechanisms included modus operandi for the appointment of SPECIAL RAPPORTEURS to examine charges of human rights abuses in discrete categories or in particular areas of the world and then prepare reports for the commission. The WORLD TRADE ORGANIZATION's Trade Policy Review Mechanism stipulates procedures for reviewing and evaluating individual member states' trade policies and their impact on the global trading system.

Examples of the use of the word "mechanism" in UN-related topics are legion. For example, there are mechanisms to realize the goals of AGENDA 21, to achieve CONFLICT RESOLUTION, and to carry into effect the aims of the LAW OF THE SEA. In 2004 the INTERNATIONAL MONETARY FUND introduced the explicitly named "Trade Integration Mechanism," which was designed to assure DEVELOPING COUNTRIES that they would receive assistance from the international community to help them adjust to any difficulties resulting from the loss of trade preferences when tariffs were lowered.

mediation

In international affairs mediation is a form of accommodation that involves an active search for a negotiated settlement to a conflict or disagreement between two or more states. Mediation specifically refers to having an agreed-upon impartial third party bring the rival disputants together and offer a settlement. The mediator may shuttle between the adversaries, call meetings, draw up an agenda, and propose solutions. In some instances the parties in disagreement may agree beforehand to accept the final solution of the mediator. The United Nations, particularly via the SECRETARY-GENERAL's office, has often been seen as a potential mediator, although usually with the full concurrence of the five PERMANENT MEMBERS OF THE SECURITY COUNCIL (P5). For example, the Secretary-General's office attempted to provide mediation in the SUEZ CRISIS of 1956, the IRAN HOSTAGE CRISIS (1979–80), and AFGHANISTAN during the 1980s. U.S. president JIMMY CARTER's activities bringing the Egyptians and Israelis together in the Camp David agreement in the late 1970s was an example of energetic mediation.

See also ARBITRATION, CHAPTER VI, CONCILIATION, CONFLICT RESOLUTION, ECONOMIC COMMUNITY OF WEST AFRICAN STATES, GOOD OFFICES, INDONESIA, ORGANIZATION OF AFRICAN UNITY, PEACEKEEPING.

membership

The United Nations is a universal international organization that, under Article 4 of its CHARTER, is open to all peace-loving states willing and capable of fulfilling their charter obligations. Founded in 1945 with 51 original members, the United Nations included 192 members by mid 2007. Switzerland and TIMOR-LESTE joined in 2002, Montenegro entered in 2006, after separation from Serbia, which in turn took over the seat formerly held by Serbia-Montenegro. The growth in UN membership—the product of COLD WAR politics, decolonization, and the desire for universality—transformed the operations and relationship of the PRINCIPAL ORGANS of the institution from those contemplated by the founding states. It also affected significantly internal UN politics and the agenda of the world body.

CHINA, the UNITED STATES, the Soviet Union, and the UNITED KINGDOM committed themselves in the MOSCOW DECLARATION of October 30, 1943, to the creation of a universal organization of "peace-loving states," defined later as those states that had declared war on the Axis powers by March 1, 1945. However, the Charter approved at the San Francisco Conference applied stipulations for membership. According to Article 4, members "must accept the obligations contained in the present Charter and, in the judgment of the Organization, are able and willing to carry out those obligations." The judgment of the organization was to be exercised by a GENERAL ASSEMBLY vote to admit the member on the recommendation of the SECURITY COUNCIL. Following the San Francisco meeting, the allies at the Postdam Conference expanded the pool of potential members by including states that had been neutral during the war, and that had followed a general policy of neutrality, even though the Charter obligated members to support mandatory ENFORCEMENT MEASURES.

As the cold war deepened in the late 1940s, the USSR and the United States invoked these conditions to block the admission of members. Only nine states, out of 31 applicants, became members between 1946 and 1955. [A listing of UN members and the years in which they achieved membership can be found in Appendix C.] A large pro-American majority in the original UN membership allowed the United States to muster the needed votes in the Security Council to block East European candidates that Washington saw as satellite communist regimes, not free to participate in the United Nations independent of Soviet control. Moscow, in turn, used its VETO 47 times prior to 1955 to keep states friendly to the United States from being admitted. The deadlock was resolved in December 1955 with what was known as a "package deal," admitting 16 nations from both the Soviet and Western blocs and thus keeping the VOTING balance little changed.

Separate from cold war politics, rapid decolonization in the 1950s and 1960s placed pressure on the organization for enlargement. Membership grew from 76 at the end of

1955 to 110 in 1962. Almost all of the new members came from the developing world. With their admission, virtually all membership requirements, other than statehood, were set aside. Many of the new members were geographically small and poor, and each often represented only a minute portion of the world's POPULATION. By the turn of the century, more than 30 members had populations under one million people. Among the smallest, Tuvalu, admitted in 2000, had a population of 10,000, and Nauru, admitted in 1999, had 11,000.

These states' ability to fulfill Charter obligations was suspect. The General Assembly, however, was willing to accept their applications if they maintained friendly relations with other states, fulfilled other international obligations that they had made, and were committed to using pacific settlement methods to resolve disputes. Worried that it had lost its majority in the world body, the United States raised some precautionary concerns about admitting states that could offer little to preserving world peace and security. At its urging, the Security Council in 1969 established a committee to consider the MINISTATE PROBLEM. The committee floated the idea of "associated" membership for some small states, but no change in membership requirements eventuated. After 1955 only a few "partitioned" states were initially barred from membership—East and West GERMANY, North and South Korea, and North and South Vietnam. The Germanies were admitted separately in 1973, and a unified Vietnam gained membership in 1977.

The growth in membership, coupled with the principle of sovereign equality that awarded an equal vote to each member, produced a new majority in the General Assembly, capable of passing sweeping RESOLUTIONS, but without the power or resources to fulfill new UN commitments. That majority also could, and did, shift the agenda of the world body from peace and security interests among the great powers to economic DEVELOPMENT concerns. The enlarged size of the world body also led to the formation of CAUCUS GROUPS, the expansion of membership on UN bodies like the ECONOMIC AND SOCIAL COUNCIL, and the proliferation of PROGRAMMES AND FUNDS for activities promoted by the new states.

The disintegration of communist regimes in Eastern Europe and of the Soviet Union itself occasioned a new surge in UN membership, raising interesting legal questions about successor states and continuing membership in the world body. When the Soviet Union dissolved in 1991, the RUSSIAN FEDERATION notified the UN SECRETARY-GENERAL that it intended to take the Soviet Union's seat on the Security Council as a PERMANENT MEMBER with the veto power. This announcement was endorsed by the other former Soviet republics, and there was no objection from members of either the Security Council or the General Assembly. Ukraine and Belarus were original UN members and thus no action needed to be taken on their membership. All of the other republics were required to apply under Article 4 for membership, and were admitted (with the exception of Georgia) on March 2, 1992. Georgia, locked in a civil war, was finally admitted the following July. In the case of Czechoslovakia (an original member of the United Nations), which ceased to exist on December 31, 1992, two successor states were admitted, the Czech Republic and the Slovak Federal Republic.

Another original UN member, the Socialist Federal Republic of Yugoslavia, was suspended from exercising its rights and privileges in the General Assembly during the 1990s for the violation of UN resolutions pertaining to the Balkans. In 1992, when several of the seceding parts of Yugoslavia were immediately admitted as new members of the United Nations, the Security Council decided that the remaining "Yugoslavia" (Serbia and Montenegro) could not assume the FORMER YUGOSLAVIA's seat and would have to apply for new membership under Article 4. Following the overthrow of President SLOBODAN MILOŠEVIĆ, the Republic of Yugoslavia was readmitted on November 1, 2000. In March 2002, leaders from the two remaining republics of the former Yugoslavia signed a PACT creating a weak confederation to be called Serbia and Montenegro. In 2006, Montenegro left the partnership and entered the United Nations as a sovereign new nation; Serbia retained the seat of the now vanished Yugoslavia.

See also APARTHEID; ARAB-ISRAELI DISPUTE; DISARMAMENT; SUSPENSION AND EXPULSION OF MEMBERS; GROUP OF 77; HAMMARSKJÖLD, DAG; HULL, CORDELL; HUMAN RIGHTS; KIM IL-SUNG; LEAGUE OF NATIONS, NATIONAL LIBERATION; NATION-STATE; NEW INTERNATIONAL ECONOMIC ORDER; NON-PERMANENT MEMBERS OF THE SECURITY COUNCIL; PASVOLSKY, LEO; ROOSEVELT, FRANKLIN D.; SCALE OF ASSESSMENTS; SOVEREIGNTY; STRUCTURE OF THE UNITED NATIONS; UNIVERSAL DECLARATION OF HUMAN RIGHTS, YALTA CONFERENCE.

Further Reading: Riggs, Robert E., and Jack C. Plano. *The United Nations. International Organization and World Politics.* Pacific Grove, Calif.: Brooks/Cole Publishing Company, 1988. Simma, Bruno, ed. *The Charter of the United Nations; A Commentary.* 2nd ed. New York: Oxford University Press, 2002. United Nations Web site: <www.un.org>.

memorandum of understanding (MOU)

A memorandum of understanding is a document establishing a legal agreement between two parties usually announcing a common purpose rather than a strict legal obligation. While it does not as a rule have the binding authority of a TREATY or contract, a memorandum of understanding is more formal than what is sometimes called a "gentleman's agreement," such as the informal agreement between the UNITED STATES and JAPAN in 1907 addressing immigration and racial prejudice. By the resultant so-called Gentlemen's Agreement, Japan was pressed not to issue passports to Japanese immigrants to the United States; in exchange, President Theodore Roosevelt agreed to exhort the schools in San Francisco not to segregate and discriminate against students of Japanese descent already in the country. A memorandum of understanding is considered more official than such an informal arrangement.

The two parties to a memorandum of understanding could be individuals within a country, businesses, a business and a government, two entities within a governmental agency, and more. In international relations, MOUs could be kept confidential (unlike treaties) and usually can go into effect without official ratification. They are also easier to revise and adapt than are treaties. An example of an MOU in international affairs was the Agreed Framework over Nuclear Weaponry in North Korea, negotiated between the United States and North Korea, October 21, 1994, in an attempt to defuse a crisis over North Korea's nuclear program. Examples within the UNITED NATIONS SYSTEM include a 1997 MOU between the CONVENTION ON BIO-LOGICAL DIVERSITY SECRETARIAT and the UNITED NATIONS CONFERENCE ON TRADE AND DEVELOPMENT (UNCTAD) to coordinate efforts to help turn protection of biodiversity into an asset for LEAST DEVELOPED COUNTRIES (LDCs), and the 1998 MOU between SECRETARY-GENERAL KOFI ANNAN and the government of SADDAM HUSSEIN by which IRAQ accepted all previous SECURITY COUNCIL RESOLUTIONS regarding the country.

See also OIL-FOR-FOOD SCANDAL.

Middle East   *See* AFGHANISTAN, ARAB-ISRAELI DISPUTE, GULF WAR, IRAN HOSTAGE CRISIS, IRAN-IRAQ WAR, MIDDLE EAST WAR OF 1967, MIDDLE EAST WAR OF 1973, SUEZ CRISIS, UNITED NATIONS INTERIM FORCE IN LEBANON, UN SECURITY COUNCIL RESOLUTION 242, UN SECURITY COUNCIL RESOLUTION 338.

Middle East War of 1967

The Middle East War of 1967 began June 5 and ended June 10. It was initiated by Israel's June 5, 1967, attack on EGYPT, IRAQ, Jordan, and Syria in which Israeli forces seized Egyptian territory in the Sinai Peninsula, Syrian territory in the Golan Heights, and the land designated by the 1947 UN partition plan for Palestine as the space for the Arab state in Palestine. There is contention as to whether Egyptian president GAMAL ABDUL NASSER's provocations (for example, his demand that the UN PEACEKEEPING force be removed from Egyptian territory) produced the regional environment for the war or whether Israel's "preemptive strikes" were a product of planned and intentioned belligerency; but what is not contested is that Israel's air force destroyed Egypt's surprised air force and through its territorial occupations tripled the size of 1949 Israel.

Two days after Israel initiated the conflict Jordan agreed to a UN SECURITY COUNCIL cease-fire RESOLUTION, as did Egypt on June 8 and Syria on June 9. Israel continued its attack and did not assent to the UN cease-fire until June 10. The cost to human life of this six-day engagement totaled 5,500 dead on the Israeli side, with Syria suffering 1,800 casualties, Jordan 3,100 casualties, and Egypt almost 18,000 casualties.

The short duration of the war precluded the Security Council from issuing any substantive resolutions. After Israel accepted the cease-fire, the Security Council became deadlocked; the Soviet Union condemned Israel's June 5th attacks on its neighbors and the UNITED STATES condemned subsequent breaches of the established cease-fire. The deadlock was tightened by American threats to VETO the proposals and resolutions emanating from non-permanent Security Council members.

This deadlock in the Security Council effectively handed the issue of the ARAB-ISRAELI DISPUTE over to the GENERAL ASSEMBLY. The futility of handling the conflict, however, spilled over into the larger UN organ and reduced its EMERGENCY SPECIAL SESSIONS into similarly ineffectual endeavors. A joint Soviet Union–Albania resolution was rejected as was an American resolution, a 17-member non-aligned resolution, and a 20-member Latin American resolution. Two resolutions, one a 26-member "humanitarian" resolution and the other a Pakistani resolution denouncing Israel's annexation of Jerusalem, were, however, passed overwhelmingly by the Assembly.

The most significant UN response to the war of 1967 was SECURITY COUNCIL RESOLUTION 242, which was adopted unanimously on November 22. This resolution was introduced by the UNITED KINGDOM and called for a withdrawal of Israel's forces from occupied territories, a termination of the states of belligerency, freedom of navigation and a settlement of the refugee problem. It also called on SECRETARY-GENERAL U THANT to designate a UN SPECIAL REPRESENTATIVE to the Middle East, later to be announced as GUNNAR JARRING.

Resolution 242 was accepted by Israel, Egypt, and Jordan but rejected by Syria. Resolution 242 signaled Jordan's and Egypt's long withheld acknowledgment of Israel's existence and, because it was premised on the idea of "land for peace," it formed one of the cornerstones for ensuing regional peace negotiations. As late as 2007 Arab nations, led by Saudi Arabia, offered peaceful relations with Israel in return for an Israeli pullback to its pre-1967 borders and the acceptance of the remaining terms of Resolution 242.

Further Reading: Ben-Ami, Shlomo. *Scars of War, Wounds of Peace: The Israeli-Arab Tragedy.* New York: Oxford University Press, 2005. Bickerton, Ian, and Carla Klausner. *A Concise History of the Arab-Israeli Conflict.* 4th ed. Upper Saddle River, N.J.: Prince Hall, 2005. Korn, David A. *Stalemate: The War of Attrition and Great Power Diplomacy in the Middle East, 1667–1970.* Boulder, Colo.: Westview Press, 1992. Meisler, Stanley. *United Nations: The First Fifty Years.* New York: Atlantic Monthly Press, 1995. Thant, U. *View from the UN.* Garden City, N.Y.: Doubleday, 1978.

— S. F. McMahon

Middle East War of 1973

October 6, 1973, was Yom Kippur, the Day of Atonement, the holiest day of the year for Jews. Syria and Egypt chose that date to attack Israel from two fronts. For three days the Arab coalition advanced; Egyptians crossed the Suez Canal, forced hundreds of Israeli troops to surrender, and recaptured land in the Sinai seized from them in the Israeli victory of 1967. Syria, in the north, nearly broke through Israeli defenses on the Golan Heights. During the first days of the war, neither the UNITED STATES nor the Soviet Union favored an immediate cease-fire RESOLUTION in the SECURITY COUNCIL. Egypt had established a line across the Suez Canal, and the Syrians were well into the Golan Heights, so neither was ready to halt its advance. Israel would not accept any cease-fire that left Arab enemies with gains on the ground. The tide of battle began to turn, however, as American assistance

flowed to Tel Aviv. On October 16, Egypt, now under duress in the field, made contact through diplomatic channels with U.S. secretary of state Henry Kissinger, who recommended a cease-fire in place to be followed by "talks under the aegis of the SECRETARY-GENERAL with a view to achieving a settlement in accordance with SECURITY COUNCIL RESOLUTION 242 in all of its parts." Two days later, the Soviet Union offered a draft Security Council resolution calling for (1) a cease-fire in place, (2) withdrawal of Israeli forces to borders implied in Resolution 242, and (3) the commencement of consultations on a peace agreement. In a Moscow meeting between Kissinger and Soviet leader Leonid Brezhnev a resolution was worked out, accepting the first and third of the Soviet proposals, but altering the second provision to a more equivocal call for the implementation of UN Resolution 242. The carefully calibrated compromise became UN SECURITY COUNCIL RESOLUTION 338 when it passed the Council at 12:50 A.M., October 22. But the attempted cease-fire did not hold, and on October 25 a message arrived from Egyptian president Anwar Sadat, who said that he would ask the United Nations, not the United States and the Soviet Union, to provide an international PEACEKEEPING force. The Security

UN Observer Force monitoring cease-fire in the Golan Heights (UNITED NATIONS/Y. NAGATA)

Council then passed Resolution 340, calling for a "return" to the original cease-fire lines as provided in Resolution 338, and for an augmentation of the international observers in the area to monitor compliance. Early Sunday morning, October 28, under the watchful eye of staff from the UNITED NATIONS TRUCE SUPERVISORY ORGANIZATION, Israeli and Egyptian military representatives faced one another in the Sinai. It was the first time in the 25 years of Israel's history that high-ranking officials from the two nations had met for direct talks.

See also ARAB-ISRAELI DISPUTE.

Further Reading: Bailey, Sydney D. *Four Arab-Israeli Wars and the Peace Process.* London: Macmillan, 1990. Bickerton, Ian, and Carla Klausner. *A Concise History of the Arab-Israeli Conflict.* 4th ed. Upper Saddle River, N.J.: Prentice Hall, 2005. Dayan, Moshe. *Breakthrough: A Personal Account of the Egypt-Israel Peace Negotiations.* New York: Knopf, 1981. Laqueur, Walter, and Barry Rubin. *The Israel-Arab Reader: A Documentary History of the Middle East Conflict.* New York: Penguin Books, 2000.

Migrant Workers Convention   *See* INTERNATIONAL CONVENTION ON THE PROTECTION OF THE RIGHT OF ALL MIGRANT WORKERS AND MEMBERS OF THEIR FAMILIES.

Military Staff Committee

Article 47 of the UN CHARTER created the Military Staff Committee to "advise and assist" the SECURITY COUNCIL when it decided to use force under CHAPTER VII's provisions for the maintenance of peace and security. Clearly meant to provide the United Nations with its own military capability, Article 47 joined Articles 42, 43, 45, and 46 in producing an extraordinary innovation over previous international organizations such as the LEAGUE OF NATIONS. The Military Staff Committee provisions also were a realization of the wartime allies' expectation that the great powers would have the responsibility and authority to act militarily through UN machinery to preserve peace in the postwar period. The drafters of the Charter also contemplated in Article 26 the committee playing a role in the development of UN DISARMAMENT programs. Yet, despite the intentions of the founders in 1945, the Military Staff Committee quickly fell into disuse, largely ignored after 1946.

The membership of the committee consists of the military chiefs of staff of the Security Council's PERMANENT MEMBERS or their representatives. Charged with "the strategic direction of any armed forces placed at the disposal of the Security Council," the committee became an early victim of the COLD WAR. The permanent members were unable to agree on the kind of forces required or the size each should contribute to the committee's command. Article 43 calls upon member states to negotiate agreements with the United Nations on the provision of national forces and military facilities to the world organization, but no agreements were ever achieved, leaving the Military Staff Committee without troops to command.

During the cold war it was unimaginable that either the UNITED STATES or the Soviet Union, both essential to the effective application of Chapter VII's military articles, would relinquish national control over their armed forces. Only in 1950, while the USSR was boycotting the Security Council, did the committee meet briefly to discuss the response to North Korea's invasion of South Korea. Once the Soviet delegate returned, however, with the weapon of the VETO, military action in the KOREAN WAR had to be taken by individual member states, authorized by pertinent Security Council RESOLUTIONS and the recommendations of the GENERAL ASSEMBLY acting in accordance with the UNITING FOR PEACE RESOLUTION. Even at the close of the cold war, the Security Council preferred to authorize member states to "use all means necessary" to repel the 1990 Iraqi invasion of Kuwait. Some discussions occurred in the committee at the time, but no effort then or in other operations during the 1990s was made to resuscitate the committee's role under the Charter.

In 1992 SECRETARY-GENERAL BOUTROS BOUTROS-GHALI alluded to the Military Staff Committee in his *AGENDA FOR PEACE,* a report to the UN membership on the new possibilities for the world body in the post–cold war era. He called upon the Security Council to negotiate agreements under Article 43 with NATION-STATES to place military forces at the disposal of the United Nations, and suggested a role in the use of those forces for the Committee—not in PEACEKEEPING operations, however, but in the application of ENFORCEMENT MEASURES against an aggressor. The Council members demonstrated no interest in Boutros-Ghali's recommendation, not even in giving the committee some capacity for contingency planning. And while Boutros-Ghali's successor, KOFI ANNAN—in his 1997 REFORM proposals—endorsed the previous Secretary-General's call for a UN rapid reaction force to meet immediate threats to the peace, he did not tie this recommendation to a revitalized Military Staff Committee. In stark contrast to expectations in 1945, Annan admitted to the gathering of world leaders at the 2000 MILLENNIUM SUMMIT that "We [the United Nations] are an organization without independent military capability," offering no recommendation to change that reality. The disregard with which the Military Staff Committee continued to be held was reflected in the summer of 2001 when its current members officially complained to the SECRETARIAT about a reallocation of its facilities. Its "changing room" at UN HEADQUARTERS, where its members changed from civilian clothes into their military uniforms prior to their regular meetings, had been converted into a "smoking lounge" for UN diplomats. As part of his recommendations to the 2005 WORLD SUMMIT, Annan proposed abolishing the committee, but the summit participants took no action, only requesting that the Security Council "consider the composition, mandate and working methods of the Military Staff Committee."

See also COLLECTIVE SECURITY, COLLECTIVE SELF-DEFENSE, GULF WAR, *IN LARGER FREEDOM*.

Further Reading: Annan, Kofi. Report of the Secretary-General: *In Larger Freedom: Towards Development, Security and Human Rights for All*. March 21, 2005, A/59/2005. Hill, Felicity. "The Military Staff Committee: A Possible Future Role in UN Peace Operations?" *Global Policy Forum*, 2001. Found at: <www.globalpolicy.org/security/peacekpg/reform/2001/msc.htm>. New Zealand Ministry of Foreign Affairs. *United Nations Handbook*. Wellington, N.Z.: Ministry of Foreign Affairs and Trade, published annually. Roberts, Adam, and Benedict Kingsbury, eds. *United Nations, Divided World: The UN's Roles in International Relations*. Oxford: Clarendon Press, 1993.

Millennium Development Goals

The MILLENNIUM SUMMIT convened in September, 2000—the GENERAL ASSEMBLY's opening session of the 21st century. Attended by the largest number of heads of state and government in history, the summit adopted several specific goals to achieve by 2015. The goals were originally proposed by SECRETARY-GENERAL KOFI ANNAN in his report to the Millennium Summit entitled: *We the Peoples: The Role of the United Nations in the 21st Century*. The Millennium Development Goals (MDGs), adopted by consensus in the General Assembly, were designed to be the centerpiece of the UN's efforts to promote DEVELOPMENT and reduce poverty in the early years of the new century. They represented the first time the international community had agreed upon explicit achievable targets. The MDGs were stated in a manner that applied to all nations, each country being required to achieve the goals within its territorial boundaries. They were based on the assumption that donor states would assist developing nations in the achievement of the targets. Indeed, the challenges addressed by the MDGs were clearly most critical for the developing world, exactly where the resources to address them were most deficient.

The summit agreed to eight goals to be achieved in all UN member states by 2015. They are listed below.

Goal 1: Eradicate extreme poverty and hunger
>   Target 1: Halve by 2015 the proportion of people whose income is less than $1 a day
>   Target 2: Halve by 2015 the proportion of people who suffer from hunger

Goal 2: Achieve universal primary education
>   Target 3: Ensure that by 2015 children everywhere, boys and girls alike, will be able to complete a full course of primary schooling

Goal 3: Promote gender equality and empower WOMEN
>   Target 4: Eliminate gender disparity in primary and secondary education, preferably by 2005, and to all levels of education no later than 2015

Goal 4: Reduce child mortality
>   Target 5: Reduce by two-thirds by 2015 the under-five mortality rate

Goal 5: Improve maternal health
>   Target 6: Reduce by three-quarters by 2015 the maternal mortality ratio

Goal 6: Combat HIV/AIDS, malaria and other diseases
>   Target 7: Have halted by 2015 and begun to reverse the spread of HIV/AIDS
>   Target 8: Have halted by 2015 and begun to reverse the incidence of malaria and other major diseases

Goal 7: Ensure environmental sustainability
>   Target 9: Integrate the principles of SUSTAINABLE DEVELOPMENT into country policies and programs and reverse the loss of environmental resources
>   Target 10: Halve by 2015 the proportion of people without sustainable access to safe drinking water
>   Target 11: By 2020, to have achieved a significant improvement in the lives of at least 100 million slum dwellers

Goal 8: Develop a Global Partnership for Development
>   Target 12: Develop further an open, rule-based, predictable, non-discriminatory trading and financial system [Includes a commitment to good governance, development, and poverty reduction—both nationally and internationally]
>   Target 13: Address the special needs of the LEAST DEVELOPED COUNTRIES [Includes: tariff and quota free access for LDC exports; enhanced program of debt relief for HIPC and cancellation of official bilateral debt; and more generous ODA (Official Development Assistance) for countries committed to poverty reduction]
>   Target 14: Address the special needs of landlocked countries and small island developing states (through the PROGRAMME of Action for the Sustainable Development of Small Island Developing States and the outcome of the 22nd SPECIAL SESSION OF THE GENERAL ASSEMBLY)
>   Target 15: Deal comprehensively with the debt problems of DEVELOPING COUNTRIES through national and international measures in order to make debt sustainable in the long-term
>   Target 16: In cooperation with DEVELOPING COUNTRIES, develop and implement strategies for decent and productive work for youth
>   Target 17: In cooperation with pharmaceutical companies, provide access to affordable, essential drugs in developing countries
>   Target 18: In cooperation with the private sector, make available the benefits of new technologies, especially information and communications

An annual report issued by the UN DEPARTMENT OF ECONOMIC AND SOCIAL AFFAIRS following the summit highlighted progress toward achieving the MDGs. Progress proved to be uneven, with the greatest difficulties in meeting the goals occurring in AFRICA. Asian states made slightly better progress. LATIN AMERICA, reflecting a higher level of development at the start of the century, was a region that generally moved toward a timely fulfillment of the goals. While progress was made in all regions, most observers expressed doubt that the targets could be achieved by 2015.

See also AGENDA FOR DEVELOPMENT; BOLTON, JOHN; BUSH, GEORGE W.; DECLARATION ON THE RIGHTS OF THE CHILD; DEVELOPMENT DECADES; ECONOMIC AND SOCIAL COUNCIL; ECONOMIC COMMISSION FOR AFRICA; ECONOMIC COMMISSION FOR LATIN AMERICA; ENVIRONMENT; HUMAN RIGHTS; *IN LARGER FREEDOM;* INTER-AGENCY COMMITTEE ON SUSTAINABLE DEVELOPMENT; INTERNATIONAL CONFERENCE ON POPULATION AND DEVELOPMENT; ISLAMIC DEVELOPMENT BANK; MILLENNIUM PROJECT; UNITED NATIONS CONFERENCE ON TRADE AND DEVELOPMENT; UNITED NATIONS DEVELOPMENT PROGRAMME; UNITED NATIONS ENVIRONMENT PROGRAMME; UNITED NATIONS VOLUNTEERS; WORLD BANK; WORLD CONFERENCES ON WOMEN; WORLD SUMMIT (2005).

Further Reading: Annan, Kofi. *We the Peoples: The Role of the United Nations in the 21st Century.* New York: United Nations, 2000. Moore, John Allphin, Jr., and Jerry Pubantz. *The New United Nations: International Organization in the 21st Century.* Upper Saddle River, N.J.: Prentice Hall, 2006. United Nations. *We the Peoples: The Millennium Summit Declaration,* New York: United Nations, 2000. UN Department of Economic and Social Affairs. *The Millennium Development Goals Report.* New York: United Nations, annually since 2001.

— *K. J. Grieb*

Millennium Project

SECRETARY-GENERAL KOFI ANNAN commissioned the UN Millennium Project in 2002, charging it with developing an explicit, feasible action plan for achieving the MILLENNIUM DEVELOPMENT GOALS announced at the MILLENNIUM SUMMIT in September 2000. The Millennium Project's independent advisory body was, in 2007, administered by a SECRETARIAT of about 20 specialists. Chaired from its inception by Columbia University professor Jeffrey Sachs, the Secretariat presented its comprehensive recommendations to the Secretary-General in January 2005. The report, entitled *Investing in Development: A Practical Plan to Achieve the Millennium Development Goals,* forwarded detailed proposals that had been developed by 10 thematic task forces. These task forces had made use of over 250 experts from the fields of science, policy-making, economics, and from the INTERNATIONAL MONETARY FUND (IMF), the WORLD BANK, other UN agen-

cies, relevant NON-GOVERNMENTAL ORGANIZATIONS (NGOs), and representatives from the private sector. The 10 themes represented in the task forces' work overlapped the MDG's eight goals to reduce poverty and hunger, boost WOMEN's rights, improve health, and stimulate DEVELOPMENT for the poorest of the world's people.

Among the project's broader recommendations were the following: (1) DEVELOPING COUNTRIES should set up definable goals and strategies to effect the MDGs; (2) strategies should stress increased public investment, official development assistance (ODA), and domestic resource mobilization; (3) implementation of strategies must be transparent and inclusive; (4) international donors should identify at least a dozen "fast-track" countries for immediate attention; (5) both developed and developing countries should concentrate on building expertise at the community level; (6) strategies should welcome and take advantage of regional initiatives; (7) donor nations should boost official direct assistance from the 2003 level of .25 percent to .44 percent by 2006, and .54 percent by 2015; (8) richer nations should open their markets to developing nations; (9) there should be increased funding for scientific research and development related to the MDGs; (10) the Secretary-General should coordinate the activities regarding the MDGs among all relevant UN organs.

The project's Secretariat continued to work through 2006 in an advisory role to support implementation of its proposals, concentrating on helping developing countries prepare national development strategies to achieve the MDGs. In early 2007 the UN Millennium Project Secretariat was integrated into the UNITED NATIONS DEVELOPMENT PROGRAMME (UNDP).

See also DEVELOPMENT DECADES; FIRST AND THIRD WORLDS; GLOBAL COMPACT.

Further Reading: Millennium Project Web site: <www.unmillenniumproject.org/>.

Millennium Summit

From September 6 to 8, 2000, the Millennium Summit took place in a special room adjacent to the delegates' entrance to UN HEADQUARTERS in New York City. Although other international meetings had counted sizable numbers of delegates, the Millennium Summit reputedly attracted the largest number of heads of state—approximately 150—to a single gathering in the history of the world. They included some 100 presidents, including the president of Switzerland, whose electorate would vote in March 2002 to become a UN member, about 50 other government leaders, three crown princes, and a few vice presidents, deputy prime ministers, and "high ranking officials," a category that included Palestinian leader YASSER ARAFAT.

Following the urgings of SECRETARY-GENERAL KOFI ANNAN, General Assembly Resolution 202 of December 17,

Heads of Government Security Council Meeting   (UN/DPI PHOTO BY MILTON GRANT)

1998, called for convening the summit as an integral part of—and to initiate—the 2000 Millennium Assembly of the United Nations. By Resolution 254 (March 15, 2000) the GENERAL ASSEMBLY decided that the summit would be composed of plenary sessions and four interactive roundtable sessions, each held simultaneously with a plenary meeting. The UN SECRETARIAT also planned for every participating head of state to be provided time to make an address to the full summit.

Criticized by the conservative American newspaper the *Washington Times* as "a non-event . . . [and] amusingly reminiscent of an elementary class photo," the summit nonetheless witnessed a total of 273 TREATY actions by participants, resulting in 187 signatures and 86 ratifications or ACCESSIONS. Among those treaties that attracted the most media attention was the CONVENTION on the Rights of the Child, which obtained nearly 60 nations' signatures—and two instant ratifications—for two new optional PROTOCOLS seeking to prevent children under 18 from being recruited into armed conflict, and to bring to an end the sale of children, child prostitution, and child pornography. Also receiving support were the CONVENTION ON THE ELIMINATION OF ALL FORMS OF DISCRIMINATION AGAINST WOMEN (57 signatures and one ratification for an optional protocol), the Rome Statute of the INTERNATIONAL CRIMINAL COURT (12 signatures and four ratifications), the International Convention for the Suppression of the Financing of TERRORISM (10 signatures and two ratifications), and the Convention on the Safety of UN Personnel (seven ratifications and accessions). Observing this prodigious activity, Mary Robinson, the UN HIGH COMMISSIONER FOR HUMAN RIGHTS (UNHCHR) mused that "ratification of [these] treaties will be the first indicator of State willingness to embrace a rights-based order in the new millennium." In fact, at the summit world leaders, in major speeches and in informal comments, reaffirmed their determination to take responsibility for the fate of the United Nations and to try to imbue the world organization with a sense of hope and action for the new millennium.

By the conclusion of the summit, the assembled nations, often with very divergent views about issues like DEVELOPMENT and HUMAN RIGHTS, overwhelmingly approved a DECLARATION of the world's hopes for the 21st century. They agreed on six "fundamental values" essential to international relations: freedom, equality, solidarity, tolerance, respect for nature, and a sense of shared responsibility. The declaration also set specific goals, including to halve by 2015 the number of people living on less than $1 a day or living in hunger or having no access to clean water, to assure that by 2015 all children complete primary school and that there is no gender inequality in education, to reduce maternal mortality by three-fourths and the deaths of children under five by two-thirds, to stop the spread of HIV/AIDS, malaria, and other infectious diseases, to achieve significant improvement in the lives of at least 100 million slum dwellers, to promote gender equality and the empowerment of WOMEN, to encourage the pharmaceutical industry to make essential drugs more widely available, and to provide the benefits of new technologies to all the world's peoples. These became the notable MILLENNIUM DEVELOPMENT GOALS (MDGs).

Some 8,000 delegates and 4,500 Secretariat employees attended the summit, and 5,500 journalists covered the gathering. About 185 meetings between government leaders took place at UN headquarters. Dozens more were held at hotels and diplomatic MISSIONS around New York City.

Among the most prominently reported of these collateral meetings or encounters were a high profile handshake between U.S. president BILL CLINTON and Cuban president Fidel Castro, and attendance by President Clinton and U.S. secretary of state Madeleine Albright at speeches delivered by Iranian president Mohammed Khatami. Secretary-General Kofi Annan, with the complicity of American and Iranian leaders, had worked with diligence to bring about the latter events. He worked up to the last minute to achieve contact between the two nations that had been locked in a pattern of distrust and diplomatic isolation since the Iranian Islamic Revolution began in 1979. The Secretary-General contacted Iranian and U.S. officials to urge the two presidents to sit through the other's major speech at the summit. President Clinton delayed talks with Vietnamese president Tran Duc Luong to remain for President Khatami's address, and Khatami arrived at the United Nations six hours earlier than scheduled to hear President Clinton. Annan also successfully encouraged Ms. Albright to attend President Khatami's address a day earlier at a UNESCO gathering.

Additionally, the various parties involved in the intractable Israeli-Palestinian negotiations, including President Clinton, Palestinian president Yasser Arafat, and Israeli prime minister Ehud Barak, met for extended discussions during the summit, and several leaders held side discussions and meetings over various other topics, including ballistic missile defense policies and all the challenges of globalization. Vladimir Putin's visit to the summit was his first trip to the UNITED STATES as Russian president, and he took the opportunity to call for a ban on militarization of space, offered to host international talks on halting an arms race in space, and engaged in one-on-one talks with a number of other world leaders.

Unfortunately, CONGO president Laurent Kabila was not in attendance, rendering any efforts at peace initiatives

in war-plagued central Africa futile, and sad news met the opening of the summit, when an armed mob of 1,000 people stormed a UN refugee operation in West Timor, INDONESIA, demolishing the office and beating to death three unarmed UN workers. Embattled Indonesian president Abdurrahman Wahid, attending the summit, promised to reassert control in West Timor, but his words could hardly placate UN employees, who had seen 193 peacekeepers and civilian workers killed in the line of duty since 1992.

Given this grisly news, it seemed appropriate that, on the eve of the summit, the Secretary-General received a set of recommendations regarding UN PEACEKEEPING policy that he was able to place before the meeting for extended discussion. The international panel making the recommendations was drawn from 10 nations, including the United States and Russia. Named for its chairman, Lakhdar Brahimi, a former foreign minister of Algeria, the BRAHIMI REPORT reflected Secretary-General Annan's new vision for a more robust UN peacekeeping approach, including enhanced funding for such operations, a new information-gathering and analysis office within the United Nations, an integrated task force for each peacekeeping mission—combining political analysis, military operations, civilian police, electoral assistance, aid to refugees and displaced people, finance, logistics, and public information—and streamlined procurement procedures. When the SECURITY COUNCIL met during the summit, the member nations' government leaders occupied the seats normally filled by appointed envoys, and the discussion focused on broadening the role of the Security Council in peacekeeping. The Brahimi Report was central to the discussion and, while there was some demur from Chinese president Jiang Zemin and President Putin regarding more vigorous and intrusive peacekeeping by the UN, a significant number of national leaders echoed President Clinton's and British prime minister Tony Blair's support for the broader view of Secretary-General Annan.

When the summit ended, sober questions remained about the practical effectiveness of such a meeting to address seriously the major problems that afflict the world. As DEPUTY SECRETARY-GENERAL LOUISE FRÉCHETTE opined, "It is easy to be cynical about these meetings and say, 'Oh, they produce nothing.' But many such gatherings have made a real difference in focusing political energy and raising political will." The summit was certainly a media event, covered each day on television and in the major newspapers of the world. "This has been the mother of all summits," said Singapore's UN representative Kishore Mahbubani. "It also confirmed that the UN provides the only viable setting to develop a village council for a global village." Secretary-General Kofi Annan may have had reason to call the Millennium Summit a "Defining Moment" for the world.

Further Reading: Crossette, Barbara. "UN Meeting Ends with Declaration of Common Values." *New York Times,* September 9, 2000. Farley, Maggie. "Millennium Summit at UN to Draw 150 Leaders." *Los Angeles Times,* September 4, 2000. Schaefer, Bret. "United Nations Non-Event." *Washington Times,* September 23, 2000. The Millennium Summit Web site: <www.un.org/millennium/summit.htm>. United Nations. *We the Peoples: The Millennium Summit Declaration.* New York: United Nations, 2000.

Milošević, Slobodan (1941–2006)

Slobodan Milošević was the most notorious figure in the civil wars that rocked the area then called Yugoslavia during the 1990s. Milošević was president of Serbia from 1989 to 1997, then from 1997 to 2000 president of the Federal Republic of Yugoslavia (the FORMER YUGOSLAVIA). He was, in addition, the leader of the Serbian Socialist Party from 1990. He was the dominating political figure in the Balkans during the last decade of the 20th century, when the area witnessed brutal violence and Yugoslavia fragmented into separate ethnic-based nations.

In May 1999, during the war in KOSOVO, the UN INTERNATIONAL CRIMINAL TRIBUNAL FOR THE FORMER YUGOSLAVIA (ICTY) indicted Milošević for crimes against humanity in Kosovo. Later the Court added charges of violations of the laws of war, breaches of the Geneva Conventions, and GENOCIDE for alleged actions in Croatia and BOSNIA. After a disputed election in October 2000, Milošević resigned. Within nine months of his leaving office security forces arrested him on domestic charges of corruption during his years in power. Soon he was extradited to The Hague, Netherlands. He remained in prison there for five years as his trial dragged on, dying on March 11, 2006, of a heart attack, within days of the conclusion of his legal ordeal.

Milošević was born in Pozarevac, Yugoslavia (now in Serbia), during the Axis occupation in World War II. Both of his parents committed suicide in the postwar period, when the multiethnic Slavic country was run by Marshal Josip Tito, a Communist and an anti-Soviet nationalist. He studied law at Belgrade University and became active in the Communist Party. He then became a businessman and banker, and traveled frequently to FRANCE and even New York, learning French and English. In 1984 he became the head of Belgrade's Communist Party. He developed an effective populist political style and championed Serb interests within the federation. He especially urged Serb control of the autonomous province of Kosovo, viewed as the ancient birth site of the Serb nation. He was elected president of Serbia in 1989, and disaffected leaders in Slovenia and Croatia, worried about Serb claims to dominance in the federation, declared independence in 1991. In 1992, Croat and Muslim POPULATIONs in Bosnia-Herzegovina seceded from Yugoslavia. A complex and vicious civil war followed. Milošević supported Serb rebels in Bosnia, who used ruthless techniques of ethnic cleansing of civilians to subdue opponents. Facing SANCTIONS from the West, Milošević agreed to the DAYTON PEACE ACCORDS in 1995 that effectively ended the Bosnian fighting. In 1997 he became president of what was left of Yugoslavia (Serbia—including the province of Kosovo—and Montenegro). The primarily Albanian population of Kosovo, opposed to rule from Belgrade, faced mounting violence from Milošević's forces who attempted to forcibly deport ethnic Albanians out of the region. In March 1999, NATO, responding to the consequent distress and bloodshed, commenced to bomb Serb military targets throughout the former Yugoslavia. In June, Milošević agreed to withdraw Yugoslav forces from Kosovo. NATO peacekeepers entered the area, soon to be followed by UN PEACEKEEPING forces. Meantime, domestic opponents mounted protests against the president and Montenegro sought autonomy within the federation and began to move toward independence. In the summer of 2000 Milošević called early elections, but when opposition candidates won the bulk of the votes and protests spilled into the streets, the president was forced to resign. He then was arrested and eventually sent to the Netherlands where he died in custody.

See also MEMBERSHIP, SUSPENSION AND EXPULSION OF MEMBERS, WAR CRIMES TRIBUNALS, UNITED NATIONS INTERIM ADMINISTRATION MISSION TO KOSOVO, UNITED NATIONS SPECIAL COMMITTEE ON THE BALKANS, UNITED NATIONS MISSION IN BOSNIA AND HERZEGOVINA, UNITED NATIONS PREVENTIVE DEPLOYMENT FORCE IN THE FORMER YUGOSLAV REPUBLIC OF MACEDONIA.

Further Reading: Cohen, Leonard J. *Serpent in the Bosom: The Rise and Fall of Slobodan Milošević.* Boulder, Colo.: Westview Press, 2002. Holbrooke, Richard. *To End a War.* New York: Random House, 1998. Meier, Viktor. *Yugoslavia: A History of Its Demise.* London: Routledge, 1999. Ramet, Sabrina P., and Vjeran Pavlakovic, eds. *Serbia since 1989: Politics and Society under Milošević and After.* Seattle: University of Washington Press, 2005. Rogel, Carole. *The Breakup of Yugoslavia and the War in Bosnia.* Westport, Conn.: Greenwood Press, 1998. Silber, Laura, and Allan Little. *Yugoslavia: Death of a Nation.* New York: Penguin Books, 1995. Udovicki, Jasminka, and James Ridgeway, eds. *Burn This House: The Making and Unmaking of Yugoslavia.* Durham, N.C.: Duke University Press, 2000.

ministate problem

Beginning in 1955 the United Nations experienced an extraordinary growth in MEMBERSHIP that increased the size of the world body from 60 member states in that year to 192 by 2008. Several of the new members came from the Third World and had achieved their statehood through the process of decolonization. Many of them were poor, weak, and small—both in territory and POPULATION. Yet, because each state has an equal vote in the United Nations, by the mid-1960s the new members constituted a working UN majority. This was worrisome to several of the great powers who argued that small states, which could not carry the international responsibilities imposed by UN RESOLUTIONS, should not be able to establish by their votes policy, commitments, and agenda for the organization.

In 1969, at American urging, the SECURITY COUNCIL established a Committee of Experts to look at the ministate problem, and to consider suggested changes such as weighted VOTING. The committee held 11 meetings and recommended that a CHARTER revision be considered to allow for "Associated" membership. The matter was put on the Council agenda in 1970, but discussions among Council members resulted in no proposed AMENDMENTS, nor in an effort to tighten membership requirements. Amending the Charter would have required GENERAL ASSEMBLY agreement, which would not have been possible given the large number of small member states. Efforts by the UNITED STATES to impose greater scrutiny in the Security Council on candidates for membership in order to determine if they could meet Article 4's requirement that a member be "able" to carry out its Charter obligations were overwhelmed by the majority's wish to admit as many states as possible. As of summer 2007, 42 of the UN's 192 members had populations under one million. When the 35 nations with one to four million people were added, these small states controlled 40 percent of the votes in the organization. The smallest of the ministate members was Tuvalu (10,000 people), followed by Nauru (11,000), Palau (19,000), Liechtenstein (32,000), and Monaco (33,000).

Under the "parliamentary" procedures of UN bodies, ministates, in addition to their votes in the PRINCIPAL ORGANS, could influence policy dramatically through their membership in CAUCUS GROUPS. Small nations that found it difficult to exert influence individually were more likely to agree on a common position representing an entire group. The most influential caucusing groups at the turn of the century were the NON-ALIGNED MOVEMENT and the GROUP OF 77, which represented the developing nations and exerted considerable influence because of the large number of such nations.

missions to the United Nations

Each member state maintains a mission at UN HEADQUARTERS in New York City. Several states also have missions at the UNITED NATIONS OFFICE IN GENEVA (UNOG), where many SPECIALIZED AGENCIES and some UN bodies have their headquarters. Diplomats from the nation's foreign service staff the mission, and representatives from other governmental ministries, including the military, are often stationed there. Their duty is to represent the concerns of their government in all UN bodies.

Missions vary in size according to the resources individual nations can budget to support them. Most missions include

from six to 18 diplomats, plus support staff, although they can range from one or two individuals to several hundred. Generally speaking, major industrialized nations maintain the larger missions at the United Nations. Individual governments determine the precise numbers and the ranks of mission personnel. Nations that maintain smaller missions often bring in additional employees on temporary assignment during busy periods, such as when the GENERAL ASSEMBLY is in session.

The head of the mission is the PERMANENT REPRESENTATIVE to the United Nations and holds the rank of ambassador. The ambassador functions as the principal representative of the nation to all UN bodies. The second-ranking individual is the deputy permanent representative. In most missions this deputy will have the rank of minister. Larger missions may include several individuals with the rank of ambassador and have the option of choosing to appoint an individual with that rank as their deputy permanent representative. Major nations often assign an individual with the rank of ambassador to represent them in the ECONOMIC AND SOCIAL COUNCIL (ECOSOC). Most missions are organized into political, economic, and social sections, each headed by a counselor to coordinate diplomatic activity in these areas. Members of the mission serve on the main committees of the General Assembly, ECOSOC and its commissions, UN subcommittees, and other bodies located at UN headquarters.

A country's representatives have a broad range of responsibilities. They deliver speeches describing their nation's viewpoints on the various issues being debated at the United Nations, and they submit reports from their nation to the various UN organs. They also engage in constant negotiations with representatives of other nations in order to shape the RESOLUTIONS and actions of each body, and to reach the necessary consensus upon which all UN bodies function. This requires expertise on a broad range of subjects, since it involves detailed negotiations regarding the content and precise phraseology of each resolution or statement. The members of the mission are also collectively responsible for reporting to their home governments on all aspects of the issues under consideration, the views of their counterparts from other nations, and the status of all proposals and actions at the United Nations.

These diplomats serve not only as representatives to the United Nations but also as representatives interacting on a daily basis with their counterparts from other governments. This feature of the post contrasts to that of ambassadors in individual nations, who interact with only a single government. It is this larger task that endows missions to the United Nations with special status and importance. Smaller nations conduct a major part of their diplomacy at the United Nations, since they often cannot afford to maintain embassies in all nations. The country's UN mission becomes its principal point of contact with the other nations of the world. The permanent representative in this case functions as the member state's representative to the world, and can be called upon to conduct negotiations unrelated to the United Nations. It is for this reason that UN representatives are often seasoned diplomats, and that, for many countries, the UN permanent representative is the second most important member of the nation's foreign service, after the foreign minister. It is not unusual for permanent representatives to ascend to the position of their country's foreign minister, or become a senior member of the government. Even in major nations, the post of permanent representative to the United Nations is considered a senior post outranking ambassadorial appointments to individual countries.

Further Reading: UN member state Web site: <www.un.org/members/index.html>.

— *K. J. Grieb*

Montreal Protocol on Substances that Deplete the Ozone Layer

The Montreal Protocol on Substances that Deplete the Ozone Layer included 191 parties as of February 2007. It supplemented the efforts of the VIENNA CONVENTION FOR THE PROTECTION OF THE OZONE LAYER by establishing the goal of using scientific knowledge and technical and economic tools to achieve total elimination of global emissions of ozone-depleting substances. The PROTOCOL was negotiated in 1987 and went into effect on January 1, 1989. For the first time, the international community set specific production and consumption limits on refrigerant and industrial substances known as chlorofluorocarbons (CFCs).

See also ENVIRONMENT, KYOTO PROTOCOL, UNITED NATIONS ENVIRONMENT PROGRAMME, UNITED NATIONS INDUSTRIAL DEVELOPMENT ORGANIZATION, WORLD METEOROLOGICAL ORGANIZATION.

Further Reading: UNEP Ozone Secretariat Web site: <www.ozone.unep.org/Treaties_and_Ratification/2B_montreal_protocol.asp>.

Moon agreement

The Agreement Governing Activities of States on the Moon and Other Celestial Bodies codified the principles relating to the moon laid out in the 1966 Treaty on the Exploration and Use of Outer Space. It was opened for signature on December 18, 1979, and went into force on July 11, 1984. The terms of the agreement were negotiated in the COMMITTEE ON THE PEACEFUL USES OF OUTER SPACE and its legal subcommittee. Excerpts from the agreement follow.

The States Parties to this Agreement,

Noting the achievements of States in the exploration and use of the moon and other celestial bodies,

Recognizing that the moon, as a natural satellite of the earth, has an important role to play in the exploration of outer space,

Determined to promote on the basis of equality the further development of co-operation among States in the exploration and use of the moon and other celestial bodies,

Desiring to prevent the moon from becoming an area of international conflict,

Bearing in mind the benefits which may be derived from the exploitation of the natural resources of the moon and other celestial bodies,

Recalling the TREATY on Principles Governing the Activities of States in the Exploration and Use of Outer Space, including the Moon and Other Celestial Bodies, the Agreement on the Rescue of Astronauts, the Return of Astronauts and the Return of Objects Launched into Outer Space, the CONVENTION on International Liability for Damage Caused by Space Objects, and the Convention on Registration of Objects Launched into Outer Space,

Taking into account the need to define and develop the provisions of these international instruments in relation to the moon and other celestial bodies, having regard to further progress in the exploration and use of outer space,

Have agreed on the following:

Article 1

1. The provisions of this Agreement relating to the moon shall also apply to other celestial bodies within the solar system, other than the earth, except in so far as specific legal norms enter into force with respect to any of these celestial bodies. . .

Article 2

All activities on the moon, including its exploration and use, shall be carried out in accordance with INTERNATIONAL LAW, in particular the CHARTER OF THE UNITED NATIONS, and taking into account the DECLARATION on Principles of International Law concerning Friendly Relations and Co-operation Among States in accordance with the Charter of the United Nations, adopted by the GENERAL ASSEMBLY on 24 October 1970, in the interests of maintaining international peace and security and promoting international co-operation and mutual understanding, and with due regard to the corresponding interests of all other States Parties.

Article 3

1. The moon shall be used by all States Parties exclusively for peaceful purposes.

2. Any threat or use of force or any other hostile act or threat of hostile act on the moon is prohibited. It is likewise prohibited to use the moon in order to commit any such act or to engage in any such threat in relation to the earth, the moon spacecraft, the personnel of spacecraft or man-made space objects.

3. States Parties shall not place in orbit around or other trajectory to or around the moon objects carrying nuclear WEAPONS or any other kinds of WEAPONS OF MASS DESTRUCTION or place or use such weapons on or in the moon.

4. The establishment of military bases, installations and fortifications, the testing of any type of weapons and the conduct of military manoeuvres on the moon shall be forbidden. The use of military personnel for scientific research or for any other peaceful purposes shall not be prohibited. The use of any equipment or facility necessary for peaceful exploration and use of the moon shall also not be prohibited.

Article 4

1. The exploration and use of the moon shall be the province of all mankind and shall be carried out for the benefit and in the interests of all countries, irrespective of their degree of economic or scientific DEVELOPMENT. Due regard shall be paid to the interests of present and future generations as well as to the need to promote higher standards of living and conditions of economic and social progress and development in accordance with the Charter of the United Nations.

2. States Parties shall be guided by the principle of co-operation and mutual assistance in all their activities concerning the exploration and use of the moon. International co-operation in pursuance of this Agreement should be as wide as possible and may take place on a multilateral basis, on a bilateral basis or through international intergovernmental organizations.

Article 5

1. States Parties shall inform the SECRETARY-GENERAL of the United Nations as well as the public and the international scientific community, to the greatest extent feasible and practicable, of their activities concerned with the exploration and use of the moon . . .

2. If a State Party becomes aware that another State Party plans to operate simultaneously in the same area of or in the same orbit around or trajectory to or around the moon, it shall promptly inform the other State of the timing of and plans for its own operations.

3. In carrying out activities under this Agreement, States Parties shall promptly inform the Secretary-General, as well as the public and the international scientific community, of any phenomena they discover in outer space, including the moon, which could endanger human life or health, as well as of any indication of organic life.

Article 6

1. There shall be freedom of scientific investigation on the moon by all States Parties without discrimination of any kind, on the basis of equality and in accordance with international law.

2. In carrying out scientific investigations and in furtherance of the provisions of this Agreement, the States Parties shall have the right to collect on and remove from the moon samples of its mineral and other substances. Such samples shall remain at the disposal of those States Parties which caused them to be collected and may be used by them for scientific purposes. States Parties shall have regard to the desirability of making a portion of such samples available to other interested States Parties and the international scientific community for scientific investigation. States Parties may in the course of scientific investigations also use mineral and other substances of the moon in quantities appropriate for the support of their missions . . .

Article 7

1. In exploring and using the moon, States Parties shall take measures to prevent the disruption of the existing balance of its ENVIRONMENT, whether by introducing adverse changes in that environment, by its harmful contamination through the introduction of extra-environmental matter or otherwise. States Parties shall also take measures to avoid harmfully affecting the environment of the earth through the introduction of extraterrestrial matter or otherwise . . .

Article 8

2 . . . States Parties may, in particular:

(a) Land their space objects on the moon and launch them from the moon;

(b) Place their personnel, space vehicles, equipment, facilities, stations and installations anywhere on or below the surface of the moon.

Personnel, space vehicles, equipment, facilities, stations and installations may move or be moved freely over or below the surface of the moon . . .

Article 9

1. States Parties may establish manned and unmanned stations on the moon. A State Party establishing a station shall use only that area which is required for the needs of the station and shall immediately inform the Secretary-General of the United Nations of the location and purposes of that station. Subsequently, at annual intervals that State shall likewise inform the Secretary-General whether the station continues in use and whether its purposes have changed . . .

Article 11

1. The moon and its natural resources are the common heritage of mankind, which finds its expression in the provisions of this Agreement and in particular in paragraph 5 of this article.

2. The moon is not subject to national appropriation by any claim of SOVEREIGNTY, by means of use or occupation, or by any other means.

3. Neither the surface nor the subsurface of the moon, nor any part thereof or natural resources in place, shall become property of any State, international intergovernmental or NON-GOVERNMENTAL ORGANIZATION, national

organization or non-governmental entity or of any natural person. The placement of personnel, space vehicles, equipment, facilities, stations and installations on or below the surface of the moon, including structures connected with its surface or subsurface, shall not create a right of ownership over the surface or the subsurface of the moon or any areas thereof. The foregoing provisions are without prejudice to the international regime referred to in paragraph 5 of this article . . .

Article 18

Ten years after the entry into force of this Agreement, the question of the review of the Agreement shall be included in the provisional agenda of the General Assembly of the United Nations in order to consider, in the light of past application of the Agreement, whether it requires revision. However, at any time after the Agreement has been in force for five years, the Secretary-General of the United Nations, as depository, shall, at the request of one third of the States Parties to the Agreement and with the concurrence of the majority of the States Parties, convene a conference of the States Parties to review this Agreement. A review conference shall also consider the question of the implementation of the provisions of article 11, paragraph 5, on the basis of the principle referred to in paragraph 1 of that article and taking into account in particular any relevant technological developments . . .

See also DISARMAMENT.

Further Reading: Moon agreement Web site: <www.unoosa. org/pdf/publications/STSPACE11E.pdf>.

A More Secure World: Our Shared Responsibilities *See* HIGH-LEVEL PANEL ON THREATS, CHALLENGES AND CHANGE.

Moscow Conference of Foreign Ministers

The first serious effort of the administration of U.S. president FRANKLIN ROOSEVELT to convince America's major allies—the Soviet Union and the United Kingdom—of the merits of a postwar international organization was made in Moscow in October 1943. At the Moscow Conference of Foreign Ministers, CORDELL HULL of the UNITED STATES, ANTHONY EDEN of Britain, V. I. Molotov of the USSR, and Foo Ping-sheung of CHINA signed the Moscow Declaration on General Security. The DECLARATION pledged continuing wartime cooperation "for the organization and maintenance of peace and security" and explicitly announced "the necessity of establishing at the earliest practicable date a general international organization."

U.S. secretary of state Hull had set up a special committee in the State Department to draw up a draft CHARTER for the new organization. By the fall of 1943 Roosevelt was prepared to have the secretary pursue the project with vigor. Hull traveled to Russia hoping to convince the Soviets that cooperation in a global organization would serve their interests. Up to that time JOSEPH STALIN's preference had been to ensure postwar military security by way of regional spheres of influence. Stalin's foreign minister, Vyacheslav Molotov, insisted on assurances from the American and British delegations that a western front in the war would be opened during 1944 and that the USSR would have freedom of action in Eastern Europe before the Soviets would consider the idea of a general international organization. Once agreement was reached on those matters, Stalin's government gave its support to the American proposal. Thus, of high significance at the Moscow conference was the commitment of the Soviet Union to the establishment of a world organization.

See also QUADRANT CONFERENCE, TEHERAN CONFERENCE.

Further Reading: Hoopes, Townsend, and Douglas Brinkley. *FDR and the Creation of the U.N.* New Haven, Conn.: Yale University Press, 1997. Moore, John Allphin, Jr., and Jerry Pubantz. *To Create a New World?: American Presidents and the United Nations.* New York: Peter Lang Publishers, 1999.

Moscow Declaration *See* MOSCOW CONFERENCE OF FOREIGN MINISTERS.

Mozambique *See* DEMOCRATIZATION, UNITED NATIONS OPERATION IN MOZAMBIQUE.

Multilateral Development Bank (MDB) *See* REGIONAL DEVELOPMENT BANKS.

Multilateral Financial Institution (MFI) *See* REGIONAL DEVELOPMENT BANKS.

Multilateral Investment Guarantee Agency (MIGA) *See* WORLD BANK.

multilateralism

Multilateralism is defined as the managing of relations among three or more states within the STRUCTURE of international institutions/organizations. Multilateralism is an organizing principle premised on the ideas of indivisibility (recognition that the effects of political and economic vicissitudes have the potential to spill over national boundaries), generalized principles of conduct (modifying behavior to conform to established norms), and diffuse reciprocity (more enduring expectation of benefits to be derived from coordination).

Multilateral activity has assumed the forms of congresses, conferences, and organizations and has addressed itself to myriad issues. Economic relations were and are the focus of such multilateral institutions as the BRET-TON WOODS agreements (establishing the INTERNATIONAL MONETARY FUND [IMF] and WORLD BANK) and the WORLD TRADE ORGANIZATION (WTO). Matters of peace and security have been the concern of the Concert of Europe, the LEAGUE OF NATIONS, and the United Nations. Other examples of multilateralism in practice are the European Union (EU), the Association of Southeast Asian Nations (ASEAN), and AFRICAN UNION (AU).

Conceptualizations and practices of multilateralism have changed and continue to change, and this morphing of multilateralism is often tied to REFORM OF THE UNITED NATIONS. Changing multilateralism and UN reform are connected because as the concept has proven malleable the practical deployment of the concept has increased. The conceptual definition has started to address demands for inclusion of non-state actors, particularly civil society organizations, and this is reflected practically in the UN's attempts to include NON-GOVERNMENTAL ORGANIZATIONS (NGOs) in its daily operations.

See also CARDOSO REPORT; HIGH-LEVEL PANEL ON THREATS, CHALLENGES, AND CHANGE; REGIONAL ORGANIZATIONS; UNITED NATIONS CONFERENCE ON INTERNATIONAL ORGANIZATION; WORLD CONFERENCES.

Further Reading: Cox, Robert. "Multilateralism and World Order." *Review of International Studies* 18, no. 2 (April 1992): 161–80. Knight, W. Andy. *Adapting the United Nations to a Post Modern Era: Lessons Learned.* London: Macmillan Press, 2000. Ruggie, John. *Multilateralism Matters: The Theory and Praxis of an Institutional Form.* New York: Columbia University Press, 1993.

— *S. F. McMahon*

N

Nairobi Conference *See* WORLD CONFERENCES ON WOMEN.

Namibia

Namibia, known until 1968 as South-West Africa, became a colony of GERMANY in 1884. With Germany's defeat in World War I, Namibia was classified under Article 22 of the LEAGUE OF NATIONS Covenant as a class "C" mandate. This designation enabled South Africa to administer Namibia as a part of its territory beginning in 1920. Directly contradicting the League's ideas of self-determination, the white government of South Africa required black Africans to carry passbooks and live on segregated reserves, took traditional lands, and appointed and dismissed black political leaders.

In 1946, the UN GENERAL ASSEMBLY (GA) passed Resolution 11(I) that encouraged all mandatory states to end their trusteeship agreements. Instead of complying, South Africa asked for UN consent to incorporate fully Namibia into its territory on grounds that the region lacked the economic and social DEVELOPMENT to achieve self-government. Refusing to consent, the GA recommended that Namibia be placed under the international TRUSTEESHIP SYSTEM (Res. 65[I]). South Africa indicated that it would not incorporate Namibia in 1947, though it would continue to apply the League of Nations mandate to it. By 1949, the government in Pretoria refused to submit reports on Namibia to the UN and formally imposed APARTHEID policies on the territory.

As a result, the GA requested that the INTERNATIONAL COURT OF JUSTICE (ICJ) issue an advisory opinion regarding the status of Namibia. In 1950, the ICJ ruled that Namibia was still under the 1920 international mandate, but that the UN could play a supervisory role over the territory. In 1956, the ICJ decided that the GA had the right to adopt RESOLUTIONS and hear petitions concerning Namibia. Yet, in a disappointing 1966 decision, the ICJ ruled by one vote that Ethiopia and Liberia (original League members) had no legal right to charge South Africa with violating the spirit of the League's mandate system through its indirect incorporation of Namibia. By 1971, the composition of the ICJ had changed, and the Court ruled that South Africa's occupation of Namibia was illegal. In 1973, Pretoria devised its own internal settlement, the Turnhalle system, which dispersed the majority black POPULATION into distinct, separate ethnic homelands. The UN rejected this proposal.

From the late 1960s until independence, the UN-recognized South-West Africa People's Organization (SWAPO) actively resisted South Africa's domination. The SWAPO army—the People's Liberation Army of Namibia (PLAN)—received arms from ANGOLA, Zambia, and the USSR. Reacting to PLAN, the South African Defense Force (SADF) stepped up its repression in northern Namibia, deployed special forces, drafted blacks into the SADF, and invaded Angola to destroy PLAN bases there. In response, Angola requested military support from Cuban troops. As violence in the region escalated in the late 1970s, the Western

Security-General Javier Pérez de Cuéllar in Namibia (UN/Photo 156770/M. Grant)

members on the SECURITY COUNCIL (the UNITED STATES, United Kingdom, FRANCE, West Germany, and Canada) tried to resolve the issue in order to avoid adopting SANCTIONS against South Africa. This Western Contact Group facilitated indirect talks between South Africa and SWAPO. The Security Council (SC) also passed two resolutions: Resolution 385 (1976), which called for a cease-fire and withdrawal of all forces to bases, and Resolution 435 (1978), which called for Namibia's independence and for free elections based on universal suffrage.

But COLD WAR politics enabled South Africa to stall Namibian independence for more than a decade. Fearing communism in Angola, the United States, during the 1980s, vetoed SC resolutions calling for mandatory sanctions on South Africa, refused to condemn SADF raids into neighboring states, and began to support militarily the UNITA (National Union for the Total Independence of Angola) rebels against the Angolan government (which was being aided by Cuban forces). Under U.S.-guided diplomatic efforts, South Africa's adherence to S/RES 385 and 435 was linked in negotiations to the removal of Cuban troops from Angola. By 1988, the high physical and monetary cost of war and

the changing relationship between the United States and the USSR led South Africa, Angola, and CUBA to sign the Geneva PROTOCOL and Tripartite Agreement. These set target dates for the implementation of S/RES 385 and 435, provided for a cease-fire, mandated South African and Cuban withdrawals from Namibia and Angola, and required free elections in Namibia.

The Security Council designed the UNITED NATIONS TRANSITIONAL ASSISTANCE GROUP (UNTAG) to assist with the independence process and to protect Namibians from South African biases during the transition. UNTAG educated and registered voters, oversaw the 1989 elections for a constituent assembly, assisted in Namibian refugee repatriation, and confirmed that troops were confined to bases. UNTAG contained 1,500 police monitors, 2,000 civilians, and 4,650 military personnel, though this last number was decreased from 7,500 at the final minute by the SC PERMANENT MEMBERS to save money. Delays prevented most UNTAG troops from being in Namibia on April 1, 1989, the official beginning date of the cease-fire. On that day, fighting broke out between SWAPO and SADF, almost derailing the peace settlement. Western pressure on South Africa and more rapid deployment of UNTAG forces helped the independence plan to continue. UNTAG declared the elections—in which 96 percent of eligible Namibians voted and SWAPO won a majority—to be free and fair. On March 21, 1990, Namibia achieved full independence and UNTAG left the country. Independent Namibia became a member of the UN in April 1990. With a total cost of $368 million, UNTAG was the first mission to go beyond traditional PEACEKEEPING by observing elections, educating voters, and assisting REFUGEES; its success served as a model for UN missions in Central America and CAMBODIA.

SWAPO continued to be the dominant political party in Namibia, winning elections into the new century. The country's first president, Sam Nujoma, served until 2005, when he was succeeded by his colleague and co-founder of SWAPO, Hifikepunye Pohamba. Namibia, with its population at about 2 million in 2005, experienced more stability than many sub-Saharan African countries, and had a respectable annual per capita income of about $7,300.

See also CHINA; COMMITTEE OF 24; CONGO; DEMOCRATIZATION; DEPARTMENT OF PEACEKEEPING OPERATIONS; ELECTION ASSISTANCE; EMERGENCY SPECIAL SESSIONS OF THE GENERAL ASSEMBLY; GOOD OFFICES; JAPAN; JURISDICTION OF THE UNITED NATIONS; ORGANIZATION OF AFRICAN UNITY; PÉREZ DE CUÉLLAR, JAVIER; SPECIAL SESSIONS OF THE GENERAL ASSEMBLY; WORLD PRESS FREEDOM DAY.

Further Reading: Cliffe, Lionel. *The Transition to Independence in Namibia.* Boulder, Colo.: Lynne Rienner, 1994. Dobbins, James, Seth G. Jones, Keith Crane, Andrew Rathmell, Brett Steele, and Richard Teltscbik. *The UN's Role in Nation-Building: From the Congo to Iraq.* Santa Monica, Calif.: RAND Corporation, 2004. Kaela, Laurent. *The Question of Namibia.* New York: St. Martin's, 1996. MacQueen, Norrie. *United Nations Peacekeeping in Africa since 1960.* London: Pearson Education Limited, 2002.

— A. S. Patterson

narcotic drugs *See* COMMISSION ON NARCOTIC DRUGS, OFFICE FOR DRUG CONTROL AND CRIME PREVENTION.

Nasser, Gamal Abdul *See* ARAB-ISRAELI DISPUTE, SUEZ CRISIS.

nation-building

Nation-building refers to purposeful efforts by an outside power or an international organization (such as the United Nations) to install or construct the institutions of national government and civil society in a dysfunctional state. Such states, frequently former colonial possessions in the Third World, often are victims of civil war, ethnic strife, or out-side interference from antagonistic neighbors. Nation-building efforts typically include military action from the outside force, and aid in establishing police functions, governance structures, educational institutions, and ethnic harmony. Sometimes nation-building is considered a pathway to establishing democratic societies with the rule of law, open elections, HUMAN RIGHTS, WOMEN's rights, and possibilities for full economic DEVELOPMENT. While the term may have pejorative overtones remindful of imperialism and colonialism, the international community has in recent years increasingly considered nation-building a necessary activity, and a reasonable extension of PEACEKEEPING and peacebuilding endeavors. Examples of UN nation-building include SECURITY COUNCIL–approved activities in AFGHANISTAN, the FORMER YUGOSLAVIA, KOSOVO, and TIMOR-LESTE. While the aforementioned examples were, as of 2008, not clearly successful, they were seen as more meritorious than similar UN nation-building initiatives in CONGO, SIERRA LEONE, and SOMALIA, where continuing or recent civil strife made governance difficult even with substantial outside support. Former SECRETARY-GENERAL KOFI ANNAN embraced features of nation-building in some of his REFORM proposals, seen, for example, in the recommendations of the HIGH-LEVEL PANEL ON THREATS, CHALLENGES AND CHANGE, which in December 2004 issued its report, *A More Secure World: Our Shared Responsibility.* When he campaigned for the U.S. presidency in 2000, GEORGE W. BUSH insisted that the UNITED STATES would no longer support nation-building, but following the terrorist attacks of September 11, 2001, and the occupation of Afghanistan, President Bush became a strong supporter of nation-building. With the invasion of IRAQ in 2003, the president also advocated U.S.-directed nation-building in that country, but by 2008 these efforts had not stemmed the internal violence and disorder in post–SADDAM HUSSEIN Iraq.

See also AGENDA FOR PEACE; ANGOLA; BOSNIA; BRAHIMI REPORT; CAMBODIA; CLINTON, WILLIAM JEFFERSON; DEMOCRATIZATION; ELECTION ASSISTANCE; NAMIBIA; RWANDA CRISIS; UNITED NATIONS INTERIM ADMINISTRATION IN KOSOVO; WORLD BANK.

Further Reading: Berdal, Mats, and Spyros Economides, eds. *United Nations Interventionism, 1991–2004.* Cambridge: Cambridge University Press, 2007. Boulden, Jane. *The United Nations Experience in Congo, Somalia, and Bosnia.* Westport, Conn.: Praeger Publishers, 2001. Dobbins, James, Seth G. Jones, Keith Crane, Andrew Rathmell, Brett Steele, and Richard Teltschik. *The UN's Role in Nation-Building: From the Congo to Iraq.* Santa Monica, Calif.: RAND Corporation, 2004.

nation-state

In the discourse of modern international affairs some countries or regions appear so dominant that the idea of co-equal nations often seems rather questionable, if not exceptional. Yet, according to Article 4 of the UN CHARTER, MEMBERSHIP in the United Nations is open to all "peace-loving" nation-states, and each is deemed equal with all other states in the world (Article 2).

A nation-state is an aggregation of citizens who share some important phenomena in common, including several or all of the following: language, history, culture, a sense of destiny, a shared religion and ethnicity, and, most importantly, a definable geographic area. Such a nation-state is considered sovereign in that its government has complete authority within its borders under INTERNATIONAL LAW and is not subject to any higher or external law or governance STRUCTURE.

The nation-state is the prevailing political entity of modern history. Although it is a fairly recent historical occurrence, it remained, at the commencement of the third millennium, the principal unit of international relations. Before the 16th century most people were congregated into either large empires—the Roman Empire and the Ottoman Empire give example—large religious entities—Christendom, for example—smaller entities, such as city-states (ancient Athens, Venice in the early modern period, Singapore in more recent times), or in ethnically based tribal entities (in the Americas, Africa, and in other localities). The nation-state developed in Europe from the 16th to the 19th centuries, first after the collapse of the Holy Roman Empire, and then, particularly with regard to GERMANY and Italy, in response to romantic notions of "national" solidarity.

The nation-state early claimed exclusive and monopolistic authority, or SOVEREIGNTY, within a defined territorial area. Early nation-states were ruled by monarchs, usually "absolute" monarchs, such as Louis XIV in 17th-century FRANCE. With this development came the emergence of modern international relations, which featured the interaction of sovereign nation-states in all variety of political and economic matters. However, it was the 19th century that witnessed the fusion of "nation" with "state," dovetailing the idea of cultural homogeneity with supreme political organization and political grouping of a peculiar people, considered the "nation." In a world of colonial powers, the desire of subjugated peoples for their own independent states produced the phenomenon of self-determination movements. U.S. president Woodrow Wilson promoted self-determination as a legal principle among the FOURTEEN POINTS proclaimed in 1918. Article 1 of the UN Charter enshrined self-determination of the nation-state as a fundamental principle of international law. In the 20th century, this notion of a people and a geographic area merged, in various parts of the world, with a notion of a homogeneous or fused nationality, ominously in "Palestine," "Israel," and the fractured parts of the FORMER YUGOSLAVIA, as well as elsewhere, threatening the survival of multinational states.

The 20th century witnessed the trend toward cooperation among nation-states in the formation of increasingly for-

mal international and supranational political organizations. Some of these were regional in nature, such as the European Union. The LEAGUE OF NATIONS, predecessor of the United Nations, was the first effort to create a "universal" international organization based on the rule of law and committed to limiting the anarchy of an international system made up of sovereign nation-states. Still, as the 21st century began, the nation-state was considered the most viable and vibrant force in international relations.

See also BOSNIA, COLLECTIVE SECURITY SYSTEM, EAST TIMOR DISPUTE, NATIONAL LIBERATION.

national liberation

Emancipating a "nation" from outside or unwanted control is the aim of national liberation movements. Thus "national liberation" refers to the efforts of a people—sometimes an ethnic group, sometimes a political party, sometimes a self-defined "nation"—to free itself from colonial control or from any kind of oppressive rule. Wars of national liberation, then, seek to realize independence from outside or repressive regimes. The American and French Revolutions have often been considered the first successful "national liberation movements" of modern history in that the first event led to the liberation of 13 colonies from an external, imperial overlord and during the French upheaval a "people" freed themselves from an internal, authoritarian monarchy. In the post–World War II period, national liberation struggles became a common phenomenon in world politics and succeeded in establishing the independence of many former colonial possessions in Africa and Asia. Examples spanned the second half of the 20th century and included ancient civilizations such as INDIA (gaining independence from the UNITED KINGDOM in 1947), former French colony Vietnam, where national liberation guerrillas fought first the French and then the Americans, and many other polities that became new states and usually were located in the geographic south.

In the 1950s and 1960s, newly liberated nations joined the United Nations, forming the majority of the UN's MEMBERSHIP. The UN CHARTER committed the world body to the principle of self-determination. At the San Francisco Conference in 1945 a DECLARATION on self-determination was included as Chapter V of the Charter. This reflected the Wilsonian principles embodied in the FOURTEEN POINTS. Typically the new states became members of the GROUP OF 77 (G-77) as well.

Other national liberation movements, usually of a leftist political persuasion, fought to overthrow their existing governments. For example, a Cuban rebellion, led by Fidel Castro, succeeded in ousting the existing, and pro-American, government in 1959 and assumed the Cuban membership in the United Nations. CUBA also became a supporter of other similarly motivated national liberation movements.

Some national liberation movements sought to resist and eliminate the "hegemonic" authority of international capitalism, fearing that external financial and commercial power eroded the national culture and subordinated the nation's peoples to the whim of distant financiers. CHINA, under the leadership of Mao Zedong, announced this intention at his Communist Party victory over the Chinese Republicans in 1949.

The Palestine Liberation Organization (PLO), founded in 1964, and led by YASSER ARAFAT from 1967 into the new century, represented several characteristics of national liberation movements. It sought to resist the intrusion of the State of Israel into territories the PLO believed belonged to the Palestinian people. In effect the PLO defined an Arab population as "Palestinian" by virtue of its residence in the geographic area of Palestine. It organized a political infrastructure and a military arm for guerrilla resistance and it led a diplomatic effort to convince the world of the legitimate national aspirations of the Palestinians. It signed international agreements and succeeded in receiving considerable support in the United Nations, particularly from nations recently successful in their own national liberation movements, achieving OBSERVER STATUS in the GENERAL ASSEMBLY in 1974. As of 2001, however, the PLO had not achieved its final aim—a completely independent NATION-STATE.

See also ARAB-ISRAELI DISPUTE, FIRST AND THIRD WORLDS, SPECIAL SESSIONS OF THE GENERAL ASSEMBLY, TERRORISM, TRUSTEESHIP COUNCIL.

Further Reading: Singh, Lalita Prasad. *India and Afro-Asian Independence: Liberation Diplomacy in the United Nations.* New Delhi: National Book Organization, 1993.

NBC-weapons *See* WEAPONS OF MASS DESTRUCTION.

New International Economic Order (NIEO)

The GROUP OF 77 developing nations (G-77) proposed the New International Economic Order in order to redress global trade imbalances and to REFORM the global trading system, which it perceived as unfair to the developing states. NIEO was proposed at the 1974 SPECIAL SESSION OF THE GENERAL ASSEMBLY on trade and DEVELOPMENT issues. The proposal described the principal problems facing the LESS DEVELOPED COUNTRIES (LDC) and concluded that only a drastic revision of global trading rules and processes would improve their lot. Beginning with the premise that the existing global trade rules had been developed by the major industrialized states before most of the developing nations received their independence, and, therefore, unfairly discriminated against LDC, the NIEO called for the replacement of the BRETTON WOODS system with a new set of rules to assure that the voices of developing nations were heard. G-77 nations

sought more favorable terms of trade for primary commodities, which, they contended, were not priced fairly in the existing trading system. They anticipated that a revaluation of trade effectively would constitute a global redistribution of wealth, their only hope to escape poverty.

The NIEO was based on the theory of "dependency," which contended that the industrialized nations had manipulated the rules to keep the developing nations permanently impoverished and "dependent" on developed nations for goods and support. The existing system underpriced primary commodities, produced mainly in impoverished developing countries, relative to manufactured goods produced principally in wealthy industrialized states. On the basis of the dependency theory Third World countries also pressed for a code of conduct for transnational corporations, and for the CHARTER OF THE ECONOMIC RIGHTS AND DUTIES OF STATES.

The NIEO was proposed at the point when the decolonization process had transformed the MEMBERSHIP of the United Nations, resulting in DEVELOPING COUNTRIES becoming a majority in the GENERAL ASSEMBLY. Newly independent states sought to blame their domestic ills on their former colonizers, and to use the forum of the United Nations to criticize world trade policies that seemed to undermine their development policies. Both the G-77 and the NON-ALIGNED MOVEMENT (NAM) promoted the NIEO as the preferred international trade regime in their strident economic debates with the developed states of the FIRST WORLD. Among other changes in the free trade system, these groups, in cooperation with the UNITED NATIONS CONFERENCE ON TRADE AND DEVELOPMENT (UNCTAD), sought, as part of the NIEO, the establishment of commodity agreements, the transfer of technology to the developing world, a generalized system of preferences on tariffs for LDC, support for the creation of producer cartels to negotiate with importing countries, and increased financial aid from the developed North to the South.

By the mid-1980s, as it became apparent that withholding production had little effect on most commodity prices, and that the key to development was foreign direct investment, developing nations modified their objectives considerably and adopted more pragmatic goals. These goals were still based on the NIEO ideology. The most radical ideas—the development of an entire new trading system and a global redistribution of wealth—were abandoned and replaced with calls for debt reduction and debt forgiveness. LDC objectives continued to include special trade privileges, such as tariff exemptions, protection for infant industries in developing nations, commodity price supports, development assistance, export diversification, and guaranteed access to the markets of industrialized countries (especially for LEAST DEVELOPED COUNTRIES). The G-77 and NAM remained committed to its goals, but were more practical and pragmatic in their proposed solutions to the problems of development.

See also DEVELOPMENT DECADES; ORGANIZATION OF AFRICAN UNITY; RIO DECLARATION; RUSSIAN FEDERATION; WALDHEIM, KURT.

Further Reading: Murphy, Craig. *The Emergence of the NIEO Ideology.* Boulder, Colo.: Westview Press, 1984. Sauvant, Karl P., and Hajo Hasenpflug. *The New International Economic Order: Confrontation or Cooperation between North and South.* Boulder, Colo.: Westview Press, 1977.

— *K. J. Grieb*

New Partnership for Africa's Development (NEPAD)

In July 2001 the 37th summit of the ORGANIZATION OF AFRICAN UNITY (OAU) formally adopted the NEPAD Strategic Framework Document, detailing several challenges to AFRICA and making recommendations to combat poverty, underdevelopment, and the marginalization of Africa in international relations. The heads of state of five African nations—Algeria, EGYPT, Nigeria, Senegal, and South Africa—received a mandate from the OAU to develop an integrated socioeconomic DEVELOPMENT framework, which became the document issued in 2001; it is described by its authors as "a vision and strategic framework for Africa's renewal." NEPAD's primary objectives are to eradicate poverty, help African countries, both individually and collectively, achieve SUSTAINABLE DEVELOPMENT and economic growth, end Africa's marginalization in the march of globalization, integrate Africa into the global economy, and empower WOMEN on the continent. Its stated "principles" include: (1) good governance, (2) African leadership and ownership of businesses, and full participation by all sectors of society in economic activities, (3) emphasizing the natural resources of the continent as well as the resourcefulness of Africa's people, (4) partnership among all Africans, (5) promoting regional and continental integration, (6) encouraging Africans' competitiveness in economic matters, (7) forging new international partnerships that reverse the unequal relationship between the FIRST WORLD and Africa, and (8) ensuring that all partnerships with NEPAD abide by the MILLENNIUM DEVELOPMENT GOALS (MDGs). These principles underlie NEPAD's Programme of Action, the priorities of which are to ensure peace and security in Africa; promote democracy and sound political, economic, and corporate governance; expand regional cooperation; enhance capacity building; and increase investment, particularly in agriculture, health, education, science and technology, and skills development. Additionally, the PROGRAMME stresses economic diversification and improving infrastructure, including information and communications technologies, transportation, and water and sanitation upgrading. Importantly, NEPAD seeks to increase direct foreign investment (including Official Direct Assistance—ODA) and

domestic savings and to further debt reduction. The Strategic Framework Document underscores that the aims of the programme depend on conflict prevention and the establishment of enduring peace on the continent. Specifically, NEPAD urges African nations to participate in a transparent "African Peer Review MECHANISM" to measure progress in achieving its aims as well as carrying out the MDGs. It also recommends coordinated positions by cooperating African nations on issues of market access, debt relief, and ODA REFORM. As of 2007, the highest authority of the NEPAD implementation authority was the Heads of State and Government of the AFRICAN UNION (AU). NEPAD's Implementation Committee reports to the AU Summit annually. A SECRETARIAT coordinates all implementation activities.

See also APPENDIX F (Declaration on the New Partnership for Africa's Development), ECONOMIC AND SOCIAL COUNCIL, ECONOMIC COMMISSION FOR AFRICA, JOINT INSPECTION UNIT, UNITED NATIONS CONFERENCES ON THE LEAST DEVELOPED COUNTRIES, UNITED NATIONS INDUSTRIAL DEVELOPMENT ORGANIZATION.

Further Reading: Adesina, Jimi O., Adebayo Olukoshi, and Yao Graham, eds. *Africa and Development Challenges in the New Millennium: The NEPAD Debate.* New York: Zed Books, 2006. Taylor, Ian. *NEPAD: Toward Africa's Development or Another False Start?* Boulder, Colo.: Lynne Rienner Publishers, 2005. NEPAD Web site: <www.nepad.org/2005/files/inbrief.php>. NEPAD Framework Document Web site: <www.nepad.org/2005/files/documents/inbrief.pdf>.

Non-Aligned Movement (NAM)

The Non-Aligned Movement is the most significant CAUCUS GROUP in the UNITED NATIONS SYSTEM. Along with the GROUP OF 77 (G-77), it represents the interests of the developing nations in global diplomacy and in all related meetings and conferences of the United Nations. Originally established to enable newly independent former colonies to resist COLD WAR pressures to affiliate with either of the two superpowers, the NAM is an informal organization without a regular SECRETARIAT. It was established at a summit conference in Belgrade, Yugoslavia, in 1961, after several preliminary meetings. The NAM, therefore, dates from the decade when the rapid end of colonialism brought independence to many African and Asian nations, most ruled by fragile governments in newly established nations. Though small when compared individually with the industrialized nations, these states collectively came to comprise the majority of the members of the United Nations. Since most could not afford diplomatic representation in all capitals, UN HEADQUARTERS became the focal point of their diplomacy and provided a means of contact with other nations and involvement in global affairs. In this situation, solidarity and joint action became essential to these nations.

The NAM was formed to coordinate cooperation in political affairs among developing nations. It sought to span the continental regional blocs. The number and diversity of its member nations in size, economies, characteristics, governments, and ideologies required it to adopt broad stances and focus on global issues. It led the movement against colonialism and APARTHEID, supported the Palestinian cause, and called for DEVELOPMENT assistance, while attempting to balance itself between the East and West blocs. While the later formation of the G-77 was intended to promote cooperation in economic matters, there was inevitably some overlap between the two groups; essentially they followed each other's lead and adopted identical stands, blurring the distinction between them. As of 2007 the NAM represented 118 member states and the Palestine Liberation Organization (a full member). The People's Republic of CHINA is not a member of the NAM, though it frequently associates itself with the group's positions.

NAM summits are held every three years, with foreign ministers' meetings in between (also held every three years so that the sessions fall midway between the summits). The summit host country becomes the leader and spokesman for the group and provides communications and coordination. The meetings (and hence the leadership) rotate among countries in Asia, AFRICA, and LATIN AMERICA, with negotiations determining the precise host.

With the end of the cold war, the NAM became the single most important political caucusing bloc at the United Nations, encompassing the largest grouping of member states. As the focus of global diplomacy shifted from the East-West cold war axis to the north-south axis based on economic well-being, the Non-Aligned Movement represented the developing and poor south in seeking concessions and assistance from the industrialized, developed North. Though critics often contended that there was no longer anyone to be non-aligned with, the NAM grew stronger and assumed a more pivotal role as the focus of global politics shifted to the North-South divide. The NAM deals with global issues, insisting that key questions be addressed in global rather than bilateral negotiations, and hence is particularly focused on and seeks prominence at the United Nations. Visitors to UN Headquarters frequently note posted schedules listing the NAM as one of the caucusing groups that meets most frequently.

The NAM stresses discussing all matters at the global level and making decisions at the United Nations by majority vote of all member states, where its members can effectively use their numbers to exert a greater influence. As a result it places particular priority on the GENERAL ASSEMBLY as a major decision-maker and regards the Assembly as the primary organ of the United Nations and the most representative body in the UN system. The NAM is the largest single VOTING bloc in the General Assembly, and its support, or at least forbearance, is required for any item to be adopted by

that body, thereby guaranteeing the nations that collectively command less economic and military power but comprise the majority of the world's inhabitants an opportunity to influence the result and to prevent the imposition of the will of the larger economic and military powers. From the point of view of the developing nations, this means the application of the democratic process to decision making to assure that the views of all members, large and small, are able to influence the outcome. The NAM is also prominent in WORLD CONFERENCES and throughout all bodies of the UN system. It influences the selection of the SECRETARY-GENERAL and presses for equitable geographical representation in all UN committees, commissions, bodies, and working groups, and in the UN staff. The NAM is also highly important in the SECURITY COUNCIL, since all developing states that are members of the council regard themselves as representatives of the Non-Aligned Movement, even more so than of their respective regions.

Nations comprising the NAM are strong supporters of the United Nations. They place particular emphasis on the economic and social portions of the UN CHARTER, seeing these issues as equal in importance to international peace and security. Consequently, the NAM seeks to give greater prominence to economic problems and assistance, and to promote greater representation of all nations and people in all UN bodies.

See also CONFERENCE ON DISARMAMENT, RWANDA CRISIS.

Further Reading: Jackson, Richard L. *The Non-aligned; The UN, and the Superpowers.* New York: Praeger, 1983. Kochler, Hans, ed. *The Principles of Non-Alignment.* London: Third World Center, 1982. Mortimore, Robert. *The Third World Coalition in International Politics.* Boulder, Colo.: Westview Press, 1984. NAM Web site: <www.nam.gov.za/>. NAM 2006 Summit Web site: <www.cubanoal.cu/ingles/index.html>.

— *K. J. Grieb*

non-governmental organization (NGO)

A non-governmental organization is any nonprofit, voluntary citizens' group which is organized on a local, national, or international level. Task-oriented and driven by people with a common interest, NGOs perform a variety of services and humanitarian functions, bring citizens' concerns to governments, monitor policies, and encourage political participation at the community level. They provide analysis and expertise, serve as early warning MECHANISMS, and help monitor and implement international agreements. Some are organized around specific issues, such as HUMAN RIGHTS, the ENVIRONMENT, or health. Their relationship with offices and agencies of the UNITED NATIONS SYSTEM differs depending on their goals, their venue, and their mandate.

The importance of working with and through NGOs as an integral part of UN information activities was recognized when the DEPARTMENT OF PUBLIC INFORMATION (DPI) was first established in 1946. The GENERAL ASSEMBLY, in its Resolution 13 (I), instructed DPI and its branch offices to "actively assist and encourage national information services, educational institutions and other governmental and non-governmental organizations of all kinds interested in spreading information about the United Nations. For this and other purposes, it should operate a fully equipped reference service, brief or supply lecturers, and make available its publications, documentary films, film strips, posters and other exhibits for use by these agencies and organizations."

Non-governmental organizations may be admitted into a mutually beneficial working relationship with the United Nations by attaining CONSULTATIVE STATUS with the ECONOMIC AND SOCIAL COUNCIL (ECOSOC). This status is based on Article 71 of the CHARTER of the United Nations and on ECOSOC Resolution 31 adopted in 1996. The rights and privileges enumerated in detail in that RESOLUTION enable qualifying organizations to make a contribution to the work programs and goals of the United Nations by serving as technical experts, advisers, and consultants to governments and the SECRETARIAT. Sometimes, as advocacy groups, they espouse UN themes, implementing plans of action, programs, and DECLARATIONS adopted by the United Nations. In concrete terms this entails their participation in ECOSOC and its various subsidiary bodies through attendance at these meetings, and also through oral interventions and written statements on agenda items of those bodies. In addition, organizations qualifying for General Category consultative status may propose new items for consideration by ECOSOC. Organizations granted such status are also invited to attend international conferences called by the United Nations, General Assembly SPECIAL SESSIONS, and other inter-governmental bodies. The participation modalities for NGOs are governed by the rules of procedure of those bodies. By June 2002, there were 2,143 NGOs in consultative status with the Economic and Social Council (ECOSOC). Several UN agencies require NGO consultation in their deliberative processes. The JOINT UNITED NATIONS PROGRAMME ON HIV/AIDS (UNAIDS) was the first UN body to welcome NGO representatives to full MEMBERSHIP on its coordinating board.

NGOs that have an informational component in their programs can become associated with the UN Department of Public Information. NGOs associated with DPI disseminate information about the United Nations to their MEMBERSHIP, thereby building knowledge of and support for the organization at the grassroots level. This dissemination includes publicizing UN activities around the world on such issues as peace and security, economic and social DEVELOPMENT, human rights, humanitarian affairs, and INTERNATIONAL LAW; and promoting UN observances and international years established by the General Assembly to focus world attention on important issues facing humanity. More than 1,500 NGOs

with strong information programs on issues of concern to the United Nations are associated with the Department of Public Information, giving the United Nations valuable links around the world.

NGOs at the United Nations have established several bodies to coordinate their activities, two of which deserve special mention. Congo, the CONFERENCE ON NON-GOVERNMENTAL ORGANIZATIONS IN CONSULTATIVE STATUS WITH THE ECONOMIC AND SOCIAL COUNCIL, serves as a representative voice of accredited NGOs before ECOSOC. Its aims are to ensure that they enjoy the fullest opportunities and appropriate facilities for performing their consultative functions, provide a forum on the consultative process, and convene meetings of member organizations to exchange views on matters of common interest. In addition, the DPI/NGO community elects an 18-member DPI/NGO Executive Committee to act in an advisory and liaison capacity to channel information and to represent the interests of NGOs associated with DPI. This committee is made up of NGOs from different parts of the world whose representatives in New York are elected for a period of two years. The Executive Committee collaborates with the DPI/NGO section on events, programs, and initiatives of mutual interest, including organization of the annual DPI/NGO conference.

See also AGENDA 21, APPENDIX F (Economic and Social Council Resolution 31 [1996] Excerpts: Consultative Relationship between the United Nations and Non-governmental Organizations; Declaration on the Elimination of Violence against Women), CARDOSO REPORT, COMMITTEE ON NON-GOVERNMENTAL ORGANIZATIONS, GLOBAL COMPACT, HIV/AIDS, INDIGENOUS PEOPLES, LAND MINES, SUBSIDIARITY, UNITED NATIONS CONFERENCE ON ENVIRONMENT AND DEVELOPMENT, UNITED NATIONS CONFERENCE ON THE HUMAN ENVIRONMENT, UNITED NATIONS DEVELOPMENT FUND FOR WOMEN.

Further Reading: Eizenstat, Stuart E. "Nongovernmental Organizations as the Fifth Estate." *Seton Hall Journal of Diplomacy and International Relations* 5, no. 2 (Summer–Fall 2004): 15–28. Foster, John W., and Anita Anand. *Whose World Is It Anyway? Civil Society, the United Nations and the Multilateral Future.* Bloomfield, Conn.: Kumarian Press, 1996. Fox, Jonathan A., and L. David Brown, eds. *The Struggle for Accountability: The World Bank, NGOs, and Grassroots Movements.* Cambridge, Mass.: MIT Press, 1998. Johns, Gary. "Relations with Nongovernmental Organizations: Lessons for the UN." *Seton Hall Journal of Diplomacy and International Relations* 5, no. 2 (Summer–Fall 2004): 51–65. Korey, William. *NGOs and the Universal Declaration of Human Rights.* New York: St. Martin's, 1998. Weiss, Thomas, and Leon Gordenker, eds. *NGOs, the UN and Global Governance.* Boulder, Colo.: Lynne Rienner, 1996. Panel of Eminent Persons on United Nations–Civil Society Relations. *We the Peoples: Civil Society, the United Nations and Global Governance.* New York:

United Nations, 2004, A/58/817. Scherl, Lea M. *Relationships and Partnerships among Governments, NGOs, CBOs and Indigenous Groups in the Context of the Convention to Combat Desertification and Drought.* Nairobi, Kenya: Environment Liaison Centre International, 1996. Willetts, Peter, ed. *The Conscience of the World: The Influence of Non-governmental Organizations in the UN System.* Washington, D.C.: Brookings Institution, 1996. Official NOG Web site: <www.un.org/dpi/ngosection/index.asp>.

— *A. I. Maximenko*

non-permanent members of the Security Council

Article 23, Chapter V, of the UN CHARTER, which deals with the MEMBERSHIP of the SECURITY COUNCIL, established five PERMANENT MEMBERS, with the rest of the members of the Council elected by the GENERAL ASSEMBLY. The elected members are referred to as non-permanent members. Originally there were six such members, but the number of non-permanent members increased to 10 by Charter amendment in 1965 in order to reflect the expanding membership of the United Nations. The non-permanent members are elected for two-year terms and are not eligible for immediate reelection, so that the membership of the Council rotates. Five non-permanent members are elected each year in the fall, at the start of the General Assembly's regular session. Non-permanent members have full powers except for the VETO, which is held only by the five permanent members.

In practice, the member states of the United Nations have agreed on a formula, established by a General Assembly RESOLUTION, to assure that the Security Council is proportionately representative of the overall UN membership. Under this formula, five of the non-permanent seats are allocated to Asia and Africa, which are combined to assure representation of the Middle East, which is not a geographical bloc and spans two continents. This formula allows the single Middle Eastern seat to alternate between Africa and Asia. Two seats are allocated to LATIN AMERICA, two more to the Western Europe and Other group (the Other category is used to add the Western democracies located outside Western Europe, and includes Canada, Australia, and New Zealand), and one to Eastern Europe. Each geographical bloc rotates its allocated Security Council seats among its members.

— *K. J. Grieb*

Non-Self-Governing Territories *See* TRUSTEESHIP COUNCIL.

North-South relations

The designations of *north* and *south* to indicate economic and political differences are roughly comparable to the terms *First World* and *Third World.* Typically, nations to the north of the equator are considered those that historically were in the forefront of economic and political modernization and benefited most by the industrial revolution. Also, colonial powers usually came from the Northern Hemisphere. Contrariwise, Third World nations and peoples are often located south of the equator, are economically underdeveloped, and often were those countries and areas colonized prior to the last half of the 20th century. Some observers employed the terms *developed* and *developing* to denote differences between nations of the North and nations of the South. Of course the designations North and South have not always been of precise accuracy in describing the complete configuration of the world's countries. Some DEVELOPING COUNTRIES, for example, are found north of the equator, and some developed nations in the south—Australia and New Zealand for example. Also, during the COLD WAR, the Soviet Union and its allies in the Soviet bloc were sometimes placed in yet another category, then called the "Second World."

Still, within the United Nations the idea of different interests and aims between the North and the South have come to have some procedural meaning. Particularly in the GENERAL ASSEMBLY and in the ECONOMIC AND SOCIAL COUNCIL, CAUCUS GROUPS have formed to promote common interests and highlight common concerns for the so-called South. For instance, the GROUP OF 77 was originally organized by Third World nations of the south as a caucus bloc. As of the turn of the century, the Group of 77 counted more than 100 countries and most of those were from the Southern Hemisphere. Several of the countries of the South also tended to be non-aligned during the cold war, neither joining Western alliances of northern states, nor Soviet-inspired alliances, such as the Warsaw PACT. These countries, becoming the majority from the 1960s on, often acted together as the largest bloc in UN organs, frequently frustrating the more powerful nations of the North who had instigated the United Nations in the 1940s, and who found it necessary to form their own caucus group, the West European and Other States bloc. During the 1970s, and with less vigor in later years, the countries of the South promoted in the United Nations the idea of a NEW INTERNATIONAL ECONOMIC ORDER in an attempt to create international measures to provide for a significant transfer of economic resources from the North to the South.

See also RIGHT TO DEVELOPMENT, SUSTAINABLE DEVELOPMENT.

Further Reading: Mortimore, Robert. *The Third World Coalition in International Politics.* Boulder, Colo.: Westview Press, 1984. United Nations Development Programme. *Human Development Report 2005: International Cooperation at a Crossroads: Aid, Trade and Security in an Unequal World.* New York: UNDP, 2005.

Nuclear Non-Proliferation Treaty (NPT)

The Nuclear Non-Proliferation Treaty (opened for signature on July 1, 1968) entered into force in 1970 after five years of negotiations at the EIGHTEEN NATION DISARMAMENT COMMITTEE (ENDC) in Geneva. The NPT, inspired by the "Irish Resolution" first introduced into the GENERAL ASSEMBLY in 1961, is often called the "cornerstone of the arms control nonproliferation regime." The PACT was the direct result of multilateral negotiations on a joint draft submitted by the UNITED STATES and the SOVIET UNION to the ENDC on August 24, 1967. The NPT's intention was to halt and then reverse the spread of independent control over nuclear weapons. It established in Article IX that only states that had acquired nuclear WEAPONS by January 1, 1967, qualified as Nuclear Weapons States (NWS). All others were considered Non-Nuclear Weapons States (NNWS) and any such state adhering to the NPT was obligated to subject its entire peaceful nuclear program to the INTERNATIONAL ATOMIC ENERGY AGENCY (IAEA) material accountancy safeguards, and to pledge only to acquire nuclear materials and equipment for peaceful purposes. Conversely the NWS, which happened to be the five PERMANENT MEMBERS of the SECURITY COUNCIL, pledged not to transfer nuclear weapons to any NNWS or to assist it in manufacturing or acquiring nuclear weapons (Article I); to share the benefits of the "Peaceful Atom" with any NNWS party to the TREATY (Articles IV and V); and to pledge to make a "good faith" effort to end the arms race at an "early date" (Article VI).

The treaty called for five-year review conferences (Article VIII) and for a conference 25 years from entry into force for the parties to the treaty to determine whether the treaty should be extended indefinitely or for a period or periods (Article X). That conference, held at the UN in 1995, reached a consensus that a majority of the parties wished to extend the NPT indefinitely. The parties also agreed to an "enhanced" review process to hold all parties "accountable" for their NPT obligations, and the NWS further committed to achieve a COMPREHENSIVE NUCLEAR TEST BAN TREATY (CTBT) by 1996. The CTBT was opened for signature on September 24, 1996. At the Sixth Review Conference in 2000, the NWS issued a statement that they were "unequivocally committed" to fulfilling "all" their obligations under the treaty. Most experts read this to be an affirmation of their agreement to reach a cessation of the nuclear arms race and universal DISARMAMENT, as called for in Article VI.

During the 1990s adherence to the NPT accelerated as long-time holdouts to the treaty like FRANCE (1992), CHINA (1992), and South Africa (1991) signed and ratified the treaty. By early 2007, only five states stood outside the treaty's framework: CUBA, INDIA, Pakistan, Israel, and North Korea (which announced its withdrawal in 2003 and conducted a successful nuclear weapons test in 2006). Nevertheless, the treaty had vociferous critics. Indian leaders decried the NPT as an unequal treaty that created an unfair caste system of nuclear haves and have-nots. Others, especially in NON-GOVERNMENTAL ORGANIZATIONS (NGOs) and among certain NNWS, objected to the "pace" with which the NWS had moved to eliminate their own weapons and specifically demanded a "date certain" for the abolition of *all* nuclear weapons. On the other hand, some NNWS party to the treaty either violated the NPT (IRAQ), attempted to withdraw from it (North Korea), or had their commitment to the treaty questioned by other parties (IRAN). Continuing pressure from non-nuclear weapons states, proliferation challenges brought by India's and Pakistan's nuclear weapons tests in 1998, and events outside the treaty's parameters, such as U.S. efforts to alter or abrogate the 1972 Anti-Ballistic Missile Treaty and doubts about the future of the CTBT lowered expectations for success at the Seventh NPT Review Conference in 2005.

See also CONFERENCE ON DISARMAMENT.

Further Reading: Bader, William. *The United States and the Spread of Nuclear Weapons*. New York: Pegasus, 1968. Larson, Thomas. *Disarmament and Soviet Policy, 1964–1968*. Englewood Cliffs, N.J.: Prentice Hall, 1969. United Nations. *The United Nations and Nuclear Non-Proliferation*. Volume 3 of the United Nations Bluebook Series. New York: United Nations Department of Public Information, 1995. *United Nations Treaty Series*. New York: United Nations. UN Disarmament Treaty Web site: <www.un.org/events/npt2005/npttreaty.html>.

— *S. L. Williams*

nuclear weapons

nuclear weapons *See* DISARMAMENT, WEAPONS OF MASS DESTRUCTION.

nuclear-weapons-free zones

Eliminating, or at least limiting, the possession and use of nuclear WEAPONS has long been a focus of international diplomacy and a frequent subject of debate and negotiations at the United Nations. In view of the COLD WAR stalemate that slowed negotiation of a NUCLEAR NON-PROLIFERATION TREATY in the 1950s and 1960s, regional groupings of states established nuclear-weapons-free zones (NFZ) as a more rapid means of limiting the possession and spread of nuclear weapons. NFZ treaties enabled non-nuclear WEAPONS states to take the initiative in nuclear DISARMAMENT. While limited to portions of the globe, these agreements were easier to reach because they were adopted in regions where none of the nuclear weapons states (that is, nations acknowledged to have nuclear weapons—the UNITED STATES, RUSSIAN FEDERATION, CHINA, the United Kingdom, and FRANCE—were located. Establishing such zones proved most difficult in regions that included states with the potential to develop their own nuclear weapons.

Nuclear-weapons-free zone treaties usually extend beyond pledges not to develop, manufacture, store, or station nuclear weapons on the territories of the signatory states. Some include test ban commitments, as well as PROTOCOLS requiring signatory nuclear weapons states to respect the provisions of the TREATY. Some of the accords contained provisions by which nuclear powers renounced the use of nuclear weapons or the threat to use them against nations in the zone.

The ANTARCTIC TREATY of 1959 was the first agreement to limit nuclear proliferation on a regional basis. Sponsored by the nuclear weapons states, the treaty banned the stationing or testing of nuclear weapons on the Antarctic continent. Signatories pledged to demilitarize Antarctica. Recognizing the fragile ENVIRONMENT of the region, the treaty also banned the dumping of radioactive wastes. Verification provisions included required inspections.

Latin American states negotiated the 1967 Treaty for the Prohibition of Nuclear Weapons in LATIN AMERICA and the Caribbean, more commonly referred to as the TREATY OF TLATLELOCO. All Latin American nations signed the treaty, but as of the turn of the century CUBA had not ratified it, the only signatory not to do so. Brazil and Argentina filed reservations, each fearing that the other would develop nuclear weapons, but they resolved their dispute in the 1990s. All five nuclear weapons states signed and ratified the appropriate protocols pledging to respect the zone.

Both Africa and the Middle East sought to develop similar agreements, but it proved far more difficult because of resistance from states in the region with the potential for nuclear weapons development. Although efforts to establish an NFZ in the Middle East continued, with annual RESOLUTIONS of the GENERAL ASSEMBLY calling for such action, the refusal of Israel to participate and its resistance to inspection prevented agreement. In response, several Arab nations declared that they could not sign a treaty regarding nuclear weapons until Israel did so. In the case of Africa, a similar problem existed with the APARTHEID regime in South Africa. The African Nuclear Weapons Free Zone Treaty, more commonly known as the TREATY OF PELINDABA, was signed finally in 1996, after the new government of South Africa renounced its right to construct nuclear weapons and announced that it had destroyed all of its nuclear stockpile. When the treaty was first proposed there was another sensitive issue that blocked agreement, namely, French nuclear tests then being conducted in the Sahara Desert. But the progress of decolonization, removing France from its former colonial possessions in north Africa, and the construction of other facilities in the Pacific (for French use) removed this impediment by the time of the treaty signing in 1996, and all five nuclear weapons states agreed to the treaty. Although all African nations signed the accord, ratifications came slowly, and in

2001 the total was still far short of the number necessary to bring it into force.

Efforts to promote a nuclear-weapons-free zone in Asia also proved problematic, due to the presence of two states, INDIA and Pakistan, that refused to renounce the possibility of developing nuclear weapons. The history of warfare between the two since gaining independence from Britain, and the ongoing tension in disputed KASHMIR province caused both to cite national security in preserving their options to develop such weapons. As a result, efforts in Asia moved from promoting a continent-wide NFZ to establishing smaller zones. The presence of the French nuclear-testing facilities in the South Pacific Islands raised particular problems but also strengthened regional resolve. The result was the South Pacific Nuclear Free Zone Treaty, more commonly known as the TREATY OF RAROTONGA, signed in 1985. This agreement encompassed the South Pacific islands states, Australia, and New Zealand. Four of the five nuclear weapons states signed the accord, with Russia not adhering. Although France signed the treaty, it later conducted a series of nuclear tests in the zone. Another Asian accord was added in 1995, with the signature of the Treaty of the Southeast Asia Nuclear Weapons Free Zone, more commonly known as the TREATY OF BANGKOK, which encompassed the members of the Association of South East Asian Nations (ASEAN). In the 1990s, after the collapse of the Soviet Union, the newly independent states of central Asia commenced negotiations on the establishment of a Central Asian nuclear free zone, although by early 2007 no treaty had resulted.

In addition to these agreements, related proposals included DECLARATIONS on the Indian Ocean as a zone of peace, and on the entire Southern Hemisphere as either a nuclear-weapons-free zone or a zone of peace. The General Assembly endorsed all such efforts and perennially included nuclear-weapons-free zones on its agenda.

See also FIRST COMMITTEE OF THE GENERAL ASSEMBLY, INTERNATIONAL ATOMIC ENERGY AGENCY.

Further Reading: Larsen, Jeffrey A., and Gregory J. Rattray, eds. *Arms Control: Toward the 21st Century.* Boulder, Colo.: Lynne Rienner, 1996. Stokke, Olav Schram, and Davor Vidas, eds. *Governing the Antarctic: The Effectiveness and Legitimacy of the Antarctic Treaty System.* New York: Cambridge University Press, 1996. Thakur, Ramesh. *Nuclear Weapons-Free Zones.* New York: St. Martin's, 1998. United Nations Department of Public Information. *The United Nations and Nuclear Non-Proliferation.* New York: United Nations Department of Public Information, 1995. ———. *The United Nations and Nuclear Non-Proliferation.* Volume III of the United Nations Bluebook Series. New York: United Nations Department of Public Information, 1995.

— K. J. Grieb

observer status

The United Nations is a universal international organization. As such, MEMBERSHIP is open only to NATION-STATES. However, in the search for universality, and in order to promote cooperation, the GENERAL ASSEMBLY (GA) and SECRETARY-GENERAL have created permanent "Observer Status" for various non-member states, regional groupings of states, and NATIONAL LIBERATION movements. Several SPECIALIZED AGENCIES have also been invited to participate in the Assembly's work, and each maintains a liaison office in New York City to facilitate that relationship. As of March 2007, there were 59 observers, 17 with MISSIONS at UN HEADQUARTERS, and 12 specialized agencies with liaison privileges. All had limited rights to participate in the work of the General Assembly and its subsidiary bodies. Without the privilege of VOTING, or submitting motions and RESOLUTIONS, observer groups could participate in debate and negotiation with member delegations, particularly when UN forums were discussing issues related to their interests and work.

The only reference in the UN CHARTER to non-members of the United Nations participating in UN activities is found in Article 35, which grants to non-member states the right to bring disputes to the attention of the General Assembly and the SECURITY COUNCIL. The creation of observer status, therefore, arose not from Charter provisions but from actions of the Assembly and the Secretary-General. States have achieved observer status by first sending a request to the Secretary-General, who in turn decided whether to grant the request. Using what came to be known as the "Vienna Formula," the Secretary-General granted observer status if the state had a high degree of diplomatic recognition and had a formal relationship with at least one specialized agency. In 2000, Switzerland and the Holy See maintained New York missions as non-member state observers. The former, however, achieved full membership in the United Nations in 2002.

Pursuant to Chapter VIII of the UN Charter, which recognizes the legitimacy of REGIONAL ORGANIZATIONS in the maintenance of peace and security and in cooperation with the United Nations, the General Assembly granted observer status to regional groupings of states at different points in its history. Observers include the ORGANIZATION OF AMERICAN STATES (Res. 253, October 16, 1948), the League of Arab States (Res., November 1, 1950), the AFRICAN UNION (Res. 475, August 15, 2002), succeeding the ORGANIZATION OF AFRICAN UNITY (OAU), which had held observer status since November 1965 (Res. 2011), the European Union (Res. 3208, November 11, 1974), the Organization of the Islamic Conference (Res. 3369, November 10, 1975), the Commonwealth SECRETARIAT (Res. 3, October 18, 1976), and the Asian-African Legal Consultative Committee (Res. 2, October 10, 1980). Other inter-governmental organizations that have observer status include the INTERNATIONAL SEABED AUTHORITY, the International Tribunal for the Law of the Sea, the International Union for the Conservation of

Nature and Natural Resources, the Caribbean Community, the African Development Bank, the Commonwealth of Independent States, the Council of Europe, the Andean Community, the ISLAMIC DEVELOPMENT BANK, the PERMANENT COURT OF ARBITRATION, the Agency for the Prohibition of nuclear weapons in LATIN AMERICA and the Caribbean, the Customs Cooperation Council, the Economic Community of Central African States, the Central American Integration System, the Association of Caribbean States, the Latin American Parliament, the Community of Portuguese-Speaking Countries, the Latin American Economic System, the International Criminal Police Organization, the Black Sea Economic Cooperation Organization, the Inter-American Development Bank, the Organization for Economic Cooperation and Development, the Organization for Security and Cooperation in Europe, the Pacific Islands Forum, the Community of Sahelo-Saharan States, and the African, Caribbean and Pacific Group of States.

The General Assembly granted observer status to national liberation movements during the 1970s and 1980s in an effort to encourage decolonization, and to endorse self-determination and statehood. The Assembly "invited" participation by groups in Africa and the Middle East, giving those movements international visibility and legitimacy. In November 1974 the Assembly recognized the Palestine Liberation Organization (PLO) as the "sole legitimate representative of the Palestinian people," and granted it observer status. In December of that year GA Resolution 3280 granted observer status automatically to all national liberation movements recognized by the Organization of African Unity. That led to UN approval of the African National Congress and the Pan-Africanist Congress as observers. Two years later the SOUTH WEST AFRICAN PEOPLE'S ORGANIZATION was added to the list of observers from the African continent. As of 2007, the PLO—by now identifying its UN observer delegation as "Palestine"—was the only remaining movement with a mission in New York.

See also ARAB-ISRAELI DISPUTE, COMMITTEE ON THE PEACEFUL USES OF OUTER SPACE, ENVIRONMENT, INTERNATIONAL ORGANIZATION ON MIGRATION, JAPAN, WORLD INTELLECTUAL PROPERTY ORGANIZATION.

Further Reading: Riggs, Robert E., and Jack C. Plano. *The United Nations: International Organization and World Politics.* Pacific Grove, Calif.: Brooks/Cole Publishing Co., 1988. Simma, Bruno, ed. *The Charter of the United Nations: A Commentary.* 2nd ed. New York: Oxford University Press, 2002. United Nations Protocol and Liaison Service. *Permanent Missions to the United Nations.* New York: United Nations, 2006.

Office for Drug Control and Crime Prevention (ODCCP) *See* OFFICE ON DRUGS AND CRIME.

Office for the Coordination of Humanitarian Affairs (OCHA)

The United Nations has always been involved in assisting and protecting the civilian victims of conflicts and natural disasters, but such activity increased in volume and complexity in the years following the COLD WAR. With the expansion of PEACEKEEPING operations to include protecting civilians and providing security for humanitarian aid workers, the United Nations found it necessary to develop new, multidimensional institutional MECHANISMS. Establishing the Department of Humanitarian Affairs (DHA) in 1992 represented the initial effort to deal with these complex humanitarian emergencies.

In 1998 DHA was expanded and renamed the Office for the Coordination of Humanitarian Affairs. It is headed by the UNDER SECRETARY-GENERAL (USG) for humanitarian affairs, who also serves as the UN's emergency relief coordinator. In the latter capacity the USG chairs the Inter-Agency Standing Committee that includes representatives of all major UN offices, SPECIALIZED AGENCIES involved in humanitarian relief, and appropriate major NON-GOVERNMENTAL ORGANIZATIONS (NGOs). On January 4, 2007, SECRETARY-GENERAL BAN KI-MOON appointed Sir John Holmes of GREAT BRITAIN to replace Jan Egeland of Norway as the OCHA director.

The mandate of OCHA is to coordinate all international humanitarian assistance, contingency planning, and field responses to unexpected emergencies. It also seeks to protect the HUMAN RIGHTS of victims. OCHA designates a UN humanitarian coordinator to oversee efforts in countries where a UN resident coordinator is not already present. The coordinator conducts negotiations with the government of the affected nation in order to assure access to the needy population and security and facilities for relief workers.

OCHA monitors humanitarian developments throughout the world, particularly in vulnerable countries, in order to provide early warning of crises. It also undertakes inter-agency coordination to set priorities for relief efforts and assistance, and tries to assure that major humanitarian issues are addressed even if they fall between the existing mandates of humanitarian organizations. OCHA provides information to help raise global consciousness about humanitarian issues and crises, and works with other agencies to coordinate inter-agency appeals to fund relief efforts. It also serves as a policy advocate for the victims of humanitarian emergencies before all UN bodies and organs.

OCHA's BUDGET for 2007 was nearly $160 million; $12.7 million of this sum came from the UN's regular budget and the rest from donations. The funds were used to support a staff of 1,064 people and to fulfill a work plan meant to assist more than 5.5 million individuals. Severe natural disasters in recent years, such as the 2004 Asian tsunami and earthquakes in KASHMIR and PAKISTAN, persuaded OCHA to issue "flash" appeals for additional resources in order to meet its needs. A portion of the contributions were placed in the Central Emergency Response Fund (CERF) to enable UN agencies to jump-start relief activities at the earliest possible moment following a disaster.

See also Afghanistan, Indonesia, Rwanda crisis, Secretariat, Senior Management Group, Somalia, Unified Task Force.

Further Reading: Inter-Agency Standing Committee. *Humanitarian Action in the 21st Century.* New York: United Nations, 2000. Weiss, Thomas G., and Cindy Collins. *Humanitarian Challenges and Intervention: World Politics and the Dilemmas of Help.* Boulder, Colo.: Westview Press, 1996. OCHA Web site: <http://ochaonline.un.org/>.

— *K. J. Grieb*

Office of Internal Oversight Services (OIOS)
See Secretariat.

Office of Legal Affairs (OLA)   *See* Secretariat.

Office of the High Commissioner for Human Rights (OHCHR)   *See* United Nations High Commissioner for Human Rights (UNHCHR).

Office of the United Nations Security Coordinator (UNSECOORD)   *See* Secretariat.

Office on Drugs and Crime (UNODC)

Founded in 1997 as the Office for Drug Control and Crime Prevention (ODCCP), UNODC was renamed on October 1, 2002. The office provides coordination in UN efforts to combat illicit drug trafficking and related organized crime activities. The Office on Drugs and Crime supervises the UN International Drug Control Programme (UNDCP) and the United Nations Centre for International Crime Prevention (CICP). It also coordinates the work of the Commission on Narcotic Drugs (CND), established in 1946 by the Economic and Social Council, the International Narcotics Control Board (INCB), a quasi-judicial body established by the 1961 Single Convention on Narcotic Drugs, and the UN Commission on Crime Prevention and Criminal Justice. UNODC has a worldwide staff of about 500. Its Headquarters is in Vienna and it has 21 field offices worldwide. It depends on voluntary contributions for its Budget. Its executive director in 2007 was Antonio Maria Costa of Italy, who also served as the Director-General of the United Nations Office at Vienna.

The UN International Drug Control Programme was founded in 1991. It provides educational materials about the dangers of drug abuse, works to strengthen international efforts against the production and trafficking of narcotic drugs, and encourages alternative Development projects and crop monitoring programs. UNDCP works closely with over 1,000 Non-Governmental Organizations to counter drug abuse around the world.

Shortly after its redesignation, UNODC faced anonymous charges of corruption concerning the travel expenditures of its senior crime prevention expert. This was followed by the resignation of a staff member who made public still further charges against the office, including the inappropriate hiring of the wife of a senior official in the Centre for International Crime Prevention, and retaliation for reporting malpractices to superiors. The Office of Internal Oversight Services (OIOS) was asked to investigate. While it cleared UNODC of corruption charges, it found serious management deficiencies and unethical behavior on the part of the crime prevention expert. OIOS recommended Reforms in how UNODC operates.

On a more positive note, UNODC led the public campaign to slow poppy cultivation in Afghanistan in 2004 and 2005. Mr. Costa met with Afghan president Hamid Karzai in January 2005 and the two agreed to issue arrest warrants for drug traffickers based on existing international Treaties. That year UNODC's ongoing efforts in Afghanistan produced the first reduction in poppy production since the 2001 toppling of the Taliban regime.

See also Declaration on the Elimination of Violence against Women, Global Compact, human trafficking, Programmes and Funds, United Nations Industrial Development Organization.

Further Reading: United Nations Office for Drug Control and Crime Prevention. *Global Report on Crime and Justice.* New York: Oxford University Press, 1999. United Nations Office for Drug Control and Crime Prevention. *World Drug Report 2000.* New York: Oxford University Press, 2001. UNODC Web site: <www.unodc.org/unodc/index.html>. UNDCP Web site: <www.undcp.org>.

Official Languages   *See* Languages, United Nations Official and Working.

Oil-for-Food scandal

On April 14, 1995, the UN Security Council established the Oil-for-Food Programme (Resolution 986) that allowed Iraq's government to export oil and to use the proceeds to import humanitarian supplies such as food and medicines. The program marked an easing of the Sanctions imposed on Iraq following the 1991 war to liberate Kuwait from Iraqi occupation. Those sanctions had imposed severe hardships on the Iraqi people while apparently not producing their desired goal: forcing the government of Saddam Hussein to comply with UN RESOLUTIONs on WEAPONS inspections and DISARMAMENT. Nearly twenty months later the program commenced with the sale of approximately $67 billion of oil. It lasted until November 2003, when all sanctions were lifted following the invasion of Iraq and the toppling of the Hussein regime. Oil sales and foreign purchases were transferred at that time to the Coalition Provisional Authority then governing Iraq.

In December 1999, U.S. deputy PERMANENT REPRESENTATIVE to the United Nations A. Peter Burleigh commended "the success of this important humanitarian effort, which has brought about a significant improvement in the living conditions for the civilian POPULATION in Iraq." Speaking to the Security Council, Mr. Burleigh also congratulated the Office of the Iraq Program established by UN SECRETARY-GENERAL KOFI ANNAN and its director, Mr. Annan's appointee, Benon Sevan, for their administration of the largest humanitarian assistance program in UN history. The UNITED STATES along with the other 14 members of the Security Council oversaw the work of Mr. Sevan and his colleagues through the 661 Committee, which approved all contracts associated with the sale of oil or the purchase of humanitarian supplies.

Under the program, Hussein's government was allowed to determine to whom the oil would be sold and from whom goods would be purchased. This was a concession to the Baghdad government. In the early 1990s the Security Council had offered to sell Iraqi oil through the United Nations in return for humanitarian materials in order to ease the impact of the sanctions. Saddam Hussein had refused the proposal. He insisted on Iraqi control. As a result of the concession, the plaudits for the program were tempered in early 2004 when an Iraqi newspaper published a list of people to whom Saddam had decided to sell oil vouchers for a profit. The list included politicians and business people in countries that were interested in lifting the sanctions at the earliest possible date. There was also some indication that Benon Sevan may have been a recipient of Hussein's largesse. Evidence soon became public that the Baghdad government was also demanding kickbacks from vendors supplying the humanitarian items for distribution in Iraq.

Driven in part by the extensive reporting of influential *New York Times* columnist William Safire, the U.S. Congress launched several committee investigations. Safire called the oil-for-food program a scam and a "great cash cow" that milked $10 billion into the pockets of contractors, traders, banks, and UN inspectors, including Kofi Annan's son, Kojo Annan, who had worked for the Swiss company Cotecna that handled many of the international transactions for the program. When he left the company he received a monthly stipend of $2,500 for many months afterward ostensibly as a "non-compete" payment. The allocations only ended in the opening month—April 2004—of the official investigation launched by his father.

The Secretary-General sought to demonstrate that the UN took the charges seriously, and would find the truth and punish anyone involved in wrongdoing. Sidestepping the normal UN investigative bodies (the OFFICE FOR INTERNAL OVERSIGHT SERVICES and the JOINT INSPECTIONS UNIT), Annan appointed PAUL A. VOLCKER, the former head of the U.S. Federal Reserve System and previous co-author of a significant UN REFORM report, to head an independent investigation. Volcker's primary targets were Benon Sevan, his deputy Teklay Afeworki, and Cotecna of Switzerland. Sevan denied all of the charges, noting that the program was monitored by the Security Council's 661 Committee. Therefore, representatives of all Council members, including the permanent members, had reviewed all transactions and given their approval through the six-year life of the program. He accused these states of overlooking dubious contracts because they benefited companies in their countries.

While Volcker's Independent Inquiry Committee, which consisted of himself, Richard Goldstone, and Mark Pieth—the latter two the former prosecutor for the WAR CRIMES TRIBUNALS for the FORMER YUGOSLAVIA and RWANDA and an expert on money-laundering in the Organization for Economic Cooperation and Development, respectively—continued its work, there were calls in the United States by prominent congressional members demanding that the Secretary-General resign. Others urged him to fire close allies in the UN bureaucracy. Neither step was Annan willing to take. Furthermore, Volcker's group refused to turn over its evidence to U.S. investigators, arguing there were no legal grounds for member states to demand the United Nations respond to domestic investigations.

Following two interim findings, Volcker's group publicly released its Final Report on September 7, 2005. The report found no reasonable evidence that the Secretary-General knew about Cotecna's payments to his son, or that he had in any way influenced the choice of the company handling the procurement process for the UN Iraq program. It concluded that Saddam Hussein's regime derived approximately $1.8 billion in illicit revenues from the Oil-for-Food Programme, far less than the $10.99 billion it procured through smuggling oil secretly across the country's borders. Volcker's committee criticized Annan and the Security Council for insufficient supervision of the program and of Mr. Sevan specifically. The committee members recommended the creation of a new UN post, that of Chief Operating Officer, to be nominated by the Security Council and approved by the GENERAL ASSEMBLY. Believing secretaries-general are traditionally selected for diplomatic and political reasons, the Volcker committee argued that operations such as the Oil-for-Food Programme require a CEO with administrative and managerial expertise and time to oversee their operation.

Secretary-General Annan fully accepted the committee's conclusions and recommendations. He acknowledged personal responsibility for the managerial shortcomings in the program. However, he noted that despite the program's failings, it had reversed the deteriorating food situation in Iraq, provided much needed medicines and other humanitarian supplies, and worked as a formula that kept a consensus in the Security Council favoring sanctions meant to keep Saddam from developing WEAPONS OF MASS DESTRUCTION. He also expressed some relief that the total losses in revenues to Hussein's government were approximately one-tenth of the amount first estimated by the U.S. government's General Accounting Office.

See also FRÉCHETTE, LOUISE; UNITED NATIONS ASSISTANCE MISSION FOR IRAQ.

Further Reading: Independent Inquiry Committee into the United Nations Oil-for-Food Programme. *The Management of the United Nations Oil-for-Food Programme: Volume 1—The Report of the Committee.* September 7, 2005. Available at <http://www.iic-offp.org/documents/Sept05/Mgmt_V1.pdf>. Malone, David M. *The International Struggle over Iraq: Politics in the UN Security Council, 1980–2005.* New York: Oxford University Press, 2006. Traub, James. *The Best Intentions: Kofi Annan and the UN in the Era of American World Power.* New York: Farrar, Straus and Giroux, 2006. Meyer, Jeffrey A., and Mark G. Califano. With an introduction by Paul A. Volcker. *Good Intentions Corrupted: The Oil for Food Scandal and the Threat to the U.N.* New York: United Nations Department of Public Information, 2006.

Open Skies Proposal   *See* QUANTICO MEETING.

optional clause

Often treaties, PROTOCOLS, and CONVENTIONS contain provisions that require specific assent by NATION-STATES before those states are subject to them, even if they are signatories to the agreement as a whole. This is often a useful device to attract support for the full agreement, while subjecting the state to a controversial provision in the convention only if it has specifically agreed to it. The most famous is Optional Clause 36 (paragraphs 2 and 3) in the STATUTE OF THE INTERNATIONAL COURT OF JUSTICE. Countries that have accepted this provision allow the Court to adjudicate legal disputes concerning (1) the interpretation of a TREATY, (2) any question of INTERNATIONAL LAW, (3) the existence of any fact that may constitute a breach of an international obligation, or (4) the nature and extent of a reparation for such a breach. In the case of the 1965 International Convention on the Elimination of all Forms of Racial Discrimination, Article 14 is an optional clause under which states agree to allow their citizens to submit complaints about domestic racial discrimination to the COMMITTEE ON THE ELIMINATION OF RACIAL DISCRIMINATION (CERD) for investigation and discussion.

See also COMPULSORY JURISDICTION.

Organisation for the Prohibition of Chemical Weapons (OPCW)

The 1997 Chemical Weapons Convention (CWC) established the Organisation for the Prohibition of Chemical Weapons in The Hague as its implementing institution. With more than 500 staff, including 200 inspectors, OPCW conducted 2,900 inspections at nearly 1,080 production and storage sites in 79 countries during its first 10 years of operation. Headed first by José Bustani, OPCW's Conference of the State Parties (COP) appointed Rogelio Pfirter of Argentina as DIRECTOR-GENERAL on July 25, 2002, after Bustani was removed from office under pressure from the UNITED STATES, which charged him with poor financial management of the organization. Pfirter was reappointed to a second term of five years in November 2005. In addition to inspections, the OPCW promotes ACCESSION to the CONVENTION, which had 182 signatories as of May 2007.

The Conference of the State Parties meets annually. As required by the CWC, the Conference of State Parties convened a review conference in April 2003, and it scheduled another for April 2008. The COP elects the Executive Council, consisting of 41 states, each serving a two-year term. Seats are allocated on an equitable geographical basis, with Africa having nine seats, three of which must go to countries with the most significant chemical industry. Asia has nine seats with four assigned again to states with extensive chemical facilities. For Eastern Europe the equivalent seats are five and one, for LATIN AMERICA and the Caribbean, seven and three, for Western European and Other States, 10 and five, and an additional seat alternates between Asia and Latin America, including the Caribbean. The Council supervises the day-to-day activities of OPCW, and has policy responsibilities between meetings of the COP.

The director-general oversees the Technical SECRETARIAT and the Scientific Advisory Board. The first of these carries out the verification provisions of the Chemical Weapons Convention, and it is assigned responsibility for aiding any state that becomes a victim of chemical warfare. Given the dual-use character of chemical agents, the Technical Secretariat must be staffed with highly trained chemists, munitions experts, and industrial specialists. The OPCW puts together teams, averaging 14 members, of these experts to inspect military and civilian facilities in the member states. The places and materials to be inspected are selected based on the DECLARATION reports each signatory is required to submit regularly to OPCW. The convention not only prohibits the manufacture and possession of CHEMICAL WEAPONS but also requires the destruction of any existing stockpiles. The CWC provides a timetable spanning 10 years during which a country must eliminate these WEAPONS. The verification teams monitor this process, and they may carry out unscheduled "challenge" inspections when other members to the agreement believe a state is violating the convention. The Scientific Advisory Board consists of independent experts and provides specialized scientific and technological recommendations to the organization.

The OPCW has had difficulty convincing states to submit, in timely fashion, their reports on chemical agents in their possession and on plans for weapons destruction. In some cases, such as that of the RUSSIAN FEDERATION, states have declared a willingness to destroy their chemical weapons but have pleaded a lack of funds for the project. States also have been slow to establish a national authority, as required by the convention, to serve as the liaison with the organization in The Hague. It has also been difficult to obtain financial contributions from parties to the TREATY, as required by the CWC. With many states in arrears, OPCW has had a chronic budgetary shortfall, limiting its work. More ominously, several CWC member states have reinterpreted the treaty provisions in an effort to limit its impact on their military programs, and some suspected chemical weapons states have refused to join the treaty, including North Korea, Egypt, Israel, and Syria. In addition to these, in 2007 IRAQ, Libya, Lebanon, ANGOLA, and SOMALIA were the only remaining non-signatory states among UN members.

See also APPENDIX F (Security Council Resolution 1540), DEPARTMENT FOR DISARMAMENT AFFAIRS, DISARMAMENT, REMEMBRANCE DAY FOR THE VICTIMS OF CHEMICAL WARFARE.

Further Reading: Moodie, Michael, and Javed Ali, eds. *Synthesis 2000: A Year in Review.* The Hague: Organization for the Prohibition of Chemical Weapons, 2001. Organization for the Prohibition of Chemical Weapons. *Chemical Disarmament: Basic Facts.* 1999 Edition. The Hague: Organization for the Prohibition of Chemical Weapons, 2000. Tucker, Jonathan B., ed. *The Chemical Weapons Convention: Implementation Challenges and Solutions.* Monterey, Calif.: Monterey Institute Studies' Center for Nonproliferation Studies, 2001. Weapons of Mass Destruction Commission. *Weapons of Terror: Freeing the World of Nuclear, Biological and Chemical Arms.* Stockholm: Weapons of Mass Destruction Commission, 2006. OPCW Web site: <www.opcw.org>.

Organization of African Unity (OAU)

In 1963, the leaders of independent African states formed the Organization of African Unity (OAU). The OAU sought to facilitate African solidarity and to encourage economic DEVELOPMENT and peace and security on the continent. The OAU secretary-general worked closely with the UN SECRETARY-GENERAL on numerous issues, and OAU members played an influential role in the United Nations. Closely linked to the UN CHARTER, OAU principles included promotion of sovereign equality, noninterference in the internal affairs of states, respect for SOVEREIGNTY and territorial integrity, peaceful settlement of disputes, and the end of colonialism in Africa. At its formation, the OAU agreed

that the UN Charter takes precedence over any OAU policy document.

The 53 OAU members gained their strength in the UN from the fact that they comprised approximately one-third of the UN MEMBERSHIP. OAU members lobbied the UN to pay attention to issues of African economic and social DEVELOPMENT and were particularly active in SPECIALIZED AGENCIES such as UNESCO (UNITED NATIONS EDUCATIONAL, SCIENTIFIC AND CULTURAL ORGANIZATION), WHO (WORLD HEALTH ORGANIZATION), UNEP (UNITED NATIONS ENVIRONMENT PROGRAMME), UNCTAD (UNITED NATIONS CONFERENCE ON TRADE AND DEVELOPMENT), UNHCR (UNITED NATIONS HIGH COMMISSIONER FOR REFUGEES), and UNDP (UNITED NATIONS DEVELOPMENT PROGRAMME). OAU members were instrumental in the 1974 GENERAL ASSEMBLY discussions of a NEW INTERNATIONAL ECONOMIC ORDER (NIEO), the development of UNCTAD, and the creation of the first DEVELOPMENT DECADE (A/16/1710; A/17/1785). In 1974, OAU members helped pass a RESOLUTION to prohibit South African participation in the General Assembly.

The OAU founders established commissions for MEDIATION, CONCILIATION, and ARBITRATION that dealt with decolonization, border disputes, interstate conflicts, and internal conflicts. The OAU carried out two significant PEACEKEEPING missions: one in 1963 to observe the conflict between Algeria and Morocco, and one in 1981 during the Chad conflict. The OAU also worked with the United Nations and other subregional organizations such as the ECONOMIC COMMUNITY OF WEST AFRICAN STATES (ECOWAS) and the Southern African Development Community (SADC) to promote peace in Liberia, the Democratic Republic of CONGO, Rwanda, and NAMIBIA. Cooperation between the UN and the OAU took the form of consultation, diplomatic support, and co-deployment of UN/OAU monitoring missions. In Western Sahara, the UN Secretary-General and the OAU used their GOOD OFFICES to facilitate a cease-fire and settlement agreement in 1988 and to set up a commission to determine eligible voters for a political referendum. In the SOMALIA conflict, OAU leaders met with factional leaders, as directed by SECURITY COUNCIL Resolution 733 of 1992; UNOSOM II also worked closely with the OAU to facilitate a political dialogue in the south. The OAU provided 50 observers in Rwanda after the 1993 Arusha Accords, which the OAU and United Nations had helped to mediate. The Security Council consulted with OAU officials after the April 1994 GENOCIDE began in Rwanda, and the OAU unsuccessfully lobbied the Security Council in December 1995 to extend UNAMIR's (UNITED NATIONS ASSISTANCE MISSION FOR RWANDA) mandate to help repatriate refugees. The OAU also helped facilitate the peace process in Liberia in 1995, working with the UN Secretary-General's SPECIAL ENVOY. As the United Nations sought to REFORM peacekeeping missions, the OAU agreed to the necessity of creating a multinational African Defense Force to respond militarily to African crises.

The growing need to respond to COLLECTIVE SECURITY challenges on the African continent and the desire to create a comprehensive development program for Africa led to calls in the late 1990s to replace the OAU with a broader REGIONAL ORGANIZATION. The process of transformation began with the OAU's Sirte DECLARATION in 1999, which committed the MEMBERSHIP to the establishment of an AFRICAN UNION (AU) modeled after the European Union. The 2000 Lomé Summit of African leaders approved the Constitutive Act for the new organization, and the 2001 Lusaka Summit decided on its STRUCTURE and procedures. In 2002 at the Durban Summit the participating governments inaugurated the African Union with the convocation of the first AU Assembly meeting.

See also BOUTROS-GHALI BOUTROS; ELECTION ASSISTANCE DIVISION; GULF WAR; HUMAN RIGHTS; JOHNSON, LYNDON; MULTILATERALISM; NEW PARTNERSHIP FOR AFRICA'S DEVELOPMENT; OBSERVER STATUS; SIERRA LEONE; TERRORISM TREATIES; TREATY OF PELINDABA; UNITED NATIONS MISSION IN ETHIOPIA AND ERITREA.

Further Reading: El-Ayouty, Yassin, ed. *The Organization of African Unity after Thirty Years.* New York: Praeger, 1994. Nyangoni, Wellington. *Africa in the United Nations System.* London: Associated University Presses, 1975. United Nations. *Cooperation between the United Nations and the Organization of African Unity, Annual Report by the General Assembly.* New York: United Nations, 1998.

— *A. S. Patterson*

Organization of American States (OAS)

Created in the wake of World War II, the Organization of American States received special recognition as a regional representative body charged by the United Nations to handle disputes between nations in the Western Hemisphere. The special status of the OAS dates from the efforts by Latin American states to protect and preserve their regional authority within the international framework of interstate and interregional relations established under the auspices of the UN CHARTER. A definition of authority that established working boundaries between the United Nations and REGIONAL ORGANIZATIONS appears in Articles 51 and 52, Chapter VIII of the Charter. These articles approved the rights of individual and COLLECTIVE SELF-DEFENSE orchestrated through regional bodies, and also limited the intervention of the United Nations in regional conflicts only after the efforts of regional bodies had been exhausted.

The OAS was officially constituted at the Ninth International Conference of American States in Bogotá, Colombia, in 1948. Initially conceived as a body that would preserve local authority in the face of potential UN interest or intervention within the Americas, the OAS became increasingly tied to the interests and actions of the UNITED STATES during the COLD WAR. OAS RESOLUTIONS often provided the U.S. government with apparent support for unilateral actions within the Western Hemisphere that it then used to counter potential SANCTIONS from the United Nations. The case of GUATEMALA in 1954, and the series of actions against CUBA between 1959 and 1964 helped create the appearance of international support for the military, diplomatic, and economic actions of the United States through resolutions approved by the OAS.

The Cuban case created conflict between the OAS and the United Nations. As the revolutionary government moved openly toward the adoption of a communist model in the early 1960s, it was sanctioned by the OAS for parting from the group's commitment to anticommunism. The OAS attempt to isolate Cuba led its representatives to seek UN involvement in its escalating conflict with the United States. While the threat of a U.S. VETO effectively blocked SECURITY COUNCIL action, discussion and debate over the U.S.–Cuba conflict challenged the authority and called into question the actions of the OAS.

As cold war tensions eased after 1972, and as regional conflicts, such as those in Nicaragua (1979) and EL SALVADOR (1980) arose, the ability of the United States to command the unanimous approval of the OAS for its actions lessened. While the OAS continued to serve as a regional body recognized by the United Nations as holding authority over disputes within the Americas, its role was no longer clearly defined. Aggrieved parties within the hemisphere increasingly turned to the United Nations rather than to the OAS to seek redress.

The potential for contention between the United Nations and the OAS first arose in relation to the U.S. invasion of Grenada in October 1983. UN condemnation of U.S. sanctions against Nicaragua as well as for its continued support of the Contra rebels in the civil war during the mid-1980s again shattered OAS consensus and led Nicaragua to seek UN support for its case in 1984. The December 1989 invasion of Panama by the United States again paralyzed the OAS and led Latin American states to use the United Nations as a forum to criticize U.S. action.

Developed as a body that reserved the right of American states to defend peace and security of the hemisphere without intervention by the United Nations, the legacy, and ultimate end of the cold war left the OAS with an unclear mission. Efforts to defend the democratically elected government of HAITI between 1991 and 1996 once again brought into question the relationship between the United Nations and the OAS, and the responsibilities of each in regional disputes. Of the six PEACEKEEPING missions sent to Haiti, five were solely UN initiatives. Only the INTERNATIONAL CIVILIAN MISSION IN HAITI (MICIVIH) had active OAS participation. In a joint effort by the United Nations and the Organization of American States, MICIVIH sought to promote respect for HUMAN RIGHTS following the departure from office of the island's military leaders.

The OAS co-sponsorship of MICIVIH reflected a new emphasis on promoting democracy. Its 1991 GENERAL ASSEMBLY meeting endorsed this trend by creating a MECHANISM, known as Resolution 1080, that required the OAS SECRETARY-GENERAL to convene the organization's Permanent Council and the members' foreign ministers within 10 days of a coup or interruption of a legitimate, elected government. Resolution 1080 was first used when the military seized power in Haiti, then in Peru in 1992, Guatemala in 1993, and Paraguay in 1996. Having contributed to democracy's restoration in Haiti, the OAS monitored the rising protests against the government of President Jean-Bertrand Aristide. In 2004, fearful of a collapse of democratic government in the island nation, the OAS Council asked the UN Security Council to take all necessary means to address the deteriorating situation. It also participated in the negotiations that led finally to Aristide's resignation and exile. Resolution 1080 provided a means for the OAS to take the initiative ahead of UN responses whenever a threat to democratic stability occurred in the Western Hemisphere. In September 2001 the OAS General Assembly went even further by endorsing a proposed Inter-American Democratic Charter that called for the SUSPENSION of a member nation if it altered its "constitutional regime," or interrupted the "democratic order." The measure was meant to forestall internal subversion of democratic systems by elected governments that were, in fact, "disguised dictatorships." OAS action came in the wake of President Fujimori's restrictions on the democratic process in Peru during the 1990s.

See also COMMITTEE OF INTERNATIONAL DEVELOPMENT INSTITUTIONS ON THE ENVIRONMENT; HAMMARSKJÖLD, DAG; JURISDICTION OF THE UNITED NATIONS; LATIN AMERICA; OBSERVER STATUS.

Further Reading: Levin, Aida L. "The Organization of the American States and the United Nations." In *Regionalism and the United Nations.* Edited by Berhanykun Andemicael, 147–224. Dobbs Ferry, N.Y.: Oceana Publications, 1979. Wilson, Larman C., and David W. Dent. *Historical Dictionary of Inter-American Organizations.* Lanham, Md.: Scarecrow Press, 1998. OAS Web site: <www.oas.org>.

— *D. K. Lewis*

Ottawa Convention   *See* CONVENTION ON THE PROHIBITION OF THE USE, STOCKPILING, PRODUCTION AND TRANSFER OF ANTI-PERSONNEL MINES AND THEIR DESTRUCTION; *see also* LAND MINES.

Our Common Future   *See* WORLD COMMISSION ON ENVIRONMENT AND DEVELOPMENT (WCED).

P

P5 *See* PERMANENT MEMBERS OF THE SECURITY COUNCIL.

Pacific Settlement of Disputes *See* CHAPTER VI OF THE UN CHARTER.

pact

From Latin *pactum*, pact is very close in meaning to COVENANT and TREATY. It is an agreement between individuals or parties. As a particular type of treaty, a pact usually binds the parties to undertake some common activity or to pursue a generally positive relationship. The notorious Nazi-Soviet "pact" of August 1939 is an example. Unlike CONVENTIONS, pacts are not open for additional signature, but require further negotiation in order to include new partners. All pacts that are made by one or more members of the United Nations must be registered with the world body, and are published in the *UNITED NATIONS TREATY SERIES.*

Pakistan *See* AFGHANISTAN, COMPREHENSIVE NUCLEAR TEST BAN TREATY, DEPARTMENT OF PEACEKEEPING OPERATIONS, INDIA, KASHMIR, UNITED NATIONS INDIA-PAKISTAN OBSERVATION MISSION, UNITED NATIONS MILITARY OBSERVER GROUP IN INDIA AND PAKISTAN.

Palais des Nations *See* GENEVA HEADQUARTERS OF THE UNITED NATIONS.

Panel on United Nations Peace Operations *See* BRAHIMI REPORT.

Pasvolsky, Leo (1893–1953)

Wartime planning for a postwar international body to keep the peace and the drafting of a charter for the proposed United Nations Organization were undertaken primarily by the UNITED STATES Department of State. Under the leadership of Secretary of State CORDELL HULL, Leo Pasvolsky and other department officials crafted the proposals and shepherded the process that produced great power agreement at the DUMBARTON OAKS CONFERENCE (1944) on the STRUCTURE and purposes of the United Nations. Joining the State Department in 1938, Pasvolsky was one of the few senior officials to participate in every phase of the UN's development leading to the successful conclusion of the 1945 UNITED NATIONS CONFERENCE ON INTERNATIONAL ORGANIZATION at San Francisco.

Prior to his service at the U.S. State Department, Pasvolsky worked at the Brookings Institution in Washington, D.C., where he published many works on interwar economics and the effects of World War I on central Europe. His writings included *The Economics of Communism with Special Reference to Russia's Experience* (1921), *Russian Debts and Russian Reconstruction* (1924), *World War Debt Settlements* (1926), *Economic Nationalism of the Danubian States* (1928), *War Debts and World Prosperity* (1932), and *Current Monetary Issues* (1933). In this period he was also a member of the Council on Foreign Relations (CFR), which, at the outbreak of World War II in Europe, launched a private effort to convince the American government to plan for a postwar successor to the ineffectual LEAGUE OF NATIONS. Pasvolsky drafted the council's proposal presented to the State Department on September 12, 1939, suggesting that the CFR form a group of experts to research postwar issues under the "general guidance" of the department. Hull accepted the idea, and the council established the War and Peace Studies Project with Pasvolsky as one of its research secretaries. A parallel structure was created within the State Department, and many CFR personnel were brought into the government. Pasvolsky was appointed director of the Special Research Division, and he became a confidant of Secretary Hull.

Hull set up a department committee for postwar planning in December 1939 with Pasvolsky as a member. The work of the committee soon came under the leadership of Under Secretary of State Sumner Welles, who joined Pasvolsky as the two strongest advocates for a new international organization. Pasvolsky was also involved in the State Department's discussions concerning an International Stabilization Fund to finance world commerce after the war. As part of the department's "Technical Committee," he helped draft the American proposals that later emerged as the BRETTON WOODS AGREEMENT, creating the major international postwar financial and monetary institutions.

In 1943 Leo Pasvolsky was given the title of "Special Adviser to the Secretary" in charge of preparatory work for the proposed international organization. Following the MOSCOW FOREIGN MINISTERS CONFERENCE in the fall, he was appointed to Hull's "Informal Political Agenda Group," which crafted the outlines of the world body based on the secretary's own draft of a "CHARTER OF THE UNITED NATIONS," written the previous August. President FRANKLIN ROOSEVELT approved the plan in February 1944, and it served as the basis of the Dumbarton Oaks discussions in the fall of that year. Pasvolsky, RALPH BUNCHE, and ALGER HISS served as the core of the U.S. preparation team for the conference. During the meeting Pasvolsky chaired the Joint Formulation Group, consisting of American, British, and Soviet officials charged with the technical drafting of the Charter. As the negotiations proceeded, it was within this group that most of the substantive discussions about the new organization occurred. Pasvolsky was particularly involved in discussions with Soviet ambassador Andrei Gromyko about the potential MEMBERSHIP of the 16 Soviet republics, and VOTING issues within the UN.

Pasvolsky accompanied Roosevelt to the YALTA CONFERENCE, and, immediately following that meeting, he went with Secretary of State EDWARD STETTINIUS to the Mexico Conference, where the United States and its hemispheric neighbors drafted the Act of Chapultepec, dealing with the thorny problems of the relationship between the United Nations and a REGIONAL ORGANIZATION. He was appointed to the U.S. delegation to the San Francisco Conference in April 1945, where he chaired the critical Coordination Committee. Taking the recommendations from each of the conference commissions and committees, Pasvolsky's group decided on the structure of the Charter and drafted the final text. When the language of recommendations was unclear, the Coordination Committee recommended changes and standardized references in the Charter on social, economic, and HUMAN RIGHTS topics. Following the conference, Pasvolsky was one of the major advocates at the ratification hearings of the U.S. Senate Foreign Relations Committee.

Before leaving the State Department in 1946 to return to the Brookings Institution, Pasvolsky served on the key committee that prepared the recommendations for the creation of the Central Intelligence Agency. Back at Brookings, he headed up the International Studies Group that developed the draft outline for the Marshall Plan and its administration once Congress had approved the European recovery program. In 1951 he initiated a study program at Brookings on the United Nations that was projected to publish seven volumes on different aspects of the world body. He began work on the first volume, *The Charter of the United Nations,* but he died in 1953 before its completion. In all, five volumes were completed after his death, including his first volume, which was written by his associate, Ruth B. Russell, and dedicated to him. It became the seminal work on the drafting of the document.

Further Reading: Moore, John Allphin, Jr., and Jerry Pubantz. *To Create a New World?: American Presidents and the United Nations.* New York: Peter Lang Publishing, 1999. Russell, Ruth B. *A History of the United Nations Charter: The Role of the United States, 1940–1945.* Washington, D.C.: Brookings Institution, 1958. Simma, Bruno, ed. *The Charter of the United Nations. A Commentary.* 2nd ed. New York: Oxford University Press, 2002. Brookings Institution archives Web site: <www.brookings.org/lib/archives.html>. National Archives and Administration searchpage Web site: <search.nara.gov/>.

Peacebuilding Commission

A serious international problem is the tendency of nations in which conflict has ended to relapse into violence. Ending conflicts through negotiations and restoring some stability with international peacekeepers address only part of the problem. Many expert commentators think that lasting

Opening minutes of the Peacebuilding Commission's inaugural session, at the UN Headquarters in New York. (UN PHOTO 120715/PAULO FILGUEIRAS)

peace requires rebuilding the troubled nation's society, dealing with the root causes of the original conflict, and moving the country from reconstruction to constructive DEVELOPMENT. The United Nations has long been interested in post-conflict political assistance to violence-ravaged countries. Developing nations have called attention to the need to establish a body specifically charged with this responsibility, since existing UN bodies and SPECIALIZED AGENCIES, acting under other mandates, have not been positioned to deal that effectively with post-conflict issues. Accordingly, a joint RESOLUTION of the SECURITY COUNCIL and the GENERAL ASSEMBLY in December 2005 established the Peacebuilding Commission. Its creation constituted one of the most dramatic REFORM efforts to improve the efficiency of assistance programs and to attend to the long-term problems resulting from internal conflicts.

Like the HUMAN RIGHTS COUNCIL, the Peacebuilding Commission was the product of lengthy negotiations regarding UN reform. It emerged from the recommendations of the 2004 HIGH-LEVEL PANEL ON THREATS, CHALLENGES, AND CHANGE, SECRETARY-GENERAL KOFI ANNAN's report, *IN LARGER FREEDOM,* proposals made by the PRESIDENT OF THE GENERAL ASSEMBLY, and the Outcome Statement of the 2005 UN WORLD SUMMIT.

In negotiations leading up to the creation of the commission, many issues arose involving the STRUCTURE, composition, powers, and review MECHANISM of the proposed body. There was also significant debate about whether it should be a new organ, or a committee of another body. The principal dispute was whether the commission should report to the Security Council, which establishes and concludes PEACE-KEEPING missions, as recommended by the Western nations, to the General Assembly, with its universal representation, as advocated by the NON-ALIGNED MOVEMENT and the GROUP OF 77, or to the ECONOMIC AND SOCIAL COUNCIL (ECO-SOC), which is responsible for development and for coordinating the specialized agencies. There was also an issue about which body would choose its members, since its designated charges appeared to overlap the functions of several of the UN's major organs. These differences were resolved only by lengthy consultations in a post–World Summit follow-up group which was co-chaired by the ambassadors of Denmark and Tanzania. The Peacebuilding Commission is considered an advisory body. It has no enforcement powers, which remain with the PRINCIPAL ORGANS OF THE UNITED NATIONS. A committee reporting to both the General Assembly and the Security Council, the Peacebuilding Commission can take up issues only on which its advice has been requested by the Security Council, the General Assembly, the Economic and Social Council, or the Secretary-General. Any individual member state can also request the commission's advice about its own situation.

The Peacebuilding Commission consists of an Organizational Committee, elected for the first time in December 2005, to oversee its activities, but it acts through individual country-specific committees set up for each situation that the Organizational Committee decides should be addressed. Country committees conduct the studies, provide advice for the unique situation of each case, assure that the country involved will be represented in discussions and decisions about its future, and consult the countries most involved in providing aid. The Organizational Committee consists of 31 member states: seven elected by and from the current Security Council MEMBERSHIP (which will usually include some of the PERMANENT MEMBERS of that body), seven elected by and from the current membership of the Economic and Social Council (which will tend to be DEVELOPING COUNTRIES), five of the 10 top providers of assessed contributions to the UN (which will include aid donors), the five top providers of military personnel and civilian police to United Nations peacekeeping operations, and seven members elected by the General Assembly.

Recognizing that development is a long term process, the Peacebuilding Commission seeks to extend the period of attention to post-conflict situations, reconstruction, institution-building, and SUSTAINABLE DEVELOPMENT. It therefore identifies and coordinates the provision of resources and financing to establish integrated strategies for post-conflict recovery, both during the presence and after the departure of peacekeeping missions. The commission promotes cooperation among political, military, humanitarian, and development actors involved in a specific country. This process is expected to improve efficiency by assuring that efforts complement each other in building toward a fixed plan, placing resource providers and aid givers together with each other and with the government of the country involved. The commission also compiles best practices from previous efforts, which can be adopted in new crises.

Original expectations were that the Peacebuilding Commission would deal with only four or five cases each year, and that the Organizational Committee would meet as often as it deemed necessary. Country committees would meet regularly and frequently, especially in the initial stages of dealing with a post-conflict nation.

The Peacebuilding Commission convened its inaugural session on June 23, 2006, meeting also as the Organizational Committee of the Whole. The commission established its rules of procedure and set its first agenda. Among other decisions, the members agreed to reconvene to consider the Security Council's request for advice on the situations in Burundi and SIERRA LEONE.

Further Reading: Peacebuilding Commission Web site: <www.un.org/peace/peacebuilding.htm>. Also see <www.un.org./News/Press/Docs/2006/pbcl.doc.htm>.

— *K. J. Grieb*

peacekeeping

Although peacekeeping is an endeavor often associated with the United Nations, it is an ad hoc undertaking that is not mentioned in the CHARTER. Peacekeeping is a concept that has evolved over the years, and the resulting changes in various peacekeeping missions account for many of the difficulties encountered by these efforts, for a great deal of misunderstanding of the United Nations, and for the rising criticism of the organization.

The founders of the United Nations did not envisage anything like peacekeeping. Consequently, while Chapter I, Article 1 of the Charter states that one of the purposes of the United Nations is "[T]o maintain international peace and security," the only methods elaborated in the Charter for achieving this objective are those of MEDIATION, investigation, and negotiation, as suggested in CHAPTER VI's provision for "pacific settlement of disputes," and the use of force by member states, as discussed in CHAPTER VII. Recognizing the need for forceful measures short of war, such as SANCTIONS, diplomats and UN staff members sought new methods to deal with the outbreak of international conflict. Peacekeeping was developed during the initial years of the UN as an action more intrusive than the peaceful settlement provisions of Chapter VI, yet short of Chapter VII's provisions authorizing member states to use force. Hence it is often referred to within the United Nations as coming under "CHAPTER VI ½."

Thus, international peacekeeping was a new concept developed by the United Nations. Since such measures had not previously taken place in history, they required the development of a new method of operation, without the benefit of previous precedents that normally govern international activity. The idea of neutral international action to facilitate peace, rather than order being maintained by the extension of war based on national interests, was a new idea. During the latter half of the 20th century, distinctive "BLUE HELMETS" worn by UN peacekeepers became a symbol of the international security system, providing an important MECHANISM to preserve the global order, ensure the survival of small states, and protect HUMAN RIGHTS. By January 2007 more than 80,000 peacekeepers were serving in multinational missions around the world. Of these, over 71,000 were military troops, 6,700 police, and 2,400 observers. The largest deployment was in the CONGO, where more than 18,000 UN personnel were stationed. The nature of these missions included humanitarian assistance, civil administration, combatant separation, and truce observation.

As initially conceived in 1948 and 1949 and practiced for the first 40 years of the United Nations, peacekeeping was a narrowly focused process with limited and specific purposes. It normally involved an international action to assist in ending an international conflict (that is, a war between states) in an entirely voluntary action, carried out with the express permission of both sides to the conflict. Peacekeepers arrived after a cease-fire agreement or other settlement had been negotiated by both parties, positioning themselves between the combatants. The sole purpose of these early peacekeeping efforts was to supervise the implementation of truce agreements and specifically to verify that both sides took appropriate actions to carry out the agreements already reached. While military personnel were involved, only light arms were carried. Peacekeepers had no enforcement powers and were directed to use force only to defend themselves. The entire operation was based on voluntary consent and the cooperation of the parties to the conflict. Indeed, peacekeepers were sent only after the UN negotiated a "Status of Forces Agreement" by which the host state granted permission to use its territory, since it remained a sovereign nation. The agreement also defined the powers of the peacekeepers, their access to facilities, and the specific territory in which they would operate. Early peacekeeping operations were conducted by the United Nations in Egypt following the 1956 SUEZ CRISIS (UNITED NATIONS EMERGENCY FORCE, UNEF), during the 1960 Congolese civil war (UNITED NATIONS OPERATION IN THE CONGO, ONUC), and in the Cypriot crisis of 1964 (UNITED NATIONS FORCE IN CYPRUS, UNFICYP).

Troops involved in these operations were drawn from countries perceived as neutral in the conflict. Indeed, during the initial decades of peacekeeping, troops from the superpowers were never involved, with every effort made to draw troops from neutral nations. More than 110 nations have contributed troops to peacekeeping missions, and the increasing use of peacekeeping clearly demonstrates that it has filled a need in the international system.

As designed and practiced for the first 40 years of the UN, peacekeeping was a neutral operation to monitor or observe the combatants' steps to disengage and pull back after a cease-fire agreement had been reached prior to the arrival of the peacekeeping mission. Initially peacekeeping was used sparingly, but over the years the number of missions proliferated as nations brought more and more disputes to the

Peacekeeping in East Timor, 2000 (UN/DPI PHOTO BY ESKINDER DEBEBE)

United Nations, and missions continued indefinitely because cease-fire agreements did not necessarily lead to negotiation of a final agreement. The costs of these peacekeeping operations were paid by all member states through a separate assessment, apart from the regular UN BUDGET, since the costs of such operations varied during any year depending on the number of crises the UN was asked to resolve. Objections to certain peacekeeping operations led to the withholding of assessment payments by many states, including major powers such as FRANCE and the Soviet Union.

The end of the COLD WAR brought an expansion of and notable changes in peacekeeping, as different types of disputes came before the United Nations. New challenges necessitated augmenting the number of troops and raising the costs of financing the increased number of operations. The 1990s saw the launching of almost three times as many peacekeeping missions as were initiated during the previous 40 years, reflecting a period of increasing security crises and greater reliance on the United Nations. Only 13 peacekeeping missions were authorized prior to 1988. From 1988 through 2000, more than 36 operations were undertaken. From 2000 to 2007 the number of UN peacekeeping personnel grew from 30,000 to 80,000. In this situation, merely raising the necessary troops and funding the costs of the operation became major concerns, in addition to conducting the missions. Other challenges included adequate training, equipping, and transporting of troops pledged by various nations. The increased number of missions also led to delays between authorization and deployment of forces, which caused further problems. Moreover, distressing scandals troubled the UN's peacekeeping operations in 2004 and 2005. Published allegations of excessive alcohol abuse and sexual improprieties among peacekeepers surfaced as SECRETARY-GENERAL KOFI ANNAN was reporting to the Security Council about internal studies of peacekeeping missions that uncovered intolerable misconduct toward local POPULATIONS and poor internal policing by the United Nations. The most serious offenses were in the Democratic Republic of the Congo (DRC), where peacekeepers were reported to have been involved in sexual exploitation of WOMEN and girls. The Secretary-General announced a "zero tolerance" policy for such practices not only in the Congo but in any UN peacekeeping operation. The SECURITY COUNCIL endorsed this policy in its reauthorization of the DRC operation.

The nature of peacekeeping, the tasks involved, and the types of disputes that peacekeepers were asked to address also changed considerably during the period following 1988. The conflicts brought to the United Nations after 1988 mainly involved domestic, that is, internal civil wars, several disputing the legitimacy of an existing government or assaulting ethnic, religious, and minority groups, as in Rwanda, SOMALIA, BOSNIA, KOSOVO, and TIMOR-LESTE. Although these conflicts often affected, or potentially affected, international peace and security, they fell outside the original scope of the

United Nations, which dealt only with international disputes and interstate warfare. But this new form of peacekeeping, or "peacemaking," involved intervening in internal domestic disputes, and they thus challenged, if not violated, a nation's SOVEREIGNTY. More important, since at least one of the parties involved in the dispute was likely a rebel movement, and not a signatory of international agreements, it could consider itself outside the scope of INTERNATIONAL LAW. Hence, the United Nations was asked to become involved in disputes outside existing norms and with a party beyond the reach of normal international measures. Attempting to settle internal disputes also often meant that peacekeepers acted without the approval of all parties to the dispute, since the United Nations normally deals with the governments of its member states. The UN Charter does not provide explicit authority for the UN to act against the sovereignty of a member state without the permission of that government. Thus, interventions in disputes involving the potential emergence of new states meant entering entirely new legal ground. Inevitably difficulties ensued, due to the challenges of an entirely new type of peacekeeping.

Modern warfare also changed, with civilians increasingly the targets of efforts by rebels using unconventional methods of warfare, and this also brought new challenges. Peacekeepers were often asked to protect refugees and guard the delivery of humanitarian aid, as well as to investigate and seek to prevent violations of the human rights of the populace. While the United Nations did indeed seek to protect basic human rights and especially to prevent crimes against humanity, peacekeepers were not equipped and never intended to fight a conflict. Once peacekeepers attempted to protect victims or segments of the population, the neutrality on which their actions had previously been based was lost, and they were invariably perceived as parties to the conflict by at least one side. Efforts to protect civilians involved unprecedented cooperation of peacekeeping forces with SPECIALIZED AGENCIES and NON-GOVERNMENTAL ORGANIZATIONS, requiring complex coordination. In addition, the new mandates often involved lengthy deployments that included not merely troops but also police officers and legal officials.

Taking on vast new responsibilities that were well beyond the original concept of peacekeeping, with little advance planning and few new resources, peacekeepers were now being asked to perform tasks that were at times contradictory. For example, protecting populations and delivering aid invariably caused a loss of the aura of neutrality. The relatively small DEPARTMENT OF PEACEKEEPING OPERATIONS (DPKO) struggled with inadequate resources trying to meet new mandates that went far beyond the original idea of peacekeeping. Secretary-General Kofi Annan appointed a panel of experts in March 2000 to study the new challenges facing UN peacekeeping operations. He hoped to avoid in future missions the errors, inefficiencies, and failures experienced in past UN efforts. Annan charged the panel with examining the ability of UN resources to meet the peacekeeping mandates given to the world body by the Security Council in recent years. He hoped the experts would complement the work of the Lessons Learned Unit in DPKO. The panel's report, issued just before the September 2000 meeting of the MILLENNIUM SUMMIT, recommended formalizing the UN's peacekeeping activities, ending ad hoc deployments, creating a new information-gathering and analysis office within the United Nations to act as a professional policy planning staff, establishing an integrated task force for each new mission, and changing definitions of self-defense to allow missions to take a more offensive posture in dangerous situations.

See also specific peacekeeping operations, listing of all peacekeeping operations in DEPARTMENT OF PEACEKEEPING OPERATIONS; AFRICAN UNION; *AN AGENDA FOR PEACE;* BRAHIMI REPORT; BUNCHE, RALPH; DEMOCRATIZATION; ECONOMIC COMMUNITY OF WEST AFRICAN STATES; ELECTION ASSISTANCE; NATION-BUILDING; PEACEBUILDING COMMISSION; PEARSON, LESTER; REGIONAL ORGANIZATIONS.

Further Reading: Dobbins, James, Seth G. Jones, Keith Crane, Andrew Rathmell, Brett Steele, and Richard Teltschik. *The UN's Role in Nation-Building: From the Congo to Iraq.* Santa Monica, Calif.: RAND Corporation, 2004. DPKO Web site: <www.un.org/Depts/dpko/dpko/index.asp>. Hill, Stephen M., and Shanin Malik. *Peacekeeping and the United Nations.* Aldershot, U.K.: Dartmouth, 1996. Moore, John Allphin, Jr., and Jerry Pubantz. *The New United Nations: International Organization in the Twenty-first Century.* Upper Saddle River, N.J.: Prentice Hall, 2004. Ontunnu, Olara A., and Michael W. Doyle, eds. *Peacemaking and Peacekeeping for the New Century.* Lanham, Md.: Rowman and Littlefield, 1996. Ratner, Steven R. *The New UN Peacekeeping: Building Peace in Land of Conflict after the Cold War.* New York: St. Martin's, 1995. United Nations. *The Blue Helmets: A Review of United Nations Peace-Keeping.* 3d ed. New York: United Nations Department of Public Information, 1996.

— *K. J. Grieb*

Pearson, Lester (1897–1972)

Lester Bowles Pearson was born in Newton Brook, Ontario, Canada. Following university studies Pearson taught history at the University of Toronto from 1924 to 1928, after which he entered the Canadian foreign service. While employed by the foreign service during World War II, Pearson became involved with precursors to the United Nations. In 1943 he was a delegate to sessions of the UNITED NATIONS RELIEF AND REHABILITATION ADMINISTRATION (UNRRA) and chaired its supplies committee. He was also included in the planning sessions of the United Nations FOOD AND AGRICULTURE ORGANIZATION (FAO) and served in 1944 as Canada's senior adviser at the DUMBARTON OAKS CONFERENCE.

In 1945 he was his nation's head delegate to the UN's founding conference in San Francisco.

In 1946 Pearson was appointed Canada's under-secretary of state for external affairs. Serving as chairman of the UN political and security committee in 1947, he played a decisive role in mediating the Palestinian crisis. From 1948 to 1956, Pearson served as head of the Canadian mission to the United Nations and was president of the seventh GENERAL ASSEMBLY during the 1952–53 session. Following Israel's attack on Egypt's Sinai Peninsula in 1956, Pearson proposed the deployment of a UN EMERGENCY FORCE (UNEF) to the Suez and volunteered a Canadian contingent of troops, thereby becoming the father of UN PEACEKEEPING. For his efforts Pearson was awarded the Nobel Peace Prize in 1957. The next year he became leader of the Liberal Party in Canada and, in 1963, prime minister, a position from which he retired in 1968.

Further Reading: English, John. *The Life of Lester Pearson: Shadow of Heaven (1897–1948) and Worldly Years (1949–1972).* Toronto: Lester and Orphen Dennys and A. A. Knopf, 1989–1992. Pearson, Lester B. *Mike: The Memoirs of the Right Honourable Lester B. Pearson.* 3 vols. Toronto: New American Library of Canada, 1972.

— *S. F. McMahon*

People's Republic of China   *See* CHINA.

Pérez de Cuéllar, Javier (1920–   )

Pérez de Cuéllar, the fifth SECRETARY-GENERAL and first Latin American to hold that office, served two terms, from 1982 to 1991. He was born in Lima, Peru, in 1920 of a family descended from Spanish nobility. Educated early in life in Roman Catholic schools, Pérez de Cuéllar developed a keen interest in Hispanic art, culture, and literature. While studying law at Catholic University in Lima, he took a position in the Peruvian Foreign Ministry as a clerk, commencing a long diplomatic career. From the mid-1940s he served successively in embassies in FRANCE, the United Kingdom, Bolivia, and Brazil, and in 1946 he was a member of Peru's delegation to the first United Nations GENERAL ASSEMBLY session. His career evinced a rapid rise within the foreign ministry. He was promoted to the rank of ambassador in 1962 and by the mid-1960s simultaneously held appointments as professor of diplomatic law at the Academia Diplomatica del Peru and professor of international relations at the Academia de Guerra Aerea del Peru, during which time he wrote *Manual de Derecho Diplomatico* (Manual of international law). He served as ambassador to Switzerland from 1964 to 1966, and, following the establishment of full diplomatic relations with the Soviet Union in 1969, he became his nation's first ambassador to Moscow, serving concurrently as ambassador to Poland.

In 1971 he became Peru's PERMANENT REPRESENTATIVE to the United Nations, serving as president of the SECURITY COUNCIL during the CYPRUS DISPUTE of 1974. In the summer of that year, a military faction overthrew the government of Archbishop Makarios in an effort to bring about union of the island with Greece. Turkey immediately ordered an invasion to protect the Turkish minority. On September 18, 1975, Secretary-General KURT WALDHEIM named Pérez de Cuéllar as his SPECIAL REPRESENTATIVE to Cyprus. Although the Cyprus dispute would persist as one of the most long-lasting concerns of the United Nations, Pérez de Cuéllar eventually convinced the leaders of the Greek and Turkish communities to initiate talks about their differences. In late 1977 he left the United Nations in order to assume the position of Peruvian ambassador to Venezuela, but in early 1979 returned to New York as UNDER SECRETARY-GENERAL for Special Political Affairs. In April 1981, Waldheim appointed him his personal representative to AFGHANISTAN and Pakistan, in an effort to defuse the tense relations between the two countries resulting from the Soviet invasion of Afghanistan in December 1979.

In 1981, at the age of 61, Pérez de Cuéllar intended to retire from his long and active diplomatic career, but events would conspire to delay his leaving the world stage. Kurt Waldheim's second term was coming to a close, and the United Nations now began the knotty process of designating a new Secretary-General. The selection was complicated by several factors. Waldheim wanted a third term, but he was vigorously opposed by several Third World countries, led by CHINA in the Security Council. The procedure provided in the CHARTER OF THE UNITED NATIONS (see Article 97) authorized the General Assembly to appoint the Secretary-General upon the recommendation of the Security Council. Since the five PERMANENT MEMBERS OF THE SECURITY COUNCIL retain a VETO, it is conceivable that a nominee could receive 14 votes yet be an unsuccessful nominee. That is, all five permanent members must accede to any nomination. Tanzania's foreign minister, Salim Ahmed Salim, was a challenging candidate to Waldheim, and he would have become the first sub-Saharan African to serve in the post. The new, conservative, RONALD REAGAN administration in Washington, resistant to the recent tilt in the United Nations toward what it perceived as Third-World radicalism, supported Waldheim, as did, interestingly, the Soviet Union. For six weeks the Security Council deadlocked on a nomination as either the UNITED STATES or China vetoed opposing candidates. Finally, upon the urging of Ugandan ambassador Olara Otunnu, president of the Security Council, both Salim and Waldheim withdrew from consideration. On December 11, 1981, the Council went into closed session for an arduous half day to consider nine candidates. By the end of the session, only one of those candidates proved acceptable to all of the permanent members—Javier Pérez de Cuéllar, who was quickly, and by acclamation, approved by the General

Secretary-General Javier Pérez de Cuéllar (UN PHOTO 169681/ J. ISAAC)

Assembly. Here appeared a diplomat from a Latin American "Third World" country, yet of a "Western" cultural tradition, who had gained the confidence of the Soviet Union while serving as ambassador in Moscow. It is likely as well that, since he was 61, no one thought he would serve more than one term. Yet he would be reelected and would serve a full 10 years.

His first major challenge involved a military confrontation between GREAT BRITAIN and Argentina over the Falkland Islands, called the Malvinas by the Argentineans, who invaded and claimed the islands in April 1982. Although his efforts at MEDIATION came to naught—by June 1982 Britain had defeated the Argentine army and reestablished control over the islands—he was widely praised in the international community for his labors. He continued with other personal initiatives, in Russian-occupied Afghanistan, in South African-occupied NAMIBIA, in LEBANON (plagued by Israeli invasion and internal civil strife), and in the Guyana-Venezuela border dispute, in the event continuing to win praise for his mediation efforts and enhancing his growing reputation as an impartial negotiator. He consistently advocated the use of the Security Council as a forum for negotiations and as the appropriate international tool to pursue PEACEKEEPING, despite the persistent lack of funding for such efforts. During his tenure as well, the United Nations continued to emphasize refugee resettlement and HUMAN RIGHTS, and the Secretary-General initiated a program to bring relief to Ethiopia during a devastating famine in the late 1980s.

Most important, it was on his watch that the COLD WAR ended, providing the United Nations with the opportunity to be transformed from an international organization paralyzed by bipolarity into an institution that could more directly affect world affairs. Suddenly, at least for the moment, an environment more reflective of great power cooperation than the world had seen in some years seemed to provide the context for successful diplomacy orchestrated by an active and principled Secretary-General. The new opportunities for the organization over which Pérez de Cuéllar presided, however, brought with them the need for additional financial resources and more personnel. The Secretary-General expanded the UN bureaucracy and lobbied for increased funding.

Unfortunately, his efforts encountered growing hostility from the U.S. government, historically the United Nations's most important supporter. The Reagan administration, having come to office the same year as Pérez de Cuéllar's first appointment as Secretary-General, reversed decades of American financial support. Demanding reforms at the UN, President Reagan limited annual assessment payments, endorsed the KASSEBAUM AMENDMENT cutting contributions to UN SPECIALIZED AGENCIES, and demanded a 15 percent reduction in the UN staff. When the United States went so far as to withdraw from UNESCO (UNITED NATIONS EDUCATIONAL, SCIENTIFIC AND CULTURAL ORGANIZATION), arguing its mission had become too highly politicized and its staff and BUDGET bloated, the confrontation reached a crisis point. UNESCO appointed a new DIRECTOR-GENERAL and cut its activities by one-third. The Secretary-General agreed REFORM and streamlining at the UN were needed. To accommodate American pressure, Pérez de Cuéllar even allowed the U.S. government's General Accounting Office (GAO) to review the work of the UN's auditing and evaluation unit. This was an unprecedented step, since nothing in the Charter allows national governments to review the management of the organization's agencies. In the end, however, none of Pérez de Cuéllar's efforts were sufficient to assuage the conservative Republican leadership in Washington.

On a brighter note for U.S.–UN relations, and with warmer relations developing between the United States and the USSR after the ascendancy of President MIKHAIL GORBACHEV, several apparently intractable international problems were resolved through initiatives by the United Nations. In southern Africa, by the summer of 1988, all parties agreed to simultaneous withdrawals of forces by CUBA and South Africa from, respectively, ANGOLA and Namibia. This opened the way for full implementation of Security Council Resolution 435, providing for a UNITED NATIONS ANGOLA VERIFICATION MISSION (UNAVEM) and the placement of the UNITED NATIONS TRANSITION ASSISTANCE GROUP (UNTAG)

in Namibia to help with the conversion to independence, achieved at the UN HEADQUARTERS in Geneva (the Palais des Nations) in December 1988. Meantime, Diego Cordovez, an assistant to the Secretary-General, worked quietly but effectively to mediate the conflict in Afghanistan and to help expedite the removal of Soviet forces from that country. At the Palais des Nations, a four-part agreement (Afghanistan, Pakistan, the United States, and the Soviet Union) was reached on April 14, 1988, providing for peace talks among the warring parties and removal of Soviet troops, which was completed by the following February.

Pérez de Cuéllar also oversaw the conclusion of the most devastating war in the post–World War II period. The IRAN-IRAQ WAR had begun in 1980 and had been characterized by extreme ferocity and brutality on both sides, resulting in hundreds of thousands of casualties. The war entered its final stages in early 1988 during the so-called war of the cities. In February, Iraqi leader SADDAM HUSSEIN ordered the bombing of an oil refinery near Tehran, and IRAN launched missiles into Baghdad in retaliation. Kurds in IRAQ demanded autonomy and Hussein bombed their villages with poison gas. The war had completely degenerated into an unacceptable barbarity, and yet it was, by all accounts, a stalemate. Reluctantly, Ayatollah Khomeini, the Iranian religious leader, allowed his government to accept UN RESOLUTION 598, calling for a cease-fire and withdrawal of forces to pre-war boundaries. The RESOLUTION had been hammered out in an all-day session of the Security Council (July 20, 1987) that included the active participation of Pérez de Cuéllar. The action was historic; the United States and the Soviet Union for the first time jointly sponsored a Security Council resolution on the MIDDLE EAST. The resolution threatened retaliation against either of the combatants if they failed to accept its terms. Pérez de Cuéllar was entrusted with the diplomatic task of obtaining compliance. Iraq at first rejected the resolution and attempted yet another offensive, but the Secretary-General persisted in talks with the foreign ministers of each side and was finally able to announce agreement on August 20, 1988. The UN Security Council was now poised to act, cooperatively, to address the international crisis created when, in August 1990, Saddam Hussein directed an Iraqi invasion of neighboring Kuwait. UN SECURITY COUNCIL RESOLUTION 678 became the juridical basis of the U.S.-led coalition that drove Iraq out of Kuwait during the GULF WAR.

Once the war was concluded in the spring of 1991, a new humanitarian challenge presented itself. At the end of March the Iraqi army launched a massive attack against rebels in the northern part of the country. The attack produced more than 200,000 Kurdish refugees fleeing to the region along Iraq's border with Turkey and 500,000 crossing into Iran. On April 5 the Security Council condemned the attacks and called upon "the Secretary-General to use all the resources at his disposal . . . to address urgently the critical needs of the refugees." The United States, with the assistance of Turkey, Great

Britain, and France, established a "no-fly" zone over the area, launched a massive humanitarian airdrop, and created protective "enclaves" inside Iraq for the Kurds. Almost immediately thereafter these powers urged the United Nations to take over administration of the enclaves. Pérez de Cuéllar was hesitant to do so without the consent of the Iraqi government. To this end he negotiated an agreement with Baghdad on April 18, 1991. With this in place the allied states ceded control of the camps to the UN. The episode proved to be another example of deft diplomacy by Pérez de Cuéllar, reminiscent of the successful approach he had used in international crises throughout his tenure as Secretary-General.

See also BRUNDTLAND, GRO HARLEM; CAMBODIA; DEMOCRATIZATION; ELECTION ASSISTANCE; ENVIRONMENT; UNITED NATIONS EDUCATIONAL, SCIENTIFIC AND CULTURAL ORGANIZATION.

Further Reading: Pérez de Cuéllar, Javier. *Pilgrimage for Peace: A Secretary-General's Memoir.* New York: St. Martin's, 1997.

Permanent Court of Arbitration (PCA)

Often referred to as the "Hague Tribunal," the Permanent Court of Arbitration was initiated in 1899 by a CONVENTION of the First Hague Conference. The PCA arose from a developing interest in MEDIATION and ARBITRATION as methods of resolving international disputes. The 19th century witnessed a growth in the practice of inserting clauses in TREATIES calling for arbitration, and legal and political leaders considered proposals to create a permanent court to handle such cases. The Hague Peace Conference of 1899, convened to discuss peace and DISARMAMENT, adopted a Convention on the pacific settlement of International Disputes and called for a permanent organization to enable the creation of arbitral tribunals. The resulting Permanent Court of Arbitration was established in 1900 and began operating in 1902 in The Hague, Netherlands. In 1913 it moved to the Peace Palace in that city, where it continues to function alongside its neighbors, the INTERNATIONAL COURT OF JUSTICE, the Carnegie Foundation (which originally provided the building), the INTERNATIONAL CRIMINAL COURT, and the HAGUE ACADEMY OF INTERNATIONAL LAW. In 2007 there were 107 countries adhering to the convention. The PCA's services were available to resolve disputes between states, between states and private parties, and disputes in which inter-governmental organizations were involved.

The court consists of a panel of jurists designated by member countries. Each country is allotted up to four appointees, all of whom are expected to be experts in INTERNATIONAL LAW; they constitute what is called that country's PCA "National Group." From the full panel of all national groups, members of each arbitration tribunal may be chosen in a particular case. A case is initiated when two or more disputants sign an agreement to submit a disagreement to binding arbitration. They may then select arbiters from the PCA's panel to hear the case, or they may ask two panelists to pick an umpire before whom a hearing will take place.

On request, the PCA offers possibilities of arbitration (its original function), CONCILIATION, fact-finding commissions, GOOD OFFICES, and mediation. It also can provide administrative support to litigants, a private courtroom and hearing facilities at the Peace Palace, and access to the Peace Palace library.

The tribunal lost much of its original importance to the PERMANENT COURT OF INTERNATIONAL JUSTICE, established by the LEAGUE OF NATIONS after World War I, which was then superseded by the International Court of Justice after World War II. However, the Permanent Court of Arbitration regularly performs a role in nominating candidates for the ICJ. At the request of the UN SECRETARY-GENERAL, the "National Groups" can propose candidates for vacant positions on the Court. From these nominations the GENERAL ASSEMBLY and the SECURITY COUNCIL elect the ICJ's judges.

See also APPENDIX E, OBSERVER STATUS.

Further Reading: PCA Web site: <pca-cpa.org>.

Permanent Court of International Justice (PCIJ)

Often called the "World Court," the Permanent Court of International Justice was established by the LEAGUE OF NATIONS, pursuant to Article 14 of the League's COVENANT. In 1920 the League Assembly unanimously approved a statute for the new court and later that year called upon the League Council to submit a PROTOCOL to League members to adopt the statute. The required number of NATION-STATES (a majority of League members) ratified it by the next year. The Permanent Court began meeting at The Hague in February 1922, but it dissolved after World War II, when its functions, JURISDICTION, and, for the most part, its statute were transferred to the new INTERNATIONAL COURT OF JUSTICE (ICJ).

Like its progeny, the PCIJ received authorization from its statute to make judgments in cases submitted to it by states in disagreement over an issue of an international character and to give advisory opinions in any matter that the League's Council or Assembly referred to it. Thus its areas of activity were more extensive than that of the older PERMANENT COURT OF ARBITRATION (PCA)—often called the "Hague Tribunal." The latter, created by the Hague Peace Conference of 1899, dealt with ARBITRATION issues solely. Also unlike the Hague Tribunal, the PCIJ was a permanently constituted body, had its own statute and rules of procedure, and had a group of permanent judges rather than a large panel of jurists from which nations might select arbiters to hear a specific case. The PCIJ began with 11 regular judges and four deputies, but in 1931 the number increased to 15. The

League Council and Assembly concurrently elected judges for nine-year terms. Nominees came from lists supplied by the Permanent Court of Arbitration, and no more than one citizen of a nation could serve at the same time. Judges were paid a salary and were barred from any occupation, government service, or legal activity other than their work on the World Court. The PCIJ had a permanent registry that served to keep records and make public all activities of the Court. The PCIJ was accessible to all states for judicial judgments in international disputes, and its statute specifically listed the sources of INTERNATIONAL LAW that were to apply to contentious cases and advisory opinions. All of these features of the PCIJ were transferred to the ICJ in 1946.

The UNITED STATES never joined the PCIJ because the U.S. Senate never ratified the original protocol. Yet an American always served on the Court's bench. By 1945, its last year, the statute of the PCIJ had an official adherence from 59 states. From 1922 until 1939, when the Court discontinued sitting, it received 66 cases, some of which were settled out of court and some left pending. Of the remaining, the Court handed down 32 judgments in contentious cases and 27 advisory opinions. Most of these, and particularly the advisory opinions, retained the sanctity of international law after the Permanent Court's demise, and were catalogued with the decisions subsequently made by the International Court of Justice. With the outbreak of World War II, the Permanent Court ceased to function, and its reputation, along with that of the League of Nations, suffered with the collapse of international order. It held its last meeting in October 1945, in order to transfer its archives and functions to the new International Court of Justice. The PCIJ's judges resigned on January 31, 1946, and election of the ICJ judges occurred the next week at the UN GENERAL ASSEMBLY's first session. April 1946 witnessed the formal dissolution of the PCIJ. Simultaneously, the ICJ, meeting at The Hague for the first time, chose as its inaugural president Judge J. Gustavo Guerrero, the last president of the PCIJ.

Further Reading: Hudson, Manley O. *The Permanent Court of International Justice, 1920–1942; A Treatise.* New York: Garland Publishers, 1972. Rosenne, Shabtai. *The World Court: What It Is and How It Works.* 5th rev. ed. Boston: Martinus Nijhoff Publishers, 1995.

Permanent Members of the Security Council (P5)

Article 23, CHAPTER V of the United Nations CHARTER specifies that five major powers shall be permanent members of the SECURITY COUNCIL. The five are the UNITED STATES, GREAT BRITAIN, FRANCE, the RUSSIAN FEDERATION, and CHINA. Article 27 of the Charter endows the five permanent members with special powers on the Council by requiring a majority of nine votes and "the concurring votes of the permanent members" for the passage of all RESOLUTIONS on SUBSTANTIVE QUESTIONS. This provision effectively gave each of the five permanent members a VETO over Security Council action. While other nations often object to the veto, it was essential in order to win the approval of the U.S. Senate to ratification of the Charter, and to convince Marshal JOSEPH STALIN of the Soviet Union—wary of the U.S. idea of a United Nations—to pledge that the USSR would join the world body.

The veto has proven controversial, but has always remained intact, since Article 108 requires that AMENDMENTS TO THE CHARTER must obtain the ratification of the five permanent members. Also, in practice the decision to consider a topic or complaint has been considered procedural, and hence not subject to veto. However, whether an issue is a procedural or substantive matter is itself a substantive question, thus giving the permanent members a "DOUBLE VETO" on items before the Council. Over time, the Council adopted the interpretation that the words "concurring vote" in Article 27 meant that there had been no negative vote by any permanent member. That is, an abstention, not being a negative, indicated concurrence, and thus does not constitute a veto.

The veto was particularly important during the early years of the United Nations, when the COLD WAR protagonists used it to prevent condemnation of their actions and prevent action against their allies. It was used not only to block resolutions but also to thwart nominations for SECRETARY-GENERAL (43 cases) and to impede the ADMISSION of new members (59 vetoes). Only by the absence of a permanent member from a Council session or the exercise of the UNITING FOR PEACE RESOLUTION could the veto be circumvented. A total of 261 vetoes were cast through April 2007. Of these, 82 occurred before 1955. Russia (the Soviet Union) cast the largest number of vetoes, with the United States casting the second largest. The use of the veto reflected the MEMBERSHIP of the United Nations, since the overwhelming majority of the Russian vetoes were cast prior to 1965, when UN membership was pro-Western. By contrast, the United States did not cast a single veto prior to 1966, and found it necessary to do so only after the waning of colonialism resulted in increased UN membership of an anti-Western majority of newly independent former colonies during the mid-1960s. Vetoes have been rare since 1990. The end of the cold war led to negotiation and consensus among the P5 on many Security Council issues. Beginning with the GULF WAR, the five powers sought to reach a common position through informal consultations on matters of international peace and security, or at least a position that would garner nothing more than an abstention by a permanent member. The U.S.-led invasion of IRAQ in 2003, however, brought new tensions to the Security Council, as only the United Kingdom among the P5 joined with Washington in defying the council's disapproval of the invasion. In following years, the P5 worked together to address issues of unwelcome nuclear developments in North Korea and in IRAN.

Just as the five permanent members have been able to block any amendment that would limit their veto power, so too they have declined to increase the number of permanent seats on the council. Since 1945, the Latin American states of Brazil and Argentina have proposed their addition to permanent membership. Other states—GERMANY, JAPAN, INDIA—have also made cases for their individual candidacies. In 2005, as part of his REFORM initiative, Secretary-General KOFI ANNAN recommended an expansion of the Security Council to 24 members. Drawing on the recommendations made in 2004 by the HIGH-LEVEL PANEL ON THREATS, CHALLENGES AND CHANGE, Annan suggested the UN membership choose between two models for expansion, the first of which would have increased the number of permanent members to 11. Annan said nothing about the veto issue or which states should gain the new status. His proposal set off a campaign by several states for a permanent seat, but the United States indicated it would only support permanent membership for Germany, and China said it would oppose any additions. As a consequence the WORLD SUMMIT in September 2005 passed without any membership amendment being put forward.

See also APARTHEID; APPEALS TO THE SECURITY COUNCIL; BOUTROS BOUTROS-GHALI; CHAPTER VII; DUMBARTON OAKS CONFERENCE; EMERGENCY SPECIAL SESSION OF THE GENERAL ASSEMBLY; GENERAL COMMITTEE; *IN LARGER FREEDOM*; KOREAN WAR; LIE, TRYGVE; SCALE OF ASSESSMENTS; TRUSTEESHIP COUNCIL; VOTING; YALTA CONFERENCE.

Further Reading: Drifte, Reinhard. *Japan's Quest for a Permanent Security Council Seat: A Matter of Pride or Justice?* New York: St. Martin's, 2000. Jensen, Erik, and Thomas Fisher, eds. *The United Kingdom, The United Nations.* London: Macmillan, 1990. Karns, Margaret P., and Karen A. Mingst, eds. *The United States and Multilateral Institutions: Patterns of Changing Instrumentality and Influence.* Boston: Unwin Hyman, 1990. Moore, John Allphin Jr., and Jerry Pubantz. *The New United Nations: International Organization in the Twenty-first Century.* Upper Saddle River, N.J.: Prentice Hall, 2006. Ostrower, Gary B. *The United Nations and the United States.* New York: Twayne, 1998. Stoessinger, John G. *The United Nations and the Superpowers: China, Russia, and America.* 4th ed. New York: Random House, 1977.

— *K. J. Grieb*

permanent observer *See* OBSERVER STATUS.

permanent representative *See* MISSIONS TO THE UNITED NATIONS.

Persian Gulf War *See* GULF WAR.

personal representative *See* SPECIAL REPRESENTATIVE OF THE SECRETARY-GENERAL.

Point Four program

Point Four of President Harry S. Truman's 1949 inaugural address urged international cooperation to teach self-help to poverty-stricken people in the underdeveloped world by providing technological knowledge and skills through private capital investment. The president argued that financial assistance was an American responsibility under Article 56 of the United Nations CHARTER, which pledged every member state to the promotion of higher standards of living and to the solution of economic and social problems. Although conceived as a weapon in the COLD WAR, the idea of economic aid to politically vulnerable areas of the world was still a novel idea confined to the Marshall Plan nations. By late 1948, the UNITED STATES offered no extensive aid to LATIN AMERICA, Asia, and Africa.

President Truman, however, felt that the absence of an aid program to the non-European world weakened American global policy. Its absence should be rectified, as he noted in his inaugural address. The brainchild of Benjamin Hardy, a State Department official, the idea of raising living standards for those peoples who would otherwise be "ripe for revolution" was brought to Truman's attention by advisers Clark Clifford and George Elsey.

An enthusiastic Truman embraced the concept for several reasons, both humanitarian and political. Point Four would encourage the extraction of critical raw materials in the noncommunist world—particularly oil, rubber, and metal ores—as well as stimulate more U.S. exports to these nations, paid for by dollars generated by investments from abroad. Finally, Point Four would contribute to the expansion and specialization of world trade; in a phrase, liberal internationalism.

Despite the president's enthusiasm for "a bold new program," the Point Four program was not easily implemented because of underfunding and a reliance on reluctant private investment. Secretary of State DEAN ACHESON recalled that the "hyperbole of the inaugural outran the provisions of the budget." Congress shared the tepid interest of the business and banking communities in the program.

Senior staffer Walter S. Salant of the Council of Economic Advisers was responsible for recognizing the inadequacies of cautious private initiatives and urged instead the principle that extensive aid from the U.S. government was necessary to strengthen the economies of the underdeveloped nations. During the course of 1949, a series of crises forced a change in the orthodox international economic thinking of the Truman administration. Although ignoring calls by public figures for an Asian Marshall Plan, policy makers began to move away from the initially cautious Point Four legislation and toward Salant's advice for exports of government capital. The administration proposed an EXPANDED PROGRAM OF

TECHNICAL ASSISTANCE (EPTA) under the JURISDICTION of the UN's ECONOMIC AND SOCIAL COUNCIL (ECOSOC).

By late 1949, the administration no longer regarded the difficulties of some underdeveloped nations as peripheral concerns. Truman's state of the union address of January 4, 1950, urged forceful government financial aid, the importance of such programs for Japanese and European economic recovery (the Marshall Plan was to end in 1952), and the critical importance of Southeast Asia as an object of economic stimulation. The Chinese revolution of October 1949 made all of these arguments compelling. The new demands placed on American foreign policy during 1949 required a more ambitious response, including capital assistance for the underdeveloped world and revitalization of commerce between the developed and underdeveloped nations. Financed by voluntary contributions, EPTA commenced operations in 1950 as the UN's single largest program. The United States initially provided 60 percent of the agency's $20 million BUDGET.

See also DEVELOPMENT, SPECIAL UNITED NATIONS FUND FOR ECONOMIC DEVELOPMENT, UNITED NATIONS DEVELOPMENT PROGRAMME.

Further Reading: Acheson, Dean. *Present at the Creation.* New York: Norton, 1969. Clifford, Clark. *Counsel to the President: A Memoir.* New York: Random House, 1991. Rotter, Andrew. *The Path to Vietnam: Origins of the American Commitment to Southeast Asia.* Ithaca, N.Y.: Cornell University Press, 1987.

— *E. M. Clauss*

population *See* INTERNATIONAL CONFERENCE ON POPULATION AND DEVELOPMENT, UNITED NATIONS POPULATION FUND.

Prebisch, Raúl (1901–1986)

Prebisch, preeminent Third World economist of the post–World War II era, was an Argentine who helped manage his nation's economy during the Great Depression of the 1930s and World War II. His approach to economic issues was essentially Keynesian; that is, he advocated government economic intervention to break the bottlenecks of capitalist DEVELOPMENT. In 1948, as a consultant, he wrote for ECLA (ECONOMIC COMMISSION FOR LATIN AMERICA, now ECLAC) the groundbreaking *The Economic Development of Latin America and Its Principal Problems* and in 1949 the first part of the annual *Survey* of the region. In these works he amassed data to demonstrate the decline of trade between LATIN AMERICA—the "periphery"—and Europe and the UNITED STATES—the "center"—by aggregating the historical trade figures of Latin America with the two other regions and analyzing the trends. He proposed implementation of import substitution measures to enable commodity producing nations to

achieve more balanced economies by becoming industrialized. In 1950 he was appointed executive secretary of ECLA. His analysis and recommendations were to influence the economic policies of most of the nations of the region for several decades. Although ECLA participated in creating the failed Latin American Free Trade Area (LAFTA), he expressed grave doubts about the rigid nature of the organization, believing that the range of difference among the levels of development of the nations of the region made that arrangement one that would have great difficulty in succeeding. The theoretical approach of ECLA under his leadership became a dominant paradigm for the Third World in general.

His own role assumed world proportions when he became the first SECRETARY-GENERAL of the UNITED NATIONS CONFERENCE ON TRADE AND DEVELOPMENT (UNCTAD) in 1963. There he played a more activist role than did the heads of most other UN organizations, promoting the interests of Third World countries according to his views. One of his major goals was to promote an integrated program for the support of an expanded number of commodity agreements that would regulate the production and sale of the principal products of developing nations. After retirement from UNCTAD in 1969 he remained active in various capacities with ECLAC and advised the government of Argentina until his death. To the end of his life his ideas continued to evolve in response to new circumstances and his own changing understanding of the problems of underdeveloped nations.

Further Reading: Meier, Gerald M., and Dudley Seers, eds. *Pioneers in Development.* New York: Oxford University Press,

UNCTAD Secretary-General Raúl Prebisch (right) (UNITED NATIONS/T. CHEN)

1984: 175–91. Pinto, Anibal. "Raúl Prebisch 1901–1986." *CEPAL Review*, no. 29 (August 1986): 9–11. Prebisch, Raúl. "A Critique of Peripheral Capitalism." *CEPAL Review*, no. 1 (1976): 9–76. ———. "Notes on Trade from the Standpoint of the Periphery." *CEPAL Review*, no. 28 (April 1985): 203–14. Solis, Leopoldo. *Raúl Prebisch at ECLA: Years of Creative Intellectual Effort*. San Francisco: International Center for Economic Growth, 1988.

— M. W. Bray

president of the General Assembly *See* GENERAL COMMITTEE.

preventive diplomacy *See* AGENDA FOR PEACE.

principal organs of the United Nations *See* ECONOMIC AND SOCIAL COUNCIL, GENERAL ASSEMBLY, INTERNATIONAL COURT OF JUSTICE, SECRETARIAT, SECURITY COUNCIL, STRUCTURE OF THE UNITED NATIONS, TRUSTEESHIP COUNCIL.

procedural committees of the General Assembly

The UN GENERAL ASSEMBLY has two permanent procedural committees: the GENERAL COMMITTEE and the CREDENTIALS COMMITTEE. The General Committee functions as the steering committee for the annual session of the General Assembly, making decisions regarding the agenda and the order in which items will be considered. It consists of the Assembly's president, 21 vice presidents, and the elected chairmen of the six main committees of the General Assembly. The Credentials Committee consists of nine members appointed at the beginning of the yearly session to consider and approve the credentials of representatives and delegations to the United Nations.

See also COMMITTEE SYSTEM OF THE GENERAL ASSEMBLY.

programmes and funds

The United Nations STRUCTURE includes a number of programmes and funds, created by the GENERAL ASSEMBLY to oversee and operate specific activities that are central to the organization's operations and purposes. Programmes and funds are differentiated from the SPECIALIZED AGENCIES in that they were created by and are part of the United Nations, whereas specialized agencies were established by separate treaties and have their own CHARTERS and executive boards. Both specialized agencies and UN programmes and funds rely on voluntary contributions from member states, and in some cases on private organizations and corporations. In addition to being formal parts of the United Nations rather than associated agencies, programmes and funds all report to both the GENERAL ASSEMBLY and the ECONOMIC AND SOCIAL COUNCIL (ECOSOC), while specialized agencies report only to ECOSOC and then exclusively for purposes of coordination with UN offices, activities, and organs.

United Nations programmes and funds include large operations that are among the principal dispensers of aid and assistance to developing countries, such as the UNITED NATIONS DEVELOPMENT PROGRAMME (UNDP). Smaller offices focus on problems of particular concern to the nations of the world. This latter group includes specialized research institutes extending knowledge regarding particular issues and assuring that the results are available to all nations. The broadest is the UNITED NATIONS INSTITUTE FOR TRAINING AND RESEARCH (UNITAR), which runs a large number of training seminars primarily for individuals from DEVELOPING COUNTRIES and new UN staff members. Others are more narrowly focused on particular specialties. They include the INTERNATIONAL RESEARCH AND TRAINING INSTITUTE FOR THE ADVANCEMENT OF WOMEN (INSTRAW), the UNITED NATIONS INSTITUTE FOR DISARMAMENT RESEARCH (UNIDIR), the UNITED NATIONS INTERREGIONAL CRIME AND JUSTICE RESEARCH INSTITUTE (UNICRI), and the UNITED NATIONS RESEARCH INSTITUTE FOR SOCIAL DEVELOPMENT (UNRISD). All conduct extensive research programs in their areas of specialty, publishing reports that are made available to the governments of member states and conducting training seminars at various locations around the world.

The United Nations has also created offices that serve particular conferences and commissions, providing the specialized information and support necessary to the implementation of their missions. They supply the policy studies needed by governments to implement the programs of action adopted by the various WORLD CONFERENCES. The INTERNATIONAL TRADE CENTRE and the Centre for Transnational Corporations offer this type of service for the UNITED NATIONS CONFERENCE ON TRADE AND DEVELOPMENT (UNCTAD). Several also have their own governing boards or regular conferences, and hence constitute separate decision-making bodies within the United Nations, but all were established by the United Nations and are considered part of it.

The programmes include several large and pivotal agencies. The Office of the UNITED NATIONS HIGH COMMISSIONER FOR REFUGEES (UNHCR), established in 1993, is the primary body that provides assistance to refugees throughout the world and protects their rights. It has more than 5,000 personnel scattered throughout the world, wherever there is a refugee crisis. The UNHCR also seeks to coordinate the work of more than 450 independent NONGOVERNMENTAL ORGANIZATIONS (NGOs) involved in refugee aid. The NGOs are designated officially as "partners" of the UNHCR. The United Nations Conference on Trade and Development promotes and represents the interests of developing nations in international trade negotiations. The UNITED NATIONS ENVIRONMENT PROGRAMME (UNEP) is the principal UN body in protecting the ENVIRONMENT. The UNITED NATIONS CHILDREN'S FUND (UNICEF) is the only UN body dedicated exclusively to the protection of children. It supports and conducts programs aimed at improving the rights of children everywhere, particularly in developing countries. It relies, like nearly all UN programmes, on voluntary contributions.

The UNITED NATIONS RELIEF AND WORKS AGENCY FOR PALESTINE REFUGEES IN THE NEAR EAST (UNRWA), one of the earliest UN offices, was established in 1949. It provides assistance to Palestinians who lost their homes and livelihood as a result of the 1948 ARAB-ISRAELI conflict, which led to the establishment of Israel and the dispersal of Palestinian refugees to the neighboring countries and throughout the Middle East, where many still remain. The UNITED NATIONS POPULATION FUND (UNFPA) is the largest multilateral source of population assistance for developing countries. It promotes efforts to improve reproductive health for WOMEN and to encourage family planning. This work reflects its commitment to women's equality, as a critical factor in slowing global birth rates. The WORLD FOOD PROGRAMME (WFP) extends food assistance to people living in poverty and emergency relief to countries and areas affected by natural and man-made disasters.

The United Nations Development Programme (UNDP), established in 1965, is one of the UN's largest and most important offices. UNDP is the world's leading source of aid to governments to assist economic and social DEVELOPMENT, drawing on voluntary contributions. Developing countries generally prefer multilateral aid, such as that made available by the UNDP, because aid from specific countries often comes with conditions that restrict the recipient's freedom of action. The UNDP operates more than 100 country offices in developing nations, which constitute the heart of UN activities in support of development. The UNDP also manages several associated funds and programmes, including the UNITED NATIONS DEVELOPMENT FUND FOR WOMEN (UNIFEM), the UNITED NATIONS VOLUNTEERS (UNV), the Office to Combat DESERTIFICATION and Drought (UNSO), the United Nations Capital Development Fund (UNCDF), the United Nations Fund for Science and Technology for Development (UNFSDT), and the United Nations Revolving Fund for Natural Resources (UNRFNRE).

The Office of the High Commissioner for Human Rights, established in 1993, is officially designated as the focal point of all HUMAN RIGHTS activities in the United Nations. It is charged with coordinating UN efforts for the promotion of civil, cultural, political, economic, and social rights. The UNITED NATIONS CENTRE FOR HUMAN SETTLEMENTS (Habitat), originally created in 1978, was designated in 1996 as the focal point for the implementation of the Habitat Agenda adopted by the Second UN Conference on Human Settlements. It works in partnership with governments and local authorities. The UNITED NATIONS UNIVERSITY engages in research and postgraduate education, and it operates a publications program for the dissemination of knowledge. It includes several institutes and specialized programs disbursed throughout the world dealing with development, the environment, and technology.

See also ADVISORY COMMITTEE ON ADMINISTRATIVE AND BUDGETARY QUESTIONS, CHIEF EXECUTIVES BOARD FOR COORDINATION, EXPANDED PROGRAM OF TECHNICAL ASSISTANCE, GLOBAL ENVIRONMENT FACILITY, HIV/AIDS, INTER-AGENCY COMMITTEE ON SUSTAINABLE DEVELOPMENT, INTERGOVERNMENTAL PANEL ON CLIMATE CHANGE, JOINT UNITED NATIONS PROGRAMME ON AIDS, LANGUAGES, SOMALIA, SPECIAL SESSIONS OF THE GENERAL ASSEMBLY, SPECIAL UNITED NATIONS FUND FOR ECONOMIC DEVELOPMENT, SUSTAINABLE DEVELOPMENT, UNITED NATIONS CONFERENCE ON ENVIRONMENT AND DEVELOPMENT, UNITED NATIONS CONFERENCE ON THE HUMAN ENVIRONMENT, UNITED NATIONS OFFICE FOR PROJECT SERVICES.

Further Reading: Moore, John Allphin, Jr., and Jerry Pubantz. *The New United Nations: International Organization in the Twenty-first Century.* Upper Saddle River, N.J.: Prentice Hall, 2006.

— *K. J. Grieb*

protocol

Protocol is a more ambiguous international term than TREATY and CONVENTION. It refers to agreed-upon rules governing diplomatic conduct or written international instruments, such as statements of principle, preliminary agreements, or authenticated minutes of an international conference, all of which might become part of a formal treaty in the future, provided the parties ratify the protocol. The KYOTO PROTOCOL of 1997 called for international agreement to cut energy emissions in the future in order to abate global warming. The protocol required formal ratification by the participating nations. It entered into force on February 16, 2005, and 169 countries and other government entities had ratified the Protocol by the end of 2006.

See also examples of protocols in AFRICAN UNION, ANGOLA, ANTARCTIC TREATY, BASEL CONVENTION ON THE CONTROL OF TRANSBOUNDARY MOVEMENTS OF HAZARDOUS WASTES AND THEIR DISPOSAL, BIOLOGICAL WEAPONS, CONVENTION ON THE ELIMINATION OF ALL FORMS OF DISCRIMINATION AGAINST WOMEN, CONVENTION RELATING TO THE STATUS OF REFUGEES, HUMAN RIGHTS COMMITTEE, HUMAN TRAFFICKING, INQUIRY, INTERNATIONAL ATOMIC ENERGY AGENCY, IRAN-IRAQ WAR, MARRAKESH PROTOCOL, MILLENNIUM SUMMIT, MONTREAL PROTOCOL ON SUBSTANCES THAT DEPLETE THE OZONE LAYER, NAMIBIA, NUCLEAR-WEAPONS-FREE ZONES, SOUTHEAST ASIA TREATY ORGANIZATION.